MONTREAL

Island City of the St. Lawrence

MONTREAL

Island City of the St. Lawrence

BY
KATHLEEN JENKINS

Doubleday & Company, Inc.
Garden City, New York
1966

Illustrations numbered 1 through 23 courtesy McCord Museum, McGill University; number 24 courtesy Cunard Line; 25 and 26 courtesy City of Montreal; and 27 courtesy National Harbours Board, Montreal.

Booklist Nov. 1, 1966 - pg. 298

48403

ACKNOWLEDGMENTS

MY THANKS must go, first of all, to the libraries in which I did the major part of my research. Mr. Jules Bazin added personal kindness to the normal services rendered by the Municipal Library of Montreal, of which he is the Director. My relationship was particularly close with two of his assistants, Miss Marie Baboyant of the Gagnon Collection of Canadiana, and Miss Cecile Saint-Jorre of the Periodicals Room. Both were endlessly patient.

The Westmount Public Library was equally helpful, for my visits to its Reference Department were virtually a daily occurrence. I was, in addition, a constant borrower. My long-term loan privileges were greatly appreciated, especially in respect to out-of-print material which I was unable to purchase for myself. It is a pleasure to express my formal thanks to Mrs. Norah Bryant and her staff.

The clipping files of the Montreal *Star* proved of great benefit in my study of modern times. For making them accessible, I am grateful to the Librarian, Mr. C. M. Lapointe. As Director of the Jewish Public Library, Mr. David Rome not only provided me with the necessary books, but in the course of several interviews, gave me much valuable information about the Jewish community.

It is with pleasure that I acknowledge my indebtedness to the McCord Museum, McGill University, for permission to use the illustrations of old Montreal, reproduced in these pages. Mrs. Isabel Barclay Dobell, the Archivist, was co-operation personified, as were the several members of the staff. The photographs of the modern city appear, courtesy of the City of Montreal; the National Harbours Board; the Cunard Steam-Ship Company.

The Public Archives of Canada has permitted me to quote from the Elgin-Grey Papers, edited by Sir Arthur Doughty. The Champlain Society has been equally generous in allowing a quotation from the Works of Samuel de Champlain, edited by H. H. Langton and W. F. Ganong.

Miss Vernon Ross, the Director of the Graduate School of Library Science at McGill University, has read large portions of my manuscript. Her pertinent comments and unending interest in my progress reflect the strength of our long-standing friendship. Mrs. Maud Stockwell and Mr. J. D. Converse were equally helpful as readers and constructive critics.

Dr. William Kaye Lamb, Dominion Archivist and National Librarian, was—as I have always known him to be—both friendly and encouraging. For advice and assistance in their several fields, I am grateful to the Reverend Edmond Desrochers, S.J.; Mr. David M. Legate of the Montreal *Star;* Mr. John D. King of the Château de Ramezay; Mr. John M. Mackenzie of the Royal Automobile Club of Canada; Mr. Raymond Vaillancourt of the National Harbours Board; Dr. Harry J. Stern of Temple Emanu-El; Dr. Joseph Kage of the Jewish Immigrant Aid Service; Dr. Trevor Lloyd of the Geography Department, McGill University; Miss Virginia Murray of the Library School, McGill University.

CONTENTS

LIST OF ILLUSTRATIONS

1. Montreal from the mountain, 1811.
2. Montreal from St. Helen's Island, 1828.
3. Port of Montreal, 1829–30.
4. Saint James Street, Montreal, 1829–30.
5. Place d'Armes, Montreal, 1829.
6. Nelson Monument, Notre Dame Street, 1830.
7. Interior of Notre Dame Church, 1839–40.
8. Notre Dame Church, 1839–40.
9. Place d'Armes, à Montreal, 1848.
10. Destruction of the Parliament House, Montreal, April 25, 1849.
11. McGill College Avenue, probably after 1850.
12. River front, Montreal, probably after 1850.
13. Montreal, Canada east, 1852.
14. The Gavazzi riots at Zion Church, 1853.
15. Bonsecours Church, 1855.
16. Shoving of ice upon no. 9 pier, Victoria Bridge, 1858.
17. Shoving of ice upon wharves in front of Montreal, 1860.
18. Staging for center tube, Victoria Bridge, 1860.
19. The harbor from custom house wharf, about 1885–89.
20. Saint-Gabriel farmhouse, Congregation of Notre Dame, 1886.
21. Ice Palace—Montreal Carnival, 1889.
22. The harbor, about 1896–1910.
23. Montreal from the mountain, 1963.
24. The harbor at dusk, 1963.
25. Maisonneuve monument, Place d'Armes, 1964.
26. Notre Dame Church, 1964.
27. Montreal, grain elevator no. 4, 1964.

MONTREAL
Island City of the St. Lawrence

Chapter 1
1535–1600

Jacques Cartier at Hochelaga. The St. Lawrence, the Island and Mount Royal.

CARTIER BUCKLED ON his armor and went ashore at daybreak, thankful after a night in the cramped quarters of the longboats, to be on the move once more. His companions were of a like mind, the half-dozen gentlemen and twenty-five sailors, each busy on that Sunday in October 1535, with his preparations for the visit to the wondrous village of Hochelaga.

The French had already enjoyed a foretaste of native hospitality, for their arrival at the Island the previous day touched off an astonishing demonstration. More than a thousand men, women, and children crowded down to the shore, dancing and making great signs of joy. In their hands they carried food, quantities of fish, and bread made of Indian corn, throwing so much of it down into the boats that the heavens seemed to rain bread.

The reception on the Sunday was more decorous, as befitted the higher rank of the participants. It began with a quiet walk along a well-trodden path, the ground covered with acorns, fallen from the oak trees which grew everywhere. As beautiful, recorded Cartier, as any forest in France. A march of about a league and a half brought them to one of the headmen, who suggested by signs that they rest beside a fire, lighted for their comfort. This they did, moving on again, after an exchange of speeches and gifts, past fields filled with the corn of the country, the Indian equivalent of the wheat of Europe.

The village as seen by Cartier and his companions was circular

in shape and ringed about by a palisade of wood, built in three
tiers like a pyramid, well lashed together and some two lances
in height. One gate only, gave access to the fifty houses within,
also of wood and covered with large pieces of bark. An open
square stood in the midst, and there the visitors were conducted,
as though about to perform a miracle play. Into this assemblage
came the chief, carried by the young men of the tribe. He was
paralyzed and deprived of the use of his limbs. It was only then
that Cartier realized other sick persons had gathered around, in
obvious expectation that he would heal them. But his reading of
a passage from the Gospel of St. John seemed to satisfy them,
and when at last he ordered the trumpets to be sounded, all the
Indians were much delighted.

After this, the party proceeded to climb the mountain, to
which Cartier gave the name of Mount Royal. From its summit,
he saw the countryside for more than thirty leagues round about.
To the north and the south, rose the mountains, and between
was the finest land it was possible to find, arable, level and flat.
Through this, flowed the Great River—later to be known as the
St. Lawrence—and beyond stretched the rapids, of the most violent sort and utterly impassable for boats. And then, after regret-
ful looks at the unknown west and much conversation by means
of signs, the long day came to an end, some of the white men
so visibly weary that their hosts picked them up and carried them
down to the shore. The farewells were brief and the departure
immediate, for fear of what Cartier called a misadventure. For no
matter how friendly the natives, he was haunted by the fear that
their feelings might change.

The historically minded reader will, of course, realize that
Cartier, the discoverer of Canada, was neither the first nor the
last adventurer, who almost by accident, stumbled upon some
portion of the American continent while searching for a passage
to the Far East. Once Europe had accepted the fact that the
world was round, the race moved off, its prize the fabulous
wealth of India and China. This was the great dream of the
age, and attempts to bring it to fruition, explain the willingness
of kings and merchants to finance the long series of voyages.
Columbus shared in it, as did his royal patrons of Spain. So too,

did his fellow Genoese, John Cabot, who served Henry VII of England.

Of Cabot, little is known, yet he deserves more than a passing mention in any study of the Canadian past. For his interests lay far from the tropical terrain discovered by Columbus, leading him in 1497 and again in 1498 to explore some part of the coasts of northeastern America, probably Newfoundland and Labrador, and perhaps Cape Breton Island.

Cabot disappears from history after the year 1499, having established a path across the North Atlantic which others quickly followed. Some at least were traders, for the fishermen of Western Europe as early as 1501, knew of the wealth to be garnered from the Grand Banks of Newfoundland. Theirs was a pious age, and the fast days of the Church not only numerous but strictly observed. The codfish became a valuable article of commerce.

Obviously, none of these fishermen—no matter what their nationality—had any desire to see European settlers in their midst. But as they came and went, inevitably each one added his mite to the store of accumulated knowledge—particularly as their landings brought them into contact with the Indians along the shore. Poor souls as these were, they welcomed the simplest adjuncts of civilization, and so there sprang up a haphazard system of barter, involving among other things, their decidedly greasy beaver robes. Out of these accidental encounters developed the fur trade, later so important to the people of Montreal.

Given this background of familiarity with the North Atlantic, the next step could not be long delayed. It was only a matter of time until someone, more thoughtful than his neighbors, would decide to investigate what lay beyond the rocky coastline, and search in its deep bays for an outlet that would permit ships to penetrate the unknown. That this inspiration came to a French citizen explains the presence of Jacques Cartier at the future site of Montreal.

The fact that France had such an eminently suitable commander for the proposed expedition, may well have induced Francis I to give it his blessing. Known to Canadian schoolchildren as the Mariner of Saint-Malo, the sobriquet indicates not only Cartier's place of birth (about the year 1491) but also his permanent home. Although details of his early life are few, it almost certainly included much experience at sea, for as his ventures in the New World were soon to show, he was a navigator of rare skill.

So far as Montreal is concerned, Cartier's first voyage in 1534 might be described as a reconnaissance, for although he sailed along the shores of Newfoundland and Labrador, discovered La Baie de Chaleur in what is now New Brunswick and claimed Gaspé for his king, storms in the Gulf of St. Lawrence halted him at Anticosti. Because of the lateness of the season, he returned to France.

The second and more famous voyage began on May 19, 1535, with the departure of three ships from Saint-Malo: *La Grande Hermine* of 120 tons; *La Petite Hermine,* just half the size; and the 40-ton *Emerillon.* This time, despite storms at sea, the entire party reached Stadacona—the modern Quebec—in safety. There the two larger vessels were left at anchor, while Cartier with a few companions, made his way upstream, sailing along under idyllic conditions from September 19 to October 2. The visit to Hochelaga, as we have seen, was equally felicitous, but the winter which followed at Stadacona, could scarcely have been worse. Suffering from the bitter cold and racked by scurvy, the survivors owed their lives to Cartier's chance discovery of a native remedy, brewed of spruce or cedar.

As for Hochelaga, this was its only appearance in recorded history. It has always provoked discussion, both as to its way of life and the fate of its inhabitants. Even its site is debatable, although most authorities place it as just south of Sherbrooke Street, adjacent to the McGill campus. Cartier's own narrative indicates, at least, that it stood part way up the slopes of Mount Royal, and hence a fair distance from the waterfront settlement of the French a century later.

The mere fact that such doubts exist, points to the early disappearance of the village. At some time—and in all probability soon after 1535—all trace of its people vanished, either wiped out by the more warlike tribes of the Five Nations, or when the soil became worn-out, in a voluntary abandonment of the spot. Of the two, the former seems the more likely, for the Indians fought with each other, long before the advent of the white man.

In any case, Cartier's visit serves as a romantic introduction to the story of Montreal. Taken in conjunction with his other discoveries in eastern Canada, it would seem of sufficient importance to have warranted some official recognition of his services to France. Nothing could have been further from what actually happened, for war with Spain and domestic strife far outweighed any nebulous plans for colonies overseas. The "diamonds" which he so carefully carried home, proved to be quartz crystal, and the "gold" iron pyrites. It was all very disappointing, and for no one more than Cartier himself, as he cooled his heels at court, waiting and hoping for a fresh commission.

In 1540, a short-lived peace in Europe led to some confused plans for a permanent establishment at Quebec. At one point, Cartier was appointed Captain General and placed in charge of the expedition; later he was demoted, and the coveted honor awarded to the Sieur de Roberval. Failing volunteers, men were taken from the jails and packed off unwillingly to the New World. As might be expected, they made such poor colonists that the whole enterprise was foredoomed to failure.

It was then that Cartier paid what may have been his last visit to the Island. Since he made no mention of Hochelaga or its people, the assumption is that they had already disappeared. A closer view of the rapids which he called the Long Sault, confirmed his earlier impression that no boat could safely navigate its rock-strewn turbulent waters. As for the few natives who greeted him along the way, he could only dismiss them as untrustworthy. For all their apparent joy, they might well have killed the party.

On this sadly suspicious note, Montreal is lost to sight for the rest of the century. Cartier died in France in 1557, a disappointed man. Whether he ever made a fourth voyage to the St. Lawrence, is open to doubt; equally questionable is Roberval's presence on the Island. No one, in official circles in France, had the slightest interest in Canada. A few private merchants traded in furs each summer along the lower reaches of the Great River but otherwise, there was silence everywhere on its shores.

Chapter 2
1600–1635

Samuel de Champlain and New France. Quebec. The quest for the beaver and the greed of the merchants. The summer fur-trading post at the Island.

SAMUEL DE CHAMPLAIN, whom posterity was to honor as the Father of New France, first saw the Great River in the summer of 1603. He was then in his early thirties, a man of excellent repute, and a veteran of ten years' service in the armies of his country. From that date onward until his death, the New World and above all the St. Lawrence Valley, became the focal point of his life, and eventually his home. In time, he was appointed its Governor, officially charged with the duties which in several capacities he had long exercised. He traveled constantly—to France, where he pleaded with indifferent or antagonistic governments for greater support for the colony—and more to his liking, into the vast and unknown hinterland encompassed by the St. Lawrence and Ottawa rivers and the Lakes beyond.

Obviously, the fame of such a man cannot be localized. Champlain belongs to Canada, and in any case, there was no permanent settlement at Montreal until after his death. Yet the records of his many visits to the Island reveal an appreciation for the natural beauty of the region, and when at the age of forty-three, he married, a more enduring local link was forged. His bride, at the age of twelve, perforce left behind in France to complete her education, was not forgotten by her husband. Cruising through the islands in the Great River, Champlain chose one, the fairest of them all and named it Ile Ste. Hélène in her honor. And so it remains to this day.

However little progress there may have been otherwise, the fur trade as Champlain first knew it, was thriving. Its basis was the beaver—the French castor—familiar nowadays as the makings for coats of great feminine appeal, but in the seventeenth century used in the manufacture of hats for men. And because the deepest and most luxuriant pelts came from the north, the merchants of the St. Lawrence enjoyed a fair measure of profit.

It was men of this caliber who, for many years, constituted the ruling class of New France. So long as successive kings were unwilling or unable to direct colonial affairs themselves, just so long did the administration remain a matter for private or company control. Moreover, the unpredictable swing of the pendulum between the extremes of monopoly and free trade, made for uncertainty and a disregard for law and order.

The word "monopoly" in modern times, is ordinarily used to denote something sinister, perhaps even illegal; it suggests price fixing and overpowerful combines. France, two hundred years ago, saw it as a means of getting something done that the government could not itself carry out; in the case of New France, a simple quid pro quo between king and merchant.

Even so, the picture presented by these trading privileges is a strange one. One season, they might be in effect, the next canceled. Awarded in perpetuity, they could be abruptly annuled; given for a single year, they might grudgingly be extended. At times they were bestowed upon an individual, more often upon a group, transforming an informal group of traders into a formal company. Nor did partnership necessarily insure harmony, for if the profits were great, the competition was fierce. Moreover, the merchants were slow to honor the conditions that formed a part of every agreement with the king. Since these ordinarily included such matters as settlement and the conversion of the Indians, it is easy to see why the early arrivals from France were pathetically few, and altogether lacking in the necessities of life.

Such was the prevailing atmosphere along the St. Lawrence at the time of Champlain's arrival. The changes came slowly, and largely as a result of his initiative. One of the more significant was the establishment of a settlement at Quebec, the modest

nucleus of a permanent French colony in North America. The
"Habitation," as constructed in 1608, consisted of a group of
buildings, surrounding a courtyard and protected by a palisade.
For the rest of his life Champlain regarded it as home—a choice
which at once brought him into closer contact with the Indians
of the neighborhood. How he reacted; what he did; what he
failed to do; his choice of tribal friends and foes; all, in the
future, were to affect Montreal.

Of the several racial groups involved at this period, those in
the northern part of the continent gradually fell within the
French sphere of influence, even as their southern kinsfolk allied
themselves with the Dutch and later with the English. The
Algonquins and Montagnais lived nearest Quebec, nomadic peoples, undisciplined, decidedly dirty and altogether unappetizing
in their habits. The Hurons, in contrast, who occupied the territory adjoining and beyond the Ottawa River, dwelt in relatively
settled villages, and made some slight show of civilization. Yet it
was the Iroquois, who by general consent, were voted the most
intelligent of the tribes. They occupied the country south of the
St. Lawrence and Lake Ontario—the Oneidas, the Onondagas,
the Senecas, the Cayugas and the Mohawks, who together made
up the Five Nations Confederacy. Their remarkable qualities as
warriors were matched with a rudimentary political sense. Notorious for their cruelty, it went hand in hand with stoical courage,
so great that even their enemies—soon to include New France—
found themselves at times, forced into an unwilling admiration of
their behavior.

Champlain quickly proved to be a past master at dealing with
the tribes, himself an accomplished orator who listened patiently
to their flowery speeches and faced with equanimity, their interminable feasts. He treated them well, meting out justice with
an impartial hand and fulfilling his promises. In return, the
Indians trusted him, to an extent enjoyed by few Europeans.
And although there was much that was repugnant in their way
of life, there was also much to be learned, and this the French
realized. At Champlain's instigation, a succession of young men
went out from Quebec to the remote villages, living as natives

and returning to act as interpreters and intermediaries between the white men and the red.

Not long after the founding of Quebec, his Indian neighbors sought Champlain's assistance in a projected raid against the Iroquois. Specifically, they wanted the support of European fire-arms, as opposed to the bows and arrows of the enemy. Their request posed a dilemma, to which probably there could only have been one answer. Champlain and two companions accompanied the Huron and Algonquin warriors, paddling south to the lake that now bears his name, and there took part in a brief battle. Everything turned out as expected, a few Iroquois killed and the rest put to flight.

To call this a battle is, of course, to exaggerate. It was a skirmish and a minor one to boot, lost and won in a remote tangle of forests and lakes. Yet historians, ever since, have looked at it with questioning eyes. Did anyone, at the time, recognize its significance? Champlain almost certainly did, being wise in the ways of the savages, but although he knew that his partisanship would bring down revenge upon the colony, he could hardly have remained neutral. Had he failed to befriend the Hurons, the warfare would have been worse than ever, for they lived along the Ottawa, the direct route to the north and hence to the richest furs. Support for them was a form of insurance, a guarantee that the pelts would be brought to the St. Lawrence, and not diverted south to Albany and the Dutch and English colonies. Nevertheless, Montreal within a few years, was to suffer from the undying enmity of the Iroquois.

It was precisely because of the fur trade that the idle talk of a second settlement took a more serious turn in the summer of 1611. If fear of the Five Nations kept the other tribes from carrying their pelts down to Quebec, then the French must go upstream to meet them at the Grand Sault on the Island.

Champlain, with a dozen boatloads of traders dogging his heels, examined the district with care. Not only the land, but the nearby waters, dangerous because of their swift currents and hidden rocks. It was not an easy choice, for there were many islands in the Great River. In the end, he returned to Cartier's Hochelaga—not to the precise spot, but to a new location on the shore. "There are many fine meadows which would feed as many cattle as one could wish, and there are all the varieties of wood which we have in our forests in France, with many vines, butternuts, plums, cherries, strawberries and other kinds of fruits, which are very good to eat . . . An abundance of fish can be caught, of all the varieties we have in France, and of many other kinds which we do not have . . . So having examined very carefully and found this spot to be one of the finest on the river, I ordered the trees of the Place Royale to be cut down and cleared off, in order to level the ground and make it ready for building."

Meanwhile, the hoped-for convoy of Indians having arrived, two hundred Hurons sat down in council with the French, exchanging gifts of beaver skins and wampum belts for hatchets and other useful tools. There are much talk of the Iroquois. Champlain, always curious, questioned his visitors about the west, parting from them in the end, in an atmosphere of mutual trust.

Events during the next few years, for Champlain, fell more or less into a pattern. By 1616 he could no longer find time to explore the new land in person, since growing responsibilities and the pressure of business kept him tied down, either in Quebec or France. It was then that his young trainees in the wilderness proved their value to the colony, for in an official sense they served as his deputies, and from their reports he kept in touch with developments in the west. Increasingly, there was reason to be worried over the chaos in the fur trade and the greed of the merchants.

The absence of any attempt to Christianize the Indians revealed the laxity of these self-same men, for although religious obligations invariably formed a part of their contracts with the king, there were no priests along the St. Lawrence. Champlain, as a devoted son of the church, had long regretted this fact, and finally he took action. In 1615, when he returned from France, four Recollet fathers accompanied him.

Strangely enough, in view of the evangelizing zeal of later years, there seems to have been some difficulty in finding volunteers for the mission field. The Recollets came from a convent near Champlain's home, and this may have been the reason for their selection. As members of an Order which stemmed from the great Franciscan brotherhood, they were mendicants who stressed the need for meditation or recollection. Not perhaps the most likely candidates for the rough life of the frontier.

Yet the Recollets brought enthusiasm to their task, as Champlain discovered when he met Father Le Caron, already busy near the Island. His celebration of Mass, to mark their reunion, was almost certainly the first in the Montreal region. The date, being June 24, could not have been more appropriate, since all French Canada today honors the feast of St. Jean Baptiste. But in 1615 the savages crowded about the altar, lost in admiration at its ornaments the like of which they had never seen before.

Clearly, by this date, a busy trading post had sprung up on the Island, although the matter of a permanent settlement still hung fire. Each summer, the place came to life, with the arrival of the Indians, their canoes loaded down with furs. Most seasons found Champlain in attendance, still asking questions and eager for knowledge of the west. Guerrilla warfare among the tribes never ceased, the Iroquois proving exceptionally troublesome near Montreal. An occasional patched-up peace yielded a short respite, only to be followed by raids which grew steadily worse, for just as the French lent their support to the Hurons, the Dutch backed the Five Nations.

As though Indian troubles in themselves were not bad enough, Champlain for the remainder of his life, found himself faced with intrigues at court, a general indifference to the welfare of the colonists, a need for supplies and reinforcements. In 1627, with the formation of the Company of One Hundred Associates, a brighter future seemed in prospect. Heading the list of members was the name of Cardinal Richelieu, and in its Charter, an obligation to colonize served to counterbalance the perpetual grant of fur-trade privileges. With this went the establishment of seigniories, which though then of little significance, suggested an extension to the New World of the feudal system of Europe.

By 1625 the Recollets had come to realize that the vastness of the Indian missions called for more priests from France, and in their need, they turned to the Jesuits for reinforcements. That summer, the first of the "black robes" reached Quebec, and although later years unfortunately brought friction, for the moment the two Orders shared living quarters.

Four years later the English, led by Admiral Kirke, captured Quebec. Despite troops from overseas that failed to arrive and a desperate shortage of food, Champlain held out to the bitter end. But the place was virtually defenseless, being no better than a trading post and its population not more than a hundred souls. In the negotiations that followed, no one attached much importance to Canada. As was the way of royalty, the kings of England and France considered that colonies existed chiefly for their own benefit. So it was that Charles I traded New France back to Louis XIII in return for an overdue payment on his wife's dowry.

The last three years of Champlain's life were happier than the past, for he served the One Hundred Associates as acting Governor of the colony. With the restoration of Quebec, there was some emigration from France, while a more harmonious atmosphere aided the general program of reconstruction. His death in 1635, fittingly, found him at home in his beloved new land.

Chapter 3

1636–1642

Ville-Marie de Montréal. The piety of the founders. Paul de Chomedey, Sieur de Maisonneuve. Jeanne Mance. May 18, 1642, the grain of mustard seed.

THE TINY SETTLEMENT which made its appearance in the summer of 1642 was not altogether the Montreal of which Champlain had dreamed. With some justification, it could be termed the creation of outsiders, whose philosophy was as alien to fur-trading New France as their names were unknown. Their emphasis on the things of the spirit, to the exclusion of monetary gains, ran counter to the pursuits of the often venal merchants. An assumption of political independence aroused jealousy in Quebec—of such intensity that it lingered on for years, a cause of friction between the two communities, and a deterrent to the mutual assistance which both so often needed.

To understand the motives which prompted the launching of this seemingly quixotic venture, it is necessary to recall events in France during the period following the death of Champlain. Under the invigorating influence of the Counter Reformation, the earlier cynicism and indifference was, in many instances, replaced by a devotion to religion and the saving of souls. The Church made notable advances, and nowhere more so than in high places. Piety was very much à la mode at court, the queen, Anne of Austria, giving a lead which society was quick to follow. The wealthy, out of their abundance, provided generously for the conversion of the heathen.

Several factors combined to transform what might otherwise have remained a vague benevolence into a specific North American mission. Some credit at least, must be accorded to Champlain himself, whose published *Voyages* revealed, not only the wonders of the new land, but the heathen darkness of its people. For no matter how great his preoccupation with worldly affairs, he never lost sight of man's spiritual welfare—thus kindling a spark of interest, soon to be fanned into a full blaze by the Jesuits.

Shortly after its return to Quebec in 1632, the Order commenced the publication of *Les Relations,* a remarkable series of volumes whose French title simply means narratives. For over forty years, these appeared annually, each issue being a compilation of on-the-spot accounts of events during the previous twelve months, sent in by the missionaries from all over the colony. Presented first to the Superior in charge at Quebec, and forwarded to the Father Provincial in Paris, the reports were carefully edited before public distribution. Their success was surprising. Readers reacted quickly to their simple tales of hardships and suffering and the stark horror of the martyrs' deaths. Human interest touches lightened their generally somber tone, anecdotes of the colonists and their families, wryly humorous glimpses of the priestly authors and their charges. Illuminating as they are to the modern student, on the fertile soil of the seventeenth century, their impact was explosive.

Jérôme de la Dauversière, it is generally believed, had some knowledge of these matters, at the time of his emergence from obscurity. He was then living at La Flèche in the Province of Anjou, a devout layman whose duties as a tax collector did nothing to tarnish his good repute in the community. The story goes that while on his knees at Mass one morning, he had a vision; miraculously, he found himself charged with the task of founding at Montreal, a hospital and an order of nursing sisters. Having no previous contact with the colony, he was able to talk easily of the Island and his mission. At the suggestion of his priest, he confided the story to a gentleman of the neighborhood, by the name of Baron de Fancamp, and together the two set off for Paris. It was near that city in 1639, that Dauversière met for the first time, a certain Abbé Jacques Olier. Without any previous introduction and before the exchange of a single word, each knew immediately the thoughts of the other. They talked of Montreal.

Of the three men who were thus linked together, each had his own peculiar contribution to make. Dauversière possessed tremendous perseverance. Having little personal fortune, he was tireless in the solution of difficulties. De Fancamp had wealth, which he lavished generously upon Montreal. Olier had long dreamed of founding a new Order of priests, and in later years, his Gentlemen of St. Sulpice were to become Seigneurs of the Island. Meanwhile, through personal connections at court, he was able to win powerful patrons for the cause.

Under these auspices, the Company of Montreal—La Société de Notre Dame de Montréal—was born. Three additional associates joined the original trio; friends of Olier, they were induced to finance the venture. By 1640, the membership had risen to forty-five and included several ladies. At their own wish most remained anonymous. Although the long-range plans were ambitious, they faced immediate problems. The three religious communities of which they dreamed—the secular priests, the nursing sisters, the teaching nuns—these were, of necessity, postponed, pending the acquisition of land and the organization of a settlement.

The Company of One Hundred Associates, still the governing body of New France, had in its service for a time, a rather unscrupulous individual by the name of Jean de Lauzon. Starting in 1636, he had contrived by devious means to become the owner of large portions of the south shore of the St. Lawrence as well as the Island itself. Just what, in the long run, he proposed to do with the property is uncertain. For the present he had returned to a more comfortable life in France, and it was there that the Montreal Associates made their first offer of purchase. This de Lauzon refused, and negotiations dragged on—to yield only after strong pleas from the Jesuits. But his price of 150,000 livres was a stiff one and the title was not clear. Months passed before the change in ownership became final.

From their actions so far, the One Hundred Associates clearly regarded the new group as a purely religious organization whose sole purpose was the conversion of the heathen. And being in financial straits itself, the senior Company insisted on retaining its monopoly of the fur trade, as well as the north shore of the Island and any forts to be built thereon. Yet some civil rights were ceded—the choice of a governor, the establishment of courts of law, the provision of defense measures.

The Montrealers realized that upon their selection of a leader, hinged the success or failure of their endeavors. In addition to assuming charge of the preparations already under way, he must, as the resident governor of the Island, be endowed with administrative ability and moral integrity of a high order. To discover such a paragon was not easy, as Dauversière appreciated, when he undertook to make discreet inquiries as to a possible candidate. In his dilemma, he sought the advice of Father Lalemant, the former Supervisor of the Canadian missions, then by a happy chance in Paris.

As it happened, the Jesuit had only lately been consulted by a young man desirous of devoting his life to service in Canada. As an earnest Christian and an experienced soldier, Paul de Chomedey, Sieur de Maisonneuve possessed the basic qualities needed for the position. To bring the two together, proved to be an easy matter. Armed with the address of Maisonneuve's hotel, Dauversière lost no time in taking up residence there, and quite casually, struck up an acquaintance with the other. First impressions being favorable, meal table talk in the presence of the other guests soon developed into a series of private conversations. There was never much doubt of the outcome.

To write dispassionately of Maisonneuve is not easy, for the more one reads the words of his contemporaries, the more praiseworthy he becomes. He was, at this date, nearly thirty years of age, the only son of a comfortably well-to-do family of Champagne. From his youth, he had served in the army, as valiant against the enemy as he was firm in his Christian faith. As he grew older, his abhorrence of dissipation and the vanities of the world, turned him into a solitary individual, who grasped at the prospect of work in Canada as a release from an uncongenial environment. He was to show himself single-minded in his labors on behalf of Montreal, and no hint of self-seeking ever marred his reputation. Puritanical he undoubtedly was, by the standards of the twentieth century, yet history was to show that he could be warmly human.

That such a man should refuse to accept any recompense, might be construed as a mere reflection of his personal wealth, yet his generosity went deeper. Dollier de Casson, writing soon after the events, reported that the Governor often went hungry, taking the good food from his own table so that his men might be fed. And when, on one occasion, he met a tailor, a fine fellow but disconsolate at having nothing to trade with the Indians, Maisonneuve cut down the curtains from his bed, to be fashioned into cloaks and bartered for furs.

In the seventeenth century, most of the vessels bound for New France, sailed from La Rochelle, and the Montreal group was no exception. The preparations, already under way, intensified with Maisonneuve's arrival. What might be termed the normal procedures, were complicated by the need to exercise care in the selection of colonists. Physical fitness and the ability to bear arms were, of course, the basic requirements; skilled artisans, particularly if unmarried, were given the preference. Of equal importance was their Catholic faith, strong enough, it was hoped, to serve as an example to the Indians.

The question of including a woman in their number, seems to have arisen suddenly—one who could look after the supplies and nurse the sick—one, moreover, willing to face the privations and dangers inseparable from pioneer life. Unknown to Maisonneuve and his companions, such a heroine was near at hand.

Judged by worldly standards, Jeanne Mance was an unlikely candidate, if for no other reason than her delicate health. Nor had she as yet found her vocation for in spite of a piety far above the average, the secluded life of the cloister held no appeal. Yet her anxiety to serve mankind, brooked no denial, and because of nursing experience gained during the civil wars, she began about 1640, to think seriously of similar work in Canada.

A consultation with Father Lalemant brought in its turn, an introduction to Madame de Bullion, and after that, events moved quickly for the two women became friends, the one a wealthy and charitable widow, the other a humble volunteer for the mission field. It was to be an association of inestimable value

to Montreal in the years ahead, an initial gift of money to found a
hospital on the Island being followed by others, all under the
veil of secrecy. For Madame de Bullion remained at her own
wish, the unknown benefactress—a polite fiction to which both
Maisonneuve and Jeanne Mance subscribed without fail.

After this auspicious send-off, Jeanne Mance set off from Paris,
traveling on horseback to La Rochelle in quest of an uncertain
future. Frail that she was, such a journey could only be an ordeal,
no less trying than her arrival at the rough seaport. To make
matters worse, her family were strongly opposed to her Canadian
plans. But a first meeting with Dauversière and Maisonneuve
restored her spirits, both men being as warm in their welcome as
they were genuinely thoughtful of her welfare.

Three ships comprised the expedition, one from Dieppe and
two from La Rochelle. Maisonneuve, with twenty-five men,
boarded one of the latter, and Jeanne Mance with another dozen
colonists, the second of the pair. Both sailed in June 1641, and
promptly encountered bad weather.

There had been little change in seagoing vessels during the
hundred years that had passed since Cartier's voyages. They were
small and decidedly uncomfortable; with sails as the only means
of propulsion, they were at the mercy of the elements. Given
fine weather and favoring winds, the crossing might be accomplished in three weeks. In the teeth of gales and high seas, it
could stretch out to several months. Food was as meager in quantity as it was poor in quality, and fresh water to drink almost
unknown. Sea sickness was the common lot, the Jesuits often
bemoaning their weakness in this respect. Privacy was non-existent, especially when storms forced the passengers down to the
shelter of the hold belowdecks. Plague and other contagious
diseases were common and mortality rates high.

In this instance, the ship bearing Jeanne Mance reached the
St. Lawrence first, its smooth waters a relief after the ordeal of
the Atlantic. As she prepared to go ashore at Quebec on August
8, she seems to have felt confident of her welcome; a common
zeal for the conversion of the heathen would surely unite all
who lived in New France.

Nothing, unfortunately, could have been farther from reality.

The first blow fell with the absence of any news of Maisonneuve. No one knew anything of his progress, and three long weeks were to pass before his arrival, safe but weary after a tempestuous passage. As for the people of Quebec during this anxious period of waiting, their cold glances and malicious words disconcerted Jeanne Mance to such an extent that only in the company of the warmhearted Madame de la Peltrie did she enjoy any sympathy or understanding.

Maisonneuve himself quickly sensed the bitter feelings, since virtually everyone from Governor de Montmagny down, inveighed against the folly of setting up yet another feeble colony and in the most perilous location imaginable. It was a viewpoint based on sound reason, for New France was feeble and beset by dangers. The entire population did not exceed two hundred, and there was a desperate need of reinforcements. Communication between Quebec and the upper river was difficult, if not impossible. The Iroquois infested all routes of travel, so insolent that Father Lejeune feared the loss of the country. "They hunt men as we do wild beasts."

The horrors of the threatened warfare were such as to make the foolish enterprise a subject of public discussion. As an alternative to Montreal, de Montmagny suggested a location on the fertile Island of Orléans. Its proximity to Quebec would make settlement relatively easy, and lighten the burden of defense. To this tempting proposition, as indeed to all the doubts and criticisms, Maisonneuve had but one response: "I have not come here to deliberate but to act. It is my duty and my honor to found a colony at Montreal, and I would go, if every tree were an Iroquois."

With this, the opposition crumbled, de Montmagny taking the lead in making amends. Because the season was late, Maisonneuve had already decided against any attempt at a permanent establishment in 1641. Instead, he proposed a short visit, for the purpose of taking formal possession of the Island in the name of his Company. The Governor, still intent on peacemaking, offered to accompany him. So it was that the two went off together with Father Vimont, carrying out their mission successfully in October.

The winter in Quebec was a quiet one, each man busy in his own way with preparations for spring and the move to Montreal. A kindly resident of Ste. Foy allowed his house to be used as their headquarters, and there the colonists grew to know each other, a necessary development in the light of the dangers ahead. There was no lack of occupation. While the carpenters constructed boats, suitable for the shallow waters of the river, others toiled at the Company's storehouse, where a great assortment of supplies had to be checked and packed. Jeanne Mance was a tower of strength in the management of the provisions, yet still found time for almost daily visits to the hospital at Sillery. There she dressed wounds and treated frostbite and chilblains, compounded her own medicines and gained experience in bloodletting.

Spring comes late in eastern Canada, and, as a consequence, the ice in the St. Lawrence is slow to disappear. Nowadays, with modern equipment, the main channels are cleared early in the season, permitting a prompt opening of navigation which contrasts sharply with the past. But so long as travel was possible only by water, just so long did each hamlet exist in isolation during the annual freeze-up. For many years, communication between Montreal and Quebec ceased entirely during the winter, while answers to letters, mailed to France during the summer, would only be received twelve months later.

Thus it is not surprising to find that in the spring of 1642, the Montrealers did not get under way until May, leaving Quebec on the eighth and camping out on shore each night, to reach the Island on the seventeenth. They moved slowly, in flat-bottomed boats and big canoes, heavily laden with supplies, propelled by oars and paddles and fighting against the current all the way. The passenger list was impressive, for de Montmagny accompanied Maisonneuve, Jeanne Mance was there and Madame de la Peltrie, Father Vimont, and the main body of the colonists— some forty-five persons in all.

The next morning they landed at Place Royale, the very spot selected by Champlain thirty years earlier. It was a glorious day, warm and sunny and the surroundings peaceful, a day set aside for prayer and thanksgiving. An altar, quickly raised, was adorned with wild flowers gathered by Jeanne Mance and Madame de la Peltrie, and at the conclusion of Mass, Father Vimont spoke prophetically. "You are a grain of mustard seed, that shall rise and grow till its branches overshadow the earth. You are few, but your work is the work of God. His smile is on you, and your children shall fill the land." It was an impressive scene, this birthday of the great city, and as the darkness fell, a touch of magic was added. For the ladies gathered fireflies and hung them in a phial before the altar.

During the days that followed, there was work for all, in the creation of a temporary encampment. Although some trees had been cut by Champlain during his visits, more clearing became necessary, de Montmagny felling the first before his return to Quebec. The timber, shaped into stakes, provided a palisade and a makeshift protection against attack. Behind it stood the tents, probably of birch bark and shaped like Indian tepees. A tiny chapel arose, primitive and rough, its only door a sheet. Everything was made of the simplest materials and in the shortest time possible.

All through the summer the construction continued while the boats plied constantly between Montreal and Quebec, ferrying supplies. New arrivals appeared, increasing the population to seventy. They were artisans for the most part, among them a clever carpenter named Gilbert Barbier, nicknamed Le Minime. Under his direction, a start was made at erecting structures of a more permanent nature, against the coming of winter. August saw the completion of a new chapel, a wooden frame building about ten feet square that was to serve the colony until 1659. It was back-breaking toil, but *Les Relations* reported the men as having sound bodies and teeth. "The air of New France is very healthy for the soul and the body."

The approach of cold weather compelled other preparations. The piles of firewood grew higher, and the first crops of corn and other vegetables were brought in from the fields. But above all, the summer and autumn provided a breathing space in which to learn the ways of the new land. As though by a miracle, the Iroquois were slow to discover the existence of Montreal, and the resultant interlude of peace was all the sweeter for being unexpected. And so the writers of the period lingered over their descriptions of the beauty of the flowers and the trees, and the musical warblings of the birds. The only jarring note, in fact, came from the mosquitoes and flies, and they were rated a perpetual nuisance.

Before the closing of navigation, there was fresh cause for joy at the news from Paris. At the Church of Notre Dame in that city, the members of the Company of Montreal had gathered in February for the celebration of a special Mass. There the Island had been dedicated to the Holy Family and placed under the protection of the Virgin Mary. Henceforth, this, the newest of the settlements of New France, proudly bore the title of Ville-Marie de Montréal.

Chapter 4

1642–1652

The start of the Iroquois wars and the long agony of the settlers. The Fort. The first Hôtel Dieu. The Letters Patent. The colony endangered.

FOR SEVERAL CENTURIES, it was the fashion among travelers to hymn the praises of Montreal's winters. French and English alike, those who had experienced the arctic rigors of the lower river enjoyed the milder temperature of the Island. Whether with reason is open to doubt, and certainly not in the case of its earliest citizens. Under the most favorable conditions, theirs was a rugged and uncomfortable existence—made infinitely worse when in December, the St. Lawrence overflowed its banks, flooding their homes and threatening their safety. Apart from taking refuge on the higher ground, there was nothing to be done except to pray. Maisonneuve planted a little cross at the water's edge, and vowed, should the river subside, to bear another and a larger one up the mountainside. This he was able to do on the Feast of the Epiphany, the danger being past. Struggling along a freshly dug track through the snow, he carried his burden to the summit, and there around a crude altar, the community assembled for a special service of thanksgiving.

Spring found the men once more at work in the fields, clearing the land in preparation for the new crops. Having lived on the Island for a year undisturbed by the enemy, they began to feel at home and to think hopefully of the future. Hence their shock when in June the war flared up—a surprise attack on six men cutting wood near the Fort. Although they fought desperately against the Iroquois, the odds were too great; three French were killed and three taken prisoner. No one had time to help them, the raid was so unexpected and over so quickly.

In this respect, the encounter set a pattern, for it marked the commencement of almost twenty years of ruthless warfare between the Five Nations and the French and their Indian allies. Intermittently and officially, there would be peace, though rarely in actuality. New France suffered, and Montreal most of all. As the fighting took its toll of lives, any vestige of normality became impossible.

For Maisonneuve in particular, the test was severe. Throughout this period of danger, he alone was the government and his the full burden of responsibility. The tributes of his contemporaries suggest that he met the challenge with success. *Les Relations* considered him especially inspired by God and divinely called to service at Montreal. Obedience, it is recorded, was a pleasure, for he was loved and respected by all. Despite differing temperaments, he fostered unity and good understanding among his people, welding them into a true community, monastic in its strict simplicity and reminiscent of the primitive church.

Fortunately the main building of the settlement had been completed several months before the first attack. The stone Fort or Château, as it was often called, was of considerable size, and flanked by the chapel and storehouse. A wooden palisade, surmounted by small pieces of artillery, lent an illusion of protection. Into its cramped space, the people now crowded, and there, except for brief respites, they lived for ten years. Outside its shelter, the strictest discipline prevailed. By Maisonneuve's order, sentries kept constant watch, and no one walked alone, no matter how tempting the summer sunshine. All were governed by the sound of the bell—including the men, bearing arms, as they came and went, morning and evening, to their work in the fields.

At least in the early days, the number of combatants on both sides was small, and their encounters did not always develop into pitched battles. The Iroquois literally haunted Montreal, lurking in the woods or crouching behind tree stumps, motionless and endlessly patient, in bands or alone, lying in wait for any unwary colonist. Father Vimont labeled them as monsters, hydras, and demons. "I would almost as soon be besieged by goblins as by the Iroquois. The latter are hardly more visible than the former. When they are far away, we think they are at our doors, and when they fling themselves on their prey, we imagine that they are in their own country."

Beyond the confines of the Island, the situation was equally grave, for the enemy seemed to be everywhere, particularly along the rivers, ready to pounce on any foolhardy traveler. Communication with Quebec was so perilous that when, later in the summer, a convoy of boats neared the Island, no one save Maisonneuve dared go down to the shore to meet them. That their passengers included sorely needed reinforcements did not lessen the fear of ambush. Yet in the leader of the new group, Montreal gained a staunch defender, for Louis d'Ailleboust, an engineer as well as a soldier, lost no time in getting to work. Uprooting the wooden stakes around the Fort, he replaced them with four stone bastions, stronger than any yet built in New France.

Thus far, there had been so few demands for nursing care that one or two rooms in the mission house had sufficed to shelter the minor injuries of pioneer life. Meanwhile, Jeanne Mance occupied herself with the supervision of the supplies and the general business of the colony. It was a situation bound to change of itself, althought not to such an extent as Madame de Bullion made possible. In a letter carried by d'Ailleboust, the unknown benefactress proposed that a hospital be built in Montreal, its cost to be met from a fund she had set aside for the purpose.

The site of the first Hôtel Dieu was chosen with care, so as to avoid any danger from floods. The four acres of ground at the corner of the present St. Paul and St. Sulpice streets stood on a slight elevation, near but above the Fort. Inside the usual palisade, the building went up, sixty feet long and twenty-five wide and all of wood. Its four compartments provided two wards for the patients and accommodation for Jeanne Mance and the attendants. Attached to one side was the chapel. Two oxen, three cows, and twenty sheep completed the establishment. Almost a year passed in its planning and construction, and its opening date of October 1644, came none too soon, in view of what lay ahead.

Throughout this period of danger the colonists derived great comfort from their dogs, whose ability to detect the presence of the enemy was nothing short of uncanny. Each morning the famous Pilotte led her pups out on a scouting foray around the Fort, turning her head from side to side, sniffing into the wind to catch an elusive scent and then barking furiously as she rushed home to raise the alarm. Not content with her own accomplishments, this stern parent trained her family along similar lines, biting without mercy those who in the daily chase preferred squirrels to Iroquois.

One morning in March, when Pilotte's barks were sharper than usual, some of the younger men begged for permission to go out and fight the elusive enemy. That they should openly speak thus, reflected some discontent at Maisonneuve's refusal to engage in open combat. Hints of cowardice had so far failed to sway the Governor, who knew only too well the weakness of his garrison.

But perhaps Maisonneuve was at last nettled by the idle talk of a few hotheads, for he prepared, surprisingly enough, to take the offensive, leading his party of thirty out from the stockade to attack the unseen foes. The walking underfoot was difficult, the winter snow turning soft and treacherous under the strong spring sun. Unskilled as yet in the use of snowshoes, the French walked into an ambush, and the blood-curdling war whoops of a hundred warriors rang out on the air.

By this date, the Iroquois had come into possession of fire-arms, and so, as Maisonneuve ordered his men to take shelter among the trees, they faced a brisk barrage of shots. Several of the French were killed or captured, and those who survived, fought on without much hope of victory. At last, when the ammunition ran out, their commander ordered a retreat, he himself bringing up the rear, apparently fearless and as steady as though on parade. Stumbling by good luck onto a rough footpath, the men raced headlong into the now thoroughly alarmed Fort.

Meanwhile outside, Maisonneuve stood firm, a pistol in each hand, keeping the attackers at bay until his party reached safety. The enemy soon identified him as the leader, and their chief singled him out for personal combat. As the redskin advanced,

Maisonneuve fired his first pistol. It missed fire. The Iroquois
leaped forward once more, only to be met by the bullets of
the second pistol. Death was instantaneous. In the confusion of
the moment, the Indians bent on rescuing the body of their chief,
Maisonneuve made good his escape. There was no more talk of
unwillingness to fight.

Although this battle was more spectacular than usual, it was
in fact only one among many brushes with the Iroquois. That
most were minor affairs made little difference to Montreal, which
remained in a state of virtual siege. The enemy controlled the
country so completely that for a time, no less than ten groups of
warriors maintained a chain of look-out posts from Three Rivers
up to Montreal and beyond. Cunning and watchful by nature,
they possessed an overwhelming superiority, for in spite of Dutch
largesse, the French so far had refused to provide guns for any
of their Indian allies.

Thus there was no hope of mounting an effective assault
against the omnipresent enemy, and even the simplest holding
operations were difficult. In all New France, the population
numbered no more than three or four hundred persons, including
women and ecclesiastics, and reinforcements were slow to arrive.

Not all the Indians who visited Montreal were enemies, for
there was always a certain ebb and flow of the friendly Hurons
and Algonquins. Their number fluctuated, depending on the
severity of the fighting and the risks involved in bringing their
canoes down the St. Lawrence. There are records of the baptism
of some of these savages, and indeed, the Jesuits in their writings,
reveal the expectation that ultimately a large population of Indians would regard the Island as their home. In this priestly
view, it was destined to become the site of a truly Christian city,
a meeting place of the white man and the red, where all could
learn the arts of peace and live in harmony with their neighbors.

Meanwhile the sponsors in France found themselves in difficulties. That some arose because of idle gossip, made their position all the more vulnerable. There seems little doubt that jealousy accounted for many of the rumors—especially since the
Company of One Hundred Associates showed itself fearful of

the rival group, active and conscientious in fulfilling their promises as the merchants had never been. But for whatever cause, the critics said openly that the Charter of Montreal should be canceled, it being presumptuous for lay people, and above all for ladies, to undertake the conversion of the heathen.

Luckily for Montreal, there had already been signs of approval from those in high places. Louis XIII, near the close of his life, wrote to de Montmagny, bidding him assist Maisonneuve in every way possible, and the same policy, carried over into the reign of Louis XIV, resulted in the Letters Patent of February 1644. Since the young king was then but five years old, the royal wishes were for the moment, expressed by his mother, the Queen Regent, acting on the advice of those who governed France during the minority.

Nevertheless, the Letters were extremely important, for they placed the Company of Montreal directly under the protection of the Crown, and provided for the first time, an official definition of the status of the community. By their spelling out the rights of the inhabitants, they confirmed the assumptions of the past—the privilege of choosing their own governors, of erecting such forts as might be necessary, of peopling the Island with colonists, French or Indian, as seemed fitting. Thus Montreal, in relation to Quebec, became an autonomous town within the boundaries of New France, in full control of its own affairs except for the fur trade. This, with all its potential profits, was still reserved for the Company of One Hundred Associates at a time when its monopoly elsewhere, was under fire.

However unpopular the One Hundred Associates may have been in the past, public discontent came to a head early in 1645. The resentment, centered at Quebec, went beyond the iniquities of the merchants to attack their general indifference to the colony's needs. As a remedy, the critics proposed the formation of a Canadian company, going so far as to send a delegation to France to state their grievances. With complete success, let it be said, for the Community of Habitants was formed—an organization to which the One Hundred Associates surrendered their exclusive trading privileges in return for a release from their obligations to colonize.

When the Associates of Montreal heard of this, they realized that the interests of their town must be safeguarded. Therefore, in their turn, they entered into an agreement with the Habitants, which after stressing the friendship between Montreal and Quebec, stated that the former should be permitted to operate a fur-trading store, the profits to be divided between the two.

It was one thing to acquire on paper the right to participate in the fur trade; to secure delivery of the pelts was another matter. The lean years wiped out the occasional windfall, and the Iroquois stranglehold on the rivers continued. For this reason de Montmagny put out peace feelers, using as a lever some captives then in the hands of the French. Rebuffed by four of the Confederacy tribes, the Mohawks surprisingly agreed to a parley. But even this partial success, resulted after September 1645, in a greater volume of furs at the Island.

The truce—which no one dared believe would be of long duration—afforded an opportunity for Maisonneuve to visit France, and for his deputy, d'Ailleboust, freedom to strengthen the fortifications. At the same time, he took advantage of the unwonted calm to encourage the local farmers in their efforts to become more self-sufficient—greatly helped, it might be added, by the example of the young Charles Le Moyne, newly returned from a four year stint at the Jesuit mission on Lake Huron.

Maisonneuve was, of course, sorely missed during his twelve months' absence, yet as events turned out, it was fortunate that he was available for meetings at Quebec and Paris. The chief topic of discussion was the Community of Habitants, all too soon fallen upon evil days. Prosperity had proved a temptation to some of its number, and criticism of their high living was rife. The climax came when the administrative members decided to increase their own salaries; Maisonneuve, the most modest of men, was shocked. His indignation was so obvious as to attract official attention, and out of this developed another set of regulations for New France.

By this decree of 1647, the control of the entire colony was vested in a three member Council, composed of the Governor General, the Governor of Montreal, and the Superior of the Jesuits, there being as yet no Bishop. In 1648, it was enlarged by the addition of three habitants, chosen to represent the people. Overshadowed for the moment by the ferocity of the newly resumed Iroquois war, the Council nevertheless represented a long step forward in the administration of New France.

When, late in 1646, two colonists were taken prisoner by the marauders, their seizure heralded the start of what has been termed, a time of troublous vexations. Once again, the fur trade petered out, and Montreal suffered anew the threat of the endlessly patient warriors, hidden and immobile, waiting only for the chance to ambush some unsuspecting soul. Maisonneuve returned, to hear that the prophets of evil foresaw the end of the settlement on the Island.

To combat these conditions, de Montmagny in 1647 organized a flying column, assigning it to patrol duties along the St. Lawrence between Montreal and Three Rivers during the fur-trading seasons. In the winter, its forty members were distributed among the several settlements, to supplement the regular garrisons. During the four years of its existence, the corps performed yeoman service.

But France considered that de Montmagny had not been sufficiently vigorous in his conduct of the Iroquois war, and so 1647 saw his recall. Maisonneuve, the first choice to replace him as Governor General, refused, and the honor then fell to d'Ailleboust, who paid his initial visit to the Island in his new role in the spring of 1649. He carried bad news from France, where the earlier enthusiasm of the Company of Montreal had vanished. Of the original group, only nine remained active, and the future looked doubtful.

Under these circumstances, Jeanne Mance acted with vigor, sailing for France in September and returning to Montreal twelve months later. In Paris, she was received by Madame de Bullion with the usual kindness, and given money for the hospital. As for the surviving Associates, she succeeded in reawakening their interest to the point that all signed a new deed, accepting mutual responsibility, thus strengthening the existing Act which bore only the names of Dauversière and de Fancamp.

But Jeanne Mance, having saved the day overseas, returned to a Montreal saddened and alarmed at the news from the west.

These were the years in which the Iroquois set out to destroy the entire Huron nation, the scene of the Jesuits' most ambitious mission. Traditional enemies, the two tribal groups had become bitter rivals in the fur trade and the weaker must go. The warriors of the Five Nations swept through village after village, killing, capturing, burning, until nothing remained. Nor was the slaughter confined to the natives, for Father Bréboeuf and Father Gabriel Lalemant met the cruel deaths of martyrdom. Montreal was powerless, and its people could only watch aghast, each day, the terrible spectacle of the Hurons, fleeing from the horrors of their homes. Having lost everything, they pressed on to Quebec, anxious only to put as much space as possible between themselves and the enemy.

Paradoxically, the decision to exterminate the Hurons, brought a respite to Montreal, for Iroquois strategy never permitted their warriors to fight simultaneously on two fronts. Any hint of peace was, of course, a mirage, but while it lasted, there was a faint air of hope on the Island. The colonists were weary of their pent-up mode of living. Obtaining concessions of land from Maisonneuve, they proceeded to clear the fields in preparation for their new homes; still grouped together near the Fort, these were to be outside the walls. The more trees they felled, the further the edge of the forest receded, so that concealment for the lurking warriors, in future, would be less easy. By 1651, the community rights on the Common received official recognition—a long narrow stretch of land along the riverbank, where the cattle grazed under the care of a watchman. A few optimists dared to hope that someday, the nearby mill might be converted to peaceful use. So far, it had served chiefly as an advanced redoubt, its loopholes pierced for muskets.

But as the summer of 1651 wore on, the falsity of all such ideas became obvious. The enemy assault on the Island broke out afresh, more furious than ever. Montreal lay exposed, kept alive from day to day by the heroism of its people. As the peril spread, d'Ailleboust kept his flying column on the move, deploying them speedily and at the points of greatest urgency, while he pleaded with France for reinforcements.

Dramatic episodes crowd the records of Montreal during these critical years. Taken as a whole, they reflect the courage of the common people, for the suffering was not confined to the military. A Huron woman working in the fields, was carried off by the Iroquois, together with two of her children. A Frenchman tending cattle, was put to death, and a woman nearby, received five or six wounds. More fortunate than most, she survived, the chronicler saying that her courage carried her through. Jean Boutard was killed when he tried to rescue his wife, Catherine, from the clutches of fifty warriors. A helpless captive, she was burned alive, after her tormentors had cut off her breasts, her nose, and her ears.

As the terrors mounted, Maisonneuve ordered his people to leave their new homes and retire into the greater safety of the Fort. Jeanne Mance abandoned the hospital, which became a military outpost with soldiers always on duty. Loopholes were cut in its walls, and the chapel served as an armory for the small cannon mounted outside. A serious struggle ensued when two hundred Iroquois, hidden in a trench, attempted to capture the building and set it on fire. The defenders, who numbered sixteen, fought all day under the command of Lambert Closse, the town major, and finally for all the odds, forced the enemy to retreat.

Whether large or small, a succession of such engagements reduced the number of Montreal's effective force to about fifty men, and neither Quebec nor Three Rivers could lend any assistance. France did not seem to realize to what extremities her people overseas had been reduced, and again the defeatists said the country must be abandoned.

It was then that Jeanne Mance again showed her good sense, for she reminded Maisonneuve her benefactress had set aside a large sum of money for the hospital. If Montreal were abandoned, obviously there would be no Hôtel Dieu. Why not use its endowment to bring out more men from France? Maisonneuve, she urged, should leave immediately for overseas, first to secure Madame de Bullion's consent to the diversion, and secondly to seek for recruits. It seemed the only solution, yet as he left, the Governor promised that if he were unable to find a hundred men, he would not return. Jeanne Mance was then to take all the colonists back to France, and leave the Island unpeopled.

For those left behind, the recall of d'Ailleboust was cold comfort, for he had always been a good friend to Montreal. In his stead, the king appointed Jean de Lauzon, the infamous owner of the Island at the time of its original settlement. Although he now professed to be well disposed to its people, his actions hardly matched his fine words. His suppression of the flying squad in 1652, fell at a time when the fighting was at its worst. But under Lambert Closse, the defense was vigorous. Heroic himself, he was an inspiration to his men, and an attack on one was regarded as an attack on all. At the sound of even a single shot, the settlers ran to rescue the person under fire.

So impossible did communication become that hearsay often took the place of facts. In the spring of 1653, after the adventures of the phantom ship, Quebec announced that Montreal had been blotted out. The pinnace, dispatched up the river by de Lauzon, sailed under strict orders to remain aloof from the Fort, unless the commander had proof that the French were still in possession. When he arrived, nothing was visible in the thick fog; anchored off in the stream, he and his men listened and peered through the mist to no avail. Then, having seen no one and heard nothing, they returned to Quebec in literal obedience to their instructions. Meanwhile, inside the Fort, several of those on duty swore they had seen a vessel in the river, a claim promptly denied by those whose vision was less keen. When later, the haze lifted, there was nothing. Surely, the doubters said, this had been a figment of the imagination.

Chapter 5
1653–1660

War and peace with the Iroquois. New recruits for the settlement. Marguerite Bourgeoys. The Parish Church. Notre Dame de Bonsecours. The Gentlemen of St. Sulpice. Disputes with Quebec. Bishop Laval. Dollard des Ormeaux.

MAISONNEUVE'S STAY in France proved to be a long one, stretching out beyond the twelve months he had thought would be sufficient. It was a time of anxiety, on both sides of the Atlantic.

The interview with Madame de Bullion went off well, and afterwards, with becoming modesty, Maisonneuve confessed himself as pleased at his own diplomacy. That she should offer no objection to the proposed diversion of hospital funds, was almost a foregone conclusion. Her second donation for the same purpose, was perhaps more unexpected. Out of 75,000 livres provided for the expedition, the unknown benefactress gave 42,000.

When Maisonneuve turned to the procurement of men, his progress was less satisfactory. Just as in 1640, he looked for piety and sound morals, over and above any trade skills—qualities not easily found in exactly the right combination. In any case, there was no longer much eagerness to go out to Montreal. Perhaps the enthusiasm for missionary work had passed its zenith. A more likely cause of the apathy lay in the exaggerated tales drifting back from New France; the severity of the winters, the cruelty of the Indians, the strong possibility of never again seeing one's home.

After considerable delay, Maisonneuve was obliged to hire the recruits more or less on their own terms. They were to emigrate under five-year contracts, their board and lodging during that period to be paid by the Company. They were, in addition, to receive full wages, according to the going rates in the different trades. A free passage home was guaranteed. In the end, one hundred and eighteen signed on, of whom sixty were laborers and plowmen, the remainder a mixed bag of artisans; carpenters, masons, shoemakers, even a pastry cook.

Shortly before their sailing date, Marguerite Bourgeoys joined the party. She was then in her early thirties, a laywoman and a teacher who had volunteered to start a school in Montreal. Like Jeanne Mance, she was a rare phenomenon in that age of piety. Both were dedicated daughters of the Church, yet both, out of strong conviction, remained in the world. Because of this freedom from the restrictions of the cloister, they—and their assistants—served early Montreal in ways that would have been impossible for organized communities of nuns. That each in later life, became closely associated with new Orders, reflected not so much a change of heart, as the growth and progress within the settlement itself. Until that happier time, ecclesiastical opposition and public criticism alike, proved powerless to alter a stand, so strongly based on reason.

But for Marguerite Bourgeoys as for the other newcomers, the 1652 voyage to New France may well have seemed interminable. Their first ship was so old and leaky that everyone feared it would sink. Returning to port, a second vessel was so full of infection that eight of the men died on the way over. That the other patients recovered, was attributed to the excellence of the nursing. Not until late in September did they land at Quebec, to be greeted by Jeanne Mance. In the extremity of her anxiety, she had come down the river in search of news.

It was a happy reunion, which even Governor de Lauzon could not entirely spoil. At first, he forbade the expedition to leave; the men were needed in Quebec. Confronted with a letter from the king, he relented although not to the point of providing transportation. The delay in finding boats, meant that Montreal was not reached until mid-November. There, it need hardly be said, the welcome more than compensated for the frustrations and difficulties.

Maisonneuve returned to a country officially at peace with

some of the tribes—a twilight zone in which events could easily move in either direction. No one could say how long such a truce might last, nor define its scope. It was a situation admirably suited to the subtle minds of the Iroquois. Sometimes in their dealings with the white man, the Five Nations acted as a unit, at others, a split into tribal groups permitted independent policies. But always, the enemy felt free to descend upon Montreal in small groups, blandly disowning if caught, any knowledge of treaties or negotiations. For this reason, the settlers remained permanently on the *qui vive,* knowing full well the dangers of ambush.

Thus the absorption of the new arrivals into the community took place in conditions less tense than in the immediate past. The transients with their five-year contracts, were in time induced to regard themselves as permanent residents. Subsequent grants of land and money spurred on this highly desirable evolution. Meanwhile their arrival was an inspiration to the older settlers, weary after a decade of hardship and danger.

There is little doubt that by this date, Montrealers were heartily tired of their life, cooped-up behind the stockade of the Fort. Their earlier attempt to leave its sheltering walls had been abortive, and the Iroquois war had wiped out much of what they had done. Now with renewed courage, they made a fresh start, helping each other in turn to build little wooden shacks on their one-acre allotments. Within a few years, a village sprang up, its forty-odd houses straggling along in two rows that faced each other across a rough track. Without any semblance of planning, they offered little that was pleasing to the eye.

This new settlement stood on higher ground than the Fort, for the latter was always uncomfortably damp and subject to flooding at high water. As time passed, the old enclosure was abandoned, and the bastions, damaged by ice, left to crumble into ruins. Instead, each house was considered a fortress, its walls pierced with loopholes, and each man pledged to go to the rescue of his neighbors whenever threatened by attack. Blockhouses at strategic points, did much to deflect the danger, while the sinking of wells at a later date, rendered unnecessary the risky sorties to the St. Lawrence for water. But still, as the farmers worked in the fields, the sentries stood on the alert; even with so-called peace, the precautions stayed in force.

The truce permitted Jeanne Mance to return to the hospital, after its long occupancy by the garrison. Maisonneuve directed the construction of a larger building, protected by two redoubts with small cannon. A double chimney at one end, made for greater comfort in the wards and kitchen. And in more ways than one, a better care of the patients became possible, since three surgeons arrived with the 1652 contingent. Undoubtedly, in the fashion of the day, they doubled as barbers, but one of their number, Etienne Bouchard, soon offered his medical services to all heads of families, the born and the unborn alike, upon payment of a small annual fee.

At the outset, Marguerite Bourgeoys lived at the Fort, supervising the Governor's household and helping in the community wherever there was need. That she should thus postpone her teaching program simply meant that there were virtually no children of school age in Montreal. During the first twelve years of the settlement there had only been ten weddings; few women could face the hardships of its life. In 1654, however, thirteen ceremonies were recorded, and thereafter their number increased steadily. When the brides arrived from France, their care gradually devolved upon Marguerite Bourgeoys. Not only did she assume the duties of a chaperone, but she took many of the girls to live with her, watching over their behavior and training them in simple household arts.

The increase in population was such as to suggest the need for a church. Although the two original chapels were still in use— the one at the Fort, the other at the Hôtel Dieu—they were already inadequate. By 1656, the foundations of the new edifice had been laid, and within two years, it was completed. Dedicated to St. Joseph, it stood near the hospital, its wooden framework embellished with a tower from which twin bells rang out the call to divine worship. Outwardly, it was more impressive than anything yet attempted, and with the election of wardens, became the Parish Church.

A stone stable nearby was turned over to Marguerite Bourgeoys; it had served earlier as a shelter for cattle. Nothing daunted, she had it cleaned and a chimney erected. The granary above, became living quarters. In these humble surroundings during the spring of 1658, Montreal's first school was opened. At the outset, the class included all the children of the settlement, Indian as well as French, Father Souart assuming the responsibility of teaching the boys.

The Chapel of Notre Dame de Bonsecours, in its original form, dates from the same period. In every sense, it was the creation of Marguerite Bourgeoys. Hers was the inspiration and hers the responsibility for seeing the project through to completion. She herself is said to have carried some of the stones placed in its foundation. The work commenced in the spring of 1657, much of the labor and material being contributed by the settlers. It progressed slowly, and was halted for a time lest there be competition with the Parish Church. Later a stone edifice replaced the first wooden structure. Yet though time has brought changes, Bonsecours Church still stands, a permanent memorial to the faith of this one woman, and the scene of divine service since about the year 1659.

At this point, it is well to remember that the improvements undertaken in the years following 1653, were carried through to completion in an atmosphere of constant uneasiness. The line of separation between peace and war was never altogether clear, and intermittent raids served as reminders of the danger. If not always mortally serious, their nuisance value was high; the warriors still stalked their prey.

Thus the alarm bell sounded in the spring of 1654 at the sight of a large flotilla of canoes descending the rapids. There was a general standing to arms, quickly relaxed as the identity of the paddlers was discerned. They were Algonquins and Hurons, the bearers of a tremendous cargo of furs. In the previous seasons, Montreal had not secured a single pelt. Two years later, another great load of beaver was brought down, this time by the Ottawas from the Great Lakes region. But it was already evident that the destruction of the Huron villages had disrupted the normal routes of trade. With so many of the intermediaries killed, the traders of New France in future, would have to go farther afield.

Although the profits of such bumper seasons went far in

redressing the precarious financial situation of the colony, they were insufficient to wipe out the accumulation of debts. Perhaps Quebec under an honest governor, might have fared better, but de Lauzon tried to monopolize the traffic. Always inclined to be jealous, he bore down especially hard on Montreal, even closing its storehouse in the older city. A series of petty restrictions made him cordially disliked by the entire country, with the result that no one regretted his decision to resign.

If such unpleasant episodes seem short-lived, they were not without significance. They occurred just as a new series of disputes broke out between Montreal and Quebec, more bitter and long-lasting than any previously recorded. At first ecclesiastical, eventually they spread through the entire area of government. The root of the argument lay in Montreal's standing as an autonomous community—located within the boundaries of New France but by no means subservient. Given such an ambiguous relationship, a clash with Quebec sooner or later, was perhaps unavoidable. That it happened to arise over the selection of priests and nursing sisters was as much as anything, due to the personalities involved.

During the quarter century that followed Kirke's occupation of Quebec, all religious ministrations remained in the hands of the Jesuits. Theirs was a heavy obligation, embracing as it did, the conversion of the savages and the spiritual care of the settlers. Naturally they had gone to Montreal in 1642, and equally naturally they had remained there as the priests in charge of the Island. It was not until the growth of population in the 1650s turned men's thoughts into fresh channels that the idea of secular clergy was born—men who would be permanent priests of the parish, rather than missionaries—who being free of strict monastic rules and vows of poverty, could hold property and administer trusts.

As yet there was no Bishop in New France, the Superior of the Jesuits in Quebec assuming such ecclesiastical control as seemed necessary. Above him and utterly remote, was the Archbishop of Rouen who claimed this new land as a part of his diocese. It was not a satisfactory arrangement, as Maisonneuve realized when in the autumn of 1656, he left for France on a

threefold mission. There, as he was well aware, the personnel
was readily available, not only for the office of Bishop, but
also to meet Montreal's need for parish priests and nursing
sisters.

In his quest for priests, it was only to be expected that Maisonneuve should turn to the Gentlemen of St. Sulpice, the Order of
secular priests founded by Abbé Olier. That the Associates
of Montreal should welcome the possible advent of the Sulpicians
was equally predictable. Fewer in number and less enthusiastic
than in 1640, they were ready to transfer some of their burdens
to the Order. There remained only the task of selection, an easy
one as it proved. Abbé Gabriel de Queylus was designated as
the new Superior in Montreal and three assistants assigned to
accompany him. He was also recommended as a suitable leader
for the yet-to-be created diocese of New France.

When this reached the ears of the Jesuits, they were roused
to opposition. Although unable to fill the episcopal office themselves by reason of their rules, they had no intention of being
governed by a member of the Sulpician Order. They wasted no
time, therefore, in putting forward the name of François de
Laval—a man who though not a Jesuit, was sympathetic to the
Order.

When Maisonneuve and the four Sulpicians reached Montreal
in the summer of 1657, they had no knowledge of the outcome
of the episcopal negotiations. Thus they plunged into a morass
of understandings, largely as a result of the erratic actions of the
Archbishop of Rouen. Queylus, he had nominated as the grand
vicar of New France, an exact duplication of the title and
authority already extended to the Superior of the Jesuits in
Quebec. Small wonder that the latter's courtesy soon turned to
anger, particularly when Queylus for some months, took charge
of ecclesiastical affairs in that city. That the latter was, by all
accounts, a tactless man, only made the situation worse.

By this date, France was ready to concede that the colony
needed a Bishop. Still to be decided was the identity of the man,
and so there followed a tug of war, the Sulpicians and the Associates of Montreal pleading the cause of Queylus, the Jesuits
as zealous for Laval.

In the end, of course, Laval emerged as the successful candidate, being consecrated as Vicar Apostolic of Canada and Bishop of Petrea in Arabia. He reached Quebec in June 1659, fully aware that he came to a country divided ecclesiastically into two camps. Several months of confusion followed, quickly worsened by another batch of contradictory letters from the Archbishop of Rouen. Expulsion seemed the only solution, and in the autumn, Queylus was ordered to return to France.

Such prompt and resolute action suggests that with the advent of Bishop Laval, a new and strong personality had appeared in Canadian life. Imperious by nature, he was a firm believer in a centralized government, particularly in church affairs. It was a creed that led him, inevitably, into a series of disputes with the officials at Quebec. But above all else, Laval clashed with Montreal, partly because he tended to favor the Jesuits over the Sulpicians, but more significantly, over the much vaunted independence of the newer settlement.

Meanwhile, the Sulpicians had settled down in Montreal. They lived to begin with, in a room at the hospital, until such time as a seminary could be constructed. Father Souart was named the permanent curé. When the Jesuits withdrew to their property across the river, the daily contacts between the two Orders became less irritating, although at no time does there seem to have been active antagonism. And because the Sulpicians formed a relatively wealthy community, unhampered by vows of poverty, they could make plans for the betterment of the church. With their arrival, the purely missionary era came to an end.

During the tension over the affairs of the Sulpicians, the needs of the hospital had been temporarily shelved. By the summer of 1658, there could be no more deferment. Eighteen months earlier, Jeanne Mance had slipped on the ice, fracturing her right arm and dislocating her wrist. Despite the care of the surgeons, the pain grew steadily worse until she was no longer able to work. Finally in desperation, she decided on a return to France, in the hope that the greater skills of the Paris doctors might give her relief.

The two women—for Marguerite Bourgeoys accompanied the helpless patient—reached Paris at Christmastime. Jeanne Mance made the journey from La Rochelle in a litter, to avoid jolting, but any hopes of recovery were soon dashed by the adverse verdict of the physicians. It was then that without any prospect of human assistance, she visited the chapel of St. Sulpice, to offer up her prayers at the tomb of the recently deceased Abbé Olier. As she held the urn containing his heart, a miracle happened. The pain ceased and the arm healed.

After this auspicious beginning, the women parted company for a time, as each proceeded with the more mundane business that must be done in France. While Marguerite Bourgeoys journeyed to Troyes in a successful search for three young women to help her as teachers, Jeanne Mance pursued a similar errand at La Flèche, the home of the Hospitalières, the nursing Order founded by Dauversière.

The travelers with their new assistants, met again at La Rochelle, where the waiting ship was already crowded with some two hundred passengers bound for Canada. They were a mixed group of soldiers and civilians, men and women, a few marriageable girls; about half were destined for Montreal. Demands for advance payment of the fares embroiled the leaders in wrangles with an unpleasant captain. The sailing date was postponed, and the crossing was one of the worst ever recorded. In its earlier service, the vessel had carried troops. Now thoroughly infected with the germs of typhus fever, it brought sickness and death to many of the new Canadians. Jeanne Mance herself was one of the worst cases, being carried ashore at Quebec more dead than alive.

Quebec's reception of the Montrealers in September 1659, was on a par with the frigidity of the past. While most of the party got away quickly, Jeanne Mance, in her extremity, remained behind. When she did recover, it was only to face Bishop Laval, adamant in his opposition to the Hospitalières of La Flèche. That he had cold reason on his side, must be admitted. Why set up a second Order of nursing sisters when one existed in Quebec? Why not consider the hospital in Montreal to be an auxiliary of the older institution in Quebec? Why not provide its staff from the same source? Moreover, the argument continued, nuns should be cloistered, whereas the new arrivals, bound by vows less strict than usual, were free to come and go in public.

In this historic confrontation, Jeanne Mance stood firm, but whether she alone could have carried the day, is questionable. The matter was finally resolved by the future disposition of money. When the Associates intimated that the endowments would be made available only to the nuns from La Flèche, Laval capitulated. Only then were Jeanne Mance and her four assistants free to carry on their work in Montreal.

With this return home safely accomplished, the Iroquois once more enter the news. The semi-peace had then persisted for several years, punctuated by rumors and a fear of treachery. Under d'Ailleboust, temporarily acting as Governor, the French resistance stiffened, Montreal taking its full share in the program of preparedness. Early in 1658, Maisonneuve issued a new set of rules—no one must go out unarmed or alone; work must be carried out in groups; houses were to be fortified; all movements to be controlled by the sound of the bell; no one must go out at night; permission was required for all hunting expeditions.

Nor were these hardships confined to the men. The fifty or so wives already in Montreal, shared with their husbands in the daily needs of the defense, and before long, the Hospitalières, too, took a like role in the community. Theirs was not an easy adjustment, for as members of good families, they had been brought up in comfortable homes. The Sisters had, in fact, landed in Canada almost destitute, having sold their equipment en route to gain the bare necessities.

Once arrived in Montreal, a room was hastily built for them at the hospital. Its walls of rough planks were by no means weatherproof, so that the wind blew through the cracks without hindrance. After a winter storm, it was often necessary to shovel out the snow that had drifted in during the night. Their food, at such seasons, was frozen; the coarse brown bread was thawed out at the fireplace. Clothes were a problem, even to the most thrifty among the Sisters. Without any means of replacing their garments, they simply added patches of whatever material was available. The story goes that once, when Maisonneuve and Madame d'Ailleboust visited the hospital, they amused them-

selves with speculations as to the original stuff of the habits. In
the end, they were unable to agree.

Naturally the Hôtel Dieu was just as much exposed to attack
as the rest of the settlement. Sometimes after dark, when the
nuns looked out, they saw the Iroquois braves in the garden,
tomahawks in hand, hoping for victims. Day or night, whenever
there was fighting, Sister Brésoles and Sister Morin ran to the
belfry to sound the alarm. Then they would come down, in
terror, expecting the end. As for Sister Maillet and Sister Macé,
they would almost faint with fear, prostrating themselves before
the Holy Sacrament, as if ready for death. But when the need
arose, the Sisters without exception, were courageous in their
care of the sick and the dying.

Thus peace or no peace, the enemy warriors still hung about
Montreal, sometimes posing as friends in quest of hospitality, at
others, picking off unsuspecting workmen. As time passed, some
of these actions, basically factual, provided the grist for legends
that gained a wide circulation. Hinting as they did at divine
intervention, it is not surprising that they won a hearing from
the credulous. Quebec, needless to say, greeted them with chilly
unbelief.

Consider for example, the case of the Iroquois, who under
cover of the truce, visited Montreal as friends, then having set
the stage, turned into enemies. In a moment of relaxation, they
launched an attack on some men busily thatching a roof. Jean
Saint Père was killed and his head carried off proudly as a
trophy of war. But, in the enemy village, to the horror of the
crowd, the head began to speak, using good Iroquois to scold
his captors and threaten vengeance from above. Even after the
skull was thrown away, the same voice was said to be audible;
there was no escaping the sound. Closely akin is the tale of
Father Le Maître, the Sulpician, killed a couple of years later,
while acting as sentry for some men working in the fields. A
momentary glance at his Breviary, and he walked into an ambush. In like manner, his head was carried off in triumph,
wrapped in his own white handkerchief. Later, the cloth was
seen to be free of any stain of blood, printed only with the
features of the murdered priest.

With the commencement of the new decade, some of the vehemence faded from the domestic disputes, under the growing Iroquois threat. Rumors and warnings from friendly Indians filled the air, while in the constant disruption of the fur trade, there were hints of trouble. Discipline was tight, and Maisonneuve demanded the closest obedience to his rules, for although the garrison had been strengthened by the recent reinforcements, it was still insufficient for any offensive move.

Early in 1660, Quebec heard bad news from an Iroquois captive at the point of death—a tale of a tremendous force of warriors, a thousand strong, poised near Montreal and awaiting the signal to attack. To his listeners, it seemed as though the entire colony was to be wiped out. Panicky themselves, they stirred the capital to action. There was a rush to strengthen long unused defenses, and to alert the scattered settlers in the neighborhood. Strangely enough, Montreal does not seem to have heard the story immediately. Yet it was, without a doubt, a small band of heroes from the Island, who by standing up to the assailants in several days of desperate fighting, became the saviors of New France.

As a preface to their feat, the reader should know that two versions exist. According to the old tradition, as printed in every school text, Dollard des Ormeaux knew of the approach of the great army, and recruited his sixteen companions for the specific purpose of pitting their tiny strength against the might of the Iroquois. It is an interpretation that has long troubled the scholars, and one that recognized no inconsistencies in date or behavior. Hence their close examination of the contemporary documents and a change in opinion. There is now fairly general agreement that Dollard was unaware of the presence of the enemy in such numbers. When he led his party out from Montreal, it was in the hope of intercepting a few canoe loads of furs. They went prepared to meet a small party of Indians, they remained to fight an army.

In any event, the beginning of May found them ensconced at the Long Sault Rapids, lying in wait for anyone coming down the Ottawa with furs. Choosing a site suitable for an ambush, they were soon joined by friends—forty Hurons and four Algonquins.

All went well until on the next day, during a brush with the enemy, two of the Iroquois escaped to carry back word of what had happened. Even then Dollard does not seem to have appreciated the full extent of the danger, for he made no attempt to strengthen an old stockade that lay back from the water.

The next day, two hundred Onondagas appeared fully armed for the attack. Taken by surprise, Dollard's party hastily left the shore, for the shelter of the stockade. After an interchange of shots, the Indians took council with themselves, and as a result, sent off a request for reinforcements. Several days of intermittent fighting followed, the Onondagas sufficiently strong to keep the French pent-up in their crude enclosure. Without food or water, Dollard and his men suffered.

On the eighth day, the Mohawks arrived, a vast fleet of canoes bearing them down the Ottawa. At the sound of their war whoops, most of the Hurons promptly deserted, leaving Dollard with his sixteen French and four Algonquins to fight the hundreds of savages. There was little that could be done, effectively, to resist their onslaught. Dollard tried to make a rude sort of grenade, but instead of landing among the enemy, it caught on the branches of an overhanging tree, only to fall back among the French themselves. The battle was short and fierce. Dollard was among the first to be killed, and other casualties followed in quick succession. There were few survivors. Five of the French, taken prisoner, were too weak to move on with their captors. They were burned on the spot.

Yet this marked the end of the Iroquois campaign for that season at least. Their own death rate was high, and having lost the initial advantage of surprise, they were not strong enough to press home the attack. Thus Dollard and his heroic band saved Montreal from the immediate threat of destruction.

Chapter 6
1660–1672

The Sulpicians as Seigneurs of the Island. Louis XIV and Colbert. New France a royal province. The Carignan-Salières Regiment. De Tracy. Maisonneuve dismissed. The destruction of the Iroquois villages. Les filles du roi. Soldier settlers. Seigniorial tenure. The town grows.

MONTREAL, IN THE months following the death of Dollard, went soberly about its business, the farmers more confident that they would be spared to reap what they had sowed, but nonetheless, eternally on the alert. Theirs was a vital task, for after the long agony of the Iroquois wars, the whole colony was short of food. Fresh supplies came from France, slowly and with no certainty as to date of delivery.

Despite its many setbacks and the casualties of the wars, the town was starting to grow. By the standards of the past, its population of 350 seemed large. Yet its outward appearance remained poor, and outsiders were apt to describe the settlement as puny.

Governor d'Argenson dismissed it as "a place which makes a deal of noise and is of little consequence." The gentleman, it might be added, was slightly miffed at the lack of deference paid to his official position.

But this reprieve, like all the others, was a short one, for in February, guerrilla fighting broke out afresh. Throughout 1661 and 1662, there were intermittent raids, with Montreal as always, the main target. Ever the makers of the expressive phrase, the Jesuits wrote feelingly of the wanton wretches, the unfortunate harpies, the evil birds of prey who haunted the Island. They caused the death of Lambert Closse, the town major and a man of unrivaled courage. Going out one morning to rescue a group of workmen, he and his twenty-five followers found themselves surrounded by some two hundred Iroquois. Against these overwhelming odds, the French fought on until the evening; all were killed. Equally tragic was the fate that befell Father Vignal, while leading a party to quarry stone for the new seminary. As their boats pulled into the shore of a nearby small island, the Iroquois rushed out from their ambush. Although a few of the French escaped, the Sulpician was killed, and later the savages roasted his body and ate the flesh.

Such was Montreal's way of life during many weary months, and one that increasingly stirred its people to anger. The loss of life; the atrocities; the whole accumulation of horrors; only the destruction of the enemy villages would bring it to an end; only thus would the colony be saved from extinction. It was a feeling of desperation, that spreading through the settlements up and down the river, touched the hearts of official Quebec. The result was an unprecedented series of appeals to France—of formal requests for reinforcements—most significant of all, the mission of Pierre Boucher, the Governor of Three Rivers. To him, in the autumn, was assigned the task of seeking a personal interview with the king. His long service to the country, it was felt, would render him a good interpreter of its needs.

That much of the criticism rife at this period should center about the One Hundred Associates, indicates how consistently in its thirty-five-year monopoly, the Company had ignored its obligations. Perhaps gossip magnified the extent of its profits, but whatever the state of its ledgers, one fact was undeniable. The Associates had been callous in their attitude to New France, and under their control, the new country had failed to develop to the extent envisaged by Richelieu and the other framers of their charter.

Meanwhile, it must be admitted that the dangers from without, did not guarantee harmony at home. Sometimes the disputes lay between Montreal and Quebec, more often between church and state. The permutations and combinations were endless, but in most cases, Laval was a participant. Hence it is all the more pleasing to find that in the summer of 1661, his first visit to the

Island passed off without incident, due honor being tendered to the Bishop as the highest ecclesiastic in the land.

There is a possibility that on this occasion, Abbé de Queylus acted as official host, for he is known to have been in Montreal. If so, the façade of good will was short lived. Several weeks earlier, the Sulpician had arrived in Quebec, the bearer of documents from Pope Alexander VII, authorizing Montreal's creation as an independent parish. Such effrontery was too much for Laval, and he reminded his opponent that the mandate of eviction was still valid. Especially did he forbid a return to Montreal—a ruling promptly disobeyed, for Queylus slipped away by canoe under cover of darkness. The ensuing argument persisted for some time, but eventually the Bishop emerged as the victor. For the second time, and under official orders, Queylus was sent back to France.

By this date also, the liquor traffic with the Indians was arousing dissension throughout the country. Everybody took sides. Although in the past, its maintenance had been stoutly defended by those who took part, others looked with horror at the growing signs of depravity. The effects of strong drink on the white man were bad enough, on his red brother, they were nothing short of catastrophic. With the arrival of Laval, the drys gained fresh strength, for in 1660, he threatened excommunication to all those involved.

As the controversy widened, there was some shifting of position. At Quebec, Governor d'Argenson went over to the side of the merchants, claiming inconsistency in some of the Bishop's actions. Since his successors in office held to the same view, there remained in that quarter at least, no further obstacles to the sale of brandy. In sharp contrast was the attitude of Maisonneuve, whose misgivings were, in 1662, translated into action. Deeply moved at the murder of a man named Desjardins—his killers known to be drunken natives—he issued an ordinance prohibiting the sale or gift of intoxicating liquor to the Indians.

Outwardly, this appeared a reasonable action and one justified by the circumstances, yet it brought Montreal into active conflict with Quebec. For Maisonneuve forbade what the older city tolerated, claiming that he did so by virtue of authority derived

from the king. Governor d'Avaugour's reply was to deny the existence of any such rights, and within a few months, showed that
he intended to stand by his claim to superior authority. When
later that autumn, Maisonneuve appeared in Quebec en route to
France, he was promptly ordered back to Montreal, as a first step
in reducing the independence of the unruly settlement.

But there was nothing frivolous in Maisonneuve's projected
visit to France, and in the end, Jeanne Mance went off alone for
discussions with the Associates of Montreal. By this date, they
had dwindled so greatly in number and influence that the only
hope lay in saving something from the wreckage. Yet in their extremity, the five survivors did not forget their obligations. When
the end seemed inescapable, they proposed, not a surrender but
a transfer—and quite naturally to the Gentlemen of St. Sulpice.

The Order was, at first, reluctant to undertake such heavy responsibilities. It was only after several meetings that an agreement was reached; as finally drafted, its clauses promised a continuation of the old semi-independence. In addition to the
transfer of land, the new seigneurs retained the cherished privileges of choosing the governor and of holding courts of justice.
Maisonneuve, during his lifetime, was to continue in office, subject of course to the pleasure of the Order. In lieu of remuneration, he was promised half of the farmland and the revenues from
the mill. His residence was to be in the seignorial manor house,
under the same roof as the Sulpicians.

However much Montreal may have welcomed this news, it
was purely local in scope, and took second place to an announcement from the king, which appeared in the same spring of 1663.
This was of a nature to hearten all who lived in New France—
on the one hand, the dissolution of the much hated Company of
One Hundred Associates—on the other, the reconstitution of the
colony as a royal province, subject to the authority of the reign-
ing monarch.

Louis XIV was at this date still a young man, and the ex-
travagances of Versailles far in the future. Born in 1638, he had
succeeded to the throne in 1643, yet it was not until the death of
Cardinal Mazarin in 1661 that the last vestiges of tutelage vanished. The youthful monarch was fortunate in the choice of his

new chief minister, for Jean Baptiste Colbert ranks high in the history of his country as an efficient and far-seeing administrator. Officially designated as the Minister of Marine, he was, in effect, the government, and his supervisory powers covered a wide field. Fortunately for Canada, they included colonies, for not the least remarkable characteristic of this new leader was his vision of the French dominions overseas. In an age and in a nation that was almost entirely Europe-based in its thinking, Colbert turned his eyes to the New World. What is more, he succeeded in communicating much of his enthusiasm to his royal master, with the result that during the next eight or ten years, New France prospered.

The reorganization of the government took place at once. As in the past, it included the Governor General, while the Bishop replaced the Superior of the Jesuits. A new official known as the Intendant, was added to their number, and he soon proved to be a key man. Although subordinate in theory to the Governor, his influence often proved to be the greater. In financial matters, the Intendant was virtually supreme, through his control of the public funds. The civil administration of the country rested in his hands, and the problems of the common people became his to solve. From his office, emanated the minor ordinances—the regulations as to fur trading, and markets, pew rents, and even matrimonial quarrels.

Under its new title of the Supreme Council, the old Council of Quebec found its numbers enlarged and its powers defined. The Governor, the Bishop, and the Intendant were all members; its Canadian representation was raised from three to five. As an advisory body, it served a useful purpose—less important however, than its sweeping jurisdiction over the administration of justice. It was as a court of appeal for the province that the Council made its most striking contribution to the public welfare.

Such were the actual changes that lent a more hopeful aspect to life during the period immediately following the royal proclamation. There was general relief that the king had assumed the leadership, while his promise of regular troops from France suggested an even brighter future. In the meantime, the stepped-up immigration scheme got under way. During the first season of the new regime, a hundred families arrived in Quebec, comprising five hundred persons added to the sparse population of the colony.

Montreal, with more at stake, greeted the news with mixed feelings. As the center of the Iroquois fighting, its people naturally welcomed the prospect of military support. But the new government—that was another matter. In the regulations concerning courts of law, no exemption was offered to Montreal, and in fact, the Sovereign Council was directed to administer all local tribunals in exactly the same way as at Quebec and Three Rivers. That this spelled trouble for the normally independent Island was evident when, in the autumn of 1663, the colony acquired a new Governor.

Saffray de Mézy was the appointee of Laval, but this did not put a stop to quarreling between the two men. History has labeled him as a bad-tempered individual, so that no one can have mourned his sudden death after only two years in office. Under his instructions, the Sovereign Council took away from the Sulpicians, all former rights in the administration of justice at Montreal. Maisonneuve was relieved of his judicial duties, and new officers appointed for the local court. When he accompanied Abbé Souart to register a protest, the two were coolly received, de Mézy going so far as to say that Maisonneuve had no standing as Governor, except as derived from him. Pinpricks these were, but only a few among many, all intended to reduce the local freedom of action whenever possible. One opinion has it that Montreal was more afraid of the exactions of Quebec than of the incursions of the Iroquois.

But during the summer of 1665, all other considerations gave place to the excitement that attended the arrival of the long-expected troops. It started in June when four companies of the Carignan-Salières Regiment landed at Quebec, and continued until by September, 1200 regulars from France, were stationed in Canada. To the watching Quebeçois, they were an amazing sight, splendid in full uniform, skilled in maneuvers, and supremely self-confident, the hardened veterans of many wars, freshly come from fighting the Turks in Hungary. Their presence alone, was enough to inspire the most timid beholder, and as for their officers—for the first time in its history, the little town had a glimpse of the glitter and color of the aristocracy. They brought with them an air of gaiety and worldliness, hitherto absent from Canadian life.

After the soldiers, came the new officials, and they too, were impressive. Daniel Rémy, Sieur de Courcelle, the Governor, was a soldier of undoubted courage and ability, who was to serve the colony faithfully. At almost any other time, he would have been outstanding, but this attribute should, perhaps, be reserved for the Intendant, Jean Baptiste Talon, the first man to hold the post and one of the greatest. On paper, his position was subordinate to the Governor, yet he was tacitly accepted as the leader. His arrival was a good omen for Montreal, for although always a resident of Quebec, and compelled by his duties to deal impartially with colonial problems, he contrived to be just in his dealings with the Island.

Outranking these permanent officials, was a third, in the person of Alexandre de Prouville, Sieur de Tracy, lieutenant general of the French territories in America. He came to the colony from service in the West Indies, and on a special mission from the king—nothing less than the destruction of the Five Nations. A chain of forts soon attested to his determination. Four were located on the Richelieu River; a fifth on an island in Lake Champlain, the main routes to the Iroquois country. By November, these had been completed and garrisoned by several companies of the Carignan-Salières men. The main body of the Regiment, meanwhile, went into winter quarters at Quebec, Three Rivers, and Montreal. On the Island, the effect of the new defense works was already noticeable, there being an amazing freedom from attack.

This happy state came to an abrupt end in October with the dismissal of Maisonneuve. Although de Tracy wrapped up his action in polite language, the tenor of his letter was unmistakable; an immediate return to France was the gist of the order. As to the reason—the simple truth points to the fact that Maisonneuve was a victim of the trend to centralized government. So long as he remained in office, the opposition to the new regime was likely to continue. Without his leadership, it might be expected to crumble.

It may well be that the man himself, recalling his relations
with Quebec, was prepared for such an eventuality. To his people, the blow was cruelly unexpected. They were powerless, and
in any case, Maisonneuve would have permitted no public protest. Thus the first Governor of Montreal, after almost twenty-five
years of faithful service, went quietly home to France, his reputation unspotted by talk of personal gain. He survived for twelve
years, living quietly in Paris, and always retaining his interest in
Canadian affairs.

Meanwhile, in their eagerness to get on with the Iroquois
war, the newcomers brushed aside all warnings from the more
weather-wise Canadians. Early January saw de Courcelle starting off from Quebec, at the head of three hundred men of the
Carignan-Salières Regiment and a hundred militia. Everything
went wrong from the start. The troops, fresh from Europe, moved
slowly; unaccustomed to snowshoes, they found themselves suffering from frostbite. Food ran low. Without any hope of obtaining fresh provisions from the wintry countryside, they were
obliged to retreat before reaching the enemy villages.

A second expedition, planned for the following summer, was
canceled in response to some half-hearted Iroquois bids for
peace. When these came to nothing, the French renewed their
preparations, and by September, were ready for a large-scale invasion of the Mohawk country. The army of thirteen hundred
men which left Quebec, was an imposing sight. French regulars,
Canadian Militia and friendly Indians traveled together in some
three hundred canoes and flat-bottomed boats—across Lake
Champlain and Lake George, portaging and marching when
necessary until their objective was reached. An enemy scout having discovered their presence, they found the villages empty.
Nevertheless, they burned them, destroying the Iroquois stocks
of food, even if they inflicted no casualties. In this way, peace
came to New France, and in such an unshakable manner that
it was to endure for twenty years.

Companies of Montrealers formed a part of both these expeditions, seasoned woodsmen who were accustomed to such conditions of fighting. De Courcelle dubbed them his "blue coats,"
from the color of their coats, sashes, and caps. Since Quebec

wore red and Three Rivers white, the local contingents could readily be identified in the joint actions that now became more common. On such occasions, the Montreal men were usually accorded the dubious honor of leading the van in attack, and bringing up the rear in retreat, having already earned the distinction of being the most efficient fighters in the country.

Charles Le Moyne, the leader of the Montreal parties at this date, was of a caliber worthy of his men. Since his return from the Indian country, he had settled down, married, and become a substantial citizen. As the seigneur of Longueuil, he was a notable landowner, and a power to be reckoned with in the expanding settlement of the Island. Yet neither increasing fame nor added wealth ever interfered with his prowess as a fighter—resulting in an enviable reputation that was carried on and enhanced by his remarkable brood of sons.

This defeat of the Iroquois in the autumn of 1666, is generally hailed as the end of the heroic age in Montreal. There can have been few to regret its passing. The Island, having suffered the most, had the greatest reason to rejoice, and even the simplest actions now took on fresh meaning. But fortunately, memories of past horrors are often short-lived, and these early Montrealers were no exception to the rule. Within an amazingly short time, they started to move into the country, spreading out along the riverbanks and wherever the land looked to be the most promising, forgetful of the fact that the Iroquois, given time, might well return to the warpath. Warnings from the more prudent went unheeded, and Colbert's praise of compact, well-planned villages met with little response.

Optimism was in the air for a few years, and changes of all kinds marked the progress of the settlement. First in point of time, and probably the most gratifying to local pride, was the king's decision, in the autumn of 1666, to confirm the Sulpicians in their full enjoyment of seigniorial rights on the Island. The Order was permitted to resume the administration of justice within the district, Quebec to remain as a higher court of appeal when needed. The privilege of choosing the local Governor, was especially prized, even if not immediately acted upon, and served to ease some of the sting caused by Maisonneuve's dismissal. The storehouse at Quebec was later reopened, and its control again vested in Montreal—an important concession so long as the lower port remained the terminus of ocean shipping. Obviously, the complete independence of the founders had to disappear as the country developed. That it was replaced by these reasonable modifications, went far in making Montreal a more satisfied partner in the New France of the future.

Equally welcome was the *rapprochement* in the religious world, where the smouldering disagreement between Bishop and Abbé had long been a cause of distress to the faithful. The road to reconciliation was opened by none other than the Archbishop of Rouen, in his renunciation of all authority over New France; signs of royal interest in Queylus insured its smooth conclusion. The latter, arriving once more in Quebec, received not only a welcome, but was appointed Vicar General in Montreal—initiating a friendship which ended only when poor health in 1671, forced the Sulpician's return to France.

By the summer of 1667, more normal conditions prevailed throughout the colony. De Tracy departed for France, and the permanent officials of peacetime resumed full direction of the government. It was then, during the course of a formal visit to Montreal, that Talon revealed the innate simplicity and kindliness of his nature. According to a contemporary report, he went from house to house, even to the poorest, asking all if they were being treated with equity and justice. When he found any need of monetary assistance, he made certain that it was forthcoming.

It was Talon too, who personally supervised the taking of the first census in 1667. As a comprehensive survey, the returns provided a useful yardstick for assessing future progress. Montreal was beginning to show a steady increase, for its population was then listed as 766 souls. Within the next five years, and after intensive immigration, the total climbed to 1500 or 1600. As everywhere in New France, the males greatly outnumbered the females, being nearly two to one.

That the women remained in the minority, was not due to any inaction, either on the part of Talon or his superiors at home. All through the program of immigration that started in 1665, emphasis was placed on the inclusion of marriageable girls from

France. Each summer, as their number increased, the weddings grew more numerous, aided by dowries from the king. Large families being the order of the day, the natural growth in population was considerable.

The brides-to-be were commonly known as *les filles du roi*—the king's daughters—from the fact that most of the earlier ones were orphans, cared for and educated at public expense. Others were selected by the curés of their parishes, and later, from a variety of sources. Much has been written of *les filles* and in some cases, the claim advanced that they were no better than they should be. Such a canard is an unhappy distortion of the truth. In point of fact, the girls were chosen with care, and considering their numbers, unsuitable candidates were surprisingly few. Marguerite Bourgeoys acted as the chaperone of those who came to Montreal, and all through her active years, her careful shepherding went on. If not on the ship herself, she received the newcomers immediately on landing, took them to lodge with her, trying meanwhile to train them as good wives and mothers.

In these circumstances, it is unlikely that many of the bachelors were averse to changing their marital status. If such did exist, they received short shrift from a paternal and all-seeing government. A series of ordinances practically made marriage obligatory, since the single man was forbidden to hunt or fish, or even to enter the bush. And by no stretch of the imagination, can family allowances be considered an invention of the twentieth century. They were inaugurated in New France, with the proviso that each year, the parents must report to the Intendant, the number of their children. When ten had been registered, an annual pension began; with twelve, its amount was increased.

It is likely that at times, the lot of *les filles* was a hard one, for compulsory marriages cannot always have been successful. But as Dollier de Casson philosophically observed, a woman need never fear her inability to win a husband in such circumstances. Moreover, he went on, the climate in Montreal seemed especially favorable to the female sex; in spite of the cold winters, only one woman had died during the past six years. From *Les Relations*, a report in similar vein told of how "tender and delicate maidens who dread a snowflake in France, are not frightened when they see mountains of them here . . . A frost would, in their well-closed houses (in France) give them a cold, while a severe and very long winter, armed with snow and ice, does them no harm, other than to keep them in good appetite."

If the brides in their own way, promised a substantial growth in population, so too, did the projected settlement of the Carignan-Salières Regiment. The authorities in France at this date, were tireless, not only in encouraging regular immigration to the colony, but in searching for other means of achieving the desired increases. Colbert, in particular, was haunted by the fear the mother country might be depopulated. Hence the decision, at the end of the Iroquois campaign, to promise grants of land to any members of the Regiment who would agree to settle permanently in the country. Four hundred officers and men took up the offer, their number later being augmented, as other reinforcements became eligible.

Geographically, most of these military settlers were located close to Montreal, as being the most underdeveloped section of the country. At such vulnerable spots on the Island as Longue Pointe, Pointe aux Trembles, Lachine, they were warmly welcomed. The same open-armed reception greeted their arrival in the still largely empty districts along the St. Lawrence down to Lake St. Peter and on the shores of the Richelieu. The modern metropolitan area still has many reminders of these army colonists; Chambly and Sorel, Verchères and Varennes, Berthier and Contrecoeur; these are but a few of the towns and villages bearing the family names of the Carignan officers.

The men who thus accepted the seigniorial grants, became a part of the system of land ownership imported from France in the days of Champlain. Much has been written on the subject. It has, at times, been described as an offshoot of the feudal system of the Old World, a statement that is as true as it is unfortunate. For the connotations of medieval feudalism are, in general, unhappy ones, conjuring up visions of down-trodden serfs and lives of poverty and misery. Stripped of its harshness, the plan was admirably adapted to the time and the place, one that gave a chain of command useful in communication, and a sense of companionship in isolation.

Seigniorial tenure, as established in the colony, was essentially a hierarchy, stretching down from the Governor (representing the king) through the seigneurs themselves, to the tenants of small holdings. It was benevolent in character and entailed few obligations. The cases of malpractice were remarkably few. In the early years, some of the grants had been staggering in size, and when conferred upon absentee landlords, produced no useful results. But as more people came into the colony, this phase passed, and the seigneurs, whether soldiers or civilians, became a readily recognized caste of society. Rarely either aristocratic or wealthy, they were usually conscientious, hard-working men, mindful of the needs of their tenants.

Exceptionally praiseworthy as landlords, the Gentlemen of St. Sulpice were active at this date in dividing up their great holdings of land on the Island. It was a deliberate policy, undertaken for purposes of defense, and followed the usual pattern of such transactions. The grants were bestowed upon local seigneurs, in return for *foi et hommage* and a commitment to clear the land within a certain time. The latter, in their turn, split up their holdings among tenants, upon payment of a nominal rent. (The common rate at Montreal was half a sou and a pint of wheat for each acre.) These tenants were officially known as *censitaires*—they themselves preferred to be called *habitants*—and the divisions of land as *côtes*—a phrase that still appears in some of the modern street names. In addition to the rent, they were obliged to use the seigniory mill for grinding their corn, and to provide a few days personal labor each year. This latter practice, known as a *corvée* seldom amounted to more than a week annually, and was not always invoked.

What all this amounted to, was that land could be had for the asking. The important part of the bargain, for both seigneur and tenant, was the clearing of the forest. Once this had been transformed into acreage for cultivation, the rest was easy. It was these seigniories that formed the thin ribbons of settlement along the rivers. Everyone wanted a frontage on the water, for ease of communication. As further subdivisions took place, the strips grew narrower and narrower, in proportion to their width. With the houses all clustered closely together along the shores, both for protection and companionship, the St. Lawrence and the smaller streams came to resemble long straggling villages.

Each seigniory was conceived of as a unit, a tiny segment in the over-all framework of the colony, and as such, subject to control by those in authority. So far as possible, it was expected to be self-sustaining, and the position of the seigneur, in relation to his tenants, was spelled out in detail—civil, military, ecclesiastical. Deferment was permitted in the case of the more onerous obligations, poverty at this date, being recognized as a serious deterrent to progress. For this reason, the construction of a mill was often postponed in the districts near Montreal, the tenants instead taking their grain to the seminary property to be ground. Although civil and ecclesiastical boundaries usually coincided, many years often passed before every seigniory had its curé or parish chapel. In matters of justice, the seigneur might appoint a judge and set up a local court. If unable to do so, cases were to be referred to a neighboring jurisdiction for decision. Montreal, for example, served as the judicial center for its outlying districts. In each seigniory or parish, the captain of militia played an important role, working closely with the Intendant, even during the brief interludes of peace.

Few of the seigneurs, it must be repeated, were rich, so that outwardly there was little to distinguish them from their tenants. In this respect, at least, the Carignan officers resembled their civilian neighbors; all toiled long hours to clear the fields in readiness for planting. Occasionally, the work was done badly or not at all, as the public notices bear witness. These contain instructions for the removal of stumps, a pickaxe being recommended as the most effective instrument. Land that had once been cleared must be kept in good order, and neglect was officially frowned on. As for the trees that had been cut down, and the timber carelessly dumped into the St. Lawrence; this, said authority, prevented navigation and obstructed communication; it must cease. Instead, the wood must be cut into logs and placed carefully in the stream, to be carried away with the melting ice in the spring.

From this period also, dates the building of the first roads and bridges in the neighborhood. These became a necessity,

once carts came into common use. When the habitants asked
for a road in a certain locality, the representatives of the seigneurs
met them at the spot indicated. Then its course would be traced.
Once this had been agreed upon, each proprietor set to work to
clear the section running through his property, using logs when
the ground was marshy. If a bridge had to be constructed, it
too, was framed of logs. The width of these early highways was
generally eighteen feet. One exception was made in the case of
the important artery bordering on the St. Lawrence. This being
used as a towpath for the horses to draw the boats up to the
rapids, was widened to thirty-six feet. As this was also the
principal means of communication between the two extremities
of the Island, those whose property faced on it, were obliged
to keep it in order.

Chapter 7
1672–1682

The first streets. Dollier de Casson. The fur trade. The annual fairs. Exploration. Coureurs de bois. *The liquor traffic. Perrot and Frontenac.*

IN MARCH 1672, Dollier de Casson with the assistance of a surveyor, laid out the first streets within the municipal limits of Montreal, tracing their course with care and marking them with posts bearing the leaden seal of the seminary. It was he who determined their width and established the location of the adjoining property lines. In some cases, tracks already in use, could be adapted, in others, new thoroughfares were needed, parallel in direction or at right angles. Notre Dame Street, abutting upon the Common, as the principal highway, was thirty feet wide. Of the rest, some were twenty-four, others only eighteen.

Most of these streets still exist. Now in the downtown section, they lie close to the river and form the heart of the financial district. Some have been widened, others to modern eyes, resemble lanes. All bear the original names chosen by de Casson. Prefixed by the word "Saint," their local significance is not easily recognized. Thus St. Paul signifies the patron saint of Paul de Chomedey, Sieur de Maisonneuve; St. Peter honors the Baron de Fancamp. St. James was so-called out of respect for the Abbé Olier, St. Gabriel for the Abbé Queylus, St. Francis Xavier for de Casson himself.

That de Casson should undertake such a task reveals how close was the relationship of Montreal with its seigneurs. As the newly appointed Superior of the Sulpicians, he was then at the commencement of a local residence that ended only with his death in 1701. In every sense of the word, he was outstanding. A giant physically, he towered above his fellows in inches as in strength. It is reported that he could hold two men in his hands. Having served in the French Army during his youth, he was the perfect choice for chaplain in the 1666 attack on the Mohawks, and subsequent partnership in several parties of exploration, served only to enhance his reputation. Of de Casson, it might be said that his heart was as big as his body; genial and cheerful by disposition, he was beloved by all. His *Histoire du Montréal,* covering the years from 1640 to 1672, was the earliest of the local histories, and so has an unusually personal approach. Both in his official capacity and as a versatile individual in his own right, the Sulpician played a leading role in the developing life of the settlement.

For this initial venture in town planning sums up, as much as any one thing can do, the changes in Montreal that followed de Tracy's humbling of the Iroquois. Up to a point, they could be expressed numerically, for a rise in population automatically compelled other adjustments. Yet they went deeper. The people were not only more numerous, but different in character from their ancestors of 1642. The partial ending of civic isolation brought strangers to the Island, whose tastes did not always accord with the austerity of the founders. The church and the conversion of the heathen—these, while remaining potent forces in the community, were no longer all important. Once the mission station became a center of trade, some separation of interests—perhaps even a conflict—was inevitable.

To some extent, the stage had been set by the officers and men of the Carignan-Salières Regiment. No better, no worse, than other professional soldiers, their unabashed liking for the things of the flesh was such as to arouse alarm among the pious. When Quebec held its first ball in 1667, the Jesuits hoped it would have no evil consequences. Followed by theatrical presentations and *bals masqués,* it suggested that the armor of Catholic puritanism was starting to crack.

Yet it was from the fur trade that most of the changes flowed. A minor factor from the earliest years, it was now the all absorbing local interest. By 1667, Montreal had gained recognition as the principal market in the country, and business at Quebec and Three Rivers fell off correspondingly. Given the geographical advantages of the Island, the trend could hardly have been otherwise, and the merchants soon learned to exploit to the full, their proximity to the Indian country, with its right of first access to the tribes of the interior. In this way, the Montrealers became the middlemen, buying from the natives and selling to the royal agents for export to Europe. Not surprisingly, they prospered.

The precise method of handling the trade was always open to question. Should the Indians be encouraged to come down to the settlements? Or should the French go upcountry to the native villages in search of the precious beaver pelts? Some of the merchants, in their eagerness to outsmart their competitors, preferred the latter, and indeed practiced it in opposition to the public good. The government, however, never wavered in its support of the alternative, and as a means to this end, decreed that an annual Fair should be held on the Island.

These fairs were, in a sense, revivals or continuations of the more sober affairs held during the great days of Champlain. Picturesque they undoubtedly were, and profitable for their sponsors, yet hardly edifying for the quiet decent folk of the settlement. Each opened with due solemnity; the Grand Council on the Common beside the river; the ritual smoking of pipes; the exchange of speeches. On the next day, the trading started, when as Parkman wrote: "Merchants of high and low degree brought up their goods from Quebec, and every inhabitant of Montreal, of any substance, sought a share in the traffic. Their booths were set along the palisades of the town, and each had an interpreter, to whom he usually promised a certain portion of the gains . . . Here was a throng of Indians armed with bows and arrows, war-clubs, or the cheap guns of the trade—some of them being completely naked, except for the feathers on their heads and the paint on their faces; French bush-rangers tricked out with savage finery; merchants and habitants in their coarse and plain attire, and the grave priests of St. Sulpice robed in black. Order and sobriety were their watchwords; but the wild gathering was beyond their control. The prohibition to sell brandy could rarely be enforced; and the Fair ended at times in a pandemonium of drunken frenzy. The rapacity of trade, and the license of savages and *coureurs de bois,* had completely transformed the pious settlement."

Nor was this the whole story, since there was always a feast for the visiting redskins. With taverns at every street corner, all doing a roaring business, they arrived well-primed and eager to enjoy the truly exotic menu awaiting them in the courtyard of the Hôtel Dieu. The recipe called first of all, for large cauldrons filled with water. Into these, went a mixture of corn, large fat dogs and cats, beaver, bears, almost any animal would do. These were grilled over the embers to remove the hair and the fur, and then boiled together for half a day. Grapes and raisins were added for flavoring, the whole cooked for several more hours, and eaten, apparently with enjoyment. The warriors, as was their habit, belched loudly in appreciation of the hospitality.

However riotous these gatherings might be, they could at least be controlled and terminated by the authorities—something that was never possible in the case of the *coureurs de bois.* The fairs enjoyed their heyday all through the seventies, and then ceased about the year 1681. Abuses had crept in on the part of the French, while changing conditions among the tribes made the celebrations less valid. But the young white men who preferred to live in the wilderness—theirs was a story without an ending. No one ever succeeded completely in legislating them out of existence.

Champlain may be claimed as the originator of the *coureurs de bois,* yet his handful of youths had been chosen deliberately and to some extent, acted as his deputies. What they did was official and highly successful, and the trouble only began when others followed in their steps, and without governmental backing. By the second half of the century, their numbers had increased to such an extent as to cause concern among the authorities, ecclesiastical as well as civil.

Since outlaws do not readily lend themselves to any form of official nose counting, few statistics on this vexatious topic have survived. At one point, the number of *coureurs de bois* is re-

ported to have risen as high as 800—this total, weighed against
a population of 10,000, represented a serious drain on the
colony's manpower, which the government tried, not too successfully, to control. Thus in 1673, no one on pain of death,
could remain in the woods for more than twenty-four hours
without a special permit. Five years later, came a ban on any
trading at all, beyond the boundaries of the colony. In 1681,
a change in policy led to the proclamation of a general amnesty
for the offenders, if they returned immediately to the settlements.
At the same time, a system of official *congés* was announced,
limited in number to twenty-five each season. Issued free of
charge, they permitted the bearer to go into the interior to
trade—with the result that the lucky holders sold off their licenses
to the highest bidder. It was an unequal battle, which authority
never won.

How many of the *coureurs de bois* were native-born Montrealers is another matter on which the records were usually
silent. That all frequented the Island is a certainty, and officialdom often accused its people of being in league with the offenders—probably with justice, for such a connection was profitable
to both parties. Life in the wilderness led to direct contact with
the Indian trappers. Ergo, the restless young men blossomed
out as fur traders, at first as individuals, and later as agents
for the Montreal merchants. If the savages were to be inter-
cepted en route to the Island, they, the regular traders, intended to insure a share in the profits.

But whether the actual trading was carried on at Montreal
or in the woods, made little difference to the liquor traffic with
the Indians. It was a subject on which the church and the state
rarely agreed. Whereas Laval threatened excommunication, successive governors argued that if the English were going to supply
rum in return for furs, the French must offer brandy. The
colony needed the trade, and the trade needed the Indians.
Without liquor, French influence over the natives was bound
to weaken, with painful results to the country's economy.

Despite this official stand, and largely due to Laval's influence,
one of the first acts of the Sovereign Council in 1663, had
forbidden the sale of liquor to the tribes. Four years later, the

ban was renewed, and heavy penalties imposed, which the
coureurs de bois blithely ignored. So the traffic persisted, even
if at times driven underground. All the clergy were adamant in
their opposition, the Jesuits, the Sulpicians, the secular priests.
Led by the Bishop, they fought to secure total prohibition—and
in the end, won, at least in theory. In 1679, the king forbade the
transportation of liquor to the Indian villages, yet this, too,
proved to be a law easily evaded.

But not all the parties who left Montreal for the west, confined
their efforts to the fur trade. Exploration was decidedly a factor
in those busy years of peace, and indeed, the precise limits of
the two could not be easily defined. In both cases, the services
of the *coureurs de bois* were invaluable. At times, the government frowned on this expansion of territory. (Colbert, for instance, never ceased to consider it dangerous.) Yet the lure of
the unknown, remained strong, and a perpetual magnet for the
adventurous. All used Montreal as a base of operations, a point
of departure, a storehouse for supplies, a source of rescue in
time of trouble. Some of the men owned houses on the Island,
living there for several years at a stretch. A few returned there
to die.

Among these fur-trading explorers, none was more famous
than Robert Cavelier, Sieur de La Salle, a Montrealer by virtue
of his brief tenure of the seigniory of St. Sulpice, better known
nowadays as Lachine—a name that in itself, provides a clue to
his dreams. For Lachine is of course, La Chine—the country
of China—a title bestowed by his contemporaries in derision of
La Salle's hope of finding the long-desired northwest passage
to the Pacific. Civilization could not hope to hold such a man
for long. In 1669, some two years after his arrival from France,
he sold the property for a good price, and thereafter used the
Island chiefly as a starting point for his long trips into the
interior.

Montreal, by this date, had a new Governor in the person of
François Marie Perrot, chosen by the Sulpicians to fill the post
left vacant by the departure of Maisonneuve. He was a captain
in the Army, his wife the niece of Talon; together, a couple that
seemed to promise well, and as such, they were made welcome.

But Perrot, alas, lost little time in putting his seigniorial land to illegal use. It lay on the island that now bears his name, at the western tip of the main Island—a strategic spot for the interception of the beaver-laden canoes before they could be taken to Montreal. There he gave shelter to the more lawless elements of the population, handing out liquor and merchandise in exchange for furs. The disorderly scenes soon became an open scandal in the community.

Thus Perrot's popularity died almost before it was born, especially as he showed himself to be haughty and violent by nature. When a delegation of leading citizens ventured to protest the irregularities taking place on his property, he flew into such a rage that he clapped their leader in jail. The next day, when de Casson on behalf of the Seigneurs, objected to such high-handed justice, there were no signs of repentance. Eventually, of course, the unhappy man was released and the incident closed. But the new Governor had showed himself to be concerned only with lining his own pockets.

Not that there was anything inherently wicked in private participation in the fur trade. In the seventeenth and eighteenth centuries, it was more or less the accepted custom for the Governor, the Intendant and the lesser officials to take advantage of their positions in this way. Even such an upright public servant as Talon is said to have engaged in trading for his own ends. Salaries were so low, that some modest supplement was well-nigh imperative. At the risk of splitting hairs, it might be suggested that the practice itself was less objectionable than the manner and extent to which it was carried out.

Quebec, in the meantime, was in the midst of a transfer of government personnel. A growing coolness between Talon and de Courcelle had led, by 1671, to an almost complete estrangement. Both, having signified their desire to retire, left the country in 1672. With Laval in France on a prolonged stay, the stage was set for the initial performance of the most colorful actor New France had yet seen—the new Governor, Louis Buade, Comte de Frontenac. It was a situation made to order for a man of his temperament.

Perhaps anyone chosen to act as the personal representative

of Louis XIV, might have succumbed to vanity; Frontenac was frankly impossible. Haughty and aristocratic by nature, he demanded absolute obedience from his inferiors in rank, and an extravagant deference to all his wishes. Nor was he an inexperienced stripling. At the age of fifty, Frontenac was a veteran of long military service and a frequenter of the royal courts.

To such a man, eternally conscious of his lofty position, any division of authority was unthinkable. Neither the Intendant nor the Sovereign Council could be allowed to dictate how the country should be run. He, and he alone, was supreme, not only in the administration of justice, but in all departments of the government. And because such a course, adhered to at all times, led him into conflict with his associates, the affairs of the country were soon in an uproar. Small wonder that Montreal and the new Governor General promptly had a falling out.

Within a few months of his arrival, Frontenac announced his intention of establishing a fort on Lake Ontario for the better control of the fur trade. Only in this way, he reasoned, could the Indians be prevented from going down to Albany with their precious loads. In addition, it would provide additional defense for the whole colony.

Any such extension of French territory ran directly counter to Colbert's instructions, as Frontenac well knew. Therefore, he urged the necessity for rapid construction; the fort must be completed before a veto could possibly arrive from France. Moreover, he proposed to make an official visit to the Indians of the Lake regions.

It was in the course of this grand progress that Frontenac made his first inspection of the Island in June 1673. His official welcome was all that the vainest man could hope for; the leading citizens waiting at the wharf to greet him; speeches and sermons; a Te Deum of thanksgiving; volleys of gunfire; formal ceremonies that meant less than nothing to the townspeople. The merchants considered that Fort Frontenac at Cataraqui (now Kingston) posed a distinct threat to their trade. How could the Indians be expected to continue downstream to the Island? What is more, these shrewd observers were already suspicious of Frontenac's personal motives. To them, his grand talk seemed little more than a front to conceal his hope of private gains.

The habitants were equally resentful, for Frontenac had requisitioned about two hundred canoes and four hundred men for his expedition. He had also ordered a *corvée*, to provide the labor needed to transport the materials for building the Fort. Accustomed as everyone was to compulsory work for only a few days each year, there was considerable anger at the first imposition which lasted a month. As other *corvées* followed, most of the summer passed in these forced levies. When the expedition finally got off at the end of June, Frontenac left behind a populace that was seething with anger. Later that autumn, when trouble broke out between the two governors, Montreal unhesitatingly rallied to the support of Perrot.

That Frontenac should take the offensive against Perrot was a measure of his determination to dominate the fur trade. Because the activities at the island seigniory threatened a division of profits, they must be stopped and their author punished. An easy weapon lay close at hand in the *coureurs de bois*, at that date forbidden to remain in the woods more than twenty-four hours without official permission. A reprimand was followed by an order restricting Perrot's authority to the Island of Montreal proper. Then came the accusation that he was permitting men to leave without having secured the necessary licenses from Quebec.

The result was a decision to make an example of two supposed offenders, Frontenac sending his lieutenant to make the arrests. A first attempt failed, the culprits having been warned in time. Retribution fell, instead, on the householder who had given them shelter; he was taken into custody in lieu of the missing *coureurs de bois*. Perrot, justifiably angered, held the Quebec agent in detention for twenty-four hours before shipping him home.

What followed was a comedy of errors, as each Governor accused the other of trespassing on his opponent's prerogatives. Frontenac went further, claiming that any resistance to his authority constituted sedition and a defiance of the king. Arrest of such a person was imperative.

Having decided eventually that guile might be more effective than force, Frontenac wrote to Perrot, suggesting a friendly visit to Quebec when their differences might be ironed out satisfactorily. To the young Abbé Fénelon went a similar letter, seeking his good offices in persuading Perrot to accept the invitation. The bait, thus dangled, proved sufficiently tempting, and the two men set off together to pay their respects to their superior. They walked into a trap, for as soon as Perrot reached the capital, he was arrested and held incommunicado until his case was brought before the Sovereign Council. The affair dragged on for eight months, the accused in custody all the while, as the Council members tried in vain to reach a decision.

Needless to say, the Abbé Fénelon was shocked by this official duplicity, and ashamed at having contributed, no matter how innocently, to the downfall of his friend. But being unable to help the captive at Quebec, he busied himself in Montreal, helping Madame Perrot obtain signatures to a petition drawn up on her husband's behalf. This, to Frontenac, was treason, even though the offender was an ecclesiastic.

But worse was to follow, for the Abbé seems to have been singularly indiscreet by nature. He was always a ready talker, but when he chose Easter Sunday to deliver an inflammatory sermon in the Parish Church, he ran headlong into trouble. Without mentioning any names, he discussed the responsibilities of a truly Christian magistrate. Such a man, he pointed out, should never use his power to further his own interests; to his people, he should act as a father to his children; there should be no imposition of unjust *corvées*.

Outspoken as this was, it might have passed unnoticed, except for the attitude of La Salle, by now a faithful follower of Frontenac. Rising to his feet in the midst of the congregation, he made signs to his friends, bidding them take heed of what was being said in the pulpit. And of course, in a report to his patron in Quebec, the whole affair was magnified beyond recognition.

The Sulpicians, understandably, through all these charges, had been studious in their desire to remain neutral. Now, disturbed at such indiscretion, on the part of one of their own number, they disclaimed responsibility. The young man, they promised, would not be allowed to preach again. But La Salle refused to let his story die. Fénelon must appear before the Sovereign Council and answer to charges of sedition.

This proved to be difficult, for Fénelon, as an ecclesiastic, denied the jurisdiction of the Council. He protested the authority of such a civil court, and claimed all manner of special rights and privileges. Once again, after lengthy sessions, the members found themselves unable to arrive at a clear decision, pleading that only the king could rule in such cases.

So now, there stood the two men—Perrot and Fénelon, the Governor and the priest—arraigned together on similar charges of treason against the Crown. No one knew how to deal with them, particularly as Perrot, incensed by his long months in jail, was growing more emphatic in his threats of royal displeasure. At last, Frontenac gave way to the extent of permitting their return to France in the autumn of 1674. From start to finish, it had been a sorry performance, and in the royal judgment, rendered the following year, there was scant comfort for the instigator of the fracas.

Perrot, it is true, was confined to the Bastille for three weeks, as punishment for having defied the king's authority, vested in the person of the Governor General. But he was promptly reinstated as Governor of Montreal, on condition of making a public apology to his superior in Quebec. It was a minor penalty, face-saving for Frontenac, and nothing more. Colbert's warning was unmistakable; no action must, in future, be taken in districts having a local governor, without advance notice. Beyond this, Frontenac was cautioned to use his power with the greatest moderation, especially in regard to the priests. For although the king forbade Fénelon's return to Montreal, he insisted on the need to show particular consideration for the Gentlemen of St. Sulpice.

As for Perrot, there is little to report that is good. He returned to Montreal, retaining his office amid a chorus of mounting scandals and public complaints. Jail sentences in Paris and Quebec had brought about no reformation, and he seems to have gone from bad to worse, in his abuse of honest men, and his encouragement of the *coureurs de bois* and the liquor traffic.

Frontenac, for his part, was soon equally embroiled with the people of Montreal. His vendetta with Perrot was simply a curtain raiser, and the subsequent unholy alliance between the two did nothing to improve matters. If the Governor General was vindictive, so was his subordinate; the town resented them both, and they, in turn, punished the town whenever possible. One unfortunate victim awoke to find all his fruit trees had been cut down overnight. Another merchant actually went so far as to claim the protection of the Sovereign Council; beaten up by Perrot himself, and robbed of his furs, the unhappy man had been driven from his home. Business, in general, was nearly at a standstill, since trading with the Indians was forbidden, except to those who supported the two governors.

Faced with such a deplorable situation, it was natural that people should complain. Without any hope of redress in their own country, they turned to France, and a steady flow of written reports and personal representations got under way. Their reward came in 1680 and again in 1681, with the arrival of commissioners, charged with the duty of investigating local irregularities. It was largely as a result of their findings that Perrot was removed from office in 1682. Perhaps it is not too much to claim also, that they contributed to Frontenac's recall in the same year.

Montreal was by no means alone, in its opposition to the Governor General. One of his strongest opponents was the Intendant, Duchesneau, who came to New France in 1675. Although their disputes originated in the division of authority between their respective posts, they soon branched out into other fields. The disorders at Montreal were common knowledge, and to the honest and conscientious Intendant, inexcusable. The Sovereign Council was in a state of smoldering indignation. Frontenac's increasing determination to dominate its members, contributed to his downfall. As for the Jesuits, there had never been any love lost. Everyone protested, and the king acted. In 1682, Frontenac was recalled, along with Duchesneau. With Perrot gone, a clean sweep had been made of the top officials of the colony.

Yet the seventies, for all their unsavory lapses from grace, did not fail to show signs of progress. Carried over into the eighties, they witnessed the modest beginnings of some of Montreal's most famous religious institutions.

Spanning the years as it did, the construction of the new Parish Church imposed a considereable burden upon the still small congregation. The planning started as far back as 1669, when Laval, during one of his pastoral visits, presided over a meeting of the inhabitants. Although all signified their approval of the project, the actual work was deferred for several seasons. There was discussion over the site, it being decided eventually to move to higher ground at the head of St. Joseph Street, facing Notre Dame. By June 1672 the transfer had been completed and the outline of the proposed structure traced. On the 29th of the same month, after vespers, a procession went up from the Hôtel Dieu chapel at the foot of the hill, to the new location. Leading it was Dollier de Casson, who as Superior of the Seminary, planted a cross in the presence of a great crowd. Next day came the laying of the five cornerstones, bearing the arms respectively of Jeanne Mance, de Courcelle, Talon, de Casson, and Perrot.

But for a long time, the completion of the church remained an unrealized dream. In 1676, a thorough canvass of the Island resulted in the collection of 2072 livres, yet even though Abbé Souart promised to furnish all the wood, funds were still insufficient. Two more years were in fact, to pass before La Paroisse —the first Notre Dame—became a reality. Built of rough stone pointed with mortar, its 140 foot length stood in the middle of Notre Dame Street, projecting out into Place d'Armes.

With the death of Jeanne Mance in 1673, the last direct link with the founders was broken. Active as always, she supervised the administration of the Hôtel Dieu until the end of her days, although after the coming of the Hospitalières in 1659, she did little actual nursing. Three in number at first, there were eighteen or twenty of these devoted women in Montreal at this time of bereavement. All still went without the barest creature comforts; when there was money, it was spent on the indigent patients, and the Hospitalières never complained.

Marguerite Bourgeoys and her three original assistants suffered similar hardships. They received no remuneration, teaching school by day, supporting themselves by means of manual labor at night. Being lay women, they had taken no vows, although people referred with affection to "La Congregation." By 1667, Montreal, realizing the importance of this educational program, petitioned the king for its acceptance as a religious Order. In 1670, Marguerite Bourgeoys herself went to France in search of more volunteers and there by good fortune, she met Colbert. In 1671, the Letters Patent were published.

Laval had always objected to any such proposal. Ever the advocate of centralization, he viewed with apprehension the establishment of a second Order of nuns. In his opinion, the Ursulines of Quebec should be strengthened, not provided with competition. Especially repugnant, too, was this concept of a religious community that was not cloistered. That the Sisters should be able to move freely among the people, was unheard of during the seventeenth century.

Yet in 1676, a group of postulants awaited the Bishop in Montreal, that at his hands, they might formally be received into La Congregation de Notre Dame. For Marguerite Bourgeoys, the ceremony stood out as a landmark in her long struggle to gain acceptance for her "Community"—an achievement no less wonderful than the renewed progress on the long deferred Chapel of Bonsecours. Pushed aside temporarily because of the greater urgency of the Parish Church, the first stone was laid in the summer of 1675.

The "Mountain Mission" also dated from 1676, a village founded by the Sulpicians, in which Christian Indians might live at peace. There, on the hillside, converts were encouraged to settle, with the promise of education for their children. All were trained in simple reading and writing, and the rudiments of the faith. The girls, in addition, received instruction in the care of the home and other domestic arts. A crude affair at first, a cluster of birchbark huts stood beside the wigwams, providing living quarters for the Sisters. M. de Belmont, the Sulpician who in 1681 became the director of the boys' school, added a little chapel, dedicated to Notre Dame des Neiges. Several years later, being fearful of an attack by non-Christian tribes, he erected a palisade around the isolated settlement, and gradually the fortifications were strengthened.

A product of the same period, the Sulpician Seminary and Chapter House was fashioned of stone, strong enough to survive nearly three centuries. Today it is honored as being the oldest building in Montreal. Dollier de Casson, about 1683, was responsible for the construction of what is now the central section. Standing on Notre Dame Street, next to the church of the same name, its façade is crowned by an ancient belfry and clock. Reputed by some authorities to be the oldest public timepiece in North America, its date is not entirely certain. It was, for more than a hundred years, the only one in Montreal.

Notwithstanding all this activity, it should not be imagined that Montreal, as yet, presented any fine picture of beauty. That there were new houses meant nothing so far as outward appearance went. As for the streets, they were the cause of great complaint, long after de Casson's initial venture. Some of the proprietors went so far as to ignore them completely, carrying on the cultivation of their land, as though in the depths of the country. The more progressive owners, who wanted to build, often found their way of access blocked. Finally, all raising of crops on the roadways was forbidden, and each man permitted to enclose his lot with stakes or hedges. Still the thoroughfares remained in such bad condition, that efforts were made to force each householder to pave out to the middle of the section immediately in front of his dwelling.

Chapter 8

1682–1689

The frontier moves westward. The English colonies. The begin-
nings of conflict, in Europe and America. Fortifications. The
Iroquois once more. The massacre of Lachine.

FRONTENAC, RECALLED TO France, was not easily forgotten in the
colony. However detestable he may have seemed to Montreal
and Quebec, he had initiated a program of expansion that was
to have a lasting effect on the history of New France. Moreover,
just as Colbert had warned, it brought danger to the vulnerable
settlements along the St. Lawrence.

By this date, of course, the frontier had passed far beyond
Montreal—at first, the one hundred and fifty miles up to Fort
Frontenac at Cataraqui—later, spreading out to the west, the
north, and the south. It was a period studded with the names of
the explorers; Père Marquette and Louis Jolliet who, in 1673, discovered the Mississippi and sailed down the river as far as the
mouth of the Arkansas; La Salle who, in 1682 and after many
tribulations, reached the mouth of the Mississippi; Daniel Grey-
solon Duluth who left Montreal in 1678, for what was to be a
lifetime spent in the northwest beyond Lake Superior. One thing
led to another—discovery, the fur trade, the construction of forts
—as the French penetrated deep into the heart of the continent.
Almost imperceptibly, they acquired an empire of vast dimensions; indefensible, if measured in terms of their limited manpower, and hence an open invitation to attack.

Happily for the colony, in the years since de Tracy's campaign, the Five Nations themselves had not been immune from
trouble. There was dissension within their ranks, and fighting

with the tribes to the west. It was once again convenient to be at peace with the French. But by the early eighties, there were ominous signs that the respite was drawing to a close.

Nor were the Iroquois alone in their hostility to the French. Another and more dangerous enemy lay to the south, in the territories peopled by the English. In their earlier days, there had been little direct contact between the two nationalities in North America. Hundreds of miles of dense wilderness made an effective barrier, and each was fully occupied with the beginnings of settlement and the difficulties of life in a new land. Both had fought Indian wars. Between the two mother countries, each beset by domestic crises, there had been no open conflict, and thus no encouragement to strife overseas.

This relatively peaceful frame of mind was now changing rapidly, as the rival colonies, freed from the anxieties of their first years, turned against each other. In the end, the long struggle between the French and the English was to be more important than any fighting with the Iroquois, and its results affected the allegiance of both races. It started quite naturally with the fur trade, in which Montreal and Albany had long been rivals, and intensified with the French move into the west, where their outposts presented a direct challenge to any English occupation. The French ambitions were boundless and their hopes high; nothing less than the control of the continent. The English, hemmed in along the eastern seaboard, were to be barred from further progress inland, by means of a ring of forts from Montreal to Louisiana.

In such a grandiose scheme, the Indians had a share, for each nation had its allies among the tribes. Not always dependable, and easily weaned away from their sponsors, the savages sensed their own importance. Wooed now by one, and now by the other, they collected presents and bribes, exchanged flowery speeches, and usually ended by selling their wares to the highest bidder. It was a game that could have serious consequences.

Although the competition everywhere grew more fierce and at times broke out into actual violence, the two countries—at least in Europe—remained officially at peace. Up to a point, any disorders in America were condoned by eyes, conveniently blind, in

Paris and London. So long as the Stuart kings remained on the throne, any definite rupture was unlikely. Charles II and his brother and successor, James II, were practically pensioners of Louis XIV. Self-interest, monetary considerations, religious ties —these conspired to keep them loyal to their friends across the Channel.

Yet it was a ticklish situation that confronted Frontenac's successor, and perhaps only Solomon, in his wisdom, could have found a satisfactory solution. Unhappily, Joseph Antoine Lefebvre de la Barre possessed few of the essential qualities. His was a strange appointment. Physically, there was little to recommend him, for at the age of sixty, he could scarcely cope with the rough life of the wilderness. Intellectually, he was in worse case, indecisive in his judgments, easily swayed by others, and thus he quickly found himself involved with a clique of merchants from Montreal and Quebec. At their behest, licenses were dealt out with a lavish hand, and the *coureurs de bois* multiplied and grew rich. Fur trading was a profitable business.

When Quebec heard that the Iroquois had declared war against the Illinois tribes, it seemed reasonable that the victims, being good allies of the French, should be supported. La Barre, all in a flutter, sent off posthaste to France for reinforcements, feeling that a full-scale campaign against the ancient enemy could not be avoided. In the meantime, he decided to try compromise.

The result was that invitations went out to the offending chiefs, summoning them to a council at Montreal. What followed was almost a farce, for the attendance was meager and the results few. If the savages were haughty, La Barre was timid, and all the presents and soothing speeches availed nothing. The breathing-space was short-lived. Conspicuous by their absence were the Senecas, the most powerful tribe in the Five Nations, able to muster as many warriors as all the others put together. Living as they did, far to the west of the Mohawks, they had not as yet felt the military strength of the French and were openly contemptuous of the Governor General.

Eventually La Barre, having decided that the Senecas must be taught a lesson, set Montreal as the rendezvous in the summer of 1684. There, two hundred troops fresh from France, met with their elderly general, who proposed to take personal command of the expedition. After dawdling along, the party reached Fort Frontenac, its numbers reinforced along the way by some hundreds of Canadians and Indians. But then the mishaps started, the men sickened by a kind of fever and the supplies running short. Having put out feelers for a peace conference, La Barre agreed to meet the Iroquois on their own ground. The results were humiliating. The French promptly abandoned their Illinois allies, and returned to Montreal, demoralized by this inept leadership. That La Barre was speedily removed from office, was cold comfort to those most likely to suffer from his mishandling of the Indian menace.

By good chance, in the person of the Intendant, New France had an honest official who possessed good sense. Jacques de Meulles inherited the thankless task of paying the bills for the ill-fated affair. Montreal and the country at large, seemed headed for financial ruin. There was little currency on hand, in the sense of coins, and the legal tender of beaver skins and grain was highly inconvenient. To meet this emergency, de Meulles issued his famous "card money"—ordinary playing cards, halved or quartered, and signed and countersigned by the appropriate officials—redeemable as more specie came in from France. Although its later and excessive use led to depreciation, card money as originally conceived, was a highly ingenious invention.

But at the best, it was an atmosphere of mistrust and confusion that greeted the new Governor General in August 1685. The Marquis de Denonville was not easily daunted. Many years of service in the armies of France, had strengthened his innate vigor and firmness, while his personal honesty presented a welcome change to the habits of his predecessors.

He came from a homeland that was changing rapidly, the fortunes of New France now less vital than ascendancy in Europe. With the death of Colbert in 1683, the great colonial era ended, for his son and successor, the Marquis de Seignelay, had little power. The king's interests had shifted away from the New World, partly because of the influence of his second wife, the pious Madame de Maintenon. Hence the government's instruc-

1. Montreal from the mountain, 1811. *(Edward Walsh)*

2. Montreal from St. Helen's Island, 1828. *(James Gray)*

3. Port of Montreal, 1829–30. *(Robert Auchmuty Sproule)*

4. Saint James Street, Montreal, 1829–30. *(Robert Auchmuty Sproule)*

5. Place d'Armes, Montreal, 1829. *(Robert Auchmuty Sproule)*

6. Nelson Monument, Notre Dame Street, 1830. *(Robert Auchmuty Sproule)*

7. Interior of Notre Dame Church, 1839–40. *(William Henry Bartlett)*

8. Notre Dame Church, 1839–40. *(William Henry Bartlett)*

tions to the new official, though broad and comprehensive, were unlikely to be backed by force, should need arise.

Ecclesiastically, Denonville made a good start toward domestic peace. Laval's wish to retire was at long last being granted; age and infirmity made it imperative. It chanced that his young successor—the Bishop-elect, Monsignor de Saint-Vallier—had come to Quebec on the same ship as the Governor General. The two became fast friends, and shared a gloomy view of Canadian life and morals. Their letters reveal them as being deeply worried at the drunkenness and the infinite number of taverns at Montreal and elsewhere; at the badly trained youths who took to the woods so as to avoid parental restraints and the guidance of the church; at the lounging idlers among the noblesse; at the women and girls, given over to vanity and immodesty of dress.

Denonville, at least, was not without personal knowledge of conditions, for one of his first duties in 1684 was the induction of a new Governor of Montreal. It was a happy occasion, for Louis Hector de Callière belonged to the tradition of Maisonneuve, a soldier popular with the people, strong in his personal integrity, and decisive in his actions. Twenty years of service in New France lay before him, at first in Montreal, and later as Governor General. His was an appointment that promised well for the Island.

In truth, the two governors, with their military backgrounds, were shocked by the universal state of unpreparedness. To their trained eyes, the straggling settlements along the St. Lawrence were ill-placed for defense, and the western outposts too remote for adequate garrisons. At the very moment when another Iroquois war seemed inevitable, men were scarce, and their lines stretched dangerously thin. Montreal looked particularly exposed, since the old fortifications had long since crumbled away through neglect and indifference.

Characteristically, de Callière took action without delay, tackling the new protective measures with such energy that at one time, six hundred men worked on their construction. Great stakes of cedar were firmly implanted in the ground, to form a palisade fifteen feet high, and equipped with watchtowers, platforms, and gates. Thus the town proper was enclosed on all sides—a statement that probably sounds better than conditions warranted. The effectiveness of such a wall was questionable, in the face of heavy musketry fire. That it would serve to deflect Indian arrows was more likely; and psychologically, it was comforting to the inhabitants. That it also happened to be costly, shocked the king into ordering its cancellation—by good luck, too late to halt the work.

Beyond the Montreal boundaries, a similar flurry of construction was put in hand, when the scattered seigniories, belatedly, realized their danger. Wooden blockhouses sprang up, dotting the landscape wherever there was a cluster of houses. Occasionally, stone was employed, as in the case of the Le Moyne estate at Longueuil, its fort of solid masonry being flanked by four towers. There was, of course, much to protect in this unusually large establishment—an elaborate manor house, a church, a mill, and a full complement of stables and outhouses. For although Charles Le Moyne the elder died in 1685, his sons carried on the high family tradition.

Yet despite this preoccupation with self-defense, Montreal sometimes found itself involved in larger issues—playing host, for example, in the late winter of 1686, to a small military party, preparing for an overland attack against the Hudson's Bay Company. A hundred men made up the group, thirty of them French Troupes de la Marine, the rest, Canadian volunteers—among the latter, three Le Moyne brothers, Iberville, Sainte-Hélène, and Maricourt, their titles derived from their seigniories. The send-off was a rousing one, de Callière reviewing the troops as they stood at attention on the riverbank. Then, as they raised their hands to swear fealty to the king, there were salutes from the Fort and cheers from the inhabitants. It need only be added that they met with complete success. When Iberville returned to Canada in 1687, only one enemy fort in the north remained untouched.

Scarcely had this expedition been dispatched, than Denonville proceeded with plans for a more ambitious campaign—nothing less than the destruction of the Iroquois villages, and especially those of the Seneca tribes. The preparations were shrouded in secrecy, in the hope of catching the enemy warriors off guard.

But as the men mustered at the special camp on St. Helen's Island, they were an impressive sight; eight hundred Troupes de la Marine, a thousand Canadians, three hundred mission Indians. More volunteers joined them en route, bringing their total strength up to three thousand. Denonville led them in person; with him went the Chevalier de Vaudreuil, the recently arrived commander of the French regulars; de Champigny, the new Intendant; de Callière, in charge of the Canadian militia. June 11 saw their departure, on the first leg of a journey made difficult by the currents of the river.

It was at Fort Frontenac, their first stopping place, that a most unfortunate incident occurred. The Intendant, de Champigny, having gone ahead of the main party, issued an invitation to the friendly Iroquois of the neighborhood. In the name of the Governor General, they were bidden to a feast. Nearly a hundred accepted, quite unsuspectingly, only to be treacherously seized, bound, and held captive by their French hosts. That their betrayal originated in Denonville's determination to keep his movements hidden, did nothing to lessen the shock. Nor did his hope of using them as hostages fare any better. The king ordered the hapless savages to France, where men were needed for the royal galleys. Their relatives thirsted for revenge.

Ironically enough, the French arrived in the Seneca country, to find the enemy alerted by a lone scout who had slipped unseen through the woods. Yet the warriors could not hope to withstand such an army for long. So it was that victory of a sort went to the invaders, who spent nine days in the villages, burning and destroying homes, crops, cattle—everything in sight went up in the flames.

Two months later saw the sequel, for during October two hundred Iroquois descended upon the upper end of the Island, killing the inhabitants and razing their homes, in what was the first of many raids against the outlying districts. To counteract the danger, Denonville pressed ahead with the construction of blockhouses in each seigniory, until eventually twenty-eight of these local strongholds contributed to the defense of Montreal. Doubling as places of refuge for the civilians and as quarters for the troops, they were of great assistance to the foolhardy habitants who had refused to take precautions against their old enemy.

Yet throughout this difficult period, Denonville and de Callière were untiring in their efforts to defend the country. All to little avail, for the Iroquois raids grew fiercer. Aided and abetted by the English of New York, the warriors were proving too strong for the slender reserves of the French. While the loss of life and of property continued to climb, the fur trade was at a standstill, and agriculture paralyzed. In this crisis, Denonville conceived of a bold scheme. If only New York could be captured, most of the difficulties in New France would come to an end. Possession of an ice-free port would revolutionize life along the St. Lawrence.

Support for these views came instantly from the leaders of Montreal. In their exposed situation, they could hardly feel otherwise. De Callière went further, for he worked out a detailed plan of operations. It embodied attacks by sea and land, and entailed careful timing. Albany, as the first target, was to be reached overland via Lakes Champlain and George; its three hundred inhabitants were feebly protected by a small fort and a few men. New York itself, with its four hundred people, would then fall an easy prey to the guns of the French warships. The Dutch, dissatisfied with their new English rulers, could be counted on for assistance. So went the reasoning—logical enough for Denonville to send de Callière to France in the autumn of 1688. The king was to be told of the plans.

The summer just past had been a hard one. Montreal remained in a state of siege, its people confined within the palisade, so providentially erected the previous year. In the outlying seigniories, the habitants took refuge in the blockhouses or crowded into the main fortification. The fields lay neglected and bare of crops.

So alarming did the prospects seem that Denonville decided to try his hand at negotiations, with the hope that through discussion, some measure of peace could be won. The result was another conference, held in Montreal in June of the same year. The chiefs of the Onondagas, the Cayugas, and the Oneidas attended, and finally they hammered out an agreement, calling for a truce, and ultimately a treaty.

Laudable as this was, any thoughts of amity were wiped out by the trouble-making proclivities of "the Rat," a chief of the Huron tribe. He feared that peace would free the Iroquois for an attack on his people. Waylaying the Senecas on their way to Montreal, he fired on them from ambush, and then laid the blame on the French for breaking their word. Needless to say, the Iroquois all went home, bent on avenging the supposed wrong.

The winter and spring of 1689 were fairly quiet at Montreal. With de Callière in France, Vaudreuil assumed command of the Island. But public vigilance slackened, for he was less strict than the absent Governor. The settlers, softened by the long years of security, were, in any case, inclined to be careless, and needed constant prodding from above.

Meanwhile, there were changes in the government. Denonville was honorably recalled, to serve a France once more facing war. It was emphasized that no criticism was implied by this abrupt summons home. As his successor, Frontenac was nominated for a second term, and October 1689 saw his arrival at Quebec in the company of de Callière. The latter's New York scheme, it might be added, was so modified and then delayed that the whole enterprise collapsed.

By that date, Montreal had other matters on its mind. Disaster had struck the Island, so violent in nature that everything else was forgotten. During a heavy hailstorm on the night of August 5, fifteen hundred Iroquois warriors crossed Lake St. Louis a little above the main settlement. At that hour, everyone was asleep in the little homes scattered about Lachine. The weather was bad and no one kept watch. The enemy closed in undetected, their war whoops the first sound of warning—attacking and slaughtering the inhabitants, men, women, children, and babes in arms. It made a shocking scene, all the worse for its suddenness; the mutilated bodies, the cries and suffering of the wounded and the prisoners, the flames eating into the houses and barns.

Denonville, who was in Montreal only a few miles away, directed everyone to seek shelter in the forts. Vaudreuil, he dispatched to the scene of the massacre, at the head of three hundred men, with orders to run no risks, and remain on the defensive. The whole community, by this time, was thoroughly aroused, and at Lachine, a crowd of eager volunteers could hardly be restrained at the sight of the Iroquois, hopelessly drunk on stolen brandy. Yet although the officers longed to attack, Vaudreuil refused. Being of a cautious nature, he interpreted the Governor's words too literally. He remained safely in the fort, sending back to Montreal for reinforcements, and even these were caught in an ambush before they reached Lachine. Everyone was terrified.

Later the same day, the Iroquois crossed back to the south shore, taking their prisoners with them. That night, from the forts, as the French watched the flickering light of the fires, they realized with horror what was happening before their eyes. Some of the poor souls were being roasted alive, and their flesh eaten. No one at Montreal had offered effective resistance, and so the massacre had proceeded unchecked.

Chapter 9

1689–1698

La petite guerre. Border raids from Montreal. The Island fearful of the English and the Iroquois. Madeleine de Verchères.

THAT FRONTENAC SHOULD be appointed for a second term of office was, in part, a measure of the urgency of the times. For all his iniquitous past, he was a man of action—perhaps even of the wisdom that grows from experience—and these were qualities sorely needed in the New France that awaited him.

So the new-old Governor General returned to Quebec, under strict orders from the king to practice moderation in all things, and to strive for a peaceful co-existence with the officials already in the country. He found, in fact, an unusually strong triumvirate attending his pleasure; de Callière, Governor of Montreal; de Champigny, the Intendant; Vaudreuil, the commander of the French forces. None were men easily trampled on. None would hesitate to oppose him in wrongdoing. Their own integrity kept them above suspicion, and all boasted influential friends at court —that unfailing road to preferment in the France they served.

Meanwhile in Europe, France and England were at war. It was a sudden change of climate, whose origins lay in the deposition of James II by a people long out of sympathy with his political and religious views. William of Orange and Mary his wife, the daughter of James, ruled in his stead—sovereigns, as were their successors, by consent of Parliament. All were adherents of the Protestant faith. The Stuarts of the male line— loyal to the ancient concept of the divine right of kings—lived

out their days in exile, pensioners and hangers-on, for the most
part, of the French court.

Overnight, the friendliness between the two nations vanished,
for William III and Louis XIV were enemies of long standing.
From this European core, the hostilities spread to India and
America. Growing out of a deep-rooted national antagonism,
the bitter struggle dragged on for years, to end finally in 1815
with the defeat of Napoleon at Waterloo.

Some historians feel that the Iroquois themselves, had a grand
design. In their opinion, the attack on Lachine was intended
as a prelude to a general assault on the country. Montreal was
to be captured and destroyed, and then the warriors would
descend the St. Lawrence to Three Rivers and Quebec, carrying
out a piecemeal devastation of the land. Whatever the merits of
such a plan, it never achieved any great measure of success.
Nothing had happened to Montreal, beyond the sadly distressing
massacre. Its people remained unharmed, within their forts and
blockhouses, and there had been no decisive impact on the
main settlement. To this extent at least, the Iroquois failed to
reach any lasting victory.

It was the end of October when Frontenac landed at Quebec,
to be greeted by the news of the massacre. At its best, this very
late autumn is seldom a pleasant season; in 1689, incessant rain
added physical discomfort to the prevailing gloom. Three or
four days sufficed for the energetic Governor General to prepare
for his departure for Montreal—accompanied, be it noted, by a
large escort. Something of the old Adam appeared in his insistence that the leading citizens of the capital were to accompany him. Thus, attended by a retinue in keeping with his
lofty station in life, he set off on what was to be a miserable
trip. Seven days in open boats, exposed to the rain and the wind;
it was a bedraggled company that reached the Island.

That Montreal should welcome its ancient foe, was by no
means surprising. Although Denonville and de Champigny were
still in residence at the Fort, the sight of a fresh face promised
relief. All that was humanly possible had been done to relieve
the townspeople, the retiring Governor General and the Intendant working ceaselessly to that end. But Frontenac was always

Frontenac, convinced that his abilities outweighed the lesser qualities of his associates. The defenses were inspected and the garrison troops reviewed with a tremendous flourish. To hear him talk afterward, anyone might think that he alone had saved Montreal from the horrors of a second Lachine.

Ironically, Frontenac's first attempts at action met with little or no success. The Iroquois—those with whom he could make contact—cold-shouldered his invitation to a council at Fort Frontenac. The prospect of peace, or a temporary reconciliation, had no appeal for the warring tribes. Even the return of their captive kinsfolk from France, did nothing to soften their hearts. Only thirteen, it might be added, had survived the hardships of their life on the royal galleys.

After the Iroquois the English, and this time, the plans yielded more visible results. Frontenac and de Callière pooled their resources, to organize three parties, based on Montreal, Three Rivers and Quebec; their objective, the settlements along the New York border.

It was January by the time the Montrealers got away, on what promised to be a hard march over snow and ice. D'Ailleboust de Mantet and Le Moyne de Ste. Hélène commanded the two hundred Canadians and Indians—all accustomed to guerrilla warfare and the rigors of winter. They reached the little village of Schenectady without incident, taking its inhabitants unawares. What followed was the usual slaughter of civilians and destruction of property; it was Lachine in reverse.

Although the raid in itself was a minor one, and valuable chiefly as a restorative of morale in Montreal, it should by no means be pushed aside as unimportant. Where one army had gone, others could follow, until the isolated English villages along the borders found themselves the targets of constant small attacks. So well recognized did this type of warfare become, that it even acquired a name—*la petite guerre*. In fact, at times, it seemed more effective than the conventional tactics of the officers trained in Europe.

Montreal, from the outset, served as the base for most of these expeditions. The proximity of the Richelieu River made it an obvious choice, since Champlain's old route down the Lakes to

the Hudson, still remained the chief highway between north
and south. Doubtless the honor pleased many of the population,
for the Island was always the meeting place of the *coureurs de
bois*. War, for such men, did not make much change in their
chosen way of life. The fighting merely became official, and the
government ceased to frown on their activities. It was only the
quiet minority—and chiefly the religious Orders—who showed
anxiety at such a widespread disregard of law and order. With
strong drink flowing freely and street brawls common, the Sulpicians experienced difficulty in keeping the peace within their
seigniory.

The regular troops from France rarely shared in the manning
of the war parties. They formed the garrisons, and were responsible for the defense of the country. Many of their officers sneered
at this unconventional mode of fighting, yet it suited the Canadian temperament. The local militia showed no hesitation at
serving with the Indians. Compulsory military service was, at
this date, an established fact in New France, and all males
between the ages of sixteen and sixty were subject to call-up.
Organized as they were, in companies grouped by seigniorial
boundaries, a man could be sure of fighting alongside his friends
and neighbors. And because he knew from experience, the effectiveness of Iroquois warfare, he was apt to copy its methods
when raiding the English settlements.

By midsummer of 1690, Frontenac was back in Montreal with
encouraging words for the inhabitants still crowded in behind
the stockade. Meanwhile, de Callière toiled on, repairing and
strengthening the defenses as best he could. But weak though
these were, their cost shocked the king. There was no justification for the expenditure of so much money. Clearly, Louis XIV
was far away from the danger zone.

August brought rumors of English plans for an invasion. In
one sense, the news came as a surprise, and yet it was an obvious
retaliation for the French raids of the previous winter. These had
roused New York to such a pitch of fury that only direct action
could give relief. New England agreed. The assault, as planned,
fell into two sections—by sea against Quebec, by land against

Montreal—a strategy that became the classic framework for all subsequent attacks on Canada.

When word came in that the enemy was approaching down the Richelieu Valley, Frontenac rushed across to LaPrairie, at the head of twelve hundred men. But the English army had almost disintegrated. The small party which under Captain John Schuyler reached the St. Lawrence, retired in the face of such strong resistance.

But if Montreal was safe, the end was not yet in sight. By October, there was word of the naval half of the expedition. Sir William Phipps and his ships were on their way to Quebec. Frontenac left at once for the capital, and de Callière followed, at the head of eight hundred troops and volunteers from Montreal. Mercifully, their services were not needed, for the season was late, and the land-sea forces had not kept in touch. The timing was poor, and the whole enterprise a dismal failure.

Although the Canadians were naturally overjoyed, their troubles continued. Evil days lay ahead of Montreal, 1691 and 1692 being particularly difficult. What with the English and the Iroquois, the weary citizens enjoyed little respite. When another small English army got as far as LaPrairie, a stubborn fight ensued, from which the Canadians emerged victorious. As for the Iroquois, their attacks went ahead almost on a round-the-clock basis. No one could hope to escape them for long. They burned farms and destroyed crops; they swooped down upon unsuspecting citizens without compunction. Fifty years had passed since the founding of Montreal, and still there was no security.

The long-drawn-out agony assumed many forms, and went far beyond the actual fighters. Everyone felt the pinch of hunger, the women and children no less than the men. For the most part, the fields lay idle, and the cattle untended. No one dared to work without guards. Flour and pork were rationed, and prices were high. When some of the supply ships failed to reach Quebec, ammunition became as scarce as provisions. A storehouse at Montreal burned, with all its contents, and heavy rains ruined the few crops on the ground. The gloom was unbroken.

Yet out of this time of desolation, the story of Madeleine de Verchères emerges—the famous heroine who, in October 1692, was fourteen years of age. During her parents' absence, she was the head of the family and in charge of the seigniory, a few miles down the St. Lawrence from Montreal. An odd little group kept her company, two young brothers, an old man of eighty, some women and children.

When Madeleine went down to the wharf on her first morning alone, forty or fifty Iroquois rushed out from their hiding place in the nearby fields. Luckily, she was too quick for her would-be captors, and their bullets missed her. Breathlessly, she reached the shelter of the fort, and the gates were slammed shut. Then came the inspection of her slender resources. Broken palisades were strengthened and the ammunition made ready. Two soldiers, hidden away in one corner, were shamed into joining her garrison, while muskets, fired through the loopholes, created an illusion of strength.

Madeleine's own courage never faltered. When a settler with his family, brought his canoe near to the landing place, she went down, musket in hand, and escorted them to safety. That night, there was a storm, the snow and the wind offering good cover for an attack. Again she contrived to appear strong. In each of the corner towers, one person stood alone; Madeleine herself, the two brothers, the old man. All through the hours of darkness, they kept up the pretense, calling out to each other as though soldiers.

Incredible as it may seem, the siege went on for seven days, and still the warriors waited, afraid to attack, but hoping to garner some French scalps. At last relief arrived in the persons of a lieutenant and forty men, sent by de Callière. Not knowing whether the fort had been taken, they approached silently. Then came the challenge *"Qui vive?"* and when Madeleine heard the French reply she ran down to meet the rescuers. As for the Iroquois, they sneaked off, to try their luck elsewhere.

As the scene of the famous *prie dieu* affair, Montreal found itself the center once more of a series of petty disputes over precedence. The participants were de Callière and Saint-Vallier, the Bishop whose high-handed ways had already made him thoroughly disliked in Quebec. With some justice, the Recollet fathers might be described as innocent bystanders, involved only because the trouble started in their new church.

It all began quite innocently at the morning service, when de Callière, according to custom, occupied the kneeling desk near the altar in the place of honor. The Bishop promptly rebuked him, on the grounds that no local official should presume to occupy the position reserved for the Governor General. When de Callière insisted that this was his right, Saint-Vallier stalked out of church. What followed was the reverse of edifying. The *prie dieu* was removed by order of the Bishop; de Callière had it replaced; the Bishop placed the church under an interdict and formally admonished the Governor and the Superior for their insubordination. For two months the church remained closed, until the Recollets on their own authority, declared it open once more, marking the occasion with appropriate ceremonies.

Strangely enough, Frontenac does not seem to have taken much active part in this particular dispute. This is not to claim that he had entirely outgrown his earlier insistence on the limelight, yet his second term was proving less turbulent than the first, at least so far as the civilian officials were concerned. Never a lover of the Jesuits, his dealings with any of the ecclesiastics were apt to grow stormy at the least provocation. In his opinion —and he could on occasion be painfully plainspoken—many of the men of religion were overzealous, and completely unreasonable in their rulings as to what constituted immodesty in dress and behavior. On such occasions, Montreal had every reason to be thankful for the moderation of the Sulpicians. Under the wise guidance of the Abbé Tronson, the Superior in Paris, the representatives of the Order strove to remain neutral in all disputatious matters.

In any event, the domestic affairs of the colony appeared picayune in the light of what was happening elsewhere. Even in his old age, Frontenac never lost his determination to expand westward, opening the great plains and the rivers of the interior to French traders and settlers. Royal instructions notwithstanding, he pressed on with his program. Orders to abandon this place or cease that activity were conveniently overlooked. New France was not to be confined to the St. Lawrence Valley.

Fort Frontenac offers a good example of his methods. Destroyed by Denonville in the dreadful months following Lachine, it had never been rebuilt. But its restoration now seemed necessary, for the encouragement of trade and the protection of the colony. That others—and notably de Champigny—opposed the move, made no difference. Seven hundred men went off from Montreal, on what was, decidedly, a debatable mission. No sooner had they left, than letters arrived from France, ordering the abandonment of the fort. It is perhaps unnecessary to add that by order of Frontenac, they were ignored.

Meanwhile the drive to the west continued to reach out far beyond the confines of the little fort at Cataraqui. If treated in detail, it is a subject that belongs less to Montreal than to Canada. Yet it was from the work of these explorers and traders that much of the local prosperity stemmed. What perhaps made their progress all the more astounding, was the fact that the Iroquois troubles continued unabated. For although as the French military strength increased, the attacks on Montreal grew smaller, they were nevertheless exasperating. Nor did the repeated attempts to secure peace, meet with much success. Frontenac was always the optimist, certain that he, at least, could come to terms with the Five Nations. The less hopeful de Callière and de Champigny consistently disagreed.

But in the summer of 1697, Frontenac decided to take the offensive. From Montreal, a war party went first to Cataraqui, and thence to the Onondaga villages. Nothing but charred ruins greeted them, for the inhabitants had burned their homes and fled. It was a futile campaign—the last, as it happened, for the aged Governor General. Carried everywhere in an armchair, his physical infirmities had not stood in the way of his personal leadership.

Early the next spring, New France heard the news of the Treaty of Ryswick. The hostilities in Europe came to an end, yet neither France nor England made any attempt to bring about a settlement of the Iroquois war. Once again, Frontenac made plans for action, this time, not to be brought to fruition. For at the end of November, after an illness of only a few days, he died at the age of seventy-eight, and was buried by his own wish in the Recollet church at Quebec.

Chapter 10

1698–1713

De Callière. A peace treaty with the Indians. The Iroquois danger ended. Rumors of English attacks. Fur-trade rivalry. Madame de Repentigny. Local ordinances.

DURING THE MONTHS that followed the death of Frontenac, France found itself faced with an embarrassing number of candidates who hoped to inherit his office. This fact, alone, was surprising enough, since ordinarily there was great difficulty in finding volunteers brave enough to accept posts in the New World. That these latest aspirants were already on the ground, so to speak—experienced officials who knew the colony—served to make the situation all the more remarkable.

By appointing de Callière as the next Governor General, France undoubtedly acted wisely. Most people were pleased, a few were jealous. The disappointed pair, for example—Vaudreuil the commander, and de Champigny the Intendant—were particularly outspoken in their criticism. Even though Vaudreuil gained promotion of a lesser sort, yet as Governor of Montreal he was still subordinate to de Callière. As for the Intendant, his letters home bristled with wild accusations of vanity and ambition.

Montreal, as might be expected, received the news with mixed feelings. Pride at de Callière's advancement offset the sadness at this loss of a staunch friend. Yet as he took up the reins of office in the capital, fresh problems faced him and weighty responsibilities. Upon his shoulders rested the future of the whole country and the welfare of its people. Inevitably there were unspoken questions, and those who worked with him, may well have harbored doubts. Where others had met failure, how could he succeed? Could anyone measure up to the enormity of the current needs?

De Callière was not slow in reassuring the doubters, for he went straight to the heart of the matter. In selecting peace with the Iroquois as his first objective, he showed courage and acumen of a rare quality. That its attainment would be difficult, he knew only too well, yet it was, nevertheless, of the most pressing urgency for New France. Somehow, the endless attacks must be halted.

The Treaty of Ryswick, by its omission of any mention of the Indian tribes, introduced a new phase into French-English relations in America. The Five Nations now claimed the right to independent action. Thus separate negotiations became necessary, if any truce were to be won, and these de Callière resolved to undertake immediately. The preliminary talks found the Iroquois deputies as plausible and subtle as ever, but this time, the French presented a firm and united front. To those who suggested Albany as the meeting place, de Callière remained unresponsive. The Indians must come to him in Montreal.

While these tortuous overtures got under way, Montreal found itself, for a brief space, occupied with other matters. The new century began on a note of sadness, for on January 12, after a short illness, Marguerite Bourgeoys died at the age of eighty. Although younger than Maisonneuve and Jeanne Mance, she seemed of their generation, and close association with the founders had left a lasting imprint on her life. Her living and ever-growing memorial was, of course, La Congregation and its thirty-nine members her spiritual daughters. That her funeral oration should be pronounced by Dollier de Casson was appropriate. The venerable Sulpician—an old friend—although well past the three score mark himself, was still active and alert.

Within a few months, the name of the aged Superior appeared in a totally different connection. During the summer of 1700, when Montreal embarked on a first attempt at canal building, Dollier de Casson played an active role in the ambitious undertaking. The barrier of the rapids, immediately above the settlement, had always created transportation problems for its residents. Though the boats and canoes hugged the north shore of the St.

Lawrence, swift currents and dangerous rocks awaited the venturesome oarsmen. Between the navigable stretches of water, lay the portages—the wearisome processes of carrying everything overland, the loading and unloading of freight. Imaginative minds had long weighed the chances of cutting a channel from somewhere near Place Royale, inland and westward to Lake St. Louis. That it remained a dream, was due to want of money.

Hence there was excitement among the navigators and traders at the news of the notarial contract signed between Gédéon de Catalogne, an engineer, and Dollier de Casson, representing the seigneurs. Under its terms, a canal was to be excavated, one mile long and twelve feet wide. The depth was to be at least eighteen inches, at the period of lowest water. Because of the narrow walls, only one canoe at a time, could pass through. The work began in October, and a costly undertaking it soon proved to be. In February, the contractor failed, after having fulfilled a large part of his agreement, and the project remained unfinished. The Sulpician revenues were insufficient to meet the additional charges, and no one else seemed interested. From time to time, there were surveys and estimates and fresh plans. Since they all came to nothing, the first Lachine Canal—moderns would call it a ditch—was never completed.

Meanwhile, the plans for the truce with the Indians made good headway. On two occasions, representative groups of chieftains arrived in Montreal, for meetings with de Callière. In July, and again in September, both parties agreed on the terms of a treaty of peace, to be ratified the following year in a more permanent agreement, embracing all the Five Nations. Throughout these often difficult tasks, the Governor General remained calm and confident of success.

Once the groundwork had been laid, the arrangements for the final conference started. Montreal was the chosen site. All through the winter of 1700–01, the Jesuits went from village to village, exhorting the tribes of the Five Nations to cast aside their enmity and sign the agreement with the French. In the early spring, there was a momentary alarm, when the Ottawas attacked the Iroquois, but with his customary aplomb, de Callière smoothed over what he termed an error. At that time, in fact, he seems to have been everywhere, organizing and working, scolding and cajoling. His foresight was evident in the total ban on the sale of liquor throughout the sessions. At best, it would be no easy task to play host to some hundreds of Indians. Sober, they might be handled, drunk they would be outrageous.

By July, everything was in readiness at the Island for the savage guests. Not only were there the Christian Indians from the mission villages, and of course, the Iroquois; representatives arrived from the Hurons, the Ottawas, the Illinois, and the Miamis, and from the strange tribes of the western plains. As the camp arose outside the walls, it was a weird sight which unfolded before the eyes of the Montrealers. Accustomed as they were to trade fairs and native visitors, it far surpassed anything that had gone before. In size as in variety, this was a council never to be surpassed.

Yet the meetings opened badly, amid a chorus of disputes and recriminations. Tribal jealousies were not easily quelled, nor hatreds, built up through many years, erased in a moment. In this tense atmosphere, "the Rat" rose to his feet—the Huron chief Kondiaronk, whose treachery in the past had spelled trouble for the French. Now all this was forgotten in the eloquence of his plea for peace. It was not a receptive audience, suspicious, touchy, dubious, yet as he pictured the blessings that would flow from the cessation of war, the applause was unanimous.

But the effort of speechmaking had proved the undoing of the sickly old man. As he sat there in his armchair, in the midst of the assembly, his voice faltered and he grew weaker. That night, at the Hôtel Dieu, he died, a Christian Indian lamented by his ancient enemies as by his friends, and they united to give him a magnificent funeral. The body lay in state, clad in an officer's uniform, as befitted the holder of an honorary commission. Sixty armed men led the cortege, followed by Huron braves in long beaver robes, their faces blackened. Six war chiefs carried the flower-covered bier to the Parish Church, and volleys of musketry signaled his burial.

A few days later, the treaty was signed. For this ceremony on August 4, the French had set aside a level stretch of ground outside the walls. Young saplings, planted in the ground, made a

fence, while a shelter at one end of the enclosure, provided
cover for the ladies. De Callière, as the Governor General, occupied a prominent position where he could be seen and heard
by all. Beside him were Vaudreuil, de Champigny and other
officers, and near at hand, the delegates of the tribes. As the
interpreters turned his words into many languages, they drew
sounds of approval. Gifts of wampum belts were exchanged,
and the calumet passed from hand to hand. Then came the
captives, restored to their own people, and at last, the signatures
—thirty-eight chieftains and the French—followed by the chant-
ing of the Te Deum.

Occasionally, the solemnity was broken by peals of laughter
from the hosts. It was fortunate that the sound, to the Indians,
seemed to be applause, so that no one's feelings were hurt. The
cause of the merriment lay in the absurdity of some of the
costumes; the eccentricity of the more distant tribes, beggared
description. A chief of the Foxes had painted his face red, and
then, having no hat, had covered his head with a rusty old wig,
disheveled and uncombed. When he wished to honor the Governor in proper European style, off came the wig as though it
were the most elegant of millinery. A chief of the Potawatomis
put the skin of a bull's head over his hair, the horns hanging
down over his ears. Yet another, an Algonquin, had turned his
hair up in the form of a cock's head, a red feather forming the
crest and hanging down.

The usual feast of stewed oxen and other delicacies, brought
the formal ceremonies to a close, and during the days that followed, de Callière held a series of audiences with the individual tribes. But the end was in sight, and none too soon, in the
opinion of the townspeople. Already uneasy at the presence of
so many unknown warriors, the summer heat of July and August
did nothing to allay their anxiety. Notoriously dirty at all times,
the Indians added smallpox and influenza to the list of their
offenses. Montreal welcomed the sound of the last farewells.

Yet this treaty was of tremendous importance to the whole
colony. Locally, it was such a turning point that a man could
mark the passing of time by the year 1701. Before that date, one
set of conditions had prevailed; afterward, a new framework

would develop. De Callière had written finis to the ever-present
fear of Iroquois attacks on the Island.

Unhappily, he did not long enjoy the new safety he had
created. For many years a sufferer from gout, he died in 1703.
Vaudreuil became Governor General, the richer for his five years'
experience in command at the Island. In the sequence of promo-
tions that followed, Montreal was once more favored. To the
office of governor, Claude de Ramezay brought long experience
in the army. Coming first to the colony in 1685, he had served
under both Denonville and Frontenac, and later as commander
of militia, showed himself to be an able deputy in the absence of
Vaudreuil. His name has become familiar in local history. The
Château de Ramezay, built in 1705 and today a museum, was,
throughout his long regime, the center of the official and social
life of the community.

But however welcome the definitive treaty with the Indians,
there was confusion in other ways. New France still grappled
with the opposing policies of expansion and concentration. At
times, the solution veered to one side, only to swing back, and
ill-advised contradictory orders from the king did nothing to
clarify the situation. Thus Montreal, in the summer of 1701,
watched with some interest the departure of an expedition led
by La Mothe Cadillac. The fort, then to be established at Detroit,
took its place in the long chain of outposts between New France
and the Mississippi. But if it was a potential protection, it was
also a drain on manpower. As to its effects on the fur trade,
Montreal continued to view the move west with alarm.

That much of the prosperity of Montreal depended on the
trade, was as true in 1701 as in earlier seasons. It was scarcely a
steady source of income. No matter how enterprising the local
merchants, they were, to a large extent, caught in the grip of
events beyond their control. Peace or war, the competition with
the English persisted, as each nation reached out far beyond the
original limits of settlement. Among the French themselves, there
was rivalry. Their compatriots, in the Hudson Bay territory as in
Louisiana, could not be counted on as allies by the Montrealers.
The more eager the new outposts for business, the more the
long-established routes of the St. Lawrence suffered.

Even when furs were plentiful, they were not always readily salable. A change in male millinery fashions, added to an oversupply of pelts, made France unreceptive to the trading needs of its colony. At the official fixed price level, the market dried up. In an attempt to deal with this twist of the situation, the merchants of Montreal and Quebec combined in 1700, to form the Company of the Colony. But the troubles persisted, and the new organization went the way of all the others. Bankruptcy followed, and a threat of general financial ruin.

Montreal bore the brunt of these uncertainties in the months that followed the Indian agreement. Inflation and loss of trade were no respecters of persons; although they might strike first at the merchants, the colony at large suffered. And effective relief in New France, could come only from one source; the government must issue new rules.

In their search for constructive policies, de Callière and Vaudreuil turned first to the problem of the *coureurs de bois*, already the subject of so many contradictory regulations. The particular one then in effect, dated from 1696, when all licenses had been canceled by royal decree. But although the king could issue sweeping edicts, he could not compel obedience. As a result, the west was full of rebellious French, who took their furs to Albany or south to Louisiana. Either way, Montreal was the loser. It was to remedy this double drain of men and trade, that the two governors proposed an amnesty, and an invitation to return to the more settled parts of the colony. By 1704, the remission was in full swing with reasonably good results. Some of the voluntary exiles came back to the St. Lawrence, but for others, the change was too late. These, living in the west, became in time, the ancestors of the métis of the prairies.

The peace with the English lasted no later than March 1702. This fresh phase of the conflict—known to history as Queen Anne's War or the War of the Spanish Succession—was more European than American, in its causes as in its progress. William and Mary were dead, and Anne was Queen of England. Her great general, Marlborough, stood at the threshold of his astounding career. Louis XIV lived on, an old man, but never averse to promoting the advancement of his royal house. The accession of a French prince to the throne of Spain, was sufficient grounds for war. Further provocation arose with the death of James II, the exiled Stuart monarch. For France to recognize his son, the Old Pretender, as James III, the rightful king of England, seemed to the people of that island, the crowning insult.

During the early stages of the conflict, Montreal enjoyed the rare experience of being far away from the scene of action. Wonderingly, its citizens watched the Iroquois retain their neutrality, refusing entanglements with both English and French. Most of the fighting took place in Acadia, where the Abenaki Indians fought the New Englanders. Although *la petite guerre* flared out anew, it made little difference to everyday life on the Island.

And there, for a short time, well cultivated fields dotted the landscape. No longer hampered by the need of guards, the farmers went about their daily work in perfect freedom. Moreover, the absence of fighting in the neighborhood, meant a temporary release from military service. Add to this, the depression in the fur trade, and the result was that Montrealers in unusually large numbers, worked on the land. Yet from 1705 onward, there were crop failures, followed by near famine conditions. Prices rose steeply, with inflation and bankruptcy adding to the distress. The vessel *La Seine* inward bound from France was captured by the English, and the loss of her cargo of provisions and merchandise brought more hardship to the colony. The story goes that only the innkeepers made fortunes at this date. No matter how diluted the liquor, it could always be sold to the Indians.

One native-born Montrealer who took constructive action in this crisis, was Madame de Repentigny. Until then, in obedience to a royal decree, all cloth used in the colony, had been imported from France—a measure designed to protect the manufacturers from competition overseas. But eventually, the restrictions were eased, under the threat of rising prices and a growing scarcity of clothing. A bad situation grew much worse with the loss of *La Seine*. Such were the circumstances that, in 1703, led this energetic lady to establish a cloth factory in Montreal which under her management prospered for ten years.

At first there was such a scarcity of weavers that anyone less determined than Madame de Repentigny would have been discouraged. She simply went out and ransomed some New England prisoners, who were expert craftsmen. It was as simple as all that. Nor was she discouraged by the want of conventional materials. Goat skins, buffalo wool, tree bark, and nettles took the place of sheep's wool, flax, and hemp. Toward the end, she was able to produce a hundred and fifty yards of cloth a day, coarse rough stuff but perfectly wearable, and dyed after a process of her own invention. A year or so later, the Sisters of La Congregation were weaving cloth for their own habits, as fine as any made in France. On the same looms they made a black fabric of a texture suitable for the soutanes of the priests.

This engaging sidelight can be matched in the ordinances issued by successive intendants. A whole series of such rules, dated 1706, are revealing in their picture of everyday things, and in the multiplicity of their detail, indicative of the mores of a paternal government. The bad conditions of the streets always aroused comment—impassable for foot passengers, let alone carts and carriages. Why were they so disgraceful? Simply because the householders dumped filth there every day, and since the slope of the roadways had been improperly laid out, the drainage was insufficient to carry off the flow.

Sunday morning had its own peculiar problems, for the great crush of people at the church doors after Mass, led to disorders. Some of the habitants, whether on horseback or in carriages, tried to make such fast getaways, that they bumped into each other, not to mention frightening the pedestrians. By 1709, the authorities decided that Montrealers were too fond of horses, rearing them to the detriment of the cattle, whose fodder they ate. In future, no one could own more than two mares and one colt; the superfluous ones were to be slaughtered. As a sort of postscript, it was regretfully noted that because of the growing use of sleighs instead of snowshoes, the new generation was becoming soft.

Liquor was such a perennial headache that there were constant attempts to regulate its use. In this particular year the government decided that no more than ten taverns in Montreal should be licensed, and even they could sell only to the French. Should they operate after nine o'clock, or cater to Indian customers, their permits were subject to confiscation.

By this date, New France in general, was showing a gratifying increase in population. Although immigration had virtually ceased after Talon's departure, the rate of natural increase remained high. *Les filles du roi* had become the mothers of large families. When property values rose sharply in response to demand, some of the seigneurs took advantage of their would-be tenants by charging high prices for land that should be free. And despite the clearly stated obligations as to settlement and clearance, some of the seigniories were still undeveloped.

As a result, 1711 saw the publication of *Les Arrêts* or the *Decrees of Marly*, in which precise rules were laid down for the transfer of land to new settlers. In addition, they authorized forfeiture in cases of failure to undertake the cultivation of the soil. A survey of the seigniories, conducted by Gédéon de Catalogne, resulted in accurate and up-to-date information on conditions. Montreal, as administered by the Gentlemen of St. Sulpice, ranked as one of the most progressive communities in the country, being well settled and the land fertile. Six parishes cared for the spiritual needs of its people—a regrettable number of whom devoted their energies to trading with the Indians!

But by this date, Montreal was once more caught up in the feverish atmosphere of war. Rumors of an English invasion filled the air, to such an extent that no one knew what was happening. Even though the stories were exaggerated, everyone sensed that the colony was unprepared. A thousand men were available to defend Montreal, two thousand at Quebec; this paltry army was the sum total of Vaudreuil's resources.

In the spring of 1711, an enemy force led by Colonel Francis Nicholson, began its advance on Montreal. Traveling the now-familiar route up Lake Champlain and the Richelieu, its progress was, of necessity, slow. As usual, there was idle talk without much foundation, so that when de Ramezay led fifteen hundred Canadians and Indians out to meet the English, he left behind a town in the utmost confusion. His own actions did nothing to clarify the situation. For when the opposing armies first made contact, it was hard to distinguish friend from foe. De Ramezay lost himself in the woods and could not find his men. Some of his Indians fired on their allies. Finally, the whole force retreated to Chambly, having accomplished nothing.

The invaders for their part, fared no better. While they awaited instructions from Boston, the fierce summer heat blazed down upon the camp. Unsanitary conditions soon exacted their usual toll of disease and death, and the survivors counted themselves fortunate in being able to retreat.

Then the rumors started again. Montreal was dismayed at the prospect of another attack, and one perhaps, reinforced by artillery fire. But although the defenders were few, they went out bravely, hoping to gain the advantage by ambushing the enemy at Chambly. To their amazement, no one appeared. Colonel Nicholson and his army had vanished.

The cause of this seeming miracle lay in Quebec, the target for an attack by sea. The fleet had been delayed in its departure from Boston, yet this was a minor problem compared to the person of the commander. Sir Hovenden Walker, although a poor navigator, thought so highly of himself that he disregarded the advice of those more experienced. Having miscalculated the currents of the St. Lawrence, he lost seven transports on the rocky coastline—so great a disaster that hundreds of bodies were washed up on shore. Thus both Montreal and Quebec were safe.

After this tragedy in the Gulf, the war in America petered out, except for minor raids, until, in 1713, the peace became official.

Chapter 11

1713–1743

Thirty years of peace. Domestic harmony. The town grows. The center of commerce. Travel by water. Local prosperity.

To THOSE AT Montreal who had witnessed the twin fiascos of Colonel Nicholson and Sir Hovenden Walker, the terms of the Treaty of Utrecht signed in 1713 came as a shock. Acadia was ceded to the British, as were all the captured forts in Hudson Bay; the possession of Newfoundland was recognized. Although the French retained the St. Lawrence and the Mississippi, the losses in the north and the east were costly. In a potentially dangerous agreement concerning the Indians, the Iroquois were conceded to be British subjects, and both England and France given freedom to trade with any or all of the tribes.

All of this was, in effect, a clear indication that America was merely one small segment of a conflict that reached out from Europe to the colonies. Minor successes in New France could insure neither total victory nor a favorable peace, so long as the menace inherent in British power remained unchecked—the navy and its control of the seas, and the greater population and strength of the colonies.

As it happened, the Treaty of Utrecht was to prove more durable than its predecessors, since England and France—and hence America—remained at peace for thirty years. In 1714, Queen Anne died, the last of the Stuart line. The House of Hanover, in the person of George I, succeeded to the throne, an alien family whose ways were unknown. No one could be sure of their permanency, so long as Stuart exiles survived, and "the king over the water" could always gain supporters. After a reign of seventy-two years, Louis XIV died in 1715; his great-grandson, Louis XV, became king at the age of five. Moreover, through much of this period, the two chief ministers, Sir Robert Walpole and Cardinal Fleury, strove earnestly to avert a renewal of the conflict.

In the years that preceded Montreal's hundredth birthday, it is pleasant to find the peace in external affairs matched by domestic harmony. The government was stable, its officers conscientious. Vaudreuil remained as Governor General until his death in 1725. His successor, the Marquis de Beauharnais, held office until 1747. At Montreal, de Ramezay served as Governor for over twenty years, being succeeded in 1724 by Charles Le Moyne, first Baron de Longueuil. If sometimes, during these lengthy terms, disputes arose, they were centered in Quebec.

But although the surface appeared placid, those in command had good cause for anxiety as they surveyed an uncertain future. Their towns lay unprotected, their resources were meager. Indifference seemed the keynote of official French policy; a government, apparently tired of its colonial possessions, was unlikely to be lavish, either in sympathetic understanding or practical help.

Such was the background for Montreal's program of fortifications, on which work actually commenced in 1722. Although preliminary plans had been in the making for years, the townspeople in general showed a surprising indifference to any talk of preparedness. If personal valor in the past, could save them from Indian bows and arrows, they seem to have felt it would be equally effective against muskets and cannon. With apparent equanimity, they not only watched de Callière's old wooden palisades fall into ruins, but often assisted nature in the process. A report dated 1717, showed half the stakes to be rotten and no door in a state fit to be shut. Openings had been cut through the wall, to suit the convenience of those who lived in the neighborhood.

Although royal authorization came through in 1716, progress was slow. The king advanced 300,000 livres to meet expenses, one-half chargeable against his own account, the balance a loan to be repaid by the seigneurs and inhabitants. Even then, there were so many contrary opinions and difficulties in securing title to the

land that Chaussegros de Léry, the engineer in charge, must have
been discouraged long before the start. The walls of his design
were of rough stone, eighteen feet high, four feet thick at the
base and three at the top. Their foundations were deep, but the
stone thus dug out, served to line the revetment. Thirteen bastions were spaced out along the four sides of the enclosure, while
five gates and five posterns gave access to the town. In the end,
the work was never completely finished, and the fortifications,
though formidable in appearance, proved to be of little value.

As to Montreal itself, de Léry considered it to be overlarge,
and so badly planned that new arrivals found difficulty in ac-
quiring building sites within the municipal limits. In his opinion,
too much space was given over to gardens in the midst of the
town. Three times as many streets might easily be fitted into the
existing area, to the advantage of all.

Rather more flattering were the views of Pierre de Charlevoix,
a Jesuit who spent the winter of 1720–21 in Montreal. He considered the town to have a pleasing appearance, being well situated, well laid out, and well built. The charm of its surroundings,
no less than of its streets, inspired a certain gaiety, which everyone felt.

Because of the manner in which the land sloped toward
the mountain, Charlevoix sensed a geographical division within
the civic boundaries. The lower town, on the riverbank, he labeled the merchants' quarter; there he grouped also the Hôtel
Dieu, the king's storehouses, and the Place d'Armes. As the
nucleus of the upper section, he named the Parish Church (more
the air of a cathedral than that of Quebec); the Seminary (solid
and commodious, rather than handsome); the residence of the
Governor, as well as most of the officers. There was, in addition,
a kind of suburb, beyond a little stream which flowed in from
the northwest; this, in time, promised to be a beautiful district.

Meanwhile, the religious institutions dominated the scene. In
addition to those belonging to the Sulpicians, Charlevoix visited
the new Jesuit church, large and well built; the convent of the
Recollets, generous in size to accommodate its numerous community. As for the house owned by the ladies of La Congregation, although one of the biggest in the town, it was already too

small for the needs of the Order. The Hospitalières, too, were
well equipped—a well-ornamented church and a spacious dwelling house—its members as in the past, indefatigable in the care of
the sick, yet themselves badly fed.

In fact, the whole settlement was starting to develop in an
astonishing fashion. Whereas in 1710, the population was only
3492, by 1740, it soared to 7710. Growing pains were unavoidable, as farms and gardens gave way to streets and town lots.
Compared to Quebec, this was a new city, and its people vigorous
and adventurous. Being free of the restrictions that of necessity
surround the seat of government, Montreal by virtue of its aptitude for business and industry was ready to assume leadership in
the colony.

Sometimes the changes were involuntary, and disastrous in
their immediate consequences. In a town still largely built of
wood, fire was a constant hazard. An unusually serious blaze in
June 1721 wiped out half the community. Within the short space
of three hours, sixty houses perished in the flames, together with
the Hôtel Dieu—the latter almost monotonous in its tragic history
of destruction—burned in 1695 and rebuilt; burned in 1721 and
rebuilt; burned in 1734 and rebuilt.

But even while the charred ruins still littered the streets, de
Léry made representations to the government on the need for
better planning and stricter regulations. As a result, the use of
wood for building purposes, was soon forbidden. All new houses
were to be constructed of stone, and roofed with slates, tiles, or
tin. They were to follow the alignment of the streets, and be two
stories in height. Whether such an ordinance at once won universal favor, is questionable, but certainly it contributed largely to
the altered appearance of the settlement. One proof of its effectiveness comes from the travelers of later date, who invariably
described Montreal as *la cité d'argent*—a nice tribute to the
shining new tin roofs.

Wood had been the obvious choice for the settler in earlier
days, when he planned his move from the first crude shelter.
There was no shortage of trees, and indeed, they grew so thickly
on the Island, that to cut one down was to assist in the clearance
of land. Carpenters were available—experienced workmen from

France—and each contingent brought a fresh quota of skilled artisans. In this way, the first frame houses made their appearance, their roofs covered with shingles; no one could deny they were fire traps. Occasionally, someone, more ambitious than his neighbors, opted for stone, a native product almost as common as timber. It was easily dug from the fields, and any inconvenience in transportation was more than offset by durability and comfort. Sometimes a combination of materials appeared, the stone rubble walls being covered with boards for protection against frost.

In almost every respect, these early houses derived their inspiration from France. There were, of course, no professional architects, so that the builders fell back upon their own memories and personal experiences for assistance in planning, and being for the most part, men from the northern provinces and of modest social rank, they erected dwellings severely simple in style and admirably suited to the Canadian scene. For however European their background, the climate soon induced modifications. Out of a healthy respect for extreme heat and cold—for frost, ice, and snow—the walls grew thicker and the foundations more solid. The roofs sloped steeply down to overhanging eaves, their angle precisely calculated to prevent heavy accumulations of snow. The windows were small, and so placed that the houses seemed to turn their backs to the prevailing winds. Large chimneys served equally generous fireplaces, whose glowing heat was often supplemented by stoves. Outwardly, there was an impression of freshness, from the often-renewed coats of whitewash on the walls.

If the exteriors were simple and in harmony with the surroundings, the same could be said of the interiors, useful rather than ornamental, and designed to meet the needs of large and active families. One spacious apartment met most of their requirements during the daylight hours, a kitchen-dining-sitting room that was well lighted, warm and hospitable—a place in which parents and children went about their duties; equally a spot in which they could relax in the company of their friends and relatives. The bedrooms, whether on the main floor or upstairs, were small and cell-like. Tiny dormer windows kept them dark and chilly, while the steep pitch of their ceilings made them a menace to the taller inhabitants.

As might be expected, necessities took precedence over luxuries. Shelter against weather and provision for heating, simple beds, tables, and chairs—this was almost all that the habitant needed. Amid the cramped quarters of the immigrant ships, there was little enough space for human beings, let alone goods and chattels. If fortunate, each family group might possess a single chest packed with clothing. Battered perhaps by the long voyage, this would still be usable in the new home, and later serve as a model for the local carpenter. To import furniture from France was so prohibitive in cost that only a few highly placed officials and ecclesiastics could afford such luxury. For the vast majority, it was a matter of using the common woods of the district—the pine, the birch, the butternut—for the fashioning of the simple household equipment, square, massive, long lasting.

Those who know the Quebec countryside today, will recognize in its ancient cottages, the tastes of a simpler age. Lovingly cared for and skillfully restored, they represent this early Canadian architecture at its best and offer some clue to the appearance of Montreal two centuries ago. Yet no one, warn the experts, can be certain of the precise nature of the urban dwellings. So greatly has the Island suffered from fire, that only the Château de Ramezay remains as an example of a gabled mansion and town house. The more modest structures have long since perished.

But at best, and quite aside from fires, early Montreal was never the home of architectural masterpieces. Rather was it a busy commercial center, whose inhabitants were less concerned with beauty than with making a good living. Many of the merchants lived above their shops or places of business, an arrangement that was convenient in the compact riverside community of the day. Considering the shocking condition of the streets, long walks could have offered little appeal. The eyes and the nose of the pedestrian constantly assailed by the foul sights and smells; his feet and his clothing wet, dirty, and spattered by the mud and the melting snow and ice; in dry weather, choked by the clouds of dust; his personal safety endangered by the reckless drivers, who monopolized the roads, even mounting the pave-

ments at times; this is the picture that emerges from the contemporary ordinances.

Perhaps in the circumstances, it was fortunate that most transportation was waterborne. After the miasma of the city streets,
the fresh clear air of the rivers and lakes afforded welcome
relief. As yet, no oceangoing vessel had braved the treacherous
stretch of the St. Lawrence above Quebec. In their place, plied
the canoes and the bateaux—up and down the river above and
below Montreal—carrying men and goods, everything in fact,
needed to sustain life, in peace as in war. Only in name did
these strong workaday transports resemble the light pleasure
craft of today. Canoes up to thirty feet in length, were commonly
used in the western fur trade; they carried a score of men and
five hundred pounds of freight. The bateaux—the flat-bottomed
boats—were larger, sometimes extending to forty-five feet and
their cargoes three times as heavy. Even in winter, the water-
courses still served as highways, their surfaces frozen solid in
the severe northern air. Sledges, snowshoes, and skates were excellent means of traveling over the smooth ice, and in fine
weather, pleasurable into the bargain.

Yet Montreal, with its burgeoning sense of civic importance,
began to talk in the early 1720s of the advantages of overland
travel to Quebec. Communication with the capital should not be
liable to interruption, whether by sudden storms, spring floods or
the autumn freeze-up that preceded the solid ice of the winter.
Postal service between the two cities—the first in Canada—had
its birth in 1721, but the construction of a road along the north
shore, was a more serious undertaking. Thus it was not until
1734 that the first wheeled vehicle traversed the intervening
miles.

During the latter years of the long peace, there was prosperity
in New France. Perhaps nowhere was this more apparent than at
Montreal, where the growth of population in itself contributed
greatly to the general activity. The construction of roads and
houses, the expansion to the suburbs, the demand for goods, these
provided work in abundance, and the promise of a more stable
future. The wars were almost forgotten and matters of hearsay to
the younger generations—and this, despite the fact that the un-

official struggle with the English went on along the eastern and
western borders. Meanwhile the local scene was all absorbing,
and there was never any danger of monotony. Fresh ventures
were always in the wind—underwritten as a rule, by the merchants, in the hope of realizing handsome profits.

Thus there is a decided Montreal flavor to the story of Pierre
Gaultier de la Vérendrye, who set off in 1731 on a search for the
Pacific. Since a monopoly of the far-distant fur trade was his only
asset, he turned, of necessity, to the merchants of the town for
advances of money, supplies, and trade goods. It was the start
of a long association, for La Vérendrye and his sons lived in the
west for twenty years. Although never successful in gaining the
final objective, his parties reached the Red River, the Assiniboine
and the Saskatchewan, Lake Winnipeg and the prairies beyond.
That they also disrupted the English trade routes was much to
Montreal's liking. Furs, brought down the St. Lawrence, put
money in everyone's pockets.

Some of the more lawless turned to smuggling—always a lucra-
tive, if risky business. Just how many persons were involved at
any one moment, is impossible to determine, but with Albany
only two hundred miles away, the temptation was great. For a
time the traffic was wide open, if the reports of English artisans
and merchants seen in Montreal, are to be believed. Although
stringent regulations put a stop to this in 1734, British goods, and
above all, scarlet cloth, were still sold in the local market.

That the Indian peace remained effective, at least along the
St. Lawrence, was perhaps due to the Mohawks, who showed no
sign of a return to the warpath. But although the great councils
and fairs were things of the past, the tribes still frequented Montreal. Charlevoix, who noted their arrival in small flotillas, wished
that their contacts with the French could be limited to the missionaries. The *coureurs de bois*, he felt, by the looseness of their
lives, created disorders among the barbarians.

A decade later, Sister Ste. Hélène painted a vivid picture of the
heathen who stalked the streets, as proud in their nudity as if
they wore good clothes. The Christians, being more discreet, were
well covered with an assortment of garments, all unwashed;
clearly cleanliness had not accompanied their godliness. So thick,

in fact, was the grime, that shaking hands was an ordeal. As for dinner at the Governor's house; "Unlucky are their neighbors, especially when they happen to be ladies." But from a safe distance, their strange hair styles and painted faces were nothing short of gorgeous—more elaborate in their war toilet, noted this keen observer, than a coquette would be. True barbarians, whatever their religion, they decked themselves out in bright colors and ornaments of necklaces and bracelets. As vain as any Frenchman, the Sister concluded.

That New France was a land sadly lacking in opportunity, has been an oft-repeated accusation from historians of differing viewpoints—perhaps with some reason. The ordered life of the farmer, the modest skill of the artisan, the small-scale operation of the merchant—these to a paternal government, constituted the legitimate occupations open to Canadians. Commissions in the regular army went almost entirely to men from France, and careers in politics were non-existent. The general level of education was poor. All things considered, it was not surprising that the young men flocked to the woods. As *coureurs de bois,* they could, at least, do what they wanted.

From this spirit of independence, a sense of nationhood was slowly emerging, in which environment tugged powerfully against heredity. No longer could it be said that the Canadians and the French of Europe were identical races, for the bonds of a common language and kinship weighed lightly against more than a century of life in the New World. As the years passed, and the number of immigrants dwindled, the native-born formed the majority group in the population. To them, Canada was home, and France an unknown distant land. Out of the dangers of the past, the sufferings and the courage, there grew a self-confidence and a certain disdain for their associates from Europe.

Progress of another order was implicit in the dissolution of the original missionary organization. In 1722, the diocese was reconstituted, with more usual grouping of independent parishes. Once these parochial boundaries were established, it seemed as though a fresh ecclesiastical era had dawned. The Sulpicians saw in it, an occasion worthy of commemoration.

The decision to rebuild and adorn La Paroisse emphasized its pre-eminence among the twenty-eight parishes on the Island. After forty years, it still evoked the admiration of all who saw it. Chaussegros de Léry, who was put in charge of the new program, produced a design that was acceptable—though scarcely inspired —but one that was never completed. For although the ornamental façade across the front was constructed according to plan, the erection of the second of his twin towers was postponed indefinitely.

Montreal, in 1694, had welcomed the formation of a second hospital—l'Hôpital Général, a house of charity for male inmates. Its founder was a layman, François Charron, who in thanksgiving for his own recovery from a serious illness, vowed to serve the poor and the infirm. All went well during the early years—so much so that the project was widened to include the training of teachers, as well as instruction in handicrafts and the technical trades. Then Charron himself died unexpectedly, at a time when the favor of official France seemed to be turning to frowns. When alleged inefficiency, in 1730, led to the cancellation of the government grant, the hospital under the existing auspices, was almost at an end.

Another chapter of the same story, had as its heroine, a young Montrealer by the name of Madame d'Youville, widowed in 1730 after an unhappy marriage. In her distress, she turned to charitable work, much of it taking the form of assistance at l'Hôpital Général. When within a few years, other like-minded women joined her in this care of the poor, they started to live together as a community, although without religious vows. An unusual way of life at that date, it provoked stones and verbal insults from an unruly mob. The accusations bandied about, which included charges of personal drunkenness as well as the sale of liquor to the Indians, led to the derisive title of *Les Soeurs Grises*—a pun on the dual meaning of the last word— either gray in colour or drunk.

The idle talk continued for some time, until the Sulpicians, wiser than most, discerned in Madame d'Youville, a person of ability, and in her little band, a possible solution to the dilemma of the hospital. The changes which came only gradually, included the adoption of a religious rule. In 1747, *Les Soeurs Grises*—the Grey Nuns—assumed control of the troubled institution; they remain one of the modern city's most honored Orders.

Chapter 12
1743–1749

La petite guerre again. Indian allies. Supplies for the western outposts. Peter Kalm. The town and its people.

THE WAR OF the Austrian Succession had been in progress for several years before England became an active participant. The news, which reached New France, in the spring of 1744, at first made little difference to the settlements of the St. Lawrence.

Notwithstanding the complacency arising from the long peace, much had been accomplished for the protection of the Island. Montreal was now a walled town, and thus more easily controlled. In times of danger, the people of the outlying suburbs could seek its shelter. A few miles away, on the banks of the Richelieu, stood the stone fort at Chambly, and farther south on the narrows of Lake Champlain, Fort St. Frédéric (known to the English as Crown Point). Both were designed as defensive works against invasion from New York.

Vital though these were to the St. Lawrence Valley, they must also be regarded as the eastern links in the long chain of French forts that stretched far into the interior. In many places, they went unchallenged, in others, such as the Ohio country, the contest between the two nations was bitter. No matter what the distance, however, Montreal knew them all, in the sense of serving as their supply base and the point of departure for men and goods. Out of this personal association, grew a familiarity beyond the average, with faraway places and their problems.

Yet it was in the Atlantic region that the major action occurred. There, the great fortress of Louisbourg on Ile Royale (now Cape Breton Island) had long posed a threat to New En-

gland shipping. With its massive stone walls and heavy arma-
ment, it appeared so impregnable as to earn the title of the Dunkirk of America. But under a joint attack by colonial militia and
the British Navy, its inherent weakness led to an astonishingly
speedy surrender. For France, the catastrophe was all the worse
for being unexpected. A counterattack was planned, only to
encounter such impediments as heavy storms and an epidemic
of typhus. After a series of such mishaps, Louisbourg remained
in the possession of its captors.

The Americans, for their part, were understandably jubilant.
Buoyed up by this victory, they made their plans for 1746. An
assault on Quebec seemed to hold promise of success, if supported by British ships, and Montreal, in its turn, heard rumors
of overland operations against the St. Lawrence settlements. But
in the end, there were delays, serious enough to prevent effective
action. For all the grand talk of the conquest of Canada, nothing
much happened.

But in another sense, Montreal was very much a part of the
war zone. Once again, *la petite guerre* was in full cry, and the
raids went back and forth across the borders, with success veer-
ing now to one side, now to the other. Although New France was
far outstripped in numbers and wealth, she possessed the ineffa-
ble advantages of unity and a central command. Of all her opponents, only New England showed a truly warlike spirit. New
York, with its large Dutch population, was at best, lukewarm,
and the states farther south, frankly indifferent.

In all these operations, big or small, the support of the Iroquois
—above all, the Mohawks—often spelled the difference between
success or failure. During the long interlude of peace, they had
made full use of their pose of neutrality. Gifts and more gifts,
and profits from fur trading, legal or illegal; these as much as the
treaties, had kept them quiet, especially when one would-be
ally could be played off against the other. With the formal declaration of war, the rival bidding rose to new heights, in terms
of diplomatic promises, outright gifts and bribes. If this at times
was a somewhat unsavory business, it was also highly necessary, and as a rule, the French handled it better than the English.
Always that is, until the advent of William Johnson.

How this Irish-born immigrant emerged from obscurity, to
become the self-appointed champion of the Five Nations, is a
tale that belongs to New York State, rather than to Canada. Yet
as an adopted member of the Mohawk tribe, he was obviously
in a position to inflict a good deal of damage on the local status
quo. Although he was anathema to the conventional British
governors and generals, Johnson showed a consummate skill in
translating neutrality into active support.

For this reason, and in spite of its proximity to Montreal, the
village of Caughnawaga found itself on the receiving end of a
good deal of attention from the British. As Christian Indians and
protégés of the Jesuits, its people were naturally pro-French. That
they were also Mohawks made their kinsfolk in New York reluctant to turn against them in war. Sometimes the American braves
visited Montreal, to be showered with presents and feted as
honored guests; returning home, they would encounter Johnson
at his most persuasive. Inconclusive this relationship was in the
1740s, inconclusive it remained—a situation that was repeated
with variations, in dealings with the western tribes. Right up
until 1760, neither European nation could ever feel absolutely
certain of support from its native allies.

Meanwhile the Canadians continued their raids on the enemy
villages, spreading terror among the civilians wherever they
turned. Saratoga was destroyed and Deerfield—two devastating
attacks that by reason of their greater size stand out from the
many nameless horrors. The net result of all this was precious
little, measured in terms of any permanent advantage. It lay instead, in the deep hatred aroused, all through New England and
New York. Where once there had been apathy—a willingness to
let the other fellow do the fighting—there were now cries for
vengeance and volunteers eager to share in the dangers. The
fiery William Shirley, Governor of Massachusetts, took as his war
cry, *"Delenda est Canada,"* a phrase echoed by many, who ignorant of Latin, shared in the conviction that North America must
be rid of the foe.

It was into this highly emotional atmosphere that the news of
the Treaty of Aix-la-Chapelle broke in 1748. Once more, European interests had called the tune. For the truce—and peace

would be a misnomer—on the strength of victories in Europe and India, restored Louisbourg to France. The New Englanders were positively choleric in their indignation. All in all, it seemed likely that the fighting would continue, with or without official sanction.

But for the moment, Montreal rejoiced. A military parade and artillery salutes marked the formal proclamation of the Treaty, and at night there were fireworks. Until long after dark, a care-free people thronged the streets, all in a mood for enjoyment.

In this mid-century lull between the wars, New France enter-tained a distinguished guest, whose shrewdly observant eyes and ready pen combined to produce a richly human picture of Cana-dian life in the closing years of the old regime. Peter Kalm was exceptionally well qualified for such an undertaking. As a citizen of Sweden, he was that rara avis, a true neutral, as welcome in the English colonies as in the French. To this, he added the gift of scientific detachment, for it was as a naturalist in quest of new varieties of plants and trees that he came to North America.

During the course of his two and a half years on this continent, Kalm progressed from Pennsylvania to New York and New Jer-sey. The summer of 1749 saw him in Canada, where as the guest of the king, he visited Montreal, Quebec, and some of the small villages along the St. Lawrence. Apparently oblivious of hard-ships, he went everywhere, including the wilderness, if there were unknown botanical specimens to be secured. He showed a similar zest for people in all walks of life, and far beyond the official circles in which ordinarily he moved.

A nice precision of thought marked his definition of Montreal—"the second town in Canada in regard to size and wealth; but it is the first on account of its fine situation and mild climate . . . The town has a quadrangular form, or rather it is a rectangular parallelogram, the long and eastern side of which extends along the great branch of the river. On the other side it is surrounded with excellent corn-fields, charming meadows and delightful woods."

The state of the defenses did not impress Kalm greatly. "It is pretty well fortified, and surrounded with a high and thick wall. On the east side it has the river St. Lawrence, and on all the other sides a deep ditch filled with water, which secures the inhabitants against all danger from the sudden incursions of the enemy's troops. However, it cannot long stand a regular siege, because it requires a great garrison, on account of its extent; and because it consists chiefly of wooden houses."

Although a Protestant, Kalm showed considerably objectivity in his approach to religion. Wisely, he confined himself to not much more than a listing of the various institutions—the church belonging to the friars of the Order of St. Sulpicius, for example, being "by far the finest, both in regard to its outward and inward ornaments, not only in this place, but in all Canada." In other respects, he was more discursive.

"Some of the houses in the town are built of stone, but most of them are of timber, though very neatly built. Each of the better sort of houses has a door toward the street, with a seat on each side of it, for amusement and recreation in the morning and evening. The long streets are broad and straight, and divided at right angles by the short ones; some are paved, but most of them are very uneven. The gates of the town are numerous; on the east side of the town toward the river are five, two great and three lesser ones; and on the other side are likewise several. The governor general of Canada, when he is at Montreal, resides in the castle, which the government hires for that purpose of the family of Vaudreuil; but the governor of Montreal is obliged to buy or hire a house in town; though I was told the government contributed toward paying the rents."

The sail down to Quebec provided Kalm with his first glimpse of rural Canada. He found the countryside delightful, and in a fine state of cultivation. Equally pleasing were the farmhouses; whether of stone or wood, all were whitewashed, and surrounded by barns and outhouses. Here and there, he noted the church spires, their height adding a touch of variety to the generally flat horizon. From one city to the other, the string of small settlements resembled a single long narrow village, so closely did the buildings hug the shore.

Visits to farms in the neighborhood of Montreal, served to confirm these favorable impressions. On all sides, he saw excellent fields of grain, running down to the water's edge. In the mild climate of the Island, apple, pear, and wild plum trees flourished. A few gardens featured grapevines, imported from France; their fruit, though pleasant to the taste, was not worth making into wine. Black currants were plentiful, and melons and pumpkins. The turnips and parsnips that grew abundantly in the fields, were stored away for winter use. Kalm noticed particularly the absence of potatoes. Apparently the Canadian farmers disliked them, laughing to him about the strange tastes of the English.

Breakfast, in the more prosperous homes, was a light repast by Swedish standards. A piece of bread, dipped in brandy, often satisfied the men, while the ladies enjoyed their coffee or chocolate. Indeed, some of them seem to have stolen a march on modern dieters, by their complete abstention from food and drink in the morning. Tea was unknown, and bread and butter seldom appeared at this early hour.

Dinner at noon, was a more substantial meal, and supper between seven and eight usually brought a repetition of the earlier menu. Soup, with plenty of bread, was followed by fresh meats, and on Fridays, by fish or eggs. Kalm, it should be remembered, was a summer visitor, so that his comments on abundance, must be treated with caution. Thus he reported fruit and vegetables plentiful, as well as cheese and milk. Sweetmeats, nuts, and preserves took the place of the puddings so popular in the English colonies, while red claret, spruce beer, and water were the drinks most commonly offered.

The individual place setting at such meals, included a plate and napkin, spoon and fork. Knives as a rule, were omitted, both ladies and gentlemen carrying their own cutlery. The common people, as observed by Kalm, lived in a much rougher fashion. They had the necessities of life, but little more. Bread with onions was their usual Friday fare; "they may be smelled when one passes by."

Although boats still served as the chief means of transportation, travel by land was on the increase, especially for short distances. Dogs pulling carts or sledges, were common; the poor man's horses, Kalm called them. The real horses he found strong and well built, although almost too numerous for the rough and narrow roads. For this reason, the government strove constantly to regulate their number and speed.

The mechanical trades were not yet as advanced as they might be. In architecture, cabinetwork, turning, and brickmaking, the French colonies lagged behind the English, probably because "scarcely any other people but dismissed soldiers come to settle here." Since most of these individuals lacked formal technical training, their skills were acquired more or less by accident. A man in Montreal, who had made himself into a clever clock- and watchmaker, without proper instruction, found himself modestly famous; his was obviously an unusual case. For the fact is, that there was a scarcity of laboring people. Although wages were high, hard work in the cities seems to have been unpopular. "Almost everybody finds it easy to be a farmer, in this uncultivated country, where he can live well and at so small an expense that he does not care to work for others."

As for the men whom he met—Kalm portrayed them as extremely civil, doffing their hats to every person they met in the streets, and thus showing a refinement unknown among the Dutch and the English. That they were also neat in their persons, is suggested by the fact that all Frenchmen in Canada shaved their beards, including the Jesuits.

Above all else, however, Peter Kalm observed the women whom he met in New France—generally handsome, well bred, and virtuous with an innocent and becoming freedom—the opinion of a laic and hence a sharp contrast to the usual clerical strictures of the period. If sometimes he was critical of female vanity, at least he was not easily shocked by anything he saw.

Thus there is exceptional interest in Kalm's description of women's dress—"very fine on Sundays, and though on the other days they do not take much pains with other parts of their dress, yet they are very fond of adorning their heads, the hair of which is always curled and powdered and ornamented with glittering bodkins and aigrettes. Every day but Sunday they wear a neat little jacket, and a short petticoat which hardly reaches half the leg, and in this particular they seem to imitate the Indian women. The heels of their shoes are high and very narrow, and it is surprising how they walk on them."

On the basis of his travels in the American colonies, the keen-eyed Swede pointed the finger of scorn at "the English women in the plantations, who have indeed taken the liberty of throwing all the burden of housekeeping upon their husbands and sit in their chairs all day with folded arms. The women in Canada on the contrary do not spare themselves, especially among the common people, where they are always in the fields, meadows, stables, etc., and do not dislike any work whatsoever. However, they seem rather remiss in regard to the cleaning of the utensils and apartments; for sometimes the floors, both in the town and the country, were hardly cleaned once in six months, which is a disagreeable sight to one who comes from among the Dutch and the English where the constant scouring and scrubbing of the floors is regarded as important as the exercise of religion itself."

A similar seesaw of praise and criticism marked Kalm's picture of the ladies of Quebec, as opposed to those of Montreal. The former, he found to be equal in good manners to the French, largely because of the annual visits of the king's ships. The residents of the newer town, deprived of this breath of sophistication by the accident of geography, "are accused by the French of partaking too much of the pride of the Indians and of being much wanting in French good breeding." A common liking for clothes was perhaps a bond between the two groups. "They are no less attentive to have the newest fashions; and they laugh at each other, when they are not dressed to each other's fancy. But what they get as new fashions, are grown old and laid aside in France; for the ships coming but once every year from thence, the people in Canada consider that as the new fashion for the whole year, which the people on board brought with them or which they imposed upon them as new."

Yet in the end, Kalm decided that the fair Montrealers were of a more becoming modesty, less volatile but more industrious. "They are always at their needlework, or doing some necessary business in the home. They are likewise cheerful and content; and nobody can say that they want either wit or charm. Their fault is, that they think too well of themselves. However, the daughters of people of all ranks, without exceptions, go to market and carry home what they have bought. They rise as soon and go to bed as late as any of the people in the house. I have been assured that, in general, their fortunes are not considerable; which are rendered still more scarce by the number of children and the small revenues in a house. The girls at Montreal are very much displeased that those in Quebec get husbands sooner than they. The reason of this is that many young gentlemen who come over from France with the ships are captivated by the ladies at Quebec, and marry them; but as these gentlemen seldom go up to Montreal, the girls there are not often as happy as those of the former place."

Chapter 13

1749–1758

The Seven Years' War. Bigot and La Friponne. Vaudreuil and Montcalm. Their rivalry. Military headquarters. The social whirl. Oswego. Fort William Henry. Civilian suffering.

THE GREAT CONFLICT, which history now knows as the Seven Years' War, had its beginning in May 1756. There was nothing particularly unexpected or mysterious in this British-French declaration of hostile intent—at least in North America where the fighting had never completely ceased. Yet it led inescapably to changes in the nature and extent of the battle front. In both camps, colonial officers and local militia found themselves largely supplanted by European-trained commanders and their battalions of professional troops.

In 1756, as in previous years, New France faced an alarming disparity of numbers and wealth; odds that were now further lengthened by widespread graft and corruption in official circles. François Bigot, the Intendant, was a notoriously evil man, whose arrival at Quebec in 1748 had been preceded by rumors not at all to his credit. An earlier term of office at Louisbourg had set suspicious tongues wagging as to the reasons for the sudden downfall of the fortress. But powerful friends at court outweighed any hint of treachery or lack of moral character, so that Bigot was free to transfer his operations to the wider opportunities of the St. Lawrence Valley.

That such a man could be promoted to high office was indicative of conditions in France. Louis XV had soon tired of the burdens of sovereignty, leaving his mistress to rule the country. From 1745 until her death nearly twenty years later, Madame de

Pompadour held the reins, and because influence counted with her more than ability, the rascals gained preferment over the honest men. To win her favor, the intelligentsia of Paris made it fashionable to sneer at the simplicity of the rustic colonials. New France, in short, became a bore—a cynical philosophy soon to be summed up by Voltaire in gibes at the land that "cost a lot and brought in little." Canada was "a few acres of snow . . . inhabitated by savages, bears, and beavers."

The real Canada, unknown to these sophisticates, was by this date, assuming a more urban character, with a quarter of the population living in towns. Quebec the political capital and Montreal the commercial center; the activities of the two complemented each other and their quarrels of the past were now largely forgotten. For a short time in the early fifties, both were busy attending to their own affairs. Although no one considered the fortifications at Montreal to be of exceptional strength, they were regarded as complete, and so long as the actual fighting remained at a distance, the routines of daily life suffered little interruption. In fact, it might be claimed that business was booming on the strength of activities in the west. The forts, the trading posts, the Indians—all received their provisions and supplies from the Island.

Thus Montreal emerged as a natural for Bigot, to share with the capital, the dubious honor of providing a center for his nefarious operations. No time was lost in finding associates in crime, as corrupt as their ringleader. The head of what might be termed the local gang, was François Victor Varin, a Frenchman of low origin, well versed in the intricacies of finance, and knowledgeable in the manipulation of public money into private pockets. He soon realized a handsome profit from his dealings with the western outposts, and since he and his friends were completely bare-faced in their roguery, it became a matter of public knowledge. So much so that the townspeople nicknamed their warehouse *La Friponne*—in English, "The Cheat."

Such a man as Bigot would have spelled disaster in any circumstances, but it was nothing short of tragic that his office should have coincided with the closing years of the French regime. At a time when the colony was fighting for its existence, treason and dishonesty sapped the strength of its people to such an extent that the whole atmosphere seemed tainted. There was nothing petty in the schemes. The Intendant and his confederates milked the country at every turn, the Canadians suffering by reason of high prices and unwarranted shortage of necessities, the king paying over and over again for the same goods, in a morass of illegal transactions. Although everyone knew of the corruption, Bigot was plausible, and even the more honest officials tolerated his villainy.

The deepening gravity of events overseas led, in May 1755, to the dispatch of fourteen ships from Brest—a convoy so important in respect to its passengers as to suggest a strong French intervention in America. Three thousand regulars were aboard, together with two newly appointed officials—the Marquis de Vaudreuil, as Governor General, and Baron Dieskau as commander. The voyage was not without excitement, for a British naval squadron which loomed up out of the fog, captured two of the transports carrying eight companies of troops. Although the remaining twelve vessels reached the St. Lawrence safely, all had received a foretaste of the enemy's seapower.

For Pierre de Rigaud, the second Marquis de Vaudreuil, the arrival in New France was by way of being a homecoming. In him, the Canadians saw the fulfillment of their long-cherished desire for a native-born leader. As the son of the former Governor, he had grown up in the country, his boyhood familiarity being reinforced by military service there. He now returned to his own people with a reputation enhanced by ten successful years as Governor of Louisiana. Well meaning, kindly and likable; these are some of the labels pinned on him by posterity. Against these, must be set the counterbalances; an indecision in moments of crisis; jealousy of his associates; a narrowness of viewpoint. Although honest himself, he showed weakness in his tacit acceptance of Bigot's dishonesty.

The war was moving closer to Montreal, and many of its men had already been claimed by the growing needs of military service. As the number of conscripts increased, the normal work on the farms slowed down almost to a halt. The harvest for the most part, went ungathered, and there was interference with the western trade. In that same eventful summer of 1755, the fighting suddenly flared up close at hand, for the Richelieu-Lake Champlain highway was always the Achilles' heel of the local defenses. There, in the wilderness, the French and the English clashed in the battle of Lake George. Dieskau, wounded and captured by the American colonials, vanished from the Canadian scene. That the victory had gone to his opponents, was due almost entirely to Sir William Johnson. His skill in the ways of the wilderness, allied with his uncanny insight into the Indian mentality, was unsurpassed.

The winter of 1755–56 was a hard one in Canada, with food shortages the inescapable sequel to the neglect of the harvest. The needs of the army took precedence over the civilian requirements. Horesemeat made its appearance in lieu of beef. Flour and bread were rationed; the initial allowance of a pound loaf per day for each person, was later reduced by half. Nor could the supplies from France be counted on, in view of the British naval activity in the Gulf. Card money fell steadily in value, largely because of the machinations of Bigot. Although public expenditures were high, the common people suffered privation.

The spring of 1756 brought a successor to the captured Baron Dieskau. Louis Joseph, Marquis de Montcalm, arrived in New France holding the royal commission of captain-general and commander-in-chief of the French forces in America. From Quebec, he pressed on without delay to Montreal, where Vaudreuil was in residence. The Governor received him graciously, and the first mutual impressions were favorable.

With closer acquaintance, the harmony vanished. Indeed the dissension grew so serious that the two men have unhappily come to personify the differences between the French and the Canadians. Much of the trouble was of their own making, and there were faults on both sides. Yet in justice, it should be remembered that they worked together in almost impossible harness. Although Montcalm was the senior in military rank, he was, for a time, obliged to take orders from the Governor General. By a change of policy, he was then placed in supreme command, a brilliant general who by training and experience, followed the traditional tactics and strategy of the professional European soldier. Vaudreuil, on the other hand, with his Canadian back-ground, favored *la petite guerre*, and knew little of the arts of war beyond the limits of colonial campaigns.

Montreal was now the miltiary headquarters of the country, and a place of great activity. Vaudreuil lived there almost permanently, as did Montcalm and his train of glittering offi-cers; the Chevalier de Lévis, his second in command; François Charles de Bourlamaque, the third in rank; Louis Antoine de Bougainville, his gifted young aide-de-camp. As befitted the residence of the Governor, the Château Vaudreuil was the center of official life. Montreal, in fact, was brilliant as never before. At night, there were balls and all manner of social gaiety, with no lack of eligible young officers from France to serve as escorts for the belles of the town.

All through the summer of 1756, the troops continued to pour in—reinforcements so numerous that within a space of a few years, six thousand regulars had been dispatched from France. Few remained permanently in Montreal. Their dispersement, to the south and west, was arranged by Vaudreuil, since his was still the deciding voice in all matters of policy.

This rather ambiguous dual command won an early success when in mid-August, after a few days' siege, Oswego fell before the onslaught of a combined French and Canadian force led by Montcalm. Thus the British intrusion into Lake Ontario came abruptly to an end, and the Great Lakes were once more wholly Canadian. Although the strategy had been Vaudreuil's the victory rested with his rival, who returned in triumph to a Mon-treal which went wild in its celebrations. Prisoners, captured pro-visions, British colors; these were the visible fruits of a daring adventure.

But unhappily for the *bonne entente*, the rejoicings were less for the general than for the man who had first conceived of the bold enterprise. Just as the French professionals earlier had their doubts of its wisdom, so were they now excluded from any share in the praise. A pastoral letter from Bishop Pontbriand, which glowed with patriotism and appreciation of Vaudreuil, included references to timid spirits. The Governor General him-self wrote to France, hymning the wonders of his victory, won in spite of the vacillating ways of his associates. Not unnaturally, Montcalm regarded all this as personal ambition.

Yet the two leaders appeared together at a reception in the parlor of the Seminary, when the guests of honor were a large group of Iroquois—the Onondagas, the Cayugas, the Senecas, and the Oneidas—whose presence in Montreal was a welcome dividend that followed the capture of Oswego. Of all the Five Nations, only the Mohawks remained firm in their allegiance to the British. Even the great Sir William Johnson could do little with their disaffected brothers. The spectacle of the fort demolished and the British troops taken captive; this was a combination striking enough to shatter their long cherished beliefs, and so they sought French protection.

Montcalm had already experienced a glimpse of the Indians when shortly after his arrival, his red allies favored him with a formal visit. Presenting him with a necklace, they exchanged compliments and besought the honor of a return call. The Frenchman found them dirty and oddly disturbing in their ways. To his wife, he wrote of their vanity, carrying mirrors to war along with their tomahawks and guns. "They would exercise the patience of an angel." Their cruelty repelled him. "Slaying women and children alike, they scalp you most skillfully, an operation from which one ordinarily dies."

But however great the rivalry, cold weather effectively put a stop to any further plans for attack. Before the snow came, Montcalm built a road over the fourteen miles from LaPrairie to St. Johns, which provided a short-cut across country to the Richelieu. Then, with the troops settled in their winter quarters, the French guests at Montreal proceeded to enjoy a season that promised gaiety and a pleasant relationship with the well-to-do townspeople.

Except for a month in Quebec, Montcalm remained in Montreal, joining with Vaudreuil and his own officers in the social life of the town. Balls, receptions, and dinners, obligatory for one of his high rank, became in the end rather tiresome. Of one such entertainment at the home of de Lévis, he wrote "the hall was brilliantly illuminated; it is as large as the intendant's; much ceremony and attentive hospitality, refreshments in abundance, all the night, of every kind and species, and the party did not leave until seven o'clock in the morning. I, however, who had given up the gay life of my stay in Quebec, went to bed at an early hour." To his wife, he complained of the high cost of such a life. "Everything is very expensive. One must live according to one's rank and I do it. Every day, sixteen persons at table." Once a week he dined with the Governor General, and "up to Lent, besides the dinners, great supper parties with ladies three times a week." He was becoming a reluctant host.

Under such circumstances, marriages were bound to be common. That winter, eight soldiers took brides, with the full consent of their commander. For the officers, it was a different matter, and official disapproval is evident in his views on imprudent alliances. Since Vaudreuil was suspected of encouraging them, another cause of disagreement was born. Most serious of all, was the excessive indulgence in gambling, when egged on by Bigot, the stakes rose to extravagant heights. And because the losses were correspondingly heavy, Montcalm tried in vain, to secure their stoppage.

Vaudreuil showed to better advantage when later in the season, he dispatched a war party south against Fort William Henry on Lake George. It was essentially a Canadian affair, and although Montcalm later pointed with pride to the stamina of his regulars, their share was minor. The hardship encountered in that cruel six weeks—forced marches over ice and snow, sleeping out of doors, a shortage of food—was more than compensated by the results. Even though the enemy refused to surrender, they were obviously shaken by this sudden incursion from the north. When as a final blow, the British ships on the lake were put to the torch, their owners had to forgo any hopes they might have cherished of themselves taking the offensive.

Small though this was, it was still a triumph, and thus impressive to the always fickle Indians. In the summer of 1757, they gathered at Montreal in their hundreds. A wild lot they were, many of them strangers from the west, and completely unversed in the ways of civilized society. As always, they added a picturesque note to the streets and public places, seeming to be especially dignified when they assembled to pay their respects to the Governor General. On such occasions, of course, they were reasonably sober, yet even so, the French officers feared the future. Bougainville, in a letter home, described them as "the fiercest of men and great cannibals," adding that he trembled to think of the horrors he might be forced to witness.

Such was the nature of the allies who shortly joined the French and the Canadians in another and more ambitious assault on Fort William Henry. As the warriors continued to pour in from the west, their numbers increased to the point that fifteen hundred out of the eight-thousand-man force, were savages. They formed a dangerously large minority, and all were thirsting for blood. The siege itself might justly be termed short and sharp; from August 1, the fighting lasted for only nine days. Unable to withstand the artillery fire of the attackers, the greatly outnumbered British garrison had no alternative but to surrender.

The defenders were a pitiful sight as they marched out from the fort—the sick, the wounded and the healthy, all unarmed and all equally unprotected, in obedience to the terms laid down by the victors. The temptation was too great for the Indians, who throughout the siege, had hovered impatiently like birds of ill omen, awaiting what they regarded as their legitimate prey. Now, with their naturally cruel instincts inflamed by liquor, they could no longer be restrained. Death and destruction took over, as the tomahawks flashed and the yelling grew wilder. The scalping knives put an end to the sufferings of the wounded, but others, still able-bodied, were reserved for the horrors of later torture. Meanwhile, the looting and plundering added to the confusion.

There can be no surprise that history considers this to have been the bloodiest of all the border massacres. Among British contemporaries, it stirred the most deep-rooted and lasting of hatreds. The Canadians, it is generally agreed, had grown callous from long association with their red allies. Scalps and loot were always the reward for native support. The attitude of the French officers is less certain. Did they stand back, baffled by the ferocity that surrounded them? Could they have averted the horror, by a firm stand before the warriors went berserk?

Montcalm himself, seems to have had some premonition of what might happen. In a summons to the British garrison, he pleaded for submission. Later, he took the lead in ransoming the prisoners. De Lévis risked his life many times over in attempts to save others, while officers of lesser rank, stood at their tents as sentries, over those they had rescued.

After this ordeal, Montcalm could hardly look upon his home-coming as a triumph. Sick at heart and discouraged, he met a cold reception from Vaudreuil. From his safe niche at Montreal, the Governor General had expected other victories, perhaps the capture of Fort Edward and an invasion of New York. Battle fatigue and shortages of food and ammunition counted for nothing, when he sent off his complaints to France.

Meanwhile, the streets of Montreal were swarming with Indians, flushed with the success of their horrible victory. As they dragged their miserable prisoners along, each tribe tried to blame the others for the massacre. The usual ransom being two kegs of brandy for each Englishman, all were soon thoroughly drunk.

What the town put up with during this fortnight, hardly bears thinking about, for the Indians, being quite impartial in their insults, were ready to take on the Canadians in lieu of other victims. Knives in hand, they threatened the passers-by, demanding guns and presents. Vaudreuil took such behavior in his stride, on the grounds that at all costs, their guests must be satisfied. That many later died of smallpox was a fitting retribution for their misdeeds. Ghouls that they were, they had gone so far as to dig up the corpses in the graveyard at Fort William Henry, only to find that all had perished earlier, in an epidemic of the dread disease.

Viewed more objectively, Fort William Henry gains significance as the moment when the fortunes of New France were at their peak. At the close of 1757, the country had good reason to be proud of its resistance to the powerful Anglo-American combination. The friction among the higher command, although serious, had not destroyed their clear thinking, and there was ample scope for the French style of fighting alongside the Canadian. Right across the colony, their forces stood firm, outguessing and outmaneuvering the more ponderous enemy. As for the Indians and quite apart from the factor of cruelty, their support was indispensable.

Yet this success, no matter how pleasing when viewed from afar, was not gained without painful cost. It is questionable whether anyone in Montreal, during those long cold months, had leisure to ponder its meaning. Of all the wartime winters so far, that of 1757–58 was the worst, with the old familiar cycle in full motion; farms neglected because of military service; scanty crops; food shortages, which were in turn, unusually serious because of the army needs. And because the Gulf was infested with British ships, prowling out of Boston and Halifax, there could be little reliance placed on supplies coming from France.

For both civilians and troops, rationing made its appearance as early as October. In December, the restrictions were tightened. Horsemeat took the place of pork, and bread almost vanished from the scene. Nothing could be distributed save with government approval, and then only under the strictest supervision. The cities were, of course, in worse case than the country, and for this reason, Montreal suffered.

What made the public misery all the more poignant was the extravagant social whirl of their prosperous neighbors. Bigot, as might be expected, was the star, his entertainments the most outrageous as well as the most costly. His guests paid dearly for their attendance at his gaming tables. Vaudreuil was complacent over the hospitality of the Intendant, lending the éclat of his presence without hesitation. Montcalm, too, although less frequently, for his conscience was troubled by the ruin of his officers. "We are amusing ourselves and thinking of nothing; all is going and will go to the devil."

In Montreal, *La Friponne*, like its counterpart in Quebec, was jammed with illegal merchandise. Everything Bigot brought in from France, although privately owned, escaped import duties by means of false declaration of royal possession. Later, it could easily be sold to the government at a handsome profit, for by a strange coincidence, the king's stores were always found to be in need of precisely those articles which happened to be in stock. Fictitious names and a discreet handling of invoices could be counted on to prevent discovery. "Canada was the prey of the official jackals."

Meanwhile, in England, great political and military changes were in the making. The long succession of spineless ministries had come to an end, their do-nothing muddle being replaced by the genius of William Pitt. To the extent of believing that the victory was to be won in America, he was a revolutionary. For this reason, troops crossed the Atlantic in numbers hitherto unknown. Moreover, Pitt held strong views as to the abilities of his generals. His insistence that promotion should be based on personal qualifications, rather than family influence, resulted in a good many new faces in the higher echelons.

In New France, the authenticity of news from the outside world, was often open to question. As carried by His Majesty's supply ships each spring and summer, it had the merit of being official, but during the long icebound winters, the isolation was almost as complete as in the days of Champlain. At all seasons, there were rumors, back and forth, between the French and the British colonies. Each side indulged in all the time-honored practices, in the hope of discovering the intentions of the enemy. An escaped prisoner of war was always a profitable source of information, once he reached his own country. Deserters, eager to gain asylum, were helpful, while hints of treachery were by no means ended. Most profitable of all, were the scouts, whether white or Indian, whose hardihood and ingenuity enabled them to carry out small raids into the other's country, not so much to kill as to reconnoiter and observe. Montreal knew such men well, for they were always active in the Richelieu-Lake Champlain territory, and it was largely because of their reports that troops began to move south in June.

The story was that the British under General James Abercromby were massing for an assault on Carillon (Ticonderoga). The fact that 15,000 men and 1000 small boats were mustered, could not easily be concealed. Montcalm led some 3400 French regulars down to assist in the defense of the flimsy and unfinished fort. Notwithstanding the odds, it was soon apparent that the outcome was by no means a foregone conclusion. The British not only lacked artillery, but they served under a commander of the

old school, whose appointment predated the Pitt regime. When
he chose to throw his men head-on against the resolute French,
they died like flies. Finally even Abercromby realized the futility
of his methods and retreated to safety.

Unhappily, the battle reawakened all the old bitterness in
Montreal, since Montcalm hailed the victory as completely
French. Without Indians and almost without Canadians, he had
defeated an army of thousands. From the safety of his headquarters, Vaudreuil merely asked why the beaten English had
not been pursued further. This marked the start of a correspondence that grew acrimonious, beyond anything yet known. When
news of its contents leaked out, everyone in town promptly took
sides.

Montcalm remained at Carillon until September, lest the English should contemplate any renewal of their attack. In an attempt at reconciliation, he sent Bougainville back to Montreal—
with some success, since the discord had, for the moment, run
its course, and was indeed soon overshadowed by developments
elsewhere. For as the bad news came in from the west and the
east, it was painfully clear that this one victory counted for little
in the steady stream of defeats.

During the summer of 1758, Louisbourg fell before another
land-sea attack, interesting as marking the first appearance of
James Wolfe on the Canadian scene. This time, the fort was
razed to the ground, never to be rebuilt. Conditions in the west
were equally serious, for the French were forced into retreat all
along the Ohio. Then suddenly, the war shifted nearer to Montreal, with the British recapture of Oswego and the occupation of
Fort Frontenac. With all communication thus broken to the west
and to Louisiana, the settlements along the St. Lawrence braced
themselves for an uncertain future. And since the British Navy
was in command of the approaches to the Gulf and the river,
the lifeline to France was frail.

The gravity of the situation forced the opposing factions at
Montreal, into an armistice. Outwardly courteous, a good deal
of backbiting went on behind the scenes, the Governor General
taking umbrage at any suggestions as to the future conduct of
the campaign. Only on one point was there complete agreement;

the king must be told of the plight of his people. For this purpose, Bougainville went to France as the personal envoy of Montcalm, while Michel Pean, one of Bigot's men, presented the views of Vaudreuil. That much accomplished, little remained in the way of immediate activity. The arrival of cold weather saw the usual dispersal of the troops to winter quarters, a process naturally repeated in the British camp. But in the retirement of the ineffective Abercromby, lay the seeds of future danger. His successor, Jeffrey Amherst, was of a different quality.

Chapter 14
1759–1760

The iniquities of Bigot. No more aid from France. The British at Quebec. Capitulation. Montreal watches and prepares to attack. Ste. Foy. The three-pronged attack on the Island. Murray, Haviland, Amherst. Defense impossible. Surrender.

THE WINTER OF 1758–59, in many ways, resembled those that had gone before. There was not enough food, and prices rose to unheard-of highs. A large part of the scanty harvest had been confiscated in the name of the king, and the horses and cattle slaughtered to provide meat for the troops. Milk was unobtainable.

In the face of this suffering, the behavior of Bigot and his hangers-on was nothing less than shameless. Their one concern was to amass personal fortunes, no matter what the cost to the country. As the man in the street watched such conduct among his betters, there were murmurs against the government, and including Vaudreuil. For this was the essential tragedy of the Governor General; although honest himself, his tolerance of corruption among his colleagues, passed all belief. "It seems that all are hurrying to make their fortunes before the loss of the colony, which many perhaps desire as an impenetrable veil to hide their bad conduct." So wrote Montcalm from the depths of his despair.

That a man of his exalted rank should withdraw from the constant round of gaiety, was a measure of his integrity. A few weeks in Quebec provided an interlude, which if not exactly carefree offered relief from the pinpricks of daily association with Vaudreuil. For the rest, in Montreal, Montcalm enjoyed many quiet hours of reading and writing in the privacy of his chamber.

Among the books of his choice, probably *L'Encyclopédie*, with
all its intellectual variety, offered the greatest relief from the
deepening gravity of the war. It is true that, so far, only a few
volumes were available, since publication, dating from 1751, was
spread out over many years. Yet there was much to enjoy in the
articles on Christianity, colony, comedy, council. And if all were
not uniformly acceptable, as he pointed out to a friend, he could
always skip what he did not wish to know or failed to understand.

But events were moving quickly toward a climax, for the ice
in the St. Lawrence broke up the beginning of April, an exceptionally early date for this normally welcome event. Willingly
or not, Montcalm and Vaudreuil were again forced into joint
consultations over the course of the new season's strategy. Although outwardly, both tried to preserve the semblance of courtesy, their mutual antipathy was only stifled, never killed. Sometimes, their subordinates indulged in expressions of partisanship,
though Montcalm in particular was known to dislike tittle-tattle.

The return of Bougainville in early May, put an end to all
thoughts of pettiness. After a fruitless winter in Paris, he arrived
in Quebec, laden with honors for everyone. Medals and promo-
tions cost the king nothing, and made a brave show. Beyond
this, a mere four hundred troops represented the reinforcements
so eagerly hoped for. Canada was now thrown back upon her
own slender resources.

Whether Vaudreuil was gratified at being made a member of
the Order of St. Louis is highly doubtful, in view of the fact
that the king had decided to transfer the supreme command to
Montcalm. In future, he was to be consulted in all matters per-
taining to administration and defense. Yet aside from wounded
pride, the change may well have made little difference to the
safety of the country, since all possible defense measures had
already been taken. Meeting now in Montreal and now in Quebec, the officers had studied the danger spots and agreed upon
the most effective counter efforts. Should anyone earlier have
harbored the thought of capitulation, he had to recall the latest
royal instructions. New France was to defend itself to the death.

Strangely enough as it now seems, what the French feared

most was a thrust up from Lake Champlain. For this reason, reinforcements were sent down to Carillon in the early spring, where Bourlamaque, with 2500 men, faced a greatly superior British force under Amherst. Actually, it was not until May that the immediacy of the threat to Quebec was realized. Although the British fleet was known to be patrolling the Gulf, its magnitude remained a secret until Bougainville and his convoy managed to slip through unobserved. Even then, there was a certain blind confidence in the river itself. With all man-made landmarks removed, and without benefit of local pilots, the French felt that alien seamen would find themselves unable to navigate its treacherous waters in safety.

Nevertheless, by the end of the month, the headquarters at Montreal was deserted. Montcalm and Vaudreuil were both at Quebec, working on last-minute plans. With them were most of the troops in the colony, both French and Canadian, and including some 1100 militia from the Island. For the civilians of Montreal, it was the start of a summer of watching and waiting, torn between hope and despair in the changing fortunes of the capital.

The British, as it happened, were slow in making their appearance. Not until the latter part of June did their seventy vessels begin their ascent of the St. Lawrence. At Quebec, an empty harbor greeted them, the French ships having moved higher up the river in the hope of avoiding capture. The siege that followed was, of course, one of the most famous episodes in Canadian history, and the details of the fighting and the flaws in strategy, have been debated endlessly ever since. Its duration was significant, since from early July until mid-September the issue hung in the balance. When the garrison ran short of food, both Montreal and Three Rivers found themselves called on for assistance. A risky business it proved to be, running the small boats down under cover of darkness, dodging enemy patrols and praying for a safe landfall.

Early in August, there was more bad news. With the surrender of Niagara, the French hold on the west was broken, while Bourlamaque's abandonment of Carillon opened the way for an early invasion up the Richelieu. To the commanders hemmed in at Quebec, the retention of the frontier line seemed vital, no

matter what the cost. To this end, they put de Lévis in charge
of the Island defenses and dispatched him up the river at the
head of eight hundred men. He proved to be an excellent choice,
doing everything possible to insure the safety of Montreal. Keeping the main body of his troops on the alert, he went out from
his headquarters on a round of inspections of the outlying posts,
the mere fact of his presence encouraging the lonely garrisons
to remember the "no surrender" policy. Nor was he too lofty in
rank to overlook such everyday matters as the harvest. Under his
orders, several hundred of his soldiers went into the fields, to
help the women and children, the priests and the nuns, bring in
the grain. Later that month, some of the local pressure eased
with the report that Amherst was unlikely, after all, to attack
that season.

But, all eyes were focused on the life and death struggle at
Quebec. The besieged capital was known to be in desperate
straits for food, yet provisioning from without the walls, had
become almost impossible. The British for their part, had met delays and disappointments. It was not until September 13 that
having gained a foothold on the north shore, they went on, that
same day, to gain the victory on the Plains of Abraham. With
both sides bereft of their leaders—Montcalm and Wolfe died in
battle—other officers assumed the direction of affairs. The French
felt it to be all important that the army should be saved, and so,
on the night following their defeat, Vaudreuil led the surviving
troops out from the citadel, on a long march up the river. They
met with no resistance, and with their safe arrival, Montreal
became the heart of New France. When the formal capitulation
of Quebec followed within a few days, everything depended on
the Island.

As the weather turned colder, it became a matter of urgency
for both sides to prepare for winter. The British, though victorious, were in worse straits than their opponents. With the enforced departure of all the ships before the freeze-up, General
James Murray, the new commander, faced a serious situation.
In a city largely destroyed by artillery fire and surrounded
by enemy territory, he had no more than six thousand poorly
equipped troops under his command. The shortage of food and

firewood was serious enough in all conscience, but sickness made everything worse. An outbreak of scurvy spread so rapidly, that it was often difficult to maintain an effective watch.

In the French camp, de Lévis had succeeded to the command after the death of Montcalm, and thus shared with Vaudreuil in the responsibilities of the defense. Naturally, they maintained undercover communications with Quebec, and so were quick to take advantage of the enemy's difficulties. Most of the French ships which had been anchored higher up the river, slipped away once the British fleet disappeared. Although several were lost in storms at sea, the majority succeeded in reaching France with their bad news.

But four of the vessels stayed to winter at Sorel, braving the dangers from ice, to serve as the nucleus for the spring offensive. All through the long dark months, while petty raids served to distract the enemy, Montreal toiled at preparations for the projected assault on Quebec. There was plenty of work for everyone —the mustering of the militia; the collection of all available arms and ammunition; the gathering of provisions; the making and mending of new and old equipment.

It was late April when seven thousand men left Montreal, their fleet of bateaux convoyed by the ships from Sorel. When reinforcements came out to join them from the villages along the shore, hopes ran high and with good reason. In a bitter fight at Ste. Foy, the British were so sharply defeated that they were fortunate in making good their retreat back to the city. Then de Lévis laid siege and waited, as did his enemies, for a glimpse of the first vessels to come up the river. Upon the nationality of those in the lead, depended the final victory at Quebec and the whole future of New France.

That Murray had foreseen just such an impasse, led him to dispatch a schooner to Halifax earlier in the season. Such being the case, there can be little surprise that the British flag appeared first over the horizon, effectively putting an end to French hopes.

By the middle of May, de Lévis and his men were in full retreat to Montreal. Against such powerful odds they could do nothing else, and as it happened, the French ships never arrived. Pursued by the British patrols, they took shelter in the Baie de

Chaleur, only to be discovered there and burned. Direct communication between Canada and France ceased.

At this moment of peril, Vaudreuil and de Lévis, forgetful of any earlier petty differences, thought only of the safety of the colony. The French holdings had shrunk down to the region surrounding Montreal, and were growing less by the hour. As the British tightened their grip on the lower river, they occupied the villages, promising a peaceful "Hands off" policy to the inhabitants who swore allegiance to King George. Since refusal brought a threat of burning—carried out often enough to provide an object lesson—the men naturally preferred to keep their homes and their lands. As a result, desertion among the Canadians posed a growing threat to the plans of the French leaders.

Thus for all their brave preparations, Vaudreuil and de Lévis inwardly could only pray for peace. There was always the hope that a treaty, negotiated by the European powers, might restore New France to its original owners. For although the outposts were manned, all around Montreal, there was a scarcity of artillery and gunpowder. The great store of provisions, so hopefully gathered together the previous winter, had been largely lost after the battle of Ste. Foy. Once again, there was barely enough food to last through until the next harvest. That the people were weary of fighting, was not to be wondered at. When the French government refused to redeem the paper money so lavishly issued by Bigot, they felt a new sense of injury. The death of Bishop Pontbriand in early June added to their already strong feeling of lonely bewilderment.

Gradually, as the scouts brought in news of the British preparations, the full bleakness of Montreal's prospects was clarified. Amherst's winter hibernation was at an end, and his plans for the final campaign readied. Three armed forces were to converge on the Island, and by their capture of the city, crush the last traces of resistance. Murray was to ascend the river from Quebec, while Haviland followed the Lake Champlain-Richelieu route. Amherst himself, with the main body of the troops, was to come down the St. Lawrence, from Oswego and Lake Ontario.

Murray with his 2200 men, left Quebec on July 14, the first of the three commanders to get under way. The miniature fleet of bateaux, gunboats, and frigates moved slowly, halting frequently to inspect the villages along both shores. The habitant defections grew apace, and trading in eggs and other farm produce took the place of fighting. Three Rivers was still well garrisoned, but the invaders passed by without stopping. Near Sorel, Murray landed, to burn a deserted village, as an object lesson for any who might be tempted to offer resistance. Hating this cruelty as he did, he wrote to Pitt, "I pray God this example may suffice, for my nature revolts when this becomes a necessary part of my duty." After that, nothing stood in his way, so that before the end of August, he was encamped just east of Montreal, awaiting word from his two fellow generals.

This early success was well matched in the steady progress of Haviland who left Crown Point on August 16 at the head of 3400 regulars, colonials, and militia. Traveling by boat, he saw nothing of the enemy until Ile aux Noix, where Bougainville was stationed with a sizable garrison. But when the British brought up their artillery, the defense crumbled, while the fall of St. Johns and Chambly cleared the last obstacles before the St. Lawrence. There, on the south shore, opposite Montreal, Haviland set up his camp. Just across the river, Murray waited, and by early September, thanks to Robert Rogers and his Rangers, the two officers were in touch with each other.

Amherst, as commander-in-chief, led the main force of ten thousand British regulars and colonial militia, supported by seven hundred Indians. They followed a circuitous route, via the Mohawk River and Lake Oneida to a rendezvous on Lake Ontario and thence down the St. Lawrence. Oswego hummed with activity throughout July, as the troops came pouring in. By August 10, they were all afloat, their 656 bateaux and 166 whaleboats presenting an impressive sight. They made steady progress, slowed down occasionally by French attempts at resistance, but never effectively halted. In this fashion, they reached the head of the rapids.

Amherst dreaded the descent of these treacherous waters, knowing that none of his men were experienced pilots. At first, everything went well, and they passed through the upper stretches in safety. Then came the raging tumult of the Cedars and the Cascades. They brought disaster. Forty-six boats were completely wrecked and eighteen damaged. Eighty-four men were drowned. After such tragedy, the quiet waters of Lake St. Louis came as a relief, and from their peaceful camp on Ile Perrot, it was but a short sail down to Lachine. Thus the third and greatest of the British armies arrived at the outskirts of Montreal, as the other two were closing in toward the city. The pincers movement, planned with such care, had succeeded, and without any major fighting.

The Montreal that the invaders saw as they mounted guard in their camps, has been described by Parkman as "a long narrow assemblage of wooden or stone houses, one or two stories high, above which rose the peaked towers of the seminary, the spires of three churches, the walls of four convents, with the trees of their adjacent gardens; and conspicuous at the lower end, a high mound of earth crowned by a redoubt, where a few cannon were mounted. The whole was surrounded by a shallow moat, and a bastioned stone wall, made for defense against the Indians and incapable of resisting cannon." Within the town, there was confusion, crowded "with noncombatant refugees. Here, too, was nearly all the remaining force of Canada, consisting of twenty-two hundred troops of the line and some two hundred colony troops; for all the Canadians had by this time gone home. Many of the regulars, especially of the colony troops, had also deserted, and the rest were so broken in discipline that their officers were forced to use entreaties instead of commands. The three armies encamped around the city amounted to seventeen thousand men."

In writing of this period, Sandham questioned whether any fortified town ever fell more easily than Montreal, for its position was desperate. A French officer described their predicament. "We were all pent up in that miserable bad place, without provisions, whose pitiful walls could not resist two hours cannonade without being leveled to the ground."

Thus it was not surprising that Vaudreuil should call a council of war on the night of September 6. Bigot proposed an immediate capitulation, obviously determined to protect both his life and his money. Yet even among the honorable men, there were few who opposed him, for no one could truthfully see any hope of success. The British seemed to be everywhere and so imposing in their strength that the townspeople refused to take up arms. Since resistance was at an end, all that remained was the discussion of terms, while the town still stood intact. Those who knew of the ruins at Quebec, had a cogent argument for speed.

At seven o'clock the next morning, Bougainville was sent to Amherst, with proposals for a truce of one month. This being refused, Vaudreuil offered to surrender, but only on his own terms. Then there were delays, while both parties argued, for the fifty-five articles as drawn up by the French, formed a lengthy document. Most of them were formal in nature, and met a quick acceptance from Amherst. Others he modified, a few he refused. Most contentious of all, was the first clause. "Twenty-four hours after the signing of the present capitulation, the English general shall cause the troops of his Britannic majesty to take possession of the gates of the town of Montreal; and the English garrison shall not come into the place, till after the French troops have evacuated it."

To Vaudreuil's insistence that his men should leave with their arms intact and all the usual honors of war, Amherst returned a categorical refusal. "The whole garrison of Montreal must lay down their arms and shall not serve during the present war. Immediately after the signing of the present capitulation, the king's troops shall take possession of the gates and shall post the guards necessary to preserve good order in the town." When Vaudreuil still pleaded for some modification, he received a reply so harsh as to rule out any hope of compromise. Evidently embittered by memories of Fort William Henry and *la petite guerre*, Amherst wrote, "I am fully resolved for the infamous part the troops of France have acted in exciting the savages to perpetuate the most horrid and unheard of barbarities in the whole progress of the war, and for other open treacheries and flagrant breaches of faith, to manifest to all the world by this capitulation, my detestation of such practices."

As the messages went back and forth between the two camps, it was clear that neither officer was willing to give way on so delicate a point of honor. The result was a deadlock, which only

Vaudreuil by his acceptance of the inevitable, could break. As Governor General of New France, his was the final responsibility, and if Montreal was to be saved from destruction, he must surrender. To de Lévis, this seemed incomprehensible, and so he asked for permission to withdraw to St. Helen's Island with all available men and munitions. A defense to the death was, in his opinion, the only course open to an officer of the French Army.

With Vaudreuil's refusal of this gallant offer, the end of the negotiations was in sight. In a difficult situation and cut off from all contact with the outside world, he had done his best to fulfill his obligations to his king, no less than to the people of the Island. There can be no belittling of this decision to surrender in September 1760. It was not a local affair, as at Quebec twelve months earlier. There, where only one city changed hands, eleven articles had sufficed for the expression of the terms. But at Montreal, fifty-five were needed, covering all manner of details, when as Amherst tersely promised, "Good order will be maintained."

Chapter 15

1760–1763

The British enter the town. Vaudreuil and the French troops leave. Military rule. The new subjects and the old. Religious questions. The British merchants remain as residents. The town lively and thriving. Local ordinances. Treaty of Paris.

ON THE MOMENTOUS morning of September 9, the scene beyond the walls of Montreal was as colorful as it was lively. There, before the wondering eyes of the townspeople, the great host of British troops lay encamped, the scarlet coats of the regulars standing out in sharp relief against the nondescript garments of the colonials, but all alike in that their weapons were at the ready in case of alarm. There, too, were the Indians, fearsome as always in the garish paint of the warpath. Everyone was on the *qui vive*, both within and without the city, eagerly watching the messengers come and go. Finally, with the word that Amherst and Vaudreuil had signed the official documents, came the realization that the peace was secure.

Hard upon the news, Colonel Haldimand arrived to take possession of one of the main gates. From that vantage point, his men deployed out through the town—the Light Infantry, the Grenadiers, and a detachment of the Royal Artillery armed with a twelve-pounder. Military bands helped to relieve the tension, when for a short time, the civilians found themselves confined to the town. So as to insure good order and prevent disputes, no one was permitted to pass through the gates except the guards and those on official business. But it was soon clear that the choice of Haldimand had been a wise one, for although an officer in the British Army, he was a native of Switzerland, whose mother tongue was French. Thus there were no problems of communication. Courteous and considerate in manner, he made an impossible situation bearable.

While the newly arrived guards assumed their duties, the British flag was raised over the small fort at the east end of the town. Meanwhile, other troops, converging on Place d'Armes, received the surrender of the garrison regiments, as one after another, they laid down their arms. Back once more in their own camp, the French paraded for the last time before de Lévis; 3132 officers and men, it has been estimated, had survived and remained loyal to the end.

At one point, there was a threat of unpleasant consequences, when Haldimand, according to custom, demanded the surrender of the French regimental colors. They had disappeared, no one quite knew where, although rumor accused de Lévis of having burned them. Understandably, the British were bitter, and Amherst threatened to have the enemy baggage searched before departure. But in the main, the difficult days passed off reasonably well, and Vaudreuil at least, seems to have been content with his decision—so much so that in the final period of their enforced association, the two commanders became friends.

September 9 brought Amherst's first general order from the camp before Montreal, hailing "the success that has crowned the efforts of His Majesty's troops and faithful subjects in America . . . and the zeal and bravery which has always been exerted by the officers and soldiers of the regular and provincial troops, and also by his faithful Indian allies." Then came his warning. "The General is confident that when the troops are informed that the country is the king's, they will not disgrace themselves by the least appearance of inhumanity, or by unsoldierly behaviour, in taking any plunder, more especially as the Canadians become now good subjects, and will feel the good effect of His Majesty's protection."

Such an assurance came none too soon, since the inhabitants were already alarmed over the presence of the Indians. From long experience of their own savage friends, they sought to have the native allies of the British sent back to their villages immediately. This the victorious general refused to do, for as he later wrote to Pitt, "Sir William Johnson has taken unwearied pains in keeping the Indians within humane bounds; and I have the pleasure to assure you, that not a peasant, woman or child, has been hurt by them, or a house burnt, since I entered the enemy's country."

Two days later, Place d'Armes was again the center of attraction, when Amherst paraded his troops before Vaudreuil, in a formal farewell prior to the French departure. For ten days, the embarkation continued, until by September 22 all were away, the former Governor General among the last. A stormy crossing awaited the *émigrés*, when they sailed from Quebec in ships provided by the British government. One vessel was wrecked, the others battered by the November gales. Their reception in France was equally chilling. Vaudreuil's report on all that had happened at Montreal, brought an icy reply, the king expressing surprise and dissatisfaction at his acceptance of such shameful conditions. Notwithstanding the diminished resources, an attack or at least a spirited defense would have insured a more honorable capitulation. So read the official censure, bad enough in itself when addressed to a man whose motives had been sincere, but made more pointed by imprisonment in the Bastille along with Bigot and his followers. Although it is true that in the trial that followed, Vaudreuil was acquitted, he died in 1764, "less from age than from sorrow." As might be expected, Bigot slandered the Canadian officers, yet for once he met a sharp rebuke from Vaudreuil, who lauded their services, their merits, and their innocence. There was, at least, some satisfaction in the verdict of the court, which not only found the Intendant and his associates guilty, but sentenced them to banishment, or the payment of heavy fines.

Meanwhile, in Montreal, the activity continued. A church parade on Sunday, September 14, brought together the British and colonial troops in a service of thanksgiving for the success of His Majesty's arms. The occasion was notable as being the first public worship conducted in the English language. The officiating clergyman was the Reverend John Ogilvie, an army chaplain who probably addressed the men out-of-doors—either at Place d'Armes, or the encampment west of the walls.

This was possibly the last gathering of all the forces, for the colonials were dismissed at an early date. Some, with Haviland, crossed to Chambly, and so down the Richelieu to Crown Point, others ascended the St. Lawrence to the forts above the rapids. Rogers, with four hundred men and bearing letters from Vaudreuil, went west to take possession of the more distant posts at Detroit and beyond. The dispersal was a logical step, for such a concentration of strength was no longer needed. Yet Amherst showed wisdom in dealing first with the colonials, since memories of border raids and guerrilla cruelties were not easily forgotten. The British regiments, who formed the local garrison, being free of these unhappy associations, were more likely to live in amity with the inhabitants.

Thus as the British commanders busied themselves with the endless adjustments, Montreal itself began to settle down into some semblance of normality. For the first time in years, the Canadians faced a winter of peace, and if not exactly happy with their new masters, they offered no overt resistance. Everyone was tired to the point of numbness. When the officers went out through the neighboring villages, the militia showed no hesitation at taking the oath of loyalty to King George. The surrender of arms presented more difficulties, although softened by the British readiness to issue permits for hunting.

Within Montreal, there were no barracks, which meant compulsory billeting. But the individual soldiers needed little more than shelter and firewood, while their small daily allowance of money for food was welcomed by the householders. Often they ate together, sharing their provisions, the new subjects and the old, as they were described in the official documents. Whereas earlier there had been a struggle to get the harvest in, the demobilization of the Canadian forces was bringing the men back to their own homes. The town, for the moment, was quiet.

General Amherst's authority was in no wise localized by his sojourn at Montreal. As commander-in-chief of the British forces in America, he had assumed personal leadership of the campaign in New France, and it was in that same capacity that he returned to his New York headquarters later in the autumn. Although he never revisited Canada, he retained nominal control of its civil and military affairs. In a series of announcements and appointments before leaving, he established the framework of the new government.

The three existing districts were retained, for purposes of administration, and placed under the direction of Thomas Gage at Montreal, Ralph Burton at Three Rivers, and James Murray at Quebec. In each parish, the captain of militia was confirmed in his position of combination policeman and justice of the peace. The trial and settlement of minor disputes was left in his hands, Amherst encouraging the Canadians to render judgments in their own affairs as far as possible. However, courts of appeal were readily available in the persons of the British officers, stationed in the various localities, and above them, the governors. The French law and customs remained unchanged.

The new governors received precise instructions from Amherst. Once the Canadians had taken the required oath, they were entitled to all the privileges of British subjects. "I would have you particularly give it in charge to the troops to live in good harmony and brotherhood with them, and avoid all differences soever." It was a promising start to the new regime on the Island, and one further enhanced by Gage's common sense in the administration of justice. Within the town, he brought together all the captains of militia to form one court, which met regularly every Thursday. The country beyond the walls was divided into five regions, based on Pointe Claire, Longueuil, St. Antoine, Pointe aux Trembles, and Lavaltrie. In each one, a panel of not less than three or more than seven militia captains sat twice monthly. Above these were three superior courts, at Montreal, Varennes, and St. Sulpice, presided over by British officers who heard appeal cases once a month. Outranking them all was Gage himself.

That British officers should be so prominent in the upper levels of government was due to the continuance of the war in Europe. Until such time as Britain and France signed a formal treaty of peace, the future status of Canada remained uncertain. Hence the army ruled the colony on a temporary basis, its primary responsibility being to keep the Canadians contented and free of rebellious ideas. Even if anyone, at this date, had wanted to amend the old laws and customs, the authority was lacking.

Yet it is precisely this period of military rule—*le règne militaire* —that has so often been the target of French Canadian criticism. Some historians have professed to see in it, a time when their ancestors were downtrodden and abused—an emotional approach, understandable but far from the facts. Instead, 1760 and the few years that followed, served chiefly to mark a pause between two widely different forms of administration. No one in America could be blamed for the uncertainty of the moment.

In some respects, the new rulers pleased the Canadians. All proclamations were announced publicly, either through the captains of militia, or by placards affixed to the church doors or other centers where the people gathered. Everyone knew what was happening and what was expected of them. Even more important was the widespread use of French, so that communication presented few problems. Almost all the clerks and court assistants were Canadian, and French was the usual language of the proceedings, unless both parties to the suit were English.

Notable also was the fact that most of the British officers spoke French with reasonable fluency, having apparently acquired their knowledge in the course of their "gentleman's" education. Other elements in the army eased the linguistic situation further; the French-speaking Swiss and French Huguenots, the latter being descendants of those who earlier had sought refuge in England. Most striking of all, however, was the bilingual aptitude of General Murray himself. Even in military circles, he was noted for the vigor of his speech. No minced oaths ever watered down the full fury of his invectives, as forceful and as free flowing, the story goes, in French as in his native tongue!

Montreal first met Murray briefly as the leader of the army based on Quebec. It had been an introduction to a personality soon to be known more intimately; it was not to lead to the warmth of unalloyed friendship. Murray was a man of strong likes and dislikes, intensely loyal to those who thought as he did, but arousing bitter enmity among his opponents. As a member of the regular officer caste, he was both Tory and aristocratic in his opinions, to the extent of despising the vulgarian traders. Yet

he had a strong sense of justice, which showed particularly in
his treatment of the defeated Canadians.

It was a foregone conclusion that such a man should clash
with the Governor of Montreal. The two men disliked each other
cordially, in part because of their personal qualities, and in part
because of Gage's seniority in military rank. Although supposedly
subordinate to Quebec, he went his own way. For he, too, was
an officer of wide experience who, in 1763, succeeded Amherst
as commander-in-chief at New York. Greatly to his credit, the
Canadians liked him, and they said so, in suitably flowery
language, on no less an occasion than the death of George II.
After the conventional expressions of regret at the death of so
eminent a monarch, they made use of a play on words, effective
only in French. For in this general, who acted rather as a father
than a conqueror, they discerned *un gage précieux*—a valuable
pledge—of the late king's affection for his new subjects.

But aside from these pleasantries, the question of the hour
was a religious one. What future could the Canadians expect
for their faith in a country officially Protestant? The matter had
received lengthy consideration in the articles of capitulation,
wherein Amherst had agreed to the free exercise of the Catholic,
Apostolic, and Roman religion. Although waiving the payment
of tithes pending a later decision, he had given permission for
the *curés* to carry out their usual parochial functions. In the
case of the religious communities, he hedged, granting to the
nuns what he refused to the priests. Whereas the former were
"preserved in their constitution and privileges," the Jesuits, the
Recollets, and the Sulpicians were bidden to await the king's
pleasure.

It had fallen to Murray in Quebec to make the first contacts
with the ecclesiastical world, and his decisions, quickly taken,
set a pattern for Montreal. On the whole, they were generous,
although in both cities the governors showed some suspicion of
the Jesuits. In this they were not alone, for, as the years passed,
the Order fell into disrepute, even in France; in Canada it
dwindled slowly to a temporary ending. The Sulpicians, on the
other hand, fared better, for their holdings of land and their
general position at Montreal remained virtually unmolested.

The relationship with the nuns was a different matter, based as it was on their devoted care of the sick and wounded, irrespective of race or creed. Thus they were treated as true sisters of mercy and deserving of all possible marks of respect. It was in this spirit that Amherst visited the Hôtel Dieu, to thank the Hospitalières for their acts of charity to his men. A gift of money and two dozen bottles of Madeira provided an earnest of his official appreciation.

But although the governors tried, so far as possible, to ease the situation, the ecclesiastical problems were very real. Routine orders to officers and men, were good so far as they went, and respectful salutes to religious processions in the streets served as a pleasant panacea. Yet the Canadians knew that theirs was a church without a leader, bereft of a Bishop who might give guidance to his puzzled flock. In time, a degree of alleviation came with the election of vicars—M. Montgolfier in Montreal and M. Briand in Quebec—but nothing could be done about the replacement and consecration of priests.

It was, in fact, this matter of the priests that caused the British many hours of anxiety. So many had come from France in the old days. Just how far their loyalty could be counted on was a moot point for years. Gage, for instance, in an official report, questioned whether men, trained in the seminaries of what was now an enemy country, could possibly lead their people into "love and affection" for the new government.

But ecclesiastical hopes and fears by no means, tell the whole story of this period of adjustment. There was, in addition, the mundane question of what to do about the flood of worthless paper money everywhere in the country. It dated back to the bad old days of Bigot, and affected rich and poor alike. Everyone held some, for in wartime, there had been no other currency, yet it had never been redeemed by the French government. No immediate solution suggested itself to the British governors. Gage did not see how France could avoid making good these bills of exchange, but years were to pass before that happened, and then only at a substantial discount.

Although these legacies from the past continued to absorb public opinion, they were quickly reshaped and intensified by influences emanating from within the ranks of the British themselves. The military men did not long remain as the sole representatives of their nation. From a very early date, their numbers were augmented by civilians—a handful of merchants and tradesmen, who having completed their wartime assignment, stayed on to become permanent citizens. In the main, they were city dwellers, a few at Quebec, but the majority and those the most influential, at Montreal.

At first, everyone welcomed the newcomers. As purveyors of food and the other necessities of life, they brought relief to a war-straitened colony. They were the sutlers, who after the fashion of the day, followed in the wake of the British Army, and performed the duties of the modern commissariat. Amherst himself, had made sure of their presence, for in an open letter to the governors of New York, New Hampshire, and Massachusetts he broadcast an invitation to Canada. Those who accepted were obviously men of vigorous purpose, strong in body, determined in mind and willing to take chances. Some hailed from the American colonies, others who were English, represented reputable London firms. Yet all in varying degrees, were tinged with the prevalent Yankee ideas of freedom and democracy, of representative government and the rights of man—dangerous radicalism, in the opinion of the military authorities. Moreover, there was the question of their religion, for all were Protestants. As a group, they did not long remain unnoticed.

But in the early years of the British occupation, the troubles at Montreal were seldom racial. The Canadians and the English seem to have lived together in comparative harmony. Perhaps it was merely bewilderment, or the tremendous disparity in numbers. For some time to come, the British population was estimated in scores rather than hundreds, while of immigration, in the modern sense, there was none. Thus it was natural that in the revival of the fur trade, the old and the new subjects should each take a share, the long-tested French expertise providing invaluable assistance for their new associates.

Once the war came to an end, Montreal's traffic with the west was quick to resume its ancient vigor. It was a welcome development, and one for which Gage claimed the credit. In the course of a rather unctuous report to London in 1762, he noted the abolition of monopolies and the removal of encumberances. Everything, he concluded, was vastly superior to the French management. Yet whatever the cause of the local prosperity, the British possession of all North America had not erased the older rivalry. The men from the St. Lawrence were still the competitors of their opposites along the Hudson and both needed the support of the Indian tribes of the interior.

As their profits grew, the merchants tended to become more aggressive and outspoken. In politics as in business, they found themselves at odds with the government, the traditional antipathy between the army and those in trade being aggravated by local conditions. That no love was lost on either side is abundantly clear from contemporary evidence, while in Murray's much quoted phrase, "a set of licentious fanatics," there lies the key to much future trouble.

Dramatic though these developments may seem from the vantage point of history, they were not reflected in the outward appearance of the town. Lively it certainly was and thriving, its three or four thousand inhabitants enjoying all the benefits of full employment. Wages were high, and a man of ability might choose his own occupation. Many elected to set up in business for themselves, to the annoyance of the regular merchants. Operating out-of-doors in casual fashion, their absence of overhead led to complaints about unfair competition.

Such haphazard street corner transactions, however, served to emphasize the congestion within the town. Montreal was still surrounded by walls, barriers to expansion that were useless in defense. Each military visitor added his voice to the swelling chorus of criticism. Captain John Knox who inspected the fortifications in 1760 found them mean and inconsiderable. Having heard so much of their massive strength, he was shocked to find, instead of the four-foot thickness of public report, dimensions not exceeding twenty inches. As for the guns, some were worm-eaten and all were small, so that in any prolonged siege the walls and the town within would have been pulverized into utter ruin.

For those who knew both cities, Montreal generally held greater appeal than Quebec. Granted that the absence of war

damage may have unconsciously affected their judgment, for
much of the land along the lower St. Lawrence had been badly
devastated. Granted also that most visitors came during the summer, when a pleasant sail up the river made them appreciative
of the beauties of nature. Those who traveled overland were less
fortunate, for the state of the road was such as to try the most
patient of souls. Haldimand was not among these, for while Governor of Three Rivers he issued some forthright orders for its
improvement. The highway, he said, was so narrow that whenever several carriages met, they blocked the traffic completely.
Lakes and sloughs resulting from heavy rain or snow made
conditions worse. Therefore, he ordained it was to be widened
to thirty feet between the woods on either side. Drainage was
to be encouraged by ditches as needed, and the earth from the
excavations thrown up into the middle so as to induce a slight
slope outward.

But to return to Montreal and the summer. In what is considered to be the first Canadian novel, Frances Brooke had the
hero of *The History of Emily Montague* describe the Island as
"a very lovely spot; highly cultivated and though less wild and
magnificent, more smiling than the country around Quebec."
Knox thought that for delightfulness of situation, he had never
seen its equal, standing as it did on the side of a hill; gentlemen's
seats on the slopes; pleasure gardens within the walls; St. Helen's
Island; the river; altogether a most agreeable landscape. Moreover, as Gage reported, "the soil produces all sorts of summer
grains . . . Every kind of pulse and other vegetables to which
I add some fruits, viz, apples, pears, plums, melons. Cider is
made here, but as yet in small quantities. In general, every fruit
tree hardy enough to withstand the severity of the winter will
produce in the summer, which affords sufficient heat to bring
most kinds of fruit to maturity."

The town proper was hardly as attractive as its environs. Still
small in area, it was not much more than a narrow strip along
the river, about a mile long and at its widest, some three hundred and fifty yards across. In the upper section, stood the buildings of the religious orders and the Parish Church. Situated on a
gentle rise toward the mountain, their spires and rooftops pro-

vided the only breaks in the skyline. The commercial district hugged the shore, and although regarded as more spacious than lower town Quebec, was not a place of great beauty. There the newly arrived merchants lived above their shops or offices. Stone was coming into its own, among the older wooden houses. None, however, offered much to the passer-by in the way of color, while the windows, shuttered in sheet iron, added to the generally forbidding picture.

The ordinances show that the government was well aware of the problems of daily life in such a town. In substance, they resembled those of New France, and certainly their sanitary precautions showed little improvement. Each person was bidden to gather together, in front of his property, the dung and other refuse that had accumulated since the previous day. It then became his responsibility to have the pile carried down to the shore and dumped into the river. Those who cleaned house by throwing filth over the walls, were warned that this, too, must go into the St. Lawrence. Owners of pigs were cautioned that these constituted a public nuisance and must be kept shut up.

Fire continued to be a major hazard. Chimneys must be swept every month, while all householders were required to keep axes and buckets handy in case of emergency. Snow removal was a problem over which the government disclaimed all responsibility. Instead, each property owner was supposed to keep the surface clear in front of his land, providing a footpath two feet wide for the benefit of the pedestrian. But traffic remained the chief danger—the furious driving through the streets which had for so long menaced those on foot. As always, it was at its worst on Sunday, when fast trotting or galloping was forbidden in the vicinity of the Parish Church. In a curiously modern approach to its control, Gage insisted on drivers keeping to the right at all times.

Life was rarely serene in so congested a town. Crimes and minor disorders kept the courts busy. Montreal lacked prison facilities, which meant that punishment was swift and often severe. There were, of course, acquittals and pardons; there were also fines and floggings and sometimes an execution. The public's enjoyment of strong drink did nothing to improve local conditions and the English governors had to deal with the same patterns of behavior as their French predecessors. It was forbidden to sell intoxicating liquor to soldiers or to savages, while the inhabitants were supposedly limited as to amount.

Yet Montreal as described by Knox had its lighter moments. "The inhabitants are gay and sprightly, much more attached to dress and finery than those of Quebec, between whom there seems an emulation in this respect; and from the number of silk robes, laced coats, and powdered heads of both sexes and almost of all ages that are perambulating the streets from morning to night a stranger would be induced to believe Montreal is entirely inhabited by people of independent and plentiful fortunes."

To this might be added Mrs. Brooke's comments about the Canadian customs in winter, especially on New Year's Day when all the beaux visited their ladies "who sit dressed in form to be kissed." In her opinion, the men looked like Friday in *Robinson Crusoe*, in their coats of beaver skins. The ladies for their part, were well covered, in their long cloth cloaks with loose hoods. Describing one in scarlet, she wrote, "the hood lined with sable, the prettiest ever seen here . . . The Canadian ladies wear these cloaks in India silk in summer, which fluttering in the wind, look really graceful on a fine woman."

Such was the Montreal which in 1762 heard the news that the long-awaited peace was at hand. The negotiations between London and Paris were, of course, vital to these men and women of the St. Lawrence Valley. What was theoretical in Europe was stern reality in Canada. It was common knowledge that an influential group in England wanted to return the country to France, retaining in its place, the tropical island of Guadaloupe. Since French opinion was similarly divided, no one knew what might happen. Yet, in the end, Canada remained British, and, early in 1763, the Treaty of Paris was signed.

Chapter 16

1763–1773

Conspiracy of Pontiac. The new civilian government. Disputes. Walker. Du Calvet. The army and the traders. Guy Carleton. The fur trade.

CLOSE ON the heels of the Treaty of Paris, the tribes of the region south of the Great Lakes rose against the white men. The Conspiracy of Pontiac—so named for one of the leaders—might be described as a renewal of *la petite guerre,* consisting as it did of a series of sudden attacks on the former French outposts, manned since 1760 by small British garrisons. Lured into the open by a treacherous show of friendship, the defenders paid dearly for their lack of preparedness. In the massacres that followed, the victims were picked off, one by one, until at last, Detroit alone, under its resolute commander, remained intact.

Admittedly, Pontiac and his followers had many grievances, yet if some were genuine, others arose out of ignorance. Basically, they objected to the British, who in Indian eyes, appeared as usurpers of all that had once been French. The soldiers in their red coats and the traders—both spoke an unknown language and were aliens. Some of the newcomers showed such greed for land as to pose a threat to the tribal hunting grounds. To this extent, the indignation was understandable. Taken up and aggravated by some of the French agents supposedly in the service of the British, the whole frontier was convinced that a fleet from France would once again sail up the St. Lawrence, bringing liberation to all. It was a legend that died hard, and three years of hard fighting passed before disbelief brought about the collapse of the rebellion.

Montreal felt the effects chiefly in its commerce. With this great territory closed to civilians, the resurgent fur trade came temporarily to an end, and even when peace was restored, the controls and restrictions remained. Because of the actions of a few agitators in the west, French Canadians as a whole, were regarded with suspicion. Their gradual ouster from positions of importance followed. With the entrée to the old southwest barred, some of the more enterprising English turned their eyes toward the more distant northwest.

In the meantime, there was the Treaty of Paris to be lived with. For those Canadians whose dislike of the new rulers was sufficient, it offered a means of escape through a return to France. An eighteen-month period of grace allowed for formal dispositions to be made at leisure, while its terminal date of August 10, 1764, marked the beginning of the new civil administration. Just how many took advantage of the opportunity has always been a debatable point. Murray put their number at about two hundred and seventy, including women and children, while Gage, writing from Montreal late in 1762, noted that so far only military and civil employees had gone. "Nor do I apprehend any emigration at the peace, being persuaded that the present inhabitants will remain under the British dominion. I perceive none preparing to leave the government or that seem inclined to do it unless a few ladies whose husbands are already in France, and they propose to leave the country when peace is made, if their husbands should not rather choose to return to Canada." Montreal was affected to the extent that most of the voluntary exiles were town-dwellers, although Sulte considered that their departure "did not disturb business and created no vacuum."

The nature of the new government was, of course, determined in London, and there the years had introduced new faces into the ranks of His Majesty's servants. William Pitt resigned in the autumn of 1762, to be succeeded by a line of short-lived ministries, who, however well meaning, were often stupid and inconsistent. Add to this, the inexperience and the stubbornness of the young George III, and it becomes apparent that Canada, to some extent, shared in the disabilities that, in the American colonies, led to the Revolution.

Thus it was not surprising that the constitution should be a strange mixture of the good and the bad. Canada was no longer Canada, and the name itself, vanished officially for a few years. In its place, stood the Province of Quebec, strangely shrunken in comparison with the old land—hardly more than a strip along the north and south shores of the St. Lawrence, terminating not far above Montreal. Beyond lay the great expanse of the "Indian Territory," lopped off from the settlements to provide a reservation for the wandering tribes of the west. Within its boundaries, colonists were forbidden, and traders restricted; the interests of the natives were paramount.

To preside over the civil administration of this truncated country, the king chose James Murray. His military authority, however, was limited to the district of Quebec. A decision of dubious value at best, it was rendered impossible by reason of the personalities involved, and remained to embarrass Murray to the end of his term. As might be expected, Montreal and the new Governor General soon found themselves at odds.

When Gage left for New York in 1763, he did so amid a cloud of good wishes, notably from the captains of militia over whom he had presided in the weekly military courts. Yet, throughout his regime in Montreal, he had consistently ignored Murray. In the path thus blazed, the new appointee followed happily, for Ralph Burton was first and foremost a soldier. A shadowy sort of person of whom little is known, he ceased to be Governor with the ending of military rule. But—and it was a large qualification —he remained in Montreal as commander of the troops in the Northern Department, taking his orders from Gage and ignoring Quebec. No successor was appointed, with the result that just when Montreal was growing in size and diversity its local government was reduced to near nothingness. The few inexperienced justices of the peace were neither willing nor able to look after the municipal affairs of the Island community. It was a farcical situation with serious implications, as no one realized better than Murray. "I beg leave further, to represent to your Lordship that a lieutenant governor at Montreal is absolutely necessary. That town is in the heart of the most populous part of the province. It is surrounded by the Indian nations and is 180 miles from the capital. It is there that the most opulent priests live, and there are settled the greatest part of the French noblesse. Consequently every intrigue to our disadvantage will be hatched there."

Although the Treaty of Paris in many ways was acceptable to the Canadians, the clauses dealing with religion pulled them up short. After coasting along freely under military rule, it came as a shock to read that they might only "profess the worship of religion according to the rites of the Romish Church as far as the laws of Great Britain permit." Just what this meant, perhaps no one could have said without profound study, but coming as it did from a Protestant nation, the restrictive purpose was clear. To Murray fell the task, however uncongenial, of bringing the new subjects into the fold.

Thus the harassed Governor General was reminded by London, that in religious disputes he must be guided by the laws, and these "prohibit absolutely all Popish hierarchy in any of the dominions belonging to the Crown of Great Britain, and can only admit of a toleration of the exercise of that religion." If, to modern ears, such words sound harsh, they become less so when judged in the context of their time. A priest caught celebrating Mass in England was liable to life imprisonment, yet no attempt was ever made in Canada to impose like penalties. A further complicating factor was officialdom's fear of treachery among the French-born clergy. It died slowly, and to it, must be ascribed much of the coldness, even of such a normally sympathetic friend as Murray.

That within a few years, a Bishop once more headed the Roman Catholic Church, was entirely due to the delicate maneuvers of Murray. While London cold-shouldered the whole proposition, he intervened or interfered, depending on the point of view. There were two possible candidates in the persons of the vicars, M. Montgolfier of Montreal and M. Briand of Quebec, and it was only after lengthy negotiations that the latter emerged as the one person acceptable to all parties. Quietly consecrated in Paris, Bishop Briand returned to Quebec in 1766, to the manifest joy of his people.

With the Canadian laity, Murray's relations were reasonably happy, especially with the seigneurs of the old regime. The phrase is significant, for the Governor was too aristocratic by nature to be at home with the masses of any race. Since his friends among the noblesse were naturally concerned with the civil disabilities under which Roman Catholics labored, their energies for the next decade were directed toward finding a formula acceptable to the government. Small modifications tended to ease the main situation, and paved the way to a gradual amelioration of the first drastic regulations of 1763.

By way of contrast, the political fortunes of the English merchants moved in reverse. Cock-a-hoop at the outset, at the bright promise of civil government, they experienced disappointments and frustrations that were nonetheless real for being in large measure the result of their own actions. They talked too much and were often intolerant—if not the whole two hundred, at least a fair percentage. Aggressive by nature, militant Protestants, and imbued with the radical views of the American colonists, they were by no means the ideal ambassadors of their race. Despite all their praise of representative government, weight of numbers counted for less than nothing. In their eagerness to secure an elected assembly, they brushed aside the claims of the 65,000 Canadians. The colony was to be ruled by and for Englishmen.

So it was that the new constitution was born into an atmosphere of discord, and nowhere worse than in Montreal. On all sides there were disputes, so embittered that encouragement to one group was invariably labeled as injustice by the other. In such vital matters as the establishment of civil courts and the appointment of judges, the king's regulations were of necessity, obeyed. All the magistrates were Protestant and the law administered was that of England. Yet, Murray's sympathies soon made themselves felt. Roman Catholics were permitted to serve on juries, and lawyers of that faith, to appear before the Court of Common Pleas—the first chinks in the solid wall of British prejudice. That they grew out of a sensible realization that alien laws could not satisfactorily replace the old French Code, in no way saved their author from abuse. The vials of wrath descended upon his head in the form of petitions and memorials sponsored by the English merchants, none of them more furious than the local breed.

Not all the troubles of the period were man-made, for devastating fires swept through the town, in the spring of 1765 and again three years later. Over one hundred houses, on each occasion, were destroyed, leaving many of their hapless tenants in a state verging on destitution. For the still small population, the costs of rebuilding and general relief seemed such a burden, that several benevolent gentlemen launched an appeal in England for assistance. Successfully, if the response of royalty was any criterion, for George III headed the subscription list with a contribution of £500.

Presumably the citizens were accustomed to such disasters, for these were neither the first nor the last in the long series of holocausts which ceased only with the acquisition of adequate fire-fighting equipment. It is tempting, nevertheless, to speculate as to the possible side effects of this destruction of houses, upon the quarrel between the military and the civilians, so much a feature of the years after 1763. Its roots lay in the tiresome necessity of billeting, a wartime obligation that became onerous with the advent of peace. For some time the trouble was latent, although minor clashes testified to the town's need for barracks. When the officers and men swaggered a bit in their contempt for the inferior status of those engaged in trade, the merchants reciprocated with sharp words on the lack of discipline in the army.

The next step in the fray came with the elevation of some of the merchants to the Bench, where as magistrates they found themselves vested with authority to turn verbal diatribes against the soldiery into stern measures against hoodlums. While not all were unjust in their rulings, a few undoubtedly were, and none more so than Thomas Walker. He was a Britisher, out of New England, so filled with the most advanced political ideas of the day as to become the archetype of the hated "Bastonnais." Bad tempered and strident in speech, he made enemies wherever he went.

The affair took a serious turn when a certain Captain Payne was assigned to rooms in a private house. Since one of the new magistrates lodged under the same roof, the owner claimed exemption. Rebuffed by the army on the grounds that such concessions applied only to property actually owned by the officials, the case went to trial before Judge Walker. He promptly found against Payne and ordered him to move. A refusal brought a commitment to jail for contempt of court. By this time, feelings ran so high in the town, that Murray summoned the offending parties to Quebec, to render an account of their behavior.

Before their departure, however, the famous "outrage" occurred when, one night at supper in his own house, Walker was attacked by a party of masked men. So furious was their assault that in the course of the melee, they cut off a piece of their victim's ear (or so he claimed later). The incident, magnified in the telling, stirred the town to such an extent that everyone looked askance at the most innocent of soldiers, and went in fear of being robbed or murdered in their beds.

Events such as these, added substance to the vague unrest in Montreal, where disputes between soldiers and civilians were fast becoming serious. So disturbed was Murray at their violence that he spent some months in the town, trying to restore law and order, and at the same time, uncover the culprits in the Walker case. It was soon clear that while the citizens might be fearful of the military, the garrison had just cause for complaint. Under the pressure of unreasonable arrests and vindictive judgments, discipline was breaking down. As to the "outrage"—and Walker was never done talking about his ear—even the posting of rewards brought no results. When the king's offer of a hundred guineas was matched from local sources, still the silence remained unbroken. Two years later, there was a sequel, when a witness came forward, prepared to identify the assailants. Although the man was a discharged soldier with a bad record, his testimony served as the warrant for a number of arrests. A verdict of "Not Guilty" satisfied the ends of justice. As for Walker, he was deposed from the Bench, only to return later in triumph, thanks to the good offices of influential friends in London.

Another facet of the feud appeared in the activities of Pierre

du Calvet, whose arrival in Montreal early in the sixties, touched
off a new series of strange incidents. In contrast to the Anglo-
American background of Walker, this man claimed French birth.
He may well have been Swiss, for he was a Protestant. Although
his career in the New World dated back to 1758, the transfer of
allegiance caused him no qualms of conscience. By 1767, he was
settled in Montreal, the proud possessor of a town house and a
country estate, while as a magistrate, he was well on the way to
becoming a prominent citizen. False modesty never being one of
his failings, he considered that he carried out his judicial duties
"with the utmost purity and disinterestedness."

Du Calvet's stories, it must be said, lost nothing in the telling
—so much so that he is now largely discredited. Contradictions
abound, interspersed with untruths. He was always in the right,
and the other fellow wrong. When a judgment went against him
in the Court of Common Pleas, he complained of the partiality of
the magistrate, John Fraser, an ex-captain in the army. Time
passed, until one day in June 1771, Du Calvet was walking back
and forth on the gallery in front of his house. "The street . . .
was full of carts that were bringing materials for the building of
a new church . . . Notre Dame de Bon Secours." At this awkward moment, Captain Fraser and his wife came along in a one-
horse chaise, and finding the way blocked, blamed Du Calvet.
With that, the insults flowed thick and fast, Fraser claiming that
his "rank and office gave him a right to speak in that tone of
authority." When Du Calvet ventured to disagree, his enemy
proceeded to chastise him, using for the purpose, a little cane,
three feet long with a leaden ball in the top. Right out on the
street, there was a free-for-all, the adversaries rolling on the
ground, and pulling each other's hair until finally separated by
the horrified onlookers.

A few quiet months ensued, at least in the physical sense, although Fraser was alleged to have said that while "one Justice
of the Peace, Mr. Walker, has had his ears cut off, another will
have his tongue cut out." Intermittently, there were minor incidents—chapters in the sad history of indignities whose climax
was delayed until the spring of 1774. At that season, Du Calvet
noted, it was customary to cut little trenches or channels in the

melting snow, to prevent its running into the cellars of the adjoining houses. This, as a good householder, he had done, being careful not to encroach on the passageway of the street. So far so good, until the evening when a cariole belonging to a certain Captain Gordon, overturned. Next day came the repercussions, for the captain in his wrath, sent a sergeant with a party of men to fill in the trench. Not content with this, they heaped "the snow together to a greater height than in the adjoining part of the street," and naturally with such a bank, the cellar was soon filled with water. When Du Calvet complained, Gordon replied with haughtiness, and neither side would apologize.

The saga of Du Calvet could be continued indefinitely, if his own report is to be believed. Despite his complaints to the Governor, the unprovoked attacks went on incessantly! Moreover, he claimed, his wife being with child, was so frightened by the soldiers that her death at the end of 1774 was due entirely to the military reign of terror!

Although the lives of these two men, by their sheer extravagance, added drama to the local scene, it would be unfair to label them as typical of the new merchant class. That, indeed, would be to accord them an honor beyond their just deserts. Troublesome though the group as a whole might be, they followed more conventional lines and with great effectiveness. For they seem to have realized, soon after the proclamation of civil government, that some of its promises would remain unfulfilled so long as Murray was in office. Having fastened upon him as the author of all that they abhorred, they set to work to secure his recall. Public meetings served as platforms for open statements of opposition, while petitions beyond number, found their way across the Atlantic. Not content with this written bombardment of the British government, they added the persuasion of personal contacts.

Eventually their lobbying met with success, for Murray to his own chagrin, was summoned home in the autumn of 1765—an honorable *congé*, but nevertheless he was hurt. Although publicly vindicated by London, he never returned to Canada. To do him justice, it must be said that he had been handed an impossible situation, wherein without the support of wise cabinet ministers, no one could have achieved success. Murray could take comfort only from his friendship with the Canadians, "the bravest and best race upon the globe."

Although Murray left Quebec in June 1766, in the peculiar fashion of the day he did not formally relinquish office until April 1768. His successor, who arrived in September, held the lesser title of Deputy Governor, while assuming the full responsibility for the administration of the country. But Guy Carleton possessed an advantage denied to Murray, in that he was accorded military as well as civil authority. Moreover, his abilities were of such a nature as to transcend rank, and later admirers have sometimes called him one of the great proconsuls of the British Empire.

Like all the early British governors, Carleton was a soldier of long experience, and having served under Wolfe at Quebec, had some slight knowledge of Canada. A native of northern Ireland, he was somewhat reserved by nature, inspiring neither the strong likes nor the dislikes that had characterized Murray's regime. A certain neutrality colored his views to begin with—an aversion to the noisy turbulence of the preceding years, and a determination to know more of the people and the reasons for their dissensions.

It was probably asking too much that such a semblance of amity should be long maintained, least of all in Montreal, that perennial storm center. There were a few pleasant exchanges to start off, Carleton going so far as to plead with London for the removal of the restrictions on trade, before plunging into an exposé of the dishonesty and corruption in government circles. This was a subject on which he held strong views, and so his shock was the greater when he realized that most officials drew their remuneration from fees instead of salaries. To set a good example was easy, and he forthwith renounced any claim to what might be regarded as his own perquisites. To deal justly with all the three hundred and fifty types of fees, was another matter. These constituted an open invitation to graft which the unscrupulous were quick to accept. Some of the worst offenders lived in Montreal, practicing "all the chicanery of Westminster

Hall," and quite unashamedly taking advantage of the Canadians' ignorance of British law.

Yet while Carleton, for domestic reasons, was swinging more and more toward the Canadians, dangers from without the country, made their support essential. There was, in the first place, that never-failing nightmare of the British rulers, the fear of an attack by France. To this was added the growing disaffection of the American colonies, for the happy fantasy of an all-British North America had quickly faded. With the removal of a hostile New France from the scene, America turned to thoughts of independence. No one knew better than Carleton that these found support in Canada.

It was in the light of such misgivings that the new Governor surveyed the defenses. He was shocked. Montreal, he dismissed as impossible; with its old walls tumbling into ruin, the town lay open to any invader. Only Quebec seemed to offer any possibility of successful resistance, and so he pleaded with London for funds to strengthen the fortifications. With this weakness in mind, Carleton found himself swinging more and more into the French Canadian orbit. What had started as a personal liking grew into a matter of political expediency, for the support of the noblesse and the clergy was essential if Canada was to be retained. That such a *rapprochement* was possible, was a tribute to both parties. For Carleton, it led inescapably to a realization that French civil law should be restored and Roman Catholic disabilities removed.

Perhaps something of Carleton's calm nature rubbed off on the old subjects during the later sixties, for although Montreal seldom found itself in complete agreement with the ruling powers, the protests were less vehement than the chaotic close of Murray's term. Within the ranks of the merchants themselves, there were changes for the better, as some of the hangers-on of the war years disappeared, to be replaced by a more sober and respectable group of men, who regarded Canada as a permanent home. Although still few in number, there was a slow but steady influx of newcomers, all in business and most of them engaged in the fur trade.

At the conclusion of Pontiac's Conspiracy, the traders resumed their activities, and by 1765–66, were ready to expand, in competition with the Americans of New York and the French of Louisiana. But the Canadians—whether French or English—found themselves hemmed in by impossible regulations. These arose out of Murray's strict policy of isolation for the Indian Territory. To protect the natives from exploitation, a white man who wanted to trade, must first secure a license from the Governor, and post security for double the value of his goods. The common practice of wintering in the Indian villages was effectively blocked by the rule that confined trading to the immediate neighborhood of the forts.

All in all, it was an ill-considered scheme, drawn up by men ignorant of actual conditions. Montreal was hard hit, and its citizens penalized in their race with the Americans. The licensing system was bad enough in itself, but what hurt most of all was the restriction of trading to the posts, practical perhaps at Detroit and Niagara, impossible at Michilimakinac, by now virtually a Montreal preserve. Distance kept the Indians away, and because they neither would nor could come down to the center, the white man simply had to go out into the wilderness.

In 1768, the government restored the wintering privilege, so eagerly sought by the Montreal men. It gave an impetus to trade, more far-flung than ever before, out to the western prairies and the great rivers of the north. But as the town took the first steps toward business on a grand scale, the merchants and the government found themselves, in other respects, still holding opposing views. So, at the start of the seventies, the old round started up again, of meetings, petitions and public statements, nonetheless significant for being in quieter mood.

By this time, even the home government admitted the need for constitutional changes. Although anxious to do the right thing, the multiplicity of views made decisions difficult. For this reason, Carleton returned to London for consultations. Yet progress was depressingly slow. During the four years of his stay overseas, the whole framework of the administration was surveyed, with a view to amendments. Much thought also went into the boundaries of the province and the control of the fur trade. Since the Boston Tea Party took place in 1773 while Carleton was still in England, the sense of urgency deepened. Canada, ten years after the Treaty of Paris, awaited uneasily for news of reforms.

Chapter 17
1773–1776

The Quebec Act and constitutional changes. Political discontent. American agents and the Congress Party. Ethan Allen. General Montgomery. Capitulation. A winter of discontent. The rebels are hated. Benjamin Franklin and the Commissioners. The American retreat.

WITH THE ENACTMENT of the new legislation in June 1774, Carleton returned to Canada, happy in the knowledge that his conciliatory views had carried the day at Westminster. After the agonizing delays, Parliament at last moved quickly, spurred to a rare unanimity by events in the American colonies. Even the most confirmed Tory ostrich could no longer ignore the obvious signs of incipient revolt. If the St. Lawrence settlements were to remain British, the Canadians must be placated.

Conceived in such circumstances, it is not surprising that the Quebec Act has been hailed as the cornerstone, the Magna Charta of French Canadian liberties. Its abandonment of the policy of anglicizing the province, represented a reversal of the Proclamation of 1763. If Quebec—or Canada—need no longer be coerced into conformity with British colonies elsewhere, official sanction could be given to usages already tolerated by Murray and Carleton. All religious disabilities were removed, and in their place, a simple oath of allegiance enabled Roman Catholics to hold office under the Crown. With the restoration of French civil law, order emerged from chaos, while the maintenance of English criminal law displeased no one. Rigorous though it now seems, it was less so than the French custom of the day.

While it is not to be supposed that such principles won unanimous approval from the English minority, the main storm center lay in the denial of an assembly. Instead of a popularly elected body, the administration of the country was vested in the Governor General and an appointed Council, which though more than twice the size of the old one, bore no resemblance to representative government. Under Carleton's leadership, it became largely French Canadian and decidedly aristocratic. All racial sympathies aside, its members were as remote from the commercial interests of the country as from the habitants themselves. That they were often less than just in their decisions did nothing to improve their relationship with Montreal.

It is true that geographically, the Quebec Act offered a sop to the merchant class, so long resentful of the special status of the Indian Territory. This was restored to Canada—less from any desire to benefit Montreal, than from a determination to save it from falling into the clutches of the rebels. In the main, the new boundary followed the line of the old French frontier, along Lakes Ontario and Erie to the Ohio and the Mississippi and thence to the north. Coming as it did when the fur traders were pressing farther afield, the change was a vital one in the development of the Island.

While some Anglo-Canadians might feel uneasy at the implications of the Quebec Act, the American colonies positively seethed with indignation. To many a good Protestant lover of liberty, the specter of an alien Roman Catholic oligarchy along the St. Lawrence must be prevented at all costs. Everything was equally repugnant, the extension of the boundaries no less than the withholding of representative government—feelings which found formal expression in the autumn of 1774, when the Congress of Philadelphia gave wide circulation to an address headed, "To the Inhabitants of Quebec." Specifically, it invited the residents of Canada to send delegates to the forthcoming session of the Continental Congress, going so far as to suggest that differences in religion should not "prejudice you against a hearty amity with us. You know that the transcendent nature of freedom elevates those who unite in the cause above all such low-minded infirmities."

What with the political discontent of the Montreal merchants

and the sullen neutrality of the farmers, the timing of this somewhat bombastic missive could hardly have been better. It proved
to be the forerunner of a winter of seditious talk, in French and
in English, spontaneous to a certain extent but most of it fo-
mented by American agents. John Brown, for example, was sent
to Montreal by the governor of Massachusetts in an attempt to
get some action. Thomas Walker rallied to the cause, and at first,
to judge by the crowds who gathered in the taverns to listen, it
seemed as though the seeds of rebellion had fallen on fertile soil.
Yet so many of the inhabitants held aloof from active participation that the success was decidedly limited. Despite all the committees and petitions, Canada sent no delegates to Philadelphia.

Brown was, of course, only one of the many skillful propa-
gandists who preached the gospel of revolution to Canadian
audiences. Appearing as they did, at such a tense moment in
local history, they were disruptive to the point that no man could
gauge his neighbors' loyalties. Carleton knew of the insidious
infiltration, but was powerless to stop it. Having sent off half his
garrison to reinforce Gage, hard pressed at Boston, he was left
with a mere eight hundred regulars to defend the whole country.

In this confused fashion, the months passed until May 1, 1775,
the date on which the Quebec Act became effective. Montreal's
celebration was a strange one. The bust of George III was
discovered, daubed with black paint and decorated with a necklace of potatoes. To this was attached a cross bearing the inscription, *"Voilà le Pape du Canada et le Sot Anglais"*—the
Pope of Canada and the English fool. The incident rocked the
little town. Amid much chatter of insolence and disloyalty, the
sum of one hundred guineas was collected and offered as a
reward. No one claimed it and the culprits were never discovered. Since the words were in French, the blame without any
proof, was generally laid at the door of the French Canadians;
these in their turn, suspected an agent provocateur.

But in any case, this was all petty scandal and loose talk—
insignificant in the swift onrush of events elsewhere, which
threatened the security of the whole country. The battle of
Lexington that spring beckoned victorious America on to new

and greater conquests. Canada and its acquisition as the fourteenth colony headed the list.

Early in May, the small British garrisons at Ticonderoga and
Crown Point surrendered to forces led by Benedict Arnold and
Ethan Allen. Once the control of Lakes Champlain and George
was assured, Allen pressed ahead with his Green Mountain boys
in the hope of taking the fort at St. Johns unawares. The whole
countryside panicked at the news, as did Montreal. The people
were stunned. Fortunately, the military authorities kept their
heads, dispatching a hundred men under Colonel Preston to the
trouble spot. But the local traitors got ahead of them, for a man
named Bindon played a two-faced role with some effectiveness.
Thanks to his warning, the Americans made good their retreat
to the south.

Twenty-five miles away in Montreal, the excitement was intense. To make matters worse, it was market day and the town
crowded with farmers and their wives, bent on selling their
provisions. When the alarm went out, everyone congregated in
the streets. Rumors grew in the telling, most of them carefully
planted by the Congress supporters. No one knew what to do or
whom to trust.

At this troubled moment, the machinations of the Congress
Party were such as to create an explosive atmosphere in Montreal. Anything might happen, as Carleton soon realized, and
indeed his prompt arrival on May 26, was a measure of his deep
personal anxiety. That he knew the full extent of the disaffection
was unlikely. Although a few of the agitators came into the open,
the majority labored in obscurity, the more dangerous for being
anonymous. There was, in fact, little at Montreal to give satisfaction to the Governor, for the defenses were useless and the
troops few. Above all, there was the cruel disappointment of
the volunteers, so painfully slow to come forward, the English
half-hearted, the French Canadians studiously neutral.

It was in this French Canadian avoidance of any share in the
conflict that Carleton faced one of the great disappointments of
his career. He had set such store by his friendship with the new
subjects, and counted on their loyalty, oblivious of the fact that
the noblesse and the clergy did not represent the entire nation.

The habitants chose to go their own way. That he considered
the minds of the people to have been tainted by cabals and
intrigues, did nothing to improve the situation. Nor did he meet
with much support when he called out the militia for compulsory service. Clearly, nothing could stir the habitants, not
even a *mandement* from Bishop Friand which threatened the
ban of the church on those who joined the invaders. If the
clergy seemed ineffectual, so did the seigneurs, for their tenants
refused obedience. Inertia it was, and perhaps for no more valid
reason than an utter weariness of war. Only fifteen years had
passed since *l'ancien régime* with all its burdens of military duty.
Since then, prosperity had strengthened the farmers' love of
their homes, *et enfin,* it was England's quarrel.

The main attack on Montreal started in September. Carleton,
who had returned to Quebec in July, where the regular administrative duties awaited him, left hastily at the news that the
invading army was encamped at Ile aux Noix, twelve miles from
St. Johns. It was a sizable force, the original thousand augmented by reinforcements to a total of four thousand. Under
the command of Philip Schuyler—soon because of illness, to be
replaced by Richard Montgomery—the progress had been rapid.
Judging by the enthusiastic welcome of the villagers along the
Richelieu, there would be no opposition, except from the forts
at St. Johns and Chambly.

Among the parties sent out to make contact with the French
Canadian supporters of Congress, was one led by Ethan Allen.
As he attended to the distribution of the official manifesto, he
found himself on the south shore of the St. Lawrence, immediately opposite Montreal. To a man of his temperament, the
prospect was tempting. Why should he not go ahead and capture the city, particularly as he had a friend, Brown, within the
walls. Whereupon and without consultation with his superiors,
he made his plans.

Unhappily for Allen, Brown deserted him at the crucial moment. When a loyal farmer brought in word of the rebel advance, Carleton ordered the gates closed, and the ladders carried in from beyond the walls. This time, at least, the volunteers
turned out. When Allen, after a rough crossing by canoe, landed

at Longue Pointe, with his little band of a hundred and fifty men, he might just as well have walked into a hornets' nest. It was a sharp little battle and quickly over, the would-be attackers obviously surprised at such resistance. Allen himself was captured and placed in irons on board ship for transport to England. Forty of his men were taken with him, and the rest killed or put to flight.

Perhaps it was this incident that impelled Carleton to take action against the rebel plotters within the town, for until then, he had been amazingly lenient. When a batch of compromising letters fell into his hands, he ordered Walker's arrest. October 5 was another dramatic evening, this time in the family farmhouse at L'Assomption. For when the warrant was served by a posse of twenty regulars and twelve Canadians, Walker decided to resist. After exchanging shots, the troops set fire to the building. The smoke almost smothered Mrs. Walker, whereupon her husband carried her to a window. Then, still in her nightdress, she lowered herself as best she could, hanging on until rescued by the soldiers. It was not until the whole floor burst into flames that Walker surrendered. The couple were given some wraps to cover their night attire, and hurried into Montreal. There Walker was charged with rebellion, and placed in solitary confinement, at first in the barracks, later for greater security on board ship.

Although the loyal citizens undoubtedly took pleasure in the fate of such men as Walker and Allen, the situation south of the St. Lawrence was less satisfactory. Thanks to the welcome of the villagers, the whole district was soon in enemy hands. Montgomery was at St. Johns, preparing to lay siege to the fort, which almost alone, barred his way to the city. Behind its walls, Colonel Preston was entrenched, a resolute commander of some six hundred men, including most of the British regulars and a hundred and twenty Canadian volunteers.

As the weeks passed in a seeming stalemate, Montgomery revealed himself as a good strategist. Winter was at hand, and he felt anxious about Quebec. So he by-passed St. Johns, only to swoop down on Chambly. A day and a half sufficed to effect its surrender. It was a sorry display of cowardice, for which the commander, the Honorable John Stafford, bore the blame. Not only were his eighty men lost to the cause, but all their provisions and ammunition; he had made no effort to destroy them.

For St. Johns as for Montreal, this was a serious blow, since Chambly, twelve miles nearer the city, controlled the line of communication. Late in October, Carleton made one last try at relief. Having assembled another levy of militia, some seven or eight hundred men were encamped on St. Helen's Island. At first, hopes ran high, when the flotilla of little boats set off for the south shore, only to fade quickly under a steady barrage of gunfire from the rebels at Longueuil. Forced to retreat by this surprise attack, the British returned to the city, with some forty or fifty men killed and as many wounded.

This was the beginning of the end, for on November 3, St. Johns capitulated. Short of food and ammunition, its defenders could not have done otherwise. There was no further opposition. Montgomery at LaPrairie, started to collect the boats in the neighborhood, preparatory to crossing the river. By the tenth, Montreal heard that he was on the way. For Carleton, this was the signal for departure, since he, as Governor General, had responsibilities to the country as a whole. At five o'clock in the afternoon, he boarded one of three armed sloops in the harbor. Nearby lay a dozen or so smaller vessels, equally ready for sailing. With him, went a hundred and twenty troops, all that was left of the British garrison. Nothing more could be done for the town. The Canadian militia were dismissed to their homes, the cannon spiked and the bateaux burned.

It was not to be a peaceful passage down the river, for contrary winds west of Sorel held the little fleet motionless for two days. To the American officers along the shore, the becalmed vessels seemed easy prey. Carleton alone, managed to escape in a small boat, with the help of a loyal Canadian named Bouchette. As for the rest, all unarmed and ill-equipped, resistance was out of the question. Promptly turned about by the rebels, they sailed back to Montreal as prizes of war. Ironically, Walker, confined in the hold of one of the ships, regained his freedom.

By this time, Montreal was firmly in American hands, for Montgomery reached Point St. Charles the morning after Carleton's departure. It was a Sunday about nine o'clock when the church-bound citizens heard the news. Although a few talked bravely of resistance, they lacked ammunition, and in any case, the Congress supporters felt themselves to be in the saddle. The treacherous Bindon, while doing sentry duty at one of the embrasures, took care to make his new loyalties clear. Thus the invaders knew that they could count on support from within the walls, and perhaps for this reason, Montgomery was cool in his reception of the twelve men delegated to discuss the capitulation. Four hours he would allow them and no more, in which to draw up and present their proposals. Then with the reminder that the weather was cold, he proceeded to occupy the Recollet suburb, and by four o'clock, had his entire force comfortably settled.

The negotiations went on until midnight, Montgomery acting in a somewhat arbitrary fashion, as the citizens—six French and six English—did their best to secure guarantees on such matters as law, religion, trade, the release of prisoners, the billeting of troops. Yet in the end, he was not ungenerous, for as he pointed out: "The City of Montreal, having neither ammunition, artillery, troops nor provisions; and having it not in their power to fulfil one article of the treaty, can claim no title to a capitulation." He then went on to grant most of their requests.

The next morning, the troops entered the city, many of them wearing the scarlet coats of the British, captured in the storehouses of St. Johns and Chambly. Although lacking in the spit and polish of the regulars, as they marched along Notre Dame Street, they were, nonetheless, proof that Montreal had passed into the hands of the Americans.

Montgomery had planned to winter in Montreal, until news from Quebec caused a change in his plans. After a grueling trek through the wilderness of the Kennebec and Chaudière rivers, Benedict Arnold had reached the capital. Since Carleton, with the British and Canadians was firmly entrenched within the town, the siege was likely to be a long one. Montgomery left on November 28, but the problem of reinforcements was not easily arranged. Montreal, St. Johns, Chambly—all had to be garrisoned from the scanty eight hundred who had agreed to

re-enlist until the spring. As for the rest, they melted away,
considering their duty at an end.

As the winter wore on, a subtle change stole over Montreal, a
faint hint of disillusionment that deepened with each week that
passed. General David Wooster, the new commanding officer,
was a stupid man who spoke his mind without much regard
for the niceties of diplomacy. He seems to have despised the
Canadians, and this, despite the fact that his first official duty
was the publication of General Washington's proclamation which
saluted them as "Friends and Brethren." "Come then, my
brethren, united with us in an indissoluble union, let us run
together to the same goal."

Whether in fact, such a hope of unity could ever have been
realized, is open to doubt. Local conditions all worked against it,
and Wooster had every reason to be nervous at the growing
hostility of the townspeople. Apart from his few known adherents, the rest were biding their time and awaiting developments. With the safety of wives and children at stake, men at
such a moment of crisis, could only follow the prevailing winds.

Money was the basic problem—not paper currency, but good
coin of the realm. So long as this was available, food and firewood
would be forthcoming. But the Canadians had long memories,
and the image of Bigot and his worthless paper still rankled.
When the Americans offered continental bills in exchange for
goods, the objections started, and since the local merchants refused to make loans, they were helpless.

Nor was the behavior of the garrison altogether reassuring.
A few of the men mutinied when ordered to Quebec, and although the ringleaders were flogged, the lack of discipline made
a bad impression. The officers tried to enforce decent behavior,
but confinement in a small town during the long winter was
bearing evil fruit. Meanwhile, the civilian population grew steadily more hostile.

In January, the complaints reached such a pitch that Wooster
posted an ordinance at the church doors, forbidding anyone to
speak against Congress, under pain of being sent out of the
province. When the loyalists refused to be silenced, the general
made plans to send them into exile at Albany. Several sleighloads

of miscreants—including the Sulpician, M. Montgolfier—were actually assembled, until the pleas of one of the rebel wives brought about a cancellation of their arrest.

The merchants were no more contented than in the past, for the abrupt stoppage of trade with the west, alienated those who might have been expected to change their allegiance. When their petition to Congress met with no response, the local authorities bore the blame for the restrictions.

No one, really, was happy, for as the interference with personal liberty continued, every section of the population felt the pressure in some way. The officers of the Canadian militia, for instance; when ordered to resign their commissions, they held a meeting of protest. Four were arrested and the rest could only submit. *Corvées* to aid Quebec were most unpopular, while domiciliary visits in search of arms made the Americans appear as oppressors. Social life was largely at a standstill, many of the citizens choosing to remain patiently at home until the inevitable denouement.

At first, the local rebels were sufficiently self-assertive to make up for the silence of the majority. Most of them were natives of the thirteen colonies, army contractors and wholesale provision dealers. Walker, Price, and Heywood were the leaders, the first-named being the only fur trader to go over to the Americans. The substantial merchants had no truck with the invaders. Thoroughly Canadian by this date, they bided their time, content with political obscurity, many of them discreetly seeking the protection of the forests.

The sense of expectancy was heightened by the course of events at Quebec, where the fighting continued throughout the winter. Montgomery went into action, convinced that the surrender would not be long delayed, and boasting, according to popular report, that he would dine in Quebec or in Hell on Christmas Day. His death was a sad blow to his followers, when on the last day of the year, a strong assault against the town, ended in failure. That the depleted forces held their positions until the spring, spoke volumes for their courage. Bitter weather and smallpox made their persistence nothing short of heroic.

With the loss of Montgomery, conditions in Montreal worsened to the point that Congress belatedly took action. A Commission was appointed in February, for the specific purpose of investigating the military situation and improving relations with the Canadians—a difficult assignment for the distinguished group that included Benjamin Franklin, Samuel Chase, and Charles Carroll, the last-named a Roman Catholic, accompanied by his brother John, of the disbanded Jesuit Order.

For Franklin in particular, at the age of seventy, it was a trying mission, as difficult physically as frustrating mentally. The journey from New York, was an arduous one, lasting from April 2 to 27, with stops at Albany and Saratoga. Long before their destination, the troubles started; Carroll vowed he had never seen worse roads or carriages. What shocked them most of all was the widespread refusal to perform the most trifling services without instant payment of gold or silver.

Perhaps they felt that the reception at Montreal made up for the rudeness of the *calèche* drivers and the ferrymen. The Americans and their friends put on a brave display, the ceremonial salute of cannon lending importance to the first meeting with Arnold at the army headquarters in the Château de Ramezay. The evening passed off pleasantly enough, in what Franklin described as decent mirth, and when the ladies and gentlemen dispersed, he found himself lodged with Walker in the finest house in the town.

Franklin and his companions were not long in deciding that their mission was unlikely to succeed. They had come too late. Although they assumed full charge of affairs, there was little to be done. Wooster, they agreed, was unfit to command, his actions having already damaged the cause of Congress. But food was as scarce as money, and although Franklin advanced £350 in gold from his own purse, it counted for nothing in the general bankruptcy. The clergy ignored them, and the Roman Catholic laity were largely hostile. Of the four hundred English-speaking Protestants, a growing number showed loyalist sympathies.

During the next few weeks, there seemed no end to the bad news. Although the Commissioners struggled manfully with the local problems, they could only conclude, in a report to Congress, that their stay was no longer of service. The first to go was

Franklin, followed within a few days by Chase and the Carrolls. By the end of May, they were all out of the country, having achieved nothing.

To his own regret, Franklin did not travel alone. Since Montreal was already hostile to American sympathizers, he felt obliged to conduct Mrs. Walker to safety. When her husband joined the party at Saratoga, their taunts were almost unbearable. Yet Franklin landed her safely at Albany, with her three wagon-loads of baggage, brought there at no expense. They parted coldly. "I think they both have an excellent talent at making themselves enemies, and I believe, live where they will, they will never be long without them."

Meanwhile the military situation deteriorated rapidly. May 6 brought the end of the siege at Quebec. The arrival of a strong British fleet was too much for the war-weary Americans. Sickly and hungry, their ranks dissolved easily, and within a few hours, everyone had vanished.

When word of this retreat traveled up the river, Arnold in command at Montreal with one or two thousand men, found himself threatened from the west. To a British captain named Forster, stationed at Ogdensburg, the moment was propitious to recapture the city. Several minor actions followed, at Cedars, Senneville, Vaudreuil, and Lachine, until the loyalists found themselves holding American prisoners in embarrassing numbers.

In the end, the assistance was hardly needed, for Carleton and Burgoyne led their troops toward Montreal. They moved quickly. By June 17 it was all over, and the evacuation of Canada complete.

Chapter 18
1776–1783

Military headquarters. Carleton and Burgoyne. British troops. Thomas Anburey. A gay life. The joys of winter. Political adjustments. Fears of American invasion. Sir Frederick Haldimand. Peace.

As THE AMERICAN occupation became a thing of the past, Montreal could count itself fortunate. Just as in 1760, the town had escaped the devastation that goes with street fighting and hand-to-hand combat. Shabby it undoubtedly looked in the strong summer sunshine and more than a little down at the heel, but to the people who lived there it was enough for the moment to be assured of food and shelter.

The severity of the human scars was less easily gauged, for with the return of the British, some at least, of the trimmers went underground. Certainly the town was quieter, with the departure of Walker and his henchmen, although it was hard to believe that his handful of noisy demagogues could have stirred up so much mischief. When Carleton drew up a list of inhabitants who "very zealously served the rebels in the winter of 1775–1776, and fled upon their leaving it," only sixteen Montreal names were included. All were American, except for Walker and Bindon. Perhaps, with justice, the roster was brief. Perhaps also, it reflected the humanity of the compiler, who was never inclined to be harsh in his treatment of prisoners.

The same official benevolence appeared in the case of Fleury Mesplet, released from jail after only twenty-six days. All the cards seemed stacked against him; a native of France with republican leanings; a former resident of Philadelphia and the

protégé of Benjamin Franklin; the printer of the 1774 inflammatory address to the inhabitants of Quebec; an agent of Congress, sent to Canada for the express purpose of establishing a
free press for the dissemination of radical publications. Having
followed the Commissioners to Montreal, he had no opportunity
before they left, to set himself up in business. The retreat of the
rebel army left him stranded, without funds and burdened by
his equipment. In such circumstances, his arrest was inevitable,
yet its brevity was a credit to British tolerance. The result was
that Montreal gained a permanent citizen and the printer of its
first books, both commissioned by the Seminary: *Reglement Con-
frérie de l'Adoration Perpetuelle,* and a tragedy to be played by
the students, *Jonatas et David.* Under his auspices, too, the first
local newspaper made its bow in 1778, *La Gazette du Commerce
et Littéraire,* a French language weekly devoted to literature.

However, it is doubtful whether the people as a whole took
much interest in such *recherché* matters as books. They were too
busy, and happy at finding money in circulation again. Although
the western fur trade, bedeviled by war and government controls, was still in the doldrums, the Island and indeed the whole
district, was alive with British regulars, from LaPrairie to
Chambly and St. Johns and the villages of the Richelieu. The
first to arrive were the men who earlier in the spring had gone
to the relief of Quebec. As more and more reinforcements appeared, Montreal was well protected, for the moment, against
sudden aggression from the south. The provisioning of such an
army was a profitable business in itself, while the local taverns
reaped a rich harvest from their thirsty patrons.

Montreal, as the largest town in the district, served as military
headquarters, since for the time being, the center of interest
had shifted away from Quebec. Carleton came and went all
summer, working with General Burgoyne on plans for the projected invasion of the American colonies. On several occasions,
there were Indians to be received, representatives of those great
tribes, which if less powerful than in days gone by, could not yet
be ignored. Late in June, three hundred Iroquois chieftains, who
foregathered with the Governor in the Jesuit church, pledged
their active support for the British cause. After much official

handshaking, the night passed in feasting and merrymaking. It seemed like old times. Three weeks later, another deputation arrived, in the persons of one hundred and eighty chiefs of the Ottawas and other western tribes. Their welcome was exceptionally warm, for they had traveled far, and while their proposal to take to the war path, was not immediately accepted, Carleton urged that they hold themselves in readiness.

By this date also, loyalist fugitives from the American colonies were starting to cross into Canada. At the outset, few were civilians. But the very day after the relief of Montreal, Sir John Johnson joined Carleton there, at the head of two hundred volunteers. As the son of the late Sir William, he soon persuaded others from New York to make an open espousal of the British cause—a process undoubtedly accelerated, after July 4, 1776, by the Declaration of Independence. For although its article on "confederation and perpetual union" left the door open for Canadians to join the thirteen colonies, it also served to drive many Tories into exile. Thus the British Army found itself the stronger for two new regiments of hard-hitting provincials—the King's Royal Regiment of New York and Butler's Rangers. By 1783, it was estimated their number had risen to three thousand.

But life was not altogether serious in Montreal, for with the advent of cold weather, the army settled down into winter quarters. The presence of several hundred officers insured a gay season, whose continuous round of festivities was strenuous enough to tax the endurance of the most hardened campaigner. Colonel Butler, for one, found the life to be more tiring than scouting; only a snowshoe tramp around Mount Royal every other day, enabled him to keep fit.

It remained for a young Irishman by the name of Thomas Anburey to provide the most detailed picture of the social life of the period. As a captain in Burgoyne's army, he spent some months in Montreal, quite obviously enjoying himself. His greatest enthusiasm was reserved for the winter, so healthy and salubrious and so different from the cold, damp air of England. He marveled at the sturdiness of the Canadians, who never stayed indoors, except during heavy storms. They were, of course, dressed for the frigid temperatures, wearing in addition to the

usual blanket coat, a pair of leggings with flaps on the outside
to prevent snow from clogging them. Gloves and a cap, both of
fur, completed the outfit, the latter made to pull down over the
ears when the strong northwest winds blew. At such times, there
was always the danger of frostbite, especially when turning the
corner of a street. The afflicted member, Anburey noted, should
be rubbed with snow and kept away from the fire.

Despite these minor discomforts, the great joy of winter lay in
the outdoor amusements. Skating, for one thing, at which the
Canadians were fast, "but the Indians dart along like lightning."
Best of all, though, was the thrill of driving carioles or sleighs
over the ice of the St. Lawrence. The vehicles in themselves
were eye-catching, painted in fantastic colors, and shaped to
imitate birds and beasts. Their height rose with the social caste
of their owners. The common people rode close to the ground,
while their superiors were elevated upon runners, often as much
as two feet above the ground.

By mid-winter, the river was frozen solid, except for a few
warm springs which never congealed. Every parish, as a safety
measure, was obliged to mark the roads with large pine trees
fixed in the ice, about ten feet apart, and these continued green
all season, "as if you were going between an avenue of firs." Although near the shore, the surface was smooth, out in the center,
it was "thrown up in prodigious hills, through which the inhabitants cut a passage to cross . . . You are surrounded with ice,
several yards high." The air was inconceivably cold, amid these
curious shapes—pyramids, cones, slabs, and some resembling
men and animals.

Under such conditions, nine miles there and nine miles back
was quite a jaunt before dinner, but the speed of fifteen miles
an hour more than made up for the distance. Every day, large
parties went off to Pointe aux Trembles, where there lived a
Dutchwoman "who makes most excellent sausages, and at whose
house it is customary to refresh with these and bottled porter.
As the north wind generally blows very sharp, you acquire a
pretty good appetite, and for my own part, I enjoyed this petit
repas in preference to my dinner."

Indoors, there was ample heat, although so arranged that no

one could be surprised at the number of conflagrations in Montreal. "A wonder it has not been totally destroyed . . . for in the winter, when the inhabitants go to bed, they make great fires in their stoves and leave them burning all night, by which means they are frequently red hot before morning . . . Imagine how very dangerous they must have been when their houses were constructed of wood; few of these are now remaining except in the outskirts of the city, the greatest part of these being built of stone."

Almost every evening, there were parties, reported Anburey, "for the Canadians resemble the French in respect to dancing." The best fun of all came at the New Year, when the men went around the city, saluting the ladies "who sit up in state for three days for that purpose." Nor was there anything half-hearted about their greetings, for after the French fashion, the kiss was bestowed "upon the cheek, when having saluted one, the lady presents the other." All of which, he concluded, was preferable to the English custom.

While the young people enjoyed themselves, their elders turned to a consideration of the affairs of the province, still far from normal. Politically, there was much to occupy the authorities, for the American occupation had caught Canada at an awkward moment of transition from one constitution to the other. Although the Quebec Act, as proclaimed in 1775, actually annulled all existing provisions for civil administration, two years elapsed before the new machinery could be set in motion. The government, such as it was, was carried on by six conservators of the peace, until the first meeting of the Legislative Council in the spring of 1777.

At Montreal, the magistrates continued to direct local affairs, for in the prevailing uncertainty, there could be no thought of change, and the merchants, normally so quick off the mark, were slow in resuming their political remonstrances. It was not until April 1778 that they again addressed themselves to London. Besides their general hatred of the Quebec Act, the refusal to permit trial by jury in civil cases worked a hardship on the growing business community. The protest was once more ineffectual.

Military affairs, in the months following the retreat of the

Americans, presented an uneven pattern. At the outset, there was a good deal of criticism of Carleton's refusal to pursue the fleeing army across the border. Yet by mid-summer, optimism was in the ascendant, for everyone knew that the carpenters were busy at St. Johns, constructing a fleet of small vessels for use on the Richelieu and Lake Champlain. Considering the amount of work expended on preparations, it was unfortunate that action was postponed until October. Although the easy occupation of Crown Point came as a pleasant surprise, the British hesitated to advance the further ten miles to Ticonderoga. The lateness of the season nullified a naval victory on the Lake, and in this way, the campaign limped abruptly to an end, provoking, in due course, another wave of talk about undue caution.

Unpleasant though this was, the future looked bright, for in the summer of 1777 a great offensive was to be mounted against the Americans. With Canada as the point of departure, and the British troops already in residence, it is not surprising to read that Carleton spent a busy winter. He and Burgoyne were good friends, and when the latter left for England, he took with him the plans so carefully worked out with the Governor.

As it happened, one of the most outspoken opponents of Carleton's military policy, was no less a person than the Secretary of State in London. In a feud of long standing, neither man concealed his scorn of the other. Clearly, Lord George Germain was a difficult man to serve. Historians have labeled him as pig-headed and inefficient, and a great supporter of the patronage system. He seized upon the American campaign as a weapon to wound his enemy. While General Burgoyne was promoted to command the expedition, Carleton's army authority was restricted to Canadian soil. It was a cruel blow, made all the worse by the government's unrealistic revision of the plans. Carleton resigned, yet faced the necessity of remaining on duty until the new Governor General should arrive.

That a man in such mortifying circumstances, should lay aside his personal feelings, was a measure of character. Carleton participated to the full in the last-minute flurry of departure, and if the battle orders seemed impractical, he held his peace. But the whole affair was disastrous. The seven thousand British and

German troops who took off in June 1777 were poorly led by officers too cocksure for their own good. As the summer advanced, the news grew progressively worse, until the October climax when Burgoyne surrendered at Saratoga.

As a result of this defeat, Montreal found itself threatened with a return to front rank in the war zone. Ticonderoga was abandoned, and with it went the control of Lake Champlain. The Richelieu Valley lay wide open, a perennial temptation to the invader, and its habitant villagers again wavered in their loyalties. The continued use of *corvées*, whether paid or unpaid, was a cause of endless complaints, for no one liked to work under compulsion.

With the threat of invasion hanging over the country, uneasiness was the keynote of the winter of 1777–78. It was equally to the fore in the spring when Sir Frederick Haldimand stepped ashore at Quebec. The new Governor General was no stranger to the country, having served under Amherst in 1760, and administrative appointments in the American colonies had, since then, given him valuable experience in civil affairs. The defense of Canada became his first charge. Under his orders, the posts along the Richelieu were strengthened, and Sorel, at the mouth of the same river, was selected as the linchpin of the entire system. Then, like all his predecessors in office, he dismissed Montreal from consideration. It would, he considered, be impossible to hold against determined attack.

Meanwhile, the actions of France in Europe provided Haldimand with additional worries. Sympathy with the new American Republic had led to a formal declaration of war against Britain. And while some of those who served under Louis XVI were lukewarm in their martial spirit, others longed to repossess the colony along the St. Lawrence. The result was that the natural nostalgia of the French in Canada was kept alive and strengthened by every possible means of intrigue. Agents both from France and the United States did everything in their power to fan the discontent.

Matters came to a head in October 1778 with a proclamation from Baron d'Estaing, the admiral of the French fleet. Dated from Boston, it sounded a clarion call to all French Canadians to remember their original loyalty. Pinned to the church doors and distributed from hand to hand, it stirred up and crystallized the vague feelings of regret for what might have been.

Because of his devoted service to Canada, it is regrettable that Haldimand should so often be described as a petty tyrant who delighted in filling the jails with innocent victims, holding them incommunicado without benefit of trial. The facts of history do not bear out such a distorted version of the career of a distinguished public servant. The internees were, in most cases, American prisoners of war, and their treatment scrupulously just to the point of kindness. As for the politicals, it has been estimated that their number did not exceed twenty, during the whole period of the war, a remarkable instance of forbearance in the light of the provocation.

The canard had its origin in the fertile brain of Montreal's man-about-town, Pierre Du Calvet, who chose to make use of his well-merited term of confinement to blacken the record of an opponent whom he detested. Always the injured innocent in his own opinion, he could conceive of no reason for his arrest in 1780. Although he remained silent about his activities in the crucial months of American occupation, he pictured himself in 1779 as constantly injured "in a shameful manner without redress." Once more, the gallery of his house was brought into play; the noisy tramping at two o'clock in the morning; the men with tomahawks or hatchets cutting the rails, not once but again and again; the soldiers armed with bayonets, who tried to force open the outside shutters. In legal matters, he fared no better, the Court of Common Pleas showing repeated injustice in the hearing of his cases. Montreal may have considered him "an honest and inoffensive man," but few responsible officials would have agreed. Hence his arrest, and hence too, his confinement at Quebec until 1783, by his own account living in the most vile surroundings, forlorn and surrounded by enemies determined to ruin him.

In truth, Du Calvet's incarceration was probably long overdue, for he had been under suspicion as an active supporter of Congress, an agent who supplied information to the enemy, an abettor of the invasion of Canada. It was only with the definite proof of his treason that the loss of liberty commenced. Moreover, his treatment was altogether lacking in the horrors he so graphically depicted, and when a few months later, some of his associates followed him into custody, Montreal seemed a quieter place.

Another citizen found himself in hot water at the same period, although it is conceivable that Mesplet was more sinned against than sinning. Never a strong moral character, association with a new editor was the cause of his downfall. Under the guidance of Valentin Jautard, he forgot his earlier caution. When the *Gazette Littéraire* strayed from its ivory tower, it became the vehicle for the opinions of Jautard. Because he was always against the establishment, the complaints were not long in coming.

Haldimand encountered the pair shortly after his arrival, both men under orders from Carleton to leave the country immediately. The eviction was suspended on condition that they take the oath of allegiance and submit all articles before publication to a government-appointed inspector. When this requirement, in turn, was disobeyed, the trouble started in earnest. M. Montgolfier, on behalf of the Sulpicians, protested at the *Gazette's* views on religious matters. An article on Voltaire was especially obnoxious. The judges considered Jautard to be a scoundrel, "defaming the king's officers and trying to throw the colony into confusion." When finally, the Governor's patience came to an end, the two men were locked up in 1779. As the war drew to a close in 1782, they succeeded in making their escape, apparently with the connivance of the authorities.

Sometimes there was less justification for the official frowns, or so the fur traders felt when they tangled with Haldimand in their efforts to gain greater mobility in the west. The limitation in the number of passes put them at a disadvantage at a time when their enterprises were already sadly diminished by the war. His closure of the Great Lakes to private shipping came as an added blow. But anxiety over the safety of the distant posts led the Governor to fear that unrestricted communication might well lead to treasonable practices. It was another example of the military outlook as opposed to the commercial, and since the issue at stake was nothing less than the preservation of the country, the Montrealers gained nothing from their protests.

A series of strange events in the spring of 1783 awakened all Haldimand's old fears as to the disloyalty of the French-born clergy. The trouble began with the arrival at Quebec of two priests from St. Sulpice in Paris. Clad in secular garb, they seemed harmless enough, and in view of the shortage of *curés*, the Bishop permitted them to proceed to Montreal. The Governor first heard of their presence in a letter from M. Montgolfier, reporting that he had admitted them to the Seminary, and asking permission to retain them permanently. This was too much. An aide-de-camp was ordered to go and fetch them, and put them on board the first ship bound for overseas.

The official ukase was quite unacceptable to the inhabitants of Montreal. Everyone, clerical and lay alike, protested, and a public meeting designated two representatives to seek an interview with Haldimand. The Seminary considered the deportation order to be an invasion of its right, and Montgolfier permitted the two men to appear in the pulpit. Since they thereupon announced that more priests would shortly be arriving from France, it was not surprising that the Governor held his ground. His objection, he announced, was not to ministers of religion but to political incendiaries, and the expulsion took place as planned.

But already the war had changed. With the surrender of Cornwallis at Yorktown in October 1781, the large-scale operations were virtually at an end. In Britain, there was a growing frustration at the continuance of the fighting. Only the stubbornness of George III kept it alive for so long, and public opinion seemed ready to accept the new United States as a separate entity. As for Canada, although plagued by invasion rumors to the bitter end, an informal suspension of military activities preceded the peace by some months. Early in 1783, there was news of the cessation of hostilities, and on September 30, after long deliberations at Paris, the formal Treaty was signed.

Chapter 19

1783–1791

Effects of the American Revolution. Location of the western boundary. The Loyalists arrive. The growing importance of Montreal in trade. The river and the harbor. A canal at Lachine. Immigration, chiefly from Scotland. The diversity of churches. Grievances of the British residents. Political crises.

THE IMPACT OF the American Revolution upon Canadian life was as profound as it was long lasting. Once the war drew to an end, the new conditions were quick to make their presence felt. Everyone in the country was affected by the disintegration of British North America. After a quarter of a century, it was hard to realize that across the border, friends had become enemies.

For most Canadians there was comfort in their country's ability to remain outside the Union. Yet who could guarantee its future status? As recently as the peace talks, Franklin had blandly suggested that cession might be desirable. A feeler this undoubtedly was, and one that met with a cool reception. But if the United States really decided on annexation, anything might happen—especially in view of the suspected presence of Congress sympathizers, scattered through the towns and the villages.

Thus the authorities, for almost a century, showed themselves to be sensitive to threats of war and invasion. British regulars garrisoned the colony, their officers co-operating with successive governors in the preservation of the national status quo. If at times, there were sound reasons for apprehension, there was also a great deal of rumor and gossip. Always, however, it was Montreal's fate to remain in the forefront, weak in a military sense, and honeycombed with sedition. Together with the susceptible

villages to the south along the Richelieu, the area geographically
formed a recognizable unit. Trouble usually seemed to originate
there, and even when Quebec and the lower river were reasonably calm, the Island seethed with conflicting opinions.

Needless to say, Canadian advisers took no part in the discussions that preceded the Treaty of Paris in 1783. Colonial
etiquette of the eighteenth century forbade any such innovation.
The omission was unfortunate, for the document as finally completed, went far beyond the formal recognition of the United
States of America, and by its sacrifice of Canadian interest,
manifested a deplorable ignorance of the geography of the country and the needs of its people.

A clear-cut example of British bungling showed up in the new
location of the western boundary, or so the Montreal fur traders
believed when they learned the full extent of what Canada had
lost. The line of demarcation lay farther north than ever before,
ceding to the United States what was often called the southwest
—the vast empty territory that stretched between the Great Lakes
and the Ohio, and beyond to the Mississippi. Given away, too,
without a vestige of military necessity, and for no better reason
than to gain American good will. By cutting right across the
canoe routes followed by the fur traders in their journeys back
and forth across the continent, the decision struck a cruel blow
at the town's main source of revenue.

Public protests began immediately, and for once, were well
received by the Governor. The news which had burst like a
bombshell in Canadian circles, was as much of a surprise to
Haldimand. But the Treaty had been signed and he was powerless. While Canada lost title to a valuable tract of land, the
merchants faced what might be the end of their business; the
more humble Montrealers feared loss of employment. Locally,
the implications were grave.

However, one clause in the agreement offered a glimmer of
hope, for the territory was to be handed over "with all convenient
speed." To Haldimand, the phrase was sufficiently ambiguous to
permit delay in his surrender of the western posts. His was a
view wider than the purely commercial. He was fearful of a
renewal of Indian warfare, and of trouble between the advancing

tide of American settlers and the native tribes. Thus he delighted
Montreal by the way in which he received the several American
agents who sought him out to arrange the details of the transfer.
All of them, without exception, went home emptyhanded, but
charmed by the courtly manners of the old soldier. How could
he possibly hand over the territory without instructions from
London? And because London discreetly refrained from any
such directive, the surrender was delayed for several years, to
become in the end a cause of friction between the two countries.

Meanwhile, the Loyalists were pouring into Canada in ever-
greater numbers. The emigration from the thirteen colonies,
which started in 1776 as a trickle of fighting men, had never
ceased. Each year thereafter, civilians and soldiers with their
families, made their way north across the border, most of them
destitute and stripped of their possessions.

While the estimates vary widely, there were probably about
50,000 of these exiles. Some went back to England, and others
sought refuge in the West Indies. Many settled in Nova Scotia
and New Brunswick, and the remainder—thousands of them—
came to Canada, either by ship from New York, or overland by
way of the Champlain-Richelieu corridor, the Mohawk River or
Niagara. All were passionate royalists, and English-speaking.
Rich and poor alike, they needed temporary shelter, and as soon
as possible, new homes and the means of earning a livelihood.

The emergency was met by the establishment of receiving
centers at Montreal and the nearby villages—a contemporary
described this section of the St. Lawrence as swarming with
Loyalists. The main settlement was located at Sorel, where a
small town of huts sprang up on land belonging to the British
government. There, in the winter of 1783–84, some seven thousand persons waited out the season of cold weather. Because the
encampments were regarded as temporary, their conditions of
life were not always satisfactory. And although most people seem
to have accepted the situation philosophically, a few, in the
opinion of one officer, had unreasonable expectations.

If there were complainers, they constituted a tiny minority in
this host of persons, on whose behalf the Governor and his deputies labored incessantly to provide food, clothing, and other ne-

9. Place d'Armes, Montreal, 1848. *(Cornelius Krieghoff)*

10. Destruction of the Parliament House, Montreal, April 25, 1849. *(E. Hides)*

11. McGill College Avenue, probably after 1850. *(John H. Walker)*

12. River front, Montreal, probably after 1850. *(John H. Walker)*

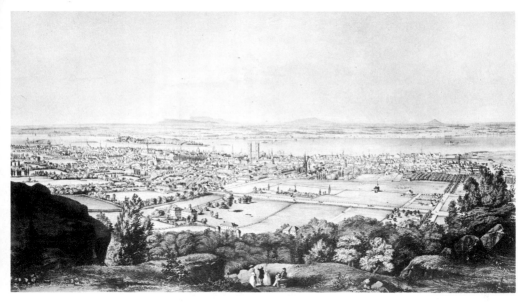

13. Montreal, Canada east, 1852. *(Edwin Whitefield)*

14. The Gavazzi riots at Zion Church, 1853. *(P. le Sueur)*

15. Bonsecours Church, 1855. *(Watercolor by Kilburn)*

cessities, until self-support again became possible. Some idea of the magnitude of the operation may be gained from one account alone, rendered by Major Nairne the officer in charge of relief in the Verchères district. It amounted to £20,000.

Temporary sustenance was only half the story. Their permanent establishment was recognized to be a matter of the utmost urgency. Most of the newcomers were farmers, who asked only that they be provided with land, and enough equipment to get themselves off to a good start. The location of the holdings was another matter, since few of the British regarded Quebec as a place in which they wanted to end their days. The predominantly French population seemed as alien as the laws, and the regulations as to land tenure especially unsatisfactory. Haldimand concurred in such views, since he considered the province to be a largely French Canadian preserve. Moreover, in the proximity of the American border, he feared a cause of future trouble. Montreal itself, was beyond the pale.

Thus the town knew the Loyalists mainly as transients. The few who remained to become residents, must have been men of strong character, to fly in the face of so much official disapproval. The majority went on to take up grants of land in what was soon to be known as Upper Canada—westward up the St. Lawrence, along the Ottawa, into the region south of Lake Ontario. Theirs was a mass migration, carefully planned and efficiently executed, and as it progressed, there was plenty to excite and occupy the Montrealers.

This great surge westward, this peopling of the empty lands, brought tremendous changes in its wake. For the country as a whole, it is no exaggeration to say that the course of its history followed an entirely new path. Canada was no longer French only, it was to be British as well; both peoples became Canadian. For Montreal, the transformation was dramatic, since the town stood at the threshold of a new and more significant role. The frontier and the forests receded into the distance. When in due course, the cleared land started to produce crops beyond local needs, the grain and other foodstuffs came down the St. Lawrence for shipment overseas. In return, the United Kingdom sent its manufactured goods in ever-growing volume, to meet the requirements of the greater population. Montreal found itself serving as the national seaport.

To the twentieth-century observer, the town hardly seemed ready for its wider importance. Man had, so far, done little to assist nature. The travelers of the day considered conditions in the harbor and the river to be deplorable. One writer in 1785, was willing to concede the pleasant and advantageous situation "if the navigation of the river had been less intricate, the harbor more commodious." So numerous were the shallows and rapids "as to cause a very strong current which cannot be stemmed without a strong easterly wind"—a serious drawback in the age of sailing vessels. The channel was so difficult that "if the greatest attention is not paid, a vessel must inevitably run on the rocks and shoals which surround it."

It is true that the channel immediately opposite the town boasted of deep water—as much as ten or fifteen fathoms. In such an anchorage, ships of four hundred tons could approach close to shore. Yet this advantage could hardly offset the immense difficulties experienced in making port. Even with all sails set and a stiff breeze, a vessel often remained stationary for an hour in the stream, off St. Helen's Island.

Twenty years later, there had been little improvement. The great depth of the stream was again noted, and the sudden declivity of the bank, forming a natural wharf upon which the vessels discharged their cargoes. But although an artificial dock had been constructed and faced with plank, it brought little real change. "The goods are all shipped from and landed upon the beach below."

Virtually every traveler from overseas related harrowing tales of the dangers of the river. In many cases, the visit to Canada started with the vessel running aground on the rocks and shoals. So complicated was the passage that ships from Europe, it was agreed, seldom made more than one voyage a season up to Montreal. On one occasion, when the pilot was thought to be intoxicated, he got into the wrong channel. The error was discovered too late, and "the ship was run broadside on one of the islands just below Montreal, though going with the wind right aft." This experience, in his first Canadian trip, so sickened the captain that he swore he would never again enter the St. Lawrence.

But one yarn in particular, was told and retold, with endless variations, doubtless for the edification of the greenhorns from England. According to one of its more extreme and apocryphal versions, "two ships arrived from England early in the year, and went up the river at the same time. The one drawing less water, I suppose, than the other, succeeded in reaching the Island of Montreal . . . but the other, not being able to stem the current, was obliged to anchor below. The successful vessel, having discharged her cargo and taken in another, sailed for England; after which, she returned to Canada the same year, with a fresh cargo, went up the river and found her companion still lying at the foot of the rapid. They afterward returned to England together."

Small wonder that most passengers, bound for Quebec, preferred the bateaux. Clumsy craft they were, but adaptable for either oars or sails, and being without a keel, they drew less water and were safer during storms. When knocked about in a sudden squall, one writer reported no injuries. For protection, the crew simply threw an oilcloth awning over the widest section. Supported by hoops, it formed a snug cabin, large enough to contain half a dozen chairs and a table.

Some attempts at improvement were already in hand above Montreal, where the long succession of rapids necessitated laborious portages, as costly as they were dangerous for passengers and freight. By order of the Governor and under the supervision of Lieutenant William Twiss, operations began in 1779, with a clearance of rocks and minor obstacles from the shallow waters near the shore. For several seasons thereafter, work proceeded on the main project, nothing less than the construction of canals and locks at Coteau du Lac, Cedars and Cascades. By modern standards, the dimensions of the "ditches" were modest—a width that never exceeded six or seven feet, and a length that varied from two to nine hundred feet. But the planning was careful and the workmanship sound. When the first walls, made of timber, proved to be anything but waterproof, they were painstakingly replaced by stone.

Haldimand's interest in the project grew out of the need to facilitate the movement of government supply boats between Montreal and the western posts. He kept a personal watch on its progress, to the point of visiting the site on several occasions. But since what was commenced under the pressures of war, terminated in the happier days of peace, it seemed likely that private traders would share in the benefits. The result was a meeting in Montreal of all who might be considered interested parties. A request for a contribution from each bateau on its passage through the canal system, met with a most gratifying response, and a toll rate of 25s was later established.

Communication of another sort caused a good deal of annoyance to the local business community, in its efforts to get back on a peacetime basis. The mail service was poor, compared to the earlier arrangements. From 1763 onward, the post offices of the country had been linked with the American colonies by means of a courier once a week to New York, and thence every month to England. Inaugurated by Benjamin Franklin, then a deputy postmaster-general, the efficiency of the system was quite remarkable until halted by the outbreak of the Revolutionary War. Canada lived through the years that followed in a state of virtual isolation, completely cut off from the world in winter, and with only an occasional vessel in from England during the summer.

Although the packet service between Falmouth in Cornwall and New York, was re-established late in 1783, the British government was slow to remember the needs of Canada. Only after vigorous protests from the merchants of Montreal and Quebec, was the courier to New York restored—under rather unhappy conditions at first, for the Americans were unfriendly. A few years later, when summer sailings were instituted between Falmouth and Halifax, slow deliveries to the inland towns cancelled out any benefits. For this reason, as relations with the United States improved, almost all correspondence from Canada to destinations in the British Isles, traveled via New York.

Outwardly, Montreal looked much the same as before the war. With monotonous repetition, the visitors commented on the narrow streets, the ruinous ancient walls, the absence of elegant buildings. The 1100 houses (including the suburbs) were not prepossessing, gloomy and forbidding by reason of their heavy iron shutters. Rents were high, to match the wages of the laborers. Walking was unpleasant, "the streets not paved, which renders the place disagreeable in bad weather, and at all times very painful to the feet from the unevenness."

But it was among the people that the changes showed most clearly. Quite apart from the Loyalists, there were other arrivals from overseas to augment the sparse British population. Not that they were numerous, nor did they represent immigration in the modern sense. The British government took a resolute stand against any such nonsense, lest the mother country be stripped of its people and the factories of the Industrial Revolution deprived of their workers. In any case, London wondered who would want to settle in the frigid arctic wastelands of Canada. Despite this somewhat discouraging dictum, some hardy souls took a chance, a few in the sixties, more in the seventies and eighties, paying their own passage, and determined to succeed in the New World. Most of them were Highland Scots, impelled to go overseas by the "clearances" of their native land. They were quick to make their presence felt in the business world of the St. Lawrence.

This growing diversity of race and temperament was nowhere more apparent than in the ecclesiastical institutions of the period. For although the newcomers were by no means unanimous in their religious beliefs, it is safe to say that for the most part, they were Protestants. Thus they would have no part in the Parish Church of Notre Dame nor the recently rebuilt Chapel of Bonsecours. Each and every denomination wanted a place of worship all its own.

At this juncture, the future status of the chapels belonging to the priestly orders was highly uncertain, as a result of the government's refusal to permit the admission of new members. Only a few aging friars survived, life tenants as it were, of the premises originally the property of their several communities. Theirs was a sad and lonely existence, a fact which made the generosity of the Recollets all the more commendable. That their chapel became available for non-Catholic services, solved some of the problems for a good many years.

The Anglicans, as members of the established Church of England, were the first tenants. One service only, each Sunday morning, with "extras" on Christmas Day and Good Friday, was the extent of their privileges. But after several years of being pushed about from pillar to post, they were in no mood, at first, to offer any complaints.

Yet much can happen in twenty years, and the Anglicans were not exempt from the general rule of change. In the latter period of their occupancy, the conditions under which they worshiped became increasingly distasteful to the congregation. Whereas earlier, the majority of the members had been drawn from the garrison, they were gradually outnumbered by the civilians. In 1768, the army chaplains gave way to a cleric of a different caliber. The Reverend David Chabrand de Lisle was a Protestant from France who had been ordained into the Anglican faith. French-speaking as he was, his presence symbolized the government's intention to anglicize the province. He was to wean the new subjects away from Roman Catholicism. It was a mission doomed to failure from the start, and it became utterly futile with the passage of the Quebec Act. His relationship with his English-speaking parishioners was almost equally unhappy.

Into this troubled atmosphere, there came in the summer of 1789, the Right Reverend Charles Inglis, first Bishop of Nova Scotia and the other British provinces, including Quebec. Although this was his first and only visit to Montreal, the episcopal presence was not easily forgotten. Not only did he preach and confirm a large number of candidates, but he took definite steps to find more suitable quarters. An inspection of the Jesuit chapel held out hopes of better conditions. Although promised earlier for use by the Anglicans, it was still a storehouse, and likely to remain so, for all the authorities cared. The ecclesiastical persuasion, however, carried the day and the Montrealers took possession. Cleaned and renovated, it was first used for divine service in December 1789. As Christ Church, it bore a name still familiar to the modern city, and the appointment of the Reverend

James Tunstall as assistant minister solved the linguistic difficulties.

Two years later, the Presbyterians became the tenants of the
Recollet chapel, remaining there for twelve months on the same
agreeable terms as the Anglicans. Since the fathers stood firm
by their refusal to accept any payment for this use of their
premises, the Scots showed their appreciation by a gift of two
hogsheads of Spanish wine, containing sixty-odd gallons each,
together with a box of candles. And because the cost of these
items amounted to £14/2/4, it is pleasing to find that the recipients "were quite grateful for the same."

The Anglicans and Presbyterians already knew each other
well, since from 1787 to 1790, there is no record of any services
conducted according to the Scottish forms. During this period,
both denominations worshiped together in an amicable fashion,
under Mr. de Lisle. For although a well-attended meeting of
Presbyterians was held in 1786, nothing seems to have come of it.

It was really the Reverend John Young who placed the church
on a more permanent footing. By September 1791, under his
guidance, an organized congregation came into being, ready to
take the necessary steps that would lead to affiliation. Since he
was a minister of the church in the United States, rather than
that of Scotland, it was to the Presbytery of Albany that the
application was directed. By 1793 sufficient progress had been
made locally to "erect" the Presbytery of Montreal—prematurely,
perhaps, for no records remain of its actual existence.

That some of the troubles were of Mr. Young's own making
appears likely, for as his chronicler discreetly remarked "he
was a man of no great strength of character." His weakness was
traceable to the great amount of dining out among the wealthy
citizens, a hard drinking group wherein unhappily, "instead of
conquering the evils of his surroundings, he was, in some degree,
conquered by them." Yet the plans went ahead. In April 1792
a lot on St. Gabriel Street was purchased for £100 (Halifax
currency) and there in the course of the year, a church was
built, sixty feet by forty-eight, with accommodation for 650
"sitters." This first Presbyterian place of worship was to exert a
strong influence on the life of the growing town, and remain a

center of much of its religious, social, and public life for fifty
years. Essentially the church of the fur traders, "its founders
and early supporters gave it a status of great influence."

Politically, 1783 stood out as a landmark. Problems, disagreements, solutions—all these to a great extent, had been held in
check, the government with some justification pleading that wartime necessities must take precedence over constitutional discussions. With the advent of peace, the excuse became inoperative, so that Haldimand, still preoccupied with the Loyalists,
found himself facing troubles of another kind. For them, he
could find no satisfactory answers, and because the British
authorities in their wisdom, sensed that his usefulness was at
an end, he returned to England in 1784.

After the usual interval, Carleton was appointed to succeed
him, commencing in 1786, a second term that was to last a
decade. In the eight years of his absence, much had happened.
The man himself had been raised to the peerage as Lord Dorchester, by which name he must henceforth be known, while as
Governor-in-Chief of all British North America, he was endowed
with powers exceeding those of any previous official. Such an
appointment might have seemed a happy augury for the future,
but unhappily it was not to be so. Dorchester had lost some of
his old self-confidence, and above all, he lacked comprehension
of the new climate in the country, and the great transformation
then in progress. As he grew older, and enfeebled in health, he
moved farther and farther away from any sympathy with its
people.

The English-speaking inhabitants of the province still lived almost entirely in the towns. Estimates of their numbers vary
greatly. Montreal—by this date probably as large as Quebec—
was credited with a population of some eight thousand, of whom
one quarter may have belonged to the minority group. The old
subjects made up what was largely a mercantile community,
with growing ambitions. Their grievances were real, and accentuated by the speculative troubles that so often follow a war.
Financial ruin threatened some of the countinghouses, just when
their relations with the courts of justice were at their worst.
Canada labored under the penalty of the so-called French com-

mercial law, long obsolete in Europe. It bore no resemblance to
the Code Marchand of France, as organized by Colbert, which
never having been introduced into New France, could not now
be invoked. The absence of an adequate and valid body of laws
placed a heavy responsibility upon judges who had neither the
learning nor the impartiality to deal wisely with the cases
brought to trial.

Thus, the political crisis in Montreal reached new heights,
the British making up in activity for what they lacked in numbers. Public meetings were held by those eager for reform, while
a constant stream of protests and petitions served to keep London, as well as the provincial capital, alert to the dangerous controversy. Some concessions were finally won—Habeas Corpus in
1784, and trial by jury in commercial cases in 1785. But this was
only the merest bite out of the monstrous, unworkable constitution, and so the pressure went on, unchecked, for an elected
assembly.

The French Canadians, on the whole, took little part in these
noisy proceedings. The purely commercial side of the agitation did not touch them intimately, for few were as yet active in
trade. In the matter of an assembly, they were either opposed or
indifferent; lacking the background and traditions of representative government, it could hardly have been otherwise. A faint
nostalgia for France still softened the air, yet without any cor-
responding admiration for the United States. The clergy at all
levels, were consistent in their allegiance to the Crown, and content in the freedom of religion and language granted by the
Quebec Act.

Despite this instinctive difference of opinion, there was little
actual bad feeling between the two races. The protests were less
against each other than against the British-appointed bureau-
cracy and the Governor. With the new decade, the storm of
political controversy grew steadily louder. London, for its part,
had for several years, been reconciled to the thought that some
changes were imperative. The only question to be solved was
their nature. The dilemma was serious, with its implications of
favoritism, either to the French Canadians, or their English-speaking fellow citizens. It was at last resolved in the Constitutional
Act of 1791.

Chapter 20

1783–1804

The fur trade. Competition. The North West Company. The development of the north. The Scots. Simon McTavish. William McGillivray. Prosperity. The Beaver Club. Rivalry at home and abroad. The Hudson's Bay Company.

"The pedlars," they were often called in derision by their rivals of the Hudson's Bay Company; they themselves preferred the proud title of *les hommes du nord*—the men of the north. Whatever the epithet chosen, however, the fur traders of Montreal hailed the coming of peace in 1783 as an opportunity for expansion. With this in mind, they proceeded to reorganize and consolidate their affairs with such aggressive self-confidence that the pulse of the whole town quickened.

There was nothing alien in such traffic per se, for its roots lay deep in the past. New France had blazed a trail which Montrealers of this later generation were quick to follow. Yet inevitably the new loyalties brought changes, as His Majesty's old subjects showed their eagerness to participate. One of the earliest of these was Alexander Henry, who served under Amherst in 1760. Then, as he later wrote, "proposing to avail myself of the new market, which was thus thrown open to British adventure, I hastened to Albany, where my commercial connections were, where I procured a quantity of goods, with which I set out, intending to carry them to Montreal."

Henry was by no means alone in his move to the west. Other merchants made their appearance, a few in the sixties suffering losses in Pontiac's rebellion, but followed by others in greater numbers during the seventies. At first, they worked chiefly in the Indian Territory south of the Great Lakes, but gradually, as the fine quality of the northern pelts became known, the more enterprising individuals shifted their operations to the northwest —a trend in which the Montrealers led the way. The results were not altogether happy, since each man was a law unto himself, working independently for his own personal gain. When overkeen competition led to friction and eventually to violence, it was agreed that co-operation was essential.

The clash of personalities did not account for all of the problems. Some were inherent in the very extent of their success. There were geographical disabilities, as the English soon discovered, a fact which was well known to their French predecessors. Whenever the supply of beaver in one district was exhausted, a move became necessary. It was always farther afield. And because a lengthening supply route from Montreal imposed higher costs, financial failure threatened the small independent traders.

Thus at the conclusion of the American war, some form of coalition was indicated, if Montreal was to retain its position as the center of the fur trade in Canada. Already the seventies had witnessed several attempts at a pooling of interests. Temporary and informal at best, they served to introduce the name of the North West Company to local history. It was to become a famous organization. Negotiations, initiated in 1783, led in January 1784 to a new and more definite pact of union.

Flexibility was its keynote. The Company, so-called, was never one in the generally accepted sense; at no time was it incorporated or granted a government charter. Instead, the partners entered into a series of agreements, whose precise scope and terms varied according to need. Even their duration was uncertain; two, three or more years. Should conditions warrant such a step, the old pact might be canceled before maturity, so that partners could be added or subtracted with relative ease, or the division of profits altered. There was no provision for the accumulation of capital.

The internal management of the concern was equally simple; its efficiency stood up well to the hard test of experience. Two types of partners were recognized. The winterers, who actually lived in the fur country, were responsible for the Company posts and for all dealings with the Indians. Whereas their main task was the procurement of the pelts, their opposites, the agents in Montreal, marketed the furs, either in London or New York. The townsmen also purchased the supplies and shipped them to the west. All in all, it was a neat dovetailing of responsibilities.

Every summer, representatives of the two groups assembled for joint sessions at the Company headquarters—in the early days at Grand Portage on the western shores of Lake Superior, and later at Fort William. The furs were brought in, and exchanged for fresh allotments of trade goods and provisions. Feasting and carousing enlivened the scene, as men of all ranks relaxed from their toil. The serious proceedings began when the partners met together in what was essentially an annual meeting. Reports on the year's activities were presented, and policies formulated for the future. The winterers voiced their opinions of the Montreal agents' actions. If a new agreement had been negotiated, their signatures were required for ratification.

The wartime regulations which hampered the Company at the outset, were unbearably galling when carried over into the post-1783 period. Yet for the most part, Montreal's protests fell on deaf ears. Haldimand and Dorchester held strangely similar and narrow views in respect to trade, so that private enterprise regained its freedom with infuriating slowness.

Transcending all else, however, the relocation of the western boundary was a menace to Montreal's future prosperity. Although Haldimand so far, had refused to surrender the posts, there was no certainty that such a policy would continue indefinitely. In the meantime, the North West Company faced the possibility of losing its headquarters at Grand Portage. Once the Americans were in possession, communication with the Saskatchewan would be broken. There might well be Indian troubles, since the tribes south of the Lakes could not be expected to accept the loss of their hunting grounds with equanimity.

Such was the boundary situation as it appeared during the winter of 1783–84. It was thoroughly discussed in Montreal. A few of the merchants retained their optimism, asserting that the new division of land would make little difference. Since settlers

would never move so far west, they could see no reason for
interference by the American government. So reasoned a group
led by James and John McGill—only to find themselves ranged
in direct opposition to Simon McTavish, Alexander Henry, and
the Frobisher brothers. The latter, who already believed that
prospects were brightest in the north, could only look with apprehension at the southern frontier. The result was another agreement, and a lordly if amicable division of the territories and the
assets between the two parties.

The appearance of these names in such a context reflects the
growing importance of one particular section of the community.
The Scots of Montreal found in the fur trade an occupation so
admirably suited to their talents that they soon dominated the
business. Thus, although French Canadians and Sassenachs
found some place in the North West Company, the roll call of
the partners often resembled a gathering of the clans.

What followed was a bewildering parade of Scottish appella-
tions, since fathers and sons, uncles, nephews, and cousins joined
forces in the new enterprise. Pitfalls lie in wait for the unwary
student of the period, for "Mac," and "Mc" are not always easily
differentiated. Thus, although Alexander Mackenzie was a cousin
and good friend of Roderick McKenzie, the patronymic was
spelled differently. The same confusion spread to the Christian
names. Within the short span of ten years, it is believed that no
fewer than four Simon Frasers served the Company. As McDon-
ald mingled with McDonell, McLeod met McLoughlin; the
Johns, the Duncans, and the Williams were as numerous.

Towering above them all stood the figure of Simon McTavish,
one of the really great men in Canadian history. Montreal met
him first in the early seventies, a youth showing, even then, signs
of unusual ability. At the end of the war, he emerged into
prominence as a partner in the North West Company and the
leading advocate of the northern venture. As agreement followed agreement, his power grew proportionately. In 1787, it
reached out beyond the Company proper; as the senior partner
in McTavish, Frobisher and Company, he headed the Montreal
firm which acted as agent for the winterers. Already the richest

man in town, he was reputed to enjoy "good wine, good oysters and pretty girls."

That McTavish had a goodly share of the clannish loyalty of his nation, was evidenced by the progress of his three McGillivray nephews. William, the eldest, who arrived in Montreal in 1784, started his career as a clerk in the employ of the North West Company. The usual novitiate in the wilderness followed, but by 1790 he had become a partner. By 1793 he was serving McTavish, Frobisher and Company in a similar capacity. However much hard work and natural ability had contributed to his rapid promotion, there were murmurs of nepotism. When Duncan appeared a few years later, the critic may well have detected further signs of favoritism. Because of his lameness, Simon, the youngest, remained in London, yet there he, too, shared in the profitable transactions of the interlocking companies.

There was little of a temporary nature in the allegiance of these fur magnates. Once they had served their terms in the northwest, they returned to Montreal as to a permanent home. Houses were acquired and furnished, and wives and children maintained in what was luxury for the place and the hour. As personal wealth accumulated, there were visits to Scotland, and reunions with relatives and friends. Sometimes there were brides to introduce to the old land, for many of the Nor'Westers married French Canadian girls, the daughters and sisters of their business associates. Most of the Scots spoke French as a matter of course, and although the majority were Presbyterian by conviction, their pews in the St. Gabriel Street kirk were matched by holdings in the Church of Notre Dame.

The Nor'Westers may have been born elsewhere, but they soon regarded themselves as Canadians. This sense of nationality entered into their dealings with the Hudson's Bay Company—"the English," they called the rival traders, as though foreigners instead of fellow countrymen. Moreover, they regarded both "the English" and "the Americans" as trespassers on the land they had inherited from New France.

The prevalence of French words in the common parlance of the trade, should therefore cause no surprise. Long after 1760, Montrealers talked of the northwest as *le pays d'en haut. Les bour-*

geois were the proprietors, *les hivernants,* the winterers. A step lower in the social scale, *les commis* were the clerks who hoped someday to be admitted as partners. *Les voyageurs* were much in evidence at certain seasons. As the canoemen, they were often called *les mangeurs de lard* or "the porkeaters," from their frugal diet of dried corn mixed with a little grease. Even *une pipe* did not always convey the usual meaning. It became a standard measurement, as on a portage—the distance covered between respites, when the hard-working voyageur had time for a rest and a smoke.

To postulate for Montreal, a wide familiarity with the fur trade, is in no sense to exaggerate. In its heyday, few families in the town remained aloof from the North West Company. The ramifications extended far beyond the managerial class, according to a report by Alexander Mackenzie. In one season, the Company had "50 clerks, 71 interpreters and clerks, 1120 canoemen and 35 guides. Of these, 5 clerks, 18 guides and 350 canoemen were employed for the summer season in going from Montreal to Grand Portage in canoes."

While much of the work was seasonal, the preparations for the annual trip west kept some Montrealers busy all the year around. The cycle had its origins with the agents, at this date, the firm of McTavish, Frobisher and Company. It was their duty in October to order the trade goods from England, eighteen months ahead of need. Transportation being leisurely and the ice in the river slow to melt, the cargoes reached Quebec only in the following spring. The bateaux brought them on to Montreal in the summer. There the goods were stored all winter at the agents' expense, sorted and repacked, and in some cases, made up into articles of clothing to suit the needs of the natives. As listed by Mackenzie, these included; "coarse woollen cloths of different kinds; milled blankets of different sizes; arms and ammunition; twist and carrot tobacco; Manchester goods; linens and coarse sheetings; threads, lines and twine; common hardware; cutlery and ironmongery of several descriptions; kettles of brass and copper and sheet-iron; silk and cotton handkerchiefs; hats, shoes and hose; calicoes and printed cottons."

The repacking was a formidable undertaking. Naturally, everything had been assembled in England according to category, that is, all the cutlery together, the tobacco in its place and the ammunition in another. Naturally, too, each bale for the winterers had to include an assortment of goods, and not necessarily in uniform quantities. The tastes of one tribe did not always correspond with those of its neighbors. Thus all the items, large and small, must be laid out with care, and protected with waterproof coverings. Weight was of prime importance, since each package must tip the scales at exactly ninety pounds and not an ounce more. This made for convenience and safety in loading the canoes, as well as for equality of burdens on the portages.

In the meantime, and while the freight was in storage at Lachine, the Company agents had been busy elsewhere. The voyageurs for the coming season must be engaged, some from Montreal, others from the neighboring villages. Such men were held in high esteem, son following father as whole families earned a meager livelihood by this back-breaking toil. By all accounts, their stamina was astounding, and their cheerfulness a source of perpetual wonder to strangers. Physically, they were short and stocky (height became a misfortune if a lad grew too tall for the canoes).

As the flotillas mustered at Lachine, they bore little resemblance to the small modern pleasure craft. *Les canots du maître* or the Montreal canoes, as used on the St. Lawrence and the Great Lakes, were the largest type, thirty-five to forty feet long and broad in proportion. Most of them were painted in gay colors and their high prows and sterns adorned with the Company flags. Of birchbark construction, they were so frail that crew and passengers had to sit motionless, hour after hour, while in transit. Their loading was a delicate maneuver, in respect to balance; when properly carried out, their capacity was amazing.

Mackenzie described the contents of a *canot du maître*. In addition to the eight or ten men with their baggage, there were: "65 packages of goods, 600 weight of biscuit, 200 weight of pork, 3 bushels of pease for the men's provision; 2 oil-cloths to cover the goods, a sail, etc.; an axe, a towing-line, a kettle and a sponge to bail out the water with, a quantity of gum, bark and watape to repair the vessel. An European, on seeing one of these slender vessels thus laden, heaped up and sunk with her gunwale within six inches of the water, would think his fate inevitable in such a boat, when he reflected on the nature of her voyage; but the Canadians are so expert that few accidents happen."

Despite its growth, Montreal was still small enough to share in the excitement inseparable from the annual departures. Most of the townspeople flocked out to Lachine to bid farewell to the travelers. Sometimes there were delays, occasioned by the social propensities of the partners who were making the journey. One such send-off was described by George Landmann of the Royal Engineers, an amusing young man somewhat given to exaggeration in his stories.

"We sat down and without loss of time, expedited the luncheon intended to supersede a dinner, during which time the bottle had freely circulated, raising the old Highland drinking propensity so that there was no stopping it; Highland speeches and sayings, Highland reminiscences and Highland farewells, with the Dioch and dorich, over and over again, was kept up with extraordinary energy, so that by six or seven o'clock, I had in common with many of the others, fallen from my seat. To save my legs from being trampled on, I contrived to draw myself into the fireplace, and sat up in one of the corners, there being no stove or grate."

Yet it was a picturesque sight as the canoes finally got under way, in their hundreds, the voyageurs, singing the old traditional songs, *A la Claire Fontaine* or *En Roulant Ma Boule.* Thomas Moore, in his *Canadian Boat Song* caught something of its plaintive atmosphere.

> *Faintly as tolls the evening chime,*
> *Our voices keep tune and our oars keep time.*
> *Soon as the woods on the shore grow dim,*
> *We'll sing at St. Anne's our parting hymn.*

In contrast to the furious activity in the west, the Montreal summers were quiet. Although the exact date was never known in advance, the canoes usually returned in September. When word of the arrival got abroad, the whole town flocked out to Lachine to greet the wanderers. On this day, above all others, there was little business transacted. As the oxcarts jolted along with their precious burdens, even a blind man could hardly mistake the furs for any other commodity. Their stench was particularly disagreeable, and the autumn weather was often warm. Beaver still headed the list, according to Mackenzie; 106,000 in one year. A ready market awaited them in England, and high prices, for men's fine quality felt hats were as fashionable as ever. The marten or sable ranked next, with 32,000 pelts. Quantitatively near the bottom came the 1800 mink; obviously, the status symbol of the twentieth century was as yet unappreciated.

By the nineties, the prosperous state of the fur trade was echoed in the town. Not only did the population show an increase, but it was more varied. Military personnel and civil servants came out from London on official business, to augment the normal arrivals from overseas. The center of activities still remained close to the river, in a blending of commercial and residential facilities. Yet the wealthier citizens had already started to abandon the long-established habit of living over the offices and shops. Thus, while the North West Company and McTavish, Frobisher and Company shared a fine new stone office and warehouse, conveniently located for access to their ships, the partners occupied separate houses or erected country seats beyond the walls.

One of the most famous belonged to Joseph Frobisher, who resided at Beaver Hall until his death in 1810. The eighty-foot-long wooden cottage stood on Coteau St. Louis, about halfway up the hill and so far out from town that dinner guests arrived in their carriages or sleighs. Its forty acres of land were partially wooded, with extensive orchards behind the house. Frobisher delighted to make presents of apples to his friends; in one season alone, fifty-eight barrels, according to the entries in his diary. Wealthy he might be, but in many respects, he was delightfully human. In the midst of his dinner parties, he noted in April that he had taken down the double windows. On another occasion, late in May, at dinner with Mr. McGill in the country, he enjoyed the new potatoes. By the middle of June, he was able to serve his own green pease at home.

Simon McTavish lived in greater style, as befitted a man known as "The Premier" or "The Marquis"—the latter the reverse of flattering, for many people found him haughty and domineering. He remained a bachelor until 1793, when, at the age of forty-three, he chose as his bride eighteen-year-old Marie Marguerite Chaboillez. They resided at first in a house on St. Jean Baptiste Street, equipped by the new owner in the most lavish fashion. £300 was spent on furniture alone, and fine carpets laid throughout.

William McGillivray followed his uncle into matrimony in 1800, when, with his Scottish wife, he took up housekeeping in quarters on St. Gabriel Street, rented from Joseph Frobisher. It was a way of life that did not satisfy him long. By 1802, he started to build a house in the suburb of St. Antoine, on farm property purchased from the Sulpicians. There, in the Château St. Antoine, near the Côte de Neiges Road to Lachine, and surrounded by magnificent views of the river and the countryside, he lived for many years, always the gracious host.

It was in mansions such as these that there dwelt what Washington Irving called "a kind of commercial aristocracy." Winter and summer alike, the festivities went on; families, friends, strangers, French- and English-speaking Canadians alike. The North West partners kept open house, to an extent that is almost beyond modern comprehension.

Men such as these made of the Beaver Club, an almost exclusive North West Company preserve. Membership was restricted to those who had wintered in *le pays d'en haut*. Founded in 1785 with an enrollment of nineteen, subsequent amendments raised the number to fifty-five. There was provision for honorary members, usually the captains of the furr (sic) ships. The Club flourished until 1804, then existed for a few years in a state of suspended animation. The year 1807 saw its resurrection—"renewed and new-modeled"—but after a decade of activity, it ceased to function. Attempts at revival in 1827 met with little success.

Thanks to some careful minutes, a good deal is known of the period from 1807 to 1817. Apart from the increase in numbers, the general pattern of the rules changed very little. As the older members died, the chosen young men took their place. In 1814

Alexander Henry was the sole survivor of the founding group. Because of his seniority, he was granted the unusual privilege of paying for his dinner only when the state of his health permitted his attendance.

Contrary to popular belief, the Beaver Club never had a headquarters of its own. Instead, each winter saw the members dining together at fortnightly intervals, in one or other of the city taverns, changing their venue from time to time, for reasons of price or service. No limitation existed on the number of guests. Each man was expected to wear his gold medal at all meetings. Inscribed with the motto "Fortitude in Distress," it was ordinarily suspended on a sky blue ribbon; in the case of death, the black of mourning was substituted. The toasts were unvarying, and always drunk in precisely the same order—The Mother of all the Saints; the King; the Fur Trade in all its branches; Voyageurs, Wives and Children; Absent Members. At their conclusion, members might leave if they wished, or remain for further conviviality. Unless indisposed, their attendance was obligatory, and private festivities on club days were forbidden.

Two famous stories have become such a recognized part of the Beaver Club tradition, that no account of its activities would be complete without their inclusion. That their veracity has been questioned by many authorities, does not make them any the less amusing.

The first, from the pen of George Landmann, tells of his invitation to dine with Alexander Mackenzie and William McGillivray, when the twenty guests assembled about four o'clock, as was the custom. At the conclusion of the meal, and after partaking of a satisfactory quantity of wine, the married men and the fainthearted withdrew. Then the survivors began their drinking "in right earnest and true Highland style, and by four o'clock in the morning, the whole of us had arrived at such a degree of perfection, that we could all give the war-whoop as well as Mackenzie and McGillivray, we could all sing admirably, we could all drink like fishes, and we all thought we could dance on the table without disturbing a single decanter, glass or plate." This, concluded Landmann, was a delusion, for everything was broken. It was a melancholy homecoming, "since all the heads and hands of the party received many severe contusions, cuts and scratches."

The second tale, as related by George Bryce, was somewhat similar. He depicted the members engaged in *le grand voyage*, a game in which all seated themselves in a row on the rich carpet, each armed with a make-believe paddle—tongs, pokers, swords, walking sticks. Then in boisterous fashion, as they went through the motions of paddling an imaginary canoe, they sang the old familiar songs of the voyageurs. A cautionary note warned that their nerves were too excited to achieve any regularity in their movements.

After such scenes of carousing, it may come as a shock to find that these same hard-headed merchants scrutinized their tavern accounts with care. On one occasion, the minutes reported the proprietor being called in "for to settle with him for the winter, but finding that he persisted in having 7/6 a bottle for his Madeira wine, we did not agree, but allowed him till Tuesday next to consider of it, and to give his final determination." It is comforting to read that the following month, they compromised at 6/6 a bottle. But for all their thrift, the price of dinners rose steadily. In 1807, it stood at 7/6; by 1814, it had risen to 15/.

In all seriousness, the actual records of the dinners do not jibe with the legends. Madeira was the usual drink preferred by the gentlemen. Laced by port and lesser amounts of ale, it may have resulted in a potion destructive of sobriety. Yet the usual breakage of wineglasses rarely exceeded three, and the members enjoyed their segars (sic), pipes, and tobacco along with the liquids.

It is doubtful, in any case, if there was much leisure for the Beaver Club, since the Nor'Westers worked under difficulties in the closing years of the century. Existing problems grew worse, as a consequence of the Jay Treaty, whereby Britain, after thirteen years delay, agreed to surrender the western posts to the United States. To the Montreal traders, the long-delayed concession, in many respects, marked the end of the road. The fact that Grand Portage was now certain to be in American territory, lent urgency to the need for a new depot. For although the pact recognized the right of each nation to navigate the waterways and to trade freely across the borders, the Company was suspicious—with good reason as events were to show.

The competition, from 1794 onward, was intensified on all fronts. In spite of their emphasis on the north, the Canadians still held a few posts in the southwest. Their retention seemed doubtful, as American traders and settlers moved into the territory. John Jacob Astor, by this date, considered himself a friend of the Montreal group, so frequent had been his visits to the town. Until 1796 the direct export of furs to the United States had been forbidden, but even so, the American contrived to clear a good profit from his transactions with London. He continued to do well, under the new ruling which permitted direct commercial intercourse between Montreal and New York—so much so that the earlier amity changed to intense rivalry, and eventually, on the Pacific coast, to downright enmity.

The situation in respect to the Hudson's Bay Company was equally grave. Although the English charter dated back to 1670, there was no trouble until the American Revolutionary War period. Ironically enough it was the strenuous program of the Nor'Westers themselves which led to the change. The main point at issue was the claim of the older Company to exclusive rights over the Bay's watershed. The Canadians riposted with the French contention that the English monopoly was limited to a narrow strip of land along its shores. At stake was the great expanse of territory in the interior, and since neither party would make concessions, the friction increased as the trade expanded. By 1794, both companies possessed forts at most of the strategic sites along the northern waterways.

Each group had some advantages. The Canadians were generally more skillful in the field, and their agents more alert to opportunities for growth. But "The Bay" held the top trump card in its ease of access, by ship directly from England to its posts in the north. Its overland routes were short. Montreal was far away, and the costs of transportation greater each season. Notwithstanding efficient operation and rigid economy, it was hard to show a profit. Thus at an early date, the Nor'Westers sought to gain transit rights by water. Despite repeated requests, they met with no success.

To overcome these handicaps, the North West Company embarked on an aggressive policy of exploration. The competition in the north and the south; the boundary relocation; the long overland hauls; the need to find fresh beaver meadows; all these factors led to the opening up of vast tracts of country. Montreal's share in the development of the west is, perhaps, one of the lesser-known facts of Canadian history, yet Montreal enterprise and Montreal money accomplished much of benefit to future generations.

It was as a partner in the North West Company that Alexander Mackenzie made his two great journeys. In the summer of 1789, traveling by way of the Slave River, Great Slave Lake, and the Mackenzie River, he reached the Arctic Ocean, an achievement which he found disappointing. He had hoped to discover the long-sought northwest passage to the Pacific. Four years later, he succeeded in reaching the great ocean, as his famous inscription recalls: *"Alexander Mackenzie, from Canada by land, the twenty-second of July, one thousand, seven hundred and ninety-three."*

Simon Fraser's fame was of a later date, although he had entered the service of the Company in 1792. It was as a partner that, in 1805, he superintended the Nor'Westers in their expansion west of the Rockies. He it was, also, who explored the Fraser River to its mouth, an extremely hazardous undertaking. David Thompson joined the Company in 1797, after some years with the Hudson's Bay men. His remarkable skill as a surveyor was promptly put to the test in a tremendous journey of four thousand miles. Moving in a great circle, he established the precise location of the new boundary. Later years saw him active beyond the Rockies, along the Columbia River, searching for a canoe route through the mountains to the Pacific.

Meanwhile, the North West Company faced ever more serious competition nearer home. It came from Montreal itself, and originated in part from a split within the Company ranks. The XY Company was essentially a local organization, deriving its popular title from the marks used on the bales of trade goods; officially, it was the New North West Company, born in 1798 of the union of two small groups. Forced out of their border posts by the American occupation, they turned their attention to the north, to such good effect that virtually all the opponents of the Nor'Westers coalesced into one unit. Sir Alexander Mackenzie, knighted by the king, was the most outstanding of the recruits. Having resigned his old partnership in 1799, he gave his name to the newcomers, when the XY Company became Sir Alexander Mackenzie and Company.

Mackenzie thus entered into active opposition to his former associates; for what reason has remained unknown. There may well have been differences with McTavish. The new company made progress, for among its partners, there were men of experience. Although a pygmy affair, it cut deeply into the fur business. At many places in the north, three rival posts confronted the others; the North West Company, the Hudson's Bay Company, and the XY Company. It was almost a case of civil war, as each group accused its rivals of inciting trouble. The growing use of rum to gain the support of the Indians, made conditions all the more serious.

The Imperial government took cognizance of the danger in 1802–03 with the passage of the Canada Jurisdiction Act. By its terms, criminal offenses committed in the Indian territories could be tried in Lower Canada. The summer of 1803 was exceptionally difficult. Price cutting and frantic bids for Indian support by all three groups, led to an impasse. No one made a profit, and Montreal was torn in two by the rival factions.

It was under such conditions that the North West Company opened its new depot in 1803. Called Fort Kaministiquia at first, the name was soon changed to Fort William in honor of William McGillivray. The enormous cluster of buildings that rose on Canadian soil about forty miles north of Grand Portage, reflected the strength of the Company. Despite the competition, McTavish still dominated the trade.

He was an extraordinary man. Notwithstanding his absorption in trade problems, McTavish found time to make plans for the erection of a grand mansion in Montreal. The old establishment on St. Jean Baptiste Street no longer seemed suitable. So it was that he chose a site high on the mountain, near the top of the street that now bears his name. McTavish supervised the construction himself, and it was in a stone cottage on the grounds, that he died suddenly on July 6, 1804, at the age of fifty-four. He was buried on the property, at so great a distance from the town that a lunch was laid out on tables in front of the house, for the refreshment of those who attended the funeral.

The death of the owner brought everything to a halt, and the house stood, weather-beaten, tenantless and unfinished until torn down in 1861. Its conception had been ambitious; a gentleman's dwelling, made of dressed limestone, with a frontage of one hundred and twenty-six feet. At each end, rose a semicircular tower, while the tin roof was fashioned on the old-fashioned "high" principle, draining from a ridgepole down to all four sides. Although empty, popular superstition supplied it with spectral tenants. People who passed by after dark, swore they had seen the ghost of McTavish, wandering through its rooms. Some said the owner had hanged himself there, and told of hearing horrible gurgling sounds. Others saw spirits dancing on the tin roof by the light of the moon.

Among the many attempts to explain the origin of all these stories, the most reasonable explanation was that put forward by a man named McMartin, who in the 1830s farmed the property around the deserted pile. He claimed that while the moon was in a certain phase, it shone on an angle of the tin roof, thus casting a bright ray of light which the superstitious thought to be Mc-Tavish's spirit.

In other ways, the death of McTavish marked the end of an era for Montreal, for the union of the two companies became possible. Within a few months of his demise, the Nor'Westers and the XY organization entered into an agreement that ended local competition.

Chapter 21

1791–1812

The Constitutional Act. An elected Assembly brings problems. France and England at war in Europe. Divided sympathies of French Canadians. Local improvements. John Molson and the steamboat "Accommodation." The Nor'Westers and the Hudson's Bay Company.

SOMETIMES THE Montreal merchants prospered in spite of what they considered adverse circumstances. The Constitutional Act was a case in point. While the fur traders proceeded with their bold ventures in the west and the north, a political transformation was under way at home, which brought them little but disappointment.

Although His Majesty's ministers had procrastinated over the constitutional amendments, in the end there was nothing half-hearted about their decisions. Just as 1774 had, to a large extent, contradicted 1763, so 1791, in its turn, brought another reversal. Henceforth the colony was to be divided into the two provinces of Upper and Lower Canada; each was endowed with a Lieutenant Governor, a Legislative Council, and most important of all, an Assembly. Such a separation, it was felt in London, would put an end to the disputes over the respective merits of the French Code Civile and English common law. Once the French Canadians were assured of the retention of their religious and civil rights, happiness would reign along the St. Lawrence. In like manner, the newly arrived Loyalists could rest content in the shelter of the English language and laws. So reasoned the Imperial Parliament, as the country plunged suddenly into the joys and responsibilities that accompany representative government. With an almost Utopian vision of the future, it was assumed that the magic of British institutions would put an end to political turmoil in Canada.

At first, London's rosy outlook seemed justified. The Act, which became effective on December 26, 1791, was greeted with applause. Montreal celebrated the day with public dinners and appropriate speeches. Relations between the French and the English citizens held promise of greater harmony. The first election, held in June 1792, was followed six months later, by the opening session of the House. Quebec, lacking as yet in a Legislative Chamber, made use of the Bishop's Palace, suitably renovated for the occasion. Four members represented Montreal; James McGill and J. B. Durocher for the west ward, Joseph Frobisher and John Richardson for the east. Having chosen Joseph Antoine Panet as Speaker, the House got down to business. A form of procedure was agreed upon, with debates to be carried out in either language. Once these initial difficulties were ironed out, affairs moved ahead smoothly.

Yet in the event, Upper Canada only, was happy. There the Loyalists rejoiced according to plan. It was otherwise in the Lower province, where with the best intentions in the world, the Imperial Parliament had created a situation more desperate than ever before. All this time, the English minorities in Montreal and Quebec had assumed that the control of the Assembly would devolve upon them. When this proved untrue, their shock was so great as to jeopardize the benevolent purpose of the Act. Cut off from their fellows by the provincial boundary, the old subjects in Lower Canada saw themselves as isolated and their growing commercial ambitions restrained by obsolete laws. Yet the new subjects, at first, were largely indifferent. The great mass of the habitants could neither read nor write, and knew very little of what went on in the world. With no parliamentary traditions to fall back upon, the transition was too sudden. The few politically conscious French Canadians were, in the main, hostile.

The news from overseas heightened the tension in domestic affairs. The French Revolution was followed by the rise of Napoleon, and 1793 saw England and France once more at war. It was the commencement of a long struggle, that except for one brief

respite, lasted until 1815. The old wistful longings of the French
Canadians were revived, and soon strengthened by the obvious
sympathy of the Americans. Within a year, Britain and the
United States came close to open hostilities. But London with its
hands full in Europe, could ill afford any such extension of the
conflict, while Washington's declaration of neutrality eased the
situation. Both sides moved with greater caution.

As in years gone by, it was doubtful whether French Canadians really wanted to join the Union. Certainly the Lower province was alive with French agents once more, with the Montreal
district the main center of disaffection. The agitation originated
with Citoyen Genêt, the representative of the French Republic in
Washington. He was an advocate of violence, who soon ran foul
of the American authorities. Yet his recall did nothing to halt the
spread of revolutionary doctrines. A pamphlet, widely circulated
in 1794, was particularly alarming. *Les Français libres à leurs
frères les Canadiens* sounded the call for an insurrection against
the alien British throne.

While no one of prominence put much faith in Genêt's sabo-
teurs, the illiterate habitants were gravely disturbed, and as
usual, the rumor mongers had a field day. Sometimes, it was the
Americans who were about to invade the country, then again the
armies of France were poised for attack. The French fleet was
preparing to sail up the St. Lawrence to liberate the oppressed
Canadians. And although the Bishop and clergy did their best
to thwart the advocates of rebellion, the stories spread like wildfire, insensibly growing with every repetition.

The unsettled conditions forced the authorities to take strong
measures for the protection of the country. As yet, there were no
civilian police, and when need arose, the British garrison troops
were called out. Their number, which varied greatly, often reflected the current state of Anglo-American relations. But since
the war in Europe prevented the dispatch of reinforcements, the
existing low of 2300 was unlikely to be strengthened from overseas.

Thus Dorchester had no recourse but to call out the militia—
with rather disappointing results at first. For although all able-
bodied men were, by law, subject to such mobilization, many of

the French Canadians professed themselves unwilling to respond. Nevertheless, the Royal Canadian Volunteer Regiment reached full strength by 1793, its two battalions serving until disbanded in 1802; the one at Quebec largely French Canadian, and the other at Montreal, English Canadian. In their scarlet uniforms with blue facings and tricorne hats with black cockades, they made a brave showing on the local parade grounds. And as American belligerency remained a strong possibility, the Canadians—French and English alike—after the turn of the century, responded well to the official program of preparedness.

The military activity was matched by a firm stand in civil matters. Arrests of the more prominent agitators in Montreal and Quebec, went far in restoring peace. In each city, moreover, the leading citizens co-operated in the formation of Constitutional Associations. Their appeals for loyal support against foreign troublemakers did much to restore public confidence and induce a respect for the law.

But Dorchester, in the closing years of the century, was a weary old man, as he himself knew only too well. His retirement in 1796 marked the end of a second term of office which had lasted a decade. The province was never happy with his immediate successors. Lack of continuity, ignorance of local conditions, an absence of sympathy; these combined to make the relationship more disastrous than the situation warranted.

For as election followed election, in the normal processes of parliamentary government, the nature of the House altered. Under the pressure of racial cleavage, the party system made its appearance. The English members, fewer in number than at first, were regarded as Tories. Newcomers appeared, in the ranks of the French, as keen lawyers and notaries replaced many of the seigneurs. Their collective temper grew more intransigent. That there were faults on both sides, seems clear—the majority, by means of public funds, striving for absolute control over the entire administration—the minority, as intolerant as ever in religion, manifestly selfish in their ambitious plans for commercial developments.

Viewed in this context of constant dispute, Montreal's civic problems acquire greater meaning. The marvel is that anything constructive was ever accomplished. Often it became a matter of the Assembly against the town, the English opposed to the French, commerce versus agriculture. The elected majority at Quebec refused to sacrifice the interests of the small rural proprietor to the apparent greed of the industrialist.

Montreal's new jail has often been cited as an early example of the diverging viewpoints. No one questioned the need for such a building, since the old one, already inadequate, had been partially destroyed by fire in 1803. Yet its financing bristled with problems, for whereas the merchants recommended that a tax be imposed upon landowners, the House placed it upon luxuries such as tea, spirits, wine, and molasses. The objectors, having petitioned the king for repeal of the obnoxious measure, proceeded to hold a dinner at Dillon's Hotel in honor of the local members, who, French and English alike, had opposed the Bill at Quebec. A report of the gathering, as printed in the *Gazette*, gave great offense in official circles. The thirteen toasts drunk on that evening, were subsequently described in the House as "a false, scandalous and malicious libel, highly and unjustly reflecting upon His Majesty's representative in this Province, and on both Houses of the Provincial Parliament." A tempest in a teapot all this was, to which nothing need be added, beyond the comment that the jail, when finally built in 1808, was, as originally scheduled, paid for by means of the import duties.

Less than a year later, another public function was held under happier auspices. On Friday, January 24, 1806, one hundred and twenty-eight persons gathered at the City Tavern to celebrate the great naval victory at Trafalgar. The news of the battle had reached Montreal in December, when an assembly was in full swing at the Exchange Coffee House, near the corner of St. Paul and St. Peter streets. "After dancing, the company had descended to the supperroom, Mr. Samuel Gerard, one of the stewards presiding. While supper was being proceeded with, a waiter brought in a packet of papers, just received from New York, containing Admiral Collingwood's despatch of the battle of Trafalgar." The sequel as related by Sandham, revealed the temper of the social élite. "When the despatches were read, loud huzzas shook the building. But the news was clouded by the fall

of the heroic Nelson, and many present, particularly ladies, were
to be seen shedding tears. Under the excitement of the moment,
the chairman proposed that a monument should be erected in
the city to the memory of Nelson, and that a subscription should
be at once opened to defray the cost. Ladies and gentlemen
pressed forward to set down their names, so that in a few minutes
a sufficient sum was subscribed . . ."

This testimonial to the great Admiral was, for many years,
Montreal's only public monument, and as such was lovingly described by virtually everyone who knew the town. The circular
limestone column, when finally completed, cost £1300. Atop its
fifty-foot height, stood an eight-foot statue of Nelson. "The like-
ness is well preserved, and the attitude judiciously chosen. The
face is directed towards the west and looks as if intently watching the termination of some great event." Some visitors from
overseas found less to admire in the posture. A sailor, they remarked caustically, should face the water at all times. Montreal,
on the contrary, had turned the hero inland, looking toward the
jail!

Meanwhile, the demolition of the town walls was very much
on the public mind. Almost from the date of their erection, the
experts had belittled their usefulness. In 1791, Captain Mann of
the Royal Engineers, reported them no longer needed as military
works, adding that their ruinous condition made them a nuisance
rather than a benefit. When no official action followed, the citizens in 1797, petitioned for their removal. Yet it was not until
1801 that the Legislature passed the necessary Act, authorizing
the work to be carried out "for the convenience, salubrity and
embellishment of the city."

In fairness to the British government, it must be added that the
delay arose, not so much from unwillingness as from uncertainty
over the rights of private citizens. The walls, when erected in
1724, had been located "partly on land the property of divers
individuals." This meant that the question of repossession had to
be settled, lest "strife and litigation became a source of detriment." For whatever reason, they went ahead so slowly that in
1813 the commissioners were still busy. James McGill, John

Richardson, Jean-Marie Rondelet, and Louis Chaboillez must long since have been weary of their task.

By this date also, the scarcity of water was a great inconvenience. Conditions were primitive and decidedly unhealthy. What had sufficed the original village was no longer adequate for the busy town. Although a few pumps stood in the public squares—Place d'Armes, the Market Place, the Jesuits' Garden—the river still remained the chief source of supply. As people moved away from its banks, transport became a problem and distance a grave hazard in case of fire. The existence of pollution can be deduced from the growth of commerce and shipping; several keen-eyed visitors criticized the unsanitary state of the harbor area.

The long winters added considerably to the difficulties. To cut holes in the ice was an unpleasant task, in the teeth of biting winds. Landmann sensed this during his brief residence in the city. The difference in the river water impressed him, the St. Lawrence beautifully clear, the Ottawa thick and turbid. Consequently, the inhabitants "used to send to a long distance from shore to procure water during the winter, and it required several test holes through the ice in order to find the nearest point at which the clear water could be obtained."

To remedy the situation, the Legislature in 1801, permitted a group of citizens to form a company under the name of the Montreal Water Works. The sequel was unhappy. "The plan proposed by the Company was to supply the city from a source in rear of the mountain, and with this in view they expended large sums of money in laying down wooden pipes. But the supply of water was so scanty, and the rude pipes so liable to leak or burst, that they failed to carry the plan into successful operation."

The danger from fire was as great as ever. When the flames broke out, the city was almost at their mercy. Incendiarism was common, and there was no fire brigade. Every householder had to keep in his house, a pair of leather buckets, and when the bell of Notre Dame sounded an alarm, he sallied out with these. Two lines of men were formed from the river, one passing down the empties, and the other the full buckets.

One of Montreal's greatest feuds with the Assembly had as its subject, the canal system of the St. Lawrence. For years, the merchants fumed to no avail over what they considered to be obstructionism of the worst order. Much of the pressure for improvements stemmed from the North West Company whose bateaux and canoes increased in number each season. Adding to the congestion was the traffic with Upper Canada, a growing factor in the local prosperity. The ability to use larger boats in the upper river en route to the Great Lakes, would facilitate the movement of goods.

In most respects, the old canals built by Twiss—the "ditches" of the last century—were unequal to the burden. They were also sorely in need of repairs. Near at hand, roared the Lachine Rapids, utterly untouched, their passage as difficult as in the days of the early French explorers. The nine miles of cartage out from the city to the head of the rapids, remained an inescapable necessity. As early as 1796, John Richardson introduced a bill in the House for the construction of a canal at Lachine. His proposal was probably premature. At all events, the motion was dropped, in view of the lack of interest.

What made these delays all the more exasperating was the progress in other maritime affairs. Among the small craft in the river, the Durham boat was coming into common use, in appearance and construction similar to the bateau, but capable of carrying five to ten times the amount of freight. A sail was hoisted in favorable winds; otherwise it was poled along by the crew.

In 1806, Philemon Wright brought the first timber raft down the Ottawa from Hull to Montreal, the pioneer in a movement that became commonplace along the rivers in the next few years. Long heavy sweeps guided the clumsy craft, made of logs fastened together with wooden pins, and bound with willow withes. A rude cabin amidships housed the crew who lived on board. Such rafts were, in the main, born of wartime necessity. Broken up at Quebec, they were loaded on ships for transport overseas. Napoleon's blockade of the Baltic states made the British Navy desperately short of timber.

But by far the most exciting event was the appearance of the first steamship, the *Accommodation,* built for John Molson on his

own property east of the town. The initial voyage, early in
November 1809, took it to Quebec in an incredibly short space of
time, "where the whole city crowded to have a look at the
nautical phenomenon."

The ship carried ten passengers, and as described by the Quebec *Mercury*, "She is continually crowded with visitants. She left
Montreal on Wednesday, at two o'clock, so that her passage was
sixty-six hours; thirty of which she was at anchor. She arrived
at Three Rivers in twenty-four hours. She has, at present, berths
for twenty passengers, which next year, will be considerably augmented. *No wind or tide can stop her*. She has 75 feet keel and
85 feet on deck. The price for a passage up is nine dollars, and
eight down, the vessel supplying provisions. The great advantage
attending a vessel so constructed is, that a passage may be
calculated on to a degree of certainty, in point of time; which
cannot be the case with any vessel propelled by sail only."

In any circumstances, this might be rated as a notable achievement, coming as it did only two years after Robert Fulton's
Clermont sailed up the Hudson. Considering the greater backwardness of Canada, it was nothing short of a triumph. Constructed entirely in this country, and using local materials and
workmen, the *Accommodation* proved that steamship service on
the St. Lawrence was practical.

Notwithstanding much research by the Molson family's biographer, little is known of the details of the building of this ship.
The work, which started in March 1809, was completed within
three months. The date of launching was August 19. After the
first triumphal voyage to Quebec, a second one followed on November 15. The winter layover was probably in the Richelieu,
near Sorel.

In its second season, the *Accommodation* was in service for
less than five months, beginning in June. Nine, or perhaps twelve
round trips were made between Montreal and Quebec. It is believed that 175 adult passengers paid for a one-way passage, resulting in gross revenues of about £450, of which £25 were
bar receipts. Thus what had cost John Molson about £2000,
yielded revenues of less than £500. The decision to build another and better vessel was apparently taken almost immediately.

The *Gazette* of November 26, 1810, carried an advertisement, giving notice of John Molson's intention to apply to the Legislature "for a law giving him the exclusive right and privilege of constructing or navigating a steamboat or steamboats . . . for the space of fifteen years." Within ten years, the family enterprise was to grow to the point of being known as the St. Lawrence Steamboat Company.

The reference to local newspapers marks another step forward in civic history. Mesplet died in 1794, a reformed character so far as politics was concerned. Having broken with Jautard, he successfully avoided controversial subjects in future. The *Gazette* as launched by him in 1785, was a bilingual publication of four pages, that sold for $3 a year. The vehicle for official proclamations and commercial announcements, it was a safe, if not original, journal, whose subscription list included the leading citizens. Yet Mesplet's personal life was never happy. He was always in financial deep water, and drink is considered to have been his besetting sin.

Meanwhile, the fur trade went ahead, expanding and prospering as though the good times would never end. Under the leadership of William McGillivray, the enlarged North West Company, after 1804, monopolized the local scene. So far as Montreal was concerned, competition was pretty well over. In view of the fact that the latest and most comprehensive of the agreements was for a period of eighteen years, stability was reasonably certain.

Imperceptibly the control of affairs had passed into the hands of the English—or more accurately the Scots—for the older practice of including French Canadians in the management group, had run its course. The Highland partners continued to dominate the social life of the town. They were the genial hosts who welcomed the strangers fortunate enough to have the entrée; they spent lavishly and were generous in worthy causes; they added color and warmth to the northern scene. Some were appointed as members of the Legislative Council, occasionally one was elected to the Assembly. Frequently they served as Justices of the Peace, and so found themselves immersed in local

judicial affairs. Generally speaking, they opposed the policies of
the French majority in the provincial House.

It has been said of McGillivray that he was not the genius his
uncle had been. But his practical experience exceeded that
of Simon McTavish, and his difficulties were on the whole,
greater. Even yet, there was no provision for the accumulation of
capital, and this, as the years passed, was probably the Company's greatest problem. Because of the long delay between
each purchase of trade goods and the matching sale of furs, the
business was conducted solely upon credits. The representatives
of the Nor'Westers, whether in Montreal, New York, or London,
had no reserves to fall back upon. The strictest of economies,
the sternest of regulations—these were imposed in the endless
struggle to secure profits.

The stiffest opposition still lay in the north, where a reawakened Hudson's Bay Company fought strenuously against the
"pedlars" so greatly despised. As a result, the profits of both
suffered a decline, the Canadians being the harder hit. Out of
this, arose a series of attempts by McGillivray to overcome the
handicap resulting from lack of access to the Bay. During 1811,
in what seems to have been a seventh try, the Nor'Westers successfully sought a charter from London. When the British government remained unmoved by these appeals, McGillivray tried
to buy Hudson's Bay Company stock. This too, was impossible.

But as the first decade of the new century neared its end,
Montreal was undeniably prosperous. Whatever may have been
the distant problems of the Nor'Westers, their presence in the
town put money in the inhabitants' pockets. Over and above
the fur trade, there was progress in other ways, since the growth
of population in Upper Canada brought added business to the
port. Some of the prosperity originated in Europe. To the extent
that the Napoleonic blockade was effective, British money
poured into Canada. Although timber was the crying need of
the moment, wheat and other commodities shared in the demands from overseas. With Quebec as the port of departure for
transatlantic cargoes, Montreal found itself busy, handling the
goods for export, and expediting their delivery to the oceangoing ships.

Meanwhile, Anglo-American relations had deteriorated, although not because of any belligerent actions on the part of Canada. One of the thorniest disputes between the two principals arose from the British claim to the right of search in American ships. When the boarding parties forcibly removed alleged deserters, war was barely averted as early as 1807. But it was not until five years later that the long-feared conflict became a fact, and only after a long series of "incidents."

When the news was received in Canada, according to Sandham, "the inhabitants at once cast aside any differences they might have among themselves, and made the most zealous display of loyalty and devotion to the British Crown, none being more ready to display their loyalty and willingness to uphold British rule in America, than were the citizens of Montreal."

Chapter 22

1812–1821

War with the United States. Uneasiness and rumors. The Americans reach Châteaguay. Colonel de Salaberry and his victory. Lord Selkirk and the Red River Colony. Rival fur traders. Demise of the North West Company. The Hudson's Bay Company in full control.

THE FIGHTING, so far as Lower Canada was concerned, at first seemed far away. Presumably a few loyal breasts swelled with pride at the efficiency of the Nor'Westers, who heard the news some days before the formal communiqué reached the country. Thanks to the excellency of this private communications system, the officials in both provinces were alerted at the earliest possible date, to the dangers of armed attack.

Yet the war, with good reason, was regarded as an affair of Upper Canada. There, the authorities feared, the largely American origin of the population, might lead to some measure of support for the enemy. That the United States command hoped for such an outcome, was evident, for General Hull led an invading army across the border, proclaiming that he brought liberation to the peaceful, unoffending Canadians. It was fortunate that the province was blessed with a leader as skillful in military strategy as he was courageous, and General Isaac Brock soon gave the lie to his rather boastful opponent by his capture of Detroit. This occupation of enemy territory was sufficiently impressive to bolster the wavering loyalty of the western Indians, and to restore the public confidence. In the first year of hostilities other American attempts against the province failed. That Brock him-

self was killed at Queenston Heights was the ultimate tragedy
of the campaign in the Niagara peninsula.

This was the background for Montreal's first direct contact
with the enemy, when in September, General Hull and his suite
passed through the city. Twenty-five officers and three hundred
men accompanied him, and all were prisoners of war. The
Herald reported that the inhabitants "were gratified with an
exhibition equally novel and interesting." The line of march was
impressive, the band of the King's Regiment preceding the General in his carriage. Behind were the captured officers and
men on foot and under escort. "It unfortunately proved rather
late in the evening for the vast concourse of visitors assembled to
experience the gratification they so anxiously looked for. The inconvenience was, however, in a great measure, remedied by the
illumination of the streets, through which the line of march
passed. . . . The General appears to be about sixty years of age,
and bears his misfortunes with a degree of resignation that but
few men in similar circumstances are gifted with."

All this excitement was hardly more than a natural reaction to
what had been locally, an uneasy summer. Many years later, an
eyewitness recalled the declaration of war as causing great depression in Montreal, "for the general belief was that the Americans would come at once and take Canada. At night, especially,
there was great alarm. Everything in the shape of a man was
pressed into service. If dogs could have carried firelocks, they
would have been taken. I saw at the sentry posts mere boys, too
weak to carry their guns, which they rested against their bases."

There had, of course, been several alarms, with rumors as usual
serving to sharpen the horrors of reality. On one occasion, General Dearborn was known to have 10,000 men massed on Lake
Champlain, ready for a descent on Montreal. Luckily, the martial
enthusiasm of his forces evaporated before the frontier was
crossed, and they returned home after a four day campaign that
saw no fighting. Yet even as the crowds gazed at the captive
Hull, they might well have feared revenge, for the Secretary of
War had declared their city to be the apple of his eye. Comfortable winter quarters and an English Christmas, he promised the troops who landed on the Island.

In the first line of defense for the colony, stood the British regulars, pathetically few when war broke out, but increasing as conditions in Europe improved. In 1812, six battalions comprised their total strength. Two years later, some 16,000 reinforcements arrived. With Wellington's final triumph in the Peninsular campaign, his veterans could be dispatched to America, and since the navy unquestionably commanded the seas, there was no fear of any break in communications.

But in the months preceding this great inflow of the professional army, the Canadians had ample opportunity to display their fighting qualities. To meet the dangers, whether real or imaginary, the militia were called out—always a tricky undertaking, but handled this time with rare skill, by the new Governor, Sir George Prevost. Even the Assembly co-operated by authorizing the mobilization of the manpower of the province, and in general, racial recriminations disappeared in the face of the common danger. Constant drilling and army discipline soon converted the amateurs into a first-class fighting force, Les Voltigeurs in particular, becoming especially famous.

A British army doctor by the name of William Dunlop professed himself greatly impressed by the local militia as they marched along, to the music of their voyageur songs, greeting their officers with an Indian war whoop, followed by shouts of *Vive le roi*. They wore capots and trousers of homespun and blue tuques, all of the same color, which added considerably to their military bearing. The gentlemen of Montreal, enrolled in two corps of artillery and sharpshooters, evoked less admiration. "If their discipline was commendable, their commissariat was beyond all praise. Long lines of carts were to be seen bearing in casks and hampers of the choicest wines, to say nothing of venison, turkeys, hams and all other esculents necessary to recruit their strength under the fatigues of war."

Posterity can only hope that the gentlemen paid for their own luxuries, since the financing of the war presented difficulties. There being no gold or silver available, Prevost issued army bills, and these, backed by the credit of the British government, remained in circulation until the end of hostilities. That paper money should be acceptable, even to the normally suspicious farmers, was no mean tribute to the man responsible.

The summer of 1813, in both provinces, was marked by a series of threats, some of a minor nature, it is true, but sufficient in number to keep the home forces on the alert. In Upper Canada, an American naval assault on York, brought destruction by fire to the public buildings of the little town, while an invasion of the Niagara peninsula forced the Canadians to retreat. Yet the defeat was not permanent, for the defenders regained the lost ground, and the close of the year saw the Americans driven back into their own country.

From the early days of the war, a campaign against Montreal, had been a feature of American strategy. The capture of the city would lead to the occupation of a wide stretch of territory, and Upper Canada might thus be starved into submission. That the attack was so long delayed, arose from the hesitation among the higher officers who felt that their shortage of troops made its success uncertain. It was not until 1813 that agreement was reached upon what was a variant of Amherst's old plan. One army under Major General Wilkinson was to descend the river, having locked up "the enemy in our rear to starve or surrender . . . to sweep the St. Lawrence of armed craft; and in concert with the division of Major General Hampton to take Montreal."

The Island city was regarded as easy prey. There were no fortifications, and few defenders. Preoccupation with the fighting in Upper Canada had immoblized a large part of the British and Canadian troops. Sizable American naval forces on Lake Champlain weighted the odds even further, yet the whole enterprise ran into trouble from the first.

The British, who were well informed as to the great build-up of strength immediately south of the border, undertook a series of delaying actions. With five gunboats from Ile aux Noix, reinforced by several hundred troops in bateaux, they made landings at Plattsburg, Burlington, and Swanton. Barracks and other military installations were burned, and a good deal of damage inflicted.

Notwithstanding these losses, Hampton led his men into Canada late in August, crossing through swampy country to a point

near St. Johns. By following the Châteauguay River to its mouth
at Lake St. Louis, he hoped to effect a rendezvous with Wilkinson. It was a hesitant sort of advance, for no one knew exactly
what lay ahead, and there was some fear of a premature encounter with the supposedly superior Canadian forces.

Prevost was at Kingston when the news broke, early in October,
but returned to Montreal at once, to call out the militia. The
town was greatly stirred, and everyone was eager to join the
fighting forces under Lieutenant Colonel de Salaberry. To him,
had fallen the responsibility for halting the enemy.

By the eighth, Hampton was near Châteauguay, some forty-
five miles from Montreal, and an equal distance from his proposed junction with Wilkinson. Estimates of his strength vary, but
it seems at the least, to have exceeded five thousand men. After
more than a year of army service, he had what was, to all intents,
a force of regulars, well drilled and equipped, even to the extent of cannon.

To challenge this formidable array, de Salaberry marched out
at the head of three hundred men—a hundred and fifty Voltigeurs, a company of Fencibles and some Indians. They proceeded to make the road impassable, with rough barriers of logs
and fallen trees, and at nearby Allan's Corners, to build a crude
blockhouse. Having done this, they waited, armed only with muskets—to be joined most unexpectedly by reinforcements on October 25, the eve of the battle. In a forced march by land and
water from Kingston, the six hundred men under Lieutenant
Colonel M'Dowell of the Lower Canada militia, reached their
objective in time to form de Salaberry's second line of defense.
The defenders now numbered nine hundred plus fifty Indians,
but they still lacked artillery.

That night, the entire American force camped on the north or
left bank of the Châteauguay River. The next morning brought
a division in their ranks, Colonel Purdy with three thousand men,
proceeding to cross and recross the stream in the hope of gaining the rear of de Salaberry's position. Meanwhile, under heavy
attack from the main body, the three hundred Canadians in the
front line fell back upon the second series of defenses. In spite
of the great disparity of numbers, they had offered a strong

resistance. Then, the story goes, de Salaberry remained at his advanced post, alone except for a boy and a bugler whom he held by the collar, forcing him to sound the advance.

By this time, the Americans had come up against M'Dowell's militia, whose presence until then, was unsuspected. There too, the bugles sounded, and the men cheered, thus restoring the confidence of the front line. When the Indians added their war whoops to the chorus, the resultant cacophony led the attackers to suppose themselves opposed by ten thousand men. They halted and fled, whereupon the Voltigeurs returned to their original position, still held by the solitary de Salaberry and his bugler.

So far, Purdy had believed himself unobserved. To be met by hot fire from M'Dowell, therefore, came as a rude surprise. When he, too, heard the bugles and the cheers, it seemed as though overwhelming forces were luring him on to certain destruction. He, in turn, retreated. But the shooting was not over, for the two American parties, in a twin case of mistaken identity, fired at each other in the confusion.

During the next few days more Americans were brought in as prisoners, while the presence of a number of bodies indicated the gravity of the defeat. Meanwhile, de Salaberry had been taken ill, and M'Dowell assumed the command.

The two men were good friends, as events soon showed, since Prevost claimed the credit for the victory—without any justification for he had been elsewhere during the battle. He was especially critical of de Salaberry, whose military reputation suffered in consequence. It remained for M'Dowell to take the matter up with the War Office on a later visit to London. At his earnest request, the record was amended, and both valiant defenders of Montreal were subsequently decorated for bravery in the field.

The action at Châteauguay, taken in conjunction with Wilkinson's defeat at Crysler's Farm, was the salvation of Lower Canada. Had de Salaberry given way, an enemy landing on the Island would have become a distinct possibility. That danger, at least for the 1813 season, was at an end.

It had, in sober truth, been a colonial victory, this battle fought against odds of four to one. Although de Salaberry and many of the officers held commissions in the Imperial army, they were Canadians, as were the Voltigeurs and Fencibles. Moreover, they were for the most part, French Canadians. One estimate has placed the number of English Canadians at about one-twentieth of the total, and the Indians about one-tenth.

Although the war dragged on for another year, Montreal was never again so directly menaced, and nothing that happened afterward could match the glory of that David and Goliath combat. Most of the fighting in 1814, was far away from the St. Lawrence Valley—in Upper Canada or localized along the Lake Champlain border. Wilkinson, it is true, attempted another invasion in March that might have reached the Island. At the head of four thousand men, he came up from Plattsburg, only to be halted at Lacolle by two hundred British, who had dug themselves into the mill, prepared for a stubborn defense. The weather turned against the invaders; ice in the river, snow on the ground, impassable roads. They were cold and they were weary, and after two hours of fighting, their ammunition gave out. Under cover of darkness, they retreated and in the morning, the British found themselves alone.

Prevost was much to the fore in this final season of warfare, exacting the full prerogatives of his office as commander-in-chief, yet without any evidence of the leadership needed for such an exalted position. Even with strong British reinforcements from overseas, he could not win the victory expected of him. In an assault on Plattsburg, with ten thousand men to back him, he made every mistake in the book; insisting that the attacks by land and sea be simultaneous; hurrying the naval commander into action against his better judgment; failing to advance by land at the same time; breaking his promises. The whole affair was a fiasco, an inglorious finale to what had never been a very glorious war. For Prevost, it brought a prompt recall to answer in London for his sins.

The Treaty of Ghent, signed on December 24, 1814, marked the formal conclusion of the conflict. Nothing was altered. The captured territory was restored, in a complete reversion to the status quo—to the great disappointment, it must be added, of the Nor'Westers, who had hoped against hope for some revision of the western boundary.

It was this Treaty that the *Gazette* described in March. "The information has not affected the public mind with any particular sensation of joy." Except for the various alarms, real and imaginary, Lower Canada had suffered little. Money was plentiful and business brisk. Ships crowded the harbor at Quebec, in quest of cargoes for a Britain still locked in bitter combat with France in Europe. Thanks to Mr. Molson's steamboats, communication with Montreal was excellent.

Montreal's feelings about war and peace may well have been somewhat divided, for violence broke out in the west, not long after the signing of the Treaty of Ghent. The summer of 1815 saw the North West Company engaged in a life and death struggle for survival, which however distant, geographically, could not be ignored in Lower Canada.

In general, the American war had been hard on the Company. To the normal difficulties involved in the shipment of furs to Montreal, there had been added new perils—attacks by the Americans, troubles with the Indians, interrupted communications. True, there were some good seasons; 1812 and 1814, for example, were tremendously rewarding in the number of pelts brought east in safety. But if it was business as usual, it was also business with a difference. The monetary gains were welcome, but underneath lay some haunting fears for the future.

Under such conditions, the border line between right and wrong may grow faint, and men's evil characteristics become accentuated. Thus the already aggressive Nor'Westers grew more so, their often callous disregard of human suffering toughened by the tensions of war. At all costs, the furs must be gathered in, and those brave enough to suggest opposition, be prepared for a ruthless trampling under foot. Rum was always certain to stimulate production, for the Indians would work to earn liquor, as for nothing else. For this reason, ten thousand gallons went upcountry from Montreal each summer, and if the natives were the worse for it, who was to care.

The North West Company was by this date, a powerful organization, formidable in its strength and stretching from the Atlantic to the Pacific. It was also exceedingly vulnerable, since a cut anywhere along the supply routes might weaken the giant beyond recovery. Realizing this, McGillivray tried yet again to secure right of access to Hudson Bay, only to be refused. The English company remained obdurate in its antagonism toward its Canadian rivals. And because the posts of the two organizations often stood side by side, there was frequent violence when quarrelsome words led to blows. Financial losses, for both, were an inescapable sequel.

Thus Lord Selkirk's decision to establish a settlement in the Red River Valley, served to exacerbate conditions already dangerous. Although there had been earlier rumors, the news broke definitely in 1811. The Scottish peer had acquired title to 116,000 square miles of territory, for a purpose completely alien to the fur trade. Moreover, the land in question, which lay directly astride the main route westward from Fort William, had been ceded by the Hudson's Bay Company without any legal justification. So, at any rate, said the Canadians, as they prepared to dispute the matter, every foot of the way. They were, after all, the rightful heirs of the French in the west.

In the vicious internecine warfare that blackened the next decade, there was no room for neutrality. Something of the same attitude holds true of the history books, so that writers' sympathies generally incline to the one side or the other. There were many angles; the personal as represented by McGillivray and Selkirk; the Company, the Nor'Westers against the men of the Hudson's Bay; agriculture and settlement in conflict with the frontier and the fur trade; perhaps even the future ousting the past. In relation to Montreal, however, there can really be only one approach, and that lies in the effect of the conflict on the town and its citizens. For the North West Company was a Montreal concern, and its chief employer of labor. No matter how eager their pursuit of personal gains, the partners provided much of the local prosperity.

Thomas Douglas, fifth Earl of Selkirk, has rightly been described as a philanthropist and a colonizer. His enemies in the North West Company called him derisively the "Bible Peer." From an early age he showed an unusual sympathy for the more unfortunate of his fellow men—a broad view which gradually crystallized into a deep concern for the sufferings of his fellow Scots, evicted from their homes by the "Highland Clearances." How to help them was a problem that haunted him, until gradually the conviction grew that only as emigrants could these men build new lives with their families. In the promotion of this ideal Selkirk discovered his life work, and he spared neither physical strength nor personal wealth in achieving the desired ends.

The first colony in Prince Edward Island, was highly successful. A second attempt, in Upper Canada, near Lake St. Clair, was less so. Brief visits to Canada in connection with these experiments, turned Selkirk's thoughts toward more distant territory. As early as 1803, and probably influenced by Sir Alexander Mackenzie, his imagination was captured by the thought of the land at what he called the western extremity of Canada, near Lake Winnipeg. It was then that Selkirk paid his first visit to Montreal, and met the leading Nor'Westers—the grandees and the nabobs as he described them. They were as always, hospitable, both in their homes and at the Beaver Club, and Selkirk as any intelligent man would, asked many questions about their business.

Marriage brought realization of his nebulous plans closer, for through the new Lady Selkirk came powerful family connections with the Hudson's Bay Company. Subsequent purchases of stock put his relatives and friends in possession of a large block of the Company's holdings, and so there was little or no opposition to the grant of land, except from the Canadians.

The first settlers were on their way almost before the gravity of the situation had been realized. Sailing at the end of July 1811 for Hudson Bay, they arrived at York Factory too late in the season for further travel. Not until the spring could they set out for their new homes, under the direction of Miles Macdonell, officially the Governor of Assiniboia. It was then that Selkirk's planning showed up for the poor thing it was. Scurvy, starvation, and death faced them, ignorant as they were of the frigid climate and the harshness of the land. Moreover, Macdonell soon proved to have been a poor choice for the post of command. No

one doubted that trouble was near, for the Nor'Westers were not
alone in their discontent. There were the métis, the half-breeds,
who had long made their homes in the district; allied with the
Indians, who could always be easily aroused, any hope of peace
was futile.

During several seasons, the survivors of the first miserable
groups were fed by the rival fur-trading companies. The Nor'-
Westers, in addition, held out the bait of free transportation to
Upper Canada, for those who wanted to escape from the unbearable hardships. It may be that eventually some modus vi-
vendi might have been agreed upon, had it not been for the
dictatorial attitude of Macdonell. His treatment of the Nor'-
Westers and the métis as though they were interlopers, became intolerable with his formal prohibition of the exports of
provisions from the territory. In this manner was launched the
"Pemmican War."

Pemmican was the dietary mainstay of the traders' diet. The
winterers and the clerks, and the voyageurs; all depended largely
upon this highly concentrated food for their sustenance. The
buffalo meat, dried and powdered, was mixed with melted fat, to
form a compact substance, easily carried and easily preserved.
Many of the men literally lived on it all winter. Since most of it
came from the disputed territory, Macdonell's embargo gave his
opponents an excuse for intervention.

During the years that followed there was nothing but misery
for everyone. When in 1818 the dispute landed in the courts its
extent may be gauged by the charges and countercharges. As
listed by the Montreal *Courant,* there were twenty-nine against
Selkirk and the Hudson's Bay Company, and one hundred and
fifty against the Nor'Westers.

Back of this, lay the Montrealers' determination to drive the
settlers out. Homes were broken up in 1815, and again in 1816
during the course of a horrible affair known as the "battle" of
Seven Oaks. Robert Semple, the new Governor of the colony,
was killed along with nineteen of his people. Selkirk, for his
part, was almost equally aggressive, for he proceeded west with
a large number of disbanded soldiers, all heavily armed. Fort
William, by his orders, was seized and ransacked, and the leading

partners, including McGillivray, arrested for high treason. That the latter were all promptly released on bail, upon their return east, did nothing to soothe their ruffled feelings.

That the normal yield of furs should have dwindled, goes without saying. A good season, once or twice, counted for very little against the costly delays and losses. On one occasion, the canoes were unable to get away from Montreal in time to complete their long journey before the freeze-up, and the men of all ranks were kept from their posts for months by the need to appear in court. Meanwhile the legal actions dragged on interminably, mainly because of Selkirk's absences and evasions. In the end the Canadians won what seems to have been a Pyrrhic victory, although a completely clear picture of the results is not easily achieved. But to fight in the courts, required money, and this McGillivray lacked. Without capital as usual, bankruptcy stared the Company in the face.

Montreal, by now, was thoroughly roused over the whole situation. The freely tendered hospitality was a thing of the past, so far as Selkirk was concerned. His health was visibly bad —so much so that the charitably minded might have discerned therein the reason for some of his strange actions. He was blessed with the most loyal of wives, for Lady Selkirk's defense of her husband was a gallant affair. Montreal knew her well, and indeed she stayed on alone after his final departure.

Popular feeling locally seems to have run strongly in favor of the North West Company, but this counted for little in the aftermath of the court judgments. During the interval of waiting, Selkirk died, and McGillivray, broken in health, was weary. The settlers remained on the prairies, and the future was black for the Canadian fur traders. They had no money, and a new agreement must be negotiated in 1822.

A minority group of the winterers grew tired of the struggle, and in their discontent, entered into a form of private understanding with their English rivals. By 1821 Simon McGillivray, in London, acting with the knowledge of his brother William, began official negotiations. Under pressure from the government, the union was achieved, and before the close of the year, Montreal heard the news.

The changes followed quickly, for the agreement proved to be a one-sided affair. The North West Company had no say in the direction of the business in future. Without money and faced with disloyalty in his own ranks, William McGillivray was helpless. Fort William was dismantled and fell into ruins, and York Factory took its place. From this date forward, the furs went out via Hudson Bay, and the Great Lakes and the St. Lawrence saw them no more. As the great brigades of canoes came to an end, Montreal lost its chief commercial asset, and two centuries of experience in the fur trade vanished overnight.

Washington Irving wrote the epitaph of the North West Company in a famous passage. "The feudal state of Fort William is at an end; its council chamber is silent and deserted; its banquet hall no longer echoes to the burst of loyalty, or the 'auld world' ditty; the lords of the lakes and the forests have passed away; and the hospitable magnates of Montreal—Where are they!"

Chapter 23

1812–1821

Domestic life. Travel. The harbor. The main streets and public buildings. Transportation. Markets. Shops. Street lights. Watchmen. Waterworks. Social life. Class distinctions. Hotels.

"LOWER CANADA seems to be as little known to the people of England as the deserts of Siberia." This was the opinion of John Lambert, a Scottish visitor to the New World in 1806. As was the case with most of his fellow Britishers who braved the perils of the Atlantic, he toured the Canadas as well as the United States, finding, on both sides of the border, as much to criticize as to praise.

After the victory at Waterloo, in 1815, these travelers grew more numerous. Some came on government business—the army or navy officers, the engineers, the doctors. Others had commercial interests, a few were gentlemen of leisure. Their backgrounds varied, as did their wealth. Whenever conditions differed from those in the mother country, the ultraconservatives were apt to be censorious; the more broad-minded enjoyed the novelty. A surprising number returned home to write and publish their memoirs. And since everyone included Montreal in any Canadian itinerary, the result is an unusual amount of local material dealing with the first quarter of the century—odd chapters buried in voluminous accounts of North American life— letters, diaries, and sketches of travel. That these were later supplemented by the recollections of two old-timers, made the record more complete. J. H. Dorwin first saw the town in 1816, T. S. Brown in 1818; each lived to a considerable age.

It is doubtful whether these early voyagers would have agreed

with the modern slogan that getting there is half the fun. Some
of the terrors of the Atlantic crossing had undoubtedly vanished, yet so long as the sailing vessel dominated the ocean
trade, wind and weather were factors to be reckoned with. Thus,
in 1818, Edward Talbot who sailed from Cork on June 13 did
not anchor off Quebec until July 27. A cabin passenger with
money enough to pay for elegant accommodations, he counted
himself lucky to escape with nothing worse than seasickness.
Twelve children, all under fourteen years, died at sea, while
as many more were buried on the islands in the lower St.
Lawrence.

There was no longer much question about the Quebec-Mon-
treal run. Everyone enjoyed the steamboats, whether as cabin
or deck passengers, and commented with wonder on their prompt
arrival. By 1819, no less than seven vessels plied the St. Lawrence,
and the competition was hot. Thomas Torrance had entered the
business several years earlier, with the *Car of Commerce,* said
to be faster and more luxurious than anything yet known. As
the owner of three ships—the *Caledonia,* the *Quebec,* and the
Telegraph—he was in a strong position to challenge the Molsons'
flagship *Lady Sherbrooke,* the new *Swiftsure,* and the *Mailsham.*

Overland travel was less comfortable. John Duncan, for example, came down from Kingston by bateau in 1818. Given head
winds, such a journey often lasted four or five days, slower than
by Durham boat but much safer. Passengers were advised to
take a supply of provisions with them, for it was not customary
to go ashore except to sleep. Equally necessary was warm clothing—cloaks and other coverings—the nights were cold, even in
summer.

Most spartan of all was the lot of those who came up the
Richelieu from Lake Champlain. As far as St. Johns, the boats,
if not elaborate, were tolerable. But the drive by carriage or
stagecoach across to LaPrairie, was a nightmare to most passengers; rough roads, bumps, holes, and often deep mud. Ahead
lay the uncertainties of the crossing to Montreal, still by canoe
or bateau, propelled by oars or sails, and hence unpredictable
as to duration. In 1816 Dorwin "was ferried across in a pine
log canoe and landed in the mud at the foot of what is now

Jacques Cartier Square." Traver VanVliet of Lacolle, as an old
man, recalled his experiences at LaPrairie in 1813. The bateau
made only one trip a day and passengers leaving Montreal had
to walk out to Point St. Charles to go on board. If the wind was
from the south, they were forced to land on Nuns' Island and
walk a mile or two to lighten the boat. Meanwhile, the crew
worked their craft along the shore with poles, keeping in the
shallow water. Such a trip often took four or five hours, and in
cold or stormy weather, was decidedly uncomfortable.

Passengers headed for the Island could at least comfort themselves with a view of the city, which at a distance "was quite
imposing. The large number of buildings, their roofs covered in
tin, glittering in the sun, was something very new to me." It had
"a showy appearance, and in summer, the circumjacent scenery
is exceedingly beautiful. Behind and to the left of the city
rises the Mountain, from which it originally took its name . . .
placed like a rampart behind the city to shield it in winter from
the unkindly blast . . . In front . . . are the tall masts of mer-
chantmen from the Thames, the Mersey and the Clyde; huge
steamboats with double chimneys; river craft of all sizes; and
enormous rafts of timber. In the middle of the stream, reposes
the island of St. Helena, encircled by a group of smaller ones;
while the unceasing sound of a small rapid which surrounds
them falls gently on the ear."

"The city, unfortunately, does not gain much upon you by a
nearer inspection." The precise phrase originated with John Duncan, but he voiced a sentiment shared by others. To start with,
there was the harbor, small but safe, once a vessel managed to
reach the Island. But the wharfs, wrote Talbot, "if such they
may be called, are in a most wretched condition. Vessels cannot
load or unload without great difficulty and excessive labor; and
to render a walk on the quays as uninviting as is consistent with
commercial enterprise, the scavengers are permitted to deposit
the whole filth of the city in their immediate vicinity."

Should this sound exaggerated, Dorwin wrote of "the river
margin almost lined with rafts and logs, but (which) otherwise
was in its natural state. There were no wharves; passengers
walked ashore on planks, goods were landed on the beach,

whether it was muddy or dry. In some places, carts were driven into the river to obtain loads of drift wood . . . Viger Garden was then a swamp, and from this a sluggish creek or ditch ran south . . . into the river . . . Its lower course was at least twenty feet deep, allowing canoes in time of high water to come up to McGill Street. Over its banks was thrown all the filth and refuse of the city, to be washed away once a year by the spring freshets."

After this, it is not surprising to find that most of the visitors enjoyed the mountain. A good road led to the summit, and although the upper part was well wooded, orchards and gardens covered the lower slopes. Vegetables and fruit grew there in abundance for the soil was fertile. The apples were unsurpassed in quality, while the cider had an excellent flavor. And all about stood the country houses, the villas, "the gentlemen's elegant seats."

But the city could not be forgotten for long. "The streets are for the greater part most inconveniently narrow . . . The dark colored limestone of which the houses are built, has a dull effect, and the massive iron shutters, folded back from almost every window and door, considerably increase the gloom." It was a small affair, bounded by Bonsecours Street on the northeast, St. James Street on the northwest, McGill Street on the southwest, and the river on the southeast, occupying about the same ground as was enclosed by the old fortifications. Within these limits, the ground was all or nearly all built over.

In this cramped space of one hundred acres, "all respectable people, with few exceptions, resided." The remains of the old town gates and walls served as its boundaries. But as the population increased, new streets were opened up, airy and of "a commodious width"—a suitable moment for the publication of the first city directory. Issued in 1819 by Thomas Doige, it not only provided an alphabetical list of merchants, traders, and housekeepers, but assigned numbers to the houses in all the streets within the town. Moreover, the suburban residents were advised that "the numbers inserted in the Directory . . . are those which they would have borne, had the numbering been continued. Every householder in those places, may now, if he

thinks proper, place the number on his house, and make it accord with the Directory, which in that particular, will not mis-
lead him."

Four of the outliers, by this date, had grown sufficiently to
merit description. The Quebec suburb, east of the city, was the
most aristocratic. It consisted of a score or two of buildings,
scattered along both sides of St. Mary Street, and extending out
beyond Molson's Brewery. A foundry and a shipyard completed
the commercial picture. Four fine residences belonged to Bishop
Mountain, Judge Reid, Baron Grant, and the Honorable John
Richardson. The St. Lawrence district, which was the most
populous, commenced at a bridge over the creek at the foot of
the street by the same name, and ran northward. "Sherbrooke
Street was then opened from St. Lawrence Street about as far
west as Bleury. In 1819 two fine new residences were built on
this street, one by Jacob Hall and the other by Thomas Torrance. They were both prominent objects to the citizens below,
and the latter, being the only cut-stone structure outside the
main city was the admiration of every passer-by . . . A foot
bridge crossed the creek at Bleury Street, and a narrow lane
ran up about as far as Dorchester Street, along which straggled
about half a dozen houses. This was called 'Flirtation Lane'
and was a favorite promenade for couples during the long twilight of the summer evenings."

St. Antoine to the west, and higher on the mountain slopes,
was obviously less advanced. It, too, started with a bridge crossing the creek at the end of St. Antoine Street, and was fairly
well built upon as far as Mountain Street. "There was only one
first-class house, that of Norman McLeod, a rich North-Wester
. . . The chief man of this company, the Honorable William
McGillivray, had a fine stone residence in Côte St. Antoine,
about the end of Dorchester Street, the most magnificent building
in the whole city." St. Anne suburb also lay to the west, although nearer the river. Much of the land was swampy, and
"other than the Lachine road, not even an attempt at road-
making." There were seven buildings scattered confusedly over
the common, and Robert Griffin, from whom Griffintown took
its name, had a soap factory near Wellington Street.

But no matter how beautiful the countryside, it is unlikely that the delights of suburban life could altogether compensate for its inconvenience. Despite the constant expansion, the center of Montreal's activities remained close to the river, its Upper and Lower Town differentiated only by a slight rise toward the mountain. The crowds, the dirt, and the noise counted for little against the charms of polite society and the urgencies of commerce.

Notre Dame Street, as the main thoroughfare, attracted a great deal of attention. Running parallel to the river, it was, as surveyed by Joseph Bouchette, 1344 yards long and 30 feet wide. In its whole length, there were only two or three shops. For the rest, it was a place of private dwellings, the aristocracy in its east end, the middle class to the west—an impressive vista, whose symmetry was marred only by the injudicious location of La Paroisse. A decided hazard this was as the traffic thickened; protruding as it did into Place d'Armes, passers-by had to go out and around the great edifice. Almost as important was St. Paul Street which, being closer to the water's edge, was well suited to commercial pursuits, both wholesale and retail. It was less impressive than its rival, being narrow and irregular in its course. At the east end, stood a gate, with a guardhouse over the top—in 1816, the last reminder of the old fortifications. The buildings were generally low as to height and forbidding in appearance, with shops and countinghouses on the ground floor, and living quarters above.

Other downtown districts were less well developed. On the upper side of St. James Street, from St. Francis Xavier to what is now Victoria Square, there was only one house, built by Benaiah Gibb. "A French gentleman lived in a stone building on the ground where the Bank of Montreal now stands, and on the site of the Merchants Bank was a small brick house, owned by Samuel Hedge, and behind it was a blacksmith's shop . . . On the other side of St. James Street were a few straggling dwellings." Beaver Hall Hill was a grassy lawn, with the old Frobisher house still standing across the summit. Everywhere to the west of Craig Street, stretched the open fields, divided by log fences. "McGill Street, opened up a short time before, as far down as the creek at St. Ann's market, had a few buildings along each side."

Although there was a good deal of criticism of the condition of these streets, Montrealers might, with some justification, claim an improvement over the old days. In 1800 an engineer had been hired to pave Notre Dame and St. Paul, and open up new roadways as needed. This he seems to have done with some success, for although Doige, in 1819, noted the shortcomings of the department in charge of the cleansing of the town, he pointed with pride to the use of flagstones on the main highways. "It is expected the whole town will soon be paved."

Others were less complacent. There was almost a waspish tone in Talbot's comments, for he found the streets narrow. "To add to the inconvenience which this occasions, the sidepaths or causeways are rendered almost impassable by a barbarous practice, which prevails in every part of the city, of erecting outside the doors, wooden steps which project three or four feet into the streets. If only two persons meet opposite one of these cumbersome piles, they will inevitably be obliged either to retrace their steps, or out of hasty complaisance, to descend into the channel, probably up to their knees in snow, or to their ankles in mud."

Recalling his early days, Dorwin admitted the absence of any drains or sewers "except the great natural one, the creek, and the water came down the spouts into the streets, and stayed there, or else ran where it pleased." There were many nuisances in the roughly paved streets, none perhaps worse than the dust, for watering carts were unknown. There were also "various kinds of roaming animals. Of the latter, the pig was the most common. On August 24, 1820, a pig sauntered into the Montreal bank, and deliberately scratched himself against the partition." Surely this must be one of the most famous porcine characters in any country's history!

Amid such congestion, transportation was a problem, as uncomfortable for the riders as it was dangerous for the pedestrians. To supplement the ordinary carts and trucks, the calèche was commonly used, "a clumsy one horse carriage with two wheels and a spring seat." Such vehicles could be hired for a modest price from the carters in the market place, who, summer and winter, looked for employment. As late as 1817 "there were but two coaches in the city, those of Lady Bowes and the Honorable John Forsythe." The mails for Upper Canada still went out to Lachine in a cart, or on horseback when the roads were bad. Thus Horace Dickenson, the Yankee carrier, created a sensation when "one fine morning in June 1820 he drove out of the city amid crowds of envious lookers-on, with two horses hitched to a large four-wheeled three-seated farmer's wagon, painted in red, the first vehicle of the kind seen in the neighborhood."

Some signs of a rudimentary "keep to the right" system had already made their appearance. Lambert remarked on this fact as early as 1808, adding that to an Englishman, the procedure appeared awkward. Noting with some surprise that legislative rulings in both Canada and the United States compelled its observance, he sought for a reason—"perhaps because drivers in winter usually jumped out of the cariole on the right side, to prevent it from upsetting in places where the road is narrow and the snow uneven."

To add to the general confusion, on Tuesdays and Fridays the farmers brought their produce into market, where they did a lively business at what were considered to be reasonable prices; much lower than at Quebec. It is probable that this differential was due to the Americans, who came across the border, loaded with provisions for sale in Canada. In addition to the usual fruit and vegetables there were quantities of fish, caught locally during the summer, but in winter, imported from Boston, packed in snow for transport in sleighs.

The conservatism of the rural mind showed in its general preference for the Old Market, which stood on what was later known as Custom House Square. There, on land used for the same purpose since the French regime, the habitants gathered in such numbers that the nearby streets were literally jammed with vehicles and people. Close by, near the Nelson Monument, stood the New Market, almost deserted, despite the superiority of its stalls. Only by persistent efforts could the special constables induce the buyers and sellers to move their stands and their horses, thus permitting traffic once more to flow freely.

Some of the liking for the older establishment may well have been due to the presence of amenities of a different kind. On the south side of the Square, a row of old women sat at tables, offering eatables for sale. Capital Street, nearby, flaunted a succession of drinking houses, whose trade went on without interruption from morning till night. The largest of these belonged to Thomas Delvecchio, commonly known as Thomas L'Italien, and its fame extended beyond the purveyance of liquor. For it boasted a clock on which small figures came out to strike the hours—"to the wonderment of all."

The more conventional shops, by comparison, sound rather drab. Whether wholesale or retail, they were small and few in number, their tiny windows affording little opportunity to show off their wares to good advantage. As a result, in good weather much of it was displayed outdoors. Many sported signs over their doors, for the benefit of the farmers who could not read. "The silvered flagon or the burnished boot would be much better understood and remembered than the most flaring and carefully gilded print."

Some shops went even further in their efforts to catch the country trade. Described as all doors and no windows, they remained open summer and winter alike, with their stock arranged outside whenever weather permitted. Beside it stood the salesmen, ready to accost any passers-by and drag them indoors, if necessary by force—perhaps the original "hard sell" in Montreal.

But vulgar arrangements of this nature held little appeal for the upper classes. One of the great events of the season was the arrival of the *Ew> Eweretta*, which usually docked in early June. Primarily a fur ship, she belonged to the North West Company. Her cargo was a varied one, including "all kinds of fancy goods, silks and ribbons, with the next year's fashions, for the citizens were always then a year behind their leaders in Paris and London."

So far, no one had given much thought to the beautification of the city. "There were no public gardens in the place, no parks, no fountains." The Nelson Monument stood alone in its grandeur, the solitary public statue in an era that admired such adornment. Some promise of improvement came in 1821 when the Governor presented to the town the ground where formerly stood Citadel Hill and the powder magazines. In honor of the donor this was called Dalhousie Square, a name which it still retains. But only a few years earlier Place d'Armes was hailed as the only publicly owned square in town. It too, was a recent acquisition, having served as a wood and hay market until 1812. For many seasons to come, a pump was its sole ornament. Champ de Mars was, of course, a parade ground, and a pleasant spot for an evening promenade. When trees were set out around its circumference, they were considered to be a great improvement. A creek ran through the mud flat, now known as Victoria Square.

The modern observer is tempted to wonder that Montrealers were content with their gloomy forbidding houses. Of the many critical visitors, none was more outspoken than Talbot. On Sundays and holidays, he wrote, "the whole city appears one vast prison; and at every noise that salutes the ear of the passing stranger, he imagines that he hears the clankings of a malefactor's chains, or pitiful moanings of an incarcerated debtor."

Most of these residences were, by now, built of stone. Within the city proper, only one structure of wood served as a reminder of earlier days. Brick was coming into fashion, although its use, at first, was restricted by a "prejudice" among the stone masons. But as local yards grew more common, the change to the new style was noticeable.

The public buildings were more impressive, and obviously a source of great local pride. To judge by the frequency of the descriptions and the glowing terms, every visitor was taken on a tour of inspection. Even the caustic Talbot conceded that they would not disgrace the finest squares in Europe—unwonted praise, which he hastily qualified by adding that the new structures "serve only to expose the older buildings, by a comparison which their present low condition cannot endure."

La Paroisse—Notre Dame Church—invariably headed the list, plain outside, but pictured in 1817 as "new fitted up, gilded and painted in the most glittering style imaginable." Next door stood the Seminary, a large structure, still surrounded by extensive grounds. There the Sulpicians taught the boys and young men of the district in such numbers, that a new Seminary was erected in the Recollet suburb to accommodate the overflow.

The Court House was on St. James Street, a large plain affair, housing the public library within its walls. "The good regulations under which it is managed, and the method in which the books are arranged, is a credit to the committee." Equally praiseworthy was the jail, substantial and spacious, built to replace the structure destroyed by fire in 1813. Since it housed both the debtors and the criminals, it is good to find that the interior was well planned for health, cleanliness, and comfort. There was less appreciation for Government House. Standing on the south side of Notre Dame Street, what is now the Château de Ramezay was dismissed as "an early specimen of the unpolished architecture of the province."

Nothing, however, attracted more attention than the English Episcopal Church, then in course of construction on Notre Dame Street. Zealous Protestants and lovers of the new style in building hailed it as "one of the handsomest specimens of modern architecture in the province." As such, its every detail merited description; the front of cut stone in the Doric style; the steeple and spire, well proportioned and covered with tin; on the summit, a large gilt weathervane, and a clock with four dials that could be seen from a distance. The interior was tasteful and neat, and painted in a chaste and appropriate manner—so overcrowded within a few years that in 1819 a gallery was added.

This was the second Christ Church, built to replace the original, destroyed by fire in 1803. "A meeting of the congregation was held within a few days, when measures were resorted to, which issued in the erection of the present handsome structure; in the meantime, the congregation were accommodated with the use of the Presbyterian Church in St. Gabriel Street." The "measures" included the appointment of a committee to meet with Dr. Mountain, the minister; the acquisition of land on which the old French prison stood formerly; the drawing of plans and the letting of the contract. "On the 21st day of June (1805), the corner stone was laid with the usual formalities, by the Lord Bishop of Quebec, who came to Montreal for the purpose." But disappointment followed, for "the funds obtained were insufficient to do more than finish the walls and the roof; and no further progress was made for some years." It was, in fact, not until October 1814, that divine service was first held in the new church.

Having regard to its size, Montreal's progress was commendable. The one hundred acres of the town proper had, with the inclusion of the suburbs, spread out over an area ten times as great. Its hundred streets contained 2500 houses, and more were going up every day. Yet in 1816 the population was a mere 16,000. Of this number, 10,000 were French-speaking and Roman Catholic; 1500 were English and chiefly Anglican; 2000 were Scotch, mostly Presbyterian; 1000 were Irish, half Roman Catholic and half Protestant; 1500 were Americans, "whose religion is politics and their God a golden eagle," wrote Talbot.

This diversity of race and religion was reflected in the crowds along the streets. There might be seen the priests of the Seminary, dignified in their black robes, and the students, in long blue surtouts with sashes of colored worsted. Sometimes there were the nuns, the beloved sisters in habits of black or gray, who, true to the wishes of the founders, remained uncloistered. Always there were the farmers or workmen, clad in serviceable gray homespun, their short black pipes a trademark of their class. If their appearance was crude, their old world courtesy won compliments from all who met them. In the background lounged the Indians, the often pathetic descendants of a once-proud race. For although the women of Caughnawaga were, in general, decently attired, the men were apt to be squalid and dirty. The young men of fashion kept themselves aloof from the throngs. It was amusing to see how they tried to be "in the London cut." The British officers, in particular, did not mix socially lest they be contaminated by trade. But they had great appeal. "The rabble flock in crowds to regimental parades; and even women, of any appearance, make a point of stepping to a march."

Montreal, "originally French, was in danger of becoming a Scotch colony before it began to be overrun by the still more hardy and adventurous sons of New England." This was the

opinion of Joseph Sansom, himself American born, who saw his
fellow countrymen as "winding themselves into all the most
active and ingenious employments." Trade was on the increase
between the two countries. Duncan saw much that was admirable
in these new comers. "So far as I have been able to discover, the
utmost harmony prevails among them and those who are by
birth subjects of our sovereign."

There was as yet no true municipal government. Since the
town was not incorporated, its affairs were administered in
common with the rest of the district. In the absence of local by-
laws or law-enforcement agencies the magistrates carried on as
best they could, aided only by a handful of civic functionaries.
But what had been effective in earlier days, no longer answered
the purpose. As the population increased, conditions got out of
hand and the roughs of the place did pretty much as they liked.
Thus a group of citizens in the summer of 1816, petitioned the
authorities "to appoint an efficient force of watchmen to patrol
the streets at night, and after much delay, in April 1818, these
began their rounds. Among their duties was to attend the lamps
and call the hours. 'Twelve o'clock and all's well' would be the
midnight cry at the corners of the streets, and so on, all night."
It is doubtful, however, if the new protective force was of much
value. The number of the constables was limited to twenty-four,
and since most were old men, armed only with long blue batons,
they could not have done much to withstand any violent assault.

Similar reasons led to the installation of street lighting, although in addition to the discouragement of crime, it was felt
that "the ladies might be induced to visit their friends more
frequently." The matter was discussed as early as 1811, when it
was agreed that "the cost would not be great, from the fact that
the lamps would only be required from the first of September to
the end of November, and from the first of March to the end of
May." But despite this thrifty suggestion, Sandham reported
"nothing was done until November 1815, when by the exertions
of Mr. Samuel Dawson and other gentlemen, that portion of St.
Paul Street west of the old market was handsomely lighted by
twenty-two lamps, fixed at fifty-four feet distance from each
other. The novelty of the thing had its effect, and hopes were

entertained that other citizens might go and do likewise. These hopes were soon to be realized, for in December of the same year, the inhabitants of the east end of St. Paul Street, determined not to be outshone by their neighbors, started a subscription among themselves, and soon collected sufficient to purchase lamps and light their portion of the street." A postscript noted that each lamp cost $7.

Another much-needed improvement got under way in 1819, when the franchise of the defunct Montreal Water Works Company was bought out by a new organization, headed by Thomas Porteous. The confusion in the town was considerable—"workmen trenching the streets to remove the logs, that had conducted the water from the mountain, to replace them with iron pipes, that were to distribute water from a reservoir on the Citadel, pumped there by an engine below Bonsecours Church, where we had all the advantages of city sewage." The new pipes, being sunk low in the ground for fear of frost, the remodelled system was welcomed as a protection against fire, especially in winter when the river was frozen over.

Attempts to improve the mails met with less success. As a part of the Postal Service of England, the province exercised no control over what went on in Canada. Montreal could merely complain, not take any action. The local office consisted of one room, about twelve feet square, on St. Sulpice Street. There were no boxes and the "general delivery" was of the crudest. "The few letters lay scattered about on a table, and had all to be looked over at each application at the door." In view of the delays and the high cost, it was hardly surprising that there were not more. One mail a week went to Upper Canada, so small that it could be carried in a single small bag. The cost per letter was 1/6. Service to Quebec at 9d, was more useful. The result was that anyone who traveled, was expected to fill his baggage with letters and parcels.

No picture of the mores of Montreal would at any period, be complete without a glimpse of its social life. As to its quality, in the early nineteenth century, opinions differed. Doige considered the town as "not overburdened with amusements." Perhaps because of his austere Scottish temperament, Duncan was more severe. "If you enjoy good eating, card playing, dancing and gaiety, you will find abundance of all. If literary society is your choice, you will discover, I am afraid, but little; if religious, still less. I was particularly struck with the extent to which card playing and dice-box abound; they seem indeed to be almost the only resource in an evening party if it is not professedly a dancing one." On the subject of his fellow Britishers, his comments were especially biting. "The greater part are eagerly intent upon the acquisition of wealth, and in general, anticipate a return to their native country to spend it, and if in their hours of intermission from other pursuits, they can glance at a novel or a fashionable poem, it is all that in most cases is attempted."

Whatever the justification of this harsh criticism, it must be said that class distinctions pervaded the town, to an extent that is shattering to any idealistic views of democracy in the New World. In the highest rank, according to Talbot, were the civil and military officers, the most respectable professional men in law, physic and divinity, together with several members of the North West Company; next came the merchants "of large fortune"; below them were the shopkeepers and more wealthy mechanics; last of all, "that class of men, which in England, is distinguished by the appellation of the lower orders."

There is no doubt that the principal partners of the North West Company considered themselves the cream of local society. They lived in a "very superior style to the rest of the inhabitants, and keep very expensive tables. They are friendly and hospitable to strangers, who are introduced to them." None was more prominent than William McGillivray, who kept open house at his spacious Château St. Antoine. After a dinner party there, Dr. Bigsby saluted his host as the great Amphitryon of Montreal. The excellent appointments and service surprised him. "I found, but did not expect to find, at Montreal, a pleasing transcript of the best form of London life . . . even in circles beneath the very first-class of official families."

That the officers of the garrison were equally hospitable, was evident from the reports of visitors who had military connections. It is to be inferred that they had no use for those engaged in the vulgar pursuits of commerce. A similar snobbishness showed itself in the select public balls, at which families in trade were blackballed if they dared to present themselves. Although Talbot considered the gentlemen to have rather a respectable appearance, he was cruel to their wives. "I have never seen more than half a dozen females in the city, who assume either the air or the dress of ladies."

Each winter, the cold weather ushered in a constant round of festivities; balls and dinner parties, public and private; New Year's calls among the young men; outdoors, the carioles, their passengers well wrapped up in great coats and fur caps, and snug under the buffalo robes. The young and strong welcomed a heavy snowfall, for it brought good sleighing. Once the river was firmly frozen over, there was a great coming and going between the town and the countryside, visits to friends, and all manner of merriment.

Spring brought all this movement to an end, for the melting snow made the country roads impassable. The city streets were almost as bad, so that a walk in the deep slush presented hazards to the pedestrian. And as the April sun grew brighter, people were forced to protect their eyes with shades of green gauze fastened to their hats.

The British visitors were never done complaining of the summer heat. Sometimes the temperatures soared into the nineties! They watched with horror the plague of houseflies and mosquitoes, and as is the way with newcomers, suffered horribly from the bites. On one tropical evening, Sansom told of cooling off in a floating bath, anchored off Windmill Point—one of the rare accounts of anything like swimming or bathing in the St. Lawrence. Informal picnics on the mountain were popular, and in the evening, there were the promenades on Champ de Mars. Largely masculine affairs they were, but even so, they rated as "an eligible place" for fashion displays.

Not all the parties took place in private homes, for the town boasted of a number of hotels and taverns. There was intense local pride in the Mansion House, a superb building, which stood on St. Paul Street. There the assemblies were held, in "a room not surpassed in size and elegance by any in the province." Originally the private residence of Sir John Johnson, it was now being improved by John Molson so as to become the most complete hotel in North America. Other establishments were less aristocratic; Clamp's Coffee House; the City Tavern where the Upper Canada merchants stayed; the Brock Tavern, preferred by the merchants from the Eastern Townships and by Americans. Others were more properly labeled as drinking houses; *Les Trois Rois,* belonging to Joseph Donegani, deriving its name from the sign which represented the three Kings of the East. A few were frankly low—patronized by voyageurs and raftsmen. St. Paul Street was disfigured by "a succession of grog shops and market people, making that neighborhood very rough."

But as Montreal moved forward into the 1820s, much of the carefree quality vanished from local life. The Beaver Club virtually folded in 1817 while the shadow of financial losses and legal anxieties made a mockery of the famed hospitality of the Nor'-Westers. So dominating a position had they occupied in municipal affairs, that few, even among the lower orders, could escape the evil results engendered by the loss of the fur trade.

Chapter 24

1821–1831

Political strife. French-English bitterness. Papineau. Immigration from Britain. Poverty of the new arrivals. Montreal General Hospital. The religious Orders. Notre Dame Church. Education. McGill College. The Bank of Montreal. Canals.

THE DEMISE OF the North West Company came upon Montreal with shattering suddenness. Within a single season, the beaver pelts had vanished, and the gaudy trade goods gone elsewhere. The warehouses, so long crowded with busy workers, were silent and empty. The Hudson's Bay Company held the monopoly of the fur trade in Canada, and ruled its affairs from London.

Probably no one suffered more in spirit than William McGillivray. Throughout his entire adult life, he had been a Nor'-Wester. He lived on in Montreal until 1824, in steadily worsening health. A visit to London, undertaken in search of a rest and change of scene, ended a few months later in death. Simon, his younger brother—the lame one—remained in Canada, a man of great kindness, whose courage and perseverance carried him through years of struggle with the tangled finances of the once prosperous McTavish, McGillivray and Company. He, too, died in London in 1840.

A reduction in staff and a reorganization of the complex activities of the fur trade—for the Hudson's Bay Company such measures were unavoidable. Wherever two rival posts had stood side by side, one must go. A few of the Canadian winterers were retained, but the majority sought other employment. The magnificent way of life, enjoyed by the partners, was a thing of the past, and some at least, ended their days in poverty.

Meanwhile, the town found itself facing serious political strife. The English-French relationship, so amicable in earlier years, became increasingly bitter. From the turn of the century, the split grew steadily worse until, by 1820, it could no longer be ignored. The harmony induced by the American war was short-lived, and peace brought a renewal of the conflict of ideas. Province-wide in scope it undoubtedly was, yet as in the past, worse at Montreal than in the capital.

Unfortunately, the governors of the day did little to soothe the hotheads of either party. Sir John Coape Sherbrooke, who followed the indecisive Prevost, was a man of great ability whose sincere desire to erase the political enmity won him universal respect. Everyone regretted that a severe stroke forced his retirement, after two years in office. The Duke of Richmond was cut from a different cloth, young and reactionary, and prone to ill-considered actions. History has remembered him chiefly for the manner of his death, which resulted from the bite of a tame fox. But the policies he instituted were continued by Lord Dalhousie, who held office from 1820 to 1828. Being a Scot and a Presbyterian, he was naturally inclined to suspect Roman Catholics, and his handling of the Assembly could hardly have been worse.

Each of these officials in turn confronted an Assembly, which if not always in opposition, was increasingly alert to its rights and privileges. The French Canadian majority had long since forgotten its early indifference or antagonism to an elected Lower Chamber. Although the British members represented wealth, and at the outset had a better knowledge of constitutional procedures, they were soon outshone by their opponents. In her sympathetic study of the period, Helen Taft Manning tells of the legend, long current, that all the French-speaking representatives were required to study Delorme's *Constitution of England*, and pass an examination on what was the only textbook then available in their own language.

This serious attention to public affairs indicated a transformation in the Assembly and, by inference, in its leaders. As the influence of the seigniorial families waned, they were replaced by the middle class—some of the latter, sufficiently affluent in due course, to become landowners themselves. And since the British merchants regarded commerce as their private preserve, the sons of French Canadian fathers turned to the professions—medicine, the church, and, above all, the law. Having received a sound classical education in the seminaries of Montreal or Quebec, they took to politics as to the manner born.

Of all the leaders, by 1820, one was recognized as the chief. Louis Joseph Papineau was born in Montreal in 1786, the son of Joseph, a man who had gained distinction as a liaison officer in the 1776 invasion. Papineau *père* represented Montreal in the House from 1792 to 1804 and from 1809 to 1814. In private life, he prospered enough to acquire the seigniory of *La Petite Nation* on the Ottawa River (now Montebello).

Thus the young Louis Joseph grew up in comfortable circumstances, an important factor at a time when members received no remuneration for their attendance at the House. His active mind, whetted by a good education, led him into politics at an early age, as Member, first for Chambly, and from 1814 to 1837, for Montreal West. That his colleagues recognized his ability was evidenced by his election as Speaker, a post which he held continuously from 1815 to 1837. There he wielded great influence, being so strategically placed that he could virtually block all legislation of which he disapproved. Needless to say, the merchants hated him on sight.

Because of the intense feelings which Papineau has always aroused, it is difficult to know what manner of man was this Montrealer of long ago. He was a fine public speaker, although one who tended to rely on an appeal to the emotions rather than on the firm constitutional stand of his more moderate associates. A lawyer by profession, he was greatly influenced by the French and the American Revolutions. There was, at least, some skepticism in religion. In later life, he suspected everything that emanated from England, even where no cause existed.

A personal glimpse of this enigmatic man comes from the pen of Dr. Bigsby, a British geologist of repute, and a fellow passenger aboard the steamer from Quebec to Montreal. He described him as "a well-dressed handsome man, standing erect, and a little above the middle size, with the black hair and eyes of France, his features regular, rather long, fine, but not ingenuous. He appeared to me subtle, persuasive, confident and eager for information. He questioned me on the subject of my rock specimens, and on geology. I told him I was only a learner. 'True; that may be,' said he, 'but un borgne is king among the blind.' In a short time, I had given him the titles and merits of all the best books on the subject, and the way to secure from London labeled cabinets of mineralogical and rock specimens. He left me high and dry. I had nothing more to tell. I wished to talk political economy with him, and perhaps a little politics, but no, there was to be nothing given in exchange. I was left courteously, but before I had received my reward, which was unpleasant."

This was the man who led the House, each session, into a dispute with the Governor over finance. At stake was the control of the provincial funds, a subject of great complexity, on which many words have been written. Until 1818 the permanent revenues of the Crown had almost sufficed to meet the ordinary expenditures of the administration. After that date, it became necessary to secure additional grants from the Assembly. The result was a steadfast refusal to vote money without a thorough item-by-item examination. For ten years, there was strife and a complete deadlock between Dalhousie and the elected members.

In this struggle for political power, the role of the Legislative Council should not be overlooked. Its few members, appointed by the Crown, were overwhelmingly English, and as such became the mouthpiece of the Montreal merchants. Die-hard Tories to a man, they invariably sided with the Governor, interjecting an element of deplorable venom into the local French-English pattern.

Naturally each group prescribed remedies for the supposed iniquities of the other. Words and phrases were bandied about in such a way as to confuse the unwary reader. Responsible government, as urged by the popular party, did not conform to modern usage. In Great Britain, then as now, it implied the existence of a Cabinet, a group of ministers responsible to the Lower House. Should a vote of confidence lead to defeat, their resignation must follow. But to Papineau and his followers, it simply meant the substitution of an elected Council for the existing appointed body.

For their part, the local Tories lent a special significance to the word "union," and by 1822 they had succeeded in gaining the ear of London. What they wanted was the reunion of the two provinces, under a single Legislative Assembly. By this means, and because of the largely Anglo-Saxon population of Upper Canada, they reasoned that Montreal would again belong to the privileged majority.

Admittedly, local differences grew so serious that some constitutional amendments seemed necessary, yet the British Cabinet, by presenting a Union Bill at Westminster, stirred up a hornets' nest in Canada. The proposal was hastily withdrawn. Both parties held public meetings at Montreal, the Unionists under John Richardson, standing pat in their own interests. But another gathering at which Denis Benjamin Viger presided, revealed the greater strength of their opponents. A committee of eighteen leading French Canadians conferred with their friends in the capital, and together they produced a monster petition, signed by 60,000 persons. Carried to London by Papineau and his ally John Neilson of Quebec, it won the day and the defeat of the English minority was complete.

Nothing daunted, the merchants cast about for an alternative. It was not long in making its appearance, being nothing less than a demand that the Island of Montreal and a strip of the adjacent territory be annexed by Upper Canada. That their first attempt met with failure, did nothing to silence the sponsors. For a decade, the suggestion hung in the air, receiving at times, some support from the Upper province. As late as 1832, a public meeting at York went on record as favoring the annexation of Montreal, for the better balance of power. Alas for their hopes, the whole affair was vetoed at the next session in Quebec.

In fact, although the merchants appeared to have lost all their battles, they gained much from the Canada Trade Act, passed by the Imperial Parliament in 1822. Basically, this was the discarded Union Bill, shorn of political allusions, but including clauses of commercial significance. Not only did it regulate the financial relationship of the two provinces, but it set up a protective tariff against American imports of such commodities as foodstuffs and timber. Previously, these had competed, on the open market, on equal terms with the native produce.

But of the 1820s in general, it can only be said that, politically, they were uneasy. Just as the friction between the French and the English grew worse, so did the disputes between the Governor and the Assembly, while in the perpetual elections that characterized the period there was every opportunity for open expressions of hatred. Since the Quebeçois were commonly known as the "lambs" and the Montrealers as the "wolves," the site of most of the trouble is clear. Papineau's activities were centered on Montreal, and on several occasions the behavior of the voters verged on the riotous. One such, in the summer of 1827, was described by a visiting naval officer.

"An election was going on in the city, and now and then there was a row in the streets, not unworthy of Covent Garden, where the public-spirited voters sometimes love to vindicate the freedom of election by trying to knock out the unpopular candidates' brains. The boys kept scampering up and down the streets, bawling out Pappineau! Pappineau! while the walls were chalked and placarded at every corner with 'Pappineau pour toujours!' and there were sundry processions through the town by mobs, which cheered one party and hissed the other, in the most approved style of party manners." As a postscript, the writer added that he found it impossible to sympathize deeply with this speculative misery, since everybody appeared so perfectly contented.

This unrest was sufficiently serious in itself to cause anxiety. It was therefore all the more unfortunate that for many years, it should coincide with an influx of immigrants from the British Isles, who by the introduction of fresh racial stocks added to the dangers of an already explosive situation.

Official London had long since forgotten its fears that emigration would depopulate the mother country. Economic depression, unemployment, poverty, and discontent, particularly in the years following the defeat of Napoleon—these had combined to unloose upon the unsuspecting American continent, such a flood of human misery as had never been seen before. The Upper province was the mecca of most of those who came to Canada. Grants of land were easily obtained by those willing to undertake the backbreaking toil of clearing the forest and tilling the soil. Certainly, the Montreal district had little to offer prospective farmers. High rentals, added perhaps to some feelings against French Canadians, sent the majority elsewhere.

Nevertheless, Montreal and Quebec, as the main ports of entry, carried a heavy burden. In most cases, the oceangoing vessels halted at Quebec, their steerage passengers then ascending the river in barges towed by steamboats. Above Montreal the journey was continued by stagecoach and boat. Numerically, their supervision was no light responsibility. In 1816, a mere 3000 arrived. Three years later, their number had climbed to 23,000. During the decade that ended in 1825, some 50,000 entered the country via the St. Lawrence, and the totals grew higher still, all through the '30s and the '40s.

By far the greater number of these immigrants had little or nothing in the way of worldly goods, and they reached Canada after lengthy sea voyages, made under shocking conditions. The effort was often too much for their frail bodies, already weakened by privation at home. Without any particular skills in the labor market, friendless and miserable, many soon became dependent on the kindness of citizens in Montreal and Quebec. And despite numerous protests, no one in the British Isles seemed to care what happened, least of all, the authorities. So the parish officials who administered the poor laws continued to dump their charges on the colonies, as heartless in their way as the ships' captains who bilked their passengers while en route.

Each governor in turn, protested to the Colonial Office, while the newspapers in both provinces publicized the general complaints. All objected, not so much to the newcomers themselves as to the scandalous manner in which the British government evaded its responsibilities. Canadians, in one way or another, were forced to pay relief charges which more properly belonged to London. As might be expected, the situation became a political football, the Montreal merchants being accused of encouraging the invasion, so as to alter the ratio of population, the French Canadians condemned as being wholly in opposition. Neither statement, it would seem, was altogether just. For although the Legislature of Lower Canada did in 1827 lodge a protest with the British officials, it was by no means alone in its stand. Similar action had already been taken in Nova Scotia, New Brunswick, and Newfoundland, while several American states proceeded to exclude ships that did not meet their requirements.

In any formal and official sense, Montreal was ill-prepared to handle the pathetic army. Private charity, of necessity, stepped into the breach, by means of such organizations as the Emigrant Association, founded in 1831 by a group of public-spirited citizens. During its first season over £750 was dispersed in assisting 4022 persons to reach their destinations. Catherine Parr Traill wrote from personal observation of the situation. "The number both of Catholic and Protestant benevolent societies, is very great, and these are maintained with a liberality of principle that does honor to both parties, who seem indeed actuated by a fervent spirit of Christian charity. I know of no place, not even excepting London itself, where the exercise of benevolent feelings is more called for, than in these two cities, Quebec and Montreal."

One such community organization had a modest beginning when in 1815, a group of charitable women banded themselves together as the Female Benevolent Society of Montreal. Being "deeply impressed with the destitute situation of the poor," they went ahead, under the leadership of Mrs. Benaiah Gibb, with practical measures of relief. Philanthropic individuals, having contributed £1200 for a soup kitchen, the ladies went further, renting a small house where the most needy cases could be provided with board and lodging. The four rooms of this "House of Recovery," thriftily equipped with discarded army bedding, soon proved too small, and a larger place was secured. Situated on Craig Street, it could care for twenty-four patients in its three wards, while an outdoor department rendered additional assistance to the poor.

Such was the origin of the Montreal General Hospital, one of the city's great institutions, which has never ceased to care for the sick since its doors first opened in May 1819. By November of the following year, it could report that 138 patients had been admitted, and 106 discharged as cured; deaths had totaled fifteen, and seventeen still remained in the hospital. Space was already at a premium. In that same month, land was purchased on Dorchester Street, in St. Lawrence suburb, and contributions sought for the erection of a permanent building. The support of such prominent citizens as John Molson and John Richardson, virtually guaranteed success, and the sum of £2000 was soon available. To the music of military bands, and with solemn Masonic ceremonies, the cornerstone was duly laid on June 6, 1821.

The new hospital, which stood in the open fields, endured all the discomforts of country living. Dependent on candles and lanterns for lighting, and hampered by an uncertain water supply, there was always fear of fire. The one and only furnace was troublesome. But it provided accommodation for seventy-two patients in its two stories, plus an attic and a basement. The cost —almost double the original estimate—was paid off in 1823, mainly due to the generosity of John Richardson. Although the same year brought a government charter and the first official grant, charitable donations provided most of the revenues. With the appointment of four doctors to its staff, all graduates of Edinburgh University, the stage was set for wider spheres of service.

The construction of the General Hospital in no way, implied a criticism of the work so long carried on by the religious Orders. Quite the contrary, for even the most ardent Protestants, in the Amherst tradition, expressed a keen admiration for the nuns. No matter how narrow their views on the Romish church, the women's communities were always exempt from criticism. But the Hôtel Dieu contained only thirty beds, while twenty-four Grey Nuns tended the mentally afflicted. The town had grown beyond them.

In the curious custom of the day, most of the male visitors to Montreal called at the convents in the course of their sightseeing. All seem to have been happy to purchase the small articles made by the nuns, as a means of augmenting their pitifully small incomes. With its revenues from France long since cut off, the Hôtel Dieu welcomed a government grant in 1823, paid on the same basis as that to the General Hospital. But no matter what the financial stringency, the patients were treated with the utmost care and tenderness. A single quotation will convey the flavor of these convents, "almost exclusively appropriated to the care of the sick. The Hôtel Dieu is a spacious hospital, managed by nuns, whose zeal in the good cause is not surpassed in any Catholic country in Europe. The Grey Sisters have another hospital . . . where the orphans who had the misfortune of losing their parents during the prevalence of cholera last year, are taken care of. It is scarcely possible to express in words the active humanity, the extreme kindness, shown by these charitable nuns toward the unfortunate children. It is equally impossible to convey a correct idea of the careful education which they give to these fatherless little ones."

For the Roman Catholics of the city, undoubtedly the outstanding event of the twenties was the building of the new Notre Dame Church—so badly needed to replace the ancient La Paroisse, whose congregation had long since outgrown the cramped dimensions of an earlier day. Architecturally, it introduced a new style to the city—what a contemporary hailed as "a chaste specimen of perpendicular gothic." Modern experts have generally regretted its departure from the native Quebeçois tradition, but given the temper of the times, the desire for a fresh inspiration, was probably inevitable.

Strangely enough, the architect was an Irish Protestant, and by virtue of residence, a New Yorker. Although it has been said of James O'Donnell that he carried on an undistinguished practice in the American metropolis, he knew how to draw up plans that suited Montreal's hunger for a church that would surpass all others in the country, if not on the continent. From the laying of the cornerstone in September 1824 until the celebration of the first High Mass in July 1829, the citizens watched the progress of the work with eager attention.

It was a fine building as Mrs. Traill saw it, although "still in an unfinished state, the towers not having been carried to the height originally intended." The extreme lightness of the architecture won her approval, and the manner in which all the features of the interior combined to form one beautiful whole. That she should miss the time-hallowing mellowness of age was only natural. "But although the new church at Montreal cannot compare with our York Minster, Westminster Abbey and others of our sacred buildings, it is well worthy the attention of travelers, who will meet with nothing equal to it in the Canadas."

This same decade witnessed some modest progress in education. Ever since 1760, it had been a thorny subject, as between the French Roman Catholics and the English Protestants, and a settlement pleasing to both, was not easily come by. Much of the friction stemmed from the official desire to anglicize the province, which however unsuccessful in fact, stirred up bad feelings on both sides.

Meanwhile, there was cause for rejoicing at the prospect of a college for Montreal—thanks to the foresight of James McGill who, on his death in 1813, bequeathed £10,000 and his country house for the purpose. In his lifetime, the benefactor was a prominent citizen, a fur trader with a wide interest in civic affairs, a member of the Assembly and later of the Legislative Council, a thoughtful man who viewed with concern, the paucity of educational opportunity in Lower Canada. Being childless, he felt able, in his last will and testament, "to give and devise all that tract and parcel of land, commonly called Burnside . . . containing about forty-six acres . . . for the purpose and advancement of learning in this province."

There were immediate difficulties, in the shape of opposition from the family of the widow, and particularly from her nephew, Francis Desrivières, the occupant of the house. He decided to hang on and contest the issue, hoping that the indolence of the authorities would leave him in possession, so that the time limit of ten years, imposed by the will, might invalidate the bequest.

At first, it seemed as though he might be right, since there were no trustees in a position to accept the legacy. It was not until 1816 that a Board was appointed, and then another four years passed before its members laid a claim. In 1820, they went to law against Desrivières, in 1821 they secured a royal charter from William IV. Three years later, four professors were appointed to serve under the first principal, the Reverend George Jehoshophat Mountain, later Anglican Bishop of Montreal. By July 24, 1829, affairs had progressed enough to permit a formal opening. Yet despite all the formal speeches and prayers which marked the occasion, it must be added that nothing more happened until 1835, when the Privy Council in London finally ruled against Desrivières.

So far, education at the school level progressed slowly. Although 1801 had seen an Act passed "to establish free schools and promote the cause of education," it remained inoperative until 1818, when the Royal Institution for the Advancement of Learning was established. Since its members were largely Protestant and its chairman was the Anglican Bishop, the Roman Catholics considered it as an instrument of proselytizing. Thus, while the administration of McGill was placed in the hands of the Royal Institution, its future otherwise, remained uncertain.

Yet the Institution met with some success in the cities. The Royal Grammar School, which flourished in Montreal from 1818 to 1843, gained an enviable reputation. Under the headmaster, Alexander Skakel, M.A., it achieved much in the teaching of English, French, Latin, and Greek languages, writing, ancient and modern geography, mathematics and natural philosophy. A report dated 1829, showed thirty-five scholars in attendance, of whom fifteen paid fees and twenty were free. The annual government allowance amounted to £60 for rent, and £200 for the headmaster.

The French Canadian schools were extremely badly off after 1760, cut off from France, the main source, both of their revenues and their teachers. The country districts suffered the most, so that often not more than half a dozen people in a parish could read or write. But the seminaries in the cities soon reopened, and after the French Revolution gained reinforcements for their teaching staffs by reason of the number of priests who escaped to Canada. Although primarily they trained youths for the priesthood, they did not confine themselves to theological subjects.

To judge by these various attempts at betterment, there was a good deal of money in circulation, despite the disappearance of the fur trade. Thanks to the colonial preference, the timber merchants flourished, and shipments of wheat were at a high level. Add to this, the countermovement of imported manufactured goods and the harbor was busy. The condition of the river grew more important, and the provision of canals vital, if this three-part traffic—the British Isles, the United States, and Upper Canada—was to be maintained.

Sometimes, private enterprise was able to initiate improvements. Banking offers a good example of a local response to a thoroughly unsatisfactory situation. In the absence of a Canadian currency, just about any coin was acceptable as legal tender, whether minted in Britain, France, Spain, Portugal, or the United States. Rates of exchange fluctuated so widely that trade was hampered by the lack of proper facilities for handling this hodge-podge of specie. It was to fill this need, that after several attempts, a group of nine merchants met together in June 1817, and signed articles of association for the formation of the Bank of Montreal. Their names included John Richardson, George Garden, George Moffatt, Thomas A. Turner, Robert Armour, James Leslie, Horatio Gates, John C. Bush, Austin Cuvillier.

They experienced no difficulty in securing subscriptions for the first issue of capital stock, in the amount of £250,000, and a rented house on St. Paul Street was soon equipped for business. Within a few weeks, the newspapers carried an announcement, "The Bank will commence operations on Monday, November 3 next, bank hours, ten to three; discount days, Tuesday and Friday; bills and notes for discount to be delivered to the cashier on the previous day." It seems safe to suppose that transactions were numerous, since four days later, the directors asked that a sentry be placed on duty.

Although the Bank was now active in the monetary field, it had as yet no legal rights. Government incorporation did not follow until May 1822—not because of any unwillingness on the part of the Assembly. The Colonial Office withheld royal assent because of doubts over the protection afforded to stockholders. Once that hurdle was surmounted, the new institution took an active share in the commercial life of the town.

But in other ways, little or nothing could be done without official permission and financial support. Hence Montreal's discontent with conditions in the St. Lawrence was repeatedly brought to the attention of the authorities. However real the need for improvements may have been in the past, they grew urgent with the loss of the fur trade. At one point, there was some hope of assistance from the British government, since that august body was in the midst of one of its periodic spurts of anxiety over Canada's deplorable lack of protection. In 1819, no less a personage than the Duke of Wellington drew up a memorandum which recommended the building of fortifications and development of the inland waterways. Other reports followed the same general lines, and although in the end, high cost proved a deterrent, a good deal of work was actually put in hand. A start was made at the construction of a citadel at Quebec, along with a strengthening of Ile aux Noix, the latter being regarded as an outer defense post for Montreal. Although the town itself gained nothing, St. Helen's Island was fortified and equipped with powder magazines, barracks, and storehouses.

The major British effort, however, was concentrated on the Rideau Canal, where work started in 1826. It proved to be expensive, this route chosen deliberately as being safer than the St. Lawrence, by reason of its distance from the American border. So far as the Lachine program was concerned, events moved more slowly, the Assembly as reluctant to make such great commitments from public funds as the Montreal merchants were pressing in their demands. After several changes of plan, the House passed a bill, in May 1821, authorizing the construction as a provincial work. The commission in charge, with John Richardson as chairman, wasted no time. On July 17, the ground was broken at Lachine with due ceremony, before a select audience. A military band was in attendance, to provide lively airs, while the distribution of beef and beer doubtless brought cheer to the laborers and farmers.

Thanks to Richardson's energy, the work went ahead steadily. It was completed in 1825 at a cost of some £115,000. In length, it was nine miles, from Montreal up the side of the Island as far as the still water at the head of the rapids. At waterline, it was 48 feet wide and at the bottom, 28 feet. There was a five-foot depth of water, a towing path, six locks, and a fall of 42 feet.

The Montrealers were almost as impatient over conditions downstream, urging upon the Assembly the need for improvements in the channel, especially in the shallow waters of Lake St.

Peter, a hazard to navigation ever since the days of Jacques Cartier. Decisions came slowly, however, so that it was not until 1830 that approval was given to "An Act to provide for the improvement and enlargement of the Harbor of Montreal." Under its provisions, the local waterfront was removed from the indifferent management of the Board of Trinity House at Quebec, and entrusted for the first time to a separate commission. For three years, its members were busy; the chairman, the Honorable George Moffatt; Jules Quesnel; Captain R. S. Piper, R.E. Wharves were built, slips for Durham boats, a revetment wall— then the money gave out. The Assembly had spent £81,000 and that was the end.

Aside from these disappointments, the river was a picturesque sight. It was, of course, a period of transition—sailing vessels mingled with steamships in the harbor, while the canoes, the bateaux, and the Durham boats were still in use. The timber rafts, too, seemed perpetually on the move, coming down past Montreal on their six-week journey from Hull to Quebec. But the towboats pointed definitely toward the future. Propelled by powerful engines, they drew the barges up from the capital in record time. At the crossing from LaPrairie, there were improvements. John Fergusson, who came up from New York in 1831, reached St. Johns in comfort. There he found two wagons waiting, to convey the passengers and mailbags across country, over a new road still in construction. A rough trip, which the coachman described as "nine miles by water, sir, and the rest by mud," and one which ended with an overnight stop at LaPrairie in a raging gale. But the next morning, he crossed by steamboat in the short space of one hour, apparently unimpeded by the shoals of ice, which late in April were still much in evidence. Add to all this, the fact that there were now ten ferries in operation to and from various parts of the Island, and it is clear that some of the old isolation was disappearing.

Chapter 25

1832–1837

The deepening political crisis. A partisan press. Daniel Tracey. Election riots. "The Massacre of Montreal." Cholera and the immigrants. Municipal incorporation. Jacques Viger. The Champlain and St. Lawrence Railroad.

THE POLITICAL TURMOIL of earlier years grew steadily worse in the thirties, with tragic results for Montreal and the countryside round about. The disagreements over the state of the harbor and the river represented only one phase of a conflict that was as complex as it was deep-seated. To label it solely as racial, would be to simplify without justification, for outside agencies often aggravated domestic misunderstandings. Among Canadians of both languages, moreover, there were moderates as well as extremists, shifting alliances and refusals to compromise. One astute visitor from overseas summed it all up as a case of restless demagogues who "excite wavering minds against the mother country."

Quebec as the capital of the province, was the scene of the formal debates, when each governor in succession, found himself locked in wordy battles with the Assembly. Finance remained the chief stumbling block to a final agreement, although neither party showed itself willing to compromise on any subject, no matter how minor. Dalhousie left the country in 1828, recalled at the earnest behest of the French Canadians, but feted by the English citizens of Montreal. "All that was eminent in the city" attended the public dinner at the Masonic Hall.

Yet the departure of Dalhousie was a turning point in the sense that the British government at last awoke from its lethargic

indifference to the colony. Although a debate in the Commons at
Westminster had no tangible results, the next administrator was
selected with care. Sir James Kempt conducted himself with
such discretion that he was regarded as the only man who had
ever handled the Canadian situation with any degree of success.
Unhappily, he had accepted the office with such reluctance that
he remained for only two years. With the arrival of the well-
meaning but ineffectual Lord Aylmer, the disputes commenced
anew. His term, which ended in 1835, was marked by constant
warfare with Papineau and the Patriotes.

It would be difficult to exaggerate the role of the press in these
years of strife. In Montreal, as in Quebec, all the newspapers
were violently partisan, and their editors and reporters, men
whose pens might have been dipped in acid, so cutting were the
phrases they used to describe their opponents. The *Gazette* and
the *Herald* were true-blue Tories, attacking Papineau with as
much vigor as they brought to their support of the merchants.
They were thus the deadly foes of the French *La Minerve* and
the English *Vindicator,* both of whom unceasingly urged their
readers to back the Patriotes, and show their devotion to the
revolutionary cause by deeds, not words. Both appeared with
their columns in mourning when Lord Aylmer visited the city.

The *Vindicator* was English in a linguistic sense only, for it
was rabidly Irish and automatically anti-British. Its founder and
editor was Daniel Tracey, a doctor of medicine whose interest in
journalism and politics gradually led to a position of prominence
in the Irish Roman Catholic community of Montreal. That such
a man should lavish abuse on the local Tories, was a foregone
conclusion, but his actions led him into trouble with the Legislative Council. Named as a co-defendant was Ludger Duvernay,
the editor of *La Minerve.* Charges of libel landed the two men
in jail at Quebec for some weeks—a high-handed punishment for
which the Montreal members of the Council were responsible,
and which inevitably paved the way for more violence.

What *La Minerve* later called the "Massacre of Montreal" began innocently enough in the spring of 1832, with the resignation
of Mr. Fisher, who, with Papineau, represented the west ward
in the provincial House. This, it should be noted, was one of

the urban constituencies included in a gentleman's agreement, whereby one member bore an English name, and one a French. And since no one had risen to challenge this amiable and informal understanding, the British residents proceeded to nominate Stanley Bagg as their candidate. A satisfactory choice, he appears to have been on the whole, and acceptable to the more moderate French Canadians. As a long-time resident and successful businessman, he was noted for his friendly spirit toward his fellow citizens regardless of language.

At this point, Tracey returned from his sojourn in jail, a hero to those who shared his radical political views. Their delight can be imagined, when he was put up as a candidate in opposition to Bagg, in a neat observance of the letter, if not the spirit, of the existing agreement as to nationality.

Elections in those days were not the well-conducted, strictly supervised affairs of modern times. Rather were they often invitations to violence—especially by reason of their duration, which in this case was about a month. Rowdiness made its appearance at an early stage, and perhaps because of this, the poll was moved from the Presbyterian Church in the Haymarket to the Engine House on St. James Street, near the Bank of Montreal on Place d'Armes. As the race moved ahead to what looked like a neck and neck finish, the supporters of Bagg complained loudly of the lawless behavior of their opponents. Unruly mobs paraded the streets, intimidating the honest voters.

There being no regular civilian police in the employ of the city, the magistrates took action at the end of April. At their order, 150 special constables were sworn in and armed with heavy staves. Most were English or Scottish. But as the balloting continued, so did the violence, worse some days than others, but always sufficient to make the authorities fearful. At last, the disorder reached such a peak that they decided to seek protection from the garrison, then under the command of Colonel Mackintosh. It was further agreed that at all times two members of the Bench should be on duty at the poll.

May 21 dawned peacefully, but by the afternoon the fighting broke out once more. The magistrates intervened personally to rescue a man from being beaten up by the mob. Then a company of troops came over from St. Helen's Island, led by their colonel himself. At three o'clock, William Robertson, a member of the Bench, read the Riot Act, while the soldiers withdrew to the porch of the neighboring church, out of the rain.

When the poll closed at five o'clock, the crowd started to get out of hand, attacking a nearby liquor store. It was this, perhaps, that led some of their number to pick up stones from a pile in use for street paving. They broke windows along St. James Street, and pelted their opponents with the impromptu missiles. Two more magistrates appeared, calling out to the troops to stop the murderous actions of the mob, and in the confusion, various authorities seem to have indicated their wish that the military should advance.

This they did without more ado, still led by Colonel Mackintosh, moving toward the Bank where the fighting was at its worst. At sight of the soldiers, the rioters started to retire in the direction of the Haymarket. Then they turned, once more throwing rocks at the bystanders in their path. The troops fired. At this the troublemakers dispersed quickly, running off along St. James Street. By six o'clock peace had been restored, and in spite of the fears of the magistrates there was no more disorder. But —in this one solitary volley—three Canadians, who had no known connection with the disturbances, were killed.

That evening, while the bodies lay exposed to the view of the curious, a coroner's inquest was held at Place d'Armes. Papineau put in an appearance, insisting that he had taken no part in the election campaign, but questioning Mackintosh as to the identity of the person who had ordered him to fire. By then, the hour was so late that the proceedings were postponed to the next day. When the jury failed to agree on a verdict, the foreman refused to allow the decision to go by a majority vote. Nevertheless, and under pressure from Papineau, the coroner ordered the arrest of the Colonel and his subordinate, Captain Temple. The counsel for the two officers promptly put in an application for a habeas corpus writ, and in due course, the proceedings of the coroner were reviewed by the judges of the Court of King's Bench, assisted by the leaders of the Montreal Bar. At their order, Mackintosh and Temple were released, and when the grand jury in its turn refused to indict them, the legal actions came to an end.

After all this it comes as an anticlimax to find that Dr. Tracey was declared the winner by a narrow margin of three or four dubious voters. But whether fraudulent or not, the victory had a hollow ring. Within a few weeks, the Irishman was dead of cholera, long before he could claim his seat.

For almost immediately after the election, tragedy of another sort struck at Montreal, and the once crowded and noisy streets were almost deserted. Spring came late in 1832, and the dreary wet weather did little to lighten the spirits of the inhabitants. Thus when the first of the immigrant ships docked at Quebec early in June, a bleak reception greeted the newcomers as they journeyed up the river.

The *Carrick*, which had sailed from Dublin with 133 passengers, told a sad story of fifty-nine deaths at sea. Within a day of its arrival, fifteen cases of cholera were reported in the capital. As one vessel after another anchored in the St. Lawrence, the pestilence spread and the mortality rates soared. As usual, the two ports of entry bore the brunt of the disaster.

There had been advance warnings of just such a catastrophe, for the disease had raged in England and Ireland the previous winter. Yet the home authorities permitted the wretched ships to sail, loaded beyond their capacity with half-starved and sickly emigrants. Private funds were hardly sufficient in Canada to deal with anything of this magnitude, and the authorities either would not or could not take action. The results were tragic. Locally, 165 cases were reported on June 20, and another 137 the following day. The deaths for the same dates numbered 88 and 77. So the story went on, until late September, by which time there had been 1904 deaths out of a total of 4420 cases. And although the government station at Grosse Isle below Quebec cared for many of the victims, the damage had already been done. Montreal in the hot summer weather, was crowded with newcomers.

Although much has been written of this visitation, nothing surpasses in vividness, the records of the two famous Strickland sisters, Mrs. Susanna Moodie and Mrs. Catherine Parr Traill.

Each, at different dates, passed through Montreal en route with
her husband to a new home in Upper Canada. Each was disappointed in the town. One noted the dirty streets, and felt "over-
powered by the noisome vapour rising from a deep open fosse
that ran along the street behind the wharf. This ditch seemed
a receptacle for every abomination, sufficient in itself to infect
a whole town with malignant fevers." Her sister understood such
feelings. "The opening of all sewers, in order to purify the place,
and stop the pestilence, rendered the public thoroughfares almost impassable, and loaded the air with intolerable effluvia,
more likely to produce, than stay the course of the plague."

Mrs. Traill commented on the people she met on her walks.
"Every house of public resort was crowded from top to bottom
with emigrants of all ages, English, Irish, and Scotch. The
sounds of riotous merriment that burst from them seemed but
ill-assorted with the haggard, careworn faces of many of the
thoughtless revellers." Both added notes of the awful ravages of
the plague, its devastating effects visible "in the darkened dwellings and mourning habiliments of all classes. An expression of
dejection and anxiety appeared in the faces of the few persons
we encountered . . . In some situations, whole streets had been
depopulated; those that were able fled panic-stricken to the
country villages, while others remained in the bosom of their
families." The death bell tolled constantly, and the display of
ready-made coffins added to the gloom. Posted up everywhere
were the advertisements for funerals "at the cheapest rate and
shortest notice."

Such disasters often breed legends, and so it was at Montreal,
where a man, known variously as "Stephen Ayre" or the "Charcoal Doctor," was believed to possess miraculous powers. No one
knew his origin, although some thought him an American who
had lived long among the Indians. A few considered him de-
ranged, and held him up to ridicule, while others dismissed him
as a quack. Certainly there was nothing attractive in his appearance, his beard unshorn, his attire tattered, and little better than
a mendicant. But those who jeered the most were apt to catch at
any nostrum in time of affliction. "He carried several small
cases suspended from his neck, containing hog's lard, maple

sugar and charcoal, with which he proclaimed he would check the fury of the disease, and exposed himself wherever his assistance was required, without receiving any remuneration . . . Whether from faith in his simple medicines, or that they actually had some effect, but they grew in repute, so that now he was esteemed by some as their guardian angel."

While no one could be sure of the power of this strange character, the fact remains that by the autumn the epidemic had run its course, after a summer which Montrealers were not soon to forget. It proved to be only the forerunner of other such visitations, which in varying severity, were to overrun Canada in the next few years. Cholera or typhus, it mattered little to those who suffered in 1832, 1834, 1847, and to a lesser extent in the '50s.

From the first, the epidemic assumed a political coloration, Lord Aylmer and his entourage being denounced publicly for their culpable negligence. With a like vehemence, the Montreal merchants stood accused of blocking preventive measures that would have led to an effective quarantine. Canada repeatedly turned to the British government for some assurance that the control of the emigrant ships would be tightened at all points of departure. Each country sought to make the other accept financial responsibility for the tremendous costs of relief. Lack of money and poor organization, in fact, were so much in evidence that a local committee in 1834 confined its approbation to the doctors and students of medicine who cared for the sick.

Sandwiched in between these two outbreaks of cholera, came a change in the local government of Montreal, for in June 1832 an Act of Incorporation received royal assent. The charter, effective the following year, divided the town into eight wards, with two representatives to be elected from each. The sixteen-man Council was in turn to elect the mayor, and was endowed, somewhat vaguely, with the same powers possessed by the magistrates in the past.

Such a measure represented a big step forward, and in that spirit, was welcomed by those citizens who had earlier hoped for some local autonomy. But unhappily, disturbed political conditions curtailed its duration. This original charter, operative for four years only, was not renewed in 1836, whereupon the city perforce reverted to the old system of rule by the magistrates.

Meanwhile, the first mayor was duly chosen in the person of Jacques Viger, a man whose interests were as much antiquarian as political. By birth and residence he was a Montrealer and had served with the Voltigeurs during the War of 1812. The collection of historical documents was his great delight, and several of his volumes of manuscript materials and illustrations have been preserved.

It was under Viger's leadership that the Council met on June 8, 1833, to establish by-laws for the future conduct of the municipality. Of the eleven rules, several dealt with the transfer of police powers from the magistrates to the Mayor and Council. The really new regulations dealt chiefly with hygiene or sanitation, and probably represented a laudable desire to reduce the hazards of infection. Thus there was a tightening of the law that forbade "throwing dirty water, ashes, soot or any dirt or filth whatever, or snow or ice from the yards, into any public squares, streets, lanes"; unhealthy or noisome privies must be cleansed, and where none existed, one must be built; proprietors in the suburbs, whose lots adjoined paved or macadamized public squares or streets, "shall scrape, clean up and place in heaps, the dust opposite their premises," the whole to be watered first and completed before ten o'clock every Saturday.

Overriding all other problems, however, the deepening political crisis held the people of Lower Canada in its grip. The fatal by-election in the spring of 1832 was followed later that year by an equally stormy session of the Legislature. Papineau and his followers seemed to go from strength to strength, and although the incessant talk of revolution induced a few moderates to withdraw their support, they could not hope to arrest the drift toward violence. True to its tradition, Montreal was the hotbed of the extremists of both parties. The city, the Island, the villages along the Richelieu—there the Patriotes were at their strongest. And since the staunchest of the Tory merchants were concentrated there also, the prospects were black.

Nor did the House at Quebec accomplish anything constructive in the way of legislation. Financial wrangles filled endless hours to no avail. The salaries of the provincial officials remained unpaid, and all government business came virtually to a standstill. Much of the 1833 session was given over to work on the famous Ninety-Two Resolutions, which in their final form, were presented to the members the following year. Papineau's influence was strong throughout their wordy and bitter clauses, filled as they were with complaints against the oligarchy then in power. But although everyone from the Governor down, served as targets for the criticism, the only real constitutional change lay in the demand for an elective Legislative Council.

The 1834 election took place in October and November, amidst generally disturbed conditions. In the west ward of Montreal the polls were closed arbitrarily before all the votes had been cast, on the plea of dangers from the mob. The Returning Officer issued an official proclamation which referred to the lack of "security to myself or the citizen electors" and declared Louis Papineau and Robert Nelson to be the victors. The opposition candidates, Mr. Walker and Mr. Donellan, protested without avail.

The general anxiety found an echo in the action taken by the Bank of Montreal, in transferring its specie to Quebec, for safekeeping in the Citadel. It evoked an irate proclamation from the Patriotes, headed *Avis aux Canadiens.* "Those of you who have bills of this bank in your possession, and who do not wish to be exposed to the risk of losing their value, wholly or in part, would do well to exchange them as soon as possible for hard coin at the Bank of Montreal." A later bank historian laconically noted that this had little effect.

That the British government was once more goaded into action, reflected the gravity of the hour. Lord Aylmer was recalled, to be succeeded by Lord Gosford, whose arrival in August 1835 might normally have suggested a brighter future for the province. Although a stranger to the Canadians, he was full of good intentions. Conciliation was to be his policy. Moreover, his appointment embodied unusual features. In addition to being Governor General, he headed a special commission appointed to investigate the state of affairs in Lower Canada. Tory Sir Charles Grey and Whig Sir George Gibbs served with him, and all three moved freely among the people as far as possible. But the provincial House studiously ignored their existence, while London had failed to give them any real legal or constitutional power. Thus their report, completed late in 1836, accomplished nothing, since events moved too rapidly for official measures to keep in step. In March of the same year, the Assembly was prorogued, to meet again in September, in a sitting that lasted exactly thirteen days. It was an exercise in futility.

A political crisis of this depth could not fail to damage the prosperity of the country, and nature herself did nothing to improve the situation. A wet summer in 1835 was followed by a poor harvest in 1836, so that rural Canada felt the pinch along with the towns. At Montreal, any hope of further improvement to the harbor or the canals was doomed to disappointment. The bank charters were running out. A severe economic depression in Great Britain and the United States made itself felt along the St. Lawrence. By the spring of 1837, the local business community was in a bad way.

But one event brightened the summer of 1836. This was the opening of the Champlain and St. Lawrence Railroad, the very first in the country, built laboriously through four difficult years at a cost of close to £35,000. Although only fifteen miles long, its run from LaPrairie to St. Johns eased the way for passengers to and from the United States. The rough and tedious drive, in deep mud or through clouds of dust, had often consumed as much as seven hours; now sixty minutes sufficed for these travelers in the new age of steam.

Small wonder then, that three hundred guests should gather on July 21, for the official ceremonies. Animosities were cast aside for the nonce, as Lord Gosford and his fellow commissioners mingled with Papineau and other members of the Assembly. Representatives of the Legislative Council, the garrison, and the merchants joined them, and Peter McGill, the Chairman of the Company acted as host. At 12:30, the little engine, the *Dorchester*, left LaPrairie at the head of two coaches, reserved for the Governor and special guests. The arrival at St. Johns was timed at 1:29. When the other two carriages drew in, horse-drawn for this once, the passengers enjoyed a buffet lunch, enlivened by Madeira, champagne, and speeches. On the return trip, all four coaches were attached to the locomotive.

In the spring of 1837, the British House of Commons at last gave serious attention to the Canadian emergency, Lord John Russell being the sponsor of what are generally known as the Ten Resolutions. Based to a certain extent on the Gosford report, they were largely unfavorable to the French Canadian party, especially in their refusal to make of the Legislative Council, an elected body.

Needless to say, the resentment in Lower Canada was intense, at this latest example of British opposition to the Patriotes. Numerous mass meetings of protest followed, one at St. Ours on the Richelieu in May being attended by some 1200 persons. In almost all cases, Papineau was the central figure. Nor were the moderates silent. Thus, on July 6, a thousand persons, French and English alike, assembled on Place d'Armes to hear the Honorable George Moffatt express disapproval of the Radicals and all their ways.

All in all, it was a sadly divided city that heard of the death of William IV on June 20, and wondered about the nature of his young successor. August 1 was the date chosen for the proclamation of Victoria as queen of British North America—a signal for her ministers to abandon any enforcement of the Ten Resolutions. The new reign was to begin with conciliation, not with repression.

But once again, the decision came too late, for that same month the House was again called into session. After a year of inaction, it was a fruitless attempt and was, in fact, abandoned after a week of argument. The temper of the French Canadian members showed in the manner of their dress, clad in gray *étoffe du pays* so as to excite the ridicule of the British population. A few went so far as to wear country style straw hats and moccasins. Some objected to taking the oath of allegiance to the new sovereign. The occasion was one of sadness, beyond the knowledge of any of those in attendance. For this was the very last meeting, and the end in this form, of the Assembly of Lower Canada.

Chapter 26

1837–1838

Les Fils de la Liberté. *The Doric Club. The loyalty of the Roman Catholic clergy. Sir John Colborne in command. The villages along the Richelieu. Fighting at St. Denis and St. Charles. Lord Durham. The prisoners at Montreal. His solution disavowed by London. His resignation.*

FACED WITH the shifting political quicksands of Lower Canada, any sign of firmness, allied with reason, comes as a relief to the student of today. One event of this nature, late in 1837, had unusual significance, marking as it did the first definite split between the Roman Catholic hierarchy and the Patriotes. As the considered opinion of the Bishop of the district, the *mandement* of October 24 aroused strong feelings, for and against, among all who heard its message.

Jean Jacques Lartigue spoke as a Montrealer to his fellow citizens. Although his was a diocese of recent creation, he knew the local picture thoroughly; ecclesiastically, as auxiliary to the Bishop of Quebec, the city had been his responsibility since 1820. It was his birthplace and the scene of his initiation into the Sulpician Order. In an informal speech to the clergy earlier that summer, he had cautioned against revolt and any violation of the laws of the land. The pastoral letter that followed set forth the moral issues involved, when brothers arrayed themselves against brothers and friends opposed friends. Bidding his flock consider seriously the horrors of civil strife, he reminded them of the blood that would flow in the streets, should violence be invoked.

Almost to a man, the *curés* heeded the advice of their spiritual leader, and by the tone of their sermons, did much to lessen the forces of revolution. Not all the reaction was as favorable. Popular demonstrations and anticlerical diatribes in the Patriote press raised tempers to boiling point. In several parishes men walked out of church when the episcopal admonition was read aloud. The *Marseillaise* was sung in defiance, and unruly crowds paraded the streets of Montreal.

The city was no stranger to such passionate convictions, for the more the revolutionary doctrines caught the fancy of the populace, the larger grew the public gatherings. The dissolution of the Assembly had been the signal for the organization of *Les Fils de la Liberté*. At a meeting on September 5, the would-be rebels chose *"En Avant"* as their motto. Military drill was instituted, and a manifesto on October 1 urged the necessity for preparedness as the first step toward the attainment of independent sovereignty.

The propagation of this dangerous creed did not go unobserved in official circles, where the administration of Lord Gosford had been strengthened in 1835 by the appointment of Sir John Colborne as commander-in-chief. Having served since 1828 as Governor of Upper Canada, the latter was no stranger to the country. He now took personal charge of affairs in the Lower province, with headquarters at first in Sorel and later in Montreal. It was an experience that enabled him in October to write prophetically. "The game which Mr. Papineau is playing cannot be mistaken and we must be prepared to expect that if four or five hundred persons be allowed to parade the streets of Montreal at night, singing revolutionary songs, the excited parties will come in collision."

Later that month the village of St. Charles on the Richelieu was the scene of yet another giant rally. With Dr. Wolfred Nelson in the chair, Papineau and his associates made their usual impassioned speeches. An array of flags flaunted such mottoes as *"The Canadians know how to die but not to surrender"* or *"Long live Papineau and the Elective System."* A tall wooden pole surmounted by a cap of liberty, underlined the revolutionary theme, while a series of seditious resolutions called on the British soldiery to desert.

An assemblage such as this could have been matched anywhere in the Montreal district, and the Sons of Liberty carried on with their drill in full view of the public. Within the city, armed patrols led by the tricolor, marched through the streets after dark. "Peaceable inhabitants . . . felt themselves insecure if they ventured out unarmed after the day closed."

To counteract these open signs of rebellion, an enormous throng of constitutionalists gathered under the lead of Peter McGill to take steps that would insure the "maintenance of good order and protection of law and property." One account placed their number at seven thousand, but at any rate all seem to have concurred in the need for preparedness if civil war was to be averted. Perhaps as a result of their endeavors, the Doric Club made its appearance, a secret society of young Britons, determined to preserve the links with the mother country.

The long-expected clash in the city came to a head on November 6, and whose was the fault, would be a question difficult to answer. It originated in a report that the Sons of Liberty intended to plant a tree of liberty on Place d'Armes. Authority quickly countered with a proclamation, calling on all citizens to refrain from any such demonstration—an appeal as promptly ignored when the Sons mustered in a tavern yard at the corner of St. James and McGill streets. A group of the Doric Club adherents gathered outside, so provocative in their behavior that some two or three hundred of their opponents emerged, armed with sticks, stones, and pistols. The outnumbered English fled, chased along St. James Street to the sound of breaking windows, but when more Club members made their appearance, the tables were turned. They drove the rebels up St. Lawrence Main Street to Dorchester, at which point they dispersed.

Official reaction followed immediately, the Riot Act being read that very afternoon. The First Royals with their artillery and field guns, marched through the streets, led by two French Canadian magistrates, Mr. Desrivières and Mr. John Donegani. But the Doric Club members were still on the prowl, although fairly quiet for a time. At six o'clock, however, they were with difficulty dissuaded from launching an attack on Papineau's house. Later that evening the more zealous of their number turned in their fury on the *Vindicator* office on St. Lambert's Hill, near Fortification Lane, gutting it completely and tossing into the street, the presses, the type, and the paper.

Admittedly this newspaper had made itself particularly obnoxious to the government supporters, its vicious attacks perhaps all the more resented for being in English. But the extent of the destruction alarmed the authorities. The guards were strengthened, and pickets assigned to St. Lawrence Main, Place d'Armes, and the Quebec suburb. The artillery patrolled in some districts, while Griffintown was watched by a body of independent mechanics.

Restrictive measures to curb further outbreaks were rigidly enforced. Colborne established himself in Montreal on November 9, and three days later a proclamation forbade all meetings for the purpose of military drill. Processions and public assemblies fell under a similar ban. Additional volunteer corps were raised, and most of the available troops concentrated in the town. A call went out to Upper Canada for reinforcements.

On November 16, warrants were issued for the arrest of twenty-six of the rebel leaders. Although some were discovered and put in jail, the principals made good their escape—notably Papineau, who fled to Dr. Nelson at St. Denis. On the same day, Lieutenant Ermatinger, with a squad of eighteen cavalrymen, was dispatched to St. Johns to arrest three agents, known to be active opponents of the government. All went well until the return journey, the prisoners being in a wagon, handcuffed, and under guard. But at Longueuil, an ambush led by Bonaventure Viger, caught the troops unawares, the rescue party several hundred strong, riding off with the captives, in high spirits at the success of their first overt act of war.

Knowing that the habitants had massed in force along the Richelieu, the military command in Montreal decided to send out a two-pronged expedition against St. Denis and St. Charles, in the hope that the rebellion might be crushed in the early stages. As a first step, Colonel Gore went down to Sorel by steamer on November 22. Backed by a force of 250 men, he was to arrest Dr. Nelson at St. Denis. It proved to be a fruitless errand, largely because of the weather. The march from Sorel took the troops over roads deep in slush and mud, their clothes alternately soaked and frozen by the sleet and icy rain. The destruction of a bridge forced them into a detour. That night, they plodded along the weary twenty-four miles, and when, next morning, they came within sight of the enemy headquarters, no one could have been less eager for battle. The fighting went on for most of the day, but by four o'clock it was obvious that any further assault would be hopeless. Gore ordered the retreat, leaving behind six of his men dead, and five wounded. Thirteen of the defenders were killed. The return march in freezing temperatures, was if anything, worse than the outward trip.

The series of disasters was by no means over, for on November 23, Captain Weir arrived at Sorel, with dispatches for Gore. Finding the colonel gone, he proceeded to try and catch up with his friends, but because of their change of route, failed to make connections. Instead, he was captured by the rebels and taken to Nelson's house, clad, so the story goes, in a civilian pea jacket over his uniform, and completely unarmed. After an assurance that he would be detained only a few hours, he was sent off in a wagon to St. Charles, guarded by Captain Jalibert. The fact that his arms were bound by a stout strap, but his legs left free, proved his undoing. At the sound of shots, Weir jumped down, hoping that he might regain his regiment. He was cut down as he ran, and murdered. Later, the body was found in the Richelieu, weighted with stones and face down in two feet of water.

Meanwhile, the second section of the attacking army, under Colonel Wetherall, was also in trouble, by reason of the weather and the state of the roads. Having left Chambly at about the same time as Gore's departure from Sorel, the several hundred men stumbled along, exhausted and hardly knowing where they were, and fearful of being caught unawares by a numerically superior enemy. A few miles from St. Charles, a halt could no longer be avoided, and it was there that they heard of Gore's defeat at St. Denis. Wetherall sent back to Chambly for reinforcements, and thus strengthened, prepared to take the offensive.

But the insurgents at St. Charles were few in number, and not too ably led by Thomas Storrow Brown, their self-styled

"General." Some rude entrenchments, hastily thrown up near the church, formed their only protection, and their zest for fighting evaporated quickly under the attack of Wetherall's troops. Only seventy rebels remained at their posts, and an hour sufficed to overcome their opposition. Thirty prisoners were taken back to Montreal by the victors.

With this battle at St. Charles, the rebellion on the Richelieu came to an end. Papineau had remained at St. Hyacinthe, awaiting its outcome. When he heard of the defeat, he took off across country with two or three followers, traveling the isolated back roads until he reached safety at Swanton in Vermont. Brown galloped ahead to St. Denis with the bad news, whereupon there was a general dispersal of the rebels. Nelson was left literally alone, to become a fugitive, hiding in the woods, and with a £500 reward posted for his capture. He was picked up on December 12 by four militiamen and imprisoned at Montreal. The flight of the leaders broke the force of the insurrection, and the countryside returned to its allegiance to the king.

But St. Denis was not allowed to escape scot-free. Gore returned there on November 30, to find that everything was quiet, yet this did not prevent the policy of retribution from being carried out. Nelson's house and distillery were set ablaze, and other property damaged. According to some accounts, the sight of Weir's corpse so infuriated the soldiers, that they sacked and burned by way of reprisal. "Remember Jack Weir" was a slogan not soon forgotten.

Elsewhere the struggle continued, for when word of Gore's repulse traveled northward, the insurgents in the county of the Lake of Two Mountains took the offensive. With the village of St. Eustache as headquarters, they passed under the nominal command of two of the Patriotes' more effective leaders; Amury Girod, a Swiss adventurer, and Dr. Chénier, a local resident whose courage aroused admiration among all who knew him.

In the two or three weeks that followed, neither side had much reason to be proud of its followers. When several hundred of the Patriotes rifled the government stores at the Indian settlement on the Lake, they secured arms and ammunition with which to terrorize the neighborhood. That they also acquired plenty of liquor, put an end to any hopes of discipline.

The troops were slow in leaving Montreal, largely because of exaggerated tales of the rebels' strength. When the two-thousand-man force finally arrived on the scene, Colborne himself assumed the command. The result was, of course, victory at St. Eustache and later at nearby St. Benoit. Chénier was slain, and Girod fled, only to kill himself in desperation so to avoid capture. Burning houses and devastation marked the path of the British—especially reprehensible in one case where the inhabitants surrendered quietly in response to Colborne's promise that their homes would be untouched.

Montreal, by this date, resembled a military camp, with half the male population performing some form of army duty. Troops had been brought in from New Brunswick and Nova Scotia and quantities of stores from Quebec. Martial law was in force, and the banks, before the close of navigation, once more sent their specie to the capital for safety. As to the city itself, the principal entrances "were fortified by strong timber and heavy gates, with loopholes on the sides to command the outer roads; the subordinate streets were also strongly barricaded, so that we had all the appearance of a town in expectation of a siege."

That the insurrection had collapsed with such relative ease, was due in part to its leaders. They were poorly organized and inclined to lean too heavily on the chances of gaining active support from the United States. When this failed to materialize, their enthusiasm vanished. But chiefly, the clergy deserved the credit for its lack of success. No one ever questioned their loyalty, and the Bishop's second *mandement* was more drastic than the first; the sacraments of the church and the rite of Christian burial were denied to unrepentant rebels.

Yet, in general, 1838 marked the start of a long period of political evolution, which, without any immediate cure for ancient animosities, channeled them gradually into fresh directions. Nor was this local, for the Canadas—and particularly the Lower province—were each, in some measure, affected by British opinions and Imperial policies. The news of the rebellion shocked the authorities into a realization that constitutional changes must be set in motion if the colony was to be retained for the Crown.

Thus in January, the constitution of Lower Canada was suspended, as an emergency measure. So that civil affairs might proceed smoothly and without interruption, their administration was vested in the Governor, assisted by a council specially appointed for the purpose. In this manner elections, with all their memories of violence, were put aside, pending further study.

Lord Gosford was recalled in February, and civil responsibilities added to Colborne's military command. The dual office was a temporary expedient, while London pondered the selection of the next representative of the Crown. It was realized that he would need unusual qualities. Not only was he to govern, in this somewhat dictatorial fashion, the province of Lower Canada and supervise the affairs of the sister province, he was also to recommend a new system of administration that might restore peace to the weary colony.

Yet attempts at insurrection were not at an end, nor all the malcontents behind prison bars. From their haven in the United States, Robert Nelson and Dr. Côté announced the setting up of a provisional government for the Republic of Canada. This meant that when they crossed the border in February, they did so as out-and-out rebels, disloyal in a fashion unknown to the earlier leaders. Although few in number, their hopes were high, being nothing less than a siege of Montreal—an ambitious design, easily thwarted by the Mississquoi militia. A hasty retreat compelled a surrender of their weapons to the American military authorities. Nevertheless, their appeal for support in the battle against tyranny gained wide circulation in the province. Published by the city newspapers, its insidious message was spread through the villages along the frontier.

Colborne did not take the threat too seriously, for in April he disbanded the volunteers. Martial law being at an end, Montreal could enjoy such a spectacle as the five hundred men from Glengarry, who paraded through the streets on the first stage of their homeward journey. Pipers headed the procession, which received loud cheers from the onlookers.

But except for the extremists, most people in Canada looked

forward hopefully to the arrival of the new Governor General and Lord High Commissioner. The appointment of such a distinguished man as Lord Durham was no matter of routine, nor had he shown any eagerness to accept the formal invitation, tendered by Lord Melbourne as Prime Minister. It was only the personal solicitation of Queen Victoria that induced a change of heart.

This man of great personal wealth had so far enjoyed a varied career. As John George Lambton, he had represented Durham County in the Commons, where the nature of his views won for him the nickname of "Radical Jack." Elevation to the peerage left him politically unchanged, as evidenced by the fact that the Reform Bill of 1832 was first drafted in his house. Service to the administration in various capacities, led to his resignation, supposedly for ill health, but in reality because of disagreements with those in power. Undercurrents of official mistrust surrounded his mission to Canada—the whole situation being worsened by his own intense pride and independence of spirit.

Such in brief was the nature of the man who stepped ashore at Quebec on May 29. The pomp and circumstance that surrounded Durham had hardly been matched since the days of Frontenac. Twenty-two persons comprised his entourage and mountains of baggage hinted at a brilliant social season. His welcome was almost universal, both parties joining in an acclaim, that if at first a formality, soon won a more secure foundation from his own conduct. For in what seemed at that juncture, an incredible gesture, he refused to reappoint the old Executive Council. So far as he was concerned, there was no room for diehard adherents of either political color. The moderates—and the French Canadians above all—were delighted to see the old clique broken up.

Yet before any constructive measures for the future could be considered, one delicate problem compelled attention. As a result of the rebellion, arrests in Lower Canada had been carried out on a wholesale scale, and the Montreal jail was crowded with political prisoners. Colborne had already released some 326, and of the 161 who remained, he believed 72 to have been deeply implicated. Clearly, these men could not be held indefinitely, but to bring them to trial would be an open bid for trouble.

While a French Canadian jury would undoubtedly find them all innocent, a British panel would impose drastic sentences. Either way, the opposition would be stung to fury.

Careful study led Durham, as though by a miracle, to a solution that satisfied well-nigh everyone concerned. From the long list of prisoners, he selected the names of eight as being the most culpable. These he decided to ask for an admission of guilt, as the basis for a new ordinance. The eight would then be banished to Bermuda, and the rest pardoned. The plan worked perfectly. Charles Buller, the Governor's secretary, came up to Montreal to interview the chosen "culprits" who found his proposition quite acceptable. From their cells they said that if Durham had been in Canada earlier, there would have been no rebellion. For the sake of future peace, they professed themselves as willing to plead guilty.

And so, on June 28, the day of Queen Victoria's coronation, the amnesty was proclaimed. While Dr. Wolfred Nelson and seven associates were readied for exile, Papineau and fifteen others, already safely outside the country, were promised death should they return. The remaining suspects received their freedom. A week later, the eight set off on the first leg of their journey, sailing to Quebec by the *Canadian* at five o'clock in the afternoon. They were a melancholy spectacle, manacled and under a heavy military escort, "the spectators much impressed at their noble bearing and great heart."

Durham's reputation as a peacemaker was now firmly established in Canada. His manner of dealing with the prisoners was as ingenious as it was merciful, and if somewhat arbitrary, no one on this side of the Atlantic, raised any protest. That unhappily, it did not conform to British law, was soon only too clear.

Meanwhile he felt himself free to proceed with other measures close to his heart. Municipal government had long been one of his interests, and in its absence from the province, he discerned some of the reasons for the uprising. The use of troops in cases of purely civil disturbance, seemed particularly unwise. Yet until this date, Montreal and Quebec had possessed nothing better than an old-style "watch." Conditions were deplorable. There-

fore, Durham took steps to provide the cities of Lower Canada
with the first police force worthy of the name.

Montrealers had a chance to meet their Governor General in
July, when the vice-regal party stopped off in the city twice,
on its way to and from Upper Canada. So enthusiastic was their
greeting that Lady Durham wrote to her mother, they outdid
Quebec. The Roman Catholic Bishop and clergy waited upon
her husband, as did a great deputation of prominent citizens.
Their presentation of formal addresses elicited fitting replies, to
the pleasure of all.

Yet this attention to ceremonial did not preclude discussions
of a more serious nature. Durham seized the opportunity to
secure opinions as to the best form of government for the future.
On one occasion, seven of the city's leading businessmen, selected by Peter McGill, heard an outline of his plans. A federation of the British provinces would, in his opinion, be the ideal
solution—that is, Upper and Lower Canada, linked in some way
with New Brunswick and Nova Scotia. This, the merchants opposed without hesitation, their preference being for a simple
union of the two Canadas. Only thus, went their reasoning,
could they achieve the political power so long denied them. The
French Canadians, as might be expected, held precisely opposite views. Under union, they could only be the losers.

But Lower Canada's likes and dislikes counted for very little
in the eyes of certain British politicians, who seized upon some
earlier doubts as to the legality of Durham's arrangement with
the prisoners, and built them up into a slashing attack on the
government in power. Lord Brougham, who led the debate in
the House of Lords, grasped the chance to humiliate the Melbourne regime, through the person of its representative in Canada. When surrender seemed the only alternative to loss of office,
the Prime Minister never hesitated. By disallowing the ordinance,
he managed to escape the full force of the storm.

Lord Durham himself knew nothing of these events at Westminster, until after his return to Quebec. The news broke in
the boldest and most shocking fashion through the medium of the
American newspapers, which reached the capital ahead of the
official dispatches. Their wild reports on the subject of England's

disgraceful indifference to the interests of her colonies, made the issue more serious than it actually was. But given Durham's disposition, resignation appeared to be the only honorable course. Tendered officially on September 25, a busy month ensued, until the sailing date of November 1.

Dispassionate legal opinions of more recent times, consider that the ordinance really was illegal. Although Durham was undoubtedly sincere in believing that the breadth of his powers permitted such a ruling, no one could actually convict men of treason without a trial. He felt keenly the personal hurt inflicted by Melbourne's betrayal, seeing in himself the scapegoat who saved the day for a government with whom he had little sympathy. Canada, in general, backed the Governor General, not only for himself, but nettled by the usual British callousness. Most of the newspapers in the Lower province supported him, *Le Canadien*, for one, letting fly with scathing comments on noble lords who, from their comfortable senatorial chairs, transformed the Canadian question into a plaything.

Burning Lord Brougham in effigy may well have relieved some of the angry feelings in Montreal. Two elaborate transparencies were carried through the streets to Place d'Armes, mounted on a carriage and followed by a coffin, equally transparent, borne by pallbearers with lighted torches. One showed his lordship seated on a jackass, his face toward the animal's tail, the other, His Satanic Majesty, pulling Brougham and Melbourne along by a cord fastened about their necks. Lest anyone fail to grasp the significance, a signpost was labeled ROAD TO HELL.

Durham worked on until the last, apparently oblivious of the mass meetings whose adherents urged him to remain. At his departure, Sir John Colborne resumed the civil authority, and two days later, the second rebellion broke out in Lower Canada—a shock to the local citizenry, less so to the authorities. The summer and autumn had brought rumors of discontent from the border counties. This time, with official preparations well in hand, there was reason to hope that the conflict would be shorter in duration and less serious.

Much of the rebels' planning was carried on from American bases, and could not be completely checked. An early display of their strength came with the attack on the *Henry Brougham*, a steamboat which plied the river with such regularity that it was easy to gauge her exact hour of arrival at any given point. Four hundred men captured her at Beauharnois, and surrounded the manor house in the village. Once again, the habitants gathered at St. Charles and St. Ours, in full expectation of American aid. When this failed to materialize, some went on to Napierville, the headquarters of Robert Nelson, the recently proclaimed President of the Canadian Republic. As they were assembling in their thousands, many armed only with pitchforks and rudely made pikes, orders sent them on to Rouse's Point, where it was said friends as well as weapons awaited them from across the border. Such hopes, of course, proved false, and after several days of confused attacks and retreats the numerically inferior British troops were too much for the insurgents, whose only hope then lay in flight.

Montreal heard the news first on November 4, and in a greatly exaggerated version. With Colborne's arrival, martial law was again invoked, and strong measures taken to combat an insurrection that actually lasted no more than a week. But although the fighting was soon over, the state of alarm persisted, and volunteers kept on the alert.

Meanwhile, arms and ammunition, hidden by the rebels, were being unearthed and brought into the city. Men suspected of disloyal leanings were arrested and lodged in the jail. They were the rank and file, for the leaders, almost without exception, made good their escape. It was a sad affair, this second outbreak, in that the participants were treated with greater severity than in 1837. Although the cells were regarded as overcrowded, precise figures are hard to come by. The Reverend Douglas Borthwick, a prison chaplain, writing forty years later, noted that in November–December 1838, some 698 men awaited trial. Colborne, late in December, reported 753 prisoners, of whom 164 had been released.

What is more certain is the fact that many were found guilty at the courts-martial which began on November 28. At one point, ninety-two stood condemned to death, although only twelve were executed; the remainder were transported to Australia. According to Borthwick, the first executions in the prison yard were greeted with incredulity, the habitants declaring that the men had not been hanged, only their effigies. This led to a change, the gallows being moved to a more public situation over the front gateway of the prison. "A great crowd lined all the streets and avenues leading to the gaol. While very many wept, others positively laughed at the awful spectacle."

Chapter 27

1839–1846

The Durham Report. Lafontaine. Lord Sydenham. Montreal the capital of the United Province. A permanent municipal charter. By-laws. Charles Dickens.

THE POLITICAL PRISONERS, still crowding the Montreal jail at the New Year, represented a tragic phase of the post-rebellion period, that might possibly lead to more trouble. A more constructive outlook, in terms of future understanding, lay in the early return of many of the leaders of the 1837 uprising. Once the Durham ordinance was disallowed, the eight in Bermuda and the voluntary exiles started individually to petition for permission to come back to Canada. And because no legal grounds for their exclusion any longer existed, they rejoined their families and resumed their normal occupations as though nothing had happened. Within a surprisingly short space of time, the community not only accepted their presence, but countenanced their re-entrance into politics.

Outstanding among these men was Louis Hippolyte Lafontaine, who in earlier years had made a name for himself in the Assembly. As a disciple of Papineau, he shared in the constitutional agitation of the 1830s, but parted from the Patriotes finally over their resort to arms. So far as the government was concerned, his moderation came too late. Feeling himself to be a marked man, he went abroad, at first to England and later to France. But when Lafontaine returned to Montreal in the summer of 1838, Colborne had him arrested, this being virtually standard practice for anyone suspected of rebel tendencies. In this instance, the Governor was forced to admit his lack of legal grounds, and the prisoner was released to become in due course one of the country's great statesmen.

Lower Canada at this date, was still in the hands of the Governor and a special council—an emergency device that had proved its worth during the 1837–38 crisis and was now extended to 1842—not, it should be said, from any desire on the part of London to impose such an arbitrary system indefinitely. Rather was it an expedient, designed to maintain the civil administration, pending the constitutional revision to be made along lines recommended by Lord Durham.

The preparation of such a comprehensive document as the famous *Report* was in itself an arduous task for a man, who, like Durham, rarely enjoyed robust health. Some assistance came from his team of "experts" but the main work was his alone. Begun on the voyage home in the autumn of 1838, it was completed in time for presentation to the British Parliament in January 1839—leaving its author so exhausted and ill that the whole Canadian experience is generally believed to have been partially responsible for his death in July 1840.

As a basis for the *Report*, Durham offered a survey of existing conditions in British North America—at considerable length for the Canadas and in briefer form for the three Maritime provinces and Newfoundland. Coupled with this went a study of the present state of discontent; an attempt to discover its underlying causes; an assignment of blame. His remedies were broad in concept, yet detailed and tailored to fit the need. In that they affected the whole country, they were of significance to Montreal.

The heart of the whole matter lay in Durham's views on responsible government, for he saw in the complete separation of the legislative and executive power of the state, an error which freed those in control from the check of representative interests. By this means, Canadians had been deprived of the rights and privileges long enjoyed in England. To restore harmony and introduce "a regularity and vigor hitherto unknown . . . It needs but to follow out consistently the principles of the British Constitution, and introduce into the Government of these great colonies those wise provisions, by which alone the working of the representative system can in any country, be rendered harmonious and efficient."

There followed the recommendation of a union of the two Canadian provinces, thus leaving the way open for the future and broader federation of which he had once dreamed. Moreover, Durham chose legislative rather than federal union, as offering the best hope of relief from the existing confusion. This "would imply a complete incorporation of the Provinces included in it under one legislature, exercising universal and sole legislative authority over all of them, in exactly the same manner as the Parliament legislates alone for the whole of the British Isles." And within this House, he recommended "the principle of giving representation, as near as may be, in proportion to population. I am averse to every plan that has been proposed for giving an equal number of members to the two Provinces, in order to attain the temporary end of outnumbering the French."

If in many ways, the *Report* showed a breadth of vision beyond the normal, the same praise cannot be extended to Durham's views on the French Canadians. Undoubtedly, he was a convert to the anglicizing policy so prevalent in Tory Montreal, and it is for this reason that his work has always been criticized. His original statements were sound. "I expected to find a contest between a government and a people; I found two nations warring in the bosom of a single state; I found a struggle, not of principles, but of races; and I perceived that it would be idle to attempt any amelioration of laws or institutions until we could first succeed in terminating the deadly animosity that now separates the inhabitants of Lower Canada into the hostile division of French and English." In this national feud he pointed out that "every contest is one of French and English in the outset, or becomes so ere it has run its course." Nor could it be otherwise. "No common education has served to remove the differences of origin and language. The associations of youth, the sports of childhood, and the studies by which the character of manhood is modified are distinct and totally different. In Montreal and Quebec there are English schools and French schools; the children in these are accustomed to fight nation against nation, and the quarrels that arise among boys in the streets usually exhibit a division into English on one side, and French on the other."

In such circumstances, Durham felt it was not surprising that feelings grew so strong that "the course of civil government is hopelessly suspended." Then came his assumption. "I entertain no doubts as to the national character which must be given to Lower Canada; it must be that of the British Empire; that of the majority of the population of British America; that of the great race which must, in the lapse of no long period of time, be predominant over the whole North American continent."

Durham had much to say of the absence of "municipal institutions of local self-government, which are the foundation of Anglo-Saxon freedom and civilization; nor is their absence compensated by any thing like the centralization of France." This failure to give the people control over their own affairs he considered to be "one of the main causes of the failure of representative government, and of the bad administration of the country." More specifically: "The want of municipal institutions has been and is most glaringly remarkable in Quebec and Montreal. These cities were incorporated a few years ago by a temporary provincial Act, of which the renewal was rejected in 1836. Since that time, these cities have been without any municipal government; and the disgraceful state of the streets, and the utter absence of lighting, are consequences which arrest the attention of all, and seriously affect the comfort and security of the inhabitants."

The contrast between Canada and the United States, Durham considered to be another cause for discontent. "On the American side, all is activity and bustle . . . On the British side of the line, with the exception of a few favoured spots, where some approach to American prosperity is apparent, all seems waste and desolate . . . The ancient city of Montreal, which is naturally the commercial capital of the Canadas, will not bear the least comparison, in any respect, with Buffalo, which is a creation of yesterday."

For much of the discontent and the backwardness, Durham blamed the British government. The Constitutional Act, he felt to be a vain delusion in its denial of adequate powers to the representative Assembly—a curious sort of blindness, which events were soon to prove, still existed at Westminster. For the Colonial Office and Parliament neither accepted the *Report* in its entirety nor hurried themselves over making any changes. Much of their collective opinion was critical.

Canadians had their first sight of the *Report* in the spring of 1839, and publicity in the newspapers gave it wide circulation. People praised its recommendations or condemned its assumptions, according to their political affiliations—the Tories of Montreal hailing this new Magna Charta as a chance to achieve all their cherished dreams, the French Canadians naturally resentful, and sensing a threat to the preservation of their rights. Yet men such as Lafontaine showed a wisdom beyond the excitement of the hour, realizing that opposition to Union would be useless. No reasonable alternative, in fact, existed; a continuation of government without representation; another rebellion; chaos and nothing gained. Thus he advocated reform by constitutional means, and an acceptance of the situation.

The Union Act, as presented by Lord John Russell in March 1840, was passed by the Imperial Parliament, and became law on July 23 of the same year. In Canada it was to become effective in February 1841. By its terms the Province of Canada was established, and given a Legislative Council, appointed for life, and an elected Assembly, composed of precisely forty-two members from the Lower province and forty-two from the Upper. Although the existing laws of each province were to be maintained, English was to be the only language used in official documents and records.

By this decree, the British authorities went on record as being opposed to Durham's recommendation of representation by population. Many Parliamentarians who were staunch upholders of responsible government in the mother country were unwilling to concede it in full measure to the colonies. What they feared was a conflict of interests for the Governor General, between his duties as a representative of the Crown, and his obligation to follow the advice of his ministers. Hence, for some years, Canada's regime labored under certain built-in disabilities.

In their selection of a new Governor General, who would prepare Canadians for these impending changes, the Cabinet for once avoided the traditional high-ranking officer. Turning to Charles Edward Poulett Thomson, they secured a man of outstanding ability, who was to show himself capable of successful work under these difficult conditions.

Although Poulett Thomson at the time of his appointment was a commoner, he was shortly raised to the peerage as Lord Sydenham, and it is by that title that history has usually known him. He was a businessman and a member of Parliament. As a friend of Durham, he held to a similar liberalism in politics, finding in free trade and tariff reform the cure for the economic ills of the mother country. This, in itself, condemned him sight unseen to the British merchants of Montreal, who thrived on British preferences. And since the French Canadians saw in him another tool of England, the marvel was that his mission turned out so successfully.

The apprehensions faded gradually, as personal contact with Sydenham brought about a better understanding of the man who was to bridge the gulf between the old ways and the new. His first visit to Montreal took place soon after his arrival in the autumn of 1839, and it was there that later, he took the oath of office as Governor General of the United Province of Canada. The date of February 10, 1841, had been carefully chosen, in a delightful blend of romance and politics. The fiftieth anniversary of the Constitutional Act was also the first anniversary of Queen Victoria's wedding. An official gathering of the leading citizens marked the occasion; all, in the words of the proclamation, were urged to be as united in sentiment as now in name.

The preceding months had brought many questions and problems, for the political developments impinged upon most aspects of provincial life. One of the first, which provoked considerable heat, was the location of the capital. In a young country such as Canada suitable accommodation was not easily come by. No mere village could hope to meet the requirements of the united legislature and its accompanying officials. Quebec and Toronto, because of the past, naturally hoped for the honor. Their elimination came about because of distance from the center of the new political unit. This decision left Montreal and Kingston in the running, with official opinion tending to favor the Upper province.

Thus Kingston became the capital and the scene of the first session of the united Legislature on June 14, 1841. It was an historic moment and an honor for the town that had been Cataraqui and Fort Frontenac. Yet, by 1843, the discussion over the seat of government once more came into the open. Many of the members professed dissatisfaction over their earlier choice. Even then there was hesitation over Montreal, largely because of Upper Canada's reluctance to cede the glory to what had been the Lower province. Logically, there could have been no other choice, for it was the wealthiest and the largest city in the country. The British government very sensibly, declined the position of umpire, except on advice from the Assembly itself. And so in November, the vote was taken, upon motion of Robert Baldwin, seconded by Louis Lafontaine, and carried 51–27, favor of the move.

Early in 1844, the government established its headquarters in the city, well in advance of the next session. Great preparations were already under way. Fortunately, in the recently built St. Ann's Market, an "eligible" building was available. Standing near the foot of McGill Street, it was greatly admired architecturally, and after alterations, made a tolerably commodious Parliament House. The butchers, the fishmongers, the poulterers, the market gardeners, and the dealers in grain—they were all turned out of their quarters in the 342 foot long structure. Two fine halls at either side, provided ample accommodation for the Assembly and the Council; in the former, five hundred spectators could be seated in the galleries.

There were other developments. The Château de Ramezay on Notre Dame Street, as the residence of the governors, had recently been the subject of complaints. Although repaired and partially modernized in the 1820s, its state apartments no longer met the needs of the greater social life of the town. Besides, it was uncomfortable to live in. So the Château was converted into government offices, and another vice-regal residence provided at Monklands. This was a small but comfortable country house, fairly high up on the western slopes of Mount Royal, and separated from the old part of the city by a three-mile carriage drive.

Unhappily, Sydenham did not live to see this move to Montreal, nor did his successor, Sir Charles Bagot. In quick succession, and after short periods of office, both men died before the completion of their tasks. Nor did the tragedy end there, for Lord Metcalfe, the first official tenant of Monklands, went home in 1845 to an almost immediate death.

But wherever the new Parliament held its sessions, problems crowded in upon it. There were so many crosscurrents and unknown factors; so many members strangers to their companions; each province wondering about the intentions of the other; the French and the English mutually suspicious; the extremists so different from the moderate Reformers and both so resolute against the Tories. Yet as one election followed another some faint signs of a pattern made their appearance, and alignments that held out some hope of future stability.

One of the most promising omens lay in the understanding that slowly came into existence between the leaders of the moderate Reformers in the two sections of the country. Robert Baldwin of Toronto and Louis Lafontaine cautiously groped their way toward a common ground. Out of this grew a firm political alliance and a personal friendship which led, inescapably, to the highest office in the land. The first fruits showed as early as the 1841 elections, for when Lafontaine met defeat in his old riding of Terrebonne, a safe seat was found for him as member for York.

Francis Hincks played an active role in the promotion of this French-English entente. The Irish-born Torontonian, while a member of Parliament, had served as Inspector General, an office in which his remarkable financial abilities won great praise. But disagreements with Metcalfe led to his temporary withdrawal from politics, and by 1844, he was settled in Montreal, as the editor of the *Pilot*, a new Reform paper which added variety to the local scene.

There were other absorbing matters to occupy the corporate mind. Montreal took a great step forward in 1840 when Sydenham and his special Council granted a second charter to the city, a successor to the original document canceled four years earlier.

With an official salutation to the mayor, aldermen, and citizens (who now numbered about 40,000), six wards were established, each to be represented by three aldermen. The following year brought a redistribution, in tribute to the municipal growth. Three city wards in future, each elected three councilors, and six suburban equivalents returned two representatives each, making a Council of twenty-two.

The first Council, as named by Sydenham, served until December 1842. The Honorable Peter McGill became mayor, and associated with him were: Jules Quesnel, Adam Ferrier, C. S. Rodier, J. G. McKenzie, C. S. DeBleury, J. M. Tobin, Olivier Berthelot, F. Bruneau, Hippolyte Guy, John Donegani, Charles Tate, J. W. Dunscomb, Thomas Philipps, Colin Campbell, Stanley Bagg, Archibald Hume, D. Handside, and William Molson. The appointment of city clerk went to J. P. Sexton. Thereafter the citizens elected the councilors, who, in turn, chose the mayor from their own ranks. Joseph Bourret succeeded to the chief office in 1843.

Theirs was a heavy task, for they inherited little from the short municipal past—a motto *concordia salus* and a coat of arms, symbolic of the varied racial origins of the citizens. The beaver, the *fleur de lis*, the rose, the thistle, and the shamrock still embellish the city today.

The councilors showed no lack of industry, for in November 1842 the by-laws of the new corporation appeared, an impressive collection that filled no less than 136 pages of a neatly printed book. The preface was engaging in its modesty. "The recent existence of our Municipal Corporation, the multiplicity of subjects for which entirely new regulations have been framed, the rapid increase of the population of the city and extension of its limits, render it impossible to judge of the propriety and fitness of all the following By-Laws, until a much longer experience shall have sufficiently tested them."

Quantitatively, Public Markets headed the list with eighty-two paragraphs, followed closely by rules for the Fire Department, Carriages for Hire, and Assessments. Much briefer treatment was accorded to such matters as Common Sewers and Drains, Sports, Chimney Duty, Storing of Gunpowder, the Weight and Quality of Bread. Hackney coaches, omnibuses, carriages or cabs, when driven at night, "unless it be moonlight" must carry in some conspicuous place, two well-lighted lamps with glass fronts and sides. Property was assessed at one shilling in the pound, on the yearly value. Taxes were levied, not only on wholesale and retail merchants, but on taverns, pawnbrokers, hawkers, dogs, theaters, exhibitions of wild beasts, and a host of other items. "No person shall swim or bathe in the river opposite or adjacent to the said city, or in the canal, or other waters adjacent to any of the bridges or avenues leading into the city, so as to be exposed to the view of the inhabitants." Football was taboo on any public thoroughfare, as well as the game commonly called shinty, or the throwing of stones or snowballs. "No person shall slide with a sled, train, traineau, or skate on any street."

The Fire Department was placed on a businesslike basis. There was in future, to be an inspector, whose salary was set at £300; he was authorized to look over all houses between the hours of ten and six, and required to keep the engines and equipment in good order. As assistants, he was to have a superintendent, a chief engineer, one or more overseers of chimney sweeping, together with a captain and lieutenant for each company of twenty or twenty-five men. Although these last served voluntarily until 1863, there were awards for attendance at fires; 10/ for a captain; 7/6 for a lieutenant; 5/ for the men.

Fire apparently was of paramount importance, for in a queer sort of transfer the police force created during Durham's administration became a "Fire Society." The office of police superintendent was abolished. Its strength as listed, included 102 men, four mounted patrols, six sergeants, and six corporals under the command of four officers. The expense, borne by the provincial government until 1851, amounted to £6000 a year. In times of emergency, the presence of the garrison continued to give some sense of protection and stability.

All things considered, Montreal in the early forties, was a prosperous city, its native spirit of enterprise boosted by the presence of the government offices as well as by the financial buoyancy of Great Britain and the United States. The constitutional changes, the progressive policies and generally effective program of the moderate Reformers—these gave rise to some hopes for a brighter national future.

Although Canadians and British alike were for many years to question the value of the ties of empire, relations with the United States usually seemed of greater immediacy. Geography alone, insured this, particularly in the case of Montreal. To compensate for the dangers of armed invasion in wartime, there was the pleasant neighborly coming and going across the border in days of peace. So greatly admired was the get-up-and-go spirit of the Yankees that it served as a model for the local merchants, if Dr. Bigsby is to be believed.

"Its inhabitants have always, as the Americans say, been on the commercial 'stampedo.' They are enterprising and active, pushing their merchandise into the most remote wildernesses, where there is the chance of a market. Montreal does not wear the heavy, sleepy air of Quebec. The social easygoing Canadian is suffering from a great invasion of American and British, who, it is to be confessed, have possessed themselves of the bulk of the upper-country trade."

American visitors were, in fact, surprisingly numerous. Business transactions undoubtedly brought many of them to Montreal. Others traveled solely for pleasure, and in order to avoid the stifling heat of the southern summers. Some, by taking advantage of the favorable tariffs, anticipated the modern tourists' zest for shopping in a foreign land. Having inspected the falls at Niagara and the fortifications at Quebec, they ordered "their stock of apparel for the year at Montreal, thus evading the frontier duty." Small wonder that the hotels were unusually fine— worthy of mention in the same breath as those of New York.

This was the city that greeted Charles Dickens in May 1842 during the course of one of his North American tours. After the usual fashion, he traveled down from Niagara Falls by steamboat and stagecoach, amazed by the floating timber rafts. They "looked like a nautical street." Montreal he considered to be pleasantly situated, and possessed of "a great variety of very good shops . . . the town is full of life and bustle . . . all the rides in the vicinity made doubly interesting by the bursting out of spring, which is here so rapid."

Morning strolls along the quays revealed the immigrants, "grouped in hundreds on the public wharfs, about their chests and boxes." Upon his return from a short visit to Quebec, the ship was crowded with them, their beds spread out between decks and blocking the passage. They were nearly all English, and had had a long winter passage out. "But it was wonderful to see how clean the children had been kept, and how untiring in their love and self-denial all the poor parents were."

Dickens stayed at Rasco's Hotel, which in spite of all claims to the contrary, was considered to be the chief resort of fashionable high life. He came at the invitation of the officers of the Coldstream Guards to take part in some amateur theatricals, then all the rage. Thus at the Theatre Royal, on Wednesday evening, May 25, three plays were performed: *Roland for an Oliver; Two O'clock in the Morning; Deaf as a Post.* Mr. Charles Dickens was billed as the stage manager, and afterwards, in a letter to a friend, he described his experience:

"The play came off last night. The audience, between 500 and 600 strong, were invited as to a party; a regular table with refreshments being spread in the lobby and saloon. We had the band of the 23rd (one of the best in the service) in the orchestra, the theatre was lighted with gas, the scenery was excellent, and the properties were all brought from private homes. Sir Charles Bagot, Sir Richard Jackson, and their staffs, were present; and as the military portion of the audience were all in full uniform, it was really a splendid scene."

Meanwhile, the merchants had taken advantage of the more favorable political climate to urge upon the government the need for an extensive program of public works. As in the past, they placed particular emphasis on the construction of canals so as to render the St. Lawrence more readily navigable from Montreal up to the Great Lakes.

A legacy of pre-Union days existed in the form of financial difficulties. Whereas the Assembly at Quebec had consistently refused to embark on costly schemes of this nature, the reverse was true of Upper Canada. An overambitious building schedule, chiefly of canals, had virtually bankrupted the province, at a time when Lower Canada remained largely free of public debt.

This was the situation that faced Sydenham, and the reason why he made strenuous efforts to secure an Imperial loan. Only when London came through with £1,500,000, payable in installments, was it possible to embark on fresh projects.

By 1843, an ambitious chain of waterways was in the making, designed to open the way for shipping from Lake Huron, through Montreal to the sea. By 1848, six new canals had been completed, and at Lachine, the existing structure enlarged to accommodate the greater size of modern vessels. As opened to traffic in 1846, this extended down to the city for a distance of eight and a half miles, its four locks overcoming a drop of forty-two feet.

What lent urgency to this program of canal building was the progress being made across the border, where "Yankee" push threatened to divert the profitable carrying trade away from Montreal. Once the Erie Canal was completed, vessels could proceed directly, from a point near Buffalo, down the Mohawk-Hudson route to New York. When it came to a comparison between that great year-round seaport and the local facilities, there was never much doubt as to the winner. Yet Montreal never ceased to give battle.

To make matters worse, there was trouble brewing in Britain. As early as 1841, the agitation for the repeal of the Corn Laws was recognized as a threat to Canadian grain, which still entered the mother country at extremely low preferential rates. When economic conditions in the British Isles grew worse, "free trade" became a popular slogan. The repeal as finally enacted in 1846, was a national necessity which dealt a heavy blow to the local mercantile community.

Thus Montreal, with the rest of the country, entered upon a period of depression when world competition endangered the profitable grain trade. To be a colony no longer seemed the perfect way of life. So, at least, some of the businessmen felt as they looked with envy upon their American neighbors. Independence of the British connection might be the solution to Canadian troubles.

Chapter 28

1846–1849

*Depression years. Ship fever. The Irish immigrants. Lord Elgin.
The Rebellion Losses Bill. Unruly mobs. The burning of the Parliament Building. Riots. Annexation manifesto. No longer the
capital.*

MONTREAL PREPARED, late in January 1847, to welcome a new
Governor General. The circumstances were not of the happiest,
for the depression which followed the repeal of the Corn Laws
was one of the worst ever experienced, and the palliatives slow
in making their appearance. The political prospects were similarly
bleak, the Imperial reluctance to permit a truly responsible form
of government, leading inescapably to frustration and public disputes. Given such handicaps, the Union could never hope to
function harmoniously.

There had been so many governors in the past, each convinced
of the rightness of his own opinions, but few great enough in
stature to meet the challenge of his office. Thus if Montreal
reserved judgment in the case of Lord Elgin, it was because of
other unhappy experiences. The man who has since gained the
accolade of history, was personally unknown to the Canadians
who awaited his arrival.

Although James Bruce, eighth Earl of Elgin and Kincardine,
came of a distinguished family, his personal wealth was modest—
largely because of his father's acquisition of the Elgin Marbles,
now in the British Museum. Several years as Governor of Jamaica,
took the place of the political career he might have enjoyed as
a commoner, and provided administrative experience that was to
be useful in Canada. His second marriage was of particular

interest to this country, for Lady Mary Louisa Lambton was the daughter of the late Lord Durham, and the niece of Lord Grey, the current Secretary of the Colonial Office.

Elgin's personal attributes were of a quality to match this impeccable background. A moderate Tory, he regarded himself as the political heir of Durham. He shared the older man's belief in the principle of responsible government, and saw in its practical application, a remedy for the Canadian ills. Happily for this country, Lord Grey held similar views, leaving Elgin free to preside over the transition with what amounted to genius. That, in so doing, he aroused considerable opposition, was perhaps not surprising—particularly in Montreal. Nor were all his troubles political.

As it happens, a before-and-after picture of the city exists—in the first instance, from the pen of Colonel Sleigh, who during the summer of 1846, saw Montreal as "occupying a position of vast commercial importance . . . Shipping of every size and nation, crowds of steamers, American and English, bateaus, canoes, timber-rafts, schooners in full sail, all covered the surface of the river; and the city, with its dark stone buildings and iron shutters, gave an impression of ancient grandeur."

He was, perhaps, a gay fellow, this visitor from overseas, who considered that Great St. James Street would reflect credit on London. "Handsome equipages, with liveried servants, dash along the streets, while well-dressed ladies, à la Parisienne, give an air to the favourite promenades of a fashionable and opulent people." Donegani's Hotel on Notre Dame Street, he rated as a magnificent establishment. "The furniture was superb, and the attendance, all French waiters, most admirable, while the cuisine was of the most *recherché* character . . . Indeed, in Montreal, you cannot fancy you are in America."

The contrast with conditions as they were twelve months later could not have been more marked. An outbreak of ship fever or typhus in 1847 introduced Montreal to another season of horror, and caused the deaths of thousands of unfortunate immigrants. Political and economic problems were, of necessity, pushed aside, their solution deferred by the sheer magnitude of the human tragedy.

Canada by this date was accustomed to the annual migration from the British Isles; 28,086 persons in 1841; 44,374 in 1842; 21,727 in 1843. Three years later, their number had climbed to 32,153. Each summer, the ports of Quebec and Montreal were busy with newcomers, the Immigrant Aid Societies assisting the officials in their reception and after-care. Although some traveled independently, the majority, as in the past, were paupers, and Upper Canada remained the favorite destination. In general, they were made welcome, a 5/ head tax providing funds for transportation, medical care and the relief of the indigent.

As might be expected, the Irish, whenever possible, headed for the United States, preferring its republicanism to the hated British domination. Of those who came to Canada, many settled in Montreal, forming a community that by 1844 comprised 9595 persons. Some belonged to the professional class—priests, doctors, lawyers, teachers. Others were laborers. Few had much reason to love the English.

That the Irish should detest their overlords, was virtually a chronic condition. At the best of times theirs was a country of appalling poverty, and whenever the potato crop failed there was hunger. Thus when 1845–46 brought a blight of such unprecedented severity that the plants rotted in the ground, the people literally starved to death in their homes. Those fortunate enough to survive, turned to emigration as their only salvation.

The advance guard made their way up the St. Lawrence in the summer of 1846, many of them destitute, but apparently healthy. Some, who arrived at the close of navigation, became public charges during the cold weather that followed. Others, departing from custom, migrated to the United States during the winter months, the extremity of their desperation urging them overseas at this inclement season. Anger led Congress to take speedy action. By March, two new Passenger Acts had received approval, increasing the fares and restricting the numbers of passengers per vessel.

The British colonies in North America could, of course, impose no such controls. All emigrants from the mother country must be admitted. Yet some of the authorities in Canada, aware of conditions overseas, watched with apprehension the approach

of spring. Destitution, bad health, dirty and overcrowded ships—
these were the breeding grounds of typhus. The quarantine
station at Grosse Isle, set up to handle the cholera of the 1830s,
was still functioning but hampered by official complacency.
When its Medical Officer asked for £3000, he received £300.

But events soon put a stop to any hope of immunity. The first
ship of the season docked at Quebec on May 17, and within a
week the disaster made itself felt. Out of 241 passengers, there
were eighty-four cases of fever, while nine persons had died at
sea. Almost every day saw the arrival of more vessels, all with
typhus on board. Anchored offshore at Grosse Isle, their number
grew so rapidly that the hospital could no longer care for the
afflicted.

However, this was mild compared to what was happening at
Montreal, as desperate officials on the lower river, strove to get
the immigrants off their hands, before the outwardly healthy
could sicken and die. All through June and July, in exceptionally
hot weather, they poured into the local port, taxing its normal
facilities far beyond capacity. The larger the crowds at Grosse
Isle, the greater the speed with which they were dispatched.

To meet the emergency, a Board of Health was set up whose
rules, on paper, seemed reasonable enough. Its members proposed a closure of the overcrowded lodginghouses, and recommended that no immigrants be permitted to land in the center
of the city. But because a Board of this nature lacked power
to enforce its regulations, the sick and the well together continued as before to arrive at the stone wharves, under the gaze of
ghoulish sightseers. Often within a single twenty-four-hour period, as many as two thousand persons came ashore, some so
far gone in their agony that they lay helpless in the open, until
death came as a release.

The theory was that these people, being in transit, would remain at Montreal for a few hours at the most. In practice, this
was impossible because of the shortage of vessels for the Upper
Canada run. And so they stayed on, often for days, awaiting
transportation that for many came too late, living in open sheds
along the riverbank at Point St. Charles. The location of these
shelters provoked much comment. When the more responsible

citizens suggested a transfer to Boucherville Island, the Board of Health ruled this out as impractical. The Point was thus a compromise, being above both the town and the Lachine Canal. To those who feared a contamination of the water supply, the municipal authorities pointed out that everyone was already drinking the filth produced by fifty thousand inhabitants. Hence it seemed unlikely that the ablutions of a few thousand more, would increase the evil!

The fever victims, in addition to all the other loathsome symptoms, gave off a stench that was most offensive. Multiplied several thousand times over, the most devoted Christian could hardly avoid drawing away in disgust. But still the volunteers came forward, saintly characters who cared for the sick and the dying, only to give up their own lives in the process. Attendance at the sheds was virtually a death sentence. Elgin had nothing but praise for the exemplary conduct of the Roman Catholic priests and Protestant clergy. As for the Sisters, no one could have rendered more devoted service, and several of the Grey Nuns succumbed as a result of their nursing.

Although cooler weather gave some grounds for hoping that the crisis was past, one death late in the season was particularly tragic. Mr. Mills, in his capacity as mayor, had done much for the plague-stricken strangers all summer. It was due to his firmness and philanthropy that the townspeople had not succeeded in tossing the sheds into the river. So wrote Lord Elgin of this estimable man, who had fallen a victim to his own zeal.

No one in the end, could say exactly what the mortality had been. In that summer of 1847, over 100,000 persons left the British Isles. By the close of the year, it was estimated that 20,000 had died in Canada; some 5000 at Grosse Isle, the others at Quebec, Montreal, Kingston, and Toronto.

Over and above the heartaches and the suffering, there remained the problem of the costs, both in public funds and private charity. At the outset, Lord Elgin sanctioned a considerable outlay on medical aid and food, for as he reported to Grey, the provincial authorities were doing everything possible to mitigate the situation. By mid-summer, he noted that five or six hundred orphans remained at Montreal, for whose sustenance, some provision must be made. In December he pointed out that many of the sick, then in hospitals, would have to remain there all winter. The towns bore the brunt of the responsibility, for the farmers in the country districts closed their doors to all newcomers suspected of harboring disease. The United States was equally inhospitable in its refusal to allow the sickly and the paupers to cross the border.

Thus Elgin urged the Imperial government to reimburse Canada for the money spent in caring for the immigrants. The provincial exchequer was in a deplorable state, its solvency secured temporarily by loans from the Bank of Montreal. Yet some months elapsed before the Colonial Office could be induced to change its mind. Finally in the spring of 1848, and after much vice-regal nudging, London agreed to meet all the 1847 charges. Cautions against lavish expenditures and admonitions as to the virtues of economy, terminated the financial crisis.

Meanwhile, under Elgin's calm guidance, the normal processes of government proceeded in an orderly fashion, his neutrality as between one party and another, a clear proof of his adherence to the doctrine of ministerial responsibility and the rule of the majority in the Legislature. The result was that when the electors in December 1847, turned against the old standbys of the Metcalfe regime, Baldwin and Lafontaine found themselves called upon to assume office. It was a momentous occasion, and a great stride forward in Canadian life. Men who ten years earlier had been numbered among the rebels, now became the advisers of the Governor General.

One person who showed no understanding of what had happened was Papineau. Although Lafontaine had secured permission for his return as early as 1843, it was only now that he took advantage of the privilege. Election to the Assembly followed, and inevitably all the old bitterness was raked out and stirred to life. Elgin he opposed, and Lafontaine he hated, calling him a traitor in speech after speech. He had learned nothing in exile, and the other Reformers feared him.

The legislative session of 1849 which extended from January 18 to May 30, opened with two official announcements, read by Lord Elgin in both French and English. In the first instance, he reported that the Imperial Parliament had repealed the clause in the Act of Union which declared English to be the only official language; in the second, he affirmed the Queen's purpose to exercise the quality of mercy in favor of all persons still liable to penal consequences for political offenses in 1837–38.

During the weeks that followed, the House went about its business with extraordinary speed and efficiency. No less than 190 Acts were passed by the members, in readiness for the royal assent. One of these in particular, the Act of Indemnification— usually known as the Rebellion Losses Bill—held tremendous constitutional significance.

The government had long intended to make reparation to the persons in both provinces who had suffered from the acts of the rebels. Even before the Union, the Legislature of Upper Canada had incorporated the plan into a Bill, setting the ceiling for damages at £40,000. This action, subsequently confirmed by the new Parliament, aroused protests in Lower Canada. Why favor one section of the country at the expense of the other?

In both cases, it was difficult to assess the damages inflicted by the troops in suppressing the outbreaks. Part of the property destroyed belonged to persons actually in arms against authority; for this, no compensation could be allowed. In other instances, when the owners were loyal adherents of Her Majesty, payment should obviously be made. There remained in between all those of questionable intent, who if not avowed rebels, had been identified in some way with the disaffected groups. The precise division between loyalty and treason was not easily determined.

It was for this reason that in 1845 a commission was appointed to conduct inquiries that might lead to a distinction between the innocent and the guilty, as well as to an estimate of the claims. Its findings were sufficiently startling, since the alleged losses totaled £240,000.

While further study was still in progress, Lafontaine determined to present the Bill as planned, although with some limitation as to the amount. On March 1, it passed easily, with a majority of 47–18. But Elgin wrote to Grey of the bad feeling everywhere, of loyalists against rebels, British opposed to French and the two provinces at odds. For the dilemma was now his. Vice-regal sanction of the measure would almost certainly result in mischief—if the worst came to the worst, it could be repaired by his own sacrifice.

As the old battles were fought all over again, Montreal resounded with cries of "No pay for the rebels," from those who considered the safety of the country to be at stake. Elgin, meanwhile, in the quiet of Monklands, deliberated as to his duty. The situation was a severe test of his faith in responsible government, yet there was little doubt as to where his duty lay. In the end, it was all resolved suddenly, because of the need for approval of other legislation. The Rebellion Losses Bill became law on the afternoon of April 25, 1849.

As word spread that the Governor was on his way into town, the "loyalist" opponents of the Bill converged on the Parliament Building. Thus when the official party entered the Chamber, it was to find the galleries packed with spectators, some of whom had been in their places for several hours. In this tense, almost hostile atmosphere, the proceedings went ahead in the usual dignified fashion, the silence unbroken until the title of the contentious item was read. Elgin's formal words of assent, given without hesitation, served as a signal for action.

At once there was an intentionally noisy exodus of the onlookers. The crowd outside was obviously in an ugly mood. Half an hour later, His Excellency emerged, to be greeted by a chorus of catcalls and groans. Eggs pelted down upon him, some of them thoroughly rotten, while stones and clubs hurled into the air added a note of danger to the attack. His open landau waiting nearby offered no protection, and its panels and upholstery were soon spattered with filth. At least one egg caught Elgin squarely in the face, and it was only the speed of the horses that got him away safely.

The mob, as he noted later, was by no means numerous—a small knot of individuals, mostly of a respectable class in society, who had come well prepared with missiles. After such rough handling, it was unlikely that the action of the St. Andrew's Society caused him much surprise. Three days later, at a special meeting, a resolution was passed, erasing his name as a patron and honorary member of the organization.

Much had happened in the interval. Within an hour of the flight to Monklands, printed notices appeared, summoning all citizens to a mass meeting on the Champ de Mars. By eight o'clock, an immense number of persons had gathered there, drinking in the inflammatory speeches and applauding the strongly worded resolutions. From talk to action proved to be a very short step. Amid loud cries of "To the Parliament Building," the unruly crew moved off, many carrying lighted torches. A cynical eyewitness noted the participation of many of Montreal's most worthy citizens.

All this time, the Assembly remained in session, its members apparently unaware of the riotous behavior in the streets. It was not until a shower of stones crashed in through the windows that they realized their danger. Their retreat came none too soon, for a dozen persons burst unceremoniously into the Chamber, one of whom, a man named Courtney, seated himself in the Speaker's chair and muttered something about the dissolution of Parliament. With that, the destruction started, broken furniture tossed about, and sticks thrown up to smash the glass globes of the out-of-reach chandeliers. Piles of papers were set alight and the gas pipes cut. An explosion followed, and then wild shouts of "Fire." The blaze spread so rapidly that within half an hour the entire structure was enveloped in a sheet of flames. No attempt was made to save the building, and indeed, the fire engines were prevented from approaching.

Only two articles were saved from the ruins. One was the silver gilt mace. Seven feet in height, it had cost £600 in 1846. The other was a portrait of Queen Victoria, which only the previous year had been brought over from London to hang above the Speaker's chair. This relic of Montreal's stormy past now hangs at the entrance to the Senate Chamber in Ottawa.

But the night of horror was not yet at an end, for the mob moved on to the house of Lafontaine, the author of the hateful Bill. Fortunately, the place was empty, for although it was not completely destroyed, the interior was ransacked. Doors were forced open and windows smashed. While some of the looters

were busy, breaking china and mirrors, others opened the wine
vaults. Out of the windows went the furniture; mahogany chairs
and tables, and bedsteads of the most costly and splendid description. Even the feather mattresses were ripped apart, and
their contents strewn in the yard.

For the rest of the week, the town remained in a state of excitement. No business was transacted. Fears for the safety of Elgin
at Monklands led to a doubling of the guards. On April 26, when
some twenty citizens were arrested on charges of arson and
sedition, a horde of three thousand persons marched along with
them toward the prison. There was talk of violence and no one
doubted there would be fighting in the streets. Rumor said the
jail was to be attacked, and the accused men rescued.

Although this, indeed, did prove to be idle gossip, trouble
broke out afresh on the following Monday. On that day, the
Assembly, in temporary session at Bonsecours Market and under
police protection, adopted an address of loyalty to the Queen,
abhorring the current outrages and approving the just and impartial conduct of Lord Elgin. When a delegation of members
proceeded to the Château de Ramezay, where the Governor
General awaited them, the crowd got so out of hand that it became necessary to read the Riot Act and clear the street with
bayonets. Elgin himself, though unhurt, was stoned as he set off
for Monklands. His brother, less fortunate, was injured as
were several of the escort. The drive home was a nightmare, the
rabble in hot pursuit having grabbed cabs, caleches and anything on wheels, and shrieking "Down with the governor general."

In his private letters to Lord Grey, Elgin could express himself
more freely than in Canada, where his official position demanded neutrality. He was especially bitter on the subject of
Montreal and its anarchical elements. "The whole row is the
work of the Orange Societies, backed by the commercial men
who desire annexation, and the political leaders who want place
. . . All French Canada is with us, but the great object is to keep
them quiet, and to prevent a collison between the races . . . Montreal is rotten to the core, and if all Canada be like it, the sooner
we have done with it, the better."

His criticism of the police force was equally trenchant. So inadequate in numbers were the men, that they stood powerless before the rioters. The ministry, in his opinion, should have made better provision for this city of 50,000 inhabitants. A paltry two policemen represented the government and seventy the municipal Corporation. It was largely due to the presence of a thousand special constables, armed with pistols and cutlasses, that complete chaos had been prevented.

Elgin himself remained quietly in seclusion, fearful that his presence in the city would reawaken the forces of disaster. It was an anxious period, with family worries added to the problems of state. For shortly after the riot, Lady Elgin gave birth to a son at Monklands.

But though posterity has agreed that this withdrawal was wise, to many of his contemporaries, Elgin's behavior appeared cowardly. Formal petitions were numerous, drawn up by members of the British community and all beseeching Her Majesty to recall this unworthy representative of the Crown. They met with no encouragement. On the contrary, June brought word that the British Parliament had formally approved of the Governor's conduct.

The Canadian Legislature, by this date, stood prorogued, although not by Elgin in person. Instead, he designated Major General Rowan, as Deputy Governor, to preside over the proceedings. As a result, the day passed off quietly without any clash between the troops and the bystanders.

Yet it was not surprising that thoughtful men urged the necessity of a move. The Colonial Secretary expressed the official viewpoint, noting "that the existence of such a spirit of insubordination in that city would appear to render it a very unfit place for the seat of the Provincial Government and for the meeting of the Legislature." Many of the members were openly unwilling to return to Montreal, a town which even before the riot Elgin considered to be a hotbed of prejudice and disaffection.

Another outbreak of violence marred the summer when Lafontaine's house was attacked for the second time. The immediate cause of the excitement lay in the arrest of certain persons, believed to have been implicated in the burning of the Parlia-

ment Building. Since all but one of the accused were promptly
granted bail, the government does not seem to have been unduly harsh. But the provocation was sufficient for the crowds
to go berserk once more, and when in the course of their
efforts to damage the Lafontaine establishment, one of their
number was killed, the funeral provided another opportunity for
a public demonstration. A vast number of malcontents attended,
wearing red scarves and ribands. Shops along the line of procession were closed. That evening witnessed a scuffle on the wharf
between an unruly bunch of youths and some mounted police,
brought over from LaPrairie to help maintain order. Fires occurred on several successive nights, in circumstances that pointed
to incendiarism.

The magistrates wanted martial law, but Elgin refused his consent—just as he rejected the idea of troops from points outside
the province. His hope was that the common sense of the moderate group might prevail over the passions of the extremists.
Finally, after much persuasion, the ineffectual Mayor issued a
proclamation, calling on all respectable citizens to assist in maintaining order. Special constables patrolled the streets, much to
the satisfaction of all who owned property. When a coroner's
jury acquitted Lafontaine of all blame in the death of the youth,
and instead found the authorities to have been remiss, some degree of calmness descended upon the city.

It had been such a queer mix-up that no one knew for sure
who were friends and who were enemies. Few, if any, French
Canadians had taken part in the riot, and many of the special
constables were drawn from their ranks. The Roman Catholic
hierarchy was as strongly loyal as in the past. Papineau stood
almost alone, his hatred of Lafontaine contributing to his distrust of all authority. Elgin himself had deep suspicions of the
Irish section of the community, already excited over rumors from
overseas of an imminent revolt in the home land. Certainly the
language of the rioters was English, and many of them were
highly respectable.

But this particular brand of trouble was pretty well at an end.
In its place, a curious crosscurrent arose with the annexation cry
raised by the British, in a complete denial of all their earlier

pledges of fealty to the Crown. To a large extent, its origins were commercial. When profits dwindled, the Imperial link held less attraction, and the loss of the colonial preference on wheat had never been forgotten.

There had been signs of discontent as far back as April, when the British American League was formed. The Honorable George Moffatt held the office of president, with headquarters at Montreal, and branches at Toronto, and other centers in Upper Canada. A meeting at Kingston in July set forth its aims—opposition to the government; a return to the protective policy; an elective Legislative Council; a general union of all British North American provinces. Outside of Montreal, however, no one showed much enthusiasm. The League as such was disbanded, although its more extreme members published a manifesto in October, *To the People of Canada*. It makes strange reading.

"Of all the remedies that have been suggested for the acknowledged and insufferable ills with which our country is afflicted, there remains but one to be considered. It propounds a sweeping and important change in our political and social condition involving considerations which demand our most serious examination. This remedy consists in a friendly and peaceful separation from the British connection and a union upon equitable terms with the great North American confederacy of sovereign states."

Some 325 names were attached to this astonishing piece of work, all of them English and many prominent in the community. Men of differing political parties lent their support, as did a mixed group of officials—Justices of the Peace, militia officers, and others holding commissions from the Crown. Papineau voiced his approval. So far as the rest of the country was concerned, it had little effect. Annexation to the United States was almost entirely a Montreal scheme, and even there its life was short. Returning prosperity soon showed itself the most effective remedy for the local defeatists.

Great Britain, for her part, was not altogether sure that she wanted to retain this troublesome colony. The Rebellion Losses Bill and the subsequent rioting, had appeared from a distance, to be more serious than in fact they were. The high cost of maintaining permanent British garrisons overseas was never quite forgotten. Both Elgin and Grey disagreed, for they considered the permanence of the British-Canadian connection as being highly advantageous to both countries.

But although the furor over annexation virtually died with the old year, Montreal lost its status as the political capital of the country. In November the government office moved to Toronto, alternating thereafter in four-year shifts between that city and Quebec. Never again did any legislature meet on the Island; federal and provincial administrations alike avoided the uncertainties of life in what was undeniably the commercial center of the nation.

Chapter 29

1850–1856

The city grows and is relatively calm. Prosperity of the merchants. The first transatlantic steamers. Allan Line. Railroad building. The Grand Trunk. A bridge across the St. Lawrence. Georges Etienne Cartier. Fires. Gavazzi riots.

THE TRANSFER OF the government offices came as a blow to the citizens, who had enjoyed the prestige inseparable from life in the capital. That the loss was due entirely to their own lawless behavior, doubtless did little to ease the civic discontent.

But happily for Montreal, the 1850s were relatively calm, as compared to the past. Twenty years of almost incessant agitation may well have led to weariness among the older men, and the younger generation showed more tolerance. There were signs of an end to the depression, so noticeable that, in December 1850, the Montreal *Transcript* could write hopefully of the future. "We are glad to see in all parts of the Province, a spirit of healthful enterprise at work . . . It is as though the colony were awakening from a long lethargy to a sense of its natural greatness."

Montreal by this date, could legitimately claim city status, for its growth had long since converted into reality, the earlier courtesy title of metropolis. Geographically, it was spreading outward, as more and more well-to-do merchants moved away from the old-style living quarters, above shops and offices. New street names made their appearance, and St. Catherine and Sherbrooke developed into popular residential thoroughfares. Racially, the 1851 census revealed a great diversity.

Natives of Canada—French origin	26,020
Natives of Canada—other origins	12,494
Natives of Ireland	11,736
Natives of Scotland	3,150
Natives of England	2,858
Natives of the United States	919
Natives of France	133
Others	405
Total	57,715

Moreover, the pace of the increase was impressive. In 1849 the population had been listed at 48,207, which implied a gain of 9508 in only two years. At that, Robert MacKay, an indefatigable compiler of directories, considered the official returns to have been underrated. Several families had failed to complete their schedules, while widespread confusion existed over the questions on religion. Only the Roman Catholics seemed certain of the nature of their faith. For the rest, he noted a regrettable lack of understanding that the Church of Scotland was Presbyterian, and the Church of England, Protestant Episcopal.

Whether MacKay's statistics were always completely accurate, is questionable, yet men of his kidney have become rich sources of contemporary information. By the middle of the century, it was possible to supplement the travelers' tales by publications that were Canadian in origin—directories, handbooks, pocket guides, almanacs. In some cases the authors remained anonymous, and those who dealt with the province as a whole, touched lightly upon Montreal. MacKay, however, was local, and for that reason, of more immediate interest. That he should also be a booster, was only to be expected. Montreal, he believed firmly, would ultimately become one of the greatest commercial emporiums in North America.

And the mere fact that the guidebooks existed, points to the most dramatic development of the whole era—the improvement in transportation. As modern trains and steamboats gradually supplanted the canoes and the bateaux, travel became less of an ordeal. It could be undertaken for pleasure, and carried out in comfort. At one step, the terrible isolation of the past two centuries was coming to an end.

Of course, winter could not yet be ignored. During its early years, the little Champlain and St. Lawrence Railway ceased operation in the cold weather, and so long as the river itself remained unbridged, there were other handicaps—the solidity of the ice, the state of the road over its surface, the exposed drive from the south shore into the city. For many seasons, the sleighs retained their pre-eminence, "of every variety of shape and pattern, many of them being also very handsome, ornamented with rich furs, and drawn by fine horses with showy harness, set off by high hoops, with silver bells on the saddles, and rosettes of ribbon or glass and streamers of colored horse-hair on the bridles, while the gay chirping sound of the bells and the nice crisp sound of the runners through the new snow have a very cheerful effect."

How different were the summers, and how enticing the prospect of travel, in such unwonted luxury and at such speed. In 1854, a variety of lake and river steamers awaited the pleasure of the wayfarer from Upper Canada. If he left Ogdensburg at eight in the morning, he reached Montreal at five o'clock the same day. Excellent connections awaited him there—comfortable boats to Quebec, and railroads to Boston, New York, and the White Mountains. Montreal naturally hoped that its attractions would induce a stopover. Hence the glamorous listing of the hotels, the enumeration of the local "sights," the descriptions of the public buildings and the elegant shops.

Inevitably, this new mode of seeing the country created difficulties for the inexperienced. Hints were offered on the subject of trunks, which should be of convenient size, "to withstand the rough handling to which they are subjected." On the main lines, these could usually be checked—it was wise to carry a small bag or satchel, containing articles of clothing for daily use. Before arriving at the stopping place, everyone should decide at which hotel they intended to stay. "The noise and solicitations of the agents of the various lines of conveyances, and different public houses at the railroad depots and steamboat landings are apt to discompose even those accustomed to it, and the inexperienced traveler is liable to be misled." A final warning carried the reminder that the comforts of home could not be expected at all times when on the road.

With progress so much in evidence during the early '50s, it will come as no surprise to find Montreal's mercantile community once more on the up-and-up, and prospering. Annexation was easily forgotten, a bogey to be given decent interment until another depression came along. The men who had either shared in or condoned the burning of the Parliament Building were once again lawabiding citizens, and Queen Victoria had defeated the President of the United States in the war of nerves.

The new optimism made its bow at the Industrial Fair, held at Bonsecours Market in October 1850. The whole of the upper portion of the building was used, the northern hall for trades and manufactures, the southern for agricultural products and machinery. Attendance was estimated at 20,000 to 30,000 for the week.

For the frivolous minded among the "immense throngs," there was a round of festivities. A dinner in the Masonic Hall, offered by the Mayor and Corporation, lent an official cachet to the opening day. A regatta on the river attracted thousands of spectators. "A grand ball was given on Friday evening, when eight hundred joined in the gay scene, and the same evening a torchlight procession came off under the management of the fire brigade. All the fire companies, with their engines, hose-reels, etc., drawn by horses richly caparisoned and decorated, formed the procession. They had a most imposing appearance, and were attended and cheered by the immense numbers gathered to view the novel spectacle. Every window and available point of sight was crowded with spectators."

The social whirl aside, the Fair possessed wider significance. It was designed as a kind of local showcase in preparation for the great International Exhibition to be held in London the following year, under the distinguished patronage of the Prince Consort. When the "Industry of the Nations" was put on display in the Empire capital, Montreal intended to be represented. Some two hundred packages were shipped overseas, the cream of the local products in themselves a means of attracting British attention to Canada.

Probably the merchants welcomed this opportunity for a closer rapport with their English counterparts, since their relations with London had been strained, in ways far beyond the purely political. The repeal of the Corn Laws led to a long agitation in which Montreal took the lead. If the Empire preference on grain was, indeed, irretrievably lost, the Canadians felt that in compensation, the crippling restrictions of the Navigation Acts should be lifted. The requirement that all trade between Great Britain and her colonies must be carried in British ships seemed indefensible. But the Imperial Parliament was slow to accept this thesis, and the much-desired amendment did not come until 1849. It made a world of difference to the St. Lawrence. On and after January 1, 1850, foreign vessels of any nation were allowed to load or unload cargoes in colonial ports, regardless of whence they came or where they were going.

So far as Montreal was concerned foreigners generally meant citizens of the United States, and although annexation was a dead issue, Reciprocity took its place. A free interchange of natural products with the Americans became the objective of the merchants. They brought pressure to bear on the Canadian government, and made their voice heard at Washington and Westminster. Their reward was the Treaty, signed in 1854, and the fruits of their victory, the vessels that crowded the port. Taking the two factors together—the repeal of the Navigation Acts and the establishment of Reciprocity—the results were, on the whole, better than had been anticipated. Moreover, Montreal soon forged ahead of Quebec, as being the most profitable meeting place for ocean and lake shipping. Transshipments spelled prosperity.

Although this showed in various ways, one of the more promising was the increase in the number and type of factories. To some extent, this was due to immigration, for the British mechanics brought with them old world skills of a high order. Machine industry gradually rose to importance, at much the same date as the completion of the Lachine Canal. Along its basin, new developments found convenient locations, close to water transportation. Thus the city started to spread out in yet another direction, since flour mills, sugar refineries, and the like each had its quota of employees.

In the person of the Honorable John Young, Montreal had a quite astonishing citizen. Not only did he have a vision of what the port might be in the future, but he possessed the ability to convert the dream into reality. Thanks to his foresight, he actually did what others had merely talked about. For his plan, presented in 1850, followed several years of effort on the part of the newly formed Board of Trade, to persuade the authorities to resume their work on the Lake St. Peter ship channel. The government, however, having spent money to little or no purpose on rather elaborate schemes, would do nothing more until Young came along with his simple but wholly practical ideas.

A transfer of jurisdiction formed the basis for his recommendations. The Montreal Harbor Commission, in his opinion, should be authorized, not only to undertake the actual work, but to finance it by borrowing. To meet the interest on the loans, Young suggested the imposition of a new tonnage duty, not to exceed one shilling per ton for all vessels drawing ten feet or more. Official approval followed quickly, and the ship owners offered no objections. Engineers, appointed by the Commission, were soon busy on a survey. Their advice to abandon the earlier attempts to cut a straight and artificial channel, meant that the natural line could be followed.

Because the sand and clay formation made for easy dredging, progress thereafter was rapid. By the close of the 1851 season, the channel had been deepened by two feet and widened to seventy-five, a year later, the depth went to fifteen feet and the width to a hundred and fifty. Simultaneous improvements at the harbor entrance, insured a fifteen-foot depth throughout. To conclude this particular record of local enterprise, it need only be said that the task of dredging this stretch of the river remained the responsibility of the Harbor Commission until 1888, at which time it was taken over by the Dominion Department of Marine and Fisheries. During the thirty-eight-year period, the depth had been increased from eleven to twenty-seven and a half feet.

When, in May 1853, the 700-ton *Genova* tied up at the stone wharves, her arrival opened up a new world for Montreal. For although small in size, she was the first transatlantic steamer to venture so far up the river. The bearer of the Royal Mail, she docked amidst great rejoicing, and that evening at a dinner at Donegani's Hotel, her captain, Walter Paton, was honored as a pioneer, and his ship saluted as a gratifying token of the country's advances. That such a voyage had been undertaken, arose from a contract between the provincial government and McLean, McLarty and Co. of Liverpool which called for fourteen sailings each season. But, unfortunately, the company soon found itself unable to maintain the service with such frequency, and the Canadians annulled the agreement.

The Englishmen, however, were scarcely missed, for that same season Hugh Allan decided to build iron vessels for the St. Lawrence trade. Montreal was their summer terminus, and Portland the winter port. This was no idle decision, for the Allan Line had been in existence since 1822. The business prospered so greatly, that the owners were ready to step in and take advantage of the general disruption caused by the Crimean War. A government contract, awarded in 1855, was filled satisfactorily. Under the newer title of the Montreal Ocean Steamship Company, these vessels carried the mails, a service which yielded an annual subsidy of $120,000. With the crossing reduced to ten or eleven days, the break with the past seemed complete.

Yet this was not altogether true, for although the new vessels were steam propelled, the old sailing fleet remained in service. As late as 1851, more than half the Great Lakes tonnage was sail, and steam came slowly on the Atlantic. Long after it was a commonplace on the St. Lawrence, it was deemed too hazardous for the ocean. Thus the two types of craft were seen locally for some years.

But no matter how pleased a Canadian might be, as he looked at the canals, the harbors, and the river, he might well wonder sometimes if such improvements had come too late. Across the border, he saw in the United States a tremendous network of railways stretching out to provide cheap and rapid transit for industry. In his own country, in 1849, there were exactly fifty miles. Shattered by the contrast, Canada in its turn, started construction. Five years later, with 800 miles completed and 2000 under way, the same Canadian might have felt pride at the extent of the achievement.

The early railroads were thought of in much the same fashion, as the portages or carrying-places. Their function was to bridge the gaps between the main waterways of the inhabited portions of the continent. For this reason, they were usually short in length, and the property of small private companies. Some existed to provide communication between the eastern and western sectors of the province, others turned toward the United States, to link up with American lines. Ordinarily, they were centered upon a city, radiating out in various directions.

In the Montreal district, the Champlain and St. Lawrence was the forerunner of modern railroad development. Ever since its modest beginning in 1836, it had eased travel across the border. By 1852 its sixteen miles of track had grown to forty-nine, extending up from Rouses Point, through LaPrairie to St. Lambert. Passengers using this route reached Boston in thirteen hours, New York in fifteen.

Plans for another international line, announced in 1846, provided grounds for rivalry between Portland and Boston as to which should be the southern terminus. Under the title of the St. Lawrence and Atlantic, it went as far as the border; on the American side, the name was reversed. Subscriptions came in freely at first, among them £125,000 from the city of Montreal. But still the management faced financial problems. By 1849, when John Young and Alexander Galt took it over, only forty miles had been built. Two years later, with the completion of several small lines, the Portland connection was assured. Montreal made it an occasion for rejoicing—a grand procession, a dinner and a ball, triumphal arches in the streets. July 1853 saw the departure of the first through train from Longueuil, bearing an excursion party that included some of the city fathers.

In the interval, other work had been completed—the eight-mile stretch of track, for example, out to Lachine. The Montreal and Champlain Railroad, opened in 1847, covered the distance in twenty-one minutes. By 1851, an extension went into service, running from Caughnawaga on the south shore down to the boundary, the two portions being linked together by a steam ferry, the *Iroquois*. Operating twelve months in the year, it was powerful enough to carry a locomotive and three loaded cars.

But the greatest development dated from 1852 when the Grand Trunk received its charter, and with this, the real period of railroad construction had its birth. Designed on a more ambitious scale than the pioneer operations, the small companies were, by degrees, absorbed into wider groupings. Whereas earlier there had been talk of a line up to Kingston, this was now to be extended to Toronto. In the east, the proposal was for tracks from Quebec to Trois Pistoles.

The Grand Trunk at its inception, leased the several lines between Montreal and Portland. One condition of this arrangement had tremendous local significance, being nothing less than the construction of a bridge across the St. Lawrence. There was nothing really new in the idea, John Young in particular having urged its adoption for several years, yet so far without success.

Several of Young's articles, published in the Montreal *Economist* for 1846, paved the way sufficiently for him to secure authorization for a survey, from the directors of the St. Lawrence and Atlantic. It was the first of several, carried out by professional engineers. All, by pronouncing a bridge to be feasible in the technical sense, gave encouragement to the often skeptical laymen. Young himself never faltered, going so far on one occasion as to advance £600 out of his own pocket, when railway funds were unable to meet the preliminary costs.

A report by Thomas Keefer, published in 1853, was particularly valuable, based as it was on long experience gained while conducting hydrographic surveys for the government. Many of his recommendations later found a place in the actual specifications, drawn up by the famous English expert, Robert Stephenson. Granted that a bridge was practicable, Keefer foresaw that its construction would pose many problems. The climate for one thing, and above all, the powerful ice "shoves" of the spring and autumn. The piers must be as few as possible, so as to offer a minimum of resistance. Openings, at least 250 feet wide, were needed to permit the passage of the timber rafts. Nor could navigation be interfered with. The original suggestion of a central drawbridge was discarded, in favor of a high level span, rising gradually from both shores, and allowing clearance for the masts of the lake boats. The relative merits of wood and stone were carefully weighed, with durability and fire-resistance winning out over lower costs. Much earnest discussion was devoted to the precise site, although generally there was not much deviation from the line actually followed downstream from Nuns' Island.

Since the Grand Trunk had a general contract with the British firm of Peto, Brassey, and Betts, the bridge was included in its terms—"when completed, to be in perfect repair, and of the best and most substantial character, and to be approved of by the said Robert Stephenson."

For although several persons shared in the planning and the construction, the chain of command started with Stephenson; contemporary statements are the authority for the fact that he alone conceived, designed, and carried out the project. Alexander Ross acted as his assistant and Chief Engineer, who supervised the work. Almost more important, locally, was James Hodges, the engineer and agent for the contractors. He actually lived in Montreal for five years, winning golden opinions for his daily superintendence of the workmen. He never ceased his care for their welfare. By his orders, doctors and chaplains were provided, while cordiality marked all his dealings with the staff.

Stephenson at this date, was fresh from the triumph of the great Menai Bridge, linking the mainland of Wales with the Island of Anglesey. Tubular in construction, it was recognized everywhere as a novel but highly satisfactory type of structure. Thus no one felt much surprise that he should advocate the same enclosed passageway for Montreal, during the course of a visit to Canada in 1853. Work commenced the following summer, the first stone being laid on July 22, 1854. It was a gala day, the principal officers of the railroad being in attendance, together with the local reporters and a large party of ladies and gentlemen. At the bottom of the coffer-dam, the stone was laid with the usual ceremonies, and still in the same odd surroundings, the guests enjoyed a sumptuous lunch, followed by a dance.

But work on the bridge continued for some years, and before its conclusion, another railroad inaugural afforded fresh oppor-

16. Shoving of ice upon no. 9 pier, Victoria Bridge, 1858. *(Lithograph by Kell Bros.)*

17. Shoving of ice upon wharves in front of Montreal, 1860. *(Lithograph by Kell Bros.)*

18. Staging for center tube, Victoria Bridge, 1860. *(Lithograph by Kell Bros.)*

19. The harbor from custom house wharf, about 1885–89. *(Photograph by Notman)*

20. Saint-Gabriel farmhouse, Congregation of Notre Dame, 1886. (*H. Bunnett*)

21. Ice Palace—Montreal carnival, 1889. *(Lithograph by Burland Litho. Co.)*

22. The harbor, about 1896–1910. *(Photograph by Notman)*

tunities for public rejoicing. With the completion of the line between Montreal and Toronto in 1856, through trains became a reality. The first to leave the local depot pulled out at 7:30 in the morning. Three first-class and three second-class coaches carried the passengers and the mail, and arrival time was ten o'clock the same evening. The spring of 1857 saw the institution of night service, the sleeping cars insuring comfort during the fifteen-hour trip.

Montreal celebrated the pioneer Toronto run with what Sandham called "a bumper." "When the eventful day dawned, the city had a most extraordinary appearance. The crowds of strangers pouring through the chief streets and thoroughfares reminded one of Cheapside or the Strand. Vehicles, too, of all kinds and descriptions, were in requisition the whole time, so that the scene of animation and interest never flagged." That evening saw a banquet and later a ball, in one of the immense rooms of the Engine Station at Point St. Charles. Four thousand persons attended—"the crush was immense." Cupids holding vases of flowers vied with the flags and shields to provide decorations. A great banner bore the inscription, *Success to Mercantile Enterprise, Railways, Telegraphs and Ocean Steam-Ships.* Other mottoes carried such reminders as *God helps them who help themselves* and *Past labour is present delight.* The whole scene glittered and sparkled, as did the later torchlight procession and the fireworks. "Cannons roared, the gratified spectators loudly cheered, and hats were waved by both young and old."

Political interest paled before these quite astounding signs of progress. When confronted by better times, Montreal's chagrin over the departure of the government vanished, even to the point of making its peace with the sorely tried Lord Elgin. When he visited the city in the autumn of 1851, what might have been an embarrassment turned out to be a personal triumph. By his invitation, the citizens gathered for the exchange of speeches, and afterward, all rushed forward to grasp his hand —including, he noted, some of the most violent of the disaffected in 1849. Thousands assembled on the quay, at his departure, to wish him Godspeed.

But Lord Elgin's residence in Canada terminated in 1854, and his successors in the vice-regal office wielded less influence. For as the years passed, Her Majesty's representatives advised the government, but did not themselves rule. So far as Montreal was concerned, the relationship became largely social.

The year 1851 brought other changes, for both Lafontaine and Baldwin retired from active politics. Montreal bade an official farewell to its distinguished son at a public dinner, held at St. Lawrence Hall in October. For the 160 French and English gentlemen who attended, it was a pleasant evening, the *Gazette* reporting that harmony and good feeling were the presiding deities of the occasion. The Honorable Mr. Morin presided, while at the opposite end of the table, Dr. Nelson did the honors. Other gentlemen acted as stewards, placing themselves at convenient intervals about the room, so that they might see to the comfort of all the guests. "The table literally groaned under the weight of every possible dainty that our markets could afford, or that could be procured from the neighboring States."

This was, in no sense, a final good-by, for Lafontaine lived in Montreal until his death in 1864. Queen Victoria honored him with a baronetcy so that it was as Sir Louis that he continued to serve his country on the Bench. Always the good citizen, he was active on various benevolent committees.

In Georges Etienne Cartier, however, the city possessed another rising political star. Although born in the Richelieu village of St. Antoine, he received his legal education in Montreal. As an early disciple of Papineau, his active participation in the 1837 Rebellion forced him into exile in the United States. A return to civil life led him into politics, and, in 1848, he was elected as the member for Vercheres. But by then his opinions had changed; as a supporter of Lafontaine, he found himself opposing Papineau. Recognition of his ability followed quickly, for in 1855 he was appointed Provincial Secretary. A close associate of John A. Macdonald, he became one of the pillars of the Liberal-Conservative party, and in 1857, the two men were chosen joint premiers of the country.

Municipal government for its part, took another step forward, when, in 1852, the right to select the mayor passed from the

Council to the people at large. Charles Wilson was the first candidate to be chosen by popular suffrage. The number of aldermen was increased, each of the suburban districts electing three representatives, as in the case of the city wards. The twenty-seven members were required to meet every three months. Prior to this date the office of mayor does not seem to have been greatly coveted, a penalty of £100 being imposed for non-acceptance of the honor.

Of the many problems faced by the civic authorities, fire was still one of the most serious. The age-long scourge had not yet been overcome. Nor was this surprising. The 1851 census showed that out of 7244 houses, 4351 were frame construction. Add to this the primitive protective measures, and the result could be accurately predicted.

The first outbreak occurred on a Saturday afternoon in June 1850, when flames spread rapidly from a carpenter's shop in Griffintown. Several buildings were blown up, to no avail. St. Stephen's Anglican Church, with its wooden spire, was a total loss, and the shingles, tossed about by the wind, were blamed for extending the area of damage. Over two hundred houses were destroyed, and five hundred families rendered homeless.

While the ground was still littered by the blackened ruins, an equally disastrous conflagration broke out in another district. This started about ten in the morning of Friday, August 23, in the premises of a livery-stable keeper on Craig Street. High breezes fanned the blaze, which in about half an hour, had moved along to the Main Street of St. Lawrence suburb, and on up to Vitre Street. Over 150 houses were lost.

As if this were not enough, two great fires in 1852 caused the loss of some twelve hundred buildings, and deprived nine thousand persons of shelter. The earlier one originated in a carpenter's shop on St. Peter Street, back of the old St. Andrew's Church. On this Sunday in early June, the whole area bounded by St. Peter, St. Francis Xavier, St. Sacrement and St. Paul streets, was laid waste. Notre Dame Church was threatened, as were the ships in the harbor. With both sides of St. Paul Street afire, the scene was terrifying. Some thirty large buildings, standing in three parallel rows, were all in flames. Soldiers aided civilians in moving the sick from the Hôtel Dieu, while others in distress searched for the missing members of their families. The noise was dreadful—the roaring of the fires, the crackling of the timbers, the shouts of the firemen, the ringing of the alarms.

The second visitation came on Thursday, July 9. From a house on the east side of St. Lawrence Main Street, the blaze spread northward, gaining extra fuel from a large lumberyard at the corner of St. Dominique. With great difficulty, the General Hospital was saved, but everything to the south burned as though of matchwood. Driven by a strong westerly wind, the flames leaped from street to street. Soon after noon, they reached St. Denis Street, its stone and wooden buildings equally powerless to resist the sheet of fire, a quarter of a mile wide. St. James Cathedral, barely thirty years old, was lost, along with the adjacent and newly built episcopal palace of Bishop Bourget.

About five o'clock, and just when everything seemed over, another alarm sounded. Sparks had been carried down to some wooden structures in the rear of Notre Dame Street. Hay's House was ignited, an immense block four stories high with a theater at the back. By ten o'clock, everything around Dalhousie Square had vanished, while the flames, moving eastward, cut a wide swathe between Lagauchetière and the river. Not until the next morning, were they checked at St. Mary's Foundry.

The need for relief was urgent, for one-fifth of the population was considered to be without resources. A committee of citizens worked closely with the civic authorities for a year. Food and clothing must be provided for the destitute, as well as shelter. The old immigration sheds at Point St. Charles were repaired, and new ones hastily constructed at Logan's Farm. Many persons had to be cared for, all through the winter. There were bills for such diverse items as firewood and hospitalization. The provincial government gave £2500; £1000 came from New Brunswick and £500 from Nova Scotia. Many of the Upper Canadian cities provided contributions, as did all manner of Roman Catholic and Protestant churches in the Lower province. Individuals in Great Britain, the United States, and Canada, shared in the burden carried by the citizens of Montreal. About £36,000 was collected, and at the end, a small balance of £250 was handed over to the city, to assist with aged widows, the blind, and the sick.

Two years later, an epidemic of cholera afflicted the city once more. Although this 1854 visitation was less severe than those of earlier summers, yet in two months, it caused 1186 deaths. Obviously, so long as immigration continued, under such over-crowded and unhygienic conditions, there could never be any guarantee of freedom. And Montreal itself, in hot humid weather, and lacking the protection of modern sanitation, all too often provided a fertile soil for the spread of disease.

Yet nothing ever dampened the spirits of the crowds permanently, for in between the fires and the cholera there was more rioting. The immediate cause of the 1853 outbreak was the presence of Alessandro Gavazzi, a former Roman Catholic priest, whose anti-Catholic lectures had gained him a Protestant following in various Canadian and American cities. His reception at Quebec on July 6, perhaps alerted the authorities as to what might happen elsewhere. In the course of a speech at the ancient capital, he was attacked in the pulpit. A scene of considerable confusion ensued, until the prompt arrival of the militia put an end to the trouble.

Montreal did not get off as easily, when, three days later, Gavazzi arrived to speak at Zion Church. Precautions had been taken, the police stationed at several strategic points, and a detachment of the 26th Cameronians nearby, should the civil arm need reinforcements. An Irish attempt to break into the church was easily repulsed, but in a second foray, the shooting started. Catholics and Protestants turned upon each other, and the proceedings got out of hand. The lecture was hastily canceled and everyone made for home.

But as the crowds passed along the streets, they were fired upon by the troops. Just who gave the order is open to doubt. Mayor Wilson, who had read the Riot Act, denied the accusation, as did Colonel Hogarth. Some said it had started at the request of a member of the mob, and that the aim was deliberately high. Whatever the truth, those making their way up Beaver Hall Hill were caught by the bullets. About forty persons were killed or wounded, although not all by the rifles of the

military. Some were struck by stones and other missiles, and
two women were almost trampled to death underfoot. Gavazzi,
himself, barely escaped with his life, being conducted by two
clergy in a closed cab down to the wharf, where the ferry carried him across to LaPrairie and safety.

Later that month, an investigation was launched into the
causes of the riot. When none of its findings were made public,
people suspected the whole story had been hushed up for political motives. There were attempts at retaliation. Several members of the regiment were waylaid and beaten up, while some
person unknown, entered the City Hall, and destroyed an oil
portrait of Mayor Wilson, by cutting out the head and shoulders.
There were dark mutterings about the Irish and St. Patrick's
Society, and other indications of religious intolerance.

Strangely enough, this unfortunate occurrence was followed
by a period of good will. Several events, from the outside world,
had sufficient effect locally to induce a sense of fellowship. At
the highest level, there was the alliance between England and
France in 1854, when the state visits exchanged by Victoria
and Louis Napoleon heralded a new era of international co-
operation.

To the French Emperor the moment seemed ripe to reopen
communications with his nation's ancient colony, with the result
that the summer of 1855 saw the arrival in the St. Lawrence of
La Capricieuse, under the command of M. de Belveze. Although
the Imperial motives were frankly commercial, the sentimental
impact was tremendous. As the first such sailing since the sad
days of 1759–60, it marked the reforging of the ancestral ties
shattered by the French Revolution. Belveze visited Montreal
briefly, and was feted at a round of dinners and receptions.

The Paris Exhibition afforded another occasion for racial *bonne
entente.* As in the case of the earlier London event, it was
preceded by an Industrial Fair in the City Concert Hall. For
five days, immense throngs of strangers flocked into the city.
"All who visited the hall expressed their great satisfaction with
what they saw, and not a few wondered to see so many and
such valuable specimens of native industry gathered under one
roof."

Not even the outbreak of war shattered this rare sense of amity, for in the Crimea, England and France fought side by side as allies. An event such as the fall of Sebastopol was a cause for rejoicing. After the year-long siege, the news of its surrender was greeted almost with disbelief. That evening, and for several days thereafter, the citizens went wild with joy.

Yet this celebration was outclassed by the scene of June 1856, when the 39th Regiment arrived in Canada. British troops were not, as a rule, universally popular, but these men, posted to Montreal on garrison duty, had lately seen service in the Crimea. Thousands of spectators who lined the quays, and the nearby windows and roofs, hailed them with deafening cheers. The vessels in port and the Montreal Artillery saluted them with roars of cannon, while military bands nearby played rousing music.

On shore, the Mayor and Corporation stood waiting. Amid speeches and more cheering, the men moved off, marching up McGill Street and along St. James to Place d'Armes, and thence to the barracks. There the heavy knapsacks were discarded, preparatory to attendance at a banquet in the City Concert Hall. "The hall was laid out for 1200 guests, and the whole regiment, together with the volunteer companies, the mayor, city council and a number of invited guests, sat down to a sumptuous repast . . . The greatest good feeling existed."

Chapter 30
1856–1861

Victoria Bridge. The Prince of Wales. Social gaiety. A city transformed. Municipal problems. Streetcars. Dualism in schools and colleges. The Sulpicians. McGill and William Dawson.

No MATTER how great the rival attractions, the new bridge, for most Montrealers, held the center of the stage. Its slow spanning of the turbulent waters was an achievement of no mean order. Long before its completion, the phrase-makers were busy, hailing it as the pride and chief joy of the city, the eighth wonder of the world, the most gigantic work of science and enterprise on the habitable globe.

Under the supervision of Mr. Hodges there was steady progress. The work was perforce, seasonal, for each winter compelled a shutdown. Ice conditions often caused anxiety, and the swift-moving timber rafts from time to time damaged the cribwork and the masonry. Most serious of all, was the hiatus caused by the Crimean War, when for nearly two years a financial crisis overseas brought the operations to a halt.

Some idea of the size of the labor force may be gained from the 1858 statistics. In that summer, it totaled 3040 men, 450 working in the stone quarries, 2090 artisans of all kinds, and even five hundred sailors. To ease their toil, they had the assistance of 6 steamers, 72 barges, 142 horses, and 4 locomotives. This small army had been hastily assembled at much the same date as their mates, who laid the main Grand Trunk line to Toronto. One estimate placed the combined groups at between 10,000 and 15,000.

Because of the actions of a few rowdies, construction work in general gained a bad reputation—one of the reasons, perhaps, why young French Canadians did not come forward in such numbers as had been anticipated. New England, already, was luring them southward. It was therefore inevitable that many of those employed on the project should come from overseas. Yet not all who arrived in Canada were the right type to "get on," in the contemporary phrase. Many of the men who swarmed into Montreal were no better off than at home. Strong arms were essential, and one good blacksmith, stonemason, or plowman, it was often said, was worth half a dozen clerks and a score of barristers.

In Hodges' opinion, the Canadians—of whatever language— were not tractable workmen. The local mechanics and laborers seemed to strike, twice a year, no matter how high the wages. Nor did their skills equal those of the English craftsmen. But against this, the newcomers suffered from the rigorous climate, and its extremes of bitter cold and fierce heat. Frostbitten ears, noses, and feet were common, and there were cases of snowblindness. During the summers, many succumbed to sunstroke.

Yet no matter how heterogeneous the work crews were, one touching incident revealed their reverence for the past. While engaged on the excavations at the Point St. Charles end of the bridge, they came upon the remains of the victims of the 1847 ship fever epidemic, six thousand of whom had been interred at the spot. To save the bodies from future molestation, they caused an enormous rock from the bed of the river, weighing seventeen tons, "to be conveyed to the spot and erected upon a pedestal of massive stonework, as a monument to preserve from desecration, the enclosed piece of ground around it. This Herculean task was brought to a close on the third of November 1859, and in the presence of a large number of persons there assembled, the ceremony of laying the stone was performed by Canon Leach, L.L.D."

By the terms of the contract, the bridge was to be completed by 1861. Long before that date, however, the Grand Trunk was feeling the burden of a highly expensive local set-up. Three ferries had been built in 1854, to convey passengers and cargo across from the south shore, and in winter, sleighs carried the freight over the ice. The latter proved especially costly, sometimes rising as high as $20,000 for carters' charges in a single season. As the volume of traffic increased, so did the pressure on the service, and always there remained the fear of losing out to some rival means of transport. Hence the offer to Messrs. Peto, Brassey, and Betts, early in 1859, of an additional fee of $300,000 if the bridge was ready for use by the end of the year.

Some acceleration of the work had already been possible, and it now gained even greater momentum. On August 5, the foundation of the last pier was ready, the stone, laid by Mrs. Hodges in the presence of three hundred guests, being lowered slowly amid cheers. A few months later saw the completion of the whole enterprise, and on December 17, the Grand Trunk took delivery of the bridge.

Judging by the traffic handled on the first five nights, the new service was sorely needed. Freight cars to the number of 292 made the crossing, carrying 11,723 barrels of flour, 1552 barrels of pork, 140 bales of cotton, 644 tons of general goods, and 39,000 feet of lumber. And although the work had been rushed in its later stages, there was nothing slipshod about the quality. The tests were severe, for a train of platform cars, 520 feet long and extending through two of the tubular sections, was loaded with huge chunks of stone, almost to the breaking point. Two powerful locomotives—later reinforced by a third—could barely drag it along to the center. There, by means of a steel wire, the span was measured while its entire length was covered by the heavy load. It deflected in the middle by no more than one and seven-eighths of an inch, and returned to its original level as soon as the train drew away.

Once the trial period was ended, the public could be admitted. Among the first were a thousand ladies and gentlemen, who in an informal preview boarded a special excursion train drawn by two engines. At a moderate speed, this reached the south shore in seven and a half minutes, and after a run of six or seven miles down the line, returned to the city. As a gala climax to a wonderful day, a champagne *déjeuner* awaited the fortunate guests.

Long before this date, however, the formal christening rites were being discussed. No routine performance by an ordinary official would satisfy either the city or the province. A sense of national pride led to more ambitious plans. On May 14, 1859, both Legislative Chambers approved an Address to the Queen, humbly praying that Her Majesty would be pleased to officiate at the opening ceremonies.

The idea of a royal tour of Canada was not entirely new. The feelings of patriotism generated by the Crimean War and the Indian Mutiny had led to some unofficial suggestions which met with no success. But now conditions were different, and although the Queen herself felt unable to accept the invitation, she designated her son, the Prince of Wales, to act in her stead.

The Prince in question was Albert Edward, who some forty years later, was to ascend the throne as Edward VII. At nineteen years of age, he was a slender youth, with a pleasant smile and a clear voice. Strict parental control had, until now, stood in the way of much personal freedom, so that the visit to Canada and the United States was a great adventure. As befitted the royal heir, he traveled with due formality; his suite, headed by the Duke of Newcastle, was a large one, and judging by Montreal his schedule was cruelly heavy. From the moment of his arrival at St. John's, Newfoundland, on July 23, 1860, until his departure from Portland, Maine, on October 20, "the Prince of Romance" received a wonderful welcome.

Excitement reigned in Montreal as the long-awaited day drew near. Everyone shared in the preparations, for no matter what other cities might claim, the opening of the Victoria Bridge was the immediate purpose of the visit. The provincial government made a grant of $20,000 to assist with a great exhibition of Arts and Manufactures. Not to be outdone, the City Council voted $2000 for the embellishment of Viger Square, and later appropriated a further sum of $10,000 for the general celebrations. New robes were ordered for the Mayor, after the style of those worn in London—a scarlet gown trimmed with ermine, a cocked hat, a chain of office and dress sword.

But the planning was not confined to those in authority. The Citizens' Reception Fund sought subscriptions from private donors, and everyone, high and low, joined in the fun. The *Gazette* wrote of the gay aspect of the city, even in the most remote districts. Streets were paved, houses painted, fences whitewashed—as if His Royal Highness intended to make domiciliary visits. Trees were planted in the principal thoroughfares and fountains appeared, as though by magic, in the public squares. The whole town was beautifully ornamented with flags, banners, flowers, evergreens, transparencies, and arches. The use of gaslight added immeasurably to the glamour. Outlets by the thousand, of this modern type of illumination, lent brilliancy to the night scene, indoors and out. So great, in fact, was the prodigality that a worried Gas Company begged the citizens to reduce their domestic consumption as much as possible.

Torrential rains delayed the party's arrival by twenty-four hours, so that Montrealers first greeted their Prince on Saturday, August 25. Wearing military uniform, he stepped smilingly ashore from the steamer *Kingston* soon after nine o'clock, to start on a grueling round of engagements, in which two days' program was compressed into one. The wind was raw and the air chilly; many of the decorations were sadly battered after the stormy night; delays and uncertainties marred the official reception. But nothing dampened the ardor of the 40,000 spectators massed along the streets and the wharves, on board the ships in the harbor, and in all the windows of the neighborhood.

The Prince made his appearance at the Victoria Bridge about half-past one. A large company of the élite of the country awaited him, the fortunate recipients of the immense invitations, eight inches square, issued by the Grand Trunk. Seated as they were, along the embankment, they saw little or nothing of the actual function. But as the guest of honor rode by in a specially built open railway car, the sun shone brightly and everyone cheered. At the commencement of the tube, a scaffold had been erected over the top. Handsome carpets adorned it, and a crimson canopy, fringed with gold lace. Mr. Hodges was in attendance, the special trowel ready and the mortar spread. A few quick taps and the six-ton stone was lowered into place. Then the Prince proceeded to the center arch, where he drove home the last rivet of silver. Luncheon followed, in a large room over the car shops at Point St. Charles, the audience, some seven or eight hundred strong, listening as the future king toasted "Prosperity to Canada."

The royal party stayed at Rosemount, the home of the Honorable John Rose, Commissioner of Public Works. A pleasant spot it was, on the lower slopes of the mountain, its three acres of parklike grounds insuring privacy. Special plantings of flowers and ornamental trees enhanced its beauty, while above the entrance gates, carved Prince of Wales feathers had been set. At night, colored lamps glowed softly, and indoors, the new décor embodied all that was most fashionable, in the richly ornate Victorian taste.

It seems unlikely that the young man had much leisure to enjoy these idyllic surroundings. Each day was filled with formalities—so strenuous as to leave the Prince utterly fatigued. On one occasion, he actually fell asleep at the dinner table. Luckily, a few events offered relief from what must often have been boredom. Saturday night, for example, when the illuminations turned the city into a blaze of color. The citizens reveled in it all, milling about in the open air until two o'clock in the morning. Great St. James Street was judged the most spectacular district, and the Bank of Montreal the most tastefully decorated of the public buildings. The latter was really splendid, its outline clearly traced by the flaming jets and its great pillars so festooned that they seemed columns of light. Gaiety ruled in the harbor, the ships hung with lamps, and rockets bursting on all sides. No wonder that the Prince wanted to see the fun. But his plain carriage did not get far, for the Mayor had forbidden all vehicular traffic that night. A conscientious constable seized the horses, and ordered the coachman to turn back. Told that the Prince himself was inside, he replied "by putting his finger to his proboscis." Thereupon the onlookers, more trusting by nature, tried to take out the horses and draw the carriage themselves. Of necessity, the impromptu jaunt came to an end.

Monday evening brought the ball, the grandest on the continent, the most superb affair of the kind ever held in Canada —the reporters had a field day. Eight short weeks ago, the cattle had grazed on the site of the wooden pavilion. It was as though a miracle had happened in the fields near the present intersection of Peel and St. Catherine streets. The building was circular in shape, three hundred feet in diameter, and its outside walls painted a dark pink. A board fence kept the curious onlookers at bay, for this was strictly a party for the upper classes. "There was a crowd, but not a jam. There was a lively scene, yet there was no confusion. There was haste at supper, yet it was not indecent."

Indoors, two thousand gas lamps lighted up the vast dome, supported by thirty-six columns. An orchestra played in the center space, while around the walls stretched a gallery, seating three thousand persons. In every direction, there were flowers and evergreens and rich draperies of crimson and gold. Fountains of rose water, eau de cologne, and lavender, sprayed the air with delicious scents. Champagne and claret flowed freely, while for the more abstemious, there was lemonade and ice water. The estimates of attendance varied—four, five, six thousand. Of the Prince's enjoyment, however, there could be no doubt, for he arrived at ten and danced almost without a break, until half-past four the next morning.

But Albert Edward departed and the highly emotional interlude ended. When the wondrous decorations came down, Montreal looked less impressive. The great fires of 1852 and 1854 had left scars, not quickly healed, and there still existed some of the decayed and decaying relics of the past. In a leading street, stood an old tottering shanty, its walls rickety and its roof falling in, its height even when built not more than that of an ordinary-sized man; alongside it, a massive structure of elaborately cut stone, haughtily frowning down on the humble neighboring tenement.

Yet the city had changed tremendously in the last few years. For one thing, it was much larger—even official circles accepted that fact. Although the fifties had been filled with extravagant talk of its phenomenal growth, it was not until 1861 that the census returns showed the guesses to have come near the mark. By the date, the temporary workers on the bridge had taken their departure, yet 91,006 persons remained behind to claim Montreal as their home. If the population could literally increase by 32,291 in a single decade, surely there was every reason to forecast a brilliant future for the metropolis.

But the transformation went deeper than numbers. The steady inflow of immigrants in recent years, had done much to alter the civic character, and the bridge building in particular had acted as a magnet for workmen of all types. Many of these families settled along the waterfront, in Griffintown or Point St. Charles, near the Grand Trunk shops. Their standard of living was low. Tenements and multiple dwellings took the place of the more generous detached houses of the past, and the gardens and open spaces of the old town vanished. At best, these people had few of the comforts and none of the luxuries of their betters, and many of them each spring, suffered the added disadvantage of the floods.

Alfred Sandham wrote of what happened in 1857, when the lower part of Griffintown was entirely submerged "and communication between the different homes was maintained by small boats. The condition of the residents in that locality was most pitiable. While a few of them belonged to the middling classes, the great proportion consisted of the very poor; the labourer who had to earn his daily bread, and his family who rendered all the aid they could to add to the common stock. Many of the male population were carters, who found their horses in from three to four feet of water on the morning of the 20th, and in many cases, their sleeping apartments were also flooded."

Four years passed, without any preventive measures. An exceptionally serious flood in April 1861, caused the St. Lawrence to rise twenty-four feet above the average level. So rapid was the overflow that several congregations at the conclusion of evening service, found their places of worship surrounded by four to six feet of water. Obviously, these periodic inundations did nothing to sweeten the air, already polluted by defective drainage. A visitor to the Theatre Royal found the odor so offensive in its vicinity that he was compelled to leave. "The public health is a least as deserving of attention as the almighty dollar."

Standing apart from all this unpleasantness, the elegant villas of the wealthy virtually surrounded the town. In ever-growing numbers, they dotted the lower slopes of the mountain, still semi-rural, their gardens and orchards pleasant legacies from the past. A fine macadamized road gave easy access to their domains, and as it encircled the summit, the panorama as of old never ceased to appeal. Nearby was the Priests' Farm, partly under cultivation, but now serving as the summer residence for the priests and pupils of the Seminary. Not far away were the new cemeteries—the first Protestant interment in "Mount Royal" taking place in 1852, and three years later, the first Roman Catholic burial in "Notre Dame des Neiges."

Yet for rich and poor alike, the central part of the town remained all important. It was an astonishing place. At every step, an observant German visitor reported that he saw buildings and institutions, just begun or just completed, in preparation for the colossal Montreal of the future, then still in its infancy. Everything new was constructed on a scale far exceeding present needs, and ground on which thirty years earlier, snipe and partridge were being shot in the bush, was now covered with comfortable dwellings and churches.

Other travelers wrote with similar enthusiasm, and if their tales are to be believed, Montreal was indeed an unusual sort of place. Its solidity—their favorite expression—originated in the generous use of stone for the construction of the wharves and the long range of buildings fronting on the river. These men pictured the city as venerable, picturesque, and flourishing; if it were in England, it would be considered a very handsome place. In bustle and activity, it far exceeded anything of its size overseas. And whereas the towns in the United States all looked alike to Europeans, this one possessed a distinct character all its own. Finally, there was Charles MacKay who saluted Montreal as the real capital of Canada, no matter what the politicians might say. Toronto, so this "distinguished poet" felt, was a thing of yesterday, a mere mushroom compared to the antiquity of the St. Lawrence ports.

The commentators, one and all, had a great deal to say about the streets. According to the testimony of one, more kindly than his fellows, they were paved, very clean and well lighted. Since there were in 1856, exactly 455 lamps in use, the twentieth century might well disagree. But Notre Dame Street aroused a more general admiration. It was a place of elegant shops and houses, its new buildings set many yards back on either side so as to make a broad way similar to that of New York. Other districts farther up the hill shared its aura of fashion. St. Antoine, Mountain, Dorchester, Sherbrooke—all boasted beautiful new residences. St. James remained the leading business center, the home of the larger banks and insurance companies.

Candor compels the admission that there were frequent breaks in this chorus of praise, as in the case of Samuel Day who wrote of what he saw in the early '60s. "In the leading streets, the pathways are composed of different materials. Here and there a small patch of flagstone, in a most dilapidated condition. A little further on was a brick pavement, not at all unsightly to walk upon, provided the bricks are not broken to pieces, rough or uneven, which was too frequently the case. Adjoining this was plankway, with the boards either rotten from age, or partially devoured by rats—a species of animal that flourishes wonderfully in a Canadian climate. The roads were equally faulty, and became impassable after much rain."

If such comments sound unduly critical, they were mild in comparison to Anthony Trollope's sarcasm. "The streets in Toronto are framed with wood, or rather planked, as are those of Montreal and Quebec; but they are kept in better order. I should say that the planks are first used at Toronto, then sent down by the lake to Montreal, and when all but rotted out, are again floated off by the St. Lawrence to be used in the thoroughfares of the old French capital." Yet the great novelist considered Montreal the chief city in Canada, let the government do what it could to foster Ottawa. "The idea of spiting a town because there has been a row in it, seems to be preposterous."

Although the citizens often added their complaints to the criticism of the visitors, there is no reason to suppose that the municipal government was either negligent or slothful. It was rather a case of limited resources in an expanding city, whose tastes were growing more sophisticated. Problems such as the water supply seemed to defy solution. The population simply outgrew the existing arrangements. Ever since the Corporation bought out the private company in 1845, there had been nothing but trouble. When the great fire of 1852 destroyed much of the old system, Thomas Keefer proposed abandoning what remained, in favor of completely new plans. These involved a canal or aqueduct, starting from a point a mile and a half above the Lachine Rapids, and extending down to the Wheelhouse. There the pumps, with a capacity of 4,000,000 gallons a day, raised the water to a reservoir on the mountainside. It was a good scheme, and designed for a population of double the size, yet it ceased to function whenever ice blocked the aqueduct. In 1862 and 1863, the supply of water was so uncertain that the ancient puncheons were once more pressed into service.

The public grumbled perpetually about the Police Department, but a report of this period indicates that any inefficiency was due to the small size of the force. Its 113 men were too few in number for the population, and not even the promise of twelve additional recruits would give much relief. "The beats are now so distant from their respective stations that in case of a row, it is impossible for men to arrive in time." Notwithstanding this handicap, the offenders brought to book totaled 12,297—drunkards, juvenile delinquents, tavern keepers who remained open on Sundays, persons connected with houses of ill fame.

At much the same date, a revolution in local transportation was taking place. The city had grown too large to get around comfortably on foot, and persons of modest means could not afford carriage hire. The Montreal and Lachine Railroad pioneered in cheap and rapid transit. From 1847 onward, its six trains daily shuttled back and forth between Bonaventure Station and the wharf from which the steamers left for Upper Canada. Each run took twenty minutes, and provided for several intermediate stops. So popular did this service become that in lieu of tickets, copper tokens were issued for the convenience of the early commuters.

Another milestone came in May 1861 with the incorporation of the Montreal City Passenger Railway. The first contract provided for the laying of tracks over a six-mile loop-line, westward from the Company stables at Hochelaga. Four cars, each drawn by two horses, made up the rolling stock; in winter, the sleighs took over. Regular service was maintained from seven in the morning until ten at night. The five-cent fare was attractive.

But the Company could not hope to escape opposition. While the householders on Great St. James Street feared that its semi-residential character would be lost, the cab-owners claimed the new tracks rendered the roadways unsafe. In the extremity of their anger, some turned to violence; they beat up the horses, stoned and broke the car windows, and placed obstructions along the right of way. Nonetheless, the venture prospered. Repeated extensions of the tracks and the purchase of additional cars brought the passengers out in ever-growing numbers. By September 1863 they had exceeded one million.

The almost immediate acceptance of the streetcars was, to a large extent, tied in with the growth of the labor force. The workingman could now live in the outskirts of the city with some assurance that neither physical infirmities nor inclement weather would impede his daily comings and goings. This great boon was, of course, shared by others—including, it may be assumed, the students whose numbers increased in step with the population.

By mid-century, the principle of dualism in education had become firmly entrenched. Once the English abandoned their futile attempts to impose Anglo-Saxon ways on an unwilling people, the necessity for a division along religious and linguistic lines became obvious. The pioneers, in both groups, faced many problems. After long struggles to conduct schools on a voluntary basis, the Education Act of 1841, by its adoption of the principle of compulsory taxation, seemed to promise relief. But although subsequent modifications—notably in 1846—restated the theory, in practice the French and the English alike, for some years more, maintained institutions largely dependent on free-will contributions.

Because of the differing requirements of the twin systems, there were many schools in the town. Some were large, some small, and the quality of their instruction varied. In certain respects, the Roman Catholics possessed advantages denied to the Protestants, for their teaching at both the elementary and higher levels rested with the religious communities. So far as Montreal was concerned, the Sulpicians were the most important. They had always taught, training candidates for the priesthood, while imparting a sound classical education to young laymen. As the number of their pupils increased, the Seminary or College down-town, proved inadequate. In 1854 they started to build the Grand Seminary, on the site of the old Mountain Fort or Fort des Messieurs. Its consecration in 1862 marked a great advance, especially when taken in conjunction with the foundation of Laval University at Quebec in 1852.

It was the Sulpicians, too, who, in 1837, invited Les Frères des Ecoles Chrétiennes—the Christian Brothers—to establish schools in Montreal similar to those conducted by the Order in France. The first four members started in a modest way, but their work with boys showed great progress. An unbiased visitor, about the year 1858, reported favorably on all that he saw. The classrooms were unusually spacious, and well arranged, and the writing and drawing lessons highly satisfactory. The instruction was carefully planned, and the general order and cleanliness pleasing. Direc-tors of European schools, he felt, might with profit, study the local methods of administration.

The Sulpicians in 1840, had welcomed an agreement, whereby Lord Sydenham gave them legal title to their seigniorial lands. Technically, the change was a slight one, for they had never been dispossessed. Yet there had been uncertainty. This having been removed, they could proceed with plans for the future. One stipulation only must be met—the annual revenue from these properties was to be spent on the propagation of the Catholic faith and the instruction of the young within the parish of Notre Dame.

An interview with the Sulpician authorities in 1858, revealed how carefully they honored their promises to the government. The Seminary still owned great sections of the Island—all the villages, several farms, and many houses. That the income was considerable, there could be no doubt, yet only a trifling balance remained at the end of the year. Most of it had been spent on the public good—the maintenance of schools and colleges, the care of the orphans, the relief of the poor.

By this date also, the Jesuits were settled in Montreal. Their arrival in 1842 came in response to an invitation from Bishop Bourget. But the prelate's hope that they might establish a college went unrealized for several years, mainly because of the Order's close connection with the Irish. During the ship fever epidemic, the Jesuits shared with the other priests of the city the task of ministering to the sick and dying.

When this time of trial was over, the Bishop asked four of the fathers, to take over the new St. Patrick's Church on Dorchester Street. Their charge was a heavy one, for estimates in 1861 placed the Irish at almost one-third of the total population. Yet these same men, in 1848, established St. Mary's College, offering in the words of their prospectus, a complete classical course in which equal attention was paid to French and English in their teaching. In many ways, they were fortunate, not least in the acquisition, at a moderate price, of John Donegani's land, south of Dorchester and close by the church. And while only thirteen pupils registered for the first session, the classes grew until St. Mary's became Loyola, the English-speaking Catholic College of Montreal.

In the Protestant community the greatest hopes for the future lay in the realm of higher education, for it is from this period that the rebirth of McGill is usually dated. The change for the better started in 1852, with a new and more favorable charter, and, three years later, William Dawson became the principal. The task that lay before him was a heavy one.

So far, the struggling college had experienced little but ill fortune. The long years of the lawsuit had been followed by more delays, so that the cornerstone of the first building was not laid until 1839. If the ceremony was impressive, the sequel was not. Guards of honor and military bands could not compensate for lack of money and disputes among those in authority. Even when completed in 1843, the two detached sections of the Arts Building were so far out from town that the classes included exactly three students. No degrees were conferred until May 1849, when Alexander Morris received a B.A. As he had been registered only since January, the record of his previous studies at Glasgow University presumably impressed the governors.

What probably saved the day was the presence of the Faculty

of Medicine. This had been "engrafted" on the college in 1829, but remained physically separate until its 1845 move into the Arts Building. But the distance was a problem and the rough country walk an ordeal. There was no money to keep the structure in good repair, and piles of stone, left over from the construction, lay about the grounds. These, being unfenced, were used by the townspeople for sports, and the professors cultivated vegetables and kept cows. A large portion of the original Burnside estate was sold. In such melancholy circumstances, the Medical Faculty moved to Côte Street in 1851, followed a year later by the Arts students, who took over the upper floor of the High School on Belmont Street.

The Nova Scotia-born William Dawson arrived to find the two ruinous buildings abandoned. They stood in the midst of a wilderness of rubbish, overgrown with weeds, where the cattle pastured at will. The rooms in which he was to live were dusty and needed repairs. His staff could easily be counted—in Law, two professors and two lecturers; in Medicine, ten professors and a demonstrator; in Arts, four professors and a lecturer. But the governors, he soon discovered, were men of courage and ability, anxious to make improvements if only there were money. Hopefully, the new principal, set off at Christmastime for Toronto, in search of financial aid from the Legislature. It was a tiring journey that lasted five days. As he crossed the river in a canoe among floating ice, he must have looked longingly at the start of the construction of the bridge. But he pressed on, via Albany, Niagara, and Hamilton, reaching the capital at last, over roads blocked with snow.

After this ordeal, it was disappointing to discover that little direct aid was forthcoming. An appeal to the citizens of Montreal met with a better response—$20,000 for the endowment of the Molson Chair of English Language and Literature, and $35,000 from other benefactors. For McGill, this was the turning point. In 1856 and because of a fire in the school on Belmont Street, the return to the campus started. The grounds were planted and proper walks installed. By 1860, fifty students in Arts were pursuing their studies in the central block of the original buildings.

McGill was not alone in its difficulties. For many years the struggle for survival among the Protestant schools precluded any ambitious hopes of expansion. The need for money lay at the root of the trouble, and each season brought a battle to secure increased grants from public funds. Judging by statistics, the government invariably emerged as the victor. For the fifteen-year period that ended in 1861, the annual receipts from the city and province combined averaged $1200. They then rose to $1810—spurred on, it would seem, by the census figures which revealed the existence of five thousand Protestant children of school age.

Because of this apathy on the part of those who controlled the public purse, private generosity stepped in to fill the breach. The High School originated with a group of citizens, who, in 1842, started to solicit subscriptions. Within a few months, they sponsored a public meeting, chaired by the Honorable Peter McGill, and this paved the way for the opening of the new institution in September 1842. Sixty-five pupils attended the classes, held in rented space at the corner of Notre Dame and St. Denis streets. Three years later came the absorption of the Royal Grammar School.

To its fifteen directors during the next decade, it must often have seemed as though for every two steps forward, they took one back. The number of pupils rose to two hundred, and then fell off, as the competition of rival establishments took its toll. A new building was erected on Belmont Street, only to be followed by grave financial embarrassments. It was then that McGill went to the rescue. From 1853 to 1863, the school functioned as a department of the college, and thus gained the benefits of Dr. Dawson's practical experience. In 1854 there came a move to Burnside Hall, at the corner of Dorchester Street and Union Avenue. Although destroyed by fire in 1856, the Hall was rebuilt, and the joint occupancy retained until 1860, when McGill's return to its own campus was completed.

The education of boys was obviously considered to be more vital than the training of girls. Woman's place was still in the home. For parents of sufficient means, however, the advertisements reveal the existence of various academies and finishing schools, all dedicated to imparting the arts of polite society.

On the whole, the Roman Catholic girls were more fortunate than their Protestant friends, for their teaching, as in the past, remained chiefly with the Sisters of La Congregation de Notre Dame. As the pupils increased in numbers, so did their instructors, while additions to existing structures and the provision of new quarters indicated the extent of their work. One of these was Monklands, which, when no longer needed as a vice-regal residence, was taken over by John Orr. He operated it as a hotel, apparently without much success. For although an omnibus ran back and forth to the city all day, it was too far out for the convenience of the traveling public. In 1854, the Order bought it for use as a pensionnat, and the rechristened Villa Maria has continued to flourish until the present day.

But schools and colleges did not represent the sum total of Montreal's investment in culture. Adult education claimed the attention of at least some citizens, taking the form of museums, libraries, lectures, and exhibitions. Foremost among these institutions was the Natural History Society, which from small beginnings in 1827, graduated by 1858 into spacious quarters at the intersection of University and Cathcart streets. A lecture room and library occupied the main floor, and upstairs there was a museum whose displays included mineralogical and geological specimens, as well as cases of birds, reptiles and quadrupeds. The weekly lectures, while well organized, did not always command attention, for they "have not at all been countenanced in the degree to which their important and interesting character has entitled them."

Perhaps it was just a matter of too many serious gatherings, for the Mechanics Institute, the Mercantile Library Association, and the Canadian Institute all sponsored regular talks by eminent professors. The subjects were literary as well as scientific. Perhaps too, the attendance improved, in view of the inspiration provided by the American Association for the Advancement of Science. In what was one of Montreal's early international conventions, the Court House offered suitable space for a week of meetings in August 1857. There was much hospitality—a soirée, given by the Natural History Society; a visit to St. Helen's Island, as guests of the officers of the garrison; a magnificent *conversazione,* offered by the Directors, Faculty, and Fellows of McGill.

Such occasions benefitted greatly from the foresight of the City Fathers, in their building of Bonsecours Market—a misnomer, if ever there was one, it being much more than a place in which to buy and sell the produce of the countryside. It was quite a new structure, begun in 1843, and fashioned of cut stone in a classic style of architecture. The extensive frontage looked toward the river, and being three stories high, its lofty dome and tin-covered roof shared with Notre Dame Church, the honors of the skyline. From the police station on the main floor, a connecting staircase went up to the municipal offices, which in the '50s included the city hall, fifty-five by forty-three feet in size, and decorated appropriately. Immediately across this central rotunda, a concert hall was available for use by the citizens.

For those who sought more gaiety, the Theatre Royal on Côte Street was generally to be relied on. This hospitable structure, rebuilt after the Hays' House fire, accommodated 1500 persons. One of its early lessees was J. W. Bickland, who engaged a stock company which presented such plays as *Peg Woffington, Rob Roy,* and *The Cricket on the Hearth.* In the winter, the Gentlemen Amateurs staged occasional performances, as did the regiments of the garrison. Visiting singers and actors usually performed there.

Thus, in mid-Victorian times, did Montreal attempt to lose the earlier stigma of being an intellectual desert.

Chapter 31

1861–1867

The American Civil War. The Trent affair. The South favored. Local prosperity. Talk of a federal union. Charlottetown and Quebec. Montreal entertains the delegates. The St. Albans raid. The trial and the fury of the North. The Fenians. The first Dominion Day.

CANADA, AT THIS date, had been British for a century, yet the mother country had never decided whether its retention was worthwhile. Successive generations of Englishmen, both in official circles and among the opposition, questioned the value of colonies. They were always expensive, and none more so than Canada. Moreover, Anglo-American relations were often embarrassed by the existence of this willfully independent possession.

Montreal always knew when London was gripped by one of these periodic fits of indifference, for the governmental views showed first in the reduction of the garrison. Rarely had the Imperial outlay for defense been lower than at the outbreak of the American Civil War in 1861. In all of British North America, there were less than 4300 regulars, of whom only 2200 were in Canada proper. Even when reinforced by 5000 volunteers, it was a puny force to withstand the apparent threat to the frontier.

The gravity of the situation was not at first realized. The attack on Fort Sumter in April was far away, if measured in miles, and the quarrel purely American. It was not until the Trent affair in November that Canadian opinions changed. The forcible removal from this British ship of the two Confederate envoys, Mason and Slidell, carried Great Britain and the United States to the brink of war. But fortunately wiser counsels prevailed. In the last days of his life, the dying Prince Consort toned down the harsh message of Lord Palmerston and his fellow ministers. Lincoln and his cabinet wanted to avert hostilities. With the return of the captives to a British vessel, the danger was averted for the moment, yet the long-term hazard remained operative, and Canada, geographically, was in the front line.

London lost no time in sending troops out to the rescue. Their December sailing date was a late one, and although the transports raced for the St. Lawrence, they arrived to find navigation closed. Turned back to the Maritimes, the 14,000 men went ashore, to face a laborious winter journey overland, through New Brunswick and up to Canada. Other reinforcements followed, until by the spring, 18,000 regulars were stationed in the province, most of them in what had been Lower Canada. So many were posted to Montreal that the barracks proved insufficent; several colleges and stores were leased by the government, and fitted out as living quarters. And since 50,000 rifles and an ample supply of ammunition accompanied the men, the local security picture brightened.

Few cities could have welcomed more devoutly the peaceful solution of the Trent crisis. The news reached Montreal on December 27, and the day following being a Sunday, there were services of thanksgiving in the churches. Meanwhile, its people had not been idle. During those few anxious weeks, they worked feverishly to repair the defects of their defenses. As Sandham described it, they "hastened to form themselves into military companies, and the papers of the day were filled with notices having prominent headings; 'Stand to your arms,' 'Defence not defiance,' and similar mottoes. The streets of the city, particularly in the evening, presented quite a military aspect. Mechanics, clerks, tradesmen and merchants might be seen hastening to the rendezvous of their several corps. Companies in almost every arm of the service—cavalry, artillery, infantry and riflemen were at once organized and commenced to drill."

But the enthusiasm of the volunteers could not always be maintained at such a high pitch. From time to time, the claims of everyday life were irresistible, whereas the regulars, of necessity, stayed at their posts. For three years, Montreal had an unusually large garrison, and was actually designated in a British report of 1862 as "the principal strategic point in the province." Yet it was still an open town. Various recommendations were put forward as to permanent fortifications, differing in content, but unanimous on the subject of expense. For this reason, the plans never got beyond the paper stage.

Thus Montreal witnessed a great deal of military activity. Special Imperial commissioners joined the regular officers in surveys of the defenses, and always the normal routines of drill and training were carried out. Occasionally there were special events, as when in July 1862 the new Governor General, Lord Monck, paid his initial visit to the city. The professionals and the amateurs co-operated, forming a double line through the streets as His Excellency passed, to the vast enjoyment of the crowd. On the next day, three thousand of their number staged a grand mimic fight at Logan's Farm.

All this time, Canadian public opinion was crystallizing in a surprising fashion. At the start of the war, people in general favored the North and the abolition of slavery. Not that the question was of burning importance locally, since the 1861 census showed that only 190 Negroes lived in the lower section of the province. Slavery, as an active force, was something extremely remote; it had been practiced in New France and during the years that followed. But after the last public sale of a slave in 1797, the system virtually came to an end, thirty years before legally abolished by the Imperial Parliament.

Yet when political and constitutional questions complicated the issue at stake, Canadians found a full understanding of their neighbors to be difficult. Tariff problems always lurked in the background and fears of American aggression. Gradually, the newspapers changed their views, and many of their readers followed suit. Lincoln himself, was personally unknown, and some of his officials were decidedly bellicose in the choice of their words. Although William H. Seward, as Secretary of State, was the chief sword rattler, he was well matched at more modest levels by men such as Joshua Giddings, the consul general at

Montreal, a tactless individual, and totally inexperienced in the niceties of diplomacy. By 1862, many of the local citizenry, in common with their fellow Canadians, were in the process of becoming firm supporters of the Confederacy. The crude partisanship of the Northern press irritated them, while friction along the border and minor "incidents" kept the dislike very much alive.

Montreal, of course, actually knew the Southerners, who, in more peaceful times, came to Canada as tourists to escape the summer heat of their own homes. They were usually persons of wealth, whose refinement of manner formed a pleasing contrast to the forceful Yankees; upper class society made them welcome. When stranded in this alien country by war, the same charm was put to work on behalf of their cause. It was only a short step to the establishment of informal Confederate headquarters in several Canadian cities, and notably at Montreal. One of its leading hostelries, the St. Lawrence Hall, actually won fame as having the only bar in the country to serve mint juleps! The result of all this was that the Southern secret service agents began to use Canada as a base for plotting hit-and-run raids against the North. Whatever they did was magnified by rumors along the frontier. So serious, in fact, did the situation become that by the end of 1863 the Canadian government was cooperating with the North in an attempt to prevent any more serious occurrences.

In domestic affairs, Montreal entered the war period in a state of satisfactory prosperity. As the financial center of the country, it took great pride in its banks, and boasted incessantly of the superiority of the Canadian system. No matter how common the failures across the border, the local institutions so far had escaped any "stoppage." Moreover, there was the wonderful new coinage, valid currency since 1860, and in the decimal system to boot—thanks largely to Montreal's Francis Hincks, who, while Minister of Finance, battled successfully with the British government on the subject of dollars and cents as opposed to sterling.

Improved communications made the lot of the businessman easier. Canada, after 1851, administered the Post Office, and although service complaints still appeared, the carriage of letters was both cheaper and speedier than under British management. In any event, the telegraph soon provided an alternative. A survey at the close of 1856 estimated the local office was then averaging 750 messages a day. Two years later came the successful laying of the Atlantic cable.

The movement of industry continued outward from the city limits—to sites along the Lachine Canal and to such remote spots as Côte St. Paul, where municipal taxation might be avoided. Transportation by land and water was excellent, and factory hands plentiful, although "inventions for the economisation of human labour therein are singularly ingenious." An early example of automation was the immense flour mill, housed in an eight-story building which could accommodate 200,000 bushels of grain in its warehouse. Elevators, worked by water-power, unloaded the barges and raised the wheat up into the bins. What would have taken a whole day, if men were employed, could be completed within an hour.

But behind this flirtation with modernity, Montreal faced serious problems. At times, there were contributory causes, such as poor harvests or economic depression in the United States. Yet the roots lay deeper. Out of the unending competition for the carrying trade of the west, Canada had emerged as the loser. Only ten or fifteen percent of the traffic passed through Montreal. Buffalo and Oswego were outstripping the local port, just as American canals and railroads bested the St. Lawrence River system.

The railroads, for their part, were no strangers to trouble. Throughout the '50s they expanded so recklessly that their mileage not only exceeded the needs of the population, but also its ability to pay. After 1860, construction almost ceased for a decade. No line could hope to escape the crisis, but the Grand Trunk, by virtue of its size and overextension, felt the pinch most of all. With its Canadian operations pretty well based on Montreal, the citizens soon became only too conscious of the difficulties. Only a few years after its grand inaugural, the Victoria Bridge found itself the target of criticism; its costs were said to be out of all proportion to the amount of traffic.

The transportation dilemma, in the broadest sense, could not be resolved by any single city in terms of its own needs. Thus the government from an early date was called upon to assist with the successive crises that arose, particularly in respect to finance, and this at a time when the United Province of Canada itself lacked the consistent policies that come from clear-cut parliamentary rule by majority. In the decade from 1854 to 1864, ten different ministries tried to rule the country. Election followed election, and there were coalitions and all manner of combinations.

Ever since its departure from Montreal in 1849, the government had been perambulating back and forth between Quebec and Toronto. This, in itself, was so unsatisfactory that the Queen was invited to select a permanent capital. Although her choice of Ottawa in 1857 pleased no one in official circles, preparations were under way for the move in the early sixties. It was unlikely to effect much improvement. The old conflict between the Upper and Lower sections of the province had never been completely healed, and the French and the English retained their mutually suspicious attitudes.

Such a situation gave form and substance to the vague ideas of federal union that had circulated earlier. At the commencement of 1864, some of the vacillation of the past vanished, and in any case, the pressure of outside events was forcing Canada's hands. Caught between the United States and Great Britain, the government of necessity followed a path that grew steadily more strait. It was in these circumstances that John A. Macdonald emerged into a position of leadership, while two of Montreal's parliamentary delegation started to play roles that were to grow more important. French Canadian Georges Etienne Cartier and Irish-born D'Arcy McGee, although political opponents, supported the new ideas.

The long-threatened crisis came to a head in the summer. The collapse of the administration, nominally led by Sir Etienne Taché, revealed the severity of the impasse in provincial affairs; its two strongest members, Macdonald and Cartier, seemed powerless to avert a breakdown. Another election would almost certainly fail to bring about any improvement. There had been too many already, and their old-fashioned open polls provoked violence without offering any solution.

It was then that the great news broke. Wonders will never cease, crowed the *Gazette*. Negotiations were in progress between the Conservatives—Macdonald, Cartier, and Alexander Galt of Sherbrooke—and George Brown of the Liberal or Reform party for the formation of a coalition government. Suddenly, events moved forward with startling speed, for the new ministry was openly committed to a program of union with the other colonies of British North America. On June 30, Lord Monck wrote to ask if its representatives might attend the forthcoming meeting at which Maritime union was to be discussed.

To understand the shock caused by this request, it should be remembered that the four British provinces bordering on the Atlantic were, to most Canadians, unknown territory. Despite repeated attempts to achieve an Intercolonial Railway, the Montreal-Halifax line was still a dream. No one would either agree on its location or put up the money. Thus overland travel was tedious and difficult, while the St. Lawrence route in summer was little used.

The Atlantic provinces had troubles of their own—not so much political as in Canada, but those born of isolation, a scattered population and poverty. Whenever times were bad, they talked vaguely of union among themselves. Nova Scotia, New Brunswick, Prince Edward Island, Newfoundland—together, the four might fare better than separately. But although a conference was supposedly scheduled for this summer, no one, in the prevailing lethargy, had as yet settled a date or a place.

Such were the preliminaries which led to Canadian participation in the sessions which opened at Charlottetown on September 1. On board the steamer *Queen Victoria,* the representatives sailed down from Quebec, fortified by the knowledge that the British Colonial Office favored their plans. At their head was Macdonald, who although not the titular leader of the administration, was the mainspring of the Confederation move. With him went Galt, the Minister of Finance; Cartier, converted after some hesitation; several junior cabinet colleagues and a secretarial staff of three; all in all, a delegation of unusual size and importance.

Events at the conference showed the strength of Macdonald's position, for what had been planned as a meeting to consider Maritime union soon became a serious discussion of the wider British North American federation. Somewhat to the bewilderment of the hosts, the Canadians held the floor, and gradually the first tentative proposals took shape—there was to be a central government, which would assume all existing debts and would in turn provide revenues for each province on the basis of population. This much accomplished, the progress seemed sufficient to warrant another and more formal gathering to open at Quebec on October 10.

Once the guests arrived at the ancient capital, Montreal took more interest in the discussions. The local population was by no means prepared to give unanimous approval to the changes. Many French Canadians feared a diminution of their rights, just as some English Canadians hesitated over the separation from Upper Canada. In fact, the absence of definite knowledge did nothing to allay the popular mistrust. Press conferences and official releases were as yet undreamed of, and the sessions remained strictly private. The *Gazette* reported that closed doors and almost Masonic secrecy was the rule at Quebec, adding caustically that the festivities were interfering with business.

Certainly any official hesitation at Montreal vanished, at hearing the news that the delegates would arrive in the city on October 28. A local planning committee sprang into action, while the sessions were still in progress at Quebec. Steadily, from day to day, facing problems and somehow managing to solve them, Macdonald led the members on to the formulation of definite Resolutions.

If any delegates still remained opposed to the idea of unity, the St. Albans raid came pat, on October 19. This explosive event, which threatened to precipitate an Anglo-American war, was the work of Confederates whose plans had been hatched at Montreal. When their group of picked men, led by Lieutenant Young, crossed the border into Vermont, they posed as Canadians while they shot up the peaceful village. Having robbed the banks of

$200,000, they returned across the border to safety, leaving behind a trail of burning houses, terrified townspeople, and civilian casualties.

The excitement that followed this news can readily be imagined. All the border towns were in utter confusion, their very real fears in no way abated by the flood of rumors. The Northern newspapers reacted violently, demanding dire punishment for the offenders. But Lord Monck acted promptly in ordering the arrest of all the raiders found in Canada, and, by October 23, fourteen were in custody at St. Johns awaiting examination. Because of the acute tension, however, they were soon transferred back to the city. Then the arguments began: Were the men Confederate troops? Was their attack an act of war? Or was it a simple bank robbery by desperadoes?

It was therefore no idle jest that led the delegates to view Confederation as a necessity for the preservation of independence. Being the weaker, the Maritimes had perhaps less to gain, and so were fearful of their rights, *vis-à-vis* the more populous Canadas. Yet slowly their differences were ironed out, so that Montreal met representatives who were prepared to go ahead with the summing up of the work of the entire conference.

They came to a city agog with preparations, and only the weather refused to co-operate on Friday October 28. Rain on the preceding evening was followed, next morning, by gale winds which ruined the public holiday. Impassable streets forced a postponement of the review of volunteers on the Champ de Mars. While some of the party toured the Geological Survey Museum with D'Arcy McGee, others inspected the fire alarm system. The speed and efficiency with which the reels responded, aroused great admiration. The evening brought a ball at St. Lawrence Hall.

Saturday was another busy day, the morning being devoted to a final revision of the Quebec Resolutions. That evening, three hundred leading citizens acted as hosts at a banquet, when all the speakers showed an encouraging forgetfulness of personal difficulties and local distinctions. But on Monday, the visitors left for Ottawa, and Montreal's immediate participation

in Confederation plans came to an end. Other matters crowded
forward to occupy the civic mind, and above all, the St. Albans
raiders.

The trial, which started on November 2, lasted for several
weeks before Judge Coursol, the crowded room in the Sessions
Court serving as a cockpit for the clash between North and
South. The accused, in the interval, had no reason to complain
of their treatment, being lodged in the jailer's own house, and
regaled on delicate foods and wines supplied by their friends.

Their opponents were apparently confident that savage retribution would be meted out to the offenders. Six charges were
listed as grounds for extradition—assault, murder, attempted
murder, robbery, attempted arson, and horse stealing. The defense, led by John J. Abbott, contended in reply that the raid
was a legitimate act of war and hence its perpetrators exempt
from extradition. After long and tedious examinations, he succeeded to the extent of gaining a thirty-day delay, for the purpose of securing further documentary evidence from Richmond.

It was when the case was resumed that the scandal arose. The
defense lawyers shifted their stand, and proceeded to challenge
the jurisdiction of the magistrate, on the score of technical defects in the British and Canadian statutes involved. After some
consideration, Judge Coursol concurred, and, on December 13,
ordered the release of the prisoners. Later that same day, they
all left Montreal by train, the stolen money restored to their
keeping, apparently with the full permission of Guillaume Lamothe, the Chief of Police.

To say that the fat was in the fire would be a gross under-
statement. Few of those in authority agreed with Coursol's decision. In the midst of ugly rumors of bribery, Cartier as At-
torney General for Canada East, suspended him and disclaimed
all responsibility. Macdonald himself was annoyed, both as a
lawyer and a politician. Coursol, he considered to have been in
error, over his assumption of the right to discharge the prisoners;
the question of jurisdiction should have been referred to the
Superior Court. The *Gazette* regretted the discharge "upon a
mere point of view."

Needless to say, the North was furious at the verdict, the press calling for an invasion of Canada, while the Senate voiced accusations of protection to criminals. Retaliatory measures were bound to appear. As of December 17, passports were required of all aliens entering the United States—a short-lived ruling that aroused much indignation in Canada until rescinded in March 1865. More seriously, that spring brought from Washington, a formal notice of intent to abrogate the Reciprocity Treaty between the two countries, as of March 1866.

The Canadian government, scrupulously neutral, did its best to offset the ill-conceived action of Coursol. Parliament voted $50,000, to be paid to the St. Albans banks, in reparation for their losses. The released raiders were pursued, and under the spur of a $200 reward for each capture, most of them were retaken, either in New Brunswick or east of Quebec. Once more, they appeared in Montreal, this time before Judge Smith of the Superior Court. His verdict, which reversed that of Coursol, was disputed by the defense counsel, and argued out at length. Eventually the case was dismissed, thus terminating Montreal's direct connection with these complex judicial procedures. When new warrants were issued on the charge of a violation of neutrality, the men were removed to Toronto for fresh hearings.

This clash with Confederate marauders did much to counteract the harsh language of the North. Public opinion underwent such a radical change that the news of the assassination of President Lincoln in April 1865, cast a gloom over Montreal. The city grieved over the tragedy, and a proclamation from the Corporation called on all to observe the day appointed for the funeral, as one of mourning.

But if this particular furor died down, the Fenians remained in the limelight. The Brotherhood dated from 1859, its organization in New York being dedicated to the cause of Irish independence. During the closing stages of the war, they turned their attention to British North America. Whether in the flesh or as phantoms, they haunted the frontier, from New Brunswick right up through the vulnerable fringe of the Canadas.

The emotional appeal of these anti-British raiders might well have had serious consequences in Canada, with its mixed population. Nowhere, perhaps, could they have hoped for greater success than in Montreal, with its thousands of Irish immigrants. Yet all remained loyal to their new country. From the first false alarm, the volunteers came forward, marching off to their military duties among excited crowds that included "even respectable people," and all classes from the richest to the humblest.

The high tide of the Fenian threat occurred in 1866, when the Canadian government, fearing trouble on St. Patrick's Day, called up ten thousand militia to guard the borders for three weeks. Just to add to the excitement locally, a store of enemy uniforms and military equipment was unearthed in a building on St. James Street. So hasty was the mobilization that the volunteer corps left Montreal about nine o'clock one night, minus many necessary articles of personal gear, and leaving behind, families entirely dependent on the army pittance. Their patriotism was contagious, for a group of citizens busied themselves with relief measures, collecting over $20,000 to provide outfits for men in need, as well as for the payment of a daily allowance of fifty cents to their wives and children.

But the country could not keep such patrols permanently on duty, and so was unprepared to meet the menace of early June. Four Montreal companies were then ordered off westward, to meet the invaders at Fort Erie, leaving behind a city determined to resist any attack. Guards were stationed along the Grand Trunk at such points as Vaudreuil, Ste. Annes, and Lachine, while others entrained for the border at Hemmingford, St. Armand, and Pigeon Hill. At the last-named hamlet, a thousand Fenians, led by General Spier, moved forward to the attack on June 7—a brief affair, from which they were soon driven back. Within a fortnight, the danger was over, and the troops returned to their homes and a great welcome.

In the United States, the authorities at St. Albans seized the arms of the fleeing rabble. With President Andrew Johnson's prompt enforcement of neutrality, their military power seemed at an end. Thus nothing more happened until 1870, when General John O'Neill renewed the attempt to free Ireland by an invasion of Canada. Having gathered together 15,000 stand of arms and 3,000,000 rounds of ammunition, he set up his headquarters at Franklin, Vermont. Deliberately, he chose May 24 as zero hour, when every Canadian volunteer was certain to be on parade in honor of Queen Victoria's birthday. Although delayed until the 25th, he proceeded to cross into Quebec under the green flag of the Irish Republic, undaunted by warnings from the Americans, and with forces smaller than he had hoped for.

Some advance warning of this attack had come through in April, from the British Minister in Washington. Montreal was once more the scene of military fervor. Recruiting was lively, and the streets gay with the sights and sounds of troops marching along to martial music. It was a finely equipped little army that faced O'Neill and his undisciplined mob. Their ranks broke as the Irishmen fled back across the border, throwing away their arms in their eager rush to safety.

When, the next day, President Ulysses S. Grant issued a proclamation forbidding such incursions into Canada, the Fenian menace at last came to an end. But it left its imprint on Canadian history, and played an important role in the creation of the new Dominion. For after this adversity, a fresh national spirit made itself felt, the people at large following the lead that had already been provided by their statesmen and politicians.

For although after the few hopeful months of 1864, progress was slower than expected, few Canadian leaders doubted the ultimate wisdom of some form of federation. They showed this at Quebec, when both Houses debated the proposals at length, and although their approval was delayed until March 10, and lacked unanimity, much of the opposition hinged on details, rather than on basic principles. Cartier expressed the sentiments of the majority, when he felt that Confederation was forced upon Canada. Looking across the border, no other course was possible, if absorption into the United States was to be avoided. D'Arcy McGee, too, pictured the acquisition of Canada as being the first ambition of the aggressive Americans; events, he warned, could be stronger than men.

But brave words such as these, found little echo in the Maritimes. When New Brunswick, in that same year, returned a hostile administration, its voters seemed merely to have given formal expression to the general indifference of the four provinces. Ostensibly, Confederation was dead when Macdonald headed a delegation to London in the spring, and when, a few months later, Ottawa became the Canadian capital, the fresh surroundings appeared powerless to prevent a return to the old ways.

Yet, events proved too strong for the men who confined themselves to parochial views and local needs. The emergence of a powerful North as the almost certain victor in the American war; the constant Fenian alarms; the loss of trade inherent in the termination of the Reciprocity Treaty—in such circumstances, the charms of isolation lessened. Egged on by successive British governments, eager to shed their costly military responsibilities, Nova Scotia and New Brunswick expressed themselves as willing to unite with the Canadas, soon to be known as the provinces of Quebec and Ontario. Together these four—Prince Edward Island and Newfoundland held aloof—hammered out the constitutional problems, and their give-and-take was flexible enough to insure success. In June 1866 the Legislature of the old United Province of Canada met for the last time.

The culmination of all these painstaking negotiations—the doubts, the fears, the prayers—came with the royal proclamation of the British North America Act on May 22, 1867. On July 1, the Dominion of Canada officially would come into existence. To Macdonald—now the Prime Minister and knighted by the Queen in honor of his achievement—the occasion called for a public holiday. Everyone, he felt, should be free to join in the ceremonies that saw them become citizens of this nation, new but still a part of the old Empire.

In their combination of military and civil activities, the Montreal plans aimed at providing something for everyone. They were less carefree than in 1860, since the banks and insurance companies frowned on gas illuminations for public buildings. But Mr. Jones Lyman came back from Boston, armed with a liberal provision of the finest set pieces ever seen in Canada, so that the evening program of fireworks at the reservoir promised to be a great success.

Fine weather greeted the early risers on the first Dominion Day. After some threatening signs of storm the previous evening, the morning breezes and bright sunshine ushered in a holiday that grew steadily hotter as the hours passed. The sounds of gunfire started long before breakfast, for the local regiments vied with each other in their desire to honor the occasion. An air of subdued bustle filled the streets, as people made their way along the dusty road to Logan's Farm. Past the public buildings, the houses, the ships in the harbor, all gayly beflagged and cheered on by the stirring music of the bands, on foot, on horseback, in carriages, all Montreal turned out to watch the great review of the troops. Officialdom was represented by the Mayor, dignified in his robes, his open carriage drawn by four white horses and with a suitable escort. Four times he read the Royal Proclamation, in French and English, always preceded by a flourish of trumpets—at Logan's Farm, Dalhousie Square, Place d'Armes, and Victoria Square.

The formalities having been observed, the afternoon and evening were free for relaxation—lacrosse games, and, of course, those wonderful fireworks. Montrealers were now Canadians, in the modern sense of the word, and their celebrations in the largest city of the land were matched to some degree in all the towns and villages of the four provinces. One citizen, a hundred years ahead of his time, was moved to write a letter to his newspaper. "Have we, as yet, a national flag? If not, are we going to have one?" And just to start the ball rolling, he suggested a design that would combine the Union Jack of Britain with the Tricolor of France.

Chapter 32

1867–1885

The commercial emporium of the new country. Wealth. The French-English chasm. The C.P.R. and the Pacific scandal. George Stephen and Donald A. Smith. Industry grows. Samuel Butler. "O God! O Montreal!"

THE DAWN of the brave new world, nationally, found Montreal as self-confident and ambitious as in the past—determined to retain its commercial and financial leadership and its pre-eminence as a communications center. Granted that Quebec City, as the capital of the province, had a political status denied to its sister metropolis, it was a steady loser as a port, and its railroad facilities were poor. As for upstart Toronto, with all its pretensions, Montreal could as yet afford to shrug them off as insignificant.

As he compiled his Directory in the year of Confederation, John Lovell wrote glowingly of the future. The Commercial Emporium of the Canadas would now develop into "the center around which the commerce of British North America will revolve." Having added six hundred names to his listing, he doubtless felt justified in boasting of the civic extension in house accommodation, population and wealth. And the widely quoted estimate of six hundred to seven hundred new dwellings a year at this period, did indeed suggest a surprising amount of construction—especially when churches, schools, and other public buildings were added to the total. Despite rising rentals, 1867 saw a steady demand for homes.

"No part of Canada shows more numerous and substantial indications of material improvements." The streets were widened, the shops revolutionized, and an air of wealth and grandeur prevailed along the main thoroughfares of the town. An overseas visitor described Notre Dame Street as flashing with plate glass and displays of jewelry and brocade. H. and H. Merrill's Dry Goods Store, he considered to be the finest in the country. Four stories high and well lighted, the front windows alone of the main floor Retail Department were twenty-two feet wide.

In any comment on the city proper, it should be remembered that a strong countermovement outward, was noticeable. Sandham wrote of what he saw in 1869. "The facilities afforded by the street railways have led to the expansion of the population toward the city limits, and even beyond them. It is difficult to mark the distinction between the city and the villages of the outlying municipalities. It is apparent that these villages must eventually form part of the city, and it would be advantageous if some preparatory arrangement were to be made for assimilating the building and sanitary laws of the municipalities to those of the city.

". . . The turnpike roads upon the Island are the finest in the Dominion and are much frequented for pleasure driving." Obviously, Sandham delighted in the disappearance of the ancient buildings, "their site now occupied by palatial stores and dwellings in almost every conceivable style of architecture. Again we find that where, a few years ago, orchards and fields of grain were planted, is now closely built upon, and the streets which have been laid out in various directions, are being rapidly filled with elegant houses."

But in one particular sense, Montreal was really made up of two cities, both within the municipal limits. St. Lawrence Main Street, running straight up from the river, was usually cited as the invisible dividing line. To the east, lived most of the French citizens, to the west, the English. And much of the civic power derived from the latter; in business, finance, and industry the English controlled the lion's share.

So great was the intellectual and spiritual chasm that strangers marveled, and two in particular, who came out from France a few years after Confederation, wrote at some length on the subject. M. Lamothe found the local Sunday to be a compromise between the Puritan ways of New England and the gaiety of

French peasants and workmen. While the Protestant quarter resembled a morgue, with its trains stopped and its taverns closed, the French were out enjoying themselves. The streetcars still ran, even around the mountain, without scandalizing the community!

Christophe Allard probed more deeply. Anyone who did not know Canadians would find it hard to realize what strangers the French and the English were. They breathed the same air and were subject to the same laws, yet knew nothing of each other. From a conversation in Montreal, he gleaned a graphic simile—a comparison with the famous double stairway at the Château de Chambord on the Loire. Just as two persons could climb its twin spirals, scarcely ever meeting, so it was with the French and the English of this continent. Farther apart than their parent races in Europe, they pressed on toward their destiny, literally as strangers, their rare social renconters yielding no true knowledge of each other.

Politically, the new regime soon took shape. A general election, within a few weeks of Dominion Day, was followed, on November 7, by the opening of the first federal Parliament in Ottawa. It was a triumph for Macdonald. Locally, there were some anxious moments, for although Cartier, by his statesmanship, had made himself one of the great founding "Fathers," he had failed to carry all French Canada with him. Nor could his personal victory in the constituency of Montreal East, conceal the opposition of the Parti Rouge. By training as well as by disposition, a good businessman, it was his fate to become a target for attacks by those who disliked the big interests, as controlled by the English.

In Montreal West, D'Arcy McGee gained the day, although not without a struggle. For when at the close of the polls, the results were announced, his opponents proceeded to attack his Central Committee Room in the Mechanics Hall. Broken windows, an attempt to force an entry, a few pistol shots—these brought out the cavalry to assist the police in dispersing the rioters.

Yet stark tragedy soon ended the life of D'Arcy McGee, for he fell before an assassin's bullet in Ottawa on April 7, 1868. Still young at forty-three, he was perhaps Confederation's most eloquent spokesman, and one, moreover, with so little thought of personal aggrandizement that he waived Cabinet rank to insure better territorial representation. His fellow Montrealers mourned his loss, and the City Council ordained a public funeral. The whole town turned out to watch the great hearse pass through the streets. Drawn by six gray horses, it bore, not only the traditional trappings of black, but the symbols of his Irish birth—his coat of arms and a silver harp, wreathed in shamrock.

Each year brought adjustments to the new nation. The ties with Great Britain loosened when, in 1870 and 1871, the last of the Imperial troops withdrew from Canada. After repeated warnings on the grounds of economy, the outbreak of the Franco-Prussian War finally goaded London into action. Thus Montreal and Quebec lost their familiar garrisons, so often in the last century, a comfort and protection in civil emergencies. In the same year, the Treaty of Washington pretty well wrote "finis" to the ancient dispute between Britain and the United States. Its terms gave little comfort to Canadians. Reciprocity remained a dead letter, to the regret of the local merchants. But when, in 1870, Manitoba became the fifth province to enter Confederation, and British Columbia followed in 1871, Montreal found itself the chief city in a Canada that stretched from the Atlantic to the Pacific.

Yet unavoidably there were growing pains—political, racial, and religious questions in which the local citizenry could not escape involvement. For in the sober afterthoughts that followed 1867, many French Canadians began to harbor serious doubts of the survival of their treasured rights and privileges. When in self-defense they developed reactionary and nationalistic ideas, most English Canadians made no secret of their resentment.

Admittedly, some of the troubles originated elsewhere, for 1873 is generally considered to have been the start of the Great Depression—the upper case letters deliberately borrowed from the history texts to emphasize its serious nature. Apart from short interludes of prosperity, the hard times in Canada persisted almost to the end of the century. That Great Britain and the United States, each in its own way, suffered financial reverses, undoubtedly darkened the local scene. Under fire from both home and foreign sources, the difficulties of the federal government often seemed to defy solution.

A foretaste of what might happen politically came with the General Election of 1872, when Macdonald and his Conservatives appealed to the country. Locally, the party strength devolved entirely upon Cartier—by this date, a man in poor health. Nonetheless, he was determined to run in his old riding of Montreal East. It was then that the discontent really came into the open, so effectively that he went down to defeat before a strange alliance of Liberals, anti-clericals, nationalists, and personal enemies.

For such a party stalwart as Cartier, a safe seat could easily be found. His physical well-being was not so readily insured. Always prone to optimism in such matters, he felt that a holiday in England, and consultations with London physicians, would restore his health. It was a hopeful frame of mind, from which he seldom departed in the months that preceded his death in May 1873.

To most Montrealers, Cartier's decease brought a sense of personal bereavement, so that the funeral provided the occasion for a popular last tribute. Many in the silent crowds wore the mourning badge of black silk ribbon, shaped as a rosette and centered with a photograph. They filled the trains coming into the city, and jammed the streets in their thousands. But the burial could not be a local event. The town overflowed with official representatives, who took their places in the procession that soon after seven o'clock, assembled at the Champ de Mars. Together they marched in such numbers that an hour and a quarter was required to pass any given point. Only a few persons absented themselves. While the *Gazette* regretted that the petty rancors of a group of politicians should follow such a man to his grave, *La Minerve* compared him to Du Guesclin, whose corpse, strapped to his charger went into battle, and won victory, even after death.

Meanwhile, the federal government found itself suffering from the same pressures that had contributed to Cartier's downfall the previous year. In that disaster, the opposition of French Canadian nationalists did not tell the whole story. The ugly rumors and charges of corruption then bandied about, had never been effectively denied, and in July 1873, a Commons Committee, investigating the "Pacific Scandal," gave them a full airing. In November, Macdonald resigned, amid a mass of party defections.

Geographically, the original cause of the *débâcle* lay far from Montreal, its basis being the terms under which British Columbia entered Confederation. A railroad to the Pacific was to be started within two years and completed within ten, otherwise the union became null and void. The local angle arose when Macdonald, in an effort to get construction under way, opened negotiations with Sir Hugh Allan. For although Americans made up most of the group that received the original Canadian Pacific charter in February 1873, Allan was a Montrealer.

Cartier at the time of the 1872 election held the position of solicitor to the Grand Trunk; after some years of this affiliation, he was highly vulnerable to attack by anyone associated with the new Company. For in all the devious discussions preceding the initial charter, the deadly rivalry between the two railroads had been only too clear—the one already strongly entrenched and giving service in eastern Canada, the other as yet only a dream on paper. Yet whenever the government proposed amalgamation, Allan's prohibitive demands foredoomed them to failure.

Nevertheless, in the heat of battle, the Conservatives—and above all, Macdonald and Cartier—took enormous sums of money from this man. Their taking, moreover, was active, rather than passive. They demanded as well as accepted, and unfortunately as it turned out, sometimes put their needs in writing. That Allan responded promptly did little good in the long run. The publication of a telegram from Macdonald, begging for $10,000 brought on the explosion that culminated in the Conservative exodus of 1873. It also killed the plans for the Canadian Pacific, as effectively as it did the government.

The election which followed served chiefly to confirm what everyone already expected. The Conservatives went out, and the Liberals came in, to be confronted immediately by a sea of troubles. Something had to be done about the Canadian Pacific, since Allan showed every indication of cracking under the sheer vastness of the project. That something soon revealed itself to be a cancellation of the contract. Those who knew the new Prime Minister were perhaps the least surprised, for Alexander Mackenzie was a cautious man, whose natural reluctance to take action, led him to look apprehensively at the commitments of his predecessor.

Yet the obligation to British Columbia, and to the west in general, remained to challenge this do-nothing policy. Thus, when no successor to Allan could be found, the government decided to entrust the construction to its own Department of Public Works. In practice, this proved to be an interminable operation. So snail-like was the progress that steel would not reach the Pacific coast for years.

While the Canadian Pacific conundrum was still unsolved, the depression grew steadily worse. Probably no single party at that juncture could have grappled successfully with the national problems, and certainly the Liberals showed little imagination in clearing up the sorry mess. What Montreal felt was indicated by a report dealing with conditions in 1877—a year of wrecks and ruins, of failures, speculations, and losses. A good harvest had briefly raised the local hopes, but by November business was dull again. Many firms went into bankruptcy. Most of the trouble, it was felt, originated with the unfair competition from the United States. American commercial travelers, enjoying free access to the Canadian markets, had managed to wrest a portion of the trade from the Montreal merchants. The government should impose customs duties of such a level as to furnish protection.

The words found an echo in Macdonald's actions, for although still in opposition, he had started to campaign for higher tariffs —the so-called National Policy, with its promise of assistance for the trade and commerce of the country. On July 8, 1877, he made a personal appearance in Montreal, receiving a welcome that was nothing short of overwhelming. Long lines of torchbearers lined the streets through which he passed, en route to Dominion Square, where thousands of citizens awaited him eagerly. The metropolis had, in fact, provided a good omen, foreshadowing the victory that returned the Conservatives to power in September 1878—the first election, incidentally, conducted under the law enacted by Parliament in 1876. In future, Canadians cast their votes by secret ballot.

Granting that Macdonald, once more the Prime Minister, took immediate steps to combat the country-wide distress, the question arises as to just how much help his measures received from the generally improved conditions of 1880–83. Certainly the tariff legislation of 1878 and 1879 had beneficial effects on the Canadian economy, and under its shelter, the Montreal business community took fresh heart.

Whether Macdonald himself had any roseate visions of the future, seems doubtful, for in the revival of his plans for the Canadian Pacific, he knew the pitfalls that awaited, not only his administration, but the country as a whole. But because magnitude alone, seldom bothered him, he went ahead, driven on by the urgency of Canada's need of this line to the west. Large-scale immigration was already opening up the prairies. If settlement was to proceed unchecked, British Columbia and the western territories must have rail communication with the east.

Such was the background for Macdonald's overtures to George Stephen, which led slowly and after much persuasion to the signing of a contract in October 1880 between the federal authorities and a new syndicate. Montreal's interest in the project could hardly have been greater, since Stephen had made his home in the city since 1850. His election as president of the Bank of Montreal in 1876 sufficiently indicated the high regard of his fellow financiers, and, he was by now, rated as the wealthiest man in town. Among his close associates, he numbered his cousin, Donald A. Smith, the head of the Canadian operations of the Hudson's Bay Company, and indeed, Montrealers made up the whole of the 1880 group, whose task was to construct a railroad whose every mile lay in Canada.

These wider horizons did not lessen Montreal's attention to its own affairs. Its civic government functioned efficiently under mayors, alternately representative of the French and the English communities. Needless to say, these officials presided over a still-growing city, whose population in the 1881 census reached the astonishing total of 140,747. At the same date, the estimated value of real estate stood at $65,978,930, and the municipal tax rate at $7.50 a head. As for the nearby villages, their exact status aroused discussion. With the population of the whole Island given as 193,171, the question naturally arose as to whether some of the smaller centers should not be included in the urban totals.

Yet even in purely municipal matters, the depression took its toll. The 1876 report of Mayor Hingston showed that conditions in the Police Force were far from healthy. Its strength was completely inadequate, and the citizens complained that the men took overlong to reach the scene of any trouble. An angry newspaper correspondent, who probed deeper into the reasons behind the "melting away" of the police and firemen, blamed it on the rate of pay. It was less than that of laborers. Complaints were voiced as to the number of beggars on the streets, at the doorways of the hotels, the steps of the churches. Their whining tones and outstretched hands did not match their generally strong and healthy appearance. Yet the official statistics show how heavy was the burden imposed by unemployment and distress. Whereas in 1875, only 2539 persons sought shelter in the police stations, by 1876 their number had risen to 12,894.

However divergent the viewpoints might be, it is probably true that all were colored by the growing industrialization of the city. A survey of 1880 showed, for example, that 32,000 persons were engaged in manufacturing, mainly in the garment trades. At the same date, the Grand Trunk repair shops in Point St. Charles employed three thousand skilled workmen. With the advent of like facilities for the Canadian Pacific and the striking development of the iron and steel industry, Montreal soon found itself to be the center for the production of locomotives and other "heavy" products.

So much of the local prosperity depended on the port and its shipping, that the 1870s and '80s brought no lessening of public concern. As in the past, there was just as much criticism as admiration, except in the case of steam. Everyone sang its praises; alone, it had not only transformed the harbor, but revolutionized the trade of the city.

Thanks to the constant dredging of the channel, oceangoing vessels of four thousand tons now ventured up the river in safety. Montreal saw itself in future as the great meeting place for rail and water transport in eastern Canada. Hence the relevance of a report from the Harbor Commission, which, in 1884, stressed the vital need to remember the national importance of the channel from Montreal down to tidewater, where under authority from Ottawa, the local group still carried on with its program of deepening.

In 1880 Andrew Robertson, as chairman of the board, pointed out that for the harbor proper, Montreal had never received one cent of federal aid. Ottawa, he felt, should relieve the Commission of any obligation for the channel debt; only thus could the river and port dues be placed on a competitive basis with New York and Boston. The generally run-down conditions mortified him—particularly in view of the increase in ocean tonnage—in 1859, it stood at 94,660 tons; in 1869, it had risen to 259,863; in 1879, it reached the astounding total of 506,969 tons. "The march and improvement of steam communication is Montreal's future."

Other writers praised Montreal for being the first port in the world to be electrified. The lights—two hundred yards apart—which extended from the mouth of the Lachine Canal to Hochelaga, made all-night loading feasible. Connections between the railroads and ships were simple, with the construction of a track along the entire length of the waterfront and level with the wharves. The latter, now four and a half miles long, abutted on deep water for most of the distance. Modern grain elevators and convenient equipment for the handling of cattle made for speed and efficiency. No unsightly warehouses disfigured the docks, while the streets facing on the river were kept as clean as a Parisian quay. Some of the western grain, of course, did not actually come ashore. Instead, the steam elevators at Kingston loaded it into barges for towage down the canals; at Montreal, these simply lay alongside the ocean vessels for a second transshipment.

The comings and goings of no less than thirteen lines of steamships showed that Montreal really had cause for its claim to maritime supremacy. During the 1880 season, some 710 sea-going vessels docked, of which 354 were steamships. The Allan Line elicited the greatest comment. Although subsidies from both the British and Canadian governments gave them a virtual monopoly, the good management of the Allan brothers contributed to their prosperity. They were excellent administrators, who hired their men by the season. Work or no work, the pay went on, thus resulting in a noticeable absence of strikes at critical moments.

Given the preponderance of the commercial instinct, it was not surprising that Montreal should sometimes find itself the butt of caustic remarks about its Philistine tastes. At almost any period, a sophisticated visitor from abroad was apt to let fly some shafts of sarcasm at the low cultural standards of the wealthy provincials. Whatever the hurt may have been to the contemporary mind, to posterity they make good reading.

Fitting neatly into this category is the tale of Samuel Butler, the English novelist whose posthumous fame rests chiefly upon *The Way of All Flesh*. He makes his appearance in these pages, by virtue of an investment in a dubious enterprise called the Canada Tanning Extract Company. It was in the hope of restoring it to prosperity that he came to Montreal in 1874. Never a good businessman, he met with little success, but in any case, he disliked his exile, far from the good friends and intellectual resources of London. What he discovered during a visit to the museum of the Natural History Society, tempted him into an unvarnished poetic expression of his scorn.

For some reason, Butler peered into a storeroom not ordinarily open to the public. There, among a miscellany of plants and snakes and insects not yet ready for the display cases, he spied two plaster casts of ancient Greek statues, one of them being a reproduction of the discus thrower, the Discobolus. Their banishment led him to question an old man working nearby. Stopping to talk of this and other matters, the oldster replied simply, "You see, they are rather vulgar." With these words, Butler had the text for his poem, "A Psalm of Montreal," first published in the *Spectator* in 1878.

Stowed away in a Montreal lumber room
The Discobolus standeth and turneth his face to the walls;
Dusty, cobweb-covered, maimed and set at naught,
Beauty crieth in an attic and no man regardeth:
O God! O Montreal!

In justice to the memory of the Victorians, it must be said that Butler's strictures appear to have been unduly harsh, in that he, a virtual stranger, condemned the whole city because of the idle words of an ignorant fellow. By way of contrast, the musical activities of the period might be cited. Although the departure of the British garrison and its band left things "somewhat dull" for a while, church choirs and instruction in the schools soon led to more ambitious plans. In December 1877 the Montreal Philharmonic presented its first concert in the Academy of Music. For some twenty years, this choir, averaging 250 voices, continued to give pleasure to its audiences, by its renditions of the great oratorios, including the works of Wagner.

At this date, moreover, the Art Association came to life in a manner that augured well for the future. It had led a rather languid existence since its inception in 1858, but with the Benaiah Gibb bequest of 1877, its permanency seemed assured. This permitted the construction of a building on Phillips Square, which had its formal opening in 1879. Prior to that date, the Association had sponsored exhibits and *conversaziones* in rented space, such as that held at the Windsor Hotel on February 15, 1878, during the presidency of Sir Francis Hincks. The Governor General, Lord Dufferin, with Lady Dufferin, honored the occasion by his presence. His Excellency showed his famous wit in his response to the address of welcome, for he presented a check for $100 to Sir Francis, calling it a written reply. "Every word upon the paper has been carefully studied. There is not a word too much in it, or a word too little."

Another memorable gathering, with distinctly intellectual undertones, was staged by McGill College in 1880 in honor of Dr. Dawson who had been principal for a quarter of a century. Three hundred and fifty guests attended a convocation and reception, at which, among other speeches, Peter Redpath announced his intention of building a museum for the college—now a vastly different institution from the desolate ruin that had first greeted Dr. Dawson. The Redpath Museum—erected at a cost of $100,000 and opened in 1882—was only the latest in a long series of private donations. In that year, forty professors and lecturers imparted knowledge to a student body of five hundred. Already there were twelve hundred graduates of the four faculties of Arts, Applied Science, Medicine, and Law. When, in 1884, the first class of eight women was admitted into the hitherto all male precincts, another era had its beginning. That such an unprecedented step could be taken was due to the generosity of Donald A. Smith; Dr. Dawson is reported to have shown no great enthusiasm.

Then there was the young William Osler, the brilliant graduate of Toronto Medical School, whose clinical work at the Montreal General Hospital started in 1870. Although post-graduate studies took him abroad for some time, by 1874, he was back in Canada and lecturing at McGill. Two years later, he received the appointment of Pathologist at the hospital, and in 1878, became its Chief Physician and Registrar of the McGill Medical School. The hospital of those days, as described by Harvey Cushing, Osler's biographer, was a modest affair of 150 beds, ill-lighted, ill-ventilated, and its nurses of the Sarah Gamp variety. But it yielded good experience at a time when McGill's medical teaching was growing in importance. When Osler left in 1884 to become Professor of Clinical Medicine at the University of Pennsylvania, Montreal's loss was great.

To this period also belongs an important step forward in French Canadian higher education. In 1876, Laval University of Quebec established a branch in Montreal; in 1881, it gained recognition from both the Holy See and from the Provincial Legislature. Its birth pangs had been considerable, chiefly because of Bishop Bourget's opposition. Something of the old rivalry between the two cities showed in his wish to establish an independent institution in Montreal, one that would not be only Catholic, but preferably Jesuit. The conflict reached the civil and ecclesiastical courts, and appeals were sent to Rome.

Meanwhile, the churches displayed remarkable energy. Each season, their number increased. By 1874, there were no less than seventy-four, or one for every two thousand of the population —leading Mark Twain, on one occasion, to remark during the course of a speech at the Windsor Hotel, that he never before had been in a city where one could not throw a brickbat without breaking a church window.

Sometimes the building programs involved a good many heart-aches. The new Anglican Christ Church was not consecrated until 1867, although construction had been under way for a decade. Unpaid debts delayed the formalities, for the congregation had carried a heavy financial load ever since fire destroyed the old structure on Notre Dame Street in 1856. Criticism of the site added to the difficulties, for the cathedral that today stands in the heart of the St. Catherine Street shopping district, was, at first, far out in the country.

Nothing, however, within the Protestant communions could compare with the great Roman Catholic cathedral whose slowly rising walls testified, unmistakably, to the strong faith and determined will of Bishop Bourget. A long and difficult history lay behind the start of construction in 1875 of a replacement for the old structure on St. Denis Street, destroyed by fire in 1852. Indifference played no part in the delay. On the contrary, for the Bishop had been zealous in his formulation of plans. Their ambitious nature showed first in the site, since the corner of Dorchester Street and Dominion Square lay in the heart of English Montreal.

The design was equally striking, being nothing less than a small-scale replica of St. Peter's in Rome. As a symbol of Montreal's close ties with the Holy See, the proposal could not have been bettered; as a problem in architecture, it presented difficulties. No great chorus of approval greeted the Bishop's decision, the local ecclesiastical taste running more to the Gothic. Some critics felt the style to be alien to the local scene, while architects expressed doubts as to the wisdom of cutting down the noble proportions of the Roman Basilica. But since the Bishop was the most strong-minded of prelates, he had his way—although his death in 1885 occurred before the completion of St. James. It still stands today, in the shadow of the skyscrapers, as the Cathedral of Mary, Queen of the World.

Chapter 33

1867–1885

Lord Dufferin and the Marquis of Lorne. Society. Winter sports. William Notman. Snowshoeing and torchlight processions. Mark Twain. Toboggans and skates. The Victoria Rink. Winter Carnivals. The Ice Palace. Summer resorts. Mount Royal a public park.

AMONG THE myriad adjustments that followed Confederation, it was not to be expected that the role of the Governor General should remain static. Gradually, the direct executive control of the colonial officials disappeared, to be replaced by the modern concept of a personal representative of the Sovereign, the purely nominal head of state in a self-governing Dominion.

It was during Lord Dufferin's term of office that many of these changes assumed definite shape. This warm-hearted Irish peer was endowed with all the wit and charm of his race; he also held strong views as to the importance of his position. When these led to what seemed like political meddling, they earned a rebuke from the Prime Minister. Thereafter the office remained largely one of ceremony, and few men could have graced it so admirably as Dufferin. Incessant travel and lavish entertainments brought him into close contact with Canadians in all walks of life, his easy informality winning friends everywhere. An eloquent orator, he could use blarney to good effect, delighting his audiences, not only in English, but in French, Latin, and Greek. He became a great booster for the country, ably assisted by Lady Dufferin.

The six years of this unusually happy tenure came to an end in 1878, amid much public lamentation—soon forgotten in the ex-

citement of greeting the new tenants of Rideau Hall, who in
quite a different way, had so much to offer Canadians. For although the Marquis of Lorne was only thirty-three years of age,
he came of an illustrious Scottish family, and was well schooled
in the tradition of service to the state. But aside from this innate
importance, marriage to the Princess Louise, fourth daughter of
the Queen, had undoubtedly added to the luster of the husband. The ardent royalists of the day saw her arrival as the
highest compliment yet paid to the Dominion, and since Her
Royal Highness proved to be a talented person in her own right
—a sculptor and painter as well as a social lioness—she gained
many admirers. That vice-regal life took on an air of formality,
was probably unavoidable, and a few critics mocked at the pretensions of the petty "court" at Ottawa.

To Montreal, the period spanned by these two regimes, brought
a fairly close and consistent association with the vice-regal
couples. Ottawa, after all, was so close and travel so easy that
no one could plead fatigue or discomfort at the journey. Moreover, being still a raw new town, the capital could not possibly
provide all the amenities of the older and more sophisticated
city. Thus the official parties visited Montreal often, to grace
ballrooms and dinner tables, to inspect the militia, to tour religious and charitable institutions, to see and be seen. The Dufferins, in particular, attended athletic contests and all manner
of games. At times, and particularly during the winter, they
went so far as to become active participants in the less strenuous
amusements.

It must be admitted that this pleasant friendship was not all-
embracing. The twin factors of class and wealth imposed limitations, so that while everyone might—and apparently did—turn
out to gaze wonderingly at the public spectacles, only the cream
of society—"upper tendom," to quote one reporter—found themselves welcome in the charmed circle. Much of the glamour,
moreover, was decidedly Anglo-Saxon; the writing of the '70s and
'80s makes this abundantly clear. "The French and the English
races flow on side by side like the two great rivers opposite the
city, which do not commingle until they reach tide."

There was nothing particularly new in Montreal's love of

sports. Rather did the fever rise to fresh heights under Lord Dufferin's favoring eye. In New France, the grim struggle for survival had prevented much enjoyment of outdoor amusements. Besides, said the Anglo-Saxons smugly, their athletic prowess could not be matched by the natives of any other country—boastful words that had some basis, in that the presence of the British garrisons had undoubtedly sparked a good many physical activities of a competitive nature. Whether stationed at Montreal or Quebec, the officers and men alike, bored by their humdrum duties, turned to matches and games as a means of passing the time.

At no season was the sporting urge greater than in the winter. The health-giving qualities of the cold climate were much written about—clear skies and a dry air, with none of the fogs or raw damp winds so wearing to invalids. "Many from the seaboard with pulmonary complaints come here for the winter." From early October to April, Montrealers could enjoy curling, snowshoeing, sleigh-driving, tobogganing, skating. As for the equipages, they appealed so much to one panegyrist that he felt only the Russians in St. Petersburg could be judged superior. The high spot of the week came on Saturday afternoon, when an endless procession of sumptuous sleighs of every description, drawn by high-steppers, bowled along the fashionable route from Victoria Square to Nelson's Monument. The lovely women passengers, wrapped in the richest furs of the Canadian forest, added greatly to the glamour.

Thus when the Dufferins came to Montreal to share in winter sports, they gave a fillip to something already in existence. The old necessities of life—the sleigh, the toboggan, the snowshoe—these became the new luxuries, and the newspapers, somewhat snobbishly, gave full coverage to the various events. Posterity can only be thankful that their lengthy columns of close-set type were broken by illustrations. Lively drawings of sports and sportsmen made their appearance in the press. Above all, there was photography, the new art in which Montreal speedily took the lead.

The man responsible for this rather special brand of fame was William Notman, a native of Scotland, whose local residence dated back to 1856. Photography, his all-absorbing passion, became his means of livelihood. By 1860, he was established in a studio on Bleury Street, already the winner of European awards, and honored "by appointment" to Her Majesty the Queen. Notman was, in fact, an artist in his chosen field, who remained an active photographer until his death in 1891.

Although at some stage in their careers, most of Canada's famous men posed before Notman's camera, the lesser lights must not be forgotten—the civic dignitaries and leading citizens; their stately wives; the gay young beaux and belles. At $2.00 a sitting, few could plead their inability to meet the cost. With the passage of time, some of the names have vanished into the mists of anonymity, but the charm and the skill remain. Notman made a clever use of scenery, over and above the conventional Victorian backgrounds of ornate furniture, and heavy drapes. For summer, he provided such props as a bridge, some rocks, a stream; for winter, fake snow made of salt, whitened the slopes and filled the air breathed by the pseudo-tobogganer. But the "composite" pictures were the most astonishing of all. One montage showed the Montreal Snowshoe Club, 250 members strong. Each man had first posed separately for his photo, which was then cut out and pasted on a master copy. This, in turn, when complete, was photographed as a whole—involving workmanship so painstaking as sometimes to require two years for completion.

The snowshoers thus immortalized belonged to the parent club in a city where such organizations abounded. It was founded in 1840, a modest affair whose first members went off each Saturday afternoon on a tramp into the country, returning after their ten or twelve mile walk to a good dinner at a St. James Street cafe. Forty years later, La Tuque Bleue found itself labeled as the most prosperous corporate body of its kind in Montreal, and as such, may serve here as the prototype of all those who came later. In their white blanket coats and leggings and blue tuques adorned with long tassels, its four hundred members stood out from the crowd. The showshoe itself, as used by these experts, embodied some modifications of the clumsy thing known to the lumberman or the hunter. Whereas the workhorse type might be as much as five feet long and two wide, the racing shoe was no more than three feet, with a breadth of ten inches. Its hickory frame and network of deer hide were "of a gossamer character." When fastened carefully to the moccasined foot, with its weight resting upon the toes and the heel left free to move up and down, a man might surmount hurdles three or four feet high without difficulty.

Most of the organized tramps had Mount Royal as their objective. From the usual rendezvous at the McGill gates on Sherbrooke Street, the members climbed, either by Peel Street or Côte des Neiges, to the "Pines." Although not far as the crow flies, it was uphill all the way; in the teeth of cold winds or snowstorms, the steady pace became a test of endurance. No wonder that the evenings ended with suppers of biscuits, cheese, and ale.

The greater leisure of the weekends permitted crosscountry runs. A typical event had as its objective the village of St. Vincent de Paul, on Ile Jésus, twelve miles from the city. Two hours and a half did the trick, thanks to a recent fall of snow which had covered the stubble and cabbage stalks. The men trudged along in Indian file, leaping fences or falling over them in a lump, a biting wind turning their whiskers and hair into fantastic ice pendants. A more ambitious outing took a dozen members to St. Andrews, a distance of forty-five miles. The weather was bad, most of the way. At seven o'clock on Friday evening they left Montreal, reaching St. Eustache about one in the morning; at seven, they were off again, arriving at their destination by three on Saturday afternoon. They found time, on the Sunday, to attend church, but on Tuesday morning, they were home once more and ready for business.

The annual races, generally held at the Lacrosse Grounds on Sherbrooke Street, were great attractions. Some seasons as many as three thousand spectators gathered to share in the fun, braving the cold with only the temporary stands for shelter. The presence of the ladies was always noteworthy, dressed in their best and looking their prettiest, their devoted admirers at hand to explain the technicalities. Although the committee did its best to keep the track clear, on one occasion at least, the crowds burst all obstacles and by their unruly behavior caused the race to be declared "of none effect." But for the most part the heats went

ahead on schedule—two miles, one mile, a thousand yards, a
hundred and twenty yard hurdle race—varied one winter, by an
event for boys under ten years. Six miniature "Hop-o'-My-
Thumbs," dressed as miniature athletes, competed for a special
medal.

Probably the most notable celebration of all took place on
January 15, 1873, when the clubs combined to stage a torchlight
procession in honor of Lord and Lady Dufferin. Those in charge
viewed the weather with apprehension, for after a fine clear
morning, snow fell all afternoon to a depth of several inches.
Swirled about by strong winds, the drifting became almost blind-
ing. But none of this dampened the ardor of the several hundred
enthusiasts who gathered that evening on Sherbrooke Street, to
await the distinguished guests.

The torches were tin pots, filled with oil and equipped with
wicks. Held high in the air by the three-foot-long handles, they
cast their flickering light over a scene of great animation. For the
spectators had gathered in their thousands, some in sleighs,
others on foot, lining the sidewalks and jamming the nearby
windows and balconies. The roadway was choked with the heavy
traffic, and the absence of police at the college gates made control difficult. But somehow a way was cleared, and His Excellency could be seen, bowing and smiling and obviously enjoying
the novel sight.

The procession moved off, west from the campus and thence up
the mountainside, the snowshoers marching along two-by-two,
at a good clip on the level stretches, more slowly on the steep
slopes. As they climbed higher, their torches could be seen from a
distance, twisting, and turning and ever-changing, lending a
fairy touch to the landscape. In the meantime, the official party
drove east to St. Lawrence Main Street, following the high road
to Mount Royal. A delay at the Toll Gate caused much annoyance
to the guests, the number of sleighs being so great and change
so provokingly slow to get, that a good half hour was lost. But
by nine o'clock, most of the party had reached Thornbury and
been greeted by their host, Mr. McGibbon. Last of all, came the
torchbearers, tired and hungry after their long climb.

Lady Dufferin, from the comfort of her sleigh, had been a

fascinated observer of all that took place. "The bright night, the snow-covered ground, hundreds of sleighs and thousands of tinkling bells, the torches and the gaiety of the whole scene, were delightful. The procession walked up the mountain, and we drove around it, watching the fiery serpent winding among the trees. The roads were excellent, and it was the first sleigh-drive I have really enjoyed. In about an hour, we arrived at a house where supper was prepared, and where we had a very amusing evening. There was a long list of toasts, and a song with a chorus was sung after each. When all was over, we got into our sleigh again, and the fresh air was delightful! The snowshoers were by this time 'jolly good fellows' and I found them rather alarming to our horses and to me; so we begged them not to accompany us home."

Occasionally, a more plebeian guest merited special attention. Such was the case when, in February 1885, the Athenaeum Club issued invitations for an afternoon reception at the Windsor Hotel in honor of Mr. S. L. Clemens and Mr. George W. Cable. Doubtless the party was an enjoyable affair, yet perhaps Mark Twain preferred the novelty of his début into local sporting circles. Although a year had passed since his election to membership in the Montreal Snowshoe Club, the exigencies of a heavy lecture tour had so far prevented any formal initiation. Now the omission could be remedied, for late one evening, the distinguished neophyte appeared at a meeting. Without more ado, his fellows went ahead with the ceremonial "bouncing" of Twain and his companions. "Welcome, Mark, to Montreal, when snow flies and the air tingles with the kindly electricity of a Canadian winter. We owe you many happy hours, let us make you happy for a little while, with blanket coat and tuque and snowshoes broad in the beam."

By the early eighties, tobogganing really came into its own— "the delight of youthful Montreal." For the benefit of the ignorant, the equipment was described as an Indian sleigh, four to eight feet long and ten to sixteen inches wide, the front end bent upward into a curve, and the flat surface covered with cushions. Because of the steep slopes of Mount Royal, Montreal was unusually well suited to this sport. Yet popularity came slowly, and for several seasons, only one club existed. But when within four years, its original thirty members became four hundred, and other organizations were born, it seemed as though the early handicap was being overcome. Admittedly, the hills in a state of nature were often rough, and for this reason everyone welcomed the new slides on Côte St. Antoine near Sherbrooke Street—one, natural, 2400 feet in length, and two artificial, 1500 feet each.

Once this development came into general use, there were grounds for hope that the hazards had been overcome. On a long smooth hill, without fences or trees, there was comparatively little danger, especially as a caretaker was always on duty to assist young ladies without male escorts. And the girls, bless their hearts, were much in evidence. Their grandmothers would have been shocked at the goings on. A pretty partner added greatly to the joys of tobogganing; "petticoated, of course, she sits in front, her skirts tucked in and feet drawn up, you behind." This was Sport Glorious.

Perhaps some of these same belles were numbered among those who enjoyed themselves on snowshoes. Naturally, they could not expect admission to the men's clubs, but no one could deny their powers of endurance. "Many a long night will they be dancing in their moccasined feet at Prendergast's or Lumpkin's, after a jolly tramp over the Mountain." Most of all, however, the fair sex seem to have liked skating. Even there, their entrée was recent, for until 1850 or 1855, no properly brought-up young lady indulged in such unseemly exercise. But once started, their numbers grew so rapidly that skating attained the status of a social accomplishment. It seems likely that the feminine influence was partly responsible for the trend to indoor rinks. For although the natural ice of the St. Lawrence had met the needs of less sophisticated times, its users were exposed to the full blast of the winter winds and the snow. Thus while ordinary folk still flocked to the improvised skating areas on the river, the canal, the vacant lots, society moved under cover.

Of all the skating establishments in Montreal, none could surpass the Victoria Rink on Drummond Street. Opened in 1862, its exclusive nature was reflected in the use of the word "club"—

an elastic term, perhaps, since in 1882, it boasted of two thousand members. The archlike roof rose to a height of 52 feet above the great stretch of ice, 200 by 80 feet in size. Around the walls, a ten-foot platform provided ample space for the onlookers, while a music gallery met the needs of the band. Windows on three sides admitted plenty of daylight, and at night five hundred gas jets gave a brilliant illumination.

The Victoria was adjudged the largest and best rink, in either Europe or America. When the Grand Duke Alexis skated there, he pronounced it superior to anything in Russia. As many as fifteen hundred or two thousand persons, including spectators, attended its countless entertainments. Lady Dufferin passed many happy hours there, both as an active participant and as a spectator. The Carnivals enchanted her. From the balcony, she and her husband watched "a fairy pantomime of gigantic size," as the gaily dressed throng wove in and out, dancing the state lancers in front of the distinguished guests. "There was one delightful old gentleman who passed us every round in some different way, acting capitally the whole time. There was an excellent and large monkey who performed for the children. There were Indians and Chinamen . . . The ladies' costumes had of necessity, short petticoats so there was every variety of peasant—Dolly Vardens, Watteaus—and very pretty they were! In fact, to an ordinary fancy ball, you have to add perpetual motion—for no one ever stands still on ice. The spectators lined the walls. We were torn away to have some supper . . . They danced another set of lancers and Sir Roger de Coverley. I am sure that if they had not turned the Governor General out, by playing 'God save the Queen,' I should never have been able to get him away, he enjoyed it so much."

Snowshoeing, skating, tobogganing—these were the three great winter sports of the era. Curling, in one instance, was dismissed as a pastime for middle-aged men, and this in spite of the existence of the Royal Montreal, whose founding date of 1807 made it the oldest club of the sort in North America. But by 1880, the Thistle and the Caledonian had made their appearance. With three rinks going strong, the local curlers found themselves com-

peting with players from Ottawa and Quebec for two silver cups
presented by the Governor General.

The very fact that this inter-city rivalry existed, in itself
created difficulties, for curling as played in the Province of Quebec, originated with the early Scottish garrisons. In those first
years, granites could not be imported, and so the ingenious troops
melted down cannon balls, shaping them in such a way as to
provide a narrow running surface. Out of this, grew a fairly
common use of "irons," and a belief in some quarters that granites led to less scientific play. While the discussion on this
weighty matter continued to vex the champions, they may have
found consolation in another local rule—the losing party of the
day must pay for a bowl of whisky toddy, to be placed in the
middle of the table, where all might partake.

In hockey, also, the early story was one of slow growth. Military in origin, it seems to have evolved from the English field
variety. As staged by the garrisons on outdoor natural ice surfaces, an undetermined number of players used field hockey
sticks and solid rubber balls. Their skates consisted of crude
metal runners attached to wooden bases and tied to the boots.
The rules were few, and often altered to suit special conditions,
but everyone, including the civilian bystanders, manifested interest.

Once again, it was the introduction of indoor rinks which
brought about the changes. The size of the teams had to be
limited, and the duration of the matches defined. The solid rubber balls became dangerous weapons, and broken windows were
common. The eager spectators, having paid entrance fees, faced
hazards. In the evolutionary period, that followed this partial
abandonment of outdoor ice, Montreal emerged into prominence.
It is said—although other towns disagree—that the first game of
ice hockey was played at the Victoria Rink on March 3, 1875. As
to the rules, there is more recognition of the claim that these
were drawn up about 1878 by three McGill students. Their code
soon won general acceptance, and early in the '80s, Canadian
youths had become such eager fans that hockey matches were
scheduled as regular features of the winter season.

By this date, the amateur sportsmen had gone far in dispelling the ancient myths of winter immobility. Well bundled up against the cold, Montrealers turned out in large numbers for the many races and exciting contests. It was all very pleasant. It was also very local. The first definite suggestion of a Carnival, with a well-organized program, apparently came from young Robert McGibbon. The annual meeting of the Montreal Snowshoe Club in February 1882, with its captive audience, provided the perfect springboard for his eager proposals. If all the clubs were to co-operate in such a venture, their united efforts would surely result in celebrations attractive to the outside world.

Even at this early date, Montreal seems to have been aware of the value of a healthy tourist traffic. At any rate, McGibbon's tentative suggestions were not allowed to die, and by autumn, active planning got under way. Since such powerful interests as the Grand Trunk and the Windsor Hotel indicated their willingness to contribute, the usual financial bugbears caused little anxiety. When other commercial firms followed their good example, the preparations picked up speed. Time was short, the opening date having been set for January 24.

So important did the program appear that the city fathers proclaimed a half holiday on this particular Wednesday. Thus everyone was free to enjoy the gala events—the curling bonspiel; the sleigh parade on Sherbrooke Street; the snowshoe steeplechase from the McGill grounds; the grand procession of all the snowshoe clubs; the inauguration of the Ice Palace. On the Thursday, Friday, and Saturday, equally crowded schedules were maintained—skating races, snowshoe races, trotting races; hockey matches and curling matches; a fancy dress carnival; a concert at Queen's Hall; a celebration in honor of Bobbie Burns' birthday.

Peel Street, being closed to traffic all week, was open for sliding in the evening; every precaution had been taken for the safety of the toboggans. The curling bonspiels were held on the St. Lawrence at the foot of McGill Street, the out-of-town rinks competing each night under the glare of twenty electric lights. The trotting races also took place on the river ice, in mile heats for sleighs. The snowshoe clubs as of old, staged their nightly processions, from Dominion Square up Windsor and Peel Street to the mountain.

Undoubtedly the great drawing card of the whole Carnival was the Ice Palace, the mammoth structure on Dominion Square, a delight to the eye in the sparkling sunlight, but at night, sheer enchantment. It was ninety feet square, with thirty foot towers at each corner, and a larger central column that rose some eighty feet. Blocks of ice composed the walls, each about forty by twenty inches, and ranging in thickness from fourteen to twenty inches. These were shaped with an ax or adze, and handled exactly as if cut stone, except that water took the place of mortar. An overlay of cedar branches made a satisfactory roof. When sprayed at such low temperatures, the water hardened into solid masses of ice.

The great moment came with the darkness. From dusk until midnight, the multicolored electric lamps illuminated the Square —on the opening night, literally black with a crowd estimated at 25,000. At eight o'clock, the snowshoers hove in sight, marching down Peel Street, the glow of their thousand torches the signal for another flood of lighting at the Palace. Roman candles and rockets added their quota of noise, and the band of the Victoria Rifles manfully struggled to make itself heard about the din.

The outstanding success of the 1883 Carnival led immediately to plans for the following year. An eloquent reporter saw its future as bounded only by the limits of the peopled globe. Montreal, he declared, to be a very paradise of winter joyousness and mirth. "By next year, we expect that the Czar will have adopted our plan as the sovereign cure for Nihilism." No less a personage than the Marquis of Lorne was moved to set down his feelings. "If they desire to see fairyland on earth, they should be present at a masquerade ball in the great skating rink, or watch the fêtes given in and around the palace built of snow blocks. If they wish themselves to join in exercise for which much practice is not necessary, they should join in one of the merry parties of the snowshoe clubs and clad in colored blanket coat, blue 'tuque' and moccasins, tramp away into the country on the bright powdery snow, coming home with blood tingling from the healthy exhilaration of the keen and taintless air."

The chief novelty of the 1884 and later Carnivals lay in a more ambitious program at the Ice Palace. The illuminations, the snowshoers, the sights, and sounds outside—all played their part in regular offensive and defensive maneuvers. Thus in future, it was the storming of the Palace that "the mighty mass of humanity" turned out to see—beyond the walls, an army of snowshoers, awaiting the signal to attack—inside, a group of committee members, reinforced by a hundred members of the Prince of Wales Rifles, equally poised for the siege. At a given signal, both parties started to fire off their rockets, the sound resembling rifle shots. "All was animation, noise, and glare." Meanwhile, the beleaguered party stood on the battlements, busily aiming balls of fire at their assailants. When some fell among the crowd and damaged the clothing, the slight contretemps only added to the excitement. More rockets flared up, and some elaborate set pieces. The snowshoers lit their torches, so that by the time of the supposed surrender, a line of living fire extended around the Square. Marching and countermarching to the tunes of rattling choruses, they moved off, fifteen hundred strong—so great a host that the advance guard had already reached the brow of the mountain when the rear ranks were just leaving the Palace vicinity. This was better than anything in Russia, including the marriage of the Duke of Edinburgh!

Colorful though these scenes may be, the Montreal picture would be incomplete without some consideration of the quieter joys of the summer. For those who had money, escape from the city heat presented no problem. Watering places of all kinds abounded. With the completion of the direct rail service to Portland and Boston, the beaches of the eastern seaboard soon became familiar territory. For those who preferred the cool bracing air of the St. Lawrence, there was some assurance of comfort. The presence of Sir John A. Macdonald at Rivière du Loup and Sir William Dawson at Metis lent a certain cachet to a whole string of villages.

More pertinent to the local story was the ring of resorts that surrounded Montreal. Since the gigantic metropolitan area of modern times was as yet undreamed of, a delightful green belt offered accommodations so near at hand that husbands and fathers could easily commute by rail. The Island and the adjacent mainland; the Great River, still largely free of industrial pollution; the small lakes of the region—both for beauty and convenience, these could not easily be surpassed. Lachine, Pointe Claire, and Ste. Annes were small centers of charming villas and country houses. Nearby Beaconsfield possessed an extra attraction in its vineyards; so successful had Messrs. Gallagher and Gautier been in their cultivation of grapes that one observer considered this to be the coming industry of the province. Over on the south shore, St. Lambert grew more popular each year, while neighboring Longueuil, a very old stopping place, still had its visitors.

For those confined to the city streets, a good many possibilities presented themselves—none more exciting than the shooting of the Lachine Rapids, a seemingly daredevil feat beloved of tourists. Yet, as described in a small guidebook of the 1870s, the whole thing smacked more of efficiency than of adventure. A man could catch a train at seven in the morning at Bonaventure Station, and at Lachine make connections with the small steamer *Beauharnois*. By nine o'clock the same morning, precisely two hours later, he was safely back in Montreal, having passed down through the treacherous waters, and thence under Victoria Bridge, and so into the harbor.

Those who preferred driving behind a good pair of horses, doubtless felt reassured by some statements culled from a similar source. Canadian carriages were kept with scrupulous neatness, and operated by obliging drivers, whose charges, unlike those in the United States, did not threaten total ruin. Extravagant souls who wanted to do the Rapids in style could, of course, drive out to Lachine in a hired carriage, instead of using the plebeian train. They could also tour Mount Royal and its cemeteries, turn east to Longue Pointe, or enjoy in comfort the stately buildings, the mansions of the wealthy, and the fine public squares, all within the confines of the city.

But a few cracks were starting to appear in the façade of class. Thanks to the new provisions for public parks, there was reason to hope that the poor in future, might enjoy some share of fresh air and open space. St. Helen's Island was one instance in which the departure of the British garrison had permitted a complete change. Its land, at first ceded to the federal government, was in turn leased to the city for a park, the public reaching its pleasant wooded acres via the steamer *Fulgate* from the wharf opposite Bonsecours Market.

Most promising of all, however, was the Corporation's acquisition of Mount Royal, for conversion into a public park. It proved to be a long and tedious process. For many years after the death of Simon McTavish, the upper slopes were used as grazing grounds for cattle, fenced in and barred from the citizens, but otherwise completely neglected. Public protests dated from the sixties, when a man named Lamothe purchased a part of the mountain and proceeded to cut down the timber and sell it for firewood. The more civic minded of the inhabitants deemed it imperative to save the summit from any such desecration. That their pressure was effective, is evident from the Act passed by the Provincial Legislature in 1869, authorizing the Corporation to borrow a sum not exceeding $350,000 for its purchase.

Nothing more happened for a year or two, but in 1873, Mayor Coursol reported progress in the expropriations. In 1874, Mayor Barnard stated that 360 acres had been acquired at a cost of $550,900; shortly afterward, he complained of continued opposition and litigation by the proprietors. This went on until January 1875, it being necessary in the interval to secure permission from the province to increase the loan to $1,000,000. On the Queen's birthday of that same year, Mayor Hingston officiated at the formal opening of the 485 acres thus far taken over, and twelve months later, he told of the completion of two miles of road, graded easily for the convenience of the public.

This is not to say that Montreal lacked organized sports during the summer, for in 1882, a wide variety of clubs existed. Cricket boasted of one organization; baseball, one, for the game was not widely played; bicycling, one, but there were seventy members. Football was more popular, with its three clubs, while the one and only golf club, established by Lord Dufferin in 1873, had a large enrollment for play on the grounds at Fletcher's Field. The single racket group had only forty adherents, fewer by far than lawn tennis, whose sixty enthusiasts made use of the grounds of the Lacrosse Club every weekday except Saturday. Not to be

forgotten was the gymnasium on Mansfield Street, where the
Montreal Amateur Athletic Association had its headquarters.
Since it possessed no bar or anything of the sort, parents were
quite satisfied to have their sons frequent the building.

Finally, there was lacrosse, once Canada's most popular game,
now to some extent forgotten. In 1882, there were no less than
nine groups in the city, the most important being the Montreal
Club with its grounds on Sherbrooke Street, and the Shamrock,
located on St. Catherine Street. Of Indian origin, the matches in
earlier years saw the white men lined up against the red. Described as requiring great speed of foot and quickness of hand,
it is considered that lacrosse, in certain respects, was the forerunner of hockey, lending its goal posts to the newer sport, and
adapting its rules to the use of skaters on ice.

Chapter 34

1885–1896

Louis Riel. Martyr or rebel? The French-English rift. Smallpox. Floods. Trains to the Pacific coast. Electric streetcars. Lady Aberdeen and her work with women. Wilfrid Laurier.

THE FACT that Louis Riel dominated the news during 1885, brought political controversy, once more, to Montreal. Instinctively, people took sides. Whereas the French-speaking citizens felt a certain affinity with the man, conceiving him to be a hero and a martyr, their fellows of the English language, saw only a rebel and a traitor, whose ultimate punishment was richly deserved.

To some extent, personal knowledge intensified the basic issue, for although Riel was born at St. Boniface, in what is now Manitoba, he was educated at Montreal. It was only after several years as a student at the Sulpician Seminary that he decided against the priestly vocation, and returned to his native west. His career, so far as public awareness went, dated from 1869 and 1870, when he led the métis of the Red River in active resistance to the Canadian government's takeover of the territory from the Hudson's Bay Company. The collapse of this uprising found him a fugitive in the United States, a country in which he was to spend a good deal of time until his final return to Canada in 1884.

Riel's exile was not altogether voluntary, for in 1875 Canada issued a warrant of outlawry against him. Yet, that spring, he slipped across the border as though nothing had happened, to walk the streets of Montreal quite openly, while he framed a manifesto to *The Métis Nation and the French Canadian Peo-*

ple. But wherever he lived, the signs of physical and mental illness could not be ignored. A growing obsession as to his mission led to a conviction that he was God's chosen instrument for the regeneration of his own people, the half-breeds of the west. Crying and shouting through many restless nights, his aberration became so serious that, in March 1876, the asylum at Longue Pointe admitted him as a patient. Two months later, "Louis R. David" was transferred to a similar institution at Beauport, to remain there until discharged in January 1878.

Rest and time having had the desired curative effects, Riel lived a more normal existence for a few years, his move to Montana taking him far from any direct association with Montreal. Yet it was this residence in the west that revived his old sympathies with the half-breeds and the Indians, caught as they were in the advancing tide of settlement. The summer of 1884 saw him cross the border into Saskatchewan, a free man once more, with the expiration of his sentence.

A winter of brooding over the undeniable grievances of his neighbors re-awakened Riel's sense of a divine calling, to such an extent that the Catholic clergy of the district grew apprehensive. Nevertheless, he went ahead with his plans, turning from peaceful agitation to violence, as his inward turmoil increased. A chance encounter with the Mounted Police in the spring of 1885, led to a surprise victory for the malcontents, a prelude to what history has termed the Northwest Rebellion. Troops, mustered speedily from all sections of Canada, insured defeat for the insurgents. With the surrender of Riel himself on May 15, his followers lost all taste for the uneven fight.

It should be emphasized that the outbreak of hostilities found all Canada reasonably united in its support of the government. French-speaking volunteers went out from Montreal as readily as did their English comrades, and Bishop Fabre set aside Friday, April 17, as a day of penitence, fasting, and prayers for their success. Headed by Mayor Beaugrand, the citizens gave generously to a patriotic fund set up to aid the families of those on active service. And although George Stephen and Donald A. Smith, each with a contribution of $1000, headed the list, there was no lack of more modest subscribers. The entire staff of *La*

Presse donated a day's pay to a total of $192. By June the receipts amounted to $21,500 and 240 families had received assistance.

Yet this civilian support was not unanimous. Two of Riel's supporters were said to be in the city, trying to stir up opposition. There were public meetings, at which some French Canadians expressed their dislike of the government's warlike policy. But, such opinions took second place to plans of another sort, for in July, the troops came home—the 65th Regiment, the Garrison Artillery, the Prince of Wales Rifles. The greatest reception went to the 65th, the gallant French Canadians who had actually shared in the fighting. They wore uniforms that were tattered, faded, and soiled, and their headgear was anything and everything. The band played *Vive la Canadienne* and the great bells of Notre Dame pealed out a welcome. Flags and decorations made a brave showing in the streets, until at last the men reached the Parish Church, packed to the doors for the singing of the Te Deum.

Meanwhile in the west, the trial of Riel opened on July 20. After eight weeks in prison, the accused entered the courtroom at Regina, to hear himself charged with waging war against the Queen, "wickedly, maliciously, and traitorously." Before an English-speaking judge and jury, the defense lawyers, sent out by French Canadian sympathizers from the east, pleaded insanity. To no avail, for the verdict of "guilty" was sustained, through all the subsequent appeals, right up to the Judicial Committee of the Privy Council. Since the Ottawa government refused a stay of execution, Riel was hanged on November 16.

The date is a memorable one, for it is often cited as the start of the great French-English rift. The short-term results were at once apparent in the storm of protests from French Canadians throughout the province. A newspaper account pictured the excitement and uneasiness in Montreal, and the dread of violence at night. Although the leaders on both sides counseled moderation, who could predict what might happen when four hundred French Canadian students resolved "to paint the town red." Through the streets they paraded, Tricolor in hand, suitably draped in black, and singing *La Marseillaise*. Sir John A. Macdonald was burned in effigy. On November 22, the Champ de

Mars was the scene of a great mass meeting of protest. Before a crowd of some 40,000 persons, thirty speakers from three separate platforms, delivered excited harangues, denouncing the government and all its ways. All that winter, the agitation continued, although without violence. Yet the racial tension, thus stirred, did not die easily; it remained alive, to become in future, a factor that could not be ignored, either by Montreal or by the nation.

The smallpox epidemic of 1885 did nothing to allay the local discontent. For some years, there had been odd cases of the dread disease, but never sufficiently numerous to convert the municipal authorities to the principle of compulsory vaccination. Thus when, in February, a Pullman porter from the Chicago train, sought admission to the Hôtel Dieu, no one took his slight skin eruption too seriously. Even when later diagnosis showed it to be smallpox, no one worried unduly.

As the contagion spread among the other patients, the city opened an isolation hospital. By the middle of April, it had admitted fifteen cases. By May 1, the Board of Health had vaccinated over 12,000 persons, but still the number of new cases mounted. Some of these, being outside the city proper, aroused grave concern; St. Jean Baptiste village, for example, refused to send its sick into the special hospital. There was newspaper criticism of the Health Department personnel, and pointed remarks as to the filth of the streets, the scavengers, the abattoirs. Montreal's death rate was said to be higher than in any other Canadian city—33.05 per 1000 in 1884, as against Toronto's 20.30.

It is probable that the tragic death of Sir Francis Hincks stirred some of the citizens into action. To avoid the spread of contagion, his friends thoughtfully arranged for a private funeral at five o'clock in the morning. By this mid-August date, estimates placed the home cases at four hundred and the hospitalized at forty. The mortality stood at 120. A decision to close the schools, was followed in September by a public demand for stern measures. The city, at last, decided upon compulsory vaccination, largely upon the insistence of Dr. William Hingston of the Hôtel Dieu. It was then that the trouble came to a head.

Many of the ignorant among the French Canadians seemed indifferent to the danger. They opposed isolation, and refused vaccination, out of a superstitious dread of the operation. Once it became obligatory, the measure took on tyrannical attributes in their eyes. Refusal to comply brought a fine of $20; the inability of the poor to pay, sent them to prison. And since not all the wisdom of the curés could convince them otherwise, they resisted with violence, an attempt to placard an infected home. The Health Officers found themselves facing a verbal barrage of abuse and vile insults. Then the mob moved on, to attack the City Hall, and a drugstore belonging to one of the vaccine distributors. They smashed windows and started several fires. A blaze on St. Catherine Street East brought out the Fire Brigade. The Chief of Police suffered injuries. In desperation, the authorities sent out an emergency call to the Victoria Rifles and other volunteer regiments. With the aid of their 1340 men, the police gained the upper hand. But when in future, the doctors of the city went from house to house to vaccinate the inmates, a military guard accompanied them.

It is difficult to say how many cases of smallpox there actually were. One account placed their number at 4771, with thousands more concealed. The deaths passed the three-thousand mark. During the epidemic, the city was pretty well quarantined from the rest of the world, and many were the wails from local businessmen about the adverse effects on passenger traffic and trade in general. Mayor Beaugrand came through the crisis like a soldier and a man. He rose from a sick bed to quell the mob, and "his martial music charmed the city into quiet."

Just as though human agencies had not stirred up enough misery, the St. Lawrence went on the rampage in a worse-than-usual flood during the spring of 1886. To some extent, there had been advance warnings, for the 1885 levels had been above average—no one knew why, although one suggestion placed the blame on the destruction of the forests near the source of the river. A systematic replanting of the trees was recommended as a palliative. Be that as it may, despite the smallpox and the Riel unrest, the civic Inundation Committee under Alderman Stevenson put in an active twelve months. A liberal expenditure of time and money resulted in a revetment wall, strongly constructed of wood. This, it was hoped, when allied with similar protective measures, would in future keep the lower town dry and untouched.

But by early April, the neighboring countryside was submerged in many places. Flood conditions prevailed along the Châteauguay, the Pike, and the Yamaska rivers. On the fourteenth of the month word came in that the habitant farmers on the south shore, were moving their livestock to higher ground—wisely, as it turned out, for St. Lambert and LaPrairie soon found themselves under four feet of water. The suffering was indescribable.

The discovery that the gauge on Commissioners Street had registered a rise of eight inches in less than twenty-four hours, came as a shock to the city proper. It was on the sixteenth that the first general ice shove took place, the water climbing slowly but inexorably, perhaps five feet in as many minutes. Meanwhile, the floes piled up on the wall, exerting such pressure that the gauge collapsed under its weight, as if made of paper. Then the water level fell off again, as it was to do several times during the next few days, seeming to play a cat and mouse game with the citizens. The ice movements were everywhere, and their course unpredictable—but never worse than when the Lake St. Louis floes broke away from Pointe Claire, only to collide with the solid mass packed in tightly, opposite the city. There was nowhere for it to go except inland, and this it did, with startling suddenness, advancing up McGill and the adjoining streets like a tidal wave.

In low-lying districts such as Griffintown and Point St. Charles, the conditions were appalling. The embankment at the Point was pierced, flooding the Grand Trunk shops and extinguishing the fires. The fifteen hundred employees were thrown out of work. Over a hundred houses were under water, so deep as to force the occupants into the upper stories. The river end of all the streets merged into one vast lake.

The central part of the town was almost as badly off, although to the admiration of all, the big dam on Commissioners Street stood firm. With a ten foot difference in the level on the two faces, Alderman Stevenson was delighted with his handiwork. But the next day, Saturday, April 17, brought a tremendous mass of ice crashing down into the shops and warehouses of the neighborhood. Neither employees nor customers had sufficient warning to get out dry-shod; instead, they were obliged to wade through ice-cold water above the knees. All the merchandise dislodged from the stores, went floating through the streets, in a weird tangle of objects.

Sunday was the most exciting day of all, the sunshine and unseasonably warm weather bringing out throngs of pedestrians to see the sights. The previous night, when another great field of ice moved downstream, the levels had climbed to the unprecedented height of 41 feet, 9 inches. At Bonaventure Station, the water rose above the seats of the cars, including eighteen brand new Pullmans. No trains could reach the city, those from New York halting as far off as Rouse's Point. But the people showed remarkable courage, getting about in all manner of improvised boats—doors, sections of counters, sidewalks, even furniture.

As a result of all this, there was a great outcry in the press about the future. The new dykes must be stronger, and of greater length, and built of stone, rather than wood. No matter how heavy the expenditure, it was justified. "The longer we shirk, the greater the costs." When the federal government announced its intention of employing competent engineers to investigate conditions and propose remedies, the prospects were better. There were discussions with the City Council and the Harbor Commission, and delegations to Ottawa; flood control measures required time and study to be completely effective. But the reports of the next few years indicated progress, so that Montreal never again suffered as in 1886.

Nationally, in these years, the Canadian Pacific found itself the focal point for a good deal of attention. Not all the comments were favorable, since the costs, long before completion, had soared far above the original estimates. The Montreal group still remained in control—Sir Donald A. Smith, better known under his later title of Lord Strathcona; Sir George Stephen, soon to become Lord Mountstephen, a financial wizard and the Company's first president; Sir William Van Horne, whose genius for construction led him from the post of general manager to become the second president; Thomas Shaughnessy, the future Baron, Van Horne's assistant and successor in the presidential office.

It was these men who, in 1885, found themselves at their wits' end for money with which to complete the line. Both in Canada and abroad, every possible source had been tapped until nothing remained. Even Sir John A. Macdonald, their doughty champion, harbored doubts of their success. As for Parliament, its open hostility to any further grants was all too apparent. Ironically enough, the Northwest Rebellion offered an avenue of escape from the impasse, since the urgent need of speedy transport for the troops brought Van Horne into action. Although a hundred miles of track were as yet unlaid, he guaranteed to get the men through to the west in record time. It proved to be no idle boast, as Montreal's 65th soon discovered; exactly one week after leaving home, the unit reached Winnipeg. So greatly did this feat impress the reluctant members in Ottawa, that the new loan, passed with hardly a dissenting voice, and on November 7, 1885, Donald Smith drove the last spike at Craigellachie.

This was how it came about that Montrealers could gather at the old Dalhousie Street Station on the evening of June 28, 1886, to bid Godspeed to the first through passenger train to the Pacific coast. The Mayor and the City Council were present as a body, on the platform, and the Victoria Rifles provided a guard of honor, when amid great excitement, the seventy passengers climbed aboard. Ahead of them stretched a journey of 140 hours over 2906 miles of tracks. With a due regard for the niceties of caste, the accommodation included colonist cars, first-class coaches, a diner named *Holyrood* and two sleepers, equipped with baths, *Yokohama* and *Honolulu*. A silken banner, presented by the Corporation of Montreal, adorned the locomotive as it pulled out, to the roar of a fifteen-gun salute and the cheers of thousands.

In planning its approaches to the city, the Canadian Pacific, perhaps unwittingly, fitted neatly into the general pattern of expansion to the west and the north. Its tracks came in along an escarpment, dividing the upper from the lower town, and thus at a higher level than the Grand Trunk right of way. Prominent citizens, whose gardens were mutilated in the process, voiced complaints to no avail. When the new Windsor Station was opened in February 1889, it, too, stood out of reach of any danger from floods. Architecturally, it was considered to be most impressive, resembling a palace more than a railroad terminus.

The great uptown movement in the retail trade was in full swing early in the '90s. St. Catherine Street became the main artery for the new shops that seemed so luxurious. Henry Morgan led the way, transferring his dry goods business from the corner of St. James Street and Victoria Square to a site next door to Christ Church Cathedral. Away out in the country, chorused the critics, but within a few years, his friends and competitors followed—Birks, Murphy, Ogilvy, Hamilton, Tooke. Only the more conservative Carsley's remained on Notre Dame Street, in an establishment long considered the largest and the finest in Canada.

Contributing greatly to this new development, was the improvement in public transport. September 1, 1892, deserves to be considered a red-letter day, for it was then that the first electric car, the *Rocket*, made its appearance—on a trial basis to begin with, along St. Catherine Street—but meeting with such success that, on Christmas Day, sixteen of the modern vehicles permanently replaced horses on the line. The next year, the Montreal Street Railway Company (successor to the City Passenger Railway) felt sufficiently satisfied with its use of electricity, to keep the service running all winter. There were to be no more sleighs, and soon no more horses. By 1894, the changeover on all lines was complete.

The usual statistics exist for this period, and may perhaps help toward an understanding of civic affairs in the final decade of the century. According to the census of 1891, the population stood at 216,650. One would-be wit, after a look at the detailed table of racial origins, ventured the opinion that the one-seventeenth who were Scottish, had as large a share in enterprise and business as any of the other nationalities of greater size. Then there were the suburbs—the villages and towns, whose added population would raise the metropolitan level to 300,000.

So went the Directory estimate, at a time when the authorities were starting to think of annexation. Hochelaga was absorbed in 1883, St. Jean Baptiste in 1886. Who could tell which would be the next? Westmount? Maisonneuve? St. Henri? Outremont?

There was no shortage of benevolent institutions in a city of such varied religious faiths. "Every congregation has its own congregational charities, every nationality has its 'home' for those of its own nationality." There were working men's societies, colonization societies, societies for prayer and good works. Withal, it was an age of great private generosity, as when in 1887 Sir Donald A. Smith and Sir George Stephen gave a million dollars for the construction of a hospital. Because their gift honored the Queen's Jubilee, it was fitting that the new institution should bear the name of the Royal Victoria at its opening in 1893.

A new Governor General presided over the inaugural ceremony, a man whose naturally compassionate nature accorded well with such an occasion. Lord and Lady Aberdeen—so harmonious a couple that it is difficult to think of them separately —brought a strong social conscience to bear on the life of the country at a time of political discontent and industrial malaise. Politically they were Liberals, and liberal also in their principles. Religion in the formal sense, meant a great deal to them—church attendance, preachers and their sermons, family prayers. Yet theirs was not a faith confined to Sundays, for it illumined all their days, through service to their fellow men.

Because of their wish to know Canadians in all parts of the country, the Aberdeens often left Rideau Hall for quite long periods of time. They spent a winter in Montreal, another in Toronto, and visited the Pacific coast. Always their interest extended far beyond the conventional official circles. Her Excellency kept a diary, human, frank, and sometimes amusing— important enough to be termed recently the best social portrait of Canada at the dawn of the twentieth century.

All else aside, it is for her work with women that Lady Aberdeen is chiefly held in remembrance today. She came to Canada already a leader in the recently organized International Council of Women; within a few months, she became its president. Informal discussions with a few women in Ontario resulted in a monster gathering at Toronto on October 28, 1893, whose audience, fifteen hundred strong, proceeded with the first steps toward the formation of a National Council of Women. When Lady Aberdeen agreed to serve as its first president, she added the national responsibility to her heavy international role. The dual task in no way fazed her.

The Montreal Council of Women dates from November 30 of the same year, when a widely attended meeting was held at the Armory. In the organization procedures that followed, Mrs. Drummond became the first president, and hence the original leader of a group that was to develop as a lasting force for good in the community, and one whose foresighted programs have followed broad and impartial lines. Thus, Montreal adhered to the pattern laid down by the founder, for it was Lady Aberdeen's constant endeavor to keep all the local Councils both inclusive and tolerant. For this reason, the Council, at an early date, adopted the habit of silent prayer at their meetings; an attempt to put their supplications into words was bound to displease one or other of the denominational groups.

The Victorian Order of Nurses was the other great community service, in whose formation Lady Aberdeen took the lead. The suggestion originated with the Vancouver Local Council, and was presented in May 1896 to the National Council of Women at its annual meeting in Montreal. Out of this concern for the welfare of the women and children in the outlying districts of the west, came the formal recommendation that an order of district nurses be established. Although envisaged at first as purely rural, Montreal and Toronto asked that the cities be included in the plan.

Meanwhile, Lady Aberdeen, who had lost no time in broaching the subject to Wilfrid Laurier, the Prime Minister, won his approval without much difficulty. In fact, he went so far as to express himself in favor of a Parliamentary grant, if a unanimous vote could be secured. The district nurses project might thus become the official National Memorial for the approaching Diamond Jubilee of the Queen. Various public meetings seemed to indicate fairly general popular support, and Lord Strathcona showed his interest.

It was at this juncture that a resolution from the Ontario Medical Association warned against "a scheme deleterious to the health of the country." Given wide newspaper publicity, its threat could not be denied. For although this largely rural medical view was based on misconceptions and was decidedly prejudiced into the bargain, the words were plausible, and shattering to the women. Lady Aberdeen, as usual, took prompt action, meeting with representative doctors in Ottawa and Toronto, to bring about ultimately a successful conclusion to the affair. The Queen, in May 1897, was graciously pleased to permit the use of her name, and, in due course, a royal charter made its appearance. Yet because of the opposition, the Order lost the Parliamentary grant envisaged by the Liberal leader. The hostility of the Conservatives had put an end to any hope of support from all parties.

To introduce in this connection a Liberal Prime Minister serves to illustrate the sweeping transformation that overtook Canada in the '90s. The Riel Rebellion, with its introduction of bitterness into the French-English relationship, marked to some extent the start of the Conservative disintegration. If any further irritant were needed, it lay close to hand in the Manitoba school question and the teaching of French in that province. What with one thing and another, the party popularity had already waned, when Macdonald's death in 1891 accelerated the ebbing of its fortunes.

By way of contrast, the story of the Liberals at the same date was one of a steady rise to prominence. That such a course should be possible, after so long a sojourn in the wilderness, was due mainly to the genius of Wilfrid Laurier, a young man who had long enjoyed a particularly close association with Montreal. The study of law at McGill was followed in 1864 by several years of legal practice in the city. Ill health, however, suggested the wisdom of a move to a smaller town, so that 1867 found him established in Arthabaska, a place destined to be home for the rest of his long life.

Laurier went first to the provincial Legislature in 1871; three years later, he moved on to the wider oportunities of the federal Parliament at Ottawa. He was in no sense, an extremist, yet membership in the Liberal party—Les Rouges—swept him into the great conflict then under way between church and state. Having lived in Montreal, he had firsthand knowledge of the rigid views of Bishop Bourget and his clergy. As a Liberal member, he soon found himself involved in the unreasonable ecclesiastical distrust and hatred of his party. Personal efforts to restore harmony gained official status, when, in 1887, his fellow Liberals chose him as their leader.

In the electoral sense, the great change dated from 1896, when a Liberal victory at the polls elevated Laurier to the office of Prime Minister. It was a position that he was to hold, without a break, for fifteen years. Lovell's Directory remarked in its dry fashion, that the once almost solidly Conservative Montreal had turned almost equally solidly Liberal.

Chapter 35

1897–1911

Prosperity. The Queen's Diamond Jubilee. The South African war. French-English differences. Henri Bourassa. "The city below the hill." The harbor. Grain shipments. Automobiles. Airplanes. The Eucharistic Congress.

IN MANY RESPECTS 1897 was a red-letter year, not only for Montreal but for the country as a whole. Prosperity returned, a seeming miracle after the interminable stagnation of the Great Depression, hinting at such bright prospects ahead that the financial and business woes of the past were easily forgotten.

Staunch Liberals hugged all the credit to themselves, since their return to power coincided with the revival of national health. Others, more impartial, held the turn for the better owed little to the politicians; it was bound to happen, regardless of the color of the government. Nevertheless, at an early date, Laurier had demonstrated his astuteness, taking over and making his own, the National Policy of the Conservatives. Under its protection, Canadian manufacturers grew rich.

There was, in addition, the opening up of the west. Immigrants poured in, a million strong from 1896 to 1913, to settle on the prairies from Winnipeg to the Rockies. The early years of the twentieth century saw wheat become the great national asset. The railroads prospered and expanded, and real estate values soared, in the wake of a land boom as tiny villages mushroomed overnight into busy towns.

In all that happened at this time, whether for good or ill, Montreal shared. With the national well-being apparently assured, its citizens flourished. Through its port passed the golden flood of grain, en route to the markets overseas, while the peopling of the west meant new and greater demands for consumer goods. And because the industrial heart of Canada lay in the St. Lawrence Valley, the local factories were busy and employment levels high.

Not surprisingly, a certain air of self-confidence appears in the writing of the period. Lovell's Directory for 1897 felt that Montreal, handling as it did, 46 percent of the country's exports and 36 percent of its imports by water, had fully justified its claim to be the national port. A report, dated 1903, stated that in eight years, the harbor's business had doubled. Although wheat remained the chief commodity, modern methods of cold storage and refrigeration led to greater exports of butter and cheese, chickens, cattle, pigs. Three-quarters of the sugar consumed in Canada was processed in Montreal, the local refineries employing five thousand men. The city served as the center for the Mediterranean fruit trade. Its factories produced such luxuries as biscuits and sweetmeats, coffee and spices, beer and canned goods. It controlled three-fifths of the dry goods trade of the nation, manufacturing and distributing cotton and woollen goods and a wide variety of clothing. A decade later, the situation showed no retrogression, with cheap power given the credit for much of the local pre-eminence. Tobacco had become the largest single industry, followed by boots and shoes and cotton. As for the harbor, although open only seven months each season, it ranked as the second largest in North America, surpassing even Boston and Philadelphia, with their uninterrupted year-round operations.

Much of this good fortune was, of course, still undreamed of, when, in June 1897, Canadians joined in the Empire-wide celebration of Queen Victoria's Diamond Jubilee. Prime Minister Laurier represented his countrymen at the official ceremonies in London, leaving his native shores as plain Mister, and returning as Sir Wilfrid. He passed through Montreal early in the month, en route to New York and the steamer *Lucania,* and although the rain came down in torrents, thousands assembled at Bonaventure Station to see him off. They cheered lustily, almost drowning out the music of the Police Band. Everyone wanted to

shake hands as he stood on the car steps, turning from one side
to another, and greeting old friends and political supporters.

The weather was particularly unsettled that June. A fashion
note recommended the purchase of a good tailor-made dress
for outdoor events. Charming though the flimsy fabrics might be,
the ladies would find them less serviceable than serge or cash-
mere, made up into skirts topped with small mess jackets. Worn
over soft vests or shirts, they could be used all summer. To make
matters worse, the condition of the streets was bad. Only twenty-
six miles had been asphalted, and even these were full of holes.
Craig Street, with its wooden pavement, was disgraceful. To
cross it on rainy days, required exceptional ability on the part of
pedestrians, who did not care to walk ankle-deep in water.

Yet just as in the past, nothing ever discouraged Montrealers
if they wished to celebrate, and this they proceeded to do in
right royal fashion. With fitting solemnity at first, June 20 being
a Sunday, special prayers and sermons in all the Catholic and
Protestant churches recalled the sixty glorious years of Her Majesty's reign. Notre Dame was crowded to the doors in the evening, for a great service of thanksgiving, attended by people of all
faiths—a most unusual occurrence.

That week, everyone who could possibly be spared took a holiday. On Monday, they "jubilated" in great style, especially
those who lived east of St. Lawrence Main Street, where the
hearty and enthusiastic turnout of the French Canadians con-
trasted oddly with the coolness of the spectators in the west
end. Was this the phlegmatic nature of the British character?
queried a reporter, for although the wind was cold and raw, the
weather might have been worse.

But as usual, the greatest attractions were reserved for the
hours of darkness. Rich and poor alike decorated their houses
while the public buildings vied with each other in the excellence of their adornment. Even the manufacturing districts entered into the spirit of the occasion. Nothing, however, exceeded
the brilliance of the stretch from Dorchester Street down to Bonaventure Station. The Windsor Hotel alone used a thousand lights,
while McGill festooned its campus with long lines of Chinese
lanterns, all lit by electricity. The demand for gas and electric

fixtures was phenomenal, one firm receiving orders for the place-
ment of 20,000 bulbs. No wonder that the streetcars could not
accommodate all the eager passengers. A great crush filled St.
Catherine Street, and a maelstrom of humanity flowed along
from Victoria Square to Place d'Armes, rendering St. James
Street impassable.

But Montreal's outburst of patriotic sentiment, however keyed
momentarily to the temper of the times, proved to be short-lived.
The once common British indifference to the colonies had long
since vanished, to be replaced by a strong, almost aggressive im-
perialism. A vision of empire it undoubtedly was, but one entirely Anglo-Saxon, and the French Canadians as the years
passed, grew restive in the face of the jingoism expressed by
many of their fellow countrymen.

Left to itself, the discord might perhaps have died away. Instead, it was so aggravated by the troubles of far-off South Africa
as to gain an unhappy immortality. The more serious the threat
of actual conflict, the greater the division of opinion. Must the
Dominion automatically support the mother country in the
event of war? Could the British government compel the Canadian militia to serve overseas? For every question, there were
two answers.

The result was that when, in October 1899, the Boers invaded
British territory, Canada found itself divided in sentiment. While
Ontario—and English-speaking Montreal—was gripped by a tremendous enthusiasm for the cause, French Canadians remained
indifferent, to the point, sometimes, of sympathy with the enemy.
Laurier was caught between twin fires. So far he had adhered to
the principle that no troops could go abroad without the consent
of Parliament. Now in partial capitulation to public pressure, his
government undertook to equip and transport for this purpose, a
volunteer force of a thousand. The first group sailed on October
30—not, it was emphasized, as an official contingent—and eventually 7300 Canadians saw service overseas.

Montreal, meanwhile, reacted pretty much according to
form. *La Patrie* asked why Canadians should go to the Transvaal
and assist in reducing its million people to subjection. The British, after all, possessed immense resources, a considerable navy

and a powerful warlike army. The *Star* for its part thundered that Canada must be kept British, and criticized Laurier, holidaymaking in Chicago, amid the murmurings of an insulted nation.

The relief of Ladysmith on March 1, 1900, sent the town wild. Under siege by the Boers since early November, its fate had provided many anxious moments for the British. Now all was over, and happily so. The church bells of Montreal pealed, and the flags went up on the public buildings and private dwellings. The Mayor decreed a civic half holiday, and at McGill, with the cancellation of lectures, the students decided to celebrate. It was all very noisy and harmless to start with, as the twelve hundred youths paraded the streets, pouring into the High School, to fill its stage, aisles and seats. On they went, plowing through the deep snow to St. James Street. By this time, the crowd had been swelled by hundreds of small boys and adult curiosity seekers; two thousand, it was estimated, pressed ahead, bearing all manner of trophies—newspaper bulletin boards, to-let notices, and signs advertising cheap sales.

Events took a more serious turn, upon arrival at the offices of the French newspapers. There being no flags on *La Presse* building, the mob broke in the door and smashed the windows. Then, led by "Generals" carrying hockey sticks, they continued as far as the City Hall. Again no flag! an omission soon remedied by the running up of a Jack about the size of a pocket hankerchief. Still all might have been well, had not the students gone on to Laval, and finding everything closed, raised two miniature flags. This was too much, and so that afternoon saw a battle between the universities, the combatants rolling over and over in the snow, their numbers growing constantly as clerks from the shops arrived on the scene. After about an hour, struggling with the wind, the snow, and the boys, the fifty policemen on duty succeeded in restoring order.

The leaders of both universities were prompt in the expression of their regrets, pointing out that McGill and Laval had always been on the best of terms. Many of those who had taken part in the riot had no connection with either institution. Laval said its loyalty was as great as anyone's, while McGill agreed that the celebrants' zeal had exceeded their discretion.

As much as anything, perhaps, it was the severity of the weather that restored peace. On March 2, Montreal was completely tied up, with every occupation subservient to snow removal. There were no trains, no public transport, no milkmen, and the streets in the upper part of the town were impassable, by reason of the ten- or twelve-foot drifts. The city employed a thousand shovelers, and could have used as many more. Westmounters went to work on showshoes, and Sherbrooke Street at eight in the morning resembled a giant "tramp." Dozens of hopeful passengers waited at Greene Avenue and St. Catherine Street for the snail-like streetcars that never seemed to come.

The Boer War in South Africa ended in May 1902, its later period, as far as Montreal was concerned, still marked by a cleavage in public opinion. Nor did the trouble end there, for the peace overseas did little to restore French-English harmony, and indeed, much of the racial division of modern times originated with these turn-of-the-century events. And the discontent in French Canada was no vague inarticulate murmur. It developed into a distinct Nationalist movement, whose members turned away gradually from their support of Laurier and his advocacy of a united country.

In Henri Bourassa, the Nationalists found not only a leader, but a spokesman of outstanding ability. By birth and education, he was a Montrealer, and a considerable part of his long life was spent in his native city. Although as the grandson of Louis Joseph Papineau, he was assured of a welcome, the strength of his own personality soon obviated any need of family influence. He entered Parliament as a Liberal in 1896, only to part company with the party over Laurier's South African war policy. As leader of the Nationalists, he remained a member of the Federal House until 1907. From 1908 to 1912 he enjoyed the more congenial atmosphere of the Quebec Legislature.

Bourassa's political activities gained much from his career in journalism. A free-lancer at first, in 1910 he founded *Le Devoir*, a Nationalist paper which he served as editor-in-chief for many years. But it is perhaps as a public speaker and pamphleteer that he is chiefly remembered today. In every Canadian dispute that marked those years of gathering clouds in Europe, his voice was raised. Many of his speeches, later printed, gained a wide circulation, and since he lived until 1952, his influence was remarkable.

But it should not be thought that Montreal spent all its time either dealing with weighty international problems or disputing with the neighbors. The city continued to grow—from a population of 267,730 in 1901 to 466,197 in 1911—two-thirds French speaking, one-third English. A good deal of wordage was devoted to the municipal government, some of it favorable, but as time passed, sharply critical. The French and the English press took common ground, their pages teeming with civic scandals, stories of bribery and corruption, the buying and selling of votes. Reform was what they wanted, as they denounced the existing City Council and urged support for the Citizens Association, in its campaign to secure a Board of Control. The results were gratifying, for in a referendum held on September 20, 1909, an overwhelming majority voted affirmatively.

Meanwhile, Mr. Justice Cannon, as Chairman of a Royal Commission appointed by the provincial government, had commenced what was to become many months of careful study of the situation. "We must find out the truth." His Report, made public in December, constituted a landmark in Montreal's governmental history. Its five hundred pages, in a blistering survey of municipal affairs since 1902, found the city to be saturated with corruption. Most aldermen had been concerned only with the private interests of themselves, their relatives and friends, and, as a result, 25 percent of the annual revenue was wasted "in boodling and abuses of all kinds."

Keen discussion followed, on all phases of this outspoken document, and when a provincial ruling confirmed the popular endorsation of a Board of Control, the reform leaders plunged into action. In the civic election, scheduled for early in 1910, they saw an opportunity to oust the notorious twenty-three members of the old Council, many of whom brazenly planned to run for office again. The budget, amounting to $24,000,000, needed honest and efficient management. The list of those who supported the reform slate included such outstanding names as

Archbishop Bruchesi, the Anglican Bishop Farthing, ex-Mayor Laporte, and Henri Bourassa. And happily, the victory on February 1 was a substantial one, the corrupt councilors of the old regime snowed under by the substantial majorities piled up by their challengers.

In other respects, Montreal was far from perfect. The young Herbert Ames pointed out some of its flaws in *The City Below the Hill,* a sociological study dated 1897. It was a strangely modern document, too advanced in its thinking, in fact, to achieve any great results. Its author considered the time had come for the wealthy citizens to cease their talk about the slums of London, the beggars of Paris and the tenement house evils of New York. Instead, they should endeavor to learn something about the conditions in their midst. The denizens of the lower town might as well be natives of Central Africa for all the upper class cared.

As an initial step toward remedying this deplorable situation, Ames told of a survey conducted in 1896, of a section of Griffintown, a square mile in area. Its residents numbered 38,000. Another 17,000 worked there, but lived outside the district. In their racial origins, these people were French, Irish, British, in almost equal proportions; in the social scale, they were more homogeneous, being of the real industrial class. Some of them were shockingly poor. Among the 7671 resident families, the average weekly wage per family was $11. In some cases, it dropped to $1.75, or twenty-five cents a day. Few could count on regular employment all year. The wharves in summer, and odd jobs during the five winter months—this was the lot of one family out of every four.

Ames discovered an abundant willingness in Montreal to help, but a pressing need of proper guidance and direction. A Central Charity Board, with a joint roll of cases, would lessen the tendency to pauperize the recipients. Meanwhile, the 1893 death rate was shocking. For all Canada, it stood at 14 per 1000; for the Province at 19; for Montreal at 25. Granted that since 1873 it had diminished by 40 percent, it was still higher than London, Paris, or New York. And while the mortality in the city above the hill was only 13 per 1000, in certain sections of Griffintown it rose to a shocking 34. There, he concluded, stood the perfect spot for an experiment in the provision of improved dwellings for the workers. A philanthropic investment, he termed it.

What Montreal did about slum clearance can best be told in the words of Mr. Henry Vivian, a British Member of Parliament and a great advocate of city beautification. After a visit in August 1910, he spoke frankly. "Unless preparations are constantly made for caring for your population, Montreal will become one of the greatest cesspools of human depravity in the world. Nothing in East London is worse than some of the conditions which I saw in Montreal yesterday, and immediate improvement is needed even at the present time."

The strangeness of the new century was accentuated in January 1901 by the death of Queen Victoria. She had reigned for sixty-four years and few people remembered any other sovereign. Memorial services in the local churches marked the passing of the old Queen. A good "press" hailed the accession of Edward VII, and when it was announced that the new heir to the throne would visit Canada later that year, Montreal's excitement knew no bounds.

Despite the elaborate preparations, the royal visit was a short one, with the arrival scheduled for the afternoon of September 18, and the departure for the morning of the twentieth. At the last minute, because of the tragic assassination of President William McKinley, all engagements of a festive nature were canceled. Even so, there was magic in the air when the train pulled in at Place Viger Station. Bright cool weather greeted the distinguished couple, the future George V in the uniform of a British admiral, his consort handsome in a close-fitting dress of a dark shade, with rich furs about her shoulders. During the drive to Lord Strathcona's mansion on Dorchester Street, the carriage passed between long lines of people, many of them in from the country, the habitants in their old-time habilments contrasting oddly with the silk hats and formal attire of the prosperous city dwellers.

It might be said of the Duke and Duchess of Cornwall, that by their visits to the local institutions of learning, they honored all the devoted pioneers, French and English alike, who had striven so long to promote the cause of education in the city. Thus at Laval, they received a wonderful welcome from Archbishop Bruchesi and the assembled clergy, and from the students an ovation wherein college yells enlivened the otherwise formal round of presentations and speeches. After the earlier years of turmoil, the university was now firmly established, still bearing the name of its parent in Quebec, but since 1889, to all intents and purposes, independent. The administration at that date presented problems, since the four faculties of law, medicine, theology, and arts were housed in as many different quarters of the city. Happily, in 1893, a new building on St. Denis Street permitted their concentration under one roof, and it was there, in 1901, that the royal reception took place.

McGill, in its turn, welcomed the Duke and Duchess. It was an historic occasion for the university, marked in the traditional manner by the conferment of honorary degrees. The Convocation Hall was a novel one, the Royal Victoria College being still new and sufficiently "advanced" to attract attention. Within its walls, the women undergraduates could follow courses of study leading to the degrees of B.A. or B.Sc., thanks to the generosity of Lord Strathcona. That farsighted advocate of their higher education had, at an earlier date, given $50,000 to the university to insure their admission. He now provided the Donaldas with a modern headquarters, contributing not only the $300,000 construction costs, but an endowment of $1,000,000.

In yet another engagement during that crowded day in 1901, the Duke opened the new wing of the McGill Medical Building, a much overcrowded institution, which in spite of additions and alterations, had long since proved inadequate. Once again, it was the generosity of private individuals that made the expansion possible—in the earlier period, Mr. J. H. R. Molson and latterly Lord Strathcona. Thus in the faculty that was at once the earliest organized and the chief pride of the university, more students could be accommodated and a broader research program undertaken.

Sir William Macdonald was another of McGill's benefactors extremely active at this time. He was an extraordinary character, whose eccentricity, no less than his generosity, was the talk of the town. Rated the richest of its citizens, Montreal had been his home since 1854. An old bachelor, Macdonald lived in a plain old house on Sherbrooke Street, near the university, driving down to business in an outmoded gig or phaeton. The story goes that he wore an overcoat, once gray, until time made it green. As for his dingy office on St. James Street, without benefit of elevators, it would have given the blues to anyone who enjoyed creature comforts.

Such was the contradictory nature of the man who gave away in his lifetime the sum of $15,000,000. A large percentage of this went to McGill. He founded and endowed the Macdonald Agricultural College at Ste. Anne de Bellevue, while on the Montreal campus his generosity to the sciences almost defied precise measurement. Aside from such philanthropies, business was Macdonald's all absorbing passion—the tobacco industry, to be precise. Yet above all else, he detested smoking; it was, he considered, a filthy habit. Hence the stories of the professors, busy in laboratories or pondering the course of their latest experiments, but always keeping a sharp watch on his movements, so that all pipes could be put out of sight as he approached.

Macdonald's lavish endowments played a large part in the success of one of McGill's distinguished scientists. For Ernest Rutherford, he built and equipped a laboratory, endowed the Chair of Physics, and provided special apparatus whenever requested. The young Cambridge graduate came to the university in 1898 at a salary of £500 a year. He had heard that Montreal was a pleasant place to live, yet from experience, soon found the cost of living to be one-third higher than in England. Rents especially, since for a small pillbox of a house he paid £100 annually.

Rutherford remained in Montreal until 1907, active, of course, as a teacher, but soon famous because of the nature of his studies. During 1902–03, in collaboration with Frederick Soddy of the Chemistry Department, he conducted experiments in radiation, making McGill for the moment the world center of research in atomic physics. In 1903, when Professor Eve (later his biographer) first met him, he was already famous. The newspapers carried stories of radium, and the radioactive theory of the break-up of atoms was a common topic. His book entitled *Radio-activity*, published in 1904, served to broaden his renown. As a result of this work at McGill, Rutherford received the Nobel prize in 1908—in chemistry, not physics, a fact that never ceased to amuse him.

While the élite of the learned world applauded these profound scientific theories, technology in a more practical manner was revolutionizing the lives of the ordinary citizens. Transportation was a case in point, wherein radical new ideas took shape, and the old methods found themselves transformed. Montreal, as the self-proclaimed communications center of the nation, was perhaps unusually sensitive to all the implications of the modern era.

So much of the city's prosperity depended on the harbor that scarcely a season passed without comment, or someone, locally, in emulation of Oliver Twist, asking for more. In 1903, a wheat-conscious writer saw Canada as the Empire's Granary and Montreal as the Spout of the Granary. The harbor, he recorded, was completely transformed, its new stone piers and wharves, vast in dimension and substantial in appearance, then nearing completion. Work was well advanced on two huge grain elevators, each with a capacity of a million bushels. But a railway man, the same year, held other views. "We have constructed a Hopper too big for the Spout." Pointing to the congestion at the wharf terminals, he declared the railroads lacked free enough access to the docks, for the prompt collection of imported freight bound for the interior. No wonder that the western traders were willing to pay extra freight haulage in the United States, for the sake of rapid delivery.

In 1909 the Canadian Annual Review reported that the development of the Montreal harbor proceeded apace. Millions were being spent on a project, whose national character had long since been recognized. By Act of Parliament, the jurisdiction of the Harbor Board was extended from sixteen miles of the waterfront to thirty-six. Montreal then handled a greater volume of business per month, than any other North American port, save New York.

Change came to the once-famous Victoria Bridge, when, in

October 1897, the demolition of the old tubular superstructure
started. The single track could no longer cope with the flow of
traffic. That for thirty-eight years, scores of trains in both directions should have crossed daily without collision, was indeed,
a proud record. But 1898 saw the new openwork spans erected
around the tube, which was afterward dismantled. Despite the
magnitude of the alterations, traffic was never halted for more
than two hours. The new structure, four times the width of the
original, carried double railroad tracks, carriageways, and foot-
paths, and the view from the car windows was magnificent.

To the railroads also, belonged much of the credit for the
opening-up of new districts. Especially was this true of the
north, where the extension of the line as far as Ste. Agathe des
Monts brought the great Laurentian area within easy reach of
the city. Tempted by the convenience of the telephone and a
rail journey of less than two hours, many people discovered, in
the beautiful lakes of this country, the perfect spot for their
cottages. In ever-growing numbers, they transported their families to the mountains, once school was out.

But the movement to the country was confined to the summer
months. So long as the shovel remained the only weapon with
which to fight the heavy snowstorms, city dwellers stayed at
home in winter. Sleighing was a necessity for those who did not
care to use the streetcars, and the possession of handsome equipages and fine horses was a recognized accompaniment of wealth.
The athletes still enjoyed their snowshoes, their skates, and their
toboggans, yet with a difference. Some of the earlier spontaneous
gaiety had vanished, to be replaced by a sophistication unknown
to their fathers. The Carnivals and Ice Palaces came to an end,
it being felt they created an erroneous impression as to the
severity of the Canadian climate. The American tourists, in their
thousands, must not think that Montreal was an arctic city in a
land of perpetual snow.

Suddenly, or so it now seems, there were automobiles in Montreal, and complaints about the condition of the roads. On
November 22, 1899, the sporting page of the *Star* carried a picture of the first car ever seen in the city. It was owned by Mr.
U. H. Dandurand, the managing director of the Queen's Park

Association. According to the caption, "yesterday afternoon, several prominent citizens were taken out for a ride in it. The vehicle created quite a sensation." As described by the Royal Automobile Club, it had large wheels and protruding springs and a platform with two seats. The steering wheel, gears, and brake levers were on the right-hand side. Other equipment included a bulb horn, carriage lamps at the side, oil and wick tail lamps, and headlights illuminated with carbide gas, carried in a cylinder.

It fell to Mr. Dandurand to set the fashion for correct motoring costume—a leather cap, pea jacket, gauntlets, goggles, and a cotton duster. The ladies wore similar dusters to protect their clothes, and on their heads, wide-brimmed hats tied with long veils. Driving was an ordeal, no matter how great the enthusiasm; it was hard to say whether the city or the country possessed the worse roads. But Mr. Dandurand persisted, soon to be joined by others. Later, he owned an electric automobile, and finally, a Pullman, the forerunner of today's trailers.

July 1904 saw the start of the Automobile Club of Canada, incorporated under the Amusement Act of the Province and authorized municipally by a city permit. Andrew J. Dawes became the first president, at a time when there were hardly a hundred cars in the province. The few that existed, were used solely for sport or amusement, never for business. Many people disliked them, which explains the applause when the City Council, on June 13, decided to exclude the new-fangled vehicles from Mount Royal Park. There should be at least one place of escape for those who preferred carriages or horseback riding. The news that Toronto automobilists were planning to run slowly to conciliate the farmers, provoked this item addressed to the local Gentlemen of the Horn. "A strong feeling is growing up against the automobile on this Island, which will result in very drastic legislation before long, if some steps are not taken to alleviate it."

Aviation in its early and primitive stages, ran closely parallel in date, to this burgeoning world of the automobile, and Montreal, in the opening decade of the century, produced a surprising number of Canadian "firsts." There was, for instance,

Larry Lesh, who, during the summer of 1907, made numerous towed glider flights from a farm near Dominion Park. These were all the more remarkable in that the pilot was not yet fifteen years old. Larry's family came from Chicago, and, during their brief residence in Montreal, he attended the High School. He built his own gliders, the first a frail model of bamboo and muslin, its wingspan 16 feet and its weight 25 pounds. But with a farm boy mounted on a horse as his only motive power, he succeeded in reaching heights up to 100 feet for a distance of 250 feet.

The airplane proper entered the picture somewhat later. When the early models made the news, the public clamored to see them at exhibitions or fairs. Their presence suggested stunts, and their pilots appeared as adventurous fellows who lived dangerously, and all too often died tragically. Montreal had an early glimpse of an airship in July 1906, when an American named Lincoln Beachey rose from the grounds of Dominion Park in a machine of his own construction. But the one-man dirigibles enjoyed only a brief popularity, and by 1910, the heavier-than-air machine had proved its superiority. It was in that year that the city had its chance to enjoy an ambitious aeronautical show.

The sponsors of the air meet formed a syndicate—E. M. Wilcox of Toronto, Duncan MacDonald of the Automobile Club, and William Carruthers of the Montreal Tramways. The site was a tract of level land north of the railway tracks near Lakeside. The five farmer-owners agreed that the fences should be leveled, and the ditches filled in. A grandstand provided space for ten thousand spectators, while another ten thousand could be accommodated on the grounds. The price of admission ranged from fifty cents up to two dollars, and twenty special trains a day from the city solved the transportation problem. A $10,000 fee was paid to the noted French aviator, Count Jacques de Lesseps; he attended in person and brought two machines. A similar sum went to the Wright brothers, who sent five famous fliers: Walter Brookins, Frank Coffyn, Ralph Johnstone, Duval La Chapelle, and Paul Miltgen. William Jennings Bryan brought his family all the way from Havana to see the fun.

The public showed keen interest from the start, and when at

one point, three machines were in the air together, their excitement knew no bounds. July 1, being Dominion Day, brought out a capacity crowd. Everyone gasped as Johnstone came down for a landing. A wingtip touched the ground, and the biplane was demolished. That the pilot should escape unharmed, seemed a miracle, and the onlookers went wild. July 2 was a Saturday, and 20,000 persons watched Brookins set a new Canadian altitude record of 3510 feet. But the big event came at 6:15 P.M., when de Lesseps left the ground, rising to a height of 2000 feet for a 35-mile flight that took him in a wide circuit over the city. He remained aloft for three-quarters of an hour, flying a Bleriot monoplane, *La Scarabee*. It was the climax of a week of thrills.

Montreal's experiences with great numbers of people in the summer of 1910 did not end with the departure of the aviators and their fans. In September, the city played host to the International Eucharistic Congress, the first in the New World to be so honored. It was a true ingathering of the faithful sons of the Church. Obviously, no precise count of the attendance could be taken; an advance estimate placed the probable total at 100,000; afterward it was said 200,000 came nearer the truth. The over-all cost was thought to be a million dollars.

The rain fell in torrents on Saturday, September 3, when the official party arrived from Quebec on board the government steamer, *Lady Grey*. At its head was the Papal Delegate, Vincenzo Cardinal Vannutelli; three hundred prelates, clergy, and laymen accompanied him. The Mayor, Dr. Guerin, who led the civic welcome, in his speech hailed Montreal as the Rome of the New World, and Canada as the place in which men and women and different nationalities, races, and creeds, lived together in harmony. The formal opening of the Congress came on the Tuesday evening, when a brilliant gathering crowded into St. James Cathedral to hear a message from the Holy Father. The practical work got under way on the Thursday. Three general meetings were held, over and above the thirteen working sessions, thus providing opportunities for the public to share in the deliberations.

The final event of the Congress was perhaps the greatest, and certainly so, in terms of popular attendance. This was the solemn procession of the Blessed Eucharist, when from two o'clock onward for four or five hours, half a million spectators packed the streets. They had been gathering all day, pouring in by train from points, hundreds of miles distant. Fifty to sixty thousand men marched along, their distinctive banners and religious emblems indicating their nationality. After the laymen, came the choirboys, a thousand of them, in red cassocks and surplices; the religious orders of the city; two thousand priests in their vestments; a hundred bishops and archbishops, splendid in copes and mitres. Finally the huge gold canopy came in sight, and under it walked Cardinal Vannutelli, carrying the Sacred Host. When the last stragglers reached Fletcher's Field, it was already dusk, so that the electric lights on the altar shone out in the gloom. And with the benediction from the Cardinal, the Congress ended—the most spectacular week, in the history of the country, according to some reporters.

Chapter 36
1911–1918

Reciprocity. Civic government and Médéric Martin. The war and local excitement. "The Vingt-Doos." Rioting. Conscription fears. Turbulence and then peace.

RECIPROCITY WAS a fighting word to Canadians in 1911. As outlined by the Prime Minister, the proposed treaty with the United States provided for free trade in natural farm produce, and low rates of duty on a variety of secondary products and manufactured goods. Urging its adoption on the grounds of increased prosperity for the nation, Laurier recalled the long and unsuccessful quest for such an agreement in the years that followed the Civil War. But as between the nineteenth and the twentieth centuries, the temper of the country had changed, so that while Congress endorsed President Taft's preliminary negotiations, Parliament did not. In fact, the question never even came to a vote in the House. Instead, as one of the main issues at stake in the federal election of September, it brought defeat to its Liberal sponsors. Somewhat surprisingly, the popular ballot gave the nod to the Conservatives, under Robert Borden.

The upset was not quite so spontaneous as it seemed, for big business, with few exceptions, opposed Reciprocity. Montreal and Toronto held strong views on the subject, their Boards of Trade voicing protests while most of the powerful industrial, financial, and railroad interests ganged up in a stiff fight against the supposed threat to their profits. All preferred the existing east-west flow of trade to the visionary north-south proposals. New York, they feared, would be the gainer at the expense of Montreal.

The Liberal ouster in Ottawa did nothing to weaken the party's strength in Quebec. Indeed, there it seemed to have acquired a political immortality, untouched by events in the outside world. From 1905 to 1920, Sir Lomer Gouin served as Premier of the province, a man to whose cautious, but progressive policies, the prevailing climate of prosperity and stability was often attributed. Montreal came to know him well as the arbiter, on many occasions, of its civic administrative problems.

The local Board of Control had come under fire almost from the moment of its inception. Its noisiest critics were the aldermen, ejected at that time, from their snug positions at the City Hall. Many, as the years passed, who regained their seats on the Council, longed for a return to the old "spoils" system, and none more than Médéric Martin, who saw in the municipal election of 1914, an opportunity for more direct action.

It should be remembered that Montreal's Chief Magistrates, from about 1840 onward, had been chosen alternatively from among the French- and English-speaking citizens. In terms of population, the arrangement was a generous one, since the latter constituted only a quarter of the total. That it had proved workable was a tribute to the generally high quality of the officeholders, and to the support of the leading citizens in both language groups. Thus as L. A. Lavalée's mayoral term drew to a close in 1914, traditionally his successor should have been an Anglo-Canadian. This was the moment at which Martin tossed his hat into the ring, causing consternation, not only on the grounds of his racial prejudice, but because of his supposed dishonesty. A somewhat reluctant George Washington Stephens was persuaded to stand as a reform candidate; prominent citizens, French as well as English, gave him their support, as did most of the newspapers. All to no avail, for Martin's spellbinding speeches gained him the popular vote, and Montreal had a new mayor.

With this changeover in municipal power, the pork barrel era returned to the City Hall—although not with complete effectiveness so long as the Board of Control retained its standing. Its abolition formed the basis of Martin's constant pleas to Quebec. Meanwhile, thoughtful citizens had good reason to fear what lay ahead, for the civic finances were in a bad way. Annual deficits came to be accepted as a matter of course, and the result was a debt load that took on frightening proportions. Public funds were spent lavishly, without any visible benefits. There were battles over the Tramways Company and troubles with the water supply; stories of dishonest contractors; padding of the payrolls; corruption in the Police Force; graft everywhere. Under the most favorable conditions, the situation would have been grave. That it came at a time when people were crowding into the cities, added to its gravity. Moreover, throughout Canada, the boom conditions showed ominous signs of an approaching demise.

Yet Lovell's Directory could still write boastfully of Montreal in 1914; the largest city in Canada; the second largest in the British colonies; the ninth in North America; the second largest port on the continent. During the seven-month season, its harbor handled one-third of the nation's commerce; the federal government was then spending $20,000,000 on its improvements. Everyone and everything shared in the expansion. The population grew in keeping with the commercial and industrial progress, and financial transactions climbed along with the value of land. Montreal was on the way to becoming a second New York, and so long as the banks remained strong, there was no real cause for uneasiness.

Contributing greatly to the buoyancy of the real estate market were the activities of that famous, if somewhat notorious, pair of railroaders, Sir William Mackenzie and Sir Donald Mann. They displayed a considerable sagacity in securing entry and terminal facilities for the Canadian Northern in several cities. Nowhere, perhaps, did it show to better advantage than in Montreal, for their purchases included the land on which now stands the Canadian National Central Station, the Queen Elizabeth Hotel, the Place Ville Marie complex. It was early in 1911 when they first acquired property along Dorchester Street, working quietly not only in this midtown location, but in their buying up of farms north of Mount Royal. On October 20, 1911, the Canadian Northern Tunnel and Terminal Company was authorized to construct a tunnel three miles long, under the mountain, together with a station and hotel at the downtown end. At first the work went ahead quickly. Then the war came, delaying completion, so that the first train did not run until October 12, 1918. But the effects of the enterprise had long been felt in other ways. Property values rose in the area along Dorchester Street, while beyond the mountain, Model City took shape as the newest suburb, later to be called the Town of Mount Royal.

In 1912 and 1913, the cost of living rose to such an extent that the Canadian Annual Review felt moved to comment on the reasons for the change. Its editor saw the masses, as well as the classes, sharing in luxurious habits and expensive tastes. The women dressed extravagantly. Labor costs mounted steadily, in business, industry, and domestic affairs. Rents were up, both for homes and offices. Official statistics showed that in the period from 1897 to 1912 the cost of food soared from an index figure of 86.2 to 152.7. In 1913 the banks issued warnings of the danger of inflation, and the value of stocks showed considerable shrinkage. Railroad earnings were down, forcing the discharge of many employees. Since the manufacturers and retailers found themselves in a similar plight, it is not surprising that the winter of 1913–14 witnessed a record number of unemployed in Montreal.

In June 1914 the newspapers headlined Home Rule for Ireland; the inquiry into the disastrous wreck of the *Empress of Ireland;* the iniquities of the municipal administration. The crop prospects were good, and the stock market more cheerful than had been the case earlier. In London, the militant suffragettes damaged the Coronation Chair. At Hammondsport, New York, John Porte of the British Navy made preparations to fly across the Atlantic, his trip financed by Rodman Wanamaker to mark the centennial of Anglo-American peace.

That summer, the grand Canadian weather sent thousands of people to the country, yet the advertisements for the town dwellers were enticing. "Mt. Royal Heights, back of the Mountain—a country home within five minutes of the city." "Here's an offer in refrigerators to make you stop and wonder—$6.50. Your ice bills will be reduced." "Urban and interurban men find the Ford a faithful friend." "Scroggie's after supper specials, on sale from 7 P.M. to 10 P.M."

Such was the local atmosphere when news came of the assassination at Sarajevo on June 28, 1914, of the Archduke Franz Ferdinand. (The results of the Ontario elections drew larger print.) But after the Austrian ultimatum to Serbia on July 23, the pace of events quickened, and Montreal found itself sharing in the world's apprehension. All the stock markets were demoralized; the Montreal and Toronto Exchanges closed. At armories throughout the city, there was tension, and the churches joined in offering prayers for peace.

The news that Germany had declared war on Russia provoked wild demonstrations in most Canadian cities. Thus Montreal was not unique when, on three successive nights at the beginning of August, its citizens gave expression to their pent-up feelings, spontaneously and quite apart from any official arrangements. On each occasion, the same general pattern prevailed, as cheering throngs paraded the streets, waving flags and singing. While no single district had a monopoly of these outbursts, they were especially noteworthy in the French quarter to the east. French Canadians comprised the majority of the marchers, Tricolors in their hats and Union Jacks in their hands. Their choice of songs reflected the same impartiality: *God Save the King, Rule Britannia,* and *La Marseillaise.*

This particular phase ended as suddenly as it began, for the city took on the semblance of an armed camp. Five hundred members of the militia assumed guard duties along the Lachine and Soulanges canals. No chance were to be taken with foreigners who might be dangerous. For the first time in its history, the port was closed, and a special force sworn in, with orders to exclude all landsmen. No vessel was permitted to enter or leave without express writ, and grain shipments to Germany were halted. The congestion in the harbor grew to abnormal proportions. Meanwhile, the British naval reserves had been recalled for duty, and French and Belgian nationals sought instructions from their respective consuls.

The rush to enlist was soon in full swing, and by late September most of the armories reported full strength or over. The earliest units to leave the city were the 1st Royal Highlanders and the Royal Montreal Regiment. On the evening of August 25, when a party of two thousand entrained for the camp at Val-

cartier, near Quebec, everyone turned out to join in the farewells. Many of the recruits wore civilian clothes, their simple
canvas kits being the only signs of military life. They were
a composite group—French Canadians of the 65th Regiment,
straight from Mass and an inspiring address from the Archbishop; members of the Victoria Rifles and of the Grenadiers.
The Highlanders, according to a newspaper account, wore
khaki! But as they swung west along St. Catherine Street to
Windsor Station, strains of *Cock o' the North* filled the air.

Shortly after the outbreak of war, several of Montreal's promi-
nent citizens put forward proposals for the formation of a French
Canadian unit. The talk—informal at first—became official when,
late in September, a delegation waited upon the Minister of
Militia in Ottawa. A government announcement followed, on
September 30, authorizing the establishment of the Royal 22nd
Regiment, at which probably no one rejoiced more than Dr.
Arthur Mignault. His had been the leading role, and his subse-
quent contribution of $50,000 for the equipment of the "Vingt-
Doos" revealed the depth of his feelings.

Sohmer Park was the setting of a tremendous public gathering
in October, convened to launch the recruiting campaign for the
new Regiment. A distinguished array of citizens graced the
platform, some in normal times, political rivals or enemies: Sir
Wilfrid Laurier, Sir Lomer Gouin, Senator Dandurand, the Honorable R. Lemieux, Lieutenant Colonel F. M. Gaudet the commanding officer, and Surgeon Major Mignault. The speeches
were of a high order. Laurier chose to recall the heroism of New
France. "You will enlist in a body, for this cause is just as sacred
as the one for which Dollard and his companions gave their
lives."

Although attendance estimates varied, a figure of twenty
thousand was frequently cited. Crowds packed the auditorium
to suffocation, while hundreds stood outside, unable to gain ad-
mittance. Good-tempered though they may have been, the police had their hands full, in controlling the exuberant youths. A
month later *La Patrie* gave the enlistments to date as 1132, with
thousands more wanting to join.

To McGill belonged the credit of being the first university in

Canada, if not in the Empire, to send a complete hospital unit to the front. Early in 1915, the organization of No. 3 Canadian General Hospital was well advanced, under the command of Lieutenant Colonel H. S. Birkett, M.D. Originally planned with a capacity of 520 beds, it was doubled in size at the request of the War Office. February of that year found Laval completing a scheme for a French Canadian medical group, similar to that of McGill. Here too, the authorities suggested changes, which resulted in the formation of a 1040 bed Base Hospital unit, led by Lieutenant Colonel G. Beauchamp.

In non-combatant activities, the Canadian Patriotic Fund took the lead. As the name indicates, its scope was national, and its purpose the relief of the families of enlisted men. The local campaign to raise $1,000,000 was launched by the Duke of Connaught, when in his capacity of President of the Fund, he addressed the Canadian Club on September 11. It would seem as though the citizens, in their eagerness, had not waited for the official signal, since reports of contributions had already been published. But in the whirlwind canvass that then started—"Every man something every day"—the objective was soon exceeded. The civic administration gave $150,000, the wealthy J. K. L. Ross, $500,000. Innumerable small sums came in from those in more modest circumstances, and the proceeds of many amateur entertainments went far in swelling the total.

The wonder was, from year to year, where Montreal found the money to subscribe so generously and to so many causes. The French and Belgian relief organizations were repeatedly featured, as was the Red Cross, and Victory Loans came along to take up any slack. A more personal type of appeal made its appearance during 1915, in connection with Britain's need for ten thousand airplanes. Hong Kong had already given $22,000, Toronto in one week alone, $4000. Was Montreal to be the tailender with only $2000? Then there were the machine guns—in the short space of seven days, Canadians contributed three hundred of them, twenty-nine from Montreal. By voluntary subscriptions, the employees of Molson's Brewery collected $1000, a record equalled by the men at Northern Electric. No wonder that the newspapers carried constant reminders of the needs of civilian institutions such as the Fresh Air Fund and the Children's Hospital.

But as the initial shock of the first months passed, the city could, to some extent, take stock of its position. Although it was soon evident that the boys would not be out of the trenches by Christmas, a full realization of the duration of the war came only slowly. "Business as usual" seemed a suitable commercial slogan, the merchants meanwhile showing an assured and quiet confidence, both as to the present and the future. There were few pessimists, especially when the British war orders started to come in. Men were obviously needed, not only for the active army, but in the munitions plants—and women too.

Even during the anxious months of 1916 and 1917, Montreal, along with other Canadian cities, was both busy and prosperous. Not, it must be said, because of any excellence on the part of its government, for complaints of civic maladministration persisted throughout the war. But in other respects, the progress was encouraging, for although building operations and real estate transactions showed a considerable decline, bank clearings ran to new record highs. The shipping figures fell off a little, but the general trade picture was good. The stock exchange was active, and there were practically no strikes. The munitions plants, running night and day, paid high wages, and there was, in fact, a shortage of labor.

In 1913 the cost of living had been rated as high; in 1914 it rose "somewhat"; in 1916 and 1917 it "leaped upwards." The price of bread climbed steadily, to match the rising cost of flour, and within less than a year, a nine cent loaf soared to thirteen. Turkeys were so scarce at Thanksgiving 1916, that chickens and ducks took their place. Bananas, at 25¢ a dozen in the spring of 1917, were offered as the cheapest foodstuff on the market, and just as nourishing as meat. Potatoes were plentiful, but expensive at $4.00 a bag. According to one report, 130,000 bags had been allowed to rot or freeze on the railway sidings during February, because the dealers wanted higher profits.

But a series of interviews with the retail shopkeepers shed a fresh light on the vexed problem of prices. Under the heading "Are the women themselves to blame?" came the statement that the cost of delivering goods had doubled in three years. Labor, feed, and harness—all three were up, and delivery by automobile was practically prohibitive. Gasoline, once 15¢ to 16¢ a gallon, was 34¢ in 1917. Meanwhile, many of the customers who had moved out to Outremont, Westmount, and Notre Dame de Grace, still expected the same service as when they lived within a few blocks of the store. Some were careless in their telephone orders—two or three calls a day from the same lady. The demand for packaged goods, rather than in bulk, upped the costs by 50 percent. Women should resurrect the market basket habit and take the goods home themselves. "But they don't."

A remarkable spirit of harmony animated French and English Montreal in the early years of the war. From Laurier down through the ranks, came expressions of varying eloquence, but all marked by a determination to participate fully. No one questioned the righteousness of the Allied cause, or so it seemed—and then, almost overnight, the attitude changed. The hows and the whys of that story soon virtually monopolized the local scene.

What might be termed an advance warning, occurred at a recruiting rally in LaFontaine Park on July 23, 1915. Five thousand people attended, all standing quietly to begin with, while the band played *O Canada*. The disturbance arose when some hundreds of men and youths hurled a barrage of stones and rotten eggs at the speakers, making it quite impossible for them to be heard. One of the special guests, Major Emile Ranger, was greatly distressed; having just returned from the front, he found such a reception unbelievable. But as the crowd tore down the patriotic posters and shouted their hatred of conscription, it was clear that the city's united front had broken.

As it happened, this one riotous evening did not have any immediate repercussions, yet few people could deny that recruits were coming forward too slowly. Once the initial rush to the colors had passed, there were signs of reluctance—and this at a time when the bloody battles in Flanders created a never-ending need for reinforcements. Although to some extent, the entire country shared in the indifference, the accusing finger pointed chiefly at the Province of Quebec, and above all, at its largest city.

The year 1916 brought no improvement, either in the local
scene or the desperate need for men overseas. Canadians, having
proved their gallantry by defending the Ypres salient, were
called on to "join in the great glory of the offensive on the
Somme." "Kitchener's Own" needed recruits—"A battalion with
a name that in itself is a call to arms." Surrounded by these appeals, Sir Alexandre Lacoste, Chairman of the French Division of
the Montreal Recruiting Association, did excellent work among
men of his own language. That his task became one of growing
difficulty was due largely to Bourassa and his anti-war propa-
ganda in *Le Devoir*. Moreover, the Nationalists possessed another excellent talking point in Ontario's refusal to permit
the teaching of French in the separate schools. One way and
another, the friction grew.

Had anyone cherished hopes for a more harmonious co-
existence, they were abruptly disillusioned by the fracas of October 4, between the police and the students of Laval. With a
considerable show of righteousness, after the event, each named
the other as the aggressor. It all started when a large body of
youths, on their way to Mass at St. James Cathedral, threw
ashcans at the streetcars and pulled down the trolleys. On Phillips Square, they wrecked a recruiting stand and tore up the
posters. In the scrap with the police that ensued, four of their
number were arrested on the charge of damaging public property.

The next day, a hundred or more of the young fighters turned
up in the Recorder's Court, singing and shouting gleefully in
support of their accused comrades. Meanwhile, seven hundred
of the students signed a statement to the effect that their actions
had been directed against the police, and only after provocation.
They were not opposed to recruiting, and then, to prove their
sincerity, when the 5th Pioneers marched past Laval, the lads
lined the streets for blocks, and applauded loudly.

Probably the serious character of the conflict had never been
more apparent than during the spring of 1917. Along with the
very real fear of a German breakthrough in the west, went the
more nebulous uncertainties of the eastern front. To those who
watched the Russian Revolution of February, followed by the

abdication of the Czar, the crack-up of a supposedly strong ally seemed the end of everything. To offset this *débâcle*, the entry of the United States into the war held great promise for the Allies—although less for the present than for the future.

Decidedly in tune with the gravity of the times was the return of Sir Robert Borden from a special Imperial War Conference in London. As Prime Minister of Canada, he had listened with some shock to the reports of the manpower crisis of the Allies, and the urgent need for reinforcements from his own country. The slow pace of the voluntary enlistments could not be denied. It was with such thoughts crowding his mind that he rose in the Commons, on May 18, to announce his government's intention of taking steps toward compulsion. The Military Service Bill received its third reading on July 24. With the royal assent on August 29, it became law, permitting the formation on October 13 of the first draft made according to its regulations.

The enactment of this measure had not been easy. Laurier, as leader of the Opposition, sought an amendment, providing for a referendum before further consideration. The French Canadian members generally took a strong stand against conscription, as did the French press. Party loyalties faltered, and especially so when negotiations got under way for the formation of a Coalition government. Laurier, having refused any share in the new Cabinet, the plans proceeded with almost no Quebec representation. With the overwhelming victory of Borden and his Unionists in the federal election of December 17, the isolation of French Canada seemed complete.

Montreal, in the meantime, had experienced a summer of great turbulence. There had been rumors of conscription for months before the actual event, and the creation of the National Service Board in October 1916 had been interpreted as a step toward the hated end. Its registration cards, sent out in an attempt to secure a census of manpower, were greeted with hostility and suspicion. Archbishop Bruchesi, announcing his personal decision to provide the required information, appealed to his priests, and to the citizens generally, to perform this act of patriotism.

Yet since Borden, at the outset, had promised that the cards would not be used to enforce conscription, his later sponsorship of the Military Service Act seemed to imply a breach of faith. Rightly or wrongly, the new law came as grist to the mill of Bourassa, persistent as always in his advocacy of Canada's withdrawal from Imperial wars and Empire government. Not surprisingly, some of his followers embarked on a more violent course of action.

There was, for example, the big rally at the Monument Nationale on May 7. Its purpose was to secure recruits for the 258th French Canadian Battalion, commanded by Lieutenant Colonel P. E. Blondin. So serious did the interruptions of the "hoodlums" become, that when a panel of distinguished speakers was literally silenced, Senator Beaubien in his anger, was moved to deliver a severe tongue-thrashing to the "gentlemen of Laval." In almost any week of that stormy season, the scene could have been duplicated. Parades of protest were as common as the orators who denounced Borden as "the tool of Downing Street," and conscription as organized murder. Minor riots usually ended in broken windows at the least, and often bloody noses into the bargain.

August was the worst month of all. Perhaps Archbishop Bruchesi had a premonition of what lay ahead, when on the eighth, he celebrated the twentieth anniversary of his consecration. In a sermon at St. James Cathedral, he recalled the concord of other days, notably at the time of the Eucharistic Congress. "Bonne entente was a Christian sentiment and it has gone." The Mayor issued an appeal to the citizens, on the grounds that anarchy in the province would only hurt the anti-conscription case, and play into the hands of its political enemies. Moreover, he warned that the city authorities would suppress with the utmost vigor that the law allowed, any attempts at disorder.

But when the royal assent of August 29 gave legal status to the Military Service Act, Montreal staged what was described as the first real clash between the police and the anti-conscriptionists. The disorder originated with some five hundred young men who attacked the *Gazette* building, smashing six plate-glass windows in a wild melée of bricks and stones. A similar assault was planned against the *Star*, but the leaders, after much pleading, managed to halt their unruly followers. Their numbers in the interval, had increased gathering up such debris as drunks and derelicts. At the Champ de Mars, the speechmaking began, each orator outdoing his neighbors in wild denunciation. A self-styled anarchist called for armed resistance. Two patrol wagons of police, who in the early stages "jogged along like sightseeing tourists," swung into action shortly before midnight. During the hour that followed, they broke up the crowd, by now a thousand strong, into little parties, and gradually got them dispersed.

The backlash was considerable. In Ottawa, the Minister of Justice stated that the meetings in Montreal were not only offenses against the Military Service Act, but seditious utterances in violation of the Criminal Code. Noting that the responsibility rested with the local or provincial authorities, he added, "they are being supplemented." As to the city itself, Deputy Chief Grandchamps stated there were to be no more parades, and "a few more demonstrations by the police will convince the rioters." Over and above such necessary threats, the moderate tones of the French Canadian leaders of church and state eventually exercised a calming influence. Early in 1918 the government showed a more conciliatory attitude toward Quebec, and during that summer Montreal co-operated willingly in the registration of all men and women over the age of sixteen. Enlistments actually increased. Thus it was a generally improved local atmosphere that hailed the news of the Allied breakthrough at Amiens. At long last, the scent of victory filled the air.

The Armistice fever gripped the city on November 7, that famous day when apparently authentic reports proved to be nothing but rumors. The later official denials had no effect whatsoever on the celebrants, bent chiefly on making a noise. From noon onward, when the news spread like wildfire, no one thought it worthwhile to return to work. What they did for the balance of the day was summed up by a reporter the next day who noted tersely that the city was a little sore in the head that morning of November 8.

Quite apart from what might happen in Europe, November 11 had already been designated a public holiday, as a feature of the Victory Loan appeal. For this reason, when the authentic news of the Armistice came in over the wires, the town had a

ready-made parade on hand. But in every respect, the later celebrations were quieter than on the seventh. Many of the citizens
gathered about the Arch in Phillips Square, given by the retail
merchants of St. Catherine Street to assist the Loan campaign,
and everyone remarked that Montreal could boast of the first
real Victory Arch in all Canada.

Chapter 37
1918–1928

The Roaring Twenties. The wets and the drys. Women and the franchise. Stephen Leacock. McGill. Université de Montréal. Loyola. Sir George Williams University. The Seaway. Bridges. Automobiles. Radio. Brother André.

WHEN, WITHIN a few months of the Armistice, the troops started to return from overseas, they found themselves at once plunged into the difficulties inherent in the transition from war to peace. The adjustment came suddenly, for whereas early in 1918 there had been a national shortage of 100,000 men, by the end of the year, unemployment was rife. Moreover, in many cities, strikes —real or threatened—heralded the break-up of the tacit labor truce which had kept the munitions plants working full blast.

In justice to those who showed their discontent, it must be admitted that living costs had continued to rise. Too few people enjoyed the much vaunted prosperity of the twenties. An average income of $1900 for a family of five meant that many Canadians lived a hand-to-mouth existence. The Department of Labor, in October 1918, reported that the weekly budget for staple foods in sixty cities, averaged $13.54, as against $11.81 in 1917 and $7.92 in 1914. Essentials such as gas, boots, and street-car tickets shared in the upward trend, and the newspapers were full of references to the exorbitant rents and profiteering landlords. Eventually, of course, as the new construction eased the housing shortage, the normal law of supply and demand took over. By 1922, also, food prices had leveled off somewhat from the peaks of 1919 and 1920, although nothing ever returned to the modest prewar values.

So much has been written elsewhere of this particular decade, that a coldblooded appraisal of its merits or demerits is not easy, in terms of a single city. Much of the material comes from American sources, and does not altogether jibe with conditions in Canada. The Roaring Twenties, the aspirin age—the era which featured the bootlegger, the speakeasy, bathtub gin and home-brew—all of this was based upon prohibition, and did not nec-essarily cross the border. This is not to deny that Canadian life changed. It did, and the local mores along with the rest of the country. Yet the atmosphere remained less hectic, the pulse steadier.

Nevertheless, in at least one respect, the postwar period wit-nessed a decided growth in American influence. Montreal, in particular, showed a keen appreciation of the tourists who came north in "unprecedented crowds." Or as a New York newspaper put it, "that Montreal is benefitting enormously through prohibi-tion in the States, is the outstanding fact observed by any visitor to the Canadian city."

Liquor control in Canada being vested in the provinces, nine separate legislative measures at this date dealt with the contro-versial "wet-dry" issue. A sense that the soldiers should be pro-tected from the evils of strong drink, had led to a series of re-strictive Orders-in-Council during 1918—temporary expedients that in peacetime might be made permanent or extended in scope. Quebec, moving more slowly than its neighbors, had so far only accepted prohibition in a modified form that permitted the sale of beer and wine. As to the future, this depended upon the results of a public referendum to be held on April 10, 1919.

In the short but vigorous campaign that preceded the voting, Montreal, because of its supposedly "wet" sympathies, became the main target of both parties. Many prominent citizens supported the Committee of Moderation, under the leadership of Joseph Quintal, president of La Chambre de Commerce; others, equally outstanding, preferred the Anti-Alcoholic League, headed by Mr. Justice Archambault. And in due course, the referendum came along, the bad weather leading a reporter to describe it as a wet day in a "wet" city, which the drys hoped to make "dry." The latter, of course, being dubious of Montreal and Quebec, pinned their hopes to the country districts. Thus their shock was great when the whole province voted so overwhelmingly in favor of beer and wine that even the moderates expressed surprise. Montreal, having produced the strongest majority of all, passed a quiet day, and at night its streets were normal.

But however sweet their victory, for many of the citizens it was insufficient. Within a year, the license officials were said to be facing a hard task, since as the law stood, anyone might import spirits from abroad. When the abuses grew worse, rather than better, the drys in the Province blamed Montreal for the failure of the legislation. With 75 percent of its people reputedly opposed to prohibition, enforcement became impossible. The result was a new Bill, brought before the Quebec House in February 1926. By its terms, a Liquor Commission was set up, with headquarters in Montreal, and endowed with almost absolute power in the handling of all alcoholic liquors. Within a twelvemonth, its members reported moderation in the city, and this is how it came about that Montreal was involved in a tremendous liquor traffic with the United States. Described widely as a convention mecca, in 1928 the city attracted a million and a half visitors.

Many of the changes that characterized the 1920s were not confined to the male sex. As was the case in other cities, the women of Montreal claimed a share in the new freedoms. Some whose participation in the war effort had led to employment in offices, shops, and factories never returned to the wholly domestic life. Whether necessary for economic reasons or not, they enjoyed the sense of independence that accompanied their work. Whereas earlier only a few exceptional students had gone to the university, higher education became more common, and not only in the cloistered halls of the Royal Victoria College. The girls penetrated into faculties at McGill, once purely masculine preserves, and attended mixed classes in Arts and Science. Meanwhile, the skirts grew steadily shorter, rising in not much more than a decade from the ankle to the knee. Bobbed hair rendered passé the wide-brimmed millinery of old with its elaborate trimming. The hatless generation had not yet arrived, but the cloches were small and comfortable on windy days. And in 1920 Birks advertised ladies' cigarette cases from Paris!

Politically, the women had less cause to be happy. Although sharing in the benefits of the wider federal franchise, they found themselves up against a stone wall of apathy and antagonism in provincial affairs. For many years, the Local Council of Women was the chief, if not the only agitator, and in 1909 its members gave official endorsement to the principle of equal rights. The war needs naturally overshadowed the cause, yet between 1913 and 1919, the Montreal Suffrage Association kept the movement alive locally, doing a tremendous amount of educational and publicity work. Dr. Grace Ritchie England, Professor Carrie Derick, Mrs. John Scott—these were the leaders whose petitions and resolutions led to interviews with the leaders of government. In 1922 the Provincial Franchise Commission seemed to offer some hope of gaining wider support, led by Mme. Gerin-Lajoie for the French section and Mrs. Walter Lyman for the English. Yet when in February they headed a delegation of four hundred Montreal women to a meeting with the Prime Minister of the Province of Quebec, Louis Taschereau, they met with a chilling reception. So long as he held office, he vowed, the women would never get the vote. But regardless of rebuffs and ridicule, the annual pilgrimages to Quebec continued, under various auspices, until in 1928, Mme. Thérèse Casgrain emerged into prominence. As the leader of what shortly became known as the League for Women's Rights, she symbolized the feminist movement in the province.

The young women were, of course, not alone in their growing desire to attend McGill. To the normal enrollment of boys straight out of high school were added the youthful veterans whose studies had been interrupted by war service. The 1919–20 session saw the registration climb to 2915. The buildings on the campus were badly overcrowded, and often in rundown condition; new construction was needed, and modern equipment. It was fortunate that at such a crucial point in its history, the university had in Sir Arthur Currie a principal whose service was to be of a memorable character. The same qualities which had lent distinction to his career as commanding general of the

Canadian Corps, now made him a leader in civilian life. Sir Arthur's record of untiring devotion to McGill, in time, assumed legendary proportions, just as his own commanding presence could never be overlooked as he passed through the campus.

The decade was a particularly happy one for another member of the McGill "family," since Stephen Leacock and Sir Arthur became firm friends. In the English-speaking world, Leacock had already gained fame as a humorist. From the first modest publication of *Literary Lapses* in 1910, he forged ahead, gaining new readers with every subsequent volume: *Nonsense Novels, Sunshine Sketches, Winsome Winnie,* and the rest. The university knew him officially as the William Dow Professor of Political Economy, and his specialized interests showed in his authorship of *The Elements of Political Science* and a number of works dealing with Canadian history. Yet it is in a more personal manner that countless former students still recall "Stevie"—the substance of his lectures long forgotten, but not the chuckling enjoyment of his own jokes, nor the twinkle in his eyes; the heavy lock of hair and the tattered remnants of a gown over his shoulder; the tie, which especially with a dinner jacket, never seemed to sit quite squarely.

The postwar years were equally eventful for Laval, Montreal's French Canadian and Roman Catholic University. With the announcement in May 1919 of its attainment of independent status, a long-cherished ambition came to fruition. For several years, the staff locally had tried to bring about a complete separation from the parent institution in Quebec, and it was on this errand that Archbishop Bruchesi journeyed to Rome. The Université de Montréal, as it was in future to be called, received its incorporation on February 14, 1920. The student enrollment in 1919–20 stood at 5495.

Unhappily, in the interval, disaster had struck at the university. A fire, which broke out on Saturday night, November 22, 1919, gutted the main building on St. Denis Street. The firemen fought the blaze for ten hours, watched by enormous crowds who turned out to see the excitement. Daylight on Sunday brought the sight of roofless stone walls and emptiness everywhere; all the equipment had been destroyed, including the costly apparatus of the medical laboratories. But as Monsignor Chartier, the rector, pointed out: "The building may be gone, but the university remains. The building can and will be replaced as soon as possible. In the meantime, the courses will go on." Several faculties and departments were homeless: Arts, Medicine, Law, Pharmacy, Veterinary Science. McGill, itself overcrowded, offered all possible assistance. This, the rector declined, being able to arrange for temporary classes in such places as the Sulpician Library and the Commercial High School.

In this tragically drastic fashion, the Université de Montréal found itself faced with challenging opportunities for future expansion. A move to a fresh site in a less congested area was soon being discussed, for its old location, spread out over a large section of the East End, had always been inconvenient. An appeal for funds realized $4,000,000 for the new institution. The government of Quebec gave $1,000,000 and a like amount to McGill; the Seminary of St. Sulpice $1,000,000; the Canadian Pacific $50,000; the government of Ontario $20,000. Other smaller gifts from English Canadians reciprocated the conciliatory attitude displayed by Premier Taschereau toward the universities, irrespective of language or religion.

There were other signs of interest in higher education. In 1916, Loyola College moved to the unfinished buildings of the new campus on Sherbrooke Street West, forced out of its inconvenient quarters on Drummond Street by want of space. Although the war and a shortage of funds delayed their completion as planned, improvised classrooms and temporary makeshifts enabled the authorities to accommodate the increased registration. A campaign for funds in 1919 provided sufficient assistance to finish the Stadium in 1924, and the Administration Center in 1927.

Sir George Williams University—so named for the founder of the Y.M.C.A. in England—made its first appearance in Montreal during the spring of 1926. The college, as it then was, grew out of an evening high school, inaugurated by the Y.M.C.A. in 1920, later more formally organized, and extended to include the first two years of college work. The classes, subsequently opened to girls as well as boys, were expanded to accommodate both day

23. Montreal from the mountain, 1963.

24. The harbor at dusk, 1963.

25. Maisonneuve monument, Place d'Armes, 1964.

26. Notre Dame Church, 1964.

27. Montreal, grain elevator no. 4, 1964.

and evening groups. By 1930, a student enrollment of 1206 was reported.

The citizens, as usual, greeted the decennial census returns with dissatisfaction. Whereas in the official statistics for 1921, the population of Montreal proper appeared as 618,000, Lovell's Directory placed it at 773,904, or with the inclusion of the suburbs, at 839,704. According to the same perhaps partial source, by 1928 it had risen to 1,032,385, or 1,176,461 for the wider area. In that year, the Municipal Board of Health reported that French Canadians made up 62 percent of the total, English Canadians 22.8 percent, Jews 7 percent, and other nationalities 7.9 percent. Although nudged continually by Toronto's growth, the country as a whole accepted Montreal as the largest city.

If a brochure, issued in 1921 by the Montreal Light, Heat and Power Co., can be taken as typical of the prevailing opinions, the city had no intention of resting on its past laurels. Tempting phrases outlined the advantages awaiting American manufacturers who opened branch plants in Canada. As for Montreal, the author described it as "a good city to live in, to work in, and to play in, and many large employers of labor are becoming appreciative of this fact more and more."

Just as in the past, however, maritime affairs attracted the greatest attention. Not content with such general statements as "one of the largest seaports in the world," most publications proceeded to give chapter and verse as to the exact nature of the local superiority. There was, for instance, that memorable day, August 19, 1920, when there had been forty-six ocean liners docked in the port—surely a record, since their aggregate value was estimated at $230,000,000. As for the grain handled from the opening of navigation up to July 1, the 25,000,000 bushels represented an increase of 100 percent over the same period in 1914.

But this claim was only the opening gun in the barrage, which all through the '20s hailed Montreal as the greatest grain port in the world. Off-seasons there undoubtedly were—for reasons beyond local control—but the efficiency of the harbor installations made the town a pivot in international commerce. Thanks to the vigilance of the Harbor Police, the waterfront was one of the most orderly and spick-and-span places to be found anywhere. As a striking contrast to conditions a generation ago, pilfering and lawlessness were totally unknown.

Just to add to the general excitement, the decade witnessed the start of serious discussions about improved transportation facilities in the St. Lawrence. Montreal's anguished cries can be imagined at the proposal to develop the resources of the river by joint action of Canada and the United States. If carried through, Toronto might be in a position to compete successfully for the ocean traffic which now halted at Montreal. Thus, when in the course of a series of public hearings, the International Joint Commission met in the city, on October 8 and 9, 1920, the opponents of the scheme held the floor. Joseph Quintal, on behalf of La Chambre de Commerce, probably expressed the sentiments of many when he showed not only a preference for an all-Canadian route, but a great fear of costs.

Montreal was not alone in its antagonism to the proposals for a deep waterway. Ports such as New York and Buffalo held similar views—in other words, the east generally feared the loss of its shipping trade to the west. Year after year, the newspaper comments continued to appear, in the several cities most concerned. The local press featured the earlier questioning as to costs and the imprudence of joint jurisdictions. The *Gazette,* in 1924, claimed "Montreal takes neither a narrow or selfish view of the subject. No apprehension has been felt that ocean ships will use the canals." But two seasons later, the Joint Board of Engineers stated firmly that the deep channel from Montreal to Lake Ontario was feasible, and in 1927, the two governments opened official negotiations.

A fire, which in August 1920 damaged the vehicular roadway of Victoria Bridge, brought home to Montreal a realization of the inadequacy of its one and only link with the South Shore. During the several days required for repairs, the citizens found themselves in an unhappy state of isolation that might have been really serious had not a heavy downpour prevented the spread of the blaze. A minor catastrophe, it was, but bad enough to touch off a public campaign for a second bridge.

From this date, the story becomes one of petitions, resolutions, and public gatherings, all calling for a bridge, or as an occasional variant, a tunnel. April 1922 saw the most imposing delegation in years—six hundred men from the city and district—leave by special train for Ottawa and an interview with Prime Minister William Lyon Mackenzie King and members of his Cabinet. The burden of their appeal, as always, told of the million people on the Island, whose sole means of communication with the South Shore showed little improvement over 1859.

Such representations brought results, if somewhat slowly. Prohibitive costs prevented any immediate follow through of the preliminary surveys which started in 1922. Thus it was not until January 1925 that work commenced on the Delorimier Street location, a joint responsibility of the provincial government, the City of Montreal and the Harbor Commission.

This particular project focused attention on one of the myriad problems faced by Montreal, in the flowering of the automobile age after the war. The provincial registration of motor vehicles jumped from 254 in 1907, to 170,000 in 1930, of which the majority belonged to the metropolis. The 350 miles of gravel and macadam roads in 1918, became 3100 in 1922, and 5000 in 1928. Yet by modern standards, it seems likely that Lovell's, in 1926–27, took a somewhat rosy view of conditions. "Montreal, being the center of a system of good roads, is a parking space for the automobiles of North America."

In all the changes imposed by this astounding increase, the Royal Automobile Club, from its headquarters in Montreal, took the lead. Its activities dated back to the primitive days of 1907 when cars were merely pleasure vehicles, and their gentlemen drivers "chauffeurs"—brave souls who must be prepared to act as mechanics, able to get out and get under, to tinker with engines or change tires. Anyone who ventured out into the country, traveled on roads that were narrow, dusty and rutted, greasy after rain and hazardous by reason of the deep ditches on either side. Bad though these conditions were, they were no worse than in the city; the *Witness* described the Montreal streets as "almost as unspeakable as the traditional Turk."

But the winter of 1912 saw a few brave souls use their cars in the city, not only on fine days, but during storms and below zero temperatures. The first Quebec Automobile Tour Book and Map made its bow in 1917, along with new speed limits—4 miles at intersections, 16 in urban centers, and 25 elsewhere. Perhaps they were not too well observed, since the number of accidents at the junction of St. James and Notre Dame streets, near the old Court House, led to the title "Dead Men's Curve." When the two thoroughfares became "one-way," it was considered a great innovation.

The newspapers of the day reflect the serious nature of the city's traffic problems—partly because of indifference on the part of the municipal authorities, partly because of ignorance. The world of automobiles was still so new. Thus, when the one-way rule was instituted, there were at first no signs at such intersections as McGill Street to warn the motorist he could not go east along St. James. Parking was already a problem in the busy downtown area. Should the cars be placed out at an angle on St. James or along the curb? Should the limit be fifteen minutes or thirty? For those who needed more time, "their chauffeurs or coachmen can drive around the block and come back again." Working under what must have been difficult conditions, the traffic constables won praise for their efficiency, and their clear-cut snappy actions. Yet in the spring of 1922, the *Star* considered the roads to be the worst kept, most dangerous, and most uneven on the continent. "To drive over them in an automobile or hack is positive torture, to cross even the most frequented is to risk limb and possible life by tripping over deep ruts and gaping holes."

Montreal's extremes of climate created additional perils. The road to Ottawa was "fearful" in October 1919. A traveler who had just driven over it arrived bedraggled and worn, and thankful to be alive. A sudden rain had infected the roads with a devilishness beyond description, and his tires were gashed and cut until he resembled the man going down to Jericho, who fell among thieves. As a relief for such conditions, the Club's Emergency Road Service, instituted in 1924, came as a godsend. It gave year-round protection, including towage for those stuck in snowdrifts or stalled by dead batteries. A Club campaign to keep the roads open in winter beyond the city limits started in 1928. Support came from some of the merchants and hotels, who felt that surfaces, clear of snow, should attract tourists. And so, all through that season, the Club battled the drifts along the highway to Rouse's Point. Snow fences were erected, and the new automatic machines tried out—not with complete success, and only at a great cost, yet good enough to persuade the provincial government to undertake the responsibility.

If in many of these stop-and-go developments in transportation, the interest was largely local, the reverse held true of the railroads. Their chronic ailments provided the country with plenty to talk about—not only the man in the street but his representatives in Parliament, and of course, the newspapers. Agreement as to a solution did not come easily, yet when faced by the probable bankruptcy of several of the companies, the government, willy-nilly, was obliged to take action. At various dates and in differing conditions, from 1917 to 1923, the story became one of amalgamations and take-overs, of finding money from the public purse, of resolving managerial headaches, of transforming erstwhile rivals into loyal allies.

The new organization, as formally incorporated in 1923, bore the title of the Canadian National Railways. Government owned, it included the Grand Trunk, the Grand Trunk Pacific, the Canadian Northern and several smaller lines—just about every railroad in the country except the Canadian Pacific. The latter, as the child of private enterprise, managed to remain aloof, becoming in future a serious competitor of the new giant enterprise. Montreal, in both cases the operating headquarters, took a lively interest in the Canadian Pacific Railway and the Canadian National Railways, for on their prosperity hinged the size of local payrolls and volume of purchasing power. The two presidents made their homes in the city—Sir Edward W. Beatty of the C.P.R. and Sir Henry Thornton of the C.N.R.—men of great ability, but so unlike in personality that eventually, in themselves, they seemed to typify their respective companies.

As an example of the innovations that could result from their struggle for new business, a C.N.R. announcement of August 1922 serves to introduce another subject of topical interest. That year, above all others, witnessed the start of a general acceptance of that wonderful invention, the wireless or the radio. Thus it was exciting to hear that the new medium was to be installed on trains running between Montreal and Toronto. Passengers could while away the time listening through their earphones to pleasant broadcast music.

Needless to say, it was the war, to some extent, that had made such progress possible; thanks to Marconi's earlier invention, signaling instruments were widely used overseas. Yet few people appreciated the scientific importance of the medium, with the result that as late as 1921 and 1922, it was still not much more than a toy, popular rather than serious. Montreal's first broadcasting station dates from this period, for after some months of experiment, the Marconi Wireless Telegraph Company started regular programs in 1920. Under the call letters CFCF, it still remains in operation. By 1922 there were enough sets in use throughout the country to induce the federal government, through its Department of Marine and Fisheries, to issue receiving licenses at a cost of a dollar.

As the radio became newsworthy, its progress can be followed in the columns of the local press. It was a great do-it-yourself era—how to build a radio set that is not too costly; anyone with ordinary intelligence can do it. Complete sets were difficult to secure and costly, but the home mechanic could buy the necessary equipment for $20 or $25. Once assembled, he could receive messages and concerts from transmitting stations within the city, and from high-powered stations as much as twenty-five miles away. At night, or when the atmosphere was clear and cold, even greater distances could be covered.

A few scraps of program information made their appearance, as radio pages or columns became more common. A listing in June 1922 included only American stations—Schenectady, Newark, Chicago, Pittsburgh, Medford, Hillside. Those without receiving sets could attend free concerts arranged by Radio Ltd. of Phillips Square; "hear music and songs by your favorite artists." Two years later, although CKAC in Montreal was listed, along with Omaha, Philadelphia, Schenectady, and New York, the information was still of the briefest.

But in other respects, the familiar landmarks of the modern city were making their appearance. At night, the great cross on

Mount Royal shone out through the darkness, marking the spot where, so many years ago, Maisonneuve had raised his own symbol of thanksgiving. The modern steel structure, which stood over a hundred feet high, was built after the design prepared by the Reverend Father Pierre Dupaignes, P.S.S. Its cornerstone, laid on June 24, 1924, by Monsignor Deschamps, Vicar General of the Diocese, coincided with the ninetieth anniversary of the St. Jean Baptiste Society.

On the northern slopes of Mount Royal, in the same year, the laying of yet another cornerstone testified to the remarkable faith of a humble Montrealer. Brother André, at this date, was close to eighty years of age, frail of physique as always, and nearing the end of a long life of service as a lay brother in the Congregation of the Holy Cross. His unswerving devotion to St. Joseph had gained for him permission in 1904 to erect a tiny chapel on the mountainside. Its dimensions soon proved too small to accommodate the pilgrims, who in ever-growing numbers, came to offer up their prayers and thanksgivings. Many, according to the reports, went away healed of their diseases. A new stone crypt, planned as an approach to a great basilica, was started in 1915, and it was this latter structure that was under construction all through the 1920s.

No disrespect is intended by a mention of the new Forum, almost in the same breath as these religious shrines. Many a good Montrealer went to the hockey games that became a regular feature of winter Saturday nights, and then attended church on Sunday mornings. Since he still follows the same routine, the Stanley Cup fervor has done no damage to higher things.

When the National Hockey League was formed in 1917, Toronto, alone in Canada, possessed artificial ice. The excitement was tremendous when Senator Donat Raymond announced his plans for the Forum in Montreal. At a cost of $1,250,000, he provided accommodation for 9500 spectators, all of whom were to be given a clear view of the playing area. The first game was played in November 1924, on a "perfect sheet of ice," and surrounded by a "regular beehive of hockey enthusiasts." For *Les Canadiens*, above all, the new rink soon became familiar ground, the scene of their triumphs.

Chapter 38

1929–1938

The stock market. Boom times and the crash. Unemployment and depression. The R-100. Camillien Houde. Responsibility for relief. Public suffering. The Neurological Institute.

SINCE, AS EVERYONE now knows, the autumn of 1929 was to become famous historically, as the great watershed between prosperity and depression, it is easy to read meanings into the news of the day that intelligent contemporaries would have laughed off as alarmist. For this is an out-of-time wisdom, its portent undreamed of by Montrealers, who, in their spirit of blithe self-confidence, differed not one whit from their neighbors in cities all over the continent.

Nor was the boom altogether a thing of mushroom growth. There was much talk of unprecedented activity on the stock markets, with the Exchange in Montreal doing business to the tune of 100,000 shares a day. Its annual reports were encouraging—over 4,000,000 transactions in 1925, over 6,000,000 in 1926, over 9,000,000 in 1927, almost 19,000,000 in 1928. Dividend disbursements were heavy, and the banks optimistic.

Each day set fresh records. By the early autumn of 1929, prices had reached incredible highs. From a unit level of 100 in 1926, industrial stocks soared to 237.3 in December 1928, and to 315.8 in September 1929. When profit taking invaded the market on September 4, a news story told airily of a light reaction, which was bound to have a beneficial effect on the whole list. And so, in fact, it seemed, for after the triple holiday of the Labor Day weekend, Montreal coursed along merrily, showing every indication of a repetition of the earlier bull drive. When Wall Street registered a short but severe decline, the local Exchange held its head above the whirlpool of liquidation, and demonstrated its ability to stand on its own feet.

But early in the following month the markets began to slide. On October 5 the Montreal Exchange looked back on a week of nervousness and liquidation. Prices dipped to new lows in the wake of acute bearish tendencies, and an accumulation of selling orders. Although billions were being lost on Wall Street, there was, at first, no widespread foreign alarm over the American situation. By the 21st, however, the severity of the New York slump could no longer be gainsaid, and as always, Canada reacted promptly.

What happened next is as much general history as local. Thursday, October 24, has been described as the most disastrous day ever experienced. So tremendous was the break that it led to panic in every city. Montreal showed losses up to thirty points in some cases, with the tape at noon running half an hour behind. When stocks of all descriptions joined in the landslide, everything crumpled, the good along with the rest. But hope died slowly, for two days later the local Exchange was said to have "weathered" an exciting week. On Monday, October 28, the financial news monopolized the headlines. New York took another plunge down to lose more billions, while locally there was a sharp turn for the better.

This seesawing between hope and despair ended in November, when security values fell below anything previously registered. Anxious clients thronged the brokerage houses, where the staffs worked long hours, and amid great confusion, attempting to bring some order out of chaos. The unlucky 13th saw rock-bottom everywhere, the final frenzied moment that killed the dreams of all who had tried to get rich quickly.

If so far, at this time of stress, conditions in Montreal differed little from those elsewhere, the same pattern held true during the months that followed. Most people, out of a belief that the breakdown was only temporary, had no prevision of the severity of the depression. Salary cuts and layoffs were common in 1930, but prosperity was always just around the corner.

Montreal had in reality, little excuse for optimism. A 50 percent drop in building activity during the first six months of 1930 could not fail to increase the number of workless. The harbor report for 1929 was like a cold douche after the highly successful season in 1928—decreases in revenue, in the number of vessels trading into the port, in the net registered tonnage of shipping, and in the exports. Much of the trouble originated in the failure of the grain crop to move normally; at approximately 90,000,000 bushels, Montreal's traffic had not been as low since 1920.

But in the spring of 1930 large-scale unemployment had not yet developed into front-page news. That it existed is apparent from the miscellany of brief items, tucked away in odd corners, below long columns devoted to other topics. So far, there was no extensive co-ordination of relief programs, and many of the voluntary agencies functioned only during the winter. Unemployment insurance did not exist, although the Montreal Trades and Labor Council recommended that an interprovincial conference be called to discuss the matter.

That summer, the municipal authorities urged all those who contemplated projects of any sort involving labor, to get started at once. Since April the city had spent $5,000,000 on public works, but the plight of the jobless grew more serious every day. Reporting on its activities during June, L'Assistance Publique experienced a considerable increase in the demands made upon it. Meals to a total of 6312 had been provided, and 1024 lodgings. Applications for charity, numbering 720, represented an unprecedented high. The Federated Charities told of the ex-company sergeant, who at the age of fifty, could find no work. He came into the office, starving and desperate, the personification of the thousands who faced almost impossible odds in their struggle for survival.

Meanwhile, there was a brighter side to life, especially for those fortunate enough to own cars. The spring of 1930 saw the completion of the new bridge to the South Shore. In the first nine days after its opening, more than 50,000 automobiles paid tolls amounting to $20,000, for the privilege of using it. Christened officially on May 24, the "Harbor" Bridge later acquired the more historic title of "Jacques Cartier," in honor of the great explorer whose 400th anniversary was celebrated in 1934. It remains today, one of the most important links in the network of communications that radiate out from the Island.

The Harbor Bridge came as a godsend to those charged with the arrangements for the visit of the *R-100*, since people in record numbers flocked across to see the giant dirigible at St. Hubert Airport. Plans for this unusual event had been in the making for months, with plenty of news items to whet the fancy of a public, already dreaming of flights across the ocean. Even at the ungodly hour of half-past two in the morning of August 1, there was drama in the moment that first glimpsed an outline of something resembling a big cigar, among the clouds. Although some of the crowd had gone home, discouraged by poor weather and the long wait, enough of the curious remained on the ground, to give a rousing welcome to the weary crew.

Soon after sunrise, the traffic became really heavy. So did the noise, as the hundreds of cars, parked in the neighborhood all night, saluted the dirigible with much honking of horns. As for the pedestrians, they were everywhere. Professional cameramen and movie-makers mingled with the ubiquitous amateur photographers, and an ample supply of such delicacies as hot dogs insured that no one would turn away hungry. On one day alone, an estimate placed the number of spectators at 100,000; special trains and 30,000 private cars transported them to the scene. Afterward it was thought that the total attendance had passed the million mark.

A contemporary note described the 615-acre site at St. Hubert as one of the finest aerodromes in the world. Whatever the future of transatlantic air travel, whether by dirigible or plane, Montreal considered itself fully prepared for all contingencies. The most prominent feature at this date was the mast, over 200 feet high, its tower equipped with electrically driven mooring machinery and elevators for passengers and freight. The 38-foot diameter of the landing platform in the head, indicated how considerable was its size. Construction costs were paid by the British government, it being agreed that Montreal was to become one in a proposed chain of bases that would permit the establishment of airship routes within the Commonwealth.

The flying time of seventy-eight hours and fifty-two minutes

was the fastest to date for an airship—and this despite a storm
in transit which damaged the port stabilizer fin. After Canadian
Vickers had effected the necessary repairs, the *R-100* took off
again on a leisurely circular flight over Ottawa, Toronto, and
Niagara which enabled the special guests to savor the delights of
such a novel mode of travel. The return to Montreal was followed, on August 13, by the trip back to England, which although successful, was never repeated. On October 5, 1930, the
sister ship, the *R-101*, crashed tragically, and later the Graf
Zeppelin—twin disasters that marked the end of the dirigibles.
Within a few years, the mast at St. Hubert was dismantled.

Come what may, however, the depression grew steadily worse,
all through 1931, 1932, and 1933. Nothing, either in Canada or
abroad, seemed strong enough to resist the downward trend. The
stock market touched its lowest point in May 1932 when the
Montreal and Toronto Exchanges showed a paper loss exceeding
a billion, as compared to 1929. In 1930 the volume of business
transacted locally stood at less than half that of 1929; in 1931,
less than half that of 1930, or less than a quarter of the 1929
levels.

Translated into human terms, these statistics meant that there
was no work for an ever-greater number of men and women.
That many families shortly needed assistance, was, of course, the
tragic sequel to the enforced idleness of the breadwinners. No
matter how generous their spirit, charitable organizations and
private individuals could no longer cope with the mass of distressed humanity. As relief costs mounted, the trend toward government intervention grew stronger, and at three levels—federal,
provincial, municipal. By a coincidence, there were new men in
power at Ottawa, Quebec, and Montreal.

After the death of Sir Wilfrid Laurier in 1919, the Liberals
chose Mackenzie King as their leader. Victory in the federal
election of 1921 made him Prince Minister—a position which except for a few months, he retained until 1930, when the Conservatives, under Richard Bedford Bennett, swept into power.
But if ever there was a Pyrrhic victory, this deserved the title,
for when conditions grew worse, despite the best efforts of Ottawa, everyone naturally blamed the government. Hence the

volte face of the electorate in 1935, which brought back the Liberals and Mackenzie King.

At Quebec, the Liberals had been more successful in clinging to power, their leader, Louis Alexandre Taschereau, having been Premier ever since Sir Lomer Gouin's retirement in 1920. Nevertheless, theirs was not a particularly healthy situation, for the overlong period in office led to lassitude, to a tolerance of abuses, and a belief that no matter what happened, the party would always win the next election. They had, as it happened, considerable cause for anxiety, because of what was happening in the ranks of the opposition. The year 1929 saw a young Montrealer by the name of Camillien Houde, become the leader of the Conservatives in the Provincial House. A vigorous personality and outspoken in his criticism of government policies, he soon made himself thoroughly disliked by his firmly entrenched opponents. Their elation can be pictured when Houde suffered such a staggering defeat in 1931, that provincial political circles knew him no more. Yet when in 1933, a lawyer from Three Rivers took over the leadership, he posed a greater threat to the Liberals. Maurice Duplessis, having reorganized the Conservatives as L'Union Nationale, led his followers to victory in 1936.

Disastrous though Houde's downfall undoubtedly appeared at the time, his local supporters could take comfort from the fact that their candidate was now free to give his undivided attention to municipal politics. Already he held a head start, having entered the mayoralty race in 1928, to gain a most gratifying victory over Médéric Martin. Triumphant again in 1930, his authority gained form and substance, by reason of the loyalty pledges of eighteen out of thirty-five aldermen.

For the rest of his life, whether in office or out, Houde remained a power to be reckoned with. Twice he suffered defeat in the civic elections that preceded the Second World War, four times he was successful—a self-made man with little formal education. From a career in banking which saw him a branch manager at the age of twenty-six, he turned to politics, becoming a member of the Quebec House at thirty-three, and Mayor of Montreal five years later. It was in this position that Houde was at his best, for he loved the city and its people, and particularly those who were poor and in need of assistance. A contemporary description hailed him as the idol of the masses, and it was they who supported him during the years in which he grappled incessantly with the problems of unemployment and relief. His later title of "Mr. Montreal" indicates the depth of the mutual affection.

In recalling the unemployment situation, it is necessary to understand that in the strict constitutional sense, the relief or care of the destitute jobless rested with the municipalities and provinces. Such an arrangement, satisfactory enough in normal times, broke down completely under the abnormal pressures of the thirties. Local needs so far outstripped local revenues, that willingly or not, the federal authorities were obliged to give subsidies. And because the lack of work was at its worst in the big cities, their stories at this date relate mainly to their endless jockeying for assistance. Montreal was no exception to the rule.

This governmental division of responsibility led to a constant round of delegations, interviews, correspondence, and inevitably to rumors. Regulations were amended and methods revised; red tape, however necessary, caused delays; hints of misuse of public funds touched off mutual accusations and scandals. Each level of authority, could, if hard pressed, discover scapegoats in the other two. The Liberals blamed the Conservatives, who promptly returned the compliment, with the recriminations loudest at election times. Fresh from the victory of 1936, Maurice Duplessis and his Union Nationale followers, trumpeted their intention of clearing up all of Montreal's relief needs. Each mayor, in turn, scorned the inertia of his predecessors.

The truth is that the magnitude of the problems virtually transcended solution. Therein lay the reason for much of the vacillation in policy, and the very human irritation at the other fellow's mistakes. For while the country, as a whole, agonized through the '30s, Montreal faced a situation of exceptional gravity. As the chief entrepôt between the grain of the west and the manufactured goods of the east, it had flourished beyond the average, when the nation prospered. Its reaction was all the sharper with the breakdown of the international trading system, for the stoppage of the normal flow of exports and imports was the undoing of its dependent ancillary industries.

February 1933, which is generally considered to have been the depth of the depression, saw Montreal's relief bills pass the million-dollar mark. One of the aldermen felt Ottawa should pay more than the one-third share agreed upon, since the city was harboring thousands of wandering unemployed from all parts of the country.

The summer brought some improvement, permitting the municipally owned Vitre Street refuge to move to smaller quarters. From a daily peak of 15,000 meals and 1800 beds for indigent men, attendance dropped to 400. Much of the pressure had been seasonal in the past, its maximum of 130,000 weekly attendance in 1932–33 having been reached during the seven days ending March 13. In a typical month, 39.11 percent of those registered had been French Canadians, 11.12 percent English Canadians, 9.35 percent from Great Britain and 40.41 percent foreigners. Single men made up 75 percent of the total, and unskilled workers (many of them foreign laborers) 68 percent. Half of the unemployed had been in Canada twenty-five years; of the other half 15 percent had less than five years residence.

Meanwhile, the more prosperous citizens gave generously of their means. The great welfare federations of today were already in existence—the Protestant, the French Catholic, the English Catholic, the Jewish—and each in turn sponsored annual appeals for support. Duly segregated according to race and religion, they mirrored the multiracial nature of the city, yet in all cases, their walls could crumble before the universal distress. Their need for funds was urgent, since government payments touched only the fringes of the relief problem. Officialdom offered no cure for the debilitating effects of those years, upon the poor and the unemployed.

But gradually—almost imperceptibly—conditions improved. Personal distress was still widespread, but at last, the trend was upward. In May 1935, Montreal reported fewer homeless men as being in need of food and shelter. Building permits in the first five months of 1935 were more than double the same period in 1934. Hope was obviously in the air that spring, though the

debate persisted as to the merits of "made" work versus direct
relief, and the monthly costs to the city still exceeded the million-dollar mark. Late in August came the cheering news of a
splendid tourist season. American cars were much in evidence,
and the hotels enjoyed the best summer since 1930.

As if tired of the subject, the depression faded out of the
leading positions in the press. There was a growing optimism in
domestic affairs—a state of mind that found no echo in foreign
news. In the late 1930s there were glaring headlines about the
failure of the League of Nations, the Spanish Civil War, Mus-
solini, Hitler, the many attempts to secure disarmament. A party
of veterans, returning from a pilgrimage to Vimy Ridge, expressed
themselves as fearful of war in Europe. Other travelers scoffed
at the idea. Meanwhile, Montreal had interests within its own
community, and more than a few anxieties.

The formal opening of the Montreal Neurological Institute on
September 27, 1934, gave to the city a new and very special kind
of hospital, and climaxed several years of planning, in which Dr.
Wilder Penfield played a leading role. Appointed Professor of
Neurology and Neurosurgery at McGill in 1928, this American-
born surgeon now became, in addition, the director of the first
institution in the world devoted exclusively to the treatment of
nerve disease. To finance such an undertaking, had not been
easy. The Rockefeller Foundation, with its grant of $1,000,000,
first gave reality to the dream; governmental support and the
generosity of a few public-spirited citizens, assured its completion. Its task, as defined by Dr. Penfield, was an inspiring one:
"the achievement of a greater understanding of the ills to which
the nervous system is heir, to the end that we may come to the
bedside with healing in our hands."

The creation of this medical research center was perhaps Mc-
Gill's greatest achievement during this period. No institution of
higher learning could hope to escape the discouragement and
lack of progress induced by the need for money. For the local
university, the decade presented exceptional difficulties, from
the administrative point of view, because of the sudden death
of Sir Arthur Currie in 1933. An interregnum followed, when

brief terms of office made continuity impossible. The fresh start dated from 1939 when Dr. Cyril James became principal.

The Université de Montréal, at this same date, faced an uncertain future, as its plans, formulated in the prosperous '20s, proved impossible of immediate fulfillment. A contract for $3,849,747, signed in 1929, promised relief for the scattered and overcrowded accommodation downtown. There were to be new buildings, on land donated by the city, fronting along Maplewood Avenue on the northern slopes of Mount Royal. A brief announcement in 1930 hinted at difficulties, and thereafter, there were constant references to the "unfinished" program. Appeals to the provincial government brought no results beyond promises and special study committees. In 1936, Premier Taschereau stated publicly that the university would be re-established on a sound basis. The following year, the Provincial Secretary announced that Quebec intended to take the necessary measures as soon as possible. The needs, as set forth then, were undeniably great—$3,500,000 for construction costs, and $600,000 annually to cover the existing deficit and meet the interest charges.

For Sir George Williams University, the depression brought fresh opportunities for development. The keen competition for jobs created a respect for higher education among young men and women, who in prosperity might have ignored it. The university, housed modestly in the Y.M.C.A. on Drummond Street, grew continually, making use of all available space for its day and evening classes. Its Day Division, which started with first- and second-year courses, added in succeeding seasons, the higher levels, until in May 1936, a small science class was graduated. These recipients of the first degrees ever granted, were soon joined by graduates in Arts and Commerce. By 1937 a total of 1238 students was registered in the university and the schools.

The St. Lawrence Seaway was another casualty of this period, although less from economic conditions than by reason of opposition within the United States. After months of discussion, the two countries, in July 1932, agreed on the terms of a treaty, providing for joint development. A report, tabled in the Commons, promised that Montreal's position as the leading ocean port in Canada would not be adversely affected—a sentiment endorsed by the Harbor Commission in a 1932 statement that the completion of the waterway "will give Montreal an overwhelming advantage over all its competitors." But in March 1934, the United States Senate refused ratification of the compact.

When it came to purely Canadian projects, the progress was better. Montreal, as the headquarters of Trans Canada Airways, took a keen interest in the fortunes of this company, formed by Act of Parliament in 1937, for the purpose of establishing a regular schedule of transcontinental flights. The federally owned airport at St. Hubert, using a radio beam of a type ultimately to provide guidance over the entire crosscountry route, was considered to be completely equipped for all-weather flying. The early part of 1938 saw various experimental flights, and in October mail, on a trial basis, was carried between Montreal and Toronto. The first dawn-to-dusk trip from Montreal to Vancouver took place on July 30, when a group of government officials, headed by the Honorable C. D. Howe, accompanied the pilot, J. H. Tudhope.

As some of the public works projects came to an end in the late thirties, it was apparent that their imaginative planners had gone far beyond the usual sewer digging and street improvements, in their efforts to provide employment. One of their more notable successes was the transformation wrought on St. Helen's Island—so extensive as to cause surprise when in June 1938, it was thrown open to the public. An unkempt piece of land had become a landscape pleasing to the eye, and wonderful to relate, at no expense to the city. The work, which kept hundreds of the men occupied for two years, came under the direct supervision of the Quebec Department of Labor, the costs being shared by the federal and provincial governments. No contractors being needed, 90 percent of the grant went on salaries and wages. Small wonder that Frederick G. Todd, the architect in charge, described his task as unusually "soul satisfying."

Unfortunately, during these years of lessening relief needs, the scenes at the City Hall were the reverse of edifying. The aldermen bickered among themselves, and accusations of graft and dishonesty were common. Duplessis virtually washed his

hands of Montreal, in 1937. Any complaints, he felt, should go
to Ottawa. When the Directory that season, estimated the population to be 1,251,864, the *Star* considered the figure to be over-
optimistic, but wrote thoughtfully of the responsibilities of the
citizens. A city of that size should set an example in municipal
administration. Instead, there was precious little to be proud
of—a state of affairs for which civic apathy was partly to blame.
When would people wake up?

Chapter 39

1939–1945

*The war and recruiting. Houde and National Registration. His
arrest. The Ferry Command. Rationing. Unrest in the city. Conscription brings riots.*

JUST AS the Labor Day weekend in 1929 had signaled the end
of the boom times in Canada, so, ten years later, the same ordinarily carefree holiday saw the outbreak of war in Europe.
Inevitably, the occasion aroused memories of the 1914 conflict.

Mentally, both government and people were better prepared
than in the days of the Kaiser, for the menace of Hitler had
been long in the making. They greeted the momentous news
soberly, as befitted their new responsibilities, for according to
the Statute of Westminster in 1931, a British declaration of war
no longer automatically included the great Dominions of the
Commonwealth. Instead, upon each rested the final decision as
to participation.

For this reason, although Sunday, September 3, witnessed the
commencement of hostilities between Britain and Germany, Canada remained at peace, pending action by its own elected representatives. Ardent imperialists might chafe at the delay, but
the Liberal administration, headed by Mackenzie King, moved
with deliberation. It was only after a special session of Parliament
that war was declared on the tenth—eliciting from the Prime
Minister a promise that his government would never introduce
conscription, and from the Honorable Ernest Lapointe, Minister
of Justice, a warning that French Canadians would never accept
such a measure. Under these auspices, a satisfactorily united
nation endorsed the decisions of its leaders.

Protective measures at Montreal multiplied rapidly. Late in August, the non-permanent militia had been called out for sentry duty at such vital points as canals, docks, and power plants. Veterans now took over this monotonous, but highly essential task, while the civic authorities conferred with the police over ways and means to prevent sabotage. The newspapers ceased to publish information on ship movements. Visitors were barred from the harbor, and the liners, with windows blacked out, slipped downstream almost furtively, to brave the perils of the Atlantic.

The sinking of the *Athenia* reflected the stark reality of the new order. She was westward bound with a full complement of returning Canadians, when attacked by a German submarine. The news caused consternation. On the fifth, the names of a few local survivors appeared, and ten days later, a train drew into Bonaventure Station, bearing 186 of those fortunate enough to be rescued. Eighteen were Montrealers, most of them without money or baggage, their only possessions the hodgepodge of garments on their backs.

But in other respects, the signs of war came slowly. A stream of air force reinforcements passed over and through the city—planes and men presumed to be en route to the east coast. The armories returned to life early in September, when local units started to recruit to full strength. The mobilization was considered satisfactory.

Exactly two weeks after Canada's entry into the war, Duplessis called an election for October 25. His claim that a ballot cast for the Union Nationale would be a vote against conscription and participation, guaranteed a bitter campaign. Montreal found itself in the thick of the battle. Speeches—in person and on the radio—were numerous, and public meetings at which local aspirants won the support of national figures. One of the most notable occurred on October 20 when 15,000 persons jammed the Forum to salute the Liberal cause. From Ernest Lapointe, they heard an impassioned plea for national unity, and an unbroken front throughout Canada, and from Adélard Godbout, the provincial leader, a blunt statement as to the need for honesty, common sense, and decency in the administration at Quebec.

Perhaps the applause on this occasion, was a good omen, and certainly the fine weather on October 25 helped to insure a good turnout at the polls in the fifteen Montreal constituencies. In the province as a whole, the Liberals captured 69 out of 86 seats, and on the Island, made a clean sweep except for St. Mary's, where Houde ran as an Independent.

The city's sense of political rapprochement gained strength from the federal election of March 26, 1940, which accorded a smashing victory to Mackenzie King and the Liberals. All the Island ridings fell to the majority party, even those traditionally Conservative and contested by veteran members. Locally, the voting was light, and followed one of the quietest campaigns in years. A belated Easter snowstorm was blamed for keeping some of the electors at home.

That spring, Premier Godbout demonstrated his intention of keeping at least one election promise. After their long struggle to obtain the provincial franchise, the women, in 1938, had won the support of the out-of-office Liberals. Now happily in power, Godbout himself presented the controversial Bill to the Legislature in April 1940. Given a majority of 67 to 9 on the second reading, its passage was certain. On that historic day, the galleries were packed. Mme. Casgrain was there, and the other suffrage leaders, to receive well-merited congratulations. For while the extension of the ballot was province-wide, the protagonists had almost without exception belonged to Montreal.

But all these local interests were quickly forgotten, in the sudden crisis created overseas by the German conquests of April, May, and June. Norway, Denmark, Holland, Belgium, France— the list of enemy-occupied countries grew tragically longer. Winston Churchill became Prime Minister, and Dunkirk proved that miracles were still possible.

The tempo of recruiting in Montreal rose to such a pitch that the army required extra office space to cope with the flow of volunteers. Enlistments were higher than at any period since the first weeks of the war. On June 19, three hundred joined up in a single day, with over a thousand applications received since the first of the week. The Victoria Rifles, ordered to mobilize for active service, reported a rush to enroll. On the home front, there was talk of possible enemy air raids, sabotage, blackouts, and first-aid posts. The Civilian Protection Committee appealed for 20,000 volunteers from the province, to safeguard civilian life and property.

Parliament, in session at Ottawa, authorized fresh measures to strengthen and extend the country's war effort. The Prime Minister, in announcing plans for a National Registration, stressed the fact of its being simply an inventory of manpower, without any sinister implications of conscription. Quebec's reaction was reasonably favorable, and the Roman Catholic hierarchy, led by Cardinal Villeneuve, urged compliance with the law. It was in this atmosphere that Montreal proceeded to organize for the actual event, scheduled for August 19 to 21.

But before that date, Houde made an announcement which shattered the calm. On August 2, he stated that National Registration, unequivocally, was a measure of conscription. "I do not believe that I am held to conform to the said law." Nor did he, when asking the citizens to follow his example, shrink from the consequences—"knowing full well what I am doing presently, and to what I expose myself."

At this open defiance, Parliament was in an uproar, particularly when the press censors attempted to suppress Houde's statement. The Conservatives criticized the government strongly. But four days later the errant Chief Magistrate was arrested as he left the City Hall. It was close to midnight, and there were no onlookers and no resistance. From the R.C.M.P. headquarters, he was taken by car and under escort, to an internment camp in Ontario, not immediately identified.

A somewhat stunned city, in general, supported the government's action. A man of Houde's position and influence could hardly have been allowed to get away with such barefaced incitement to revolt against the law of the land. Le Devoir stated that the Mayor, having acted like a fool, deserved what he got. La Presse saw French Canadians, traditionally on the side of law and order, as shocked by his defiance. When the Registration Offices opened, everyone quietly complied with the controversial ruling.

Painful though these events undoubtedly were, their significance was less than might have been expected. Earlier that year, in a drastic move to avert civic bankruptcy, the Quebec Municipal Commission had assumed control of the metropolis. Temporarily at least, the Mayor became a figurehead and the aldermen political nonentities. Under these conditions, Adhémar Raynault took office in December, the winner of a confused and wordy election.

Yet all administrations, whether good or bad, still suffered from the crushing burden of relief costs. An estimated expenditure, between 1930 and 1942, of $52,310,789—whether for direct aid or public works—represented the monstrous legacy of the past. It was an impossible situation, brightened only by the expansion of the war industries after 1940. Thus, when a directive from Quebec, dated March 31, 1941, warned the municipalities that no further contributions to direct relief would be forthcoming, it coincided with a startling drop in Montreal's needs. A year later, only 297 families, representing a total of 1609 persons, still drew subsistence allowances.

Housing needs, in the spring of 1942, presented the city with a headache of major severity. The City Improvement League in April, feared a shortage of 39,000 dwellings for unskilled labor, and 12,000 for the skilled trades and white-collar group. The real crisis came with the approach of May 1, Montreal's traditional moving day. Even people with money failed to find living accommodation—a few flats or apartments, at rentals that started at $75 a month, and nothing cheaper.

Aroused by a flurry of headlines which emphasized the dramatic suddenness of the emergency, the civic authorities moved into action. The order went out to clear space in markets, public halls and police stations for use as temporary shelters. Confronted by estimates that placed the homeless families at anywhere from one to twelve thousand, the City Planning Department confirmed the critical need for low-cost dwellings. Of those presently occupied, 15 percent were graded as slums, and given the small amount of new construction, their number was bound to increase.

After this build-up, it comes as an anticlimax to discover that on May 4, no more than twenty-seven families had resorted to the municipal shelters. Yet theirs was only a fraction of the story, for welfare agencies rendered assistance on a generous scale, while families and friends doubled up, sharing limited quarters, despite good wages. The months that followed evoked many words on such subjects as slum clearance, reforms in the building by-laws, new and salubrious housing. There was no action.

The fact remains that all through these years far too many Montrealers struggled with little or no success to find decent accommodation for their families. To make matters worse, the war plants, with their offers of steady work and good wages, tempted outsiders into a move to the city. They found jobs more easily than houses. At the same time, income-tax collections soared to a point where they surpassed the returns from Toronto, rising from $72,586,271 in 1940–41 to $188,008,311 in 1941–42.

Needless to say, official censorship prevailed in all matters relating to the armed forces, as well as to sea or air movements overseas. For this reason, there was little general knowledge of what may be justly termed Montreal's unique contribution to the Allied cause. Only an occasional terse statement alluded to the ferrying of planes across the Atlantic, and sometimes vague rumors penetrated the "walls have ears" attitude.

A newspaper story, which appeared after V-E Day, told of the postal and aviation experts, who three months before the war, met in London to discuss an all-year-round transatlantic mail service. Much to Canada's regret, the plan was shelved as not feasible during the winter. But with hostilities, the crying need of the R.A.F. for aircraft, prompted a second look at what, so recently, had been deemed impossible.

The original plans of the British government called for the use of ships to transport planes—at best, a slow and laborious process, and one extremely vulnerable to enemy undersea attack. While the official mind still grappled with the problem, Sir Edward Beatty, president of the C.P.R., and Morris Wilson, president of the Royal Bank of Canada, called together a group of Canadians, who, on their own initiative and using private funds, proceeded to buy fifty American aircraft as an experiment. The first seven of these Hudson bombers, dispatched via Gander on Armistice Day, 1940, reached Britain safely after flights of less than ten hours. When the remaining forty-three, in turn, made equally felicitous landings, the Atlantic Plane Ferry Organization was born, a purely civilian enterprise which paved the way for the later military command. ATFERO, as it was generally called, operated on a shoestring. Two stenographers and two male clerks staffed the office in Windsor Station. Co-operation came from the Federal Department of Transport, and technical assistance from the British Overseas Airways. Canadians, Britishers, and Americans made up the roster of pilots, most of them civilians and highly experienced.

ATFERO developed so rapidly that government control soon followed. In May 1941 the Canadians surrendered the reins to the British Ministry of Aircraft Production, for what proved to be a brief tenure. A few weeks later, President Roosevelt agreed to allow American service personnel to deliver planes anywhere in North America, on condition that the handover be made to a military rather than a civilian authority. As a result, on July 20, ATFERO became the R.A.F. Ferry Command, and shortly after, Air Chief Marshal Sir Frederick Bowhill arrived in Montreal to take charge. At that date, about 170 civilian pilots were engaged in flying two- and four-motored bombers across, and so far, with one exception, all had arrived safely. The plane carrying Sir Frederick Banting crashed in Newfoundland.

After this transfer, the ferry service expanded in size, complexity and territory covered. Planes from Montreal flew regularly across the North Atlantic, developed the South Atlantic route, and pioneered a Pacific service to Australia. Losses continued to be small, when compared to the expected 10 percent. By the time the 12,000th crossing had been made, they amounted to less than one-half of one percent. Under Sir Frederick, the Ferry Command progressed from the dispatch of bombers to Great Britain, to a delivery of anything, anywhere—from high service personnel to Mosquitoes, and from tank parts to frogs. Eventually, every transocean plane leaving Montreal, carried an all-up load of 60,000 pounds. By early 1944 the Command had logged a distance equal to a return trip to the moon, delivered 12,000,000 letters overseas without losing one, as well as thousands of pounds of vital freight and hundreds of passengers.

Yet all this growth and diversification demanded a greater degree of organization at the center. In April 1943 the Ferry Command became No. 45 (Atlantic Transport) Group of R.A.F. Transport Command, with Sir Frederick as Air Officer Commander-in-Chief, and headquarters in Britain. During the four years up to October 1944, some 25,000 planes were flown across from North America, most of them in the last eighteen months. Often as many as a hundred left Montreal within a single day, some of the Liberators going nonstop, the 3700 miles to North Africa. A shuttle service for the return of the air crews became a necessity. Those flying to the Azores could be back in Montreal within twenty-one hours; to Rabat in French Morocco, in forty-five hours; the "big fellows," going to India, in six or seven days, after 17,000 miles in the air.

Not surprisingly, the airfield at St. Hubert proved unable to handle the tremendous traffic in bombers, a fact which precipitated a removal to Dorval, ten miles west of the city. There, in 1941, the Department of Transport bought 394 acres of land, and proceeded to convert an abandoned race track and some level farmland into the headquarters of the Ferry Command. Subsequent purchases raised the total to two thousand acres, with still greater acquisitions at a later date.

With this move accomplished, the R.C.A.F. could be left in undisputed possession of St. Hubert, for in September 1941 a civilian airport was opened at Dorval, located at "a respectful distance" from the hush-hush building. The first airliner to arrive had already made a perfect landing on August 31. Civilian air travel, in fact, was growing beyond all expectation, for when in April 1939 T.C.A. commenced daily passenger and mail service between Montreal, Toronto, and Vancouver, one plane each way was sufficient. Within a year, heavy bookings necessitated an increase to two flights.

This was the period also which saw all Canadians involved in the rationing of essential commodities. By setting up the Wartime Prices and Trade Board in September 1939 the federal government paved the way for the later developments. The following year, the Board's powers were extended to include housing, a measure which led to rental controls, and greater security for the tenants. In December 1940 a general ceiling on commodity prices became effective, and rationing started on January 24, 1942, with limitations on sugar consumption. At various dates, thereafter, butter, tea, coffee, preserves, and meat were added to the list.

Poor weather in Montreal accompanied the advent of gasoline rationing at seven o'clock in the morning of April 1, 1942. The measure had been preceded by some months of voluntary restrictions, aimed at a reduction in consumption. None had been completely successful, even when cash and carry was the rule for all purchases of gasoline, oil, or other lubricants. The large shops, by reducing their deliveries to one a day, gave considerable assistance. But although in the late summer of 1941 a fortnight's survey of the district showed a 15 percent saving, still there was too much pleasure driving. Motorists, asked to reduce their speed to forty miles an hour, did not always comply. Rationing could no longer be avoided. As the warfare on the Atlantic grew worse, by April 1945 the allowance was down to 120 gallons, except in the case of cars used for business.

The newspapers gave great prominence to the air-raid precautions. A blackout, which in November 1941 covered the whole province, although neither complete nor total, was twice as good as an earlier experiment. The third, in February 1942, while marred by a few infringements, was the best yet. By 1943 preparations had advanced sufficiently to stage another without advance warning. The date of April 28 was announced, but not the hour and every citizen was reminded that his compliance was compulsory.

But those in charge sometimes found the public apathy disappointing. Amid a growing fear of enemy planes, Montreal, in 1942, needed but could not find ten thousand Civilian Protection wardens to undergo training. Pleas of this nature, endlessly repeated, lent color to the words of a young flying officer, who, in 1943, could not get over the fact that Canada was enjoying such peace. Everywhere in Montreal, he saw lights burning, an amazing number of private cars on the roads, plenty of things in the shops, and not a scar on any building. Most wonderful of all, people walked along the streets without looking apprehensively skyward.

Although Canada's contribution in materials had reached mammoth proportions after two years of war, there was growing uneasiness over the rate of enlistment for overseas service. This remained completely voluntary, as opposed to the compulsory training for home defense laid down by the National Resources Mobilization Act of 1940. Once again, the old cry arose about the Province of Quebec and its poor record. There were questions in Parliament, and public criticisms of Ottawa's anticonscription policy. The result was a governmental announcement of a plebiscite to be held on April 27, 1942, for the purpose of securing a release from its past commitments and self-imposed restrictions. "Conscription if necessary, but not necessarily conscription," was the Prime Minister's summation of the situation.

Montreal's unrest now came into the open. Where earlier, there had been vague French Canadian fears of conscription, these crystallized into public meetings of protest, staged by various nationalist organizations. One such event, on March 23, saw nine arrests for participation in riots. Throughout the north and east districts, traffic was blocked, trolleys pulled down, and windows broken in shops, automobiles, and streetcars—all to the accompaniment of shouts of *"A bas la conscription."*

Early that month, Brooke Claxton, the Liberal member for St. Lawrence-St. George, sent out a letter urging all his constituents to vote "yes." His hope was to see a united Canada emerge from a victorious war. On the sixteenth, the *Star* queried all the federal members representing the Island, (including French Canadians). The returns showed them to be unanimous in asking for an affirmative ballot. The Prime Minister, during a stopover between trains, reinforced their appeal. It seemed as though party lines, as well as racial divisions, had been swept away.

What actually happened, proved how ill-founded were all such hopes, for while in the other eight provinces, the vote went four to one for "yes," it could muster no more than a 28 percent support in Quebec. Although nine of the Island ridings swung over to the ayes, they stood alone in the province. The split was almost entirely between the eastern and western districts of Montreal, or in other words between the French and the English.

As it happened, the plebiscite made no immediate difference to conditions of service within the armed forces. The government, having secured its mandate, took no action, nor, barring an emergency, was the Prime Minister likely to give his consent to any measure that might threaten national unity. Nevertheless, a deterioration set in along the familiar racial lines, the growing French Canadian anti-war sentiment being partially a reaction to English-Canadian charges that Quebec was not doing its bit. All of this was, of course, difficult to prove or disprove.

The year 1944 brought in its train a sense of expectancy, of great events pending. The pre-invasion air offensive of the spring, and the tremendous build-up of armaments—some guess as to their extent could be gauged from the fact that the local munitions plants put out an urgent call for more workers. So great was the need for shells, that two thousand extras, mostly women, could be used immediately. And perhaps because the first landings, that memorable June, were made in France, both French and English glowed with pride at their country's share in the war of liberation.

But when the first enthusiasm waned, the differences remained. Montreal had its riots—never as severe or as widespread as in 1917—but troublesome nonetheless. This was the era of the zoot suits, those eccentric and flashy habiliments whose manufacture was literally forbidden by law. The knee-length coats with their great padded shoulders, and the equally voluminous trousers—these required too much cloth, when wool was in short supply. The wearers made nuisances of themselves, clashing in the streets with anyone in uniform, particularly if he belonged to the navy.

There was a wild night early in June, when beer bottles and bricks filled the air in the dance hall district, near St. Catherine and St. Lawrence Main streets. This time, neither sailors nor zoot suiters made up any part of the mob of five hundred who battled with the police, but in anybody's hands revolvers and truncheons made dangerous weapons. After such *mêlées*, it is not surprising to read of the formation of combined police teams —four man provost squads, representing the army, the air force, the navy, and the city. These groups, assigned to duty at the weekends and on pay-nights, were highly successful in combating the rowdiness and the constant scuffles between civilians and servicemen.

More or less in the midst of all this, Camillien Houde returned to his own people. During the four years of his absence, his family and friends had repeatedly tried to secure his release. Successful at last, they gave him a tumultuous welcome one night in August, packing the Central Station so tightly that the hero of the hour was lifted off his feet by the surge of the crowd. When within a few months, he bested Adhémar Raynault in the mayoralty race, it was obvious that "Mr. Montreal" had lost none of his spellbinding qualities.

But the troubles of this eventful year were by no means at an end. Until late that summer, both government and people remained satisfied with the progress of the war. D day had come and gone, and the long-awaited breach made in Fortress Europe. The scent of victory was in the air, and all and sundry talked of plans for the postwar period. So far as Canada knew, the voluntary recruiting system continued to fill the needs.

If this was complacency, it was soon shattered, for J. L. Ralston, the Minister of National Defense, went to Europe at the end of September, only to find casualties much higher than anticipated. Faced by the grave need for reinforcements, he became convinced of the necessity for conscription—and specifically, for the sixty thousand men, the so-called "zombies," who then comprised the N.R.M.A. force on duty in Canada. Ralston returned home, to face a hostile Prime Minister, whose guiding principle, then as always, was the preservation of French-English unity. After a Cabinet meeting on November 1, he resigned—or was dismissed by his Chief—to be succeeded by General A. G. L. McNaughton. The latter, not yet a Member of Parliament, entered upon his duties firmly persuaded that the voluntary method could still be made to work. When the results of a few weeks proved the falsity of his hopes, Mackenzie King, in a sudden move, plumped for conscription, and the measure passed the Commons on December 7.

Already Montreal had experienced restiveness. After a meeting in St. James Market on November 29, some two hundred youths went through the streets in the financial district, breaking windows along the way. The police, short of men, were outnumbered twelve to one. But the discontent was more apparent than real. On the whole, French Canadians accepted their policy defeat with good grace, so that the country approached the end of hostilities with a minimum of bad feelings.

To read of the events of V-E Day is to realize how relatively little the war in the Pacific meant to the singing, cheering, weeping Montrealers who thrilled to the message of peace on May 7. The sequel was more significant. Within twenty-four hours, no fewer than fifty-four vessels in the harbor were handling grain, consigned to Britain and the starving countries of liberated Europe. The movement, the heaviest in years, kept the local crews working day and night until the end of the season.

Chapter 40

THE POSTWAR YEARS

The metropolitan area. The Seaway. Place Ville Marie and the skyscrapers. Jean Drapeau. Music. The theater. A multicultural city. The Jewish community. Ecumenical developments. Paul Emile, Cardinal Léger.

MONTREAL PROPER, according to the 1951 census, had a population of 1,021,520; the Island that bears the same name, 1,320,232; the metropolitan area, 1,358,075. Ten years later, and using identical territorial measurements, the totals stood at 1,191,062; 1,747,696; 2,109,509. With justice, the decade could be described as one of growth, although less within the city limits than scattered through the circumjacent fringes.

For almost three centuries Montreal was synonymous with a small section of the Island, a compact breed of town with recognizable boundaries. Notwithstanding the endless local pride in the new streets and fine buildings, its acreage was never impressive. Beyond the mountain, the farmlands and orchards lingered on, a pleasant rural setting for holiday outings. As for excursions across the river to the north or south shores, they were not to be undertaken lightly.

The expansion—so familiar a phenomenon of modern times everywhere—was as much residential as industrial. Its chief instrument was the automobile. Slow-paced at first, the move out from the central core has picked up speed since 1945, and the result is today's amorphous belt of semi-urban territory, whose focus is the city proper.

Opinions differ as to the precise extent of the metropolitan area, and the absence of any official legal formula adds to the diffi-

culty. What might be termed a convenient definition originates
with the federal government, and because Ottawa's "census
tract" provides statistics not otherwise available, merits a place
in these pages. In addition to Montreal, it includes the smaller
communities on the Island, as well as a selective grouping along
the South Shore, on Ile Jésus and in the Ile Perrot-Deux Mon-
tagnes district.

Until recently, these cities and towns had no common administrative program, and the shape of things to come remains prob-
lematical. Within their boundaries, there are acres and people
enough for several municipalities, and whatever the final solution,
there is no thought of a single megalopolis. The shadow of an
often acrimonious past hangs over the present. For many years,
Montreal's official policy toward its neighbors swung between
the extremes of complete indifference and outright annexation;
the suburbs, meanwhile, asked only to be left alone, and confirmed in the right to run their own affairs. This they have generally done with efficiency, although a few have succumbed to
overambition and the resultant debts. Their variety is remarkable.
One unit has a population close to 80,000, several fall below the
one-thousand mark. Some date back to the nineteenth century
and take pride in their record, a handful are no older than the
latest housing development. Civic poverty exists, not far geographically from concentrations of wealth, and the governmental
expertise is uneven.

Yet there are signs of a growing spirit of entente—of regional
planning—not only among the suburbs themselves, but in their
attitude to Montreal. Inconclusive as yet, they justify hopes that
the big stick of compulsion will give way to voluntary agreements, based upon "common sense, open discussion, and reasonable negotiation." Of the many issues at stake, none are more
pressing than mass transportation, and an acceptance of responsibility for facilities which ultimately benefit the whole area, may
well broaden out into a comprehensive scheme for administrative
co-ordination.

The full implications of this growth were, of course, undreamed
of immediately after the war. With Camillien Houde once more
installed as Mayor, his sojourn in the internment camps of Peta-

wawa and Fredericton, to all outward appearance, might never have happened. As the official greeter in an era when conventions developed into big business, His Worship proved to be a consummate actor whose speeches, in English as in French, delighted his audiences.

But the transition to a peacetime economy had its more serious aspects. Thousands of workers, jobless with the sudden closure of the war plants, entered the labor market at a time when the servicemen started to return from overseas. University and college registrations soared, as the youthful veterans took full advantage of the federal aid available for their further education. The housewives, meanwhile, still grappled with rationing; well into 1947 such items as meat and sugar remained on the restricted list. Rising costs figured prominently in the news, with the gradual removal of price ceilings on food.

Of all the decontrols, none proved more troublesome than rents. Frozen for many years at prewar levels, a 10 percent increase in the case of new tenants seemed an inflationary move, and as such, aroused great resentment. For housing was still a problem, and its solution the main concern of interested community organizations—as indeed it has remained, in terms of low-cost dwellings and slum clearance.

Traffic was the other pressing topic of the hour, and everyone rushed to voice his complaints. A civic report, dated 1948, put its finger on some of the reasons for the strangulation, for although since 1929 the number of private cars and publicly owned trams had risen to match the 30 percent increase in population, the 850 miles of streets had only become 852.

Yet if delays and inaction threatened to hinder civic progress, they had at least, the saving grace of being local. The St. Lawrence Seaway, on the other hand, was not only national but international, and thus subject to political pressure on both sides of the border. In the case of the United States, this meant stiff opposition in both Senate and Congress. By their continued refusal to endorse the Treaty, signed by the two powers in 1941, the American legislators successfully blocked further co-operation.

Toward the close of 1951, and impelled by his country's industrial expansion, Prime Minister Louis St. Laurent outlined to the Commons his proposals for independent action. These included the creation of a Seaway Authority whose terms of reference would be based upon an all-Canadian location for the giant enterprise. Armed with this official statement, Ottawa resumed the endless round of negotiations with Washington, and the result, at long last, was a new agreement, duly ratified by both parties.

The Seaway as thus envisaged, set out to make it possible for oceangoing vessels, by a series of locks and canals, to penetrate into the heart of the continent. Its entrance lay at St. Lambert, opposite Montreal, a deliberate choice which enabled the Authority to by-pass the overcrowded main waterfront, with its costly tangle of power lines and industrial installations. Even at that, there were difficulties, largely because of the need to maintain uninterrupted communication with the South Shore, both during and after the period of construction.

For this reason, the engineers faced an exceptional challenge at the start of their plans to raise the level of the bridges, so as to give a clearance of 120 feet. The modus operandi in the case of the Jacques Cartier span involved the use of jacks, each with a lifting capacity of 500 tons. The six-inch hoists, repeated hundreds of times along the sections affected, called for precision of a high order, yet except for one single period of four hours in the early morning of October 20, 1957, vehicular traffic moved as usual. Victoria Bridge called for different treatment, since with the new height, the gradient would have been too steep for the trains. As a hundred or so crossed each day, and no stoppage to the service could be contemplated, an alternative span from midstream to the South Shore became necessary. A lock with a vertical lift at each end, permitted the rail and canal transport to flow simultaneously.

Yet the civic interest in the international waterway went far beyond the structural feats in the vicinity of the Island. Before, during, and after Montreal never ceased to speculate, and often to worry, as to what might happen to its port, and by inference to the local prosperity. The mere thought of ships from overseas docking at Toronto aroused shudders—so much so that as late as

1958 there were pessimistic reports on the impending change in traffic patterns. Benefits there might well be, but the city, it was feared, faced significant losses in the general cargo business.

But for good or for evil, the completion of the Seaway constituted a turning point in the history of the harbor. Already impressive as to size and quality of its docking facilities, a construction program got under way at the close of 1958, whose cost eventually was to run far above the estimated $65,000,000. With what success can be judged from a news item, featured in 1963 under the caption, *Harbor Emerges Winner In Big Seaway Gamble.* The story could be continued indefinitely, for 1962 was rated the second best year in the history of the port; in September 1964 it appeared to be headed for the biggest season ever. To these records, must be added the headway in winter navigation, as each spring has found the port open at a date earlier than in the past. The April 7 achievement of 1949 became February 28 in 1963 and January 4 in 1964. A seventy-day closure in 1962–63, dwindled to a mere seven in 1963–64. That the ships are not ordinary craft, scarcely needs emphasis, for strong construction and special reinforcements are needed to buck the ice in the river.

As the chosen headquarters of two new aeronautical bodies, Montreal found itself, shortly after the war, labeled as the Geneva of North America. The International Civil Air Organization, being an agency of the United Nations, had for its object the regulation of world flying and the formulation of a code—an ally and yet quite different from the co-operative group known as the International Air Transport Association. As the representatives of the airlines of the world, its staff worked on technical problems, whose solution would insure safe, regular, and cheap flying.

However much the distinction lent to the local scene by ICAO and IATA, the introduction of economy fares brought air travel within reach of modest pocketbooks. After 1945 civilian flights out of Montreal multiplied rapidly, their destinations as often overseas as domestic. By no stretch of the imagination could their landing place at Dorval be considered impressive. Its unsightly buildings, many of temporary wooden construction, were legacies of the war; all were inadequate. Each season, the public complained, until at last Ottawa announced its airport expansion program would commence in 1956. Formally opened in December 1960, the $30,000,000 project was an occasion for great rejoicing.

Given Montreal's long-term pre-eminence in the communications world, it seems fitting that a railroad should have sponsored what is generally considered to be the city's greatest redevelopment scheme. For although Place Ville Marie by no means stands alone, it has by its sheer drama succeeded in capturing the public interest, while as befits a pioneer, it has given birth to a flattering family of imitators.

To several generations of Montrealers, the hole on Dorchester Street served as a by-word, the epitome of utter futility. The property of the Canadian National, it formed a part of the holdings acquired by Mackenzie and Mann in 1911–12, its improvement halted by two wars and a depression. Not that anyone, during the booming twenties, doubted the need for a modern terminal. But arguments as to location and the merits of "union" facilities, raged until 1938, when the federal government, as part of its unemployment assistance, proceeded to construct the Central Station.

It was chiefly Sir Henry Thornton, who, during his term as president, foresaw the potentialities of the site as a whole. Piecemeal development and haphazard construction, he ruled out in favor of a master plan, which would include the use of the aerial rights over the depressed trackage surrounding the station. This policy, kept alive by his successors, began to bear fruit when the Queen Elizabeth Hotel opened for business in April 1958.

Place Ville Marie, as a unit, was an ambitious undertaking, exceeding any similar plan then in Canada, and reputedly more costly than Rockefeller Center. Designed by I. M. Pei and Associates, this city within a city lies on the north side of Dorchester Boulevard, immediately opposite the hotel and the station. Its heart is the forty-two story cruciform office building that was ready for occupancy in 1962; four smaller structures and a shopping center, one floor below the street level, complete the complex.

A few blocks to the west rises the Bank of Commerce tower,

and to the east, the Canadian Industries block. These, with Place Ville Marie, are the giants of the Boulevard—a modern thoroughfare, which in three years has seen ten major buildings erected within a half mile distance of each other. And each season, as the skyscraper fever continues to spread, so, too, does the human density mount, in what has been described as the busiest corridor in Canada.

The present exodus from the downtown districts is, of course, merely a repetition of what Montreal has been doing for several centuries. The first move away from the discomforts of the riverfront was followed by others, each one climbing a little higher up the slopes of Mount Royal. Yet this latest wave, in the opinion of the experts, does not foreshadow a desertion of the long-famous St. James Street. Instead, they predict the emergence of two "cores," the commercial and the industrial, and regard Place Victoria as a link between the different levels. This—the newest of the high rise projects—has already gained impressive neighbors, suggesting to an ebullient reporter in 1964 that "Quebec Building Booms In Billions."

If because of these additions to the skyline, it seems as though the city of the mid-1960s bears little resemblance to the guise of the early '50s, the same holds true of its administration. The transformation in municipal politics could hardly have been greater. Camillien Houde retired from public office in 1954, and with his disappearance, a whole era ended. New men assumed the direction of affairs, with policies geared to the future.

So thoroughly has Jean Drapeau identified himself with the city over which he presides that his fellow citizens sometimes find it hard to remember the days in which he was an unknown quantity. He first caught the public eye in the early '50s when, as a crusading young lawyer, he played a leading role in the prosecution of certain members of the Police Department, charged with tolerating commercialized vice on a wholesale scale. Their conviction attained, he contested the mayoral election of 1954, emerging the victor, yet with a reform program that could not be fully implemented. Without sufficient backing in the Council, it was perhaps not surprising that he should be defeated in 1957. Three years later, he returned to power, and this time, with majority support. The Drapeau regime had started in earnest.

This does not mean that the Mayor's actions have won universal approval. There have been disagreements as to policies and methods, and undoubtedly, these will continue. Yet few deny his leadership, the general tone of civic integrity he has induced, his positive approach to local problems, his imaginative program of improvements. For Montreal, in the mayoral opinion, is a pacesetter, and "in the midst of its most stimulating period in history. Already one of North America's greatest cities, it is moving ahead bodily with enthusiasm and dynamism to become a leading world metropolis."

For at least half a century, Montreal has talked of the need for a subway, and no one now living would venture to guess how many plans are gathering dust in the archives. A protest of the '50s, typical of many, waxed eloquent over "the procrastination, inaction and comprehensive inability of the Executive Committee to find or even recommend a solution to the city's mass transportation problem." Yet nowhere, perhaps, would underground facilities be more welcome, for the average annual snowfall of 110 inches is equalled only by Leningrad among the great population centers of the world. It need only be added that construction, virtually on a round-the-clock basis, has been the rule since 1962. With a completion target of 1966, the subway is Montreal's top priority project.

But however great the current emphasis on modernity, no survey would be complete without a salute to those who treasure the past. Whether the authorities, left to themselves, would have taken the necessary steps to preserve the old quarter of the city is questionable. Certainly, the initiative came from a small group of public-spirited citizens who expressed their anxiety as to the fate of the dwindling number of historic houses, miraculous survivors of an almost forgotten yesterday. Their crusade—slow moving at first—has gained such momentum that Le Vieux Quartier has become fashionable.

Once roused, however, the civic administration has been quick to accept the challenge of the old city—showing by the appointment of the Jacques Viger Commission, its recognition of the difficulties. Primarily an advisory group, the Commission members have pressed ahead with their desire to put teeth in the ruling that would prevent the wanton destruction of the tumbledown dwellings. With the co-operation of the provincial government into the bargain, the onrush of garages and parking lots seems to have been arrested. Private enterprise has done much, and the city carries on with the restoration of the waterfront district.

The Arts and Intellectual Life

To such an extent has the political protest of French Canada claimed the limelight in recent years, that few people outside the province have any conception of the Quiet Revolution now under way, in other aspects of its corporate existence. Certain it is that no sketch of present-day Montreal would be complete without some mention of its vigorous intellectual and artistic life, decidedly unusual in flavor, and so emphatically the hallmark of the '60s.

Yet this does not imply that Montreal's culture is unilingual. On the contrary, within the civic boundaries, the French and the English traditions have developed in a manner that is unique so far as Canada is concerned. Both have been enriched by an admixture of European strains. Translated into statistics this means that, in 1961, a total of 1,353,480 persons claimed French ethnic origins; 41 percent were bilingual. Those of English stock numbered 377,625, of whom 26.94 percent reported a knowledge of both languages. A third group of "other" racial descent, totaled 378,404; 31.68 percent were similarly gifted.

Although some part of this quickening of the spirit dates back to 1940 and the fall of France, its acceleration is essentially modern. Mayor Drapeau senses in this, a challenge. "No city can truly call itself a metropolis unless its cultural development keeps pace with—indeed surpasses—its growth in stone and steel, its population and industry. Without the arts, the city has no soul; it is but a giant which eats and sleeps and works, achieving little with the mind."

Nor are these merely idle words, to judge by the Greater

Montreal Arts Council. Born in 1955, it was the brain child of
the then untested First Magistrate, just as its continuance reflects
his abiding interest. That its program resembles those of similar
organizations elsewhere, need cause no surprise, and the difficulties are well-nigh universal. Rather is it the governmental
level which sets this particular group apart from the majority of
its fellows. Municipal taxation provides its revenues, and its
annual grants go to local community organizations.

It is perhaps not altogether accidental that the lion's share of
the Council funds should normally be awarded to music in its
several forms. For of all the performing arts, it makes the widest
appeal to a bilingual city. In winter as in summer, indoors and
out, there are concerts and recitals enough to satisfy the most
dedicated enthusiast, instrumental as well as vocal and their
sponsors as varied as their programs.

For the Montreal Symphony Orchestra, the completion in 1964
of La Grande Salle of Le Place des Arts represented a definite
turning point in an often difficult existence. Eye-catching architecture, excellent acoustics, and a seating capacity of 3000—these
form a glittering contrast to the more Spartan accommodation of
an earlier era. The first ensemble to bear this name presented its
opening concert in the autumn of 1930; four years later came Les
Société des Concerts Symphoniques; combined, the two evolved
into the modern Orchestra.

It is generally agreed that what has happened to the French
language theater during the past twenty-five years mirrors more
than anything else the new liveliness of Quebec's culture. Where,
before 1940, there was nothing, an average season now brings as
many as thirty-five presentations, and almost without exception,
they originate in Montreal. In the French theatrical world, the
city ranks next to Paris and Brussels, while in North America, its
dramatic productiveness is surpassed only by New York. An
evolving public taste has kept pace with the growth in numbers,
and the "boulevard" type of performance no longer has a monopoly. To a large extent, the drawing-room comedies have been
replaced by the great classical dramas, the plays of political protest, and a sometimes bewildering array of *avant-garde* productions.

This is the world which today cherishes the memory of Père Emile Legault of the Congregation de Sainte-Croix, who by his launching of Les Compagnons de Saint Laurent in 1938 became the great pioneer of the renaissance. His actors were amateurs but the high quality of their repertoire won for them a young and eager following. The company flourished, that is until its financial problems became insuperable, and then unhappily, as a unit, it ceased to exist.

Yet Père Legault and his players left behind a living tradition that has been perpetuated since 1951 by Le Théâtre du Nouveau Monde. Almost without exception, its founders received their training as members of Les Compagnons, and Jean Gascon, the original director, still remains at the helm. Molière in particular, as presented by Le Nouveau Monde, has brought him fame.

Undoubtedly the best-known individual in this quarter century of theater is Gratien Gélinas, who, whether as actor, dramatist, or director, has achieved a fame that is peculiarly his own. By virtue of long residence, he is a Montrealer, and it is there that by far the greater part of his work has been done—starting with the satiric Revues, wherein each season from 1938 to 1947, before packed houses for weeks on end, he played the title role of Fridolin.

Fridolin was the boy of the streets, and it was the story of his reactions to the world around him which year after year brought tears and laughter to the audiences. Essentially, in character, he resembled the hero of Gélinas' first serious play, *Ti-Coq*, which enjoyed a long run in 1948. In this guise, he was the little soldier, caught up in a war he could not understand. But unhappily, he did not export well; an English version met with little success outside the province, and lasted a mere three performances on Broadway.

Meanwhile, other companies and personalities crowd forward in Montreal, each for some specific reason seeming to justify individual mention. Le Rideau Vert claims to be the only permanent theater in Canada producing from September to June each season a play a month, every night in the week, with a Sunday matinee as well. Back of this lies a history of endless difficulties, heroically surmounted by the director and founder,

Mme. Yvette Brind'Amour. Le Théâtre Internationale de Montreal—La Poudière—is justly proud of being the only international theater in the country. Its playhouse is a converted powder magazine on St. Helen's Island, and there, before audiences of no more than 150, and without the stability of a regular company, Mme. Jeanine Beaubien offers an astonishing range of productions in French, English, Italian, Spanish, and German. Canada's two official tongues are much in evidence also, at the National Theatre School, which since its inception in 1960 has offered a three-year course in both languages to students from all parts of the country. Indeed, as the directors are careful to point out, the school is colingual, rather than bilingual, and there is no attempt to convert French actors into English, or vice versa.

To turn from these scenes of activity to a survey of the English language theater is to walk from light into near-darkness. In the second half of the twentieth century, and apart from intermittent campus productions, it is almost extinct—partly because of public apathy. Too many seasons in the past have seen some modest venture come and inevitably go, an imaginative project born, only to die.

In all fairness, however, it must be said that failing audiences and inadequate funds were only a part of the story. Other factors—unpredictable and beyond the control of managements—contributed to the lengthening mortality list. Take the Montreal Repertory Theatre as an example, its life span extending from 1930 to 1961, and in its heyday, rated one of the most successful little theater groups on the continent. Yet when and why the rot set in is not easily determined. Alone, it might have been overcome; complicated by housing needs and a disastrous fire, survival became impossible.

The Mountain Playhouse was another casualty, much regretted and through no fault of its own. Thanks to the imaginative direction and sheer hard work of Norma Springford, it thrived for more than a decade, and its theater, atop Mount Royal, was a pleasant oasis on warm summer evenings. But the little building was old and unsafe by modern standards. Officially condemned as a firetrap, the ukase went out in 1964 for its demolition.

To appreciate Montreal's standing in French language publishing it is necessary to recall the German occupation of Paris in 1940. Before that date no one took much interest in the production of works of a literary character or the promotion of French Canadian authors—that is, until the Nazi armies marched up the Champs-Elysées.

The abrupt termination of literary exports from France created a crisis to which French Canadian publishers reacted decisively. (Most of them, it might be added, belonged to Montreal.) By means of a special agreement with the federal government, they secured permission to make photo reproductions of any French book, the royalties therefrom to be held in trust by Ottawa for the duration of the war. The domestic market prospered, and as successive areas of the French Colonial Empire were liberated, so did the overseas markets expand. It was big business until the restoration of France in Europe and the shortage of dollars, ended the boom.

Yet stimulated by this short-lived flurry abroad, the local section survived—if not always in the most robust state of health. As of today, thanks to the forceful policies of the companies involved, Montreal retains its lead in French book publishing and sales on this continent. Trade circles rate it a "good" book city— not in any moral sense, but because of the ratio of purchases to population. Bookstores are numerous, at least by North American standards, and their stocks in French and in English as extensive as they are catholic in their variety.

That many of the books thus offered for sale should be local in origin, serves as an introduction to Montreal's authors. In both of the city's languages, they write fluently on almost any subject, drawing their inspiration from personal backgrounds as varied as the potential purchasers. To discuss them adequately, in terms of a paragraph or two is to attempt the impossible.

But the appeal—to the novelist—of the Montreal environment is something that cannot be overlooked. Increasingly, he seeks to understand, and to interpret to the outside world, a way of life that is neither "typical" nor "average," measured against the civic neighbors.

Among the representatives of the English tradition, no one has achieved greater fame than Hugh MacLennan, by birth a

Nova Scotian but by long residence, a Montrealer. Two of his most successful works feature the local scene—*Two Solitudes* whose title in itself has become a classic expression of the two peoples and *The Watch that Ends the Night* whose soaring sales reflect a widespread interest in the theme.

Prominent in the French language cadre, *Bonheur d'Occasion* gained for its author the Prix Femina of France in Europe. Gabrielle Roy has written many novels, some—indeed the majority—set in her native Province of Manitoba. Yet none are as moving as this portrayal of family life in a working class quarter of Montreal. From the troubles of such a group, Mlle. Roy has woven her narrative, strong but infinitely tender, and one, moreover, that carries with it a sense of personal identification—based, one assumes, upon the fact of her own experiences in the city.

Yet however promising the present—whether for literature or the creative arts in the French language—there remains an unspoken question as to the road ahead. Not to be answered by the generation now in control, its direction, its intellectual wealth or poverty, may well depend on what is now happening in the field of education. For although much still remains at the paper stage —proposals that are nothing short of revolutionary—enough has been accomplished to suggest that the future will not be a carbon copy of what is past and done with.

The Jewish Community

The displaced persons of the postwar years who chose Montreal as their destination overseas found themselves in a city already the home of many European immigrants of an earlier day. For the westward flow of people, originally all British, had started by the mid-nineteenth century, to assume a more varied character, as a succession of wars and pogroms drove the potential victims to seek a haven in the New World. Hopeful in most cases of entering the United States, a sizable minority spilled over into Canada. Those who remained permanently in Montreal often did so for reasons that were economic as much as anything; further travel was costly.

The amalgam resulting from these successive generations of "New Canadians" in all their ethnic variety has played a significant role in the creation of the international and cosmopolitan atmosphere, so beloved of the copywriters. Intangible to some extent, the innumerable boutiques and restaurants that line the streets, ambitious or modest as the case may be, all lend a subtly foreign nuance to the local air.

But this is, after all, a generality, and may be expressed in terms of cities elsewhere. More pertinent is the fact that the Montreal ethos, so different from that of its neighbors, inescapably affects the lives of all who live there, regardless of racial origin. In some cases, conditions may be more congenial than in the wholly English-speaking sections of the country—the Italians, for instance, whose Roman Catholic faith and Romance tongue together create a natural affinity with French Canadians. For others, however, by offering—perhaps compelling—a choice, the city presents challenges, unknown beyond the province.

At almost any time and under any circumstances, the language question can generate heated debates in Montreal, with the latest immigrants as much involved as the native born. Within the confines of what is supposedly a stronghold of bilingualism, the 1961 statistics prove the falsity of any such dream. For 462,260 persons spoke English only; 826,333 French only; 776,603 used both tongues; 44,313 knew neither French nor English.

Not surprisingly, the anglicized and anglicizing character of Greater Montreal has been the target of sharp criticism by thoughtful French Canadians. An ability to speak English, they point out, is virtually a *sine qua non* for promotion in local business circles. Add to this, the tremendous pressure exerted by English-speaking North America as a whole, and their apprehension becomes understandable. Small wonder that French Canadians, who comprise 64.2 percent of the population, contribute 71.4 percent of the bilinguals in the metropolitan area. Small wonder either, that the majority of the newcomers, for reasons of expediency, choose English as the language most likely to be useful in their future careers.

Against this sometimes troubled background and the unanswered questions that lie ahead, the Jewish community may profitably be studied in terms of Montreal. A composite of many races, it includes descendants of those who fled the atrocities of the Czar, no less than the survivors of the Nazi holocaust—yet all united by a faith that sets them apart from the Roman Catholic-Protestant traditions of their neighbors. With a population estimated at 105,000 to 110,000, they occupy the third place numerically in the city, being exceeded only by the French— and Anglo-Canadians themselves. As of today, they form not only the oldest but the largest such group in the country, and as such, play an important part in all that pertains to Canadian Jewry.

The origins of this community can be stated with rare precision, since Jews were barred from New France. Thus, when in 1759 and 1760 they first came to Canada, they did so under British auspices—either in the armies of General Amherst, or as merchants, who at the conclusion of the war, brought in food and other necessities from the American colonies to supplement the scanty local stocks. It was with the decision of some of these soldiers and civilians to remain permanently in Montreal, that the history of Canadian Jewry commenced.

A colony founded in this manner, must obviously be small in size, and by reason of its geographical isolation, close-knit in a setting that was otherwise entirely Christian. But aside from their distinctive religion, these men associated freely and on equal terms with their English and Protestant fellows. British by birth as they were, all had close ties with the familiar Anglo-Saxon world. They settled down in Montreal and prospered, although without any perceptible increase in numbers; after seventy years of residence, they totaled no more than fifty-two.

A new phase opened in 1840, with the arrival of immigrants from eastern and central Europe. Small-scale at first, the movement acquired floodlike proportions by 1880, to reach a peak in the pre-1914 era, and then to decline in the face of war and government restrictions. The British-oriented families were soon outnumbered by the later influx—Yiddish-speaking for the most part, mingled with Hebrew, Russian, or German. The totals rose sharply. In 1881, the Jewish population of Montreal stood at 814 and the national at 2443; in 1911 it had risen to 27,948 out of a national level of 74,564.

The names of many of the earliest Canadian Jews reflected Spanish and Portuguese origins, which predated their British allegiance, and went far in determining the precise form of their religious observances. When, in 1768, they organized Shearith Israel, the first congregation in what is now Canada, they did so in conformity with the Sephardic Rite, as then practiced in London and New York. By 1777, they had strengthened their position sufficiently to erect a synagogue on St. James Street, and from that date onward their story is one of progress. In 1960, what is now the Spanish and Portuguese Synagogue moved to the present site on Maplewood Avenue.

For such a small community, the provision of a permanent rabbi was often impossible, a thoroughly unsatisfactory situation which ended in 1847 with the appointment of the Reverend Abraham de Sola. Even then—at the age of twenty-one—this British-born scholar was recognized as a man of great learning, and in the years that lay ahead, he was to become a strong and invigorating force in Canadian Jewry. Appointed Professor of Hebrew and Oriental Languages at McGill, he brought to his lifelong tenure of this academic post, the same intellectual quality that was such a feature of his rabbinical office. An honorary L.L.D. from the university in 1858, provided further evidence of his standing in the city. Even more unusual was the tribute accorded to him in 1872 by President Grant. In any circumstances, an invitation to deliver the prayers at the opening of the United States Congress might be considered an honor. That it should be bestowed upon one who was not only a Jewish minister but a British subject, was a compliment deservedly considered as unique.

The Montreal which Dr. de Sola knew—he died in 1882—has been described as tolerant to the point of friendship and respect, in its attitude to the Jews. Yet this relationship had not always existed in political affairs. British subjects though they were, they lacked some of the rights and privileges that normally went with such a status, including election to Parliament. To secure these became the great objective of some of the public-spirited members of the community. Petition followed petition, in the first quarter of the nineteenth century, until in 1832, the Bill of Emancipation put an end to the disability.

By mid-century, the Jews of Montreal shared in all the civil and political rights enjoyed by their Christian associates. As early as 1837, two of their number, Moses Judah Hays and Benjamin Hart, had been appointed as magistrates for the district. With the more formal organization of municipal government, they could view with pride the election of Samuel Benjamin to the City Council in 1849. But within their own ranks, the immigration from Europe was bringing changes. So many of the newcomers needed assistance, that charity on an individual basis, soon proved inadequate. Relief schemes of a more formal nature, made their appearance, notably in 1863 under the title of the Young Men's Hebrew Benevolent Society. In 1890 this became the Baron de Hirsch Institute, in honor of the British philanthropist of that name, whose gift of $20,000 permitted a greatly widened program for the future.

The cleavage between the old and the new sections of the community was already apparent in purely religious matters. The incorporation in 1846, of a separate congregation of "English, German, and Polish Jews" brought the Ashkenazic ritual to Montreal for the first time. Shaar Hashomayim as it was later called, at the outset, occupied a building on St. Constant Street; several subsequent removals brought it in 1922, to Cote St. Antoine Road.

Shearith Israel and Shaar Hashomayim were alike, however, in the sense of being orthodox in their beliefs, as indeed the whole community was at that time. Nevertheless, 1882 saw the establishment of Temple Emanu-El, "a progressive congregation," that remained for over forty years the sole representative of Reform in the province. A modest birth led eventually to the present site at Sherbrooke Street and Elm Avenue.

At first, almost all the Jews lived in the central part of the city, a concentration that not only matched the compact character of old Montreal, but yielded them companionship. This was especially important for those of European origin, who derived comfort from the sights and sounds of the familiar traditions and language. The neighborhood they favored, up to the outbreak of World War I, extended up the slope from Craig Street and was centered upon St. Lawrence Boulevard, stretching for about six blocks on either side of this traditional dividing line between the French and the English sectors. The move, which started about 1914, was mainly northward, still following the St. Lawrence axis, but before long, swinging off in a westerly direction, to the suburbs of Outremont, St. Laurent and the like. The community institutions followed suit, and by 1941, not a single synagogue or Jewish school remained in the area south of Sherbrooke Street.

That this exodus was in general, one which took families out of ancient tenements and a depressed section of the city, is probably self-evident. Time had done much for the immigrants, whose necessitous condition on arrival had posed the problem of relief. Younger generations grew up, educated in local schools and universities, and wholly Canadian in their outlook. The original peddlers and small shopkeepers gained at least a modest success; factory workers acquired new skills and promotion followed. Jewish enterprise has led to Montreal's pre-eminence in such industries as the dyeing and finishing of furs, and the manufacture of clothing.

A Jewish journalist in Toronto, who sees his kinsfolk as being placed in a position between the hammer of the French majority and the English minority, concludes that they have been pushed by historical developments into becoming an appendix to the Protestant and English group—perhaps with some truth, for when the immigrants from Europe started to learn the language of their new country, they chose English, almost without exception. Yet a significant variation in this hitherto normal practice, appears in the disclosure that more than five thousand French-speaking Jews from the Mediterranean area have settled in Montreal during the past few years. Without friends or relatives in Canada, their reception and after-care is currently the most pressing problem facing the Jewish Immigrant Aid Service.

The "Year of the Golden Jubilee" in 1964, saw several of the community organizations pass the half-century mark—notably

the Jewish People's Schools, numbered among the twenty private
institutions, which under several names, are attended by some
25 percent of the Jewish children in the city. As originally conceived, their purpose was to provide the elements of Jewish
education in the late afternoon, after attendance at the regular
public schools. It was not until 1928 that the change to full-
time work began, in all the subjects followed in the regular cur-
riculum, as well as in Hebrew and Yiddish—resulting in what has
been described as one of the few quadrilingual teaching centers
in North America.

That these "private" schools have so greatly altered during the
twentieth century, while increasing in number, suggests a certain discontent with the public system. By one of the anomalies
of the dual educational system, inherited from the past, Jewish
children in the eyes of the law, count as Protestants. Continued
into the present day, the ruling has been the cause of endless
friction, notably over the question of Jewish representation on
the Protestant school boards. Happily, and after much negotiation, the trouble is in the course of being resolved.

The Canadian Jewish Congress, re-activated in 1933 as a result
of Hitler's rise to power, has its headquarters in Montreal. Occupying a central position in Canadian Jewry, it enjoys also a
local relationship that is close, almost personal. Thus its leadership in the hassle over education is only one facet of a program that is comprehensive to the point of becoming international—embracing not only the problems that beset its people in
Canada, but also those of Jews overseas. It is a singleness of
purpose, especially dear to the heart of Montreal, whose work
on behalf of modern Israel, has assumed almost legendary
proportions.

L'Envoi

A special service in Notre Dame Church, one wintry evening
early in 1965, illustrates as well as any single event can do, the
changing ecclesiastical climate of the city. Organized by the
Roman Catholic Ecumenical Center of the Archdiocese, the con-

gregation, fifteen hundred strong and representing a diversity of faiths, mingled their voices in French and English prayers for unity among Christians. A priest hailed it as an historic event, and a Protestant minister considered it a miracle.

That any such gathering would have been considered impossible fifteen or twenty years earlier, points directly to the leadership of Paul Emile Léger, the distinguished Sulpician who became Archbishop of Montreal in 1950. January 1953 saw him, at the age of forty-nine, created a Cardinal, the first Montrealer ever to be so honored. Predictably, the public rejoiced, and not only in Roman Catholic circles, for, as an editorial in the *Star* observed, the influence and good works of His Eminence went far beyond those of his own faith.

This anonymous journalist was, perhaps, more perceptive than he knew, since few Montrealers at that date, could have understood fully the nature of their Cardinal. True, as he came increasingly into the public ken, there were stories of his kindliness and charity toward his fellow men. But these, at first, could be shrugged off by skeptical Protestants as no concern of theirs. And because of these perfectly natural feelings, it has taken time and patience for *ce prestigieux Cardinal* to gain general acceptance from his own city.

Yet the name of Cardinal Léger is today virtually synonymous with liberal churchmanship, not only in Montreal but far beyond the boundaries of Canada. Active participation in the sessions of the Vatican Council, as convened by John XXIII and more recently by Paul VI, has lent an international flavor to his life, and non-Christians as well as Christians have been quick to appreciate the breadth of his vision.

This does not mean that church unity will come to pass in Montreal, either today or tomorrow. Roman Catholics are no more unanimous in their support of the ecumenical dialogue than are their "separated brethren." There are local obstacles, many of them legacies of the city's often stormy past, and the "solitudes" have been as much ecclesiastical as racial. But some, at least, of the ancient intolerance has vanished, and largely because of the example set by the man who ranks as a Prince of the Church.

BIBLIOGRAPHY

Bibliographical Note

The raw materials for many books lie buried in Montreal's eventful past, and this means that the conscientious bibliographer faces difficulties in respect to the citation of his sources. Since my own work is designedly popular, I have avoided what might seem an unduly meticulous report of my research, and offer instead a carefully chosen record of the materials which I have found to be useful.

My list falls naturally into two parts—the one purely local, the other Canadian or North American. No one, it might be said, ever wrote descriptively of the colony as a whole, without a survey of its commercial metropolis. That I should present brief and seemingly ephemeral publications side by side with the more comprehensive and scholarly texts, reflects my belief that each, in its own fashion, provides an insight into the mores of our civic ancestors. For those readers who decide to delve deeper, I have included the moderns—my contemporaries, whom I have ordinarily bypassed, not wishing to tread too closely in their footsteps.

There remains only the need to outline my studies in other media. I have perused the city newspapers diligently, particularly the *Gazette* and the *Star*, finding in their columns much that is revealing of people and events long since passed into history. Periodical articles, in both French and English have been equally helpful, while an assortment of reports on municipal affairs, has shown how enduring are the problems of local government. Finally, and underlying everything else, I have been an inveterate user of reference tools, primarily to verify dates and facts, but often as a species of dividend, to discover fresh angles. There is, indeed, no end to the Montreal story.

Montreal

ADAMS, FRANK DAWSON, A History of Christ Church Cathedral. Montreal, 1941.

AMES, HERBERT, "The City Below the Hill"; a Sociological Study. Montreal, 1897.

THE ARTS IN MONTREAL; a Report of a Survey of Montreal's Artistic Resources; published by the Junior League. Montreal, 1956.

ATHERTON, WILLIAM HENRY, History of the Harbour Front of Montreal. Montreal, 1935.

——, Metropolitan Montreal, being v. 1 & 2 of The Storied Province of Quebec. Toronto, 1931.

——, Montreal, 1535–1914. 3 v. Montreal, 1914.

BANK OF MONTREAL, Centenary, 1817–1917. Montreal, 1917.

BEAVER CLUB, Minutes of Proceedings, 1807–1827. Unpublished manuscript.

BECKER, L. M., Jewish Education in Montreal. Montreal, 1951.

BECKET, HUGH W., The Montreal Snow Shoe Club . . . 1840 to the Present Time. Montreal, 1882.

BERTRAND, CAMILLE, Histoire de Montréal. Montréal, 1935.

BLANCHARD, RAOUL, L'ouest du Canada Français; v. 1, Montréal et sa Region. Montréal, 1953.

BORTHWICK, J. DOUGLAS, History of the Montreal Prison, 1784 to 1886. Montreal, 1886.

——, History of Montreal, Including the Streets. Montreal, 1897.

BOSWORTH, NEWTON, Hochelaga Depicta. Montreal, 1839.

BOXER, F. N., Hunter's Hand Book of the Victoria Bridge. Montreal, 1860.

BROWN, THOMAS STORROW, Montreal Fifty Years Ago. (in *New Dominion Monthly*, March 1870).

BRUCHESI, JEAN, De Ville-Marie à Montréal. Montréal, 1942.

BURTON, KATHERINE, Brother André of Mount Royal. Notre Dame, 1952.

CAMPBELL, REV. ROBERT, A History of the Scotch Presbyterian Church, St. Gabriel St. Montreal, 1887.

CHAMBERS, ERNEST, The Book of Montreal. Montreal, 1903.

CHARRON, YVES, P.S.S., Mother Bourgeois, 1620–1700; trans. by Sister Saint Godeliva. Montreal, 1950.

CLARKE, ADELE, Old Montreal; John Clarke, His Adventures, Friends and Family. Montreal, 1906.

COLLARD, EDGAR A., Oldest McGill. Toronto, 1946.

——, Montreal Yesterdays. Toronto, 1962.

——, A Tradition Lives, the Story of the *Gazette*. Montreal, 1955.

COOPER, JOHN IRWIN, The Blessed Communion. Montreal, 1960.

——, History of the Montreal Hunt. Montreal, 1953.

——, Montreal, the Story of Three Hundred Years. Montreal, 1942.

CROSS, HAROLD W., One Hundred Years of Service with Youth; the Montreal Y.M.C.A. Montreal, 1951.

DENISON, MERRILL, The Barley and the Stream; the Molson Story. Toronto, 1955.

DE VOLPI, CHARLES AND WINKWORTH, P.S., Montreal, a Pictorial Record, 1535–1885. 2 v. Montreal, 1963.

DOIGE, THOMAS, An Alphabetical List of Merchants, Traders and Householders Residing in Montreal. Montreal, 1819.

DOLLIER DE CASSON, A History of Montreal, 1640–1672; trans. by Ralph Flenley. Toronto, 1928.

DORWIN, J. H., Montreal in 1816; Reminiscences. (in Montreal *Star*, Feb. 5, 1881).

DUDEK, LOUIS, Montréal, Paris d'Amérique, Paris of America. Montreal, 1961.

THE EMANU-EL STORY, 1882–1960; published by Temple Emanu-El. Montreal, 1960.

FORAN, J. K., Jeanne Mance. Montreal, 1931.

FROBISHER, JOSEPH, Journal, 1806–1810. Unpublished manuscript.

GEOGRAPHIA MAP CO. LTD., Famous Guide to Montreal. New York, 1955.

GIBBON, JOHN MURRAY, Our Old Montreal. Toronto, 1947.

GOAD, CHARLES E., Atlas of the City of Montreal. 2 v. Montreal, 1881, 1890.

GRAHAM, FRANKLIN, Histrionic Montreal, Annals of the Montreal Stage. Montreal, 1902.

GRAND TRUNK RAILWAY, Montreal in 1856, a Sketch Prepared for the Opening of the Grand Trunk Railway in Canada. Montreal, 1856.

GRAY, CLAYTON, Conspiracy in Canada. Montreal, 1957.

——, The Montreal Story. Montreal, 1949.

HAM, GEORGE H., The Miracle Man of Montreal. Toronto, 1922.

HANDBOOK FOR THE CITY OF MONTREAL and Its Environs, Prepared for the Meeting of the American Association for the Advancement of Science. Montreal, 1882.

HEMSLEY, RICHARD, Looking Back. Montreal, 1930.

HENDRIE, LILIAN M., Early Days in Montreal and Rambles in the Neighborhood. Montreal, 1932.

HINSHELWOOD, N. M., Montreal and Vicinity. Montreal, 1903.

HISTORIC MONTREAL, Past and Present; a Portfolio of Pictures. Montreal, n.d.

HOTEL GUESTS' GUIDE FOR THE CITY OF MONTREAL. Montreal, 1874.

KITTSON, ARTHUR, The Saga of Sherbrooke Street, 1853–1949. Montmagny, 1949.

KNOTT, LEONARD, La Place. Montreal, 1962.

LACOSTE, ABBÉ NORBERT, Les Characteristiques Sociales de la Population du Grand Montréal. Montréal, 1958.

LANGFORD'S GUIDE TO THE CITY OF MONTREAL. Montreal, 1867, 1869.

LA ROQUE, HERTEL, Camillien Houde. Montreal, 1961.

LAVALEE, OMER S. A., The Montreal City Passenger Railway Co. Montreal, 1961.

LEACOCK, STEPHEN, Leacock's Montreal; ed. by John Culliton. Toronto, 1963.

LEGGE, CHARLES, A Glance at the Victoria Bridge and the Men Who Built It. Montreal, 1860.

LIGHTHALL, W. D., Montreal After Two Hundred and Fifty Years. Montreal, 1892.

McBAIN, A. R., The History of the High School of Montreal. Montreal, 1950.

MacDERMOT, H. E., A History of the Montreal General Hospital. Montreal, 1950.

MacKAY, ROBERT W. S., The Stranger's Guide to the Island and City of Montreal. Montreal, 1848.

McLACHLAN, R. W., Fleury Mesplet, the First Printer at Montreal. Ottawa, 1906 (Royal Society of Canada).

McLEAN, ERIC, The Living Past of Montreal; illus. by R. D. Wilson. Montreal, 1964.

MacLENNAN, HUGH, ed., McGill, the Story of a University. Toronto, 1960.

McNAMEE, GEORGE, Memoirs, 1905–1958. Unpublished manuscript (Royal Automobile Club).

McROBIE, WILLIAM ORME, Fighting the Flames! Montreal, 1881.

THE MONTREAL ALMANACK or Lower Canada Register, 1829, 1830, 1831.

MONTREAL AMATEUR ATHLETIC ASSOCIATION, Souvenir of the New Club House. Montreal, 1905.

MONTREAL BOARD OF TRADE, Montreal, the Splendour of Its Location. Montreal, 1909.

MONTREAL. CITY, By-laws, Rules, Regulations and Ordinances of the Common Council. Montreal, 1883.

MONTREAL CITY PLANNING DEPARTMENT, How Our Streets Got Their Names; comp. by Paul Gauthier & Georges F. Seguin. Montreal, 1961.

MONTREAL DIRECTORY, published as MacKay's from 1842–43 and as Lovell's from 1868 to current date.

MONTREAL. HARBOUR, Montreal, Harbour City; an exhibition arranged by the Montreal Port Council, the City of Montreal & the National Harbours Board. v. 1, 1535–1867, v. 2, 1860–1964. Montreal, 1963, 1964.

MONTREAL INDUSTRIAL COMMISSION, Montreal the Metropolis of Canada. Montreal, 1931.

MONTREAL LIGHT, HEAT AND POWER CONSOLIDATED, Montreal the Centre of Canadian Industrial Activity. Montreal, 1921.

MONTREAL (periodical), Montreal '64 and '65. (Published monthly by the City of Montreal, 1st issue, May 1964).

MONTREAL POCKET GUIDE, 1905–06.

MONTREAL RESEARCH COUNCIL, The Impact of the St. Lawrence Seaway on the Montreal Area. Montreal, 1958.

MONTREAL YEAR BOOK, 1930.

MORIN, VICTOR, Fleury Mesplet. Montreal, 1939.

——, Old Montreal with Pen and Pencil; illus. by Charles W. Simpson. Montreal, 1929.

MURRAY'S ILLUSTRATED GUIDE TO MONTREAL AND VICINITY. Montreal, 1893.

NEW GUIDE TO MONTREAL AND ITS ENVIRONS. Montreal, 1851.

OFFICIAL GUIDE TO MONTREAL, prepared for the meetings of the 12th International Geological Congress, Montreal, 1913.

OLMSTED, FREDERICK LAW, Mount Royal, Montreal. New York, 1881.

PARRATT, JOHN, comp., Montreal Pictured and Described. Montreal, 1889.

PERCIVAL, W. P., The Lure of Montreal. Rev. ed. Toronto, 1964.

PICK, ALFRED JOHN, The Administration of Paris and Montreal. Montreal, 1939.

RENAUD, CHARLES, L'Imprévisible Monsieur Houde. Montréal, 1964.

REVUE FRANÇAISE (periodical), Montréal, 1963 (special issue).

ROSENBERG, LOUIS, Canadian Jewish Population Studies. v. 4, The Jewish Population of Montreal . . . Growth & Changes in Distribution. v. 5, The Jewish Community of Montreal . . . Population Characteristics. Montreal, 1954, 1955.

SANDHAM, ALFRED, Montreal and Its Fortifications. Montreal, 1874.

——, Ville-Marie, or Sketches of Montreal. Montreal, 1870.

SCRAP BOOKS, on Snowshoeing and Other Winter Sports, as Well as Lacrosse; comp. by Will H. Whyte. Montreal, 1869.

SLATTERY, T. P., Loyola and Montreal. Montreal, 1962.

SMITH, F. CLIFFORD, The Montreal Water Works, Its History from 1800–1912. Montreal, 1913.

TANGHE, RAYMOND, Géographie Humaine de Montréal. Montreal, 1928.

——, Montréal. Montréal, 1936.

TATA, SAM, Montreal; text by Sam Low and photographs by Sam Tata. Toronto, 1963.

TERRILL, FREDERICK WILLIAM, A Chronology of Montreal, 1752–1893. Montreal, 1893.

TOMBS, LAURENCE CHALMERS, The Port of Montreal. Montreal, 1926.

WEIR, ARTHUR, Art Work on Montreal. Montreal, 1898.

WILSON, LAWRENCE, comp., This Was Montreal in 1814, 1815, 1816, and 1817; as culled verbatim from the Montreal *Herald*. Montreal, 1960.

WINDSOR HOTEL GUIDE to the City of Montreal and for the Dominion of Canada. Montreal, 1890.

General

ABBOTT, MAUDE E., History of Medicine in the Province of Quebec. Montreal, 1931.

ABERDEEN, ISHBEL, MARCHIONESS OF, Canadian Journal . . . 1893–1898; ed. by John T. Saywell. Toronto, 1960 (Champlain Society).

ALLARD, CHRISTOPHE, Promenade au Canada et aux Etats-Unis. Paris, 1878.

ANBUREY, THOMAS, Travels Through the Interior Parts of America. 2 v. London, 1789.

ARFWEDSON, C. D., The United States and Canada in 1832, 1833 and 1834. 2 v. London, 1834.

ARMSTRONG, ELIZABETH, The Crisis of Quebec, 1914–1918. New York, 1937.

BABBAGE, E. F., Phat Boy's Racy Description of the St. Lawrence River and Its Environs. Rochester, 1887.

BAEDEKER, KARL, The Dominion of Canada. Leipsic, 1900 and 1922.

BIGSBY, JOHN J., The Shoe and Canoe . . . or Pictures of Life in the Canadas. 2 v. London, 1850.

BISHOP, MORRIS, Champlain, the Life of Fortitude. New York, 1948.

BONNYCASTLE, SIR RICHARD, The Canadas in 1841. 2 v. London, 1841.

BOUCHER, PIERRE, Canada in the 17th Century; trans. by Edward Montizambert. Montreal, 1883.

BOUCHETTE, JOSEPH, A Topographical Description of the Province of Lower Canada. London, 1815.

——, The British Dominions in North America. 2 v. London, 1831.

BOURINOT, JOHN GEORGE, Lord Elgin. Toronto, 1906 (Makers of Canada).

BOYD, JOHN, Sir Georges Etienne Cartier . . . a Political History from 1814 until 1873. Toronto, 1914.

BRADLEY, A. G., Lord Dorchester. Toronto, 1907 (Makers of Canada).

——, The United Empire Loyalists. London, 1932.

BREBNER, JOHN B., The Explorers of North America, 1492–1806. London, 1933.

BRIDLE, AUGUSTUS, Sons of Canada. Toronto, 1916.

BROOKE, FRANCES, The History of Emily Montague. London, 1769.

BRYCE, GEORGE, Mackenzie, Selkirk, Simpson. Toronto, 1906 (Makers of Canada).

BURT, ALFRED LEROY, The Old Province of Quebec. Toronto, 1933.

CAMPBELL, MARJORIE WILKINS, McGillivray, Lord of the Northwest. Toronto, 1962.

——, The North West Company. Toronto, 1957.

CAMPBELL, PATRICK, Travels in the Interior Inhabited Parts of North America, 1791–1792; ed. by H. H. Langton. Toronto, 1937 (Champlain Society).

CANADA. PUBLIC ARCHIVES, The Elgin-Grey Papers, 1846–52; ed. by Sir Arthur Doughty. 4 v. Ottawa, 1937.

CANADIAN GUIDE BOOK. v. 1, Eastern Canada & Newfoundland, by Charles G. D. Roberts. New York, 1891–93.

CARTIER, JACQUES, Voyages; published from the originals, with translations by H. P. Biggar. Ottawa, 1924.

CHAMPLAIN, SAMUEL DE, Works; trans. & ed. by H. H. Langton & W. F. Ganong. 6 v. Toronto, 1922–36 (Champlain Society).

CHARLEVOIX, REV. P. F. X., History and General Description of New France; trans. by Dr. John Shea. 6 v. London, 1902.

CHEVRIER, LIONEL, The St. Lawrence Seaway. Toronto, 1959.

CHISHOLM'S ALL ROUND ROUTE AND PANORAMIC GUIDE OF THE ST. LAWRENCE. Montreal, 1874.

CLEVERDON, CATHERINE LYLE, The Woman Suffrage Movement in Canada. Toronto, 1950.

COKE, E. T., A Subaltern's Furlough. London, 1833.

COLBY, CHARLES W., Canadian Types of the Old Regime, 1608–1698. New York, 1908.

COLLARD, EDGAR A., Canadian Yesterdays. Toronto, 1955.

COOPER, LEONARD, Radical Jack, the Life of the First Earl of Durham. London, 1959.

COWAN, HELEN I., British Emigration to British North America; the First Hundred Years. Rev. ed. Toronto, 1961.

CRAIG, GERALD, ed., Early Travellers in the Canadas, 1791–1867. Toronto, 1955.

CREIGHTON, DONALD, The Empire of the St. Lawrence. Toronto, 1956.

——, John A. Macdonald. 2 v. Toronto, 1952, 1955.

CURRY, RALPH, Stephen Leacock. New York, 1959.

CUSHING, HARVEY, The Life of Sir William Osler. 2 v. Oxford, 1925.

DAVISON, G. M., The Travellers' Guide Through the Middle and Northern States and the Provinces of Canada. Saratoga Springs, 1840.

DAWSON, R. MACGREGOR, The Conscription Crisis of 1944. Toronto, 1961.

DAWSON, SAMUEL EDWARD, The Saint Lawrence Basin and Its Border-lands. New York, 1905.

DAWSON, SIR WILLIAM, Fifty Years of Work in Canada. London, 1901.

DAY, SAMUEL PHILLIPS, English America, or Pictures of Canadian Places and People. 2 v. London, 1864.

DE BRUMATH, A. LEBLOND, Bishop Laval. Toronto, 1906 (Makers of Canada).

DECELLES, ALFRED, Papineau; Cartier. Toronto, 1906 (Makers of Canada).

DE ROOS, F. F., Personal Narrative of Travels in the United States and Canada in 1826. London, 1827.

DICKENS, CHARLES, American Notes. London, 1842.

DUCALVET, PETER, The Case of DuCalvet of Montreal. London, 1784.

DUFFERIN AND AVA, Harriet, Marchioness of, My Canadian Journal, 1872–1878. London, 1891.

DUNCAN, JOHN M., Travels Through Parts of the United States and Canada in 1818 and 1819. 2 v. Glasgow, 1823.

DUNLOP, DR. WILLIAM, Recollections of the War of 1812. Toronto, 1908.

DURHAM, JOHN GEORGE LAMBTON, FIRST EARL, Report on the Affairs of British North America. Toronto, 1840.

ECCLES, W. J., Frontenac, the Courtier Governor. Toronto, 1959.

ELLIS, FRANK H., Canada's Flying Heritage. Toronto, 1954.

EVE, A. E., The Life and Letters of the Rt. Hon. Lord Rutherford. Cambridge, 1939.

FAILLON, ABBÉ, Histoire de la Colonie Française en Canada. 4 v. Villemarie, 1866.

FAUTEUX, AEGIDIUS, Introduction of Printing into Canada. Montreal, 1930.

FERGUSSON, ADAM, Practical Notes Made During a Tour in Canada, 1831. Edinburgh, 1834.

FLEXNER, JAMES T., Mohawk Baronet, Sir William Johnson of New York. New York, 1959.

FORSTER, JOHN, The Life of Charles Dickens. 2 v. London, 1872–74.

FRANKLIN, BENJAMIN, The Life of Franklin, written by himself and ed. by John Bigelow. 3 v. Philadelphia, 1898.

FRASER, HUGH, A Trip to the Dominon of Canada. Halifax, 1883.

FRASER, JOHN, Canadian Pen and Ink Sketches. Montreal, 1890.

GARNEAU, F. X., History of Canada from the Time of Its Discovery Till the Union Year, 1840–41; trans. by Andrew Bell. Montreal, 1862.

GIBBON, JOHN MURRAY, Canadian Mosaic. Toronto, 1938.

——, Steel of Empire; the Romantic History of the Canadian Pacific. Toronto, 1955.

GODLEY, JOHN R., Letters from America. 2 v. London, 1844.

GOWANS, ALAN, Church Architecture in New France. Toronto, 1955.

——, Looking at Architecture in Canada. Toronto, 1958.

GRANT, GEORGE MONRO, Picturesque Canada. Toronto, 1882.

GRAY, JOHN MORGAN, Lord Selkirk of Red River. Toronto, 1963.

GREAVES, IDA, The Negro in Canada. Montreal, 1930.

GUILLET, EDWIN C., The Great Migration. Toronto, 1937.

HADFIELD, JOSEPH, An Englishman in America, 1785, being a diary ed. by Douglas S. Robertson. Toronto, 1933.

HALL, BASIL, Travels in North America, 1827 & 1828. 3 v. Edinburgh, 1830.

HAMILTON, EDWARD P., The French and Indian Wars. New York, 1962.

HARPER, J. RUSSELL, Everyman's Canada; paintings & drawings from the McCord Museum of McGill University. Ottawa, 1962.

HART, ARTHUR DANIEL, ed., The Jew in Canada. Toronto, 1926.

HEAGERTY, J. J., The Romance of Medicine in Canada. Toronto, 1940.

HENRY, ALEXANDER, Travels & Adventures in Canada & the Indian Territories, 1760–1776. New York, 1809.

HERIOT, GEORGE, Travels Through the Canadas. London, 1807.

HODGETTS, A. B., Decisive Decades. Toronto, 1960.

HUNTER, WILLIAM S., Panoramic Guide from Niagara Falls to Quebec. Montreal, 1857 & 1869.

INNIS, HAROLD A., The Fur Trade in Canada. Rev. ed. Toronto, 1956.

IRVING, WASHINGTON, Astoria. 3 v. London, 1836.

JAMIESON, A. B., Chartered Banking in Canada. Toronto, 1953.

JEFFERYS, C. W., The Picture Gallery of Canadian History. 3 v. Toronto, 1942.

JESUIT RELATIONS and Allied Documents, 1610–1791; with English trans. by Reuben Gold Thwaites. 73 v. Cleveland, 1896–1901.

KAGE, JOSEPH, With Faith and Thanksgiving. Montreal, 1962.

KALM, PETER, Travels into North America; trans. from the Swedish by John Reinhold Forster. London, 1772.

KINGSFORD, WILLIAM, History of Canada. 10 v. Toronto, 1887.

KNOX, CAPTAIN JOHN, An Historical Journal of the Campaigns in North America, 1757, 1758, 1759, 1760. London, 1769.

KOHL, J. G., Travels in Canada; trans. from the German by Mrs. Percy Sinnett. London, 1861.

LA BRIÈRE, L. DE, L'autre France; Voyage au Canada. Paris, 1886.

LAMBERT, JOHN, Travels Through Canada and the United States of North America, 1806, 1807, 1808. 2 v. London, 1814.

LAMOTHE, H. DE, Cinq mois chez les Français d'Amerique. Paris, 1880.

LANCTOT, GUSTAVE, A History of Canada. 2 v. Toronto, 1963, 1964.

LANDMANN, GEORGE THOMAS, Adventures and Recollections. London, 1852.

LA ROCHEFOUCAULT-LIANCOURT, DUC DE, Travels Through the United States . . . with an authentic account of Lower Canada, 1795, 1796, 1797; trans. by H. Neuman. London, 1799.

LEACOCK, STEPHEN, Baldwin, Lafontaine, Hincks. Toronto, 1907 (Makers of Canada).

LEGGO, WILLIAM, The Administration of the . . . Earl of Dufferin. Montreal, 1878.

 LESCARBOT, MARC, The History of New France; with an English trans. by W. L. Grant. 3 v. Toronto, 1907–1914 (Champlain Society).

LONGLEY, RONALD STEWART, Sir Francis Hincks. Toronto, 1943.

LORNE, JOHN DOUGLAS, MARQUIS OF, Canadian pictures, Drawn with Pen and Pencil. London, 1892.

MACADAM, CAPTAIN J. T., Canada from the Lakes to the Gulf. Montreal, 1881.

MCILWRAITH, JEAN, Sir Frederick Haldimand. Toronto, 1906 (Makers of Canada).

MACKAY, CHARLES, A Tour in the United States and Canada. London, 1859.

MACKAY, DOUGLAS, The Honourable Company; a History of the Hudson's Bay Company. Toronto, 1936.

MACKENZIE, ALEXANDER, Voyages from Montreal Through the Continent of North America. Philadelphia, 1802.

MACTAGGART, JOHN, Three Years in Canada, 1826, 1827, 1828. 2 v. London, 1829.

MAHON, R. H., Life of General the Hon. James Murray. London, 1921.

MANNING, HELEN TAFT, The Revolt of French Canada, 1800–1835. Toronto, 1962.

MARMIER, XAVIER, Les Etats-Unis et le Canada. Tours, 1875.

MASSON, L. R., Les Bourgeois de la Compagnie du Nord-Ouest. 2 v. Quebec, 1889.

MOODIE, SUSANNA, Roughing It in the Bush. London, 1852.

MORISSET, GERARD, L'Architecture en Nouvelle-France. Quebec, 1949.

MORTON, ARTHUR S., Sir George Simpson. Toronto, 1944.

MORTON, W. L., The Kingdom of Canada. Toronto, 1963.

MURRAY, HUGH, An Historical and Descriptive Account of British America. 3 v. Edinburgh, 1839.

NEW, CHESTER, Lord Durham. Oxford, 1929.

NUTE, GRACE LEE, The Voyageur. New York, 1931.

ONTARIO & ST. LAWRENCE STEAMBOAT CO., The Great Northern Route; a Handbook for Travellers. Buffalo, 1854.

PALARDY, JEAN, The Early Furniture of French Canada; trans. from the French by Eric McLean. Toronto, 1963.

PARKMAN, FRANCIS, France and England in the New World. 1865–1892.

PHILLIPS, CHARLES E., The Development of Education in Canada. Toronto, 1957.

POWER, TYRONE, Impressions of America, 1833, 1834, 1835. 2 v. London, 1836.

PRESTON, T. R., Three Years Residence in Canada, 1837 to 1839. London, 1840.

QUEBEC (PROVINCE). MINISTERE DES AFFAIRS CULTURELLES, Collection Art, Vie et Sciences au Canada Français. 6 v. Quebec, 1964.

    1. Panorama des lettres Canadiennes-françaises, par Guy Sylvestre.

    2. Le théâtre au Canada français, par Jean Hamelin.

    3. La peinture moderne au Canada français, par Guy Viau.

    4. La vie musicale au Canada français, par Annette Lasalle-Leduc.

    5. La vie des sciences au Canada français, par Cyrias Ouellet.

    6. L'essor des sciences sociales au Canada français, par Jean-Charles Falardeau.

REYNOLDS, LLOYD G., The British Immigrant. Toronto, 1935.

ROME, DAVID, comp., Jews in Canadian Literature; a bibliography. Montreal, 1962.

ROSENBERG, LOUIS, Canada's Jews; a Social & Economic Study. Montreal, 1939.

ROSS, MALCOLM, ed., The Arts in Canada. Toronto, 1958.

RYERSON, EGERTON, The Loyalists of America & Their Times. 2 v. Toronto, 1880.

SACK, BENJAMIN G., The History of the Jews in Canada. Montreal, 1945.

SANSOM, JOSEPH, Travels in Lower Canada. London, 1820.

SHAW, ROSA L., Proud Heritage; a History of the National Council of Women in Canada. Toronto, 1957.

SHORTT, ADAM, Lord Sydenham. Toronto, 1908 (Makers of Canada).

SKELTON, ISABEL, The Life of Thomas D'Arcy McGee. Gardenvale, 1925.

SKELTON, OSCAR DOUGLAS, Life & Letters of Sir Wilfrid Laurier. 2 v. Toronto, 1921.

SLEIGH, B. W. A., Pine Forests and Hackmatack Clearings. London, 1853.

SMALL, H. B., Canadian Handbook & Tourists' Guide. Montreal, 1866.

SMITH, WILLIAM, History of the Post Office in British North America, 1639–1870. Cambridge, 1920.

SPENDLOVE, F. ST. GEORGE, The Face of Early Canada; Pictures of Canada Which Have Helped to Make History, Toronto, 1958.

STACEY, C. P., Canada and the British Army. London, 1936.

STANLEY, GEORGE F. G., Canada's Soldiers. Rev. ed. Toronto, 1960.

——, Louis Riel. Toronto, 1963.

STEVENS, G. R., Canadian National Railways. 2 v. Toronto, 1960, 1962.

SULTE, BENJAMIN, A History of Quebec. Montreal, 1908.

TALBOT, EDWARD ALLEN, Five Years Residence in the Canadas. London, 1824.

THARP, LOUISE HALL, The Baroness and the General. Boston, 1962.

THOMPSON, NORMAN, Canadian Railway Development from the Earliest Times. Toronto, 1933.

TOUR OF THE PRINCE OF WALES Through British America & the United States, by a British Canadian. Montreal, 1860.

TRAILL, CATHERINE PARR, The Backwoods of Canada. London, 1846.

TRAQUAIR, RAMSAY, The Old Architecture of Quebec. Toronto, 1947.

TROLLOPE, ANTHONY, North America. New York, 1862.

TUCKER, GILBERT NORMAN, The Canadian Commercial Revolution, 1845–1851. New Haven, 1936.

URQUHART, HUGH, Arthur Currie. Toronto, 1950.

WADE, MASON, The French Canadians, 1760–1945. Toronto, 1955.

WAITE, P. B., ed., Confederation Debates in the Province of Canada, 1865. Toronto, 1963.

——, The Life and Times of Confederation, 1864–1867. Toronto, 1962.

WALLACE, W. S. ed., Documents Relating to the North West Company. Toronto, 1934 (Champlain Society).

——, The Pedlars from Quebec and Other Papers on the Nor'-Westers. Toronto, 1954.

WARBURTON, ELIOT, Hochelaga, or England in the New World. 2 v. London, 1846.

WELD, ISAAC, JR., Travels Through the States of North America & the Provinces of Upper & Lower Canada, 1795, 1796, 1797. London, 1799.

WHITELAW, WILLIAM M., The Maritimes and Canada Before Confederation. Toronto, 1934.

WICKETT, S. MORLEY, ed., Municipal Government in Canada. Toronto, 1907.

WILLIAMS, W., Appleton's Railroad & Steamboat Companion. New York, 1848.

WILLIS, N. P., Canadian Scenery; illus. from drawings by W. H. Bartlett. London, 1842.

WILLOUGHBY, WILLIAM H., The St. Lawrence Waterway. Madison, 1961.

WINKS, ROBIN W., Canada and the United States; the Civil War Years. Baltimore, 1960.

WOODHAM-SMITH, CECIL, The Great Hunger; Ireland, 1845–1849. New York, 1962.

WRONG, GEORGE M., Canada and the American Revolution. Toronto, 1935.

——, The Rise and Fall of New France. 2 v. Toronto, 1928.

INDEX